Handbook of Research on Strategy Process

T0314168

Edited by

Pietro Mazzola

Professor of Management, IULM University, Milan, Italy

Franz W. Kellermanns

Associate Professor of Management, University of Tennessee, Knoxville, USA and an Associated Professor, WHU-Otto Beisheim School of Management, Vallendar, Germany

Edward Elgar
Cheltenham, UK • Northampton, MA, USA

Published by
Edward Elgar Publishing Limited
The Lypiatts
15 Lansdown Road
Cheltenham
Glos GL50 2JA
UK

Edward Elgar Publishing, Inc.
William Pratt House
9 Dewey Court
Northampton
Massachusetts 01060
USA

A catalogue record for this book
is available from the British Library

Library of Congress Control Number: 2010925939

ISBN 978 1 84844 044 9 (cased)

Typeset by Servis Filmsetting Ltd, Stockport, Cheshire
Printed and bound by MPG Books Group, UK

Contents

Contributors

Joseph H. Astrachan, Ph.D., is Wachovia Eminent Scholar Chair of Family Business, Professor of Management and Entrepreneurship, Executive Director of the Cox Family Enterprise Center, and a founder of the internationally accredited Executive MBA for Families in Business at the Coles College of Business, Kennesaw State University near Atlanta, Georgia, USA. In addition he is Distinguished Research Chair of Family Business at Loyola University Chicago's Business School, USA. Astrachan is editor of the scientific publication the *Journal of Family Business Strategy* (an Elsevier title) and past editor of *Family Business Review*. He is also editor of the *Family Business Casebook Annual*, which publishes the best in teaching and educational family business cases.

Ofer H. Azar received his Ph.D. in economics from Northwestern University, Chicago, USA and joined the Department of Business Administration at Ben-Gurion University of the Negev, Israel afterwards, where he now serves as the Head of the Multidisciplinary Specialty. He was a guest editor of a special issue and is an associate editor on the *Journal of Economic Psychology*, and he serves as the Chairperson of the Executive Committee of the International Confederation for the Advancement of Behavioral Economics and Economic Psychology (ICABEEP). His research deals with various topics in behavioral economics, experimental economics, business strategy, industrial organization and applied microeconomics, and has appeared in various journals, including the *Journal of Industrial Economics, Journal of Economic Behavior and Organization, Journal of Economics and Management Strategy* and *Economic Inquiry*.

Osvald M. Bjelland is Chairman of the Anglo-Scandinavian advisory firm Xyntéo and Chairman of the Performance Theatre Foundation. In 2009 he was a visiting scholar at Stanford University, USA. His doctoral research at the University of Leeds, UK focused on the use of information technology to transform information-intensive organizations. Currently both his consulting and his research focus on how organizations can achieve low-carbon growth and innovation.

Michael R. Braun is an Assistant Professor of Management at the University of Montana, USA. His academic research interests involve the exploration of diverse organizational forms and their related structures and strategies during periods of uncertainty and decline. He also investigates strategies required to navigate recessionary environments. Michael received his doctorate in strategic management from the University of Massachusetts at Amherst, USA.

David M. Brock is an Associate Professor at the Guilford Glaser School of Management, Ben-Gurion University, Israel and a visiting professor at the Sy Syms School of Business, Yeshiva University, New York, USA. Previously he taught at the University of Auckland Business School, New Zealand, North Carolina State University, USA and the University of North Carolina at Chapel Hill, USA. He is currently guest editor for special issues of the *Journal of International Management* and *Journal of Management Studies*, and previously edited a special issue of *Management International Review*. Recent work includes modeling expatriate deployment and national culture (*Journal of International Business Studies*) and studies of the internationalization effectiveness tradeoffs of global law firms (*Journal of International Management* and *International Business Review*).

Frank C. Butler is an Assistant Professor of Management at the College of Business at the University of Tennessee at Chattanooga, USA. He received a Ph.D. in strategic management from Florida State University, USA. His research interests include merger and acquisition integration and corporate governance.

J. Ignacio Canales is a Senior Lecturer in Strategy (equivalent to Associate Professor in the USA) at the University of Glasgow Business School, UK. Previously he was at the University of St Andrews, UK after having received his Ph.D. in management from Instituto de Estudios Superiores de la Empresa Business School in 2004. His research focuses on the strategy-making process, the roles managers play within such process and strategic entrepreneurship as well as subsidiary strategy. His work has been published in *Long Range Planning*, the *Journal of Management Studies* and *Advances in Strategic Management*.

Erick P. C. Chang (Ph.D. Mississippi State University, USA) is an Assistant Professor of Management at Arkansas State University, USA. His research has been published in the *Journal of Business Venturing*, *Entrepreneurship Theory and Practice*, *Journal of Business Research* and *Family Business Review*. His achievements include: finalist for the 2008 National Federation of Independent Business Dissertation Award, the Triple Crown for Ph.D. Student research awards at Mississippi State University in 2007 and a Fulbright scholarship from 1995 to 1997.

James J. Chrisman is Professor of Management, Adkerson Notable Scholar and Director of the Center of Family Enterprise Research at Mississippi State University, USA. He holds a joint appointment as a Research Fellow with the Center of Entrepreneurship and Family Enterprise at the University of Alberta School of Business, Canada.

Vittorio Coda is Full Professor of Strategic Management at Bocconi University, Italy. He has also been senior faculty member of the Strategic Management Area at SDA Bocconi University since its foundation in 1974. He was Chairman of the SDA Bocconi School of Management from 1981 to 1996. Before becoming Full Professor at Bocconi, he held positions at the University of Urbino, Italy (from 1965 to 1967) and the University of Venice, Italy (from 1967 to 1976). He is a member of the editorial board and of the scientific boards of many Italian academic journals. He was President of the Accademia Italiana di Economia Aziendale which launched and sponsored the *Journal of Management and Governance*. His research mainly focuses on strategy appraisal, corporate values and entrepreneurship.

Alvaro Cuervo-Cazurra is a faculty member in the Sonoco International Business Department of the University of South Carolina, USA. He received a Ph.D. from the Massachusetts Institute of Technology, USA and another from the University of Salamanc, Spain. He studies the internationalization of firms with a special interest in developing-country multinational companies. He also analyses governance issues with a special interest in corruption. His research has received numerous awards and appears in leading academic journals such as the *Academy of Management Journal*, *Journal of International Business Studies*, *Research Policy* and *Strategic Management Journal*, and in several edited books. He serves on the editorial boards of leading journals such as the *Global Strategy Journal*, *Journal of International Business Studies*, *Strategic Management Journal* and *Organization Studies*. His geographical area of expertise is Latin America.

Gregory G. Dess (Ph.D., University of Washington, USA) is presently the Andrew Cecil Endowed Chair in Management at the University of Texas at Dallas, USA. His primary research interests are in strategic management, entrepreneurship and knowledge management. He has published numerous articles in leading academic journals such as the *Academy of Management Journal*, *Strategic Management Journal*, *Academy of Management Review*, *Strategic Management Journal* and *Administrative Science Quarterly*. Much of his work has also appeared in leading practitioner journals such as *Organizational Dynamics, Academy of Management Executive, Business Horizons* and *Long Range Planning*. He presently serves on several editorial boards including the *Strategic Entrepreneurship Journal* and *Journal of Business Venturing*. In 2000, he was inducted as one of 33 charter members of the *Academy of Management Journal*'s 'Hall of Fame'.

Martin J. Eppler holds the Chair in Media and Communications Management at the University of St. Gallen, Switzerland and is the Managing Director of the University's Media and Communications Management Institute. He is also a guest professor at the Helsinki School of Economics/Aalto University in Finland and at the Central University of Finance and Economics in Beijing, China, and has been a senior visiting fellow at the Department of Engineering at Cambridge University, UK. His research focuses on knowledge communication and visualization in management (particularly in strategy contexts), and employs experimental methods as well as classification approaches. He has published eight books and more than 80 articles in journals such as *Organization Studies, Long Range Planning, Harvard Business Manager,* the *Journal of Brand Management, Information Visualization, European Management Journal, The Information Society* and the *IEEE Transactions*. He has been advisor to international firms and organizations such as the United Nations, Ernst & Young, Philips, Swiss Re, and Daimler, as well as different public institutions.

Steven W. Floyd is a Professor of Strategic Management and Director of the Institute of Management at the University of St. Gallen, Switzerland. Dr. Floyd's research and consulting focus on corporate entrepreneurship and the strategic management process. The work investigates such issues as involving middle-level managers in strategy development, creating shared strategic understanding and commitment, and managing the evolution of strategic initiatives. His research has been published in such journals as *Academy of Management Review, Academy of Management Journal, Strategic Management Journal, Journal of Management, Journal of Management Studies, Entrepreneurship: Theory and Practice, Journal of International Business Studies, Journal of Organization Behavior, Organization Studies, Long Range Planning* and the *Academy of Management Executive*. Dr. Floyd is a past member of the Board of Directors of the Strategic Management Society and a general editor of the *Journal of Management Studies*. He serves on the editorial boards of several other leading journals, including the *Strategic Management Journal, Academy of Management Journal* and *Journal of Management*.

Paul N. Friga is an Associate Professor at the Kenan-Flagler School of Business at the University of North Carolina (UNC) at Chapel Hill, USA, where he teaches and researches management consulting and strategy. He is the recipient of the Indiana University (IU) Trustee Teaching Award, IU Kelley School Business Innovative Teaching Award, and the UNC Kenan-Flagler Business School Ph.D. Teaching Award. He co-chairs the Strategic Management Society task force on teaching strategy. Dr. Friga's work has been published in the *Academy of Management Learning and Education*, *Research Technology Management*, and two books by McGraw-Hill, *The McKinsey Mind* (2001) and *The McKinsey Engagement* (2008). He completed his Ph.D. and MBA at the University of North Carolina at Chapel Hill and previously worked as a consultant for PricewaterhouseCoopers and McKinsey. He has also earned Certified Public Accountant and Certified Management Accountant designations. Dr. Friga has consulted for numerous large (Fortune 100), mid-size and entrepreneurial companies as well as universities and not-for-profit organizations.

Guo-hui Sun is a Professor of Marketing, Dean of Business School of the Central University of Finance and Economics (CUFE) in China, and Vice-President of the China Marketing Association (CMAU). He received his Ph.D. from the Central University of Finance and Economics (CUFE), Beijing, China. His academic fields are in strategic marketing and global integration strategy. His textbooks *International Business Management* and *International Marketing* were awarded China National Textbook of the Eleventh Five-Year Plan in 2006. In 2009, he became a beneficiary of 'Supporting Program For Excellent Talents in the New Century' sponsored by the China Education Ministry.

Thomas Hutzschenreuter (Ph.D., Leipzig Graduate School of Management, Germany) is Dietmar Hopp Professor of Corporate Strategy at WHU– Otto Beisheim School of Management in Vallendar, Germany. His research interests include corporate growth, paths of internationalization and diversification, and strategy processes. He serves as Academic Director of Doctoral Studies at WHU.

P. Devereaux (Dev) Jennings is the Winspear Professor of Business at the Alberta School of Business, Canada, where he teaches strategy and organization theory. Dev is currently pursuing research in three areas: environmental strategy and regulation, nanotechnology patents and high-tech start-ups, and family business dynamics. His professional duties include co-editor of *Strategic Organization*, field editor for *Journal of Business*

Venturing and editorial board membership on *Administrative Science Quarterly*. Over the years, his work with diverse co-authors has been published in *Administrative Science Quarterly*, the *Academy of Management Journal*, the *Academy of Management Review* and the *American Journal of Sociology*. He received his Ph.D. and M.A. at Stanford University, USA and his B.A. at Dartmouth College, Hanover, USA.

Franz W. Kellermanns is Associate Professor of Management at the College of Business at the University of Tennessee (Knoxville), USA. He holds a joint appointment with the INTES Center for Family Enterprises at the WHU–Otto Beisheim School of Management, Vallendar, Germany. He received his Ph.D. from the University of Connecticut, USA. His research interests include strategy process and entrepreneurship with a focus on family business research. He is an associate editor of *Family Business Review* and has published in journals such as the *Journal of Management, Journal of Management Studies, Journal of Organizational Behavior, Journal of Business Venturing, Entrepreneurship Theory and Practice, Family Business Review* and *Academy of Management Learning and Education*. He is a co-editor of the recent book *Innovating Strategy Process* in the Strategic Management Society Book Series. He further serves on the editorial boards of *Entrepreneurship Theory and Practice*, the *Journal of Management Studies, Strategic Entrepreneurship, Journal, Family Business Strategy* and the *Journal of Management*. He is currently a guest editor for a special issue of *Small Business Economics*.

Ingo Kleindienst (Ph.D., WHU–Otto Beisheim School of Management, Vallendar, Germany) is Assistant Professor of Strategy Processes at WHU–Otto Beisheim School of Management. His research interests include strategy processes, paths of internationalization, and mergers and acquisitions.

Markus Kreutzer is Assistant Professor of Strategic Management at the University of St. Gallen, Switzerland. He serves as Executive Director of the Excellence Initiative on 'Responsible Corporate Competitiveness' (RoCC), a multidisciplinary initiative at the same university. He has published his research in outlets such as *Long Range Planning* and *Harvard Business Manager*. His research interests are in the area of strategy process, organizational control and coordination, and alliance strategy.

Scott F. Latham after working in the software industry for over a decade received a Ph.D. in business policy and strategy. His dissertation focused on the .com crash, specifically the strategies that successful companies employed to survive. His general research and consulting interests focus on the process of creative destruction – the interplay of innovation, entrepreneurship and the business cycle that transforms industries. His research has been published in a wide array of top academic journals and more practitioner-oriented outlets.

Christoph Lechner is a Chaired Professor of Strategic Management at the University of St. Gallen, Switzerland, Managing Director of its Institute of Management, Academic Director of its Ph.D. Program in strategy and management, and Head of its Excellence Initiative on 'Responsible Corporate Competitiveness' (RoCC). He has written five books and published his research in outlets such as the *Academy of Management Journal, Journal of Management, Journal of Management Studies, Long Range Planning, MIT Sloan Management Review, Wall Street Journal* and *Harvard Business Manager*. He is a member of the editorial boards of the *Strategic Management Journal, Journal of Management Studies, Long Range Planning* and *Journal of Strategy and Management*. Co-authored papers won the SMS Best Conference Paper Prize and the Sumantra Ghoshal Research and Practice Award at the Academy of Management Conference, Atlanta, USA in 2006. He has led executive education programs for leading companies in the USA, Europe and Asia, and is a member of the board of directors of two public listed firms in Europe.

G. T. (Tom) Lumpkin is the Chris J. Witting Chair of Entrepreneurship at Syracuse University in New York, USA. His primary research interests include entrepreneurial orientation, social entrepreneurship, opportunity recognition, family business and strategy-making processes. He is a globally recognized scholar whose research has been published in the *Academy of Management Review, Academy of Management Journal, Entrepreneurship Theory and Practice, Journal of Business Venturing, Strategic Entrepreneurship Journal, Journal of Management, Organizational Dynamics* and *Strategic Management Journal*. Tom currently co-edits the Advances in Entrepreneurship, Firm Emergence, and Growth book series with Jerry Katz. He also serves on the editorial boards of the *Strategic Entrepreneurship Journal, Entrepreneurship Theory and Practice, Journal of Business Venturing* and *Family Business Review*, and regularly reviews for other top journals in his field. Recently, Tom co-authored the fifth edition of a textbook entitled *Strategic Management: Creating Competitive Advantages* with Greg Dess and Alan Eisner. Tom received his Ph.D. in business administration from the University of Texas at Arlington, USA and MBA from the University of Southern California, USA.

George E. Manners, Ph.D., is Professor of Accounting and Management at the Coles College of Business, Kennesaw State University near Atlanta, Georgia, USA. He has had decades of experience as an educator, a consultant and a business executive. His primary expertise is in strategy development, organization design, operational modeling, management accounting and the management of technology. His industry base is broad, including electronics, chemical, pulp and paper, financial services and health systems. He is senior author of *Managing Return on Investment* and has over 40 articles in a wide range of journals. Dr. Manners has occupied tenured positions at Rensselaer Polytechnic Institute, Troy, New York, USA and Clemson University, South Carolina, USA.

Gaia G. Marchisio, Ph.D., is Assistant Professor of Management in the Management and Entrepreneurship Department at the Coles College of Business, Kennesaw State University (KSU) near Atlanta, Georgia, USA. At KSU Gaia teaches both management and family business (both undergrad and grad). She is also a faculty associate of the Coles College Cox Family Enterprise Center, world leader center in family business research. Gaia's research primarily concerns corporate entrepreneurship, burnout and strategic planning in family business. She has a number of publications, co-authoring several articles on family business issues in international academic journals and professional magazines.

Martin L. Martens is an Associate Professor of Management at the John Molson School of Business at Concordia University in Montreal, Canada. He received his Ph.D. from the University of British Columbia, Canada in 2002. His primary research focus is an investigation of the internal and external social forces that cause a firm to restructure itself when faced with new or unfamiliar environmental circumstances, with a focus on firms going through the initial public offering process. His research into sustainability includes an investigation into how industries react to a social crisis that affects their public image and uses the British Columbia leaky condo crisis as the focal social issue. He also has a strong interest in leadership and Sir Ernest Shackleton's 1914–16 Trans-Antarctic Expedition. His leadership case on Shackleton's expedition has been used at more than two dozen major universities around the world. Dr. Martens previously was a newspaper production manager at the Hawaii Newspaper Agency in Honolulu. Outside of business academia, he has investigated volcanoes and solar eclipses. He spent a month inside a volcano in Kamchatka, Russia and has watched total solar eclipses in several locations around the world.

Pietro Mazzola is Full Professor at IULM University, Milan, Italy. He is also senior faculty member of SDA Bocconi School of Business, Italy. He held visiting positions and teaching assignments at the Kennesaw State University, USA, Helsinki School of Economics, Finland and University of British Colombia, Canada. He is a member of the editorial board of *Family Business Review* and of the *Journal of Family Business Strategy*. He works as ad hoc reviewer for *Long Range Planning* and *California Management Review*. He has been involved as scientific advisor in the preparation of the Strategic Plan Listing Guide of the Milan Stock Exchange (*Strategic Plan Guide*, 2003). His research focuses on strategic planning, family business and financial communication. His works have appeared or are forthcoming in *Long Range Planning*, the *Family Business Review*, *Entrepreneurship and Regional Development* and *Small Business Economics* among others. With Salvatore Sciascia, he recently received the *Family Business Review* best article award (2008).

Anders Melander is Associate Professor in Business Administration at Jönköping International Business School, Sweden. He defended his thesis, *Industrial Wisdom and Strategic Change in the Swedish Pulp and Paper Industry 1945–1990* in 1997. In the period 2000–2007 Anders managed a national business development program targeting small and medium sized companies (see more on www.krAftprov.nu). His research focuses on strategy development and strategy processes in small and medium sized companies.

Leif Melin is Professor of Strategy and Organization and the founding Director of CeFEO, Center for Family Enterprise and Ownership, at Jönköping International Business School, Sweden, where he also has served as Dean and Managing Director. His research interests are in the field of strategizing and organizing, especially the role of ownership and leadership in strategic change applying the strategy-as-practice perspective. He has published in international journals and book volumes, including the *Strategic Management Journal*, *Journal of Management Studies*, *Strategic Organization*, *Long Range Planning* and *Family Business Review*, and the recent book *Strategy as Practice: Research Directions and Resources*. He serves on the editorial boards of several international journals.

Esra Memili is a Ph.D. student in management and a Research Assistant in the Center of Family Enterprise Research at Mississippi State University, USA. Her research interests include family business, entrepreneurship and strategy.

Mario Minoja is an Associate Professor of Strategic Management at the University of Modena and Reggio Emilia, Italy. He is also a Contract Professor at Bocconi University, Italy and has been a visiting scholar at the Norwegian School of Management–BI. His research and theoretical interests include ambidextrous organizations, firms operating in industrial districts, corporate social responsibility and its integration in competitive strategy, stakeholder theory, and antecedents and detection of managerial frauds.

Edoardo Mollona graduated in Strategic Management at Bocconi University, Milan, Italy and received a Ph.D. degree in strategic management and decision sciences at the London Business School, UK. He is currently Associate Professor in the Faculty of Mathematical, Physical and Natural Sciences at the University of Bologna, Italy, where he teaches business economics and dynamics of complex organizations. His research interests focus on the application of modeling and simulation techniques to strategic management and organizational theory. In particular, Edoardo Mollona conducts research on evolution and strategic change in large organizations, and on the changing nature of firms in knowledge-based economic contexts.

Mattias Nordqvist is Associate Professor in Business Administration at Jönköping International Business School, Sweden, where he is also Associate Dean and founding Co-director for the Center for Family Enterprise and Ownership. His research has appeared in several international journals and edited books. He is a founding associate editor of the *Journal of Family Business Strategy* (Elsevier) and has served as a Co-director for the Global STEP (Successful Transgenerational Entrepreneurship Practices) Project founded by Babson College, USA where he is still a visiting scholar.

Anil Patel is an Honorary Research Scholar with the Department of Management at the Terry College of Business, University of Georgia, USA. He serves as a long-range planner and corporate strategist in the Strategy and Integration Office at the HQ, US Army Corps of Engineers in Washington, DC. He is involved with strategic management, strategic studies and assessments, and strategic analysis. His experience extends to the private and public sectors, covering the fields of strategic management, scenario thinking, market planning, financial and technology management, public policy and legislative affairs. He is a Brookings Congressional Legis Fellow who served in the United States Congress. He holds an Executive Master of Science from the University of Maryland and Bachelor of Business Administration from the University of Georgia,

USA. He has attended the Executive Programs at The Wharton School, University of Pennsylvania, USA.

Terry B. Porter (Assistant Professor of Management) received her Ph.D. degree in management from the University of Massachusetts, USA, where her research focused on dynamic capabilities and strategic change in the case of corporate environmentalism. Her research interests include strategic processes, corporate environmentalism, complex adaptive systems, business and sustainability, and identity. An Olympic cross country skier, she enjoys outdoor sports and recreation of all kinds, and gardening, woodworking and cooking.

Annette L. Ranft is the Jim Moran Associate Professor and Department Chair of Management at the College of Business at Florida State University, USA. Her research interests are in the areas of merger and acquisition integration, strategic leadership and corporate governance. She is the author of articles published in such journals as the *Academy of Management Review*, *Academy of Management Executive*, *Organization Science*, *Journal of Management*, *Journal of International Business Studies* and *Journal of Business Research*. She received a Ph.D. in strategic management from the University of North Carolina at Chapel Hill, USA.

Patrick Regnér is an Associate Professor of Strategic Management at the Stockholm School of Economics (SSE), Sweden. Patrick's research is focused on strategy creation and change; including origins of strategy, strategy renewal, exploration/exploitation tradeoffs and strategic management in practice. Current research efforts focus on processes, practices and perceptions underlying organizational capabilities. He has published in journals such as the *Strategic Management Journal*, *Journal of Management Studies* and *Advances in Strategic Management*. Patrick is a member of the editorial board of *Strategic Organization* and *Organization Studies*. He has previously been a Co-director of the Institute of International Business at SSE and the Academic Dean of the International Graduate Program at SSE. Patrick has taught strategy at undergraduate, M.Sc., MBA, Executive MBA and Ph.D. levels for many years. He has directed the SSE Advanced Management Program and taught in numerous executive programs as well as in many firm-specific programs for publicly listed companies and for state owned ones. Patrick has worked and consulted with many public and private as well as not-for-profit organizations.

Chester W. Richards, Ph.D., is Adjunct Professor of Strategy and Quantitative Methods at Kennesaw State University in Atlanta, USA.

His previous publications include *If We Can Keep It* (2008), on post-Iraq national security, and *Certain to Win: The Strategy of John Boyd Applied to Business* (2004). He is a retired colonel in the United States Air Force and holds a Ph.D. in mathematics from the University of Mississippi, USA.

Amir Sasson is an Associate Professor at the Norwegian School of Management–BI. He has served on the faculty of University College Dublin, Ireland and has been a visiting scholar at Stanford University, USA. His research interests include the strategic management of mediating organizations and the strategic behavior of mediating actors. His theoretical interests range from network economics, economics of banking and interorganizational financial risk sharing, to social network theory and ambidextrous organizations. His most recent contributions have been published in *Organization Science*, the *Journal of Management Studies* and *Strategic Organization*.

Torsten Schmid is a postdoc. and lecturer in Strategic Management at the University of St. Gallen in Switzerland. He has published in both academic and practitioner outlets, including a review on strategy process research from a middle management perspective in the *Journal of Management*, co-authored with Bill Wooldridge and Steven Floyd. His research focuses on issues of corporate entrepreneurship and strategy process in large, diversified corporations, including such topics as the evolution of strategic initiatives, the development of entrepreneurial competences and the enactment of power.

Jennifer C. Sexton is a doctoral student in strategic management at the College of Business at Florida State University, USA. Her research interests are in the areas of innovation, strategic leadership, knowledge-based perspectives, and merger and acquisition integration.

Markus Venzin is an Associate Professor at the Management Department of Bocconi University, Italy and a Senior Lecturer at SDA Bocconi, Italy. He serves as Director of the Master of Science in International Management program at Bocconi University. He is the initiator and Director of the new flagship Senior Executive Program at SDA Bocconi. He chaired the organizing committee of the Academy of International Management Conference 2008 at Bocconi University, and he has held visiting positions and teaching assignments at the University of Michigan, USA; Fudan University, Shanghai, China; Copenhagen Business School, Denmark; Essec, Paris, France; ESADE, Barcelona, Spain; Steinbeis

University, Berlin, Germany; and St. Gallen University, Switzerland. Professor Venzin conducts research projects with firms that cover their internationalization strategies, the management of their subsidiary networks, their global knowledge management systems, and the development of formal planning and control processes. His current research interests include global knowledge-sharing systems in the cement industry, internationalization processes of retail banks, export strategies of small and medium sized firms, innovation and cross-border commercialization of financial service products, and the logic and processes behind cross-border mergers and acquisitions among banks. His latest book, *Internationalization of Financial Services Firms: How Successful Firms Design and Execute Cross-Border Strategies*, was published by Oxford University Press in January 2009.

Alain Verbeke is a Professor of International Business Strategy and holds the McCaig Research Chair in Management at the Haskayne School of Business, University of Calgary, Canada. He was previously the Director of the MBA program at Solvay Business School, University of Brussels (VUB), Belgium. He has also been a visiting professor at Dalhousie University, Canada, the University of Toronto, Canada and the Université Catholique de Louvain, Belgium, as well as an Associate Fellow of Templeton College, University of Oxford, UK. He is presently an Academic Associate of the Centre for International Business and Management, Judge Business School, University of Cambridge, UK.

Jorge Walter is an Assistant Professor in the School of Business at the George Washington University, USA. His research interests include strategic decision making, knowledge/technology transfer, social networks and social capital. He has examined these topics in the context of entrepreneurial firms, interfirm alliances and high-technology industries. Dr. Walter's research has been presented at numerous national and international conferences, was nominated for the 2004 Strategic Management Society Best Conference Paper Prize, and has been published in the *Academy of Management Best Paper Proceedings*, the *Journal of Management*, the *Journal of Management Studies*, the *Journal of Business Research* and *Organization Science*. Dr. Walter currently serves as a member of the editorial board of the *Journal of Management*.

Duane Windsor, Ph.D. (Harvard University, USA) is the Lynette S. Autrey Professor of Management in the Jesse H. Jones Graduate School of Business at Rice University, Houston, USA. He has been a member of the Rice faculty since 1977. He is currently editor of the quarterly journal *Business and Society*, founded in 1960 and sponsored by the International Association for Business and Society (IABS). He served as program Chair and head of IABS and then of the Social Issues in Management (SIM) Division of The Academy of Management, a leading professional association for scholars dedicated to creating and disseminating knowledge about management and organizations. Dr. Windsor has published a number of books and monographs, and a large number of scholarly papers appearing in journals, edited books, and proceedings or as conference presentations. Much of his recent work focuses on corporate social responsibility and stakeholder theory. His articles have appeared in such journals as *Business and Society*, *Business Ethics Quarterly*, *Cornell International Law Journal*, *Journal of Corporate Citizenship*, *Journal of International Management*, *Journal of Management Studies*, *Journal of Public Affairs* and *Public Administration Review*.

Robert Chapman Wood is Professor of Strategic Management in the College of Business at San Jose State University, California, USA. His research focuses on innovation processes in large organizations, on processes by which high-performing institutions emerge within human systems, and on approaches that will allow for-profit firms to organize to address societal problems such as possible global warming. Wood completed his doctoral studies at Boston University, USA and a post-doctoral fellowship at Harvard Business School, USA. Prior to his career as an academic, Wood was a journalist whose work appeared in such publications as *Forbes* and the *Financial Times* of London.

Bill Wooldridge is a Professor of Strategic Management at the Isenberg School of Management at the University of Massachusetts, Amherst, USA. His research interests in strategy process are motivated by the perspective that much of what constitutes strategy takes place within middle and operating, as opposed to top, levels of management. Current research projects explore how strategy is constructed through linked interactions between and across layers of management, and how individual-level competences and practices combine and cumulate into organizational-level capabilities. His research has been published in leading academic journals including the *Strategic Management Journal, Journal of Management, Academy of Management Executive, Journal of Management Studies* and *Entrepreneurship: Theory and Practice*. He is the co-author of two books on the strategy process. At the Ph.D. level he teaches a seminar in strategy process research and for undergraduates and MBA students offers a course on sustainable business strategies.

Li Yang is a lecturer at the management school at China Women's University in China. She received her Ph.D. from the Central University of Finance and Economics (CUFE), Beijing, China. She spent half a year as a visiting researcher at the University of Lugano in Switzerland. In addition to strategy implementation and strategic consensus, her current research interests include marketing strategy.

Paul A. Zandbergen is an Associate Professor in the Department of Geography at the University of New Mexico, USA. He obtained his Ph.D. in Resource Management and Environmental Studies in 1998 at the University of British Columbia in Vancouver, Canada. He has held positions as Assistant Professor at York University in Toronto, Canada and at the University of South Florida in Tampa, USA. Prof. Zandbergen is a Geographic Information Scientist with interests in both the fundamentals of GI Science as well as the applications of geospatial technologies to several fields, including water resources, spatial ecology, environmental health and criminal justice. His current research focuses on issues of scale, error and uncertainty in spatial analysis, as well as on the robustness of spatial analytical techniques.

Introduction
Pietro Mazzola and Franz W. Kellermanns

The editors of the *Handbook of Research on Strategy Process* are proud to add to the literature produced by Edward Elgar Publishing that brings together leading researchers in the field and allows younger, emerging scholars to showcase their research and explore new directions. The editorial team, which joined forces in 2008, selected 24 papers from among numerous excellent proposals and have organized them into four parts.

We would like to extend our heartfelt thanks to our authors, not only for their wonderful ideas and contributions but also for their willingness to work within very tight deadlines. We are also grateful to Francine O'Sullivan of Edward Elgar Publishing for her support and superb collaboration. Last but by no means least, our thanks to Claudia Gabbioneta and Diane Adams, who were immensely helpful in the editorial process. Before we discuss the organization of the book in more detail, we want to briefly reflect on strategy process research.

The distinction between strategy process and strategy content can be traced back to the great thinkers of strategic management, among them Chandler (1962), Ansoff (1965) and Andrews (1971). While strategy content focuses on the subject of the decision, strategy process focuses on actual decision making and its associated actions (Huff and Reger, 1987). Strategy process research examines the process underpinning strategy formation and implementation. Researchers in this area have demonstrated that strategy arises from the forces and activities that drive or counteract changes driven by human actions.

Strategy process has traditionally focused on top management team research (e.g., Barr, Stimpert and Huff, 1992; Bourgeois, 1980; Fredrickson and Mitchell, 1984). However, over time, the role of other organizational levels (e.g., middle management) and other units of analysis (e.g., strategic initiatives) (e.g., Bower, 1970; Burgelman, 1983; Kanter, 1982; Mintzberg and Waters, 1985; Wooldridge and Floyd, 1990) has received more attention in the literature (Hutzschenreuter and Kleindienst, 2006). The contents of this handbook reflect the growing scope and locus of strategic process research. The authors represent a multitude of disciplinary backgrounds, which affords us insights into the intellectual cutting edge of the field. Although aimed primarily at the academic community, many of the contributions speak to a wider audience.

The first section of our handbook includes essays that explore the current state of strategy process research as a whole and several challenging issues within this line of inquiry, pointing at areas for future research. The second section focuses on a central topic in the strategy literature, i.e., deliberate strategies (Mintzberg, 1987). Managerial and organizational factors affecting strategy implementation, as well as the challenges of putting strategy into practice, are closely examined. The contributions included in the third section analyse another fundamental topic of strategic management research, i.e., emergent strategies (Mintzberg, 1987). These essays focus on the antecedents and characteristics of emerging (entrepreneurial) initiatives. Finally, the essays in the fourth section explore strategy processes taking place either in different types of organizations (public, family businesses) or in different organizational circumstances (alliances, acquisitions, internationalization).

FIRST SECTION: REFLECTIONS

The essays included here review the strategy process literature, examine neglected or contested issues, and suggest possible areas for future research.

Azar and Brock offer a rich overview of strategy process research and a 'hall of fame' list of the most influential articles and authors in this area. They analyse the 200 most-cited articles in *Long Range Planning* (*LRP*) and the *Strategic Management Journal* (*SMJ*) over the period 1980–2004 and find that strategy process represents 67 percent of articles in *LRP* and 27 percent of those in *SMJ*. However, they also discover that the relative impact of strategy process research compared with other strategy areas has declined over time, and that the average impact of a strategy process article is smaller than that of other strategy articles. These apparently conflicting results lead them to conclude that although strategy process is now a well-established, internally consistent field of research, some of the questions raised deserve further investigation.

In this respect, Kleindienst and Hutzschenreuter argue that the topic of managerial discretion has received limited attention in the strategic management literature. In line with Finkelstein and Peteraf (2007), the authors differentiate between its origin and determinants. They maintain that managerial discretion depends first and foremost upon managerial cognition, as managers must be aware of an option in order to consider it, and that, as cognition changes over time, so does managerial discretion. The task environment and the internal organization, which most prior research has held responsible for the creation of options, are here seen as determinants rather than origins. The authors claim that task environment and internal organization determine which potential courses of action are available to a manager. Therefore, a high discretion context allows for multiple courses of action and a low discretion context restricts the number of potential actions. As the context is likely to change, the constraints imposed on managerial discretion vary over time.

Windsor focuses on another topic which has attracted surprisingly little attention, i.e., the internal politics of strategy process. He argues that, despite active efforts in this area, research tends to be fragmented, isolated and spread across several disciplines. He identifies, organizes and assesses these relatively disparate literatures in an attempt to establish a more coherent political dimension of strategic management. In addition, he identifies four areas into which continuing research is desirable through theory and model development, empirical testing and qualitative case studies: politics of strategy formulation, implementation and evaluation; moral issues in organizational and office politics; politics of resource allocation processes; and politics of promotion tournament competition (and similar phenomena) within organizations.

Melander, Melin and Nordqvist describe the 'strategic arena' approach for increased understanding of the internal dynamics of strategic change and how strategy processes are organized. Accordingly, strategic change is generated through dialogues between the actors that populate the strategic arena on a number of possible and arising strategic issues, with strategic action as the outcome. This approach attempts to overcome several limitations. First, whereas most strategy process research is based on second-hand and retrospective reports, the strategic arena approach focuses on real-time studies. Second, this approach considers all actors that influence the strategy process, where previous research has emphasized the importance of the CEO and the top management team. Third, rather than clearly separating process and content, this approach promotes their integration. Finally, it offers a conceptualization of strategy process that has potential for further theorizing, while most research has resulted only in rich descriptions.

Regnér combines strategy process research and the resource-based view of the firm. The author contends that social interests and interactions that underlie many contextual influences on strategy making are of importance for imitation possibilities and their subsequent economic consequences. He identifies four types of social barriers (i.e., cognitive, normative, motivational and political) that may frustrate attempts to imitate the strategy-making process of competitors. This essay contributes to the literature by showing how strategy process research not only may assist in describing and explaining how strategies develop generally, but may also be of great value when examining the specifics of how imitation behavior and firm heterogeneity develop. In addition, the author expands imitation impediment explanations by providing details of imitation barriers that involve social complexity.

Similarly, the conceptual framework developed by Coda and Mollona brings together strategy process research and a system dynamics approach (Forrester, 1961; Morecroft, 2007; Sterman, 2000). The authors focus in particular on the tension between top-down and bottom-up strategy processes and the role played by top managers in molding emergent patterns of strategic behavior. They connect both types of processes and identify a number of feedback structures that capture different strategic sub-processes. In addition, they explain the role played by managers in starting, fueling or disrupting these processes.

Schmid, Floyd and Wooldridge integrate the strategy process literature with research on the micro-foundations of strategic management. The authors argue that micro-level research leverages lessons learned in prior strategy process research conducted from a middle management perspective. Although the authors acknowledge that middle management research represents only one of several possible relevant approaches, they contend that this line of research possesses all the characteristics needed to fulfill its two basic imperatives: the need for grounding in an explicit and consistent theory of process and the need for realistic assumptions about human nature and managerial agency. A middle management perspective offers a more nuanced elaboration of the social embeddedness of human behavior, a more comprehensive anthropology that acknowledges the multifaceted character of human nature, and a more complex understanding of performance–outcome linkages.

SECOND SECTION: DELIBERATE STRATEGIES

These essays examine a key topic of strategic management research, i.e., deliberate strategies (Mintzberg, 1987). Four essays focus on the managerial and organizational factors that affect strategy implementation. The fifth illustrates the challenges of putting deliberate strategies into practice.

In their extensive review of the literature on strategy implementation, Yang, Sun and Eppler identify two types of studies: those highlighting the importance of individual factors and those that emphasize the 'big picture' of how such factors interrelate. In the first stream, they isolate nine recurring, individual factors and classify them as soft, hard or mixed. Soft factors (i.e., people oriented) include those who execute strategy, communication activities and closely related implementation tactics, and consensus on and commitment to the strategy. Hard (or institutional) factors include organizational structure and administrative systems. Mixed factors encompass the way in which the strategy was developed and articulated (strategy formulation), as well as the relationships among different units or departments and different strategy levels. The second stream of research analyses factors from a holistic or big picture perspective, either through their simple categorization or by relating them in an (often graphic) framework.

Wood and Bjelland focus on one of the nine factors identified by Yang *et al.*, i.e., implementation tactics. The authors review five alternative models of strategic reorientation processes and conclude by suggesting under what circumstances managers might choose an appropriate process. The first, standard model builds upon the work by Lewin (1951) and identifies three stages: unfreeze, change and refreeze. Strategic reorientation can also be achieved by changing the boundaries of the firm. Managers can launch a transformation by acquiring other companies that change the firm's resource portfolio or by spinning off units, so that the newly created firm can focus on a single business. Managers can create an ambidextrous organization, which includes two different units: one that can exploit a well-established business and one that can explore something radically new. There is also discovering and implementing clear, simple business concepts, a model that hinges upon the 'Good to Great' process documented by Collins (2001). Finally, recent research suggests that managed organizational change processes exist in which improvisational transformation plays a key role.

Wooldridge and Canales investigate a second factor influencing effective implementation, i.e., reciprocal actions between and across managerial levels. The authors draw from six case studies to inductively develop a model asserting associations among managerial interplay, strategic legitimacy and the realization of strategy. Managerial interplay is defined as the entire set of social interactions (both vertical and lateral) regarding strategy that generate reciprocal actions between and across managerial levels. It is through these interactions that the mutual validation and legitimization of strategy, by top- and lower-level managers, occur. Legitimacy, in turn, influences consistency between the originally intended strategy and realized strategy.

Sasson and Minoja focus on a third factor, i.e., the organization's commitment to a deliberated strategy. More precisely, the authors investigate whether exploration and exploitation volatility in organizational engagement may result in poor implementation and, thus, poor performance. The study provides evidence that volatility hampers the learning required for the attainment of ambidexterity, rendering the organization unable to reap the benefits of simultaneously executing exploration and exploitation. In addition, it demonstrates that ambidexterity mediates the relationship between volatility and firm performance.

Finally, Friga provides a vivid first-hand account of the challenges of putting strategy into practice. This essay contributes to the growing literature on the process or practice of strategy by adopting a micro-based perspective of the strategy process. Leader of the consulting unit of the University of North Carolina at Chapel Hill, the author adopts an experiential learning approach to strategy formulation and implementation, which requires the identification of theory, application to an actual phenomenon and reflection upon the process. In his essay, he moves from theory to application to reflection, in an insightful account of what makes strategy work.

THIRD SECTION: EMERGING STRATEGIES

The third section focuses on a topic at the core of much strategy research, i.e., emergent strategies (Mintzberg, 1987). Three essays investigate the antecedents and characteristics of entrepreneurial initiatives. The fourth describes the process that leads to the emergence of strategic initiatives.

Lechner and Kreutzer examine current knowledge on strategic initiatives and identify five elements that characterize their essence. First, strategic initiatives are temporary, meant to last until they fulfill their purpose or are discontinued by management. Second, they require a coordinated effort within the organization. Third, they are designed to explore new territories rather than exploit existing ones. Fourth, initiatives require organizations to alter their resources and capabilities. Fifth, they represent major undertakings that expose organizations to a high degree of internal and external risk and uncertainty. Based on these five characteristic elements, the authors define strategic initiatives as temporary, coordinated undertakings for renewing or expanding the capabilities of an organization that have the potential to substantially impact its evolution and performance. The authors also develop an organizing framework for illustrating research on strategic initiatives based on four components. The first encompasses all factors of the organizational context in which initiatives emerge and develop. Depending on initiative type, these factors might support or impede their evolution. The second component deals with all managerial practices and activities of organizational actors pursuing these initiatives. The third component consists of environmental context factors. The fourth covers performance implications. The framework is also useful in identifying areas for future research.

One area that seems to deserve further attention is the study of the factors that affect managers' propensity to engage in entrepreneurial initiatives. In this respect, Chrisman, Verbeke and Chang use prospect theory to argue that managers' willingness to assume the risk associated with entrepreneurial initiatives is dependent upon the role they assume in the entrepreneurial process. According to the authors, in deciding whether to take entrepreneurial initiatives, managers are subject to two forms of bias. The first, bias duality, refers to the tendency of corporate managers to perceive risk as desirable or undesirable according to the role they assume in the entrepreneurial process. Managers may indeed play different roles in different entrepreneurial initiatives depending on both their level in the organization and the source of the initiative. In turn, these roles determine the frame for a mental accounting of the risk of entrepreneurship. The second, bias reversal, refers to the tendency of managers to alter their mental accounting of the risk associated with an entrepreneurial initiative in accordance with changes that occur in their roles. The authors conclude that managers' biases toward the risk of corporate entrepreneurship vary according to their roles in the entrepreneurial process, and these variations affect initiative evaluation and implementation challenges.

Memili, Lumpkin and Dess explain managers' propensity to behave entrepreneurially as a result of entrepreneurial orientation. In line with prior research, the authors argue that entrepreneurial orientation – the processes, practices and decision-making styles that help firms identify and capture entrepreneurial opportunities – is the driving force of corporate entrepreneurship. Firms with a strong entrepreneurial orientation tend to enjoy competitive advantages when pursuing entrepreneurial activities of all kinds. According to the authors, entrepreneurial orientation is a multi-dimensional phenomenon consisting of autonomy, innovativeness, risk taking, pro-activeness and competitive aggressiveness. Autonomy is defined as the independent action of an individual or a team in bringing forth an idea or a vision and carrying it through to completion, as well as the ability and will to be self-directed in the pursuit of alternatives. Innovativeness represents a firm's tendency to pursue creative and novel solutions to challenges confronting the firm, including the development and enhancement of products and services, as well as new administrative techniques and technologies for performing organizational functions. Risk is perceived as exhibiting variation in the distribution of outcomes, their likelihoods and their subjective values. It is measured either by non-linearities in the revealed utility for money or by the variance of the probability distribution of possible gains and losses associated with a particular alternative. Pro-activeness encompasses not only alertness to unnoticed opportunities, but also efforts to capture these opportunities through monitoring and influencing trends, developing forward-looking activities and acting assertively regarding future needs or changes. Competitive aggressiveness represents a firm's propensity to directly and intensely challenge its competitors to achieve entry or improve position to outperform industry rivals in the marketplace.

Collectively, these studies describe the emergence of entrepreneurial initiatives as a complex process involving a number of interacting elements. According to Porter, such a process is best illustrated using concepts and ideas taken from complexity theory. The author asserts that complexity theory and complex adaptive systems provide an integrative framework that offers a robust platform for understanding the adaptive responses of firms in the face of the turbulence currently affecting most industries and environments. The adoption of such a theoretical framework implies the recognition that everything is process, as complex systems, by definition, continually evolve. In addition, conceptions of the organization's surrounding environment have to accommodate the ideas that change is universal, traditional boundaries are breaking down, and environments are increasingly information-intense, hyper-competitive and rapidly evolving (D'Aveni and Gunther, 1994).

FOURTH SECTION: SPECIAL TOPICS

The contributions here explore strategy processes taking place either in different types of organizations (e.g., public, family businesses) or in different organizational circumstances (e.g., alliances, acquisitions, internationalization).

In his essay, Walter provides an excellent review of the empirical literature on decision processes in the realm of strategic alliances and suggests several promising avenues for future research. To more systematically evaluate the accumulated body of knowledge, the author structures his review according to the framework proposed by Rajagopalan *et al.* (1993), which identifies six factors that characterize decision-making processes in strategic alliances. Any strategic decision process is embedded in both the alliance partners' external environment (first factor), such as environmental uncertainty, and the (inter)organizational environment (second factor), which comprises previous collaborations, alliance structure, partner diversity, and so on. Even within a specific collaboration, however, decision processes may vary according to differences in decision-specific factors (third factor), such as joint task complexity. These three factors influence not only the process by which decisions are made, but also decision characteristics. The decision process itself can be categorized by characteristics (fourth factor), such as procedural rationality, conflict and justice. These are associated with both process outcomes (fifth factor), such as commitment, attachment and learning, and economic outcomes (sixth factor), including alliance survival, flexibility and performance.

Ranft, Butler and Sexton argue that, while there is a rich body of research on mergers and acquisitions, research specifically examining process issues during acquisition integration is more limited and somewhat disjointed. A careful analysis of this literature reveals different dimensions of the acquisition integration process: (1) resource reconfiguration during integration, (2) autonomy and speed of integration, (3) learning, retention and communication, and (4) sensemaking and behavioral considerations. The authors maintain that there are significant gaps in our understanding of how these dimensions interact and can be effectively managed for acquisition success. They also suggest potential avenues for future research.

Cuervo-Cazurra examines the current state of research on the internationalization process, discusses challenges to traditional arguments and identifies areas of research that have previously been neglected. The author develops a framework which summarizes and integrates the key findings of prior research. Managers and their knowledge and attitude are the key drivers that determine how the characteristics of the firm, the network of the firm, the country of operation and worldwide conditions affect the internationalization process. This process takes different dimensions depending on answers to several questions. (1) Why: selling abroad, which is the commonly accepted underlying assumption of most studies, and buying from abroad, which is associated with new activities such as offshoring and the expansion of multi-national corporations (MNCs) into developing countries. (2) What: includes not only the start-up process and increased commitment in a country, but also diversification of operations and, in some cases, exit strategy. (3) How: refers to selecting between methods such as contracts, greenfield operations (internal development), alliances and acquisitions. (4) Where: refers to selecting the order of countries in which to begin operations. (5) When: refers to timing in terms of speed and pace.

Once the internationalization process has been completed, MNCs need to learn how to involve subsidiaries in strategic decision-making processes and find the right balance between subsidiary initiatives and central control. Venzin argues that power plays a pivotal role in driving strategy processes in multi-national firms. He maintains that both paternalistic and liberal management styles can co-exist, and that MNCs need to learn how to switch from one style to another depending on the desired knowledge process. While bureaucracies are more likely to foster efficient knowledge exploitation and strategy implementation, organized anarchies tend to be more effective in knowledge exploration and strategy creation. He concludes by inviting managers to reflect on the effects that static and clustered power have on knowledge exploration.

Braun and Latham focus on the gloomier subject matter of strategy process during situations of organizational decline. They argue that, while scholars maintain a low, yet steady, output of studies investigating causes and consequences of organizational decline, the manner in which the strategic process unfolds remains, to a large degree, underexplored. The authors examine different causes of decline (both internal and external to the firm) and how these causes can differently impact decision-makers' perceptions and framing of strategic responses to initiate turnaround. They argue that decision-makers' characteristics, predispositions and cognitive models significantly affect the decline process. They also consider the role of decisions concerning firm resources, leadership, governance and other strategic elements, as well as the role of various stakeholders, such as middle management, suppliers and competitors, in influencing the sequence of actions to accomplish turnaround. Finally, they theorize as to what extent the relationships among managerial perceptions, strategic formulations and organizational actions are influenced by additional considerations, both internal and external to the firm, and how those dynamic interactions affect firm outcomes.

Jennings *et al.* and Patel investigate strategy processes in public organizations. Jennings, Zandbergen and Martens argue that, although many of their features are consistent with private sector organizations and strategy processes, public sector organizations differ substantially in a few areas. They maintain that strategy in public sector organizations is normally derived primarily from their network of stakeholders and external controlling agencies and secondarily from their top management team, and that public sector organization strategies rely heavily on formal legitimacy. As a consequence, strategy processes can be better understood by adopting an institutional view. The authors argue that, from an institutional perspective, process strategy entails not only the focal firm's strategy, but also the related sets of strategies pursued by similar organizations. According to this view, a strategy is created by a key field member and then adopted by some, but not all, field members, leading to different success rates. This diffusion process is rarely smooth because it is based on the competitive positioning and counter-positioning of firms, each trying to garner social legitimacy and/or economic success. The authors elaborate on and exemplify these arguments by examining public sector process strategy in the domain of water management.

Patel examines how federal government organizations adopt strategic management concepts. The author describes their strategic management system as an interlocking set of strategic processes, including planning, programming, budgeting, executing and controlling activities. These activities enable multiple levels within the organization to achieve alignment (i.e., 'internal fit') as well as 'external fit' with applicable statute(s) enacted by the United States Congress, executive orders mandated by the Executive Office of the President, and directives and guidelines issued by various governmental Departments (e.g., Defense).

Finally, Astrachan, Richards, Marchisio and Manners suggest a new strategic management approach for family businesses. The authors elucidate a conceptual framework developed by John Boyd known as the 'OODA loop' and describe its relevance to entrepreneurial and family businesses. In its essence, the OODA loop describes an interactive (decision-maker and environment), non-sequential process that allows adaptability in making critical decisions in unpredictable, constantly changing environments. Agility – defined as the ability to keep one's dynamic world view more closely matched to the external world than that of an opponent or competitor – is a key concept that can apply to any form of conflict or competition, including business. Time is another important element, as the quicker the OODA loop is executed, the more quickly errors in orientation can be noticed and corrected, the more agile the organization can be in tracking the environment and discovering both customers' needs and changes in their preferences, and the faster the organization can respond to such changes. The authors believe that this framework is relevant to family businesses for a number of reasons. First, Boyd stresses the importance of the moral bonds that tie an organization together; moral bonds are prominent in family businesses. Second, the ultimate purpose of any system is to survive on its own terms and increase its capacity for independent action in a threatening and confusing world; the concepts of 'survival' and 'own terms' well fit family businesses. Third, organizations that want to adopt strategies described by the OODA loop need cultures that enable them to act and adapt more quickly than their competition. Prior research has shown that strong culture is a trait commonly associated with family businesses.

SUMMARY

Our book represents an impressive line of work that highlights the importance of strategy process. The authors examine family businesses, non-family firms, educational institutions and government organizations, and provide contextualized accounts of strategy process in specific organizational settings. Thus, this book serves as a reminder of the omnipresence of strategy process and the importance of gaining additional knowledge in this area. We hope to inspire readers to build on this research and further our understanding of the field.

REFERENCES

Andrews, K. R. (1971), *The Concept of Corporate Strategy*, Homewood, IL: Richard D. Irwin.

Ansoff, H. I. (1965), *Corporate Strategy: An Analytical Approach to Business Policy for Growth and Expansion*, New York: McGraw-Hill.

Barr, P. S., J. L. Stimpert and A. S. Huff (1992), 'Cognitive change, strategic action and organizational renewal', *Strategic Management Journal*, **13**: 15–36.

Bourgeois, L. J. (1980), 'Performance and consensus', *Strategic Management Journal*, **1**: 227–248.

Bower, J. L. (1970), *Managing the Resource Allocation Process*, Boston, MA: Harvard Business School Press.

Burgelman, R. A. (1983), 'A process model of internal corporate venturing in the diversified major firm', *Administrative Science Quarterly*, **28**: 223–244.

Chandler, A. (1962), *Strategy and Structure*, Cambridge, MA: MIT Press.

Collins, J. C. (2001), *Good to Great*, New York: Harper Business.

D'Aveni, R. and R. Gunther (1994), *Hypercompetition: Managing the Dynamics of Strategic Maneuvering*, New York: The Free Press.

Finkelstein, S. and M. Peteraf (2007), 'Managerial activities: A missing link in managerial discretion theory', *Strategic Organization*, **5**(4): 237–248.

Forrester, J. W. (1961), *Industrial Dynamics*, Cambridge, MA: Productivity Press.

Fredrickson, J. W. and T. R. Mitchell (1984), 'Strategic decision process: Comprehensiveness and performance in an industry with an unstable environment', *Academy of Management Journal*, **27**(2): 399–423.

Huff, A. and R. K. Reger (1987), 'A review of strategic process research', *Journal of Management*, **13**: 211–236.

Hutzschenreuter, T. and I. Kleindienst (2006), 'Strategy-process research: What have we learned and what is still to be explored', *Journal of Management*, **32**(5): 673–720.

Kanter, R. M. (1982), 'The middle manager as innovator', *Harvard Business Review*, **60**: 95–105.

Lewin, K. (1951), *Field Theory in Social Science*, New York: Harper & Row.

Mintzberg, H. (1987), 'Crafting strategy', *Harvard Business Review*, **4**: 66–75.

Mintzberg, H. and J. A. Waters (1985), 'Of strategies, deliberate and emergent', *Strategic Management Journal*, **6**: 257–272.

Morecroft, J. D. W. (2007), *Strategic Modelling and Business Dynamics. A Feedback Systems Approach*, Chichester: John Wiley and Sons.

Rajagopalan, N., A. M. A. Rasheed and D. K. Datta (1993), 'Strategic decision processes: Critical review and future directions', *Journal of Management*, **19**(2): 349–384.

Sterman, J. D. (2000), *Business Dynamics. System Thinking and Modeling for a Complex World*, Irwin Chicago, IL: McGraw-Hill.

Wooldridge, B. and Floyd, S. W. (1990), 'The strategy process, middle management involvement, and organizational performance', *Strategic Management Journal*, **11**: 231–241.

PART I

REFLECTIONS

1 The development of strategy process research and the most influential articles and authors
Ofer H. Azar and David M. Brock

INTRODUCTION

As we celebrate 40 years since the establishment of *Long Range Planning* (*LRP*), and 30 years since the first publication of the *Strategic Management Journal* (*SMJ*) and the *Journal of Business Strategy* (*JBS*), it is a good time to reflect on the development of the strategy field in general, and in particular on one of the main research areas in the field: the strategy process. Several articles have attempted to define the scope of the strategy field, to examine what has influenced it and to evaluate its development; see, for example, Evered (1983); Summer et al. (1990); Rumelt et al. (1994); Phelan et al. (2002); Nag et al. (2007); and Hambrick and Chen (2008). Common approaches in these earlier articles have been collecting data from prominent scholars and counting 'Strategy' published in management journals.

Our goal in this chapter is to focus on research on the strategy process (Huff and Reger, 1987; Pettigrew, 1992) and examine how it has changed over the years, evaluate its impact relative to other areas of strategy research, and offer a 'Hall of Fame' list of the most influential articles and authors in this area. We do so by studying a list of the most influential articles published in strategy journals during the field's formative years. We focus in our analysis on articles published in *LRP* and *SMJ*. These two journals are leaders in the two styles of academic research on strategy, with *LRP* representing an applied, practitioner-oriented approach[1] and *SMJ* representing a more theory-driven, academic-oriented approach. Our analysis does not include strategy articles that appeared in general management journals, because we want to avoid the controversial and possibly arbitrary decisions of which articles belong to the strategy field. Because *LRP* and *SMJ* focus on strategy, it is reasonable to assume that any article they published can be considered a strategy article. We use data on the top-cited articles in *LRP* and *SMJ* to analyse the impact and characteristics of articles about the strategy process and also to compare them with articles in other areas of strategy.

The rest of the chapter is organized as follows. The next section describes the data and our methodology. Then the extent and impact of strategy process research compared with other strategy areas are analysed. The following section examines quantitative article characteristics such as the number of authors, pages and references in various periods. The most-cited articles and authors are then presented, and the last section concludes.

DATA AND METHODS

To choose which journals to analyse, we wanted to have journals that satisfy two criteria. First, they have to be included in the Social Sciences Citation Index (SSCI) for at least 20 years. The SSCI is a database that covers over 1700 leading scholarly social sciences journals in more than 50 disciplines, including many management journals. Inclusion in the SSCI is necessary not only because it testifies about the good quality of a journal, but also because the SSCI is the source of information about citations to the journal's articles, which is essential for our analysis.

Second, we limited attention to journals that focus on strategic management and did not consider strategy articles that appeared in general management journals. The reason is that including general management journals implies that we have to decide for each article whether it is about strategy or not. The results are then sensitive to our personal opinions about what is strategy and to arbitrary decisions about how much an article has to deal with strategy in order to be classified as a strategy article.

LRP and *SMJ* are the only journals that satisfied the two criteria. *LRP* has been included in the SSCI since 1968 except for 1970; *SMJ* has been covered since its inception in 1980. The only other strategy journals that are covered by SSCI (*Advances in Strategic Management*, *Journal of Economics & Management Strategy* and *Technology Analysis & Strategic Management*) are covered only from 1994 or later (which does not leave a sufficient number of years to examine the development of research over time). Moreover, there are additional reasons for not including these journals: *Technology Analysis & Strategic Management* and the *Journal of Economics & Management Strategy* are dedicated to very specific niches of strategy research (as opposed to *LRP* and *SMJ*), and in particular to niches that are not very related to the strategy process, which is our focus. *Advances in Strategic Management*, on the other hand, is an annual publication and not a regular journal.

When choosing which period to analyse, we decided to start in 1980

Table 1.1   *Percentage of articles dealing primarily with the strategy process*

Period / Journal	1980– 1984 (%)	1985– 1989 (%)	1990– 1994 (%)	1995– 1999 (%)	2000– 2004 (%)	Total (%)
LRP	85	80	65	40	65	**67**
SMJ	50	20	15	30	20	**27**
Combined	68	50	40	35	43	**47**

because this is the year in which *SMJ* was first published. Because we use citations to identify the most influential strategy articles, we need to leave enough time for articles to get a chance to be cited. Thus we only include articles published no later than 2004. We then divided the period 1980–2004 into five consecutive periods of five years in order to analyse changes over time.

In order to determine what were the most influential articles we used the common measure of citations received by the article. When an article is cited, it usually implies that it has contributed to the relevant literature, and therefore the number of citations that an article receives is a commonly used indication of its significance. Citation counts are also often used to evaluate the quality and contribution of a researcher, an institution or a journal. We use the SSCI database to examine the number of citations received by each article published in *LRP* and *SMJ* over the period 1980–2004. For each five-year period, we then constructed a database that includes the 20 most-cited articles that appeared in *LRP* and the 20 most-cited ones from *SMJ*.

Each of these 200 articles (40 in each five-year period) then went through a process of classification as follows: A definitional description of 'strategy process research' (versus other research categories like 'strategy content' – see Azar and Brock (2008) was formulated against which articles could be classified. These definitions were based on those reported in Nag et al. (2007). Thus process research includes 'Planning, innovation, learning, structuring, alliance formation, implementation, scenarios, forecasting and environmental scanning'. The classifications were done by a strategy professor with over 20 years' experience in this field. The method included studying relevant sections of each article to decide for each whether its primary research focus was included in the strategy process category. Table 1.1 presents a summary of how the articles were classified for each journal, for each of the five-year periods and in total.

THE EXTENT AND IMPACT OF STRATEGY PROCESS RESEARCH COMPARED WITH OTHER STRATEGY AREAS

Early review articles on strategic management emphasized the centrality of and distinction between content research (e.g., Fahey and Christensen, 1986; Montgomery, 1988) and process research (e.g., Boal and Bryson, 1987; Huff and Reger, 1987). Our analysis, reported in Table 1.1, also supports the importance of the strategy process as one of the core areas of strategic management. About two thirds of *LRP* articles and over a quarter of *SMJ* articles in the sample are concerned mainly with strategy process topics. The most common topics of the most highly cited articles concerned issues of 'strategy making' – for example, Hambrick (1982), Miller and Friesen (1983), Mintzberg and Waters (1985), Prahalad and Bettis (1986), Rosenkopf and Nerkar (2001) and Schwenk (1984) – and 'learning' – for example, Anand and Khanna (2000), Hamel (1991), Lane et al. (2001), Levinthal and March (1993) and Winter (2000).

In *LRP* we see a particularly strong focus on the strategy process in the 1980s. These articles often involved topics such as environmental scanning, scenarios and other strategic planning tools. In the 1990s, *LRP* articles include a broader variety of approaches to organizational and managerial issues and to functional processes. The percentage of *LRP* articles on the strategy process generally declined between 1980 and 1999, but in 2000–2004 we see a large increase in this percentage compared with the previous period (65 percent versus 40 percent). In *SMJ* the percentage of strategy process articles is lower than in *LRP*. It is particularly high in 1980–1984 (50 percent) but then it drops to 15–30 percent in the other periods. Still, this is a significant percentage showing the importance of the strategy process.

The relative impact of strategy process articles compared with articles on other topics can be evaluated by analysing the citations received by the articles in the sample. Table 1.2 reports the total number of citations received by strategy process articles and by the other articles in the sample for the various periods. The percentage of citations received by strategy process articles is generally declining over time in both journals, with the increase from 1995–1999 to 2000–2004 being an exception in *LRP* and the increase from 1990–1994 to 1995–1999 being an exception in *SMJ*.

Because the number of citations received is affected by the number of articles in each area, it is also interesting to examine whether the per-article impact of strategy process articles is declining over time. Table 1.3 reports the average number of citations per article. Here the picture is more complex. In both *LRP* and *SMJ* we can see an increase in per-article

Table 1.2   Total number of citations

Period Journal and topic	1980– 1984	1985– 1989	1990– 1994	1995– 1999	2000– 2004	Total
LRP – strategy process	335	395	348	153	170	**1401**
LRP – other topics	47	129	224	268	124	**792**
LRP – % strategy process	**88%**	**75%**	**61%**	**36%**	**58%**	**64%**
SMJ – strategy process	1066	1096	1035	1335	282	**4814**
SMJ – other topics	2536	3555	4603	3523	1673	**15890**
SMJ – % strategy process	**30%**	**24%**	**18%**	**27%**	**14%**	**23%**

Table 1.3   Average number of citations per article

Period Journal and topic	1980– 1984	1985– 1989	1990– 1994	1995– 1999	2000– 2004	Total
LRP – strategy process	19.7	24.7	26.8	19.1	13.1	**20.9**
LRP – other topics	15.7	32.3	32	22.3	17.7	**24**
LRP – ratio process/other	**1.25**	**0.76**	**0.84**	**0.86**	**0.74**	**0.87**
SMJ – strategy process	106.6	274	345	222.5	70.5	**178.3**
SMJ – other topics	253.6	222.2	270.8	251.6	104.6	**217.7**
SMJ – ratio process/other	**0.42**	**1.23**	**1.27**	**0.88**	**0.67**	**0.82**

citations of strategy process articles until 1990–1994, and then a decrease. This is also the general pattern in articles not on the strategy process, with the exception of the decrease from 1980–1984 to 1985–1989 in *SMJ* and the decrease from 1985–1989 to 1990–1994 in *LRP*.

Table 1.4   Average number of citations per article per year since publication

Period Journal and topic	1980– 1984	1985– 1989	1990– 1994	1995– 1999	2000– 2004	Total
LRP – strategy process	0.8	1.2	1.8	1.8	2.5	**1.5**
LRP – other topics	0.7	1.7	2.1	2.1	2.9	**2.1**
LRP – ratio process/ other	**1.14**	**0.71**	**0.86**	**0.86**	**0.86**	**0.71**
SMJ – strategy process	4.3	12.8	22.8	19.9	10.9	**12.1**
SMJ – other topics	10.6	11.5	18.7	24.9	15.4	**16.5**
SMJ – ratio process/ other	**0.41**	**1.11**	**1.22**	**0.80**	**0.71**	**0.73**

Note: Average number of citations per year is computed for each article separately by dividing the number of citations the article received by the number of years since its publication (until 2007). This number is then averaged over the relevant articles.

Next, let us examine what is the average impact of strategy process articles versus other articles. The ratio between the average per-article number of citations in strategy process articles and this number in other topics is also provided in Table 1.3. This ratio shows that in *LRP* the impact of a strategy process article was higher than that of other articles in 1980–1984, but this was reversed after 1985. This ratio in *LRP* is then relatively stable from 1985, in the range of 0.74–0.86. In *SMJ*, the pattern is different. We see a large increase (almost by a factor of three) in the ratio between the first two periods, then some stability, and a reduction in this ratio after 1990. The overall impact, given in the 'Total' column, indicates that over the period 1980–2004, in both journals the impact of a strategy process article was lower than that of other articles.

While the increase in the per-article citations of strategy process articles until 1990–1994 suggests unambiguously that in 1980–1994 later articles became more cited than earlier ones (on average), the interpretation of the decrease since then is more difficult. It may be a result of later articles having less time to get cited. Therefore we report in Table 1.4 the number of per-article citations per year since publication (see the details in the Note for the table). In *LRP* we can see that indeed once the number of years in which an article could be cited is taken into account, there is no decrease in the impact of strategy process articles – this impact goes up with time, from 0.8 in 1980–1984 to 2.5 in 2000–2004. The same pattern is documented for other *LRP* articles. In *SMJ*, on the other hand, even after accounting for the number of years since publication, there is a decline in the impact of strategy process articles after 1990–1994 (after an increase until this period); for other articles the decline starts after 1995–1999.

Comparing the impact of strategy process articles with other articles, the patterns are generally similar to those in Table 1.3. In particular, in *LRP* we find that strategy process articles are more influential in 1980–1984 but this is reversed later; and in *SMJ* the ratio between the impact of strategy process to other articles increases until 1990–1994 but declines afterwards. Over the entire period 1980–2004 we see again that strategy process articles have a lower impact than other articles.

ARTICLE QUANTITATIVE CHARACTERISTICS: NUMBER OF AUTHORS, PAGES AND REFERENCES

So far we have examined how the extent of research on the strategy process and its impact changed over time, in general and in comparison with articles not dealing with the strategy process. Now we turn to analyse how several other characteristics of strategy process articles, namely the number of authors, pages and references, changed over time. Table 1.5 reports the results.

Regarding the number of authors, in *LRP* we see a stability of about 1.4–1.5 authors per article until 1994, and then a gradual increase up to

Table 1.5   Characteristics of strategy process articles

Period / Journal	1980–1984	1985–1989	1990–1994	1995–1999	2000–2004
Average number of authors					
LRP	1.5	1.4	1.5	1.8	2.1
SMJ	1.5	2.0	1.7	1.3	2.0
Average number of pages					
LRP	8.8	8.8	11.6	9.6	20.1
SMJ	18.0	15.0	18.3	20.0	20.0
Average number of references					
LRP	17.5	17.3	17.9	12.8	36.7
SMJ	37.3	56.0	63.0	75.0	59.0

2.1 in 2000–2004. In *SMJ* it is hard to discern any systematic pattern. The number of pages of each article is relatively stable in *LRP* until 1999 (between 8.8 and 11.6 on average), although it is higher in 1990–1994 than in the other periods before 1999. However, in 2000–2004 we see a remarkable increase to 20.1 pages per article; this increase is a result of the change in editorial policy in *LRP* towards being more academically oriented and less practitioner oriented. In *SMJ* the number of pages is relatively stable in all periods, with 1985–1989 being an exception, with only 15 pages on average (compared with 18–20 in the other periods). The number of references in *LRP* is stable in the first three periods (around 17–18 references), is particularly low in 1995–1999 (12.8) and increases dramatically in the last period to 36.7 – again as a result of the journal's change to a more academic orientation. In *SMJ* the number of references doubled from 1980–1984 to 1995–1999 (75.0 versus 37.3 references), but then declined to 59.0 in 2000–2004. The increase until 1999 might have resulted from changing expectations about how extensive the literature review should be, or from the body of knowledge increasing over time, resulting in a larger number of relevant articles to cite.

STRATEGY PROCESS MOST-CITED ARTICLES AND AUTHORS

Now we turn to establishing the 'Strategy Process Hall of Fame'. Table 1.6 presents the most-cited strategy process articles. Because earlier articles have more time to get cited, it is more informative to examine the most-cited articles separately for each five-year period. We can see that even though articles from the 1980s had more time to get cited than later articles, the three most-cited articles are from the 1990s (Grant, 1996; Hamel, 1991; Levinthal and March, 1993). Further, none of the eight most-cited articles is from the 1980–1984 period. In addition, the dominance of *SMJ* over *LRP* is clear: in each period, all *SMJ* citations are higher than those for *LRP*.

Finally, let us examine the most prolific authors in strategy process. In the case of a co-authored article written by N authors, each author is credited for $1/N$ of the citations. This is the common practice in the literature (e.g., Scott and Mitias, 1996; Dusansky and Vernon, 1998; Coupe, 2003; Kalaitzidakis et al., 2003). The idea behind this practice is that when an article is written by several authors, the total credit for the article should not be different from a single-author article, and therefore the credit should be divided among the authors. This also reflects the idea that when the article has more authors, the work is divided between them

Table 1.6   Most-cited articles on the strategy process

Journal	Authors	Title	Year	Times cited
		1980–84		
SMJ	Miller, D.; Friesen, P.H.	Innovation in conservative and entrepreneurial firms – 2 models of strategic momentum	1982	171
SMJ	Miller, D.; Friesen, P.H.	Strategy-making and environment – the third link	1983	163
SMJ	Schwenk, C.R.	Cognitive simplification processes in strategic decision-making	1984	151
SMJ	Hambrick, D.C.	Environmental scanning and organizational strategy	1982	120
SMJ	Dutton, J.E.; Fahey, L.; Narayanan, V.K.	Toward understanding strategic issue diagnosis	1983	111
SMJ	Armstrong, J.S.	The value of formal planning for strategic decisions – review of empirical research	1982	79
SMJ	Hambrick, D.C.	Strategic awareness within top management teams	1981	74
SMJ	Ansoff, H.I.	Strategic issue management	1980	68
SMJ	Lyles, M.A.	Formulating strategic problems – empirical analysis and model development	1981	67
SMJ	Bourgeois, L.J.; Brodwin, D.R.	Strategic implementation – 5 approaches to an elusive phenomenon	1984	62
		1985–1989		
SMJ	Mintzberg, H.; Waters, J.A.	Of strategies, deliberate and emergent	1985	344
SMJ	Prahalad, C.K.; Bettis, R.A.	The dominant logic – a new linkage between diversity and performance	1986	336
SMJ	Huber, G.P.; Power, D.J.	Retrospective reports of strategic-level managers – guidelines for increasing their accuracy	1985	242

Table 1.6   (continued)

Journal	Authors	Title	Year	Times cited
SMJ	Dutton, J.E.; Duncan, R.B.	The creation of momentum for change through the process of strategic issue diagnosis	1987	174
LRP	Gummesson, E.	The new marketing – developing long-term interactive relationships	1987	84
LRP	Scott, M.; Bruce, R.	5 stages of growth in small business	1987	38
LRP	King, W.R.	How effective is your information-systems planning?	1988	37
LRP	David, F.R.	How companies define their mission	1989	33
LRP	Schnaars, S.P.	How to develop and use scenarios	1987	29
LRP	Nueno, P.; Oosterveld, J.	Managing technology alliances	1988	21
		1990–1994		
SMJ	Hamel, G.	Competition for competence and inter-partner learning within international strategic alliances	1991	487
SMJ	Levinthal, D.A.; March, J.G.	The myopia of learning	1993	404
SMJ	Gioia, D.A.; Chittipeddi, K.	Sensemaking and sensegiving in strategic change initiation	1991	144
LRP	Bolwijn, P.T.; Kumpe, T.	Manufacturing in the 1990s – productivity, flexibility and innovation	1990	43
LRP	Johnson, G.	Managing strategic change – strategy, culture and action	1992	40
LRP	Talwar, R.	Business reengineering – a strategy-driven approach	1993	35
LRP	Premkumar, G.; King, W.R.	Assessing strategic information-systems planning	1991	35
LRP	Campbell, A.; Yeung, S.	Creating a sense of mission	1991	28

Table 1.6   (continued)

Journal	Authors	Title	Year	Times cited
LRP	Mintzberg, H.	Rethinking strategic planning. 1. pitfalls and fallacies	1994	26
LRP	Piercy, N.; Morgan, N.	Internal marketing – the missing half of the marketing program	1991	23
		1995–1999		
SMJ	Grant, R.M.	Toward a knowledge-based theory of the firm	1996	497
SMJ	Powell, T.C.	Total quality management as competitive advantage – a review and empirical study	1995	249
SMJ	Sanchez, R.; Mahoney, J.T.	Modularity, flexibility, and knowledge management in product and organization design	1996	165
SMJ	Christensen, C.M.; Bower, J.L.	Customer power, strategic investment, and the failure of leading firms	1996	164
SMJ	Dyer, J.H.	Effective interfirm collaboration: how firms minimize transaction costs and maximize transaction value	1997	131
SMJ	Sanchez, R.	Strategic flexibility in product competition	1995	129
LRP	Whittington, R.	Strategy as practice	1996	27
LRP	Willcocks, L.; Fitzgerald, G.; Feeny, D.	Outsourcing it – the strategic implications	1995	20
LRP	Godet, M.; Roubelat, F.	Creating the future: the use and misuse of scenarios	1996	19
LRP	Lane, D.; Maxfield, R.	Strategy under complexity: fostering generative relationships	1996	19
		2000–2004		
SMJ	Anand, B.N.; Khanna, T.	Do firms learn to create value? the case of alliances	2000	93
SMJ	Rosenkopf, L.; Nerkar, A.	Beyond local search: boundary-spanning, exploration, and impact in the optical disk industry	2001	69

Table 1.6   (continued)

Journal	Authors	Title	Year	Times cited
SMJ	Lane, P.J.; Salk, J.E.; Lyles, M.A.	Absorptive capacity, learning, and performance in international joint ventures	2001	65
SMJ	Winter, S.G.	The satisficing principle in capability learning	2000	55
LRP	Teece, D.J.	Strategies for managing knowledge assets: the role of firm structure and industrial context	2000	40
LRP	Volberda, H.W.; Baden-Fuller, C.; Van den Bosch, F.A.J.	Mastering strategic renewal – mobilising renewal journeys in multi-unit firms	2001	22
LRP	Mezias, J.M.; Grinyer, P.; Guth, W.D.	Changing collective cognition: a process model for strategic change	2001	15
LRP	Miles, R.E.; Snow, C.C.; Miles, G.	The Future.org	2000	15
LRP	Sadler-Smith, E.; Spicer, D.P.; Chaston, L.	Learning orientations and growth in smaller firms	2001	13
LRP	Calori, R.; Baden-Fuller, C.; Hunt, B.	Managing change at Novotel: back to the future	2000	9

and therefore it is fair to give an author more credit for a single-authored paper than for a co-authored one. Overall, the 94 strategy process articles in the sample were authored by 137 different authors. Table 1.7 reports the ranking of the top 50 in terms of total citations (with adjustments for co-authorship as explained above). However, because authors of early articles had more time to get cited than authors of later articles, another meaningful measure of an author's impact is to count the average number of citations received per year. This is done by dividing the number of citations an article received by the number of years since its publication (until 2007), and then taking for each author the sum of the per-year citations of

Table 1.7   Most-cited authors on the strategy process

Rank of total citations	Author	Total citations	Total citations per year	Rank of total citations per year
1	Grant, R.M.	515.0	46.98	1
2	Hamel, G.	487.0	30.44	2
3	Powell, T.C.	249.0	20.75	3
4	Mintzberg, H.	215.0	11.13	8
5	Sanchez, R.	211.5	18.25	4
6	Levinthal, D.A.	202.0	14.43	5
6	March, J.G.	202.0	14.43	5
8	Hambrick, D.C.	194.0	7.65	13
9	Prahalad, C.K.	176.0	10.67	9
10	Waters, J.A.	172.0	7.82	12
11	Bettis, R.A.	168.0	8.00	10
12	Friesen, P.H.	167.0	6.82	17
12	Miller, D.	167.0	6.82	17
14	Schwenk, C.R.	151.0	6.57	21
15	Dyer, J.H.	131.0	13.10	7
16	Dutton, J.E.	124.0	5.89	23
17	Huber, G.P.	121.0	5.50	27
17	Power, D.J.	121.0	5.50	27
19	Lyles, M.A.	88.7	6.19	22
20	Duncan, R.B.	87.0	4.35	31
21	Gummesson, E.	84.0	4.20	32
22	Mahoney, J.T.	82.5	7.50	14
23	Bower, J.L.	82.0	7.45	15
23	Christensen, C.M.	82.0	7.45	15
25	Armstrong, J.S.	79.0	3.16	36
26	King, W.R.	75.8	3.88	33
27	Chittipeddi, K.	72.0	4.50	29
27	Gioia, D.A.	72.0	4.50	29
29	Ansoff, H.I.	68.0	2.52	38
30	Winter, S.G.	55.0	7.86	11
31	Anand, B.N.	46.5	6.64	19
31	Khanna, T.	46.5	6.64	19
33	Fahey, L.	44.3	1.82	42
33	Narayanan, V.K.	44.3	1.82	42
35	Johnson, G.	40.0	2.67	37
35	Teece, D.J.	40.0	5.71	26
37	Kirton, M.J.	39.0	1.70	45
38	Talwar, R.	35.0	2.50	39
39	Nerkar, A.	34.5	5.75	24

Table 1.7   (continued)

Rank of total citations	Author	Total citations	Total citations per year	Rank of total citations per year
39	Rosenkopf, L.	34.5	5.75	24
41	David, F.R.	33.0	1.83	41
42	Thomas, P.S.	32.0	1.19	66
43	Bourgeois, L.J.	31.0	1.35	50
43	Brodwin, D.R.	31.0	1.35	50
45	Jain, S.C.	29.0	1.26	62
45	Schnaars, S.P.	29.0	1.45	47
47	Whittington, R.	27.0	2.45	40
48	Eden, C.	23.0	1.35	49
49	Cooper, A.C.	22.0	0.85	79
49	Goldsmith, N.	22.0	1.38	48

Note: For a co-authored article written by N authors, each author is credited for $1/N$ of the citations. The per-year number of citations is computed by dividing the number of citations the article received by the number of years since its publication (until 2007). Both rankings (total citations and total citations per year) are among the 137 authors included in the sample.

the papers (adjusted for co-authorship). This measure and the ranking of authors based on it are also reported in Table 1.7.

CONCLUSIONS

The main goals of this chapter have been to analyse the relative impact of strategy process research over time and to rank the most influential articles and authors in this area. To do so we analysed the 200 most-cited articles in *LRP* and *SMJ* over the period 1980–2004. We find that the strategy process is a very central research area in both journals: 67 per cent of the most-cited articles in *LRP* and 27 per cent of those in *SMJ* deal primarily with topics related to the strategy process. However, we also find that, in most periods, the relative impact of strategy process research compared with other strategy areas has declined over time. In addition, the average impact of a strategy process article is smaller than the average impact of other strategy articles (see Table 1.4). This is likely a leading indicator of the trend mentioned above, namely the general decline in strategy process research relative to other topics. This decline is quite natural: as a field matures it is expected that central/core topics like process will attract less attention relative to emerging topics; and in fact we see that newer areas such as the resource-based view of the firm and organizational types (like joint ventures and networks) gained prominence in the 1980s and beyond (Azar and Brock, 2008).

Putting the numbers and trends aside, there is no doubt that issues of the strategy process remain crucial to strategic management. Although Mintzberg (1994b) warns that strategic processes may often be like rain dances – in that they are more concerned with the quality of the planning (dancing) than the resulting strategic outcome (rain) – his call underlines the centrality of the topic, and simply warns scholars to keep the essence in focus. Thus we may be intrigued by state-of-the-art approaches to scenarios or forecasting, but should not lose sight of the fundamental connections between these strategy processes, the quality of information absorbed by planners, and their appropriate interpretation into plans and strategies. While the era of skepticism in planning processes in general (see Mintzberg, 1994a, b) seems to have passed, Brock and Barry (2003) emphasize how planning systems need to be aligned to strategy for overall organizational effectiveness.

As the strategy field approaches maturity and the above-mentioned anniversaries of key strategy journals come and go, it is natural to look back as well as forward. Studies such as this one that look back over the field's development are valuable because they enable a wider audience to understand a field's evolution, constituent parts and research approaches (also see Acedo et al., 2006; Baum, 2009; Cummings and Daellenbach, 2009; Hambrick and Chen, 2008; Podsakoff et al., 2008; Shane, 1997). The list of most-cited articles might be useful for any researcher entering the strategy field and others who become interested in the strategy process area to make sure they are aware of these highly influential articles.

Future research should investigate which areas of the strategy field are underdeveloped relative to the needs of key constituents. For example, it may be that top managers need more direction to help them in issues of planning process, while MBA students need better content constructs. Another idea for future research is to conduct studies similar to the research reported here, on other areas of strategy – as well as on other areas of management. It may be interesting to know which fields in strategy and management were published more frequently than others and which areas were cited more often. What are the topics in which interest declined over time, and is there a common characteristic to all of them (and similarly for topics that gained interest)? Do we identify a change in the topics covered in top strategy and management journals when the journals' editors change? Finally, a natural idea to be implemented in another decade or two is to re-examine the development of strategy process research in light of the additional years of data available by that time.

We want to end by discussing some of the limitations of this study. As we mentioned above, we did not consider strategy articles that appeared in general management journals, because including general management journals requires deciding for each article whether it is about strategy or not. The results will then be sensitive to our personal opinions about what is strategy and to arbitrary decisions about the extent to which an article has to deal with strategy in order to be considered a strategy article. Nevertheless, the fact that much strategy research is published in general management journals and those are not covered in our study is a limitation that we should bear in mind. Another limitation is that our scope was such that we did not classify the strategy process articles into finer categories. Such research that looks at the sub-areas of the strategy process literature may be interesting to conduct in the future. Also, we looked only at the most-cited articles. The justifications for doing so were that classifying articles is time consuming and should be done by someone very knowledgeable in the field (i.e., we did not want to delegate this task to a research assistant); and that these highly cited articles obviously influenced the field much more than their little-cited counterparts. Nevertheless, one should remember that the study is based on these highly cited articles and not on all articles published by *LRP* and *SMJ* during 1980–2004. A study that includes a larger sample of articles with a less stringent criterion for inclusion than we employed will require a lot of work but may yield some additional insights we could not obtain with our sample. Finally, the lack of authentication of the article classification mechanism is another limitation of this study.

NOTE

1. *LRP* reoriented itself towards a more scholarly approach in 2002. Because we analyse the period 1980–2004, however, *LRP* generally represents the more applied approach to strategy research.

REFERENCES

References marked with an asterisk are those that appear in Table 1.6 (most-cited articles on the strategy process).
Acedo, F. J., C. Barroso, C. Casanueva and J. L. Galan (2006), 'Co-authorship in management and organizational studies: an empirical and network analysis', *Journal of Management Studies*, **43**(5): 957–983.

*Anand, B. N. and T. Khanna (2000), 'Do firms learn to create value? The case of alliances', *Strategic Management Journal*, **21**: 295–315.

*Ansoff, H. I. (1980), 'Strategic issue management', *Strategic Management Journal*, **1**(2): 131–148.

*Armstrong, J. S. (1982), 'The value of formal planning for strategic decisions – review of empirical research', *Strategic Management Journal*, **3**(3): 197–211.

Azar, O. H. and D. M. Brock (2008), 'A citation-based ranking of strategic management journals', *Journal of Economics & Management Strategy*, **17**(3): 781–802.

Baum, J. (2009), 'Editorial: The seven year itch', *Strategic Organization*, **7**(1): 5–10.

Boal, K. B. and J. H. Bryson (1987), 'Representations, testing and policy implications of planning processes', *Strategic Management Journal*, **8**: 211–231.

*Bolwijn, P. T. and T. Kumpe (1990), 'Manufacturing in the 1990s – productivity, flexibility and innovation', *Long Range Planning*, **23**(4): 44–57.

*Bourgeois, L. J. and D. R. Brodwin (1984), 'Strategic implementation – 5 approaches to an elusive phenomenon', *Strategic Management Journal*, **5**(3): 241–264.

Brock, D. M. and D. Barry (2003), 'What if planning were really strategic? Exploring the strategy-planning relationship in multinationals', *International Business Review*, **12**(5): 543–561.

*Calori, R., C. Baden-Fuller and B. Hunt (2000), 'Managing change at Novotel: Back to the future', *Long Range Planning*, **33**(6): 779–804.

*Campbell, A. and S. Yeung (1991), 'Creating a sense of mission', *Long Range Planning*, **24**(4): 10–20.

*Christensen, C. M. and J. L. Bower (1996), 'Customer power, strategic investment, and the failure of leading firms', *Strategic Management Journal*, **17**(3): 197–218.

Coupe, T. (2003), 'Revealed performances: Worldwide rankings of economists and economics departments, 1990–2000', *Journal of the European Economic Association*, **1**: 1309–1345.

Cummings, S. and U. Daellenbach (2009), 'A guide to the future of strategy? The history of long range planning', *Long Range Planning*, **42**(2): 234–263

*David, F. R. (1989), 'How companies define their mission', *Long Range Planning*, **22**(1): 90–97.

Dusansky, R. and C. J. Vernon (1998), 'Rankings of U.S. economics departments', *Journal of Economic Perspectives*, **12**: 157–170.

*Dutton, J. E. and R. B. Duncan (1987), 'The creation of momentum for change through the process of strategic issue diagnosis', *Strategic Management Journal*, **8**(3): 279–295.

*Dutton, J. E., L. Fahey and V. K. Narayanan (1983), 'Toward understanding strategic issue diagnosis', *Strategic Management Journal*, **4**(4): 307–323.

*Dyer, J. H. (1997), 'Effective interfirm collaboration: How firms minimize transaction costs and maximize transaction value', *Strategic Management Journal*, **18**(7): 535–556.

Evered, R. (1983), 'So what is strategy?', *Long Range Planning*, **16**: 52–72.

Fahey, L. and H. K. Christensen (1986), 'Evaluating the research on strategy content', *Journal of Management*, **12**: 167–183.

*Gioia, D. A. and K. Chittipeddi (1991), 'Sensemaking and sensegiving in strategic change initiation', *Strategic Management Journal*, **12**(6): 433–448.

*Godet, M. and F. Roubelat (1996), 'Creating the future: The use and misuse of scenarios', *Long Range Planning*, **29**(2): 164–171.

*Grant, R. M. (1996), 'Toward a knowledge-based theory of the firm', *Strategic Management Journal*, **17**: 109–122.

*Gummesson, E. (1987), 'The new marketing – developing long-term interactive relationships', *Long Range Planning*, **20**(4): 10–20.

Hambrick, D. C. (1981), 'Strategic awareness within top management teams', *Strategic Management Journal*, **2**(3): 263–279.

*Hambrick, D. C. (1982), 'Environmental scanning and organizational strategy', *Strategic Management Journal*, **3**: 159–174.

Hambrick, D. C. and M.-J. Chen (2008), 'New academic fields as admittance-seeking social movements: The case of Strategic Management', *Academy of Management Review*, **33**: 32–54.

*Hamel, G. (1991), 'Competition for competence and inter-partner learning within international strategic alliances', *Strategic Management Journal*, **12**: 83–103.

*Huber, G. P. and D. J. Power (1985), 'Retrospective reports of strategic-level managers - guidelines for increasing their accuracy', *Strategic Management Journal*, **6**(2): 171–180.

Huff, A. and R. Reger (1987), 'A review of strategic process research', *Journal of Management*, **13**: 211–236.

*Johnson, G. (1992), 'Managing strategic change – strategy, culture and action', *Long Range Planning*, **25**(1): 28–36.

Kalaitzidakis, P., T. P. Mamuneas and T. Stengos (2003), 'Rankings of academic journals and institutions in economics', *Journal of the European Economic Association*, **1**: 1346–1366.

*King, W. R. (1988), 'How effective is your information-systems planning?', *Long Range Planning*, **21**(5): 103–112.

*Lane, D. and R. Maxfield (1996), 'Strategy under complexity: Fostering generative relationships', *Long Range Planning*, **29**(2): 215–231.

*Lane, P. J., J. E. Salk and M. A. Lyles (2001), 'Absorptive capacity, learning, and performance in international joint ventures', *Strategic Management Journal*, **22**: 1139–1161.

*Levinthal, D. A. and J. G. March (1993), 'The myopia of learning', *Strategic Management Journal*, **14**: 95–112.

*Lyles, M. A. (1981), 'Formulating strategic problems – empirical analysis and model development', *Strategic Management Journal*, **2**(1): 61–75.

*Mezias, J. M., P. Grinyer and W. D. Guth (2001), 'Changing collective cognition: A process model for strategic change', *Long Range Planning*, **34**(1): 71–95.

*Miles, R. E., C. C. Snow and G. Miles (2000), 'The Future.org', *Long Range Planning*, **33**(3): 300–321.

*Miller, D. and P. H. Friesen (1982), 'Innovation in conservative and entrepreneurial firms – 2 models of strategic momentum', *Strategic Management Journal*, **3**(1): 1–25.

*Miller, D. and P. H. Friesen (1983), 'Strategy-making and environment – the third link', *Strategic Management Journal*, **4**: 221–235.

*Mintzberg, H. (1994a), 'Rethinking strategic planning. 1. Pitfalls and fallacies', *Long Range Planning*, **27**(3): 12–21.

Mintzberg, H. (1994b), *The Rise and Fall of Strategic Planning*, New York: The Free Press.

*Mintzberg, H. and J. A. Waters (1985), 'Of strategies, deliberate and emergent', *Strategic Management Journal*, **6**: 257–272.

Montgomery, C. A. (1988), 'Guest editor's introduction to the special issue on research in the content of strategy', *Strategic Management Journal*, **9**: 3–8.

Nag, R., D. C. Hambrick and M.-J. Chen (2007), 'What is strategic management, really? Inductive derivation of a consensus definition of the field', *Strategic Management Journal*, **28**: 935–955.

*Nueno, P. and J. Oosterveld (1988), 'Managing technology alliances', *Long Range Planning*, **21**(3): 11–17.

Pettigrew, A. M. (1992), 'The character and significance of strategy process research', *Strategic Management Journal*, **13**(Winter Special Issue): 5–16.

Phelan, S. E., M. Ferreira and R. Salvador (2002), 'The first twenty years of the Strategic Management Journal', *Strategic Management Journal*, **23**: 1161–1168.

*Piercy, N. and N. Morgan (1991), 'Internal marketing – the missing half of the marketing program', *Long Range Planning*, **24**(2): 82–93.

Podsakoff, P. M., S. B. MacKenzie, N. P. Podsakoff and D. G. Bachrach (2008), 'Scholarly influence in the field of management: A bibliometric analysis of the determinants of university and author impact in the management literature in the past quarter century', *Journal of Management*, **34**(4): 641–720.

*Powell, T. C. (1995), 'Total quality management as competitive advantage – a review and empirical study', *Strategic Management Journal*, **16**(1): 15–37.

*Prahalad, C. K. and R. A. Bettis (1986), 'The dominant logic – a new linkage between diversity and performance', *Strategic Management Journal*, **7**: 485–501.

*Premkumar, G. and W. R. King (1991), 'Assessing strategic information-systems planning', *Long Range Planning*, **24**(5): 41–58.

*Rosenkopf, L. and A. Nerkar (2001), 'Beyond local search: Boundary-spanning, exploration, and impact in the optical disk industry', *Strategic Management Journal*, **22**: 287–306.

Rumelt, R. P., D. Schendel and D. J. Teece (1994), *Fundamental Issues in Strategy: A Research Agenda*, Boston, MA: Harvard Business School Press.

*Sadler-Smith, E., D. P. Spicer and L. Chaston (2001), 'Learning orientations and growth in smaller firms', *Long Range Planning*, **34**(2): 139–158.

*Sanchez, R. (1995), 'Strategic flexibility in product competition', *Strategic Management Journal*, **16**: 135–159.

*Sanchez, R. and J. T. Mahoney (1996), 'Modularity, flexibility, and knowledge management in product and organization design', *Strategic Management Journal*, **17**: 63–76.

*Schnaars, S. P. (1987), 'How to develop and use scenarios', *Long Range Planning*, **20**(1): 105–114.

*Schwenk, C. R. (1984), 'Cognitive simplification processes in strategic decision-making', *Strategic Management Journal*, **5**: 111–128.

Scott, L. C. and P. M. Mitias (1996), 'Trends in rankings of economics departments in the U.S.: An update', *Economic Inquiry*, **34**: 378–400.

*Scott, M. and R. Bruce (1987), '5 stages of growth in small business', *Long Range Planning*, **20**(3): 45–52.

Shane, S. A. (1997), 'Who is publishing the entrepreneurship research?', *Journal of Management*, **23**: 83–95.

Summer, C. E., R. A. Bettis, I. H. Duhaime, J. H. Grant, D. C. Hambrick, C. C. Snow and C. P. Zeithaml (1990), 'Doctoral education in the field of business policy and strategy', *Journal of Management*, **16**: 361–398.

*Talwar, R. (1993), 'Business reengineering – a strategy-driven approach', *Long Range Planning*, **26**(6): 22–40.

*Teece, D. J. (2000), 'Strategies for managing knowledge assets: The role of firm structure and industrial context', *Long Range Planning*, **33**(1): 35–54.

*Volberda, H. W., C. Baden-Fuller and F. A. J. van den Bosch (2001), 'Mastering strategic renewal – mobilising renewal journeys in multi-unit firms', *Long Range Planning*, **34**(2): 159–178.

*Whittington, R. (1996), 'Strategy as practice', *Long Range Planning*, **29**(5): 731–735.

*Willcocks, L., G. Fitzgerald and D. Feeny (1995), 'Outsourcing it – the strategic implications', *Long Range Planning*, **28**(5): 59–70.

*Winter, S. G. (2000), 'The satisficing principle in capability learning', *Strategic Management Journal*, **21**: 981–996.

2 Shifting focus from the determinants to the origin: the foundations of a dynamic view of managerial discretion
Ingo Kleindienst and Thomas Hutzschenreuter

INTRODUCTION

One of the most pervasive issues in the strategic management literature is the question of whether organizational adaptation is environmentally or managerially derived. In particular, at issue is the question of whether managers matter and, if so, under what circumstances (Boyd and Gove, 2006). In response to the two opposing views that have historically developed – that is, voluntarism (Andrews, 1971; Child, 1972) and determinism (Aldrich, 1979; Hannan and Freeman, 1984) – Hambrick and Finkelstein (1987) proposed the concept of managerial discretion. The concept was developed to represent the degree to which managers possess latitude of action, thereby reconciling the aforementioned two polar views.

Over the past two decades the concept of managerial discretion has proven to be very appealing conceptually and has been widely cited in leading strategic management journals.[1] However, as Keegan and Kabanoff (2008) have pointed out, the difficulty of operationalizing managerial discretion has led the concept to perhaps have far less impact on the strategic management literature to date than it should have (Ketchen et al., 2008). This assessment was further corroborated by Boyd and Gove's (2006) review, revealing a total of only 16 studies that have empirically explored managerial discretion.

Even more striking is the fact that to date no study has taken a dynamic view of managerial discretion, despite the fact that Hambrick and Finkelstein (1987: 403) called for the development of such a temporal, dynamic view. However, as Finkelstein and Peteraf (2007: 244) have emphasized, the question of how discretion changes over time is

> an important question, not only because the effects of discretion have been found to be substantial in subsequent research, but also for the more general reason that much theory on strategic organization implicitly assumes a static model of the world, even though it is quite evident that change is endemic to strategy.

Again, it is likely that the focus on the determinants of discretion at the expense of an understanding of discretion is the main reason why such a dynamic view has not yet evolved (Keegan and Kabanoff, 2008).

Finally, it appears that since its introduction to the literature, scholars have neglected to theoretically advance the concept of managerial discretion. Other concepts in the field, for example the dynamic capability concept (Teece et al., 1997), have continuously been refined and/ or extended (see for example Eisenhardt and Martin, 2000; Arend and Bromiley, 2009; Helfat and Peteraf, 2009). Managerial discretion, however – with the notable exception of Finkelstein and Peteraf (2007) – has not yet been the subject of such work.

Therefore, the objective and the contribution of the present paper are twofold. First, on a general level we intend this paper to fuel a theoretical debate on the concept of managerial discretion. This is likely to lead to its refinement and/or extension, opening up the possibilities for new research avenues. Second, in particular we intend the paper to provide an initial answer to Hambrick and Finkelstein's (1987) 20-year-old call to develop a dynamic view of managerial discretion. To do so, we introduce the crucial distinction between the determinants and the origin of discretion. This takes into account that, following the original conceptualization, managerial discretion first and foremost depends upon the manager's cognition. In doing so, we abandon mainstream research on managerial discretion and follow Finkelstein and Peteraf's (2007) reasoning, according to which any development of a dynamic view of discretion must depart from the manager. Hence, while prior research (see, for example, Finkelstein and Hambrick, 1990; Abrahamson and Hambrick, 1997; Finkelstein and Boyd, 1998) has almost exclusively explored managerial discretion at the industry and organizational level of analysis, respectively, we argue for a shift in focus towards individual level analysis.

This paper is organized as follows. In the next section we briefly describe the original concept of managerial discretion. We then introduce the crucial distinction between the determinants and the origin of discretion, before outlining the fundamental building blocks of a dynamic view of managerial discretion. Finally, we provide some suggestions for future research concerning the dynamic view of managerial discretion and close the paper with a brief conclusion.

THE CONCEPT OF MANAGERIAL DISCRETION

Managerial discretion is a multilevel construct encompassing the environmental, the organizational and the individual levels. However, while there are linkages between the levels of analysis, each level's impact on discretion may be analysed independently in a ceteris paribus fashion (Hambrick and Finkelstein, 1987; Finkelstein and Peteraf, 2007). At the core, the concept of managerial discretion argues that situational determinants such as task environment, internal organization and managerial characteristics define the scope of control managers have over their organization's form and fate. In particular, Hambrick and Finkelstein (1987: 378–379) reason that a manager's degree of discretion

> is derived from three sets of factors familiar to organizational researchers: environmental, organizational, and individual managerial characteristics. Namely, a chief executive's latitude of action is a function of (1) the degree to which the environment allows variety and change, (2) the degree to which the organization itself is amenable to an array of possible actions and empowers the chief executive to formulate and execute those actions, and (3) the degree to which the chief executive personally is able to envision or create multiple courses of action.

The effects of the task environment on organizations and managers have been well documented in the literature (Thompson, 1967; Porter, 1980). Task environments are likely to differ along a multitude of characteristics affecting the manager's degree of discretion. Following Hambrick and Finkelstein (1987), these characteristics include product differentiability, market growth, industry structure, demand instability, quasi-legal constraints and powerful outside forces. Consequently, the degree of discretion is positively related to the ambiguity in means–ends relationships within the task environment.

In contrast, the manager's degree of discretion derived from the internal organization depends upon the existence and strength of factors that inhibit the organization's ability to change. In this context, inertial forces (Hannan and Freeman, 1977) such as size, age, strong culture and capital intensity have been argued to reduce discretion. In contrast to inertial forces, resource availability has been argued to increase discretion. Strategic actions, such as the acquisition of a competitor, developing a new product, setting up a production facility in a foreign country and the like, require substantial financial and non-financial resources. Hence, high levels of slack provide the manager with a wide range of potential actions he would not be able to act on in the absence of slack resources (Cyert and March, 1963).

Finally, a manager's personal characteristics such as aspiration level, commitment, tolerance of ambiguity or locus of control impact the degree of discretion. These personal characteristics are important since they determine the degree to which the manager is able to generate and consider multiple courses of action. As Hambrick and Finkelstein (1987: 387) have argued, a 'manager's discretionary set is constrained by his or her ability to cognitively process different alternatives simultaneously. As well, some actions may be ruled out simply because they are beyond the manager's cognitive bounds'. Consequently, the higher the number of possible courses of action the manager is able to envision, the higher the degree of discretion available to the manager.

Given that the degree of discretion refers to the manager rather than to the organization (Hambrick and Finkelstein, 1987), the aforementioned determinants can be distinguished into endogenous and exogenous determinants. Being inherent in the manager, managerial characteristics represent an endogenous determinant. In contrast, task environment and internal organization are exogenous determinants, providing the context in which the manager operates.[2]

DISTINGUISHING BETWEEN DETERMINANTS AND ORIGIN

The study of Finkelstein and Peteraf (2007) provides an interesting starting point to introduce the distinction between the determinants and the origin of managerial discretion. To the best of our knowledge, the authors are the first to explicitly acknowledge the difference between the discretion of a manager and the discretion of the context in which the manager operates. Moreover, they not only differentiate between endogenous and exogenous determinants of discretion but also allow for the degree of discretion imposed by endogenous and exogenous determinants to be different. For example, Finkelstein and Peteraf (2007: 243) elaborate that 'high-discretion managers do have the potential to act even when they sit in low-discretion organizations or environments' and 'high-discretion managers can find outlets for that discretion regardless of environmental and organizational constraints because they can select from among an array of potential activities that vary in their degree of discretion'. Although Finkelstein and Peteraf (2007) explicitly refer to this important distinction, they do not provide any reasoning why they do so.

Carefully reviewing Hambrick and Finkelstein's (1987) original study, we will subsequently provide a rationale for the importance of differentiating between the manager and the context, thereby highlighting the importance of individual level analysis. In doing so, we will show that it might even be more useful not to refer to endogenous and exogenous determinants, but rather to the origin and the determinants of managerial discretion.

At the outset of their study, Hambrick and Finkelstein (1987) define discretion as 'latitude of managerial action' and comment on the requirement that discretion involves potential actions which can realistically be converted into actions. More important, however, they elaborate that discretion resides within the manager and is a function of the manager's cognition. In particular they state that 'the manager must be aware of an option for it to be part of the discretionary set' (Hambrick and Finkelstein, 1987: 373).

The statement is important for various reasons. First, it introduces *awareness* as a basic prerequisite for the existence of managerial discretion. Second, speaking of *option*, it becomes evident that discretion is inextricably linked to an issue. Third, the notion of *discretionary set* implies that the degree of managerial discretion may be conceptualized as the number of options of which the manager is aware.

It is likely that we all have an intuitive understanding of what the word 'awareness' means. For many purposes, this intuitive meaning may be sufficient. However, in trying to characterize the importance of awareness in the concept of managerial discretion, it seems appropriate to develop a more precise idea of what is meant by the term 'awareness'. According to *The Penguin Dictionary of Psychology* (Reber and Reber, 2001), awareness is briefly defined as 'an internal, subjective state of being cognizant or conscious of something'. Cognizant or conscious, in turn, indicates general information, wide knowledge, interpretative power or vigilant perception (Neufelt and Guralnik, 1989). Hence, on the one hand the definition stresses awareness as an internal state of the manager, being directed towards something and connected to the available information and knowledge. On the other hand, awareness emphasizes consciousness, thereby precluding anything that may occur unconsciously.

The basic building block of discretion is the option, that is, a potential course of action (Hambrick and Finkelstein, 1987). These options, however, are not given, but are the result of a manager's cognitive endeavor to envision potential actions in order to resolve a given strategic issue (Dutton and Duncan, 1987). Hence, the degree of discretion that is available to a manager depends first and foremost upon his ability to perceive, create and envision multiple options. Everything else constant, the more options the manager is able to envision, the higher his degree of discretion and vice versa. Consequently, given that options are the basic building block of discretion, and that these options are the result of a cognitive endeavor, the manager himself can be conceptualized as the source, that is, the origin of discretion.

The task environment and the internal organization represent determinants of managerial discretion. In contrast to the manager, the

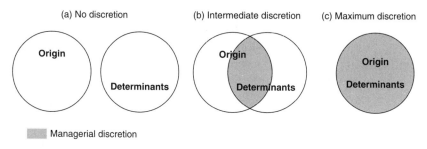

Managerial discretion

Figure 2.1   *The relationship between origin, determinants and degree of discretion*

determinants are not responsible for the creation of options. Rather task environment and internal organization determine whether or not potential courses of action a manager is able to envision lie within the zone of acceptance of powerful parties. Thereby, a high discretion context allows for multiple courses of action to be acted on, while a low discretion context restricts the number of potential actions.

Take, for example, the case of an organization being active in a regulated market. In order to cope with the decreasing profits of the organization, a manager may envision the option 'increase price' as a potential course of action. However, it is likely that legal constraints in the regulated market inhibit the manager to increase the price. Hence, although the manager was able to envision a potential course of action, his degree of discretion did not increase due to the low discretion context. The relationship between the manager as the origin of discretion (individual level of analysis), the determinants (environmental and organizational levels of analysis) and the resulting degree of discretion are summarized in Figure 2.1.[3]

Based on Hambrick and Finkelstein's (1987: 378) notion that a manager 'who is aware of multiple courses of action that lie within the zone of acceptance of powerful parties is said to have discretion', different types of the degree of managerial discretion can be distinguished (cf. Figure 2.1). On the one hand, albeit this is likely to be a theoretical rather than a practical possibility, the manager may face no discretion at all (alternative a). The absence of discretion, in turn, may be due to two reasons. First, it could be that the manager is unable to envision a single option. However, since options, that is, potential courses of action, form the basic building block of discretion, it is evident that the inability to envision options may result in having no discretion at all. Second, although the manager may be able to envision a multitude of options, it is theoretically possible that all of these options fall outside the zone of acceptance. Having no overlap between the set of options the manager is able to envision and the set of options that fall into the zone of acceptance, the manager has no discretion.

The preceding reasoning draws on the aforementioned original conceptualization of the relationship between a manager's awareness and the zone of acceptance, according to which managerial discretion is the intersection of a manager's awareness and the zone of acceptance. Interestingly, however, Finkelstein and Peteraf (2007) have argued that a manager's choice of potential actions can never be fully constrained, thus providing the manager with the opportunity to act on courses of action that lie outside the zone of acceptance.

On the other hand, it may be that the manager faces the maximum degree of discretion (alternative c). This is the case when all of the options the manager is able to envision fall into the zone of acceptance of powerful parties. In other words, the manager would be able to act upon every single option. It is important to note, however, that the manager's degree of discretion would not change, even if the determinants would allow for additional options to be acted on. This is because an option that is contained within the zone of acceptance, given that the manager is not aware of the option (that is, it is not contained within the manager's discretionary set) does not affect his overall degree of discretion.

In most cases, however, the manager's actual degree of discretion is likely to reflect the scope of the intersection between the set of options the manager is able to envision and the set of options approved by the determinants (alternative b). Thus, while the manager may be able to envision a wide variety of options, only those options that fall into the zone of acceptance contribute to the manager's degree of discretion. Consequently, the scope of overlap between the set of options the manager is able to envision and the set of options approved by the determinants, defines the manager's actual degree of discretion.

Figure 2.1 elucidates the relationship between voluntarism, determinism and managerial discretion. According to alternative (a) in Figure 2.1, the manager is unaware of a single option that falls within the zone of acceptance. Hence the manager has no options to choose from. In the absence of managerial choices, however, the development of the company is completely determined. At the other end of this continuum (alternative c), the manager is able to choose and act on every single option he is able to envision. Consequently, the development of the manager's company is dependent only upon the manager's choice of options. In other words, the determinants represent a manager's maximum amount of voluntarism. In between these two polar positions, discretion reflects those options that are restricted from the determinants, but at the same time the manager is able to voluntarily choose from.

The preceding distinction is important since it addresses an issue overlooked by previous research. Studies such as Hambrick and Abrahamson (1995), Rajagopalan and Finkelstein (1992) and Finkelstein and Boyd (1998) have measured managerial discretion at the industry and organizational level. Focusing on the determinants of discretion, rather than on the origin, these studies have made an oversimplifying implicit assumption. It is assumed that the manager is able to envision the full scope of potential courses of action approved by the context. However, it is neglected that the manager may not be able to envision the entire set of potential courses of action, which the determinants would approve to be acted on. Consequently, what is measured by focusing on the determinants is the maximum potential degree of discretion a manager can have in a given context, rather than the actual degree, reflecting the manager's ability to envision multiple courses of action (Hambrick and Finkelstein, 1987).

Consider, for example, an MBA student who has just finished his studies and is ready to enter the job market. After applying for various positions, receiving various offers and sorting out his favorites, the student is finally to decide between the following two offers from the 'standard' low and high discretion industries (Keegan and Kabanoff, 2008). The first offer is from a large company in the oil and gas production industry. In contrast, his second offer concerns a job in a small, dynamic company in the computer software industry. According to the mainstream research on managerial discretion, the MBA student, by entering the company from the oil and gas production industry, would have a low degree of discretion. In contrast, everything else equal, entering the computer software industry, research would suggest that the same MBA student has a high degree of managerial discretion (Abrahamson and Hambrick, 1997). However, given that managerial discretion resides within the manager and is a function of his cognition (Hambrick and Finkelstein, 1987), there is no reason why the degrees of discretion originating from the MBA student, that is, his ability to envision different courses of potential action, should ex ante be different.

In summary, two important conclusions can be drawn from the preceding reasoning. First, it is important to distinguish between the origin and the determinants of managerial discretion. Envisioning and creating a set of potential strategic courses of action, the manager is the source, that is, the *origin* of managerial discretion. In contrast, contextual factors, such as task environment and internal organization, define which of the options the manager is able to envision, are approved. Hence, in contrast to the manager, contextual factors do not create discretion by actively envisioning additional options, but rather *determine* the scope of discretion.

Second, focusing on the determinants of managerial discretion, research addresses the maximum potential degree, rather than the actual degree of a manager's discretion. Hence, rather than focusing on the determinants, future research should focus on the manager himself and, in particular, his ability to envision potential courses of action. In doing so, it may also be possible to develop a dynamic view of discretion as called for by Hambrick and Finkelstein (1987) some 20 years ago. In the next section, we will provide some basic ideas on the development of such a dynamic view.

THE FOUNDATION OF A DYNAMIC VIEW

In their original study, Hambrick and Finkelstein (1987: 402–403) asked:

> how does discretion change over time? What are the mechanisms for and outcomes of changed discretion? Does a CEO's discretion tend to increase as he or she gains influence over his or her tenure, or does it tend to lessen through commitment processes and organizational aging? How do such changes unfold?

and concluded that 'a temporal, dynamic view of discretion is what we eventually need'.

More than two decades have passed without published research addressing these important aspects of managerial discretion. Hence the question arises why research in the past failed to do so? Searching for possible answers, we come to the conclusion that the field's one-sided focus on the determinants may be an important, if not the main, reason for this failure.

Boyd and Gove's (2006) review not only revealed the limited empirical application of managerial discretion, but also that almost all empirical studies focused on the determinants of managerial discretion. In fact, only one empirical study, the one by Carpenter and Golden (1997), emphasized the cognitive aspect of discretion by focusing on the perceived level of managerial discretion. To explore the degree of discretion resulting from task environment or internal organization, a variety of different indicators were used. For example, Datta et al. (2005) used capital intensity, growth, R&D intensity and industry volatility, while Haleblian and Finkelstein (1993) used R&D intensity, growth, advertising intensity, instability and regulation to assess the degree of discretion at the industry level. Measuring discretion at the level of the organization, Finkelstein and Boyd (1998) used R&D intensity, advertising intensity, demand instability, capital intensity, concentration and regulation, while Boyd and Salamin (2001) as well as Rajagopalan (1997) used the strategic orientation, following the Miles and Snow (1978) typology. While those studies have for sure increased our understanding of how discretion affects various organizational phenomena, the focus on the determinants inhibited a dynamic investigation.

As can easily be seen, each of the indicators is expected to change over time with respect to both the strength and the direction of their effects (Finkelstein and Peteraf, 2007). However, some indicators have a positive (for example, R&D intensity, advertising intensity and growth) while others have a negative (for example, capital intensity, regulation, concentration) effect on the degree of discretion. Therefore an overall assessment of how managerial discretion changes over time based on the simultaneous consideration of various indicators is a complex undertaking and is likely to have precluded the development of a dynamic view in the past. However, as can be seen in Figure 2.1, change in managerial discretion over time is not restricted to change in the determinants. Rather, managerial discretion may also change over time, when the amount of potential courses of action the manager is able to envision and that are contained within the zone of acceptance, increases or decreases. Managerial discretion may also increase when the zone of acceptance decreases, but at the same time the number of those potential actions the manager is aware of, which are contained in the zone of acceptance, increases, and vice versa.

Hence in the following we shift focus from the determinants to the origin of discretion, that is, the manager's ability to envision multiple potential courses of action. In other words, our approach differs from established research in the field insofar as we abandon the analysis at the environmental and organizational levels of analysis and explore managerial discretion at the individual level of analysis (cf. Figure 2.2). Doing so is likely to enable us – and future researchers following this approach – to develop a dynamic view of managerial discretion. The rationale to do so is twofold. On the one hand, the manager is the most important building block in the concept of managerial discretion. On the other hand, by focusing on the manager's cognition, researchers circumvent the aforementioned problem of simultaneously considering directly opposing effects on discretion.

The degree of discretion originating from the manager has been argued to be 'a product of experience, scanning, and insight' (Hambrick and Finkelstein, 1987: 373). Hence a dynamic view of managerial discretion that departs from the manager must be able to explain how experience, scanning and insight change over time. In particular, such a view should be able to outline how these changes relate to the manager's ability to envision multiple options.

Experience refers to the manager's accumulation of knowledge or skill, which results either from direct participation in events or activities (Weick, 1979) or emerges from the interaction of a stimulus and the mind of the manager (Vandenbosch and Higgins, 1996). Crucial to the

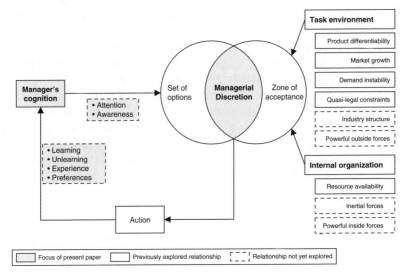

Figure 2.2   The role of managerial cognition in a dynamic view of managerial discretion

accumulation of knowledge is learning, which occurs when through the processing of information the range of potential behaviors of an entity is changed (Lovell, 1980; Huber, 1991). It is important to note at this point, that learning refers to the potential change of behavior only, rather than to the behavioral change itself. Hence, in the context of managerial discretion, learning is likely to enable the manager to add an additional potential course of action to his already existing discretionary set. In this basic understanding, learning has a positive effect on discretion. The more experience a manager has acquired over the course of his career, the more potential courses of action he is able to envision and, thus, the higher his degree of discretion.

However, recent research on organizational learning (Finkelstein and Haleblian, 2002; Hayward, 2002) has questioned the implicit assumption that experience is always positive. The pioneering study of Haleblian and Finkelstein (1999), for example, has shown that under specific conditions, organizations may mistransfer experience from past events to subsequent but different ones. Although the study of Haleblian and Finkelstein (1999) refers to a phenomenon at the organizational level, their arguments are based on the behavioral learning theory at the individual level (Ellis, 1978). Hence it is highly probable that the finding that experience may have a downturn is also relevant on an individual level. For example, the early work of Thorndike (1898) has shown that rewarded behavior tends to persist and strengthen, while punished behavior tends to diminish and weaken. In other words, a manager is likely to envision and act on potential courses of action that have proven to be successful in the past, while those courses of action that have proven to be unsuccessful, may be pushed to the back of the manager's mind or even be unlearned. Similarly, Hambrick and Fukutomi (1991: 730) have argued that after some time in office, a CEO is likely to select 'those elements that seem to work the best and are the most comfortable'. In other words, while learning may enable the manager to envision new potential courses of action, the consequences that arise from acting on these courses of action, may result in unlearning options (Thorndike, 1898; Hedberg, 1981). As a consequence, there is no simple relationship between experience and discretion. Rather, depending upon the outcomes of individual courses of action, learning may either increase or decrease the manager's overall degree of discretion.

Scanning, that is, the manager's information accumulation behavior, is also expected to affect the degree of discretion (Hambrick and Finkelstein, 1987). Based on the premise that the information acquired is used to envision multiple potential courses of action, a positive relationship between the amount of information and the degree of discretion is assumed. However, research has shown that, due to the symbolic nature of information, often more information is gathered than used (Feldman and March, 1981). Hence a surplus of information gathered on a specific issue will not affect the manager's discretion positively. Rather, with regard to the manager's limited information processing capacity (Simon, 1945; Miller, 1956), it is likely that an overload of information concerning a specific issue will prevent the manager from processing with information on other issues, thereby reducing the manager's discretion.

More important, however, research has shown that a manager's scanning behavior is not constant over time. Aguilar (1967), for example, has shown that newly appointed managers gathered their information from both internal and external sources. However, over the course of their tenure, managers were found to increase their use of internal sources, at the expense of external sources. Miller (1993) has argued that many managers become increasingly confident of their grasp of the challenges they are facing. Consequently, they feel a declining need over time to thoroughly scan and gather information about their operations and environments (Miller, 1991). Finally, Hambrick and Fukutomi (1991) have argued that the sources of a manager's information become increasingly narrow and restricted since subordinates and staff filter the content of the information according to the manager's needs. Relying on narrower and more finely filtered information over the course of his tenure, the manager increasingly restricts himself from envisioning new and distant (Cyert and March, 1963) potential courses of action.

Closely linked to experience and scanning is insight, that is, the manager interpreting and making sense of the available information. A core premise of cognitive psychology (Tolman, 1948) is that individuals come to any task with mental models. According to Johnson-Laird (1983) a mental model can be conceptualized as internal symbolic representation of the environment or specific aspects of the environment. The mental model – also termed cognitive map, schema, givens or frames of reference (Huff, 1990; Walsh, 1995) – includes the individual's definitions, procedures, examples, and so on concerning the respective aspect of the environment. Consequently, mental models determine how the individual will interpret, incorporate and synthesize environmental stimuli and even whether or not cues will be noticed and used. Hence a core task of mental models is to make knowledge and information processing more efficient by making it unnecessary to construct understanding of environmental stimuli from scratch each time similar stimuli are encountered (Vandenbosch and Higgins, 1996). Directing the gathering and processing of stimuli, mental models enable individuals to learn by filling gaps in both information and memory, and to construct updated models of the environment. According to Maier (1945) this dynamic learning can emerge from two different strategies to problem solving: reproductive and productive thought.

Reproductive thought occurs whenever an individual encounters a problem similar to one that he or she has solved in the past. In such cases individuals apply previously successful strategies that are stored in the mental model to solve the problem. In contrast, productive thought and, by that, learning, occurs whenever the individual encounters a problem with new aspects. Individuals restructure and reshape previous experience, trying to solve the problem. In doing so, the individual's mental model is adjusted, and gaps in both information and memory are filled and stored for future use (Lovell, 1980).

However, research has shown that radical changes in mental models are rare. Moreover, being based on historical events rather than on current ones (Kiesler and Sproull, 1982) and having emerged over time, a manager's mental model is rather fixed, showing only limited elasticity (Collins and Gentner, 1987). Consequently, by employing his mental model in order to understand the situation he finds himself in, the manager is restricted in his ability to envision new potential courses of action. However, rather than increasing the number of potential options, the manager's mental model may at times prevent the manager becoming aware of all potential courses of action of which he has knowledge. As research has shown, managers sometimes escalate their commitment to a chosen course of action (Staw, 1981; Ross and Staw, 1993). In doing so, managers are likely to search for information that corroborates their course of action, while ignoring information that reflects negatively on the chosen course. Hence, as a result of such a perceptual distortion, the manager will only be able to envision and become aware of a limited set of potential options although under normal conditions a wide variety of potential courses of action would be contained within the manager's discretionary set.

Several studies have argued that managers pass through various phases during their time in office (Hambrick and Fukutomi, 1991; Miller, 1991; Henderson et al., 2006). As Hambrick and Fukutomi (1991) have argued, these phases are characterized by differences in the manager's commitment to a paradigm, the degree of task knowledge, the task interest, and the breadth and depth of information used. However, having a strong influence on experience, scanning and insight, differences in these characteristics over time will inevitably have an impact on the manager's ability to envision potential courses of action, that is, the manager's degree of discretion. Hence, coming back to the outset of this section, it seems evident that a dynamic view of managerial discretion must depart from the manager, that is, the origin, rather than from the determinants. In the next section, we therefore provide some initial suggestions for future research.

A RESEARCH AGENDA

As a refinement of the upper-echelons theory (Hambrick and Mason, 1984), the manager takes a central position within the concept of managerial discretion (Hambrick, 2007; Finkelstein et al., 2009). Nevertheless, to date research has mostly neglected the manager's role within the concept, emphasizing instead the role of task environment and internal organization. However, in order to develop a dynamic view of discretion, the focus has to be shifted from the determinants to the manager, that is, the origin of discretion (Finkelstein and Peteraf, 2007).

Since managerial discretion is first and foremost the result of the manager's ability to envision different potential courses of action, a dynamic view of discretion must explore if, why and how this ability changes over time. Hence we call for a more explicit cognitive emphasis in the development of a dynamic view of managerial discretion (Huff, 1990; Walsh, 1995; Porac and Thomas, 2002).

Although learning has become a prominent topic in strategic management, almost all research focuses on the organizational level (Levitt and March, 1988; Levinthal and March, 1993; Nonaka, 1994; Zollo and Singh, 2004; Nadolska and Barkema, 2007). In contrast, hardly any study in the field of management is available that focuses on the individual level process of learning. However, building on the premise that discretion is the product of experience, scanning and insight, we need to know how managers learn in order to understand how the manager can enlarge his discretionary set. In this context a variety of questions have to be addressed. What are the requirements for a manager to learn? How does the manager store the information learned? How can stored information be accessed in the future, that is, how is it activated? Does learning affect the manager's discretion through the development of individual preferences? Explaining how managers learn is one of the fundamental issues that have to be addressed in order to develop a dynamic view of discretion. Hence to address these questions researchers are likely to build on the insights provided by cognitive and behavioral psychology.

To date, there has been no application of the concept of awareness in strategic management research. However, the related construct of 'attention' has been applied in a variety of studies. For example, building on the premise that what managers do depends on what issues they focus their attention on, Ocasio (1997) developed the attention-based view of the firm. Using managerial attention, Levy (2005) showed that organizations were more likely to be globally diversified when the top managers allocated their attention to organizations' external environments. Similarly, Bouquet (2005) found a concave relationship between the managers' attention to global issues and organizational performance. Considering the studies on managerial attention already available, it seems appropriate that future research should in a first step try to explore the relation between the concept of awareness and the concept of attention. Early work in cognitive psychology, such as Broadbent's (1958) filter theory or Kahneman's (1973) capacity theory, seems to provide a promising starting point for this endeavor.

By definition, the development of a dynamic view of managerial discretion requires the application of longitudinal rather than cross-sectional research settings. In this context, a case-based research approach seems most appropriate (Yin, 2003) since, as Eisenhardt (1989) has argued, case-study research is a strategy that focuses on understanding the dynamics present within a setting. Having access to a manager over a longer period of time, a real-time case study (for example, Montealegre, 2002) would enable the researcher to explore how the manager learns, how the awareness of potential courses of action changes over time, and whether or not individual preferences have an impact on the manager's degree of discretion, by precluding him from considering all potential options of which he has knowledge.

While the preceding ideas for future research are on a rather general level, we will subsequently provide some more detailed ideas on how to explore changes in a manager's level of discretion. A first step towards a research program on the dynamics of managerial discretion could be starting to monitor how a manager's assessment of potential courses of action develops over time. In particular, researchers may want to confront managers with a diverse set of common organizational problems (Cowan, 1990). For each of these problems the manager is then to note the potential courses of action which he would consider to resolve the respective problem. The number and diversity of potential courses of action could then be interpreted as a proxy for the manager's level of discretion. Using semi-structured interviews, additional information could be obtained, such as whether or not the manager had encountered a similar problem in the past, whether or not he had applied a potential course of action in the past and, if so, whether the course of action led to a satisfying or annoying result. Repeating this procedure over time would enable researchers to uncover whether, how and why the manager's knowledge of potential courses of action changed. A change as a result of learning, unlearning or the development of preferences would indicate a change in the level of managerial discretion.

A more sophisticated approach would require researchers to apply cognitive mapping techniques. Cognitive mapping techniques are methods used to assess the structure and the content of mental models (Axelrod, 1976; Huff, 1990; Eden, 1992). Daniels et al. (1995), for example, developed the visual card sort technique, which could be used to assess a manager's mental model. In the first stage, the element-eliciting stage, a manager would be asked to name all potential courses of action for a specific organizational problem. The potential courses of action would then be written on cards. In the second stage, the respondent would be asked to sort the cards on a surface in front of himself, such that those potential courses of action he perceives to be most suited for resolving the issue are placed more closely together. Finally, the respondent would be asked why he placed the cards in this manner. The visual card sort technique provides a quick and face valid way of representing the potential courses of action known by the manager and the potential relationships between these different courses of action. Repeating this procedure over time would provide insights on how the manager's mental model and, by that, his awareness of potential courses of action changes over time.

In most cases, however, it is likely that the researcher does not have access to a manager over a long period of time. However, using secondary data, it may nevertheless be possible to explore changes in the manager's mental model and, thus, the dynamics of managerial discretion. As research has shown, company documents such as speeches or letters to the shareholders contain a portion of the author's mental model at the time the document was created (Carley, 1997) and can be used to explore what is central to the manager's mind (Sapir, 1944; Whorf, 1956; Huff, 1990). Carley (1997), for example, has developed an automated approach for extracting the mental model from a text based on the program automap. Applying text analysis to different texts over time, which were authored by the same manager, researchers may be able to identify what potential courses of action the manager is aware of, how the awareness of options changes, and how changes in the manager's degree of discretion unfold over time.

CONCLUSION

Developed more than two decades ago, the concept of managerial discretion has not only proven to be theoretically important in its own right, but it has also helped to explain a variety of organizational phenomena such as management tenure and turnover, and management compensation (Finkelstein et al., 2009). However, although the concept has been widely cited in the strategic management literature, it seems that the concept has had far less impact on the strategic management literature to date than it should have (Keegan and Kabanoff, 2008).

To date, the field has almost exclusively explored managerial discretion at the environmental and organizational levels of analysis. We have argued in this paper, that this one-sided focus is one of the main reasons for both the limited impact of and the inability to develop a dynamic view of discretion.

Consequently, we challenge researchers to reconsider the concept of managerial discretion as past research has neglected the role of the manager. Hence in contrast to mainstream research on discretion, we have argued to shift focus: from the determinants that restrict discretion to the manager as the source of discretion. It is the contention of this paper that in order to theoretically extend and/or refine the concept of managerial discretion a shift in the level of analysis towards the individual is needed. After all, discretion first and foremost requires the availability of potential courses of action to choose from. In the absence of awareness of alternatives, the manager has no discretion. Therefore, we believe that it is important to stress the cognitive foundation of managerial discretion. Accordingly, taking a cognitive perspective on discretion is likely to enable researchers to explore how a manager's ability to envision potential courses of action changes over time. In particular, we have outlined that future research should explore mechanisms, such as learning, unlearning, experience or preferences, which enable or prevent a manager to envision multiple potential courses of action. It is evident that an empirical investigation on the dynamics of managerial discretion must take a longitudinal approach. Further developing the ideas presented in this paper, researchers may be able to seize the call made by Hambrick and Finkelstein (1987) and develop a temporal, dynamic view of managerial discretion.

NOTES

1. In July 2009 the Scopus database listed a total of 234 citations for the 13-year period between 1996 and 2008. Amongst others, the study of Hambrick and Finkelstein (1987) was cited in the *Strategic Management Journal* (32), *Academy of Management Journal* (25), *Journal of Management* (17), *Academy of Management Review* (11), *Organization Science* (9), *Leadership Quarterly* (8), *Journal of Management Studies* (7), *Administrative Science Quarterly* (5), *Organization Studies* (5) and *Journal of Applied Psychology* (5).
2. Some of the characteristics that make up the internal organization, such as size or culture, are subject to be influenced and/or changed by the manager. Thus these characteristics could also be considered to be endogenous. However, we follow the psychological distinction between endogenous and exogenous to distinguish characteristics that lie within the individual and those that lie outside the individual.
3. One might argue that managerial characteristics are also some kind of determinants. However, we introduce the distinction between origin and determinants to highlight the active as opposed to the passive role, respectively. Origin is used to point to the active role the manager plays in envisioning/creating potential courses of action. Conversely, the notion of determinants is used to emphasize the passive role of task environment and internal organization within the concept of managerial discretion.

REFERENCES

Abrahamson, E. and D. C. Hambrick (1997), 'Attentional homogeneity in industries: The effect of discretion', *Journal of Organizational Behavior*, **18**(Supplement 1): 513–532.
Aguilar, F. J. (1967), *Scanning the Business Environment*, New York: Macmillan.
Aldrich, H. (1979), *Organizations and Environments*, Englewood Cliffs, NJ: Prentice-Hall.
Andrews, K. R. (1971), *The Concept of Corporate Strategy*, Homewood, IL: Irwin.
Arend, R. J. and P. Bromiley (2009), 'Assessing the dynamic capabilities view: Spare change, everyone?', *Strategic Organization*, **7**(1): 75–90.
Axelrod, R. M. (1976), *Structure of Decision*, Princeton, NJ: Princeton University Press.
Bouquet, C. (2005), *Building Global Mindsets: An Attention-Based Perspective*, New York: Palgrave Macmillan.
Boyd, B. K. and S. Gove (2006), 'Managerial constraint: The intersection between organizational task environment and discretion', *Research Methodology in Strategy and Management*, **3**: 57–95.
Boyd, B. K. and A. Salamin (2001), 'Strategic reward systems: A contingency model of pay system design', *Strategic Management Journal*, **22**(8): 777–792.
Broadbent, D. E. (1958), *Perception and Communication*, New York: Pergamon Press.
Carley, K. M. (1997), 'Extracting team mental models through textual analysis', *Journal of Organizational Behavior*, **18**: 533–558.

Carpenter, M. A. and B. R. Golden (1997), 'Perceived managerial discretion: A study of cause and effect', *Strategic Management Journal*, **18**(3): 187–206.

Child, J. (1972), 'Organizational structure, environment and performance: The role of strategic choice', *Sociology*, **6**(1): 1–22.

Collins, A. and D. Gentner (1987), 'How people construct mental models', in B. Holland and N. Quinn (eds), *Cultural Models in Language and Thought*, Cambridge: Cambridge University Press, 243–265.

Cowan, D. A. (1990), 'Developing a classification structure of organizational problems: An empirical investigation', *Academy of Management Journal*, **33**(2): 366–390.

Cyert, R. M. and J. G. March (1963), *A Behavioral Theory of the Firm*, Englewood Cliffs, NJ: Prentice-Hall.

Daniels, K., L. de Chernatony and G. Johnson. (1995), 'Validating a method for mapping managers' mental models of competitive industry structures', *Human Relations*, **48**(9): 975–991.

Datta, D. K., J. P. Guthrie and P. M. Wright (2005), 'Human resource management and labor productivity: Does industry matter?', *Academy of Management Journal*, **48**(1): 135–145.

Dutton, J. E. and R. B. Duncan (1987), 'The influence of the strategic planning process on strategic change', *Strategic Management Journal*, **8**(2): 103–116.

Eden, C. (1992), 'On the nature of cognitive maps', *Journal of Management Studies*, **29**(3): 261–265.

Eisenhardt, K. M. (1989), 'Building theories from case study research', *Academy of Management Review*, **14**(4): 532–550.

Eisenhardt, K. M. and J. A. Martin (2000), 'Dynamic capabilities: What are they?', *Strategic Management Journal*, **21**(10/11): 1105–1121.

Ellis, H. C. (1978), *Fundamentals of Human Learning, Memory, and Cognition*, Dubuque, Iowa: W. C. Brown Co.

Feldman, M. S. and J. G. March (1981), 'Information in organizations as signal and symbol', *Administrative Science Quarterly*, **26**(2): 171–186.

Finkelstein, S. and B. K. Boyd (1998), 'How much does the CEO matter? The role of managerial discretion in the setting of CEO compensation', *Academy of Management Journal*, **41**(2): 179–199.

Finkelstein, S. and J. Haleblian (2002), 'Understanding acquisition performance: The role of transfer effects', *Organization Science*, **13**(1): 36–47.

Finkelstein, S. and D. C. Hambrick (1990), 'Top-management-team tenure and organizational outcomes: The moderating role of managerial discretion', *Administrative Science Quarterly*, **35**(3): 484–503.

Finkelstein, S. and M. A. Peteraf (2007), 'Managerial activities: A missing link in managerial discretion theory', *Strategic Organization*, **5**(3): 237–248.

Finkelstein, S., D. C. Hambrick and A. H. Cannella (2009), *Strategic Leadership: Theory and Research on Executives, Top Management Teams, and Boards*, New York: Oxford University Press.

Haleblian, J. and S. Finkelstein (1993), 'Top management team size, CEO dominance, and firm performance: The moderating roles of environmental turbulence and discretion', *Academy of Management Journal*, **36**(4): 844–863.

Haleblian, J. and S. Finkelstein (1999), 'The influence of organizational acquisition experience on acquisition performance: A behavioral learning perspective', *Administrative Science Quarterly*, **44**(1): 29–56.

Hambrick, D. C. (2007), 'Upper echelons theory: An update', *Academy of Management Review*, **32**(2): 334–343.

Hambrick, D. C. and E. Abrahamson (1995), 'Assessing managerial discretion across industries: A multimethod approach', *Academy of Management Journal*, **38**(5): 1427–1441.

Hambrick, D. C. and S. Finkelstein (1987), 'Managerial discretion: A bridge between polar views of organizational outcomes', in B. M. Staw and L. L. Cummings (eds), *Research in Organizational Behavior*, Greenwich, CT: JAI Press, 369–406.

Hambrick, D. C. and G. D. S. Fukutomi (1991), 'The seasons of a CEO's tenure', *Academy of Management Review*, **16**(4): 719–742.

Hambrick, D. C. and P. A. Mason (1984), 'Upper echelons: The organization as a reflection of its top managers', *Academy of Management Review*, **9**(2): 193–206.

Hannan, M. T. and J. Freeman (1977), 'The population ecology of organizations', *American Journal of Sociology*, **82**(5): 929–964.

Hannan, M. T. and J. Freeman (1984), 'Structural inertia and organizational change', *American Sociological Review*, **49**(2): 149–164.

Hayward, M. L. A. (2002), 'When do firms learn from their acquisition experience? Evidence from 1990–1995', *Strategic Management Journal*, **23**(1): 21–39.

Hedberg, B. L. T. (1981), 'How organizations learn and unlearn', in N. C. Nystrom and W. H. Starbuck (eds), *Handbook of Organizational Design*, Oxford: Oxford University Press, 3–27.

Helfat, C. E. and M. A. Peteraf (2009), 'Understanding dynamic capabilities: Progress along a developmental path', *Strategic Organization*, **7**(1): 91–102.

Henderson, A. D., D. Miller and D. C. Hambrick (2006), 'How quickly do CEOs become obsolete? Industry dynamism, CEO tenure, and company performance', *Strategic Management Journal*, **27**(5): 447–460.

Huber, G. P. (1991), 'Organizational learning: The contributing processes and the literatures', *Organization Science*, **2**(1): 88–115.

Huff, A. S. (1990), *Mapping Strategic Thought*. Chichster, UK: Wiley.

Johnson-Laird, P. N. (1983), 'Mental models in cognitive science', *Cognitive Science*, **4**: 71–115.

Kahneman, D. (1973), *Attention and Effort*, Englewood Cliffs, NJ: Prentice-Hall.

Keegan, J. and B. Kabanoff (2008), 'Indirect industry- and subindustry-level managerial discretion measurement', *Organizational Research Methods*, **11**(4): 682–694.

Ketchen, D. J., B. K. Boyd and D. D. Berah (2008), 'Research methodology in strategic management: Past accomplishments and future challenges', *Organizational Research Methods*, **11**(4): 643–658.

Kiesler, S. and L. Sproull (1982), 'Managerial response to changing environments: perspectives on problem sensing from social cognition', *Administrative Science Quarterly*, **27**(4): 548–570.

Levinthal, D. A. and J. G. March (1993), 'The myopia of learning', *Strategic Management Journal*, **14**(8): 95–112.

Levitt, B. and J. G. March (1988), 'Organizational learning', *Annual Review of Sociology*, **14**: 319–340.

Levy, O. (2005), 'The influence of top management team attention patterns on global strategic posture of firms', *Journal of Organizational Behavior*, **26**(7): 797–819.

Lovell, R. B. (1980), *Adult Learning*, New York: Wiley.

Maier, N. R. F. (1945), 'Reasoning in humans: III. The mechanisms of equivalent stimuli and of reasoning', *Journal of Experimental Psychology*, **35**: 349–360.

Miles, R. E. and C. C. Snow (1978), *Organizational Strategy, Structure, and Process*, New York: McGraw-Hill.

Miller, D. (1991), 'Stale in the saddle: CEO tenure and the match between organization and environment', *Management Science*, **37**(1): 34–52.

Miller, D. (1993), 'Some organizational consequences of CEO succession', *Academy of Management Journal*, **36**(3): 644–659.

Miller, G. A. (1956), 'The magical number seven, plus or minus two: Some limits on our capacity for processing information', *Psychological Review*, **63**(2): 81–97.

Montealegre, R. (2002), 'A process model of capability development: Lessons from the electronic commerce strategy at Bolsa de Valores de Guayaquil', *Organization Science*, **13**(5): 514–531.

Nadolska, A. and H. G. Barkema (2007), 'Learning to internationalise: The pace and success of foreign acquisitions', *Journal of International Business Studies*, **38**(7): 1170–1186.

Neufelt, V. and D. B. Guralnik (eds) (1989), *Webster's New World Dictionary*, Cleveland, OH: Webster's New World.

Nonaka, I. (1994), 'A dynamic theory of organizational knowledge creation', *Organization Science*, **5**(1): 14–37.

Ocasio, W. (1997), 'Towards an attention-based view of the firm', *Strategic Management Journal*, **18**(6): 187–206.

Porac, J. F. and H. Thomas (2002), 'Managing cognition and strategy: Issues, trends and future directions', in A. M. Pettigrew, H. Thomas and R. Whittington (eds), *Handbook of Strategy and Management*, London: Sage Publications, 165–181.

Porter, M. E. (1980), *Competitive Strategy*, New York: Free Press.

Rajagopalan, N. (1997), 'Strategic orientations, incentive plan adoptions, and firm performance: Evidence from electric utility firms', *Strategic Management Journal*, **18**(10): 761–785.

Rajagopalan, N. and S. Finkelstein (1992), 'Effects of strategic orientation and environmental change on senior management reward systems', *Strategic Management Journal*, **13**(5): 127–142.

Reber, A. S. and E. S. Reber (2001), *The Penguin Dictionary of Psychology*, London: Penguin Books.

Ross, J. and B. M. Staw (1993), 'Organizational escalation and exit: lessons from the Shoreham nuclear power plant', *Academy of Management Journal*, **36**(4): 701–732.

Sapir, E. (1944), 'Grading: A study in semantics', *Philosophy of Science*, **11**: 93–116.

Simon, H. A. (1945), *Administrative Behavior: A Study of Decision-Making Processes in Administration Organizations*, New York: The Free Press.

Staw, B. M. (1981), 'The escalation of commitment to a course of action', *Academy of Management Review*, **6**(4): 577–587.

Teece, D. J., G. Pisano and A. Shuen (1997), 'Dynamic capabilities and strategic management', *Strategic Management Journal*, **18**(7): 509–533.

Thompson, J. D. (1967), *Organizations in Action*, New York: McGraw-Hill.

Thorndike, E. L. (1898), *Animal Intelligence: An Experimental Study of the Associative Processes in Animals* (*Psychological Review Monograph Supplements, No. 8*), New York: Macmillan.

Tolman, E. C. (1948), 'Cognitive maps in rats and men', *Psychological Review*, **55**(4): 189–208.

Vandenbosch, B. and C. Higgins (1996), 'Information acquisition and mental models: An investigation into the relationship between behaviour and learning', *Information Systems Research*, **7**(2): 198–214.

Walsh, J. P. (1995), 'Managerial and organizational cognition: Notes from a trip down memory lane', *Organization Science*, **6**(3): 280–321.

Weick, K. E. (1979), *The Social Psychology of Organizing*, Reading, MA: Addison-Wesley Publishing Company.

Whorf, B. L. (1956), 'Science and linguistics', in J. B. Carroll (ed.), *Language, Thought and Reality: Selected Writings of Benjamin Lee Whorf*, Cambridge, MA: MIT Press, 207–219.

Yin, R. K. (2003), *Case Study Research: Design and Methods*, Thousand Oaks, CA: Sage Publications.

Zollo, M. and H. Singh (2004), 'Deliberate learning in corporate acquisitions: Post-acquisition strategies and integration capability in U.S. bank mergers', *Strategic Management Journal*, **25**(13): 1233–1256.

3 The politics of strategy process
Duane Windsor

Strategic management theory and practice concern managerial decision making within long-term objectives for the organization. The scope of topics falling within the discipline of strategic management is quite broad. Two distinct foci of research attention by organizational level exist. Macro strategy research emphasizes organization-level strategy content; micro strategy research emphasizes intra-organizational activity affecting strategy formulation, implementation and evaluation processes. The study of strategy content, concerning what managers decide to do, is dominated by economic conceptions. This macro-level research focuses on senior executives, boards of directors and unit heads. Strategy process, concerning how managers behave and units function at all levels of organizational structure, is dominated by psychological and sociological conceptions. Micro-level research extends attention to lower-level managers and small groups. Process research is studying practices and activities in detail as micro sources of or intra-organizational influences on strategy content.

The process orientation, emphasizing micro-level practices and activities, has helped open the door for revitalization of systematic study of internal politics at both macro and micro levels of organizational decision making. (External politics concerns environment–organization interaction in the forms of business–government and external–stakeholder relations.) The role of internal politics is still a neglected, or at least under-explored, dimension of strategy process. There was a classic literature on organizational (i.e. internal) politics, but early attention tended to decline in relative importance as economic and psychological–sociological conceptions matured. Scholars and practitioners understand that organizational politics is ubiquitous in the two general forms of office politics (i.e. interpersonal politics) and intra-organizational politics (i.e. inter-unit and intra-group politics). There is appreciation that both forms of internal politics may involve possibilities of collaboration (i.e. relationships, alliances and trust), competition (i.e. promotion and resource allocation tournaments) and conflict (which may be functional or dysfunctional depending on circumstances). There is active research into various aspects of what is grouped here as internal politics of strategy process, but those efforts are fragmented, or isolated, and spread across several disciplines without much integration or coordination. These fragmented research agendas do not sum to broad momentum or elicit much recognition from mainstream strategy literature. Relatively little attention has yet focused on strategy content or process, as distinct from capital budgeting, promotion tournaments, political tactics, networking, group dynamics and similar specific topics. Study of strategy politics, viewed as an integrated research topic, is as a result underdeveloped theoretically and empirically. Politics is a ubiquitous process activity occurring with intended strategies (i.e. managerial planning and top-down change management) and emergent strategies (i.e. opportunity discovery and bottom-up resource allocation processes). Political skill is a key set of practices of theoretical importance in organizational decision making for managers and groups.

This paper proposes several value-added contributions to theoretical and practical understanding of strategy process, and the implications for strategy content, through focusing systematic attention on the role of internal politics. The very diffuseness of research efforts has been a key barrier to recognition of strategy politics. There are various strands to systematizing study of office politics and intra-organizational politics of strategy process. One contribution of this paper is to identify at least some of those strands and place them in a proposed working relationship to one another. This political dimension cuts across macro-level strategy content and micro-level strategy process. Politics has some relationship to all the main topics grouped within the discipline of strategic management. Leadership involves authority and influence. Organizational structure may reflect political as much as economic and sociological considerations. A political perspective is diffuse for research purposes. This paper identifies, organizes and assesses several relatively disparate literatures – still widely neglected from a holistic viewpoint but recently expanding – bearing on politics of strategy process. What is provided here is an effort to marshal various fragmented, or isolated, research efforts into a more coherent political dimension of strategic management. Some overarching conceptual framework for the politics of strategy process is desirable. A first-cut effort is offered in the form of Table 3.1 (see facing page). Another contribution of this paper is to offer some critical assessment of specific research efforts from a holistic as well as a technical viewpoint. Approaches taking strictly economic, psychological or sociological perspectives should be examined as well from a political viewpoint to consider strengths and weaknesses of each approach. Another contribution of the paper is to suggest future research opportunities that can be usefully explored in developing a political theory and practice of strategy process.

A classical literature on organizational (i.e. internal) politics developed in the 1970s (MacMillan, 1978) and can be traced to Cyert and March's (1963) behavioral theory of the firm and Jay's (1968) statement of

Table 3.1   Antecedents, consequences, and research opportunities

Antecedents	Consequences	Research opportunities
Conditions and events		
Failing strategy	Inter-unit conflict	How do conditions and
Mergers and	Morale and trust effects	events affect perceptions
acquisitions		of politics, willingness
New CEO	Reallocation of resources	to participate, various
Slack resources	Room to maneuver	decision processes, ethics
Strong ethical climate	Avoidance of bribery	violations, etc.?
Individual actor		
Attitudes and beliefs		How do individual
Cognitive myopia		actor characteristics
Distrust	Negative politics	affect perceptions
Emotions	Office politics	of politics,
Mistrust		leadership and
Motivation	Commitment effects	strategy, willingness
Perceptions of politics		to participate,
Tolerance for failure	Constructive	commitment to the
	confrontation	organization, etc.?
Trust	Reporting of ethics issues	
Management practices		
Dysfunctional conflict	Intra-organizational	How can leaders
	politics	promote trust,
Constructive		tolerance for failure
confrontation		and a sense of fair play?
Delegation and	Participation and morale	How can leaders
empowerment		design constructive
Influence exercise	Less reliance on authority	confrontation in
Micromanagement		place of dysfunctional
Willingness to	Constructive	conflict or groupthink?
cannibalize	confrontation	What principles can help
		managers decide
		when to micromanage
		positively?
Processes and activities		
Capital budgeting	Misallocations	Can we develop
processes		optimum models for
Incentives	Expect A, get B	processes affecting
Unit head selections	Less qualified rise	resource allocation,
Performance	Morale and trust effects	unit head selections,
evaluation		promotions,
system		evaluations and
		planning?

Table 3.1   (continued)

Antecedents	Consequences	Research opportunities
Promotion system	Office politics	Will budget-less
Strategic planning	Centralization or	approaches decrease
processes	decentralization	negative politics?
Organization		
Authority structure	Top-down dominance	What is a useful
Culture and	Inter-unit conflict	behavioral model of
subcultures		intra-board relations
Governance structure	Board dominated by CEO	and interaction with
Organizational purpose	Clear mission	CEO?
Organizational	Misaligned with strategy	Can positive politics
structure		improve strategic
Strategy (content)	Uncertain options	choice?

managerial Machiavellianism. Jay (1968: 3) suggested 'a tenable political theory of business enterprise' and that business and government are 'two very similar branches of the same subject' in a way that might prove superior to a purely economic theory of business enterprise (Jensen, 2002). This political perspective helped open up the 'black box' of the organization. The resulting literature included Bower (1986), Pettigrew (1973, 1977), Tivey (1978), Bower and Doz (1979) and Narayanan and Fahey (1982). A political perspective informed the business policy movement of that era focused on managerial functions and practices. Research attention to micro-level phenomena is coming back into favor.

The 1980s and 1990s witnessed the rise of strategic management theory, more narrowly focused on what has become the economics of internal capability/resource development (i.e. organizational supply) and external opportunity identification/exploitation (i.e. market demand creation and capture). That strategy content orientation placed process-oriented research, including organizational politics, on lower priority. Office and intra-organizational politics have a negative connotation of personal or partisan gain through undesirable political methods and tactics, opinion manipulation and factional scheming for power and influence seemingly at odds with the economic rationality of company wealth creation.

Strategy process research (Johnson et al., 2003) has reopened the potential for fruitful study of organizational politics viewed as micro-level practices and activities (Vigoda-Gadot and Drory, 2006). Such study separates naturally into multiple tracks or tasks difficult of integration: appropriation of gains, delegation and empowerment, informal networks, conflict management, promotion tournaments, power and influence (Kotter, 1985; Pfeffer, 1992), persuasion, participation and resource allocation processes (Noda and Bower, 1996). An open problem is how to integrate these components with strategy formulation, implementation and evaluation (Bower and Gilbert, 2005). Executives engaged in direction setting and change management must rely on authority, incentive, persuasion and politics. The long-run check on their conduct is market reality (Khurana, 2002). Subordinates engaged in selling projects or strategic initiatives are seeking to influence executives. Cases and other studies are providing more insight into this two-way process of influence (Friedrich, 1963; Collier et al., 2004). A continuous tournament over strategic initiatives, as well as for individual opportunities and unit resources, is a set of repeated games with partial turnover of players (Kobayashi, 2007). Real strategy options are controversial choices under high uncertainty (Karnani, 2008) involving legitimacy building and development of shared mental maps. Such approaches may now help facilitate theoretical re-integration of a political perspective into strategic management.

This paper begins with basic observations concerning strategy process theorizing and the conflicting positive and negative views of politics. The paper then marshals four key themes into which continuing research is desirable through theory and model development, empirical testing and qualitative case studies. These four themes sequentially are: politics of strategy formulation, implementation and evaluation; moral issues in organizational and office politics; politics of resource allocation processes; and politics of promotion tournament competition within organizations. There are rich opportunities for research from diverse perspectives of economics, game theory, marketing, organizational studies, political science, psychology, sociology and strategy. The paper discusses some of these research opportunities, before ending with a summary and conclusion section.

STRATEGY PROCESS THEORIZING

The strategy literature is not internally unified. There has been debate over importance and relationship of industry structure, core competencies and the resource-based view (RBV) in providing sustainable competitive advantage. Industry structure theory, associated with the pioneering work of Michael E. Porter, assigns much of causal explanation for competitive positioning and advantage to the industry level of analysis. Some industries are more profitable long term and a key strategic problem is to block entry by competitors. Core competency theory, associated with the pioneering work of C. K. Prahalad and Gary Hamel, assigns much of causality to firm-level innovations. RBV, pioneered by Birger Wernerfelt and Jay Barney, traces causality to the firm's resources (broadly defined) combined to form capabilities. This expanding body of strategy literature, strongly influenced by economics, has come to focus on dynamic capabilities of firms innovating within changing environmental conditions.

The important thing for politics of strategy process (Pettigrew, 1992) is that uncertainty of dynamic change and management disagreement over real options leave fertile ground for 'politics'. A real option is the right, but not obligation, to acquire expected cash flows by making an irreversible investment under uncertainty on or before the date the opportunity expires. The difference between a right and an obligation generates the option value. Much of the analytical methodologies for strategizing arguably lack the essential element of strategic insight. As a result, both strategy formulation and implementation will tend to be chaotic and messy (Campbell and Alexander, 1997). This chaos, embedding real option controversies, is arguably the heart of strategizing. Karnani (2008) makes the case that controversy is the only way to make strategic choices, because competitive advantage cannot be simple in a competitive and changing marketplace (Luehrman, 1998). The firm internally has to make difficult choices in formulation, implementation and evaluation under conditions of uncertainty. A key managerial problem is to surface this conflict for positive resolution. Strategic dynamics may thus involve managed or staged chaos (Burgelman, 2002).

Burgelman reconciles competing 'structure follows strategy' and 'strategy follows structure' theories as follows. Strategic process comprises strategic activities of managers at multiple levels in a firm. Strategic activities are either induced by the current concept of firm strategy or are autonomous of that concept. The proportional balance between induced and autonomous activities is empirical and contingent. Large, resource-endowed firms are likely to embed entrepreneurial activities finding expression as autonomous activities. Burgelman (1996) illustrated a process model of strategic business exit decisions by Intel's decision to leave its core dynamic random access memory (DRAM) business. Intel redirected resources and competencies towards what were perceived as more viable business options. This explanation links nicely to a theory of strategy making as iterated processes of resource allocation (Noda and Bower, 1996). This theory is sometimes termed the 'Burgelman–Bower resource allocation process (RAP) model', which ties strategy implementation and evaluation to micro-level decisions and rewards.

Literature has begun to focus on micro strategy and strategizing studied through an activity-based view. This literature seeks to shift attention from macro-level strategizing to detailed operational processes and practices (or activities) underlying strategic outcomes (Johnson et al., 2003). One can discern here distinctions among motives, choices and outcomes. An activity perspective tends to blend theory and practice together. While an economic perspective emphasizes parsimony and generalizability, study of practices and activities involves sociological investigation of reality in great detail (Jarzabkowski and Whittington, 2008).

In managing strategic change, organizational (internal) politics – divisible into office politics and intra-organizational politics – is one of several tools of choice. 'Politics' is awkward to define. Customary definition includes governance (e.g. allocation and use of authority), political methods and tactics (e.g. power and influence) and factional scheming for any of the former. Politics carries both negative and positive connotations. Western managers may feel uncomfortable psychologically and morally with power and politics concepts (Lewis, 2002). The reality is that they engage in political action in various ways. Political action is simply more obvious during strategic change periods. The case of Beiersdorf-Lechia S.A. in Poznan, Poland (Blazejewski and Dorow, 2003) is illustrative. The Beiersdorf group reacquired in 1997 a former subsidiary, expropriated by the Polish Communist regime after World War II. In two years, Beiersdorf radically transformed a state-owned enterprise operating as an inefficient, production-oriented conglomerate into a profitable, market-oriented consumer goods firm. The authors propose a comprehensive model of organizational transformation that combines micro-level change management and organizational politics. An aspect of change management and business reengineering efforts has been an emphasis on empowerment, meaning delegation of decision-making authority and initiative to employees at lower levels in companies. 'Despite all the talk and the change programs, empowerment is still mostly an illusion' (Argyris, 1998: 98).

POSITIVE AND NEGATIVE POLITICS

Any basic management text contains materials on power and influence as well as on leadership and authority. Organizational politics connotes how decisions are made and how conflicts are handled. Office politics connotes how individuals compete and maneuver. Intra-organizational politics connotes how inter-unit and intra-group conflicts are handled. There are competing negative and positive views of either category of internal politics.

The negative view portrays politics as undesirable because manipulative and factional. Politics has been analogized to warfare and to organized crime. Machiavelli's *The Prince* is invoked (Buskirk, 1974;

McAlpine, 2000). This negative view emphasizes politics as pursuit of power (Lord, 2003). Bullying is a form of destructive leadership (Ferris et al., 2007). However, 'Power is a very difficult problem with which to deal in the theory of organization' (Crozier, 1964: 145). It is awkward to differentiate, under conditions of concealment, subtlety and uncertainty, among authority, coercion, command, control, influence, manipulation and power in organizations. Any can be functional (facilitating action) and dysfunctional (generating conflict). A myth of the 'corporate political jungle' itself may have political value (Klein, 1988). In layoff conditions, negative politics may intensify (Gary, 2002).

Burns (1978) advanced a positive view of leadership and politics that has gained traction. Perception and understanding of phenomena and tactics noted above are now different (Gary, 1996). Emphasis has shifted to appropriate use of office and intra-organizational politics to promote group welfare. A 'quiet' leadership model features persuasion through selling of good options or ideas (Khurana, 2002). Selling, a dimension of impression management and brand management in marketing and public opinion, is both cognitive and affective (McFarland, 2004). A good idea does not sell itself. There must be senior management buy-in and support in other departments. Selling is especially important when business units compete for tight resources. An organization may be modeled as a prisoners' dilemma. Individuals and units in conflict must cooperate for joint production. Design of structures, incentives and climates for positive influence as distinct from coercion or competitive gaming is a key research path.

POLITICS OF STRATEGY FORMULATION, IMPLEMENTATION AND EVALUATION

The job of executives is as much politics, conflict management, influence and motivation as strategic choice, organizational architecture and resource allocation. Key decisions are unique rather than repetitive and routine (Banfield, 2003). The firm is a political arena (Mintzberg, 1985) and managers need political competence (Hayes, 1984): 'running a company is like politics. You are always trying to balance interests and personalities and trying to keep people motivated' (Bower and Weinberg, 1988: 50–51, citing Jean Riboud, then Chief Executive Officer, or CEO of Schlumberger). 'Managers of today's multinationals are not so much economic decision makers as they are governors of a social and political strategic management process' (Bower and Doz, 1979: 165). Pettigrew (1977, 1992) emphasized specifically that strategy formulation is a political process, in the boardroom as well as in management (see Van Ees et al.,

2009). Enron illustrates how management can undermine and corrupt the board of directors and the internal and external advisors (e.g. auditors and lawyers). Corporate identity formation, illustrated at a Brazilian telecommunications company, Telemig, may reflect a political dimension of power relations, resource mobilization and legitimacy struggles (Rodrigues and Child, 2008).

The main emphasis in this section is on relationship conflict: who disagrees with whom, how, when and why. Variations in multiple political relationships and tactics are rich. Managerial process and leadership are not well understood. A useful interpretation of executive strategies for tough times is Phillips' (1992) study of Lincoln's practices and activities. Relationships may involve politics and hidden agendas (Atkinson and Butcher, 2003). Absence of trust may undermine managerial effectiveness. Pettigrew (1975) suggested that in client–consultant and consultant–consultant relationships a consultant's influence is conditioned on possession and tactical use of five power resources characterized as expertise, control over information, political access and sensitivity, perceived stature and group support. A resource view ties to the RBV approach to strategic management theorizing.

In focusing on relationships among actors, groups and units, it is important to keep in mind that politics and conflict may be different phenomena (Eisenhardt and Bourgeois, 1988) incorrectly conflated. While politics is ubiquitous, not all politics need be conflict. In this differentiation, politics is observable (even if covert) actions by individuals to enhance influence (i.e. persuasion and motivation of others) and power (i.e. capacity to affect outcomes). There are various approaches for doing so (such as coalition formation, lobbying, cooptation, information control and hidden agendas). Conflict is open expression of disagreement. Politics is thus different from direct influence tactics such as forthright discussion and information sharing. Eisenhardt and Bourgeois' study of eight firms in the microcomputer industry suggested that politics as defined above occurred more when power was centralized and tended to reduce organizational performance. Conflict can occur over many things, including strategic direction and resource allocation. A significant body of literature has emerged concerning how to manage conflict functionally. More research and hypothesis testing are needed to help isolate specific conditions, options and outcomes.

Institutional and organizational structures affect the decision of how to decide (Engel and Weber, 2007). Individuals can choose from a plurality of problem-solving modes, including technology, experts or groups. Engel and Weber propose a model of problem-solving modes in order to help identify access points for intervention. Hierarchy may serve to channel influence activities or power struggles. Multi-divisional (M-form) structures may involve both lower influence costs than single-tier structures and more scope for organizational conflict as well as more executives to be influenced (Inderst et al., 2007). The M-form organization helps to decentralize conflict to the divisional level and to limit that conflict to a small number of actors, strategizing in teams (Paroutis and Pettigrew, 2007) and competing over a fraction of the overall corporate resources and outcomes. At the same time, the M-form may generate free-rider problems in rent seeking. How to balance these conflicting considerations is basically unknown. Research is desirable to help identify the relationships in varying organizational structures.

A body of literature concerns influence tactics and employee perceptions of organizational and office politics (Chang et al., 2009). Advice on influence tactics and impression management is available (Krackhardt and Hanson, 1993; Reardon, 2001). There are studies of acquisition of strategic policy influence by lower-level employees (Bouquet and Birkinshaw, 2008; Cohen and Bradford, 2005: 278, concerning Apple; Hamel, 2000, concerning IBM). A rich field for study is the development and testing of ethically proper tactics for dealing with office politics. McFarland (2001) suggests four 'bulletproof strategies' for a positive approach. For example, how to 'politick' depends on the company culture and involves care in choosing friends within the company. Sussman et al. (2002) study self-serving political communications tactics. Reported data suggest that encoding and transmitting self-serving political messages depend on the target (e.g. boss, subordinate or peer) and the channel (e.g. face-to-face, telephone, memo or e-mail). There are few comparative case studies and difficulties with case study methods.

Longitudinal investigation may be desirable to study the relationship of influence tactics and perceptions of intra-organizational politics (Vigoda and Cohen, 2002). Such investigation is difficult and resource intensive. There may be important intermediate linkages and process issues lying between tactics and perceptions. There are also considerations of person–organization fit and whether personal expectations are met.

A growing literature studies perceptions of organizational politics. That the two general forms of internal politics are likely conflated is a difficulty for interpretation and theory building. A meta-analysis of 79 independent samples from 59 studies (published and unpublished) aggregated just over 25,000 individuals (Miller et al., 2008). The meta-analysis suggests strong negative relationships between perceptions of organizational politics and job satisfaction or organizational commitment. The meta-analysis suggests moderately positive relationships between perceptions of organizational politics and job stress or turnover intentions. The relationship of perceptions to job performance is not significant. Some moderators in these relationships were age, public versus private sector and international cultural differences. A multiple-foci approach is likely useful in understanding relationships between politics and organizational outcomes. Maslyn and Fedor (1998) reported that, controlling for relationship with one's supervisor, perceptions of politics at the organizational (i.e. macro) level predicted turnover intentions while perceptions of politics at the group (i.e. micro) level predicted organizational citizenship behavior. Both foci predicted organizational commitment. What has been left unanswered is whether negative politics can prevail at one level and positive politics at another level in the same organization; and how transformation from one perception to another can be engineered.

In addition to relationship conflict, there can be task conflict. Units and individuals may be assigned, inadvertently or deliberately, overlapping responsibilities that promote task competition and conflict. Data for 69 academic departments in six important Canadian universities indicate that intra-departmental task and relationship conflict are associated with perceptions of political climate. Individual-level role conflict, rather than departmental or disciplinary antecedents, was a predictor of department-level politics (Darr and Johns, 2004). These various findings suggest that there is an overarching conceptualization, involving multiple antecedents and consequences, that is not yet available in the literature. It is therefore difficult to assess the implications of specific research findings.

Task conflict and shared responsibility might be used positively rather than negatively. Burgelman (2002: 54, 66, 71, 102–103, 368) reports how Intel has emphasized a culture of disagreement followed by employee commitment in order to emphasize knowledge (i.e. expertise) over hierarchy. This approach of constructive confrontation may be beneficial rather than dysfunctional. Dynamic capability theory predicts that some firms will be better at exploring new markets and new technologies (Danneels, 2008). Organizational antecedents of such advantageous capabilities may include constructive conflict and willingness to cannibalize (i.e. shift resources), as well as environmental scanning, tolerance for failure and slack resources (Danneels, 2008). These practices are aimed at generating a continuing flow of innovations and continuing organizational adaptations to environmental changes.

A survey of 250 British managers reported their experience and perceptions of organizational politics (Buchanan, 2008). Most respondents viewed politics as both ethical and necessary. They attributed various dimensions (effectiveness, change, resources and reputation) to political tactics. Frequently experienced tactics were networking, key supporters, power broker relationships, bending rules and self-promotion.

Misinformation, rumor mongering and blackmail files were reported as rare. These respondents were willing to behave politically, act ruthlessly and practice reciprocity to political behavior by others. From a more critical perspective, there are issues of respondent bias; and accepting respondent views that regard necessity as ethical remains problematic. The findings suggest that positive techniques occurred much more frequently than negative techniques.

Research suggests positive and negative effects of participation in the processes of strategy formulation implementation and evaluation. The positive effects may be shared vision, greater rationality and greater adaptiveness. The negative effects may be more intensive politics, greater cultural inertia and increased constraints. A survey of over 6000 managers (Collier et al., 2004) found that reported levels of participation improved the positive effects just noted. Managers also found strategy process less top-down, less influenced by politics and not so affected by internal culture or constraints. In general, participation tends to have positive rather than negative effects. More critically, how specific organizational conditions and actor attitudes/beliefs shape these views needs more investigation.

MORAL ISSUES IN ORGANIZATIONAL AND OFFICE POLITICS

An actor's choice between and the consequences of positive and negative politics have ethical implications (Cavanagh et al., 1981; Lee, 1998). Bad leadership, while possibly effective in the short run in accord with Machiavelli's predictions, focuses on negative politics and abuse of others (Kellerman, 2004). In businesses, bad leadership approaches may generate ethical issues and long-term performance issues. Franco Bernabè's transformation of the Italian energy company Eni is an example of morally grounded leadership focused on positive politics and inspiration of personnel (Hill and Wetlaufer, 1998). Behnam and Rasche (2009) emphasize that strategic choice involves reflection on moral issues. A process approach tends to emphasize how strategic management and ethical reflection are related in detail. Conflict between individual incentives and organizational outcomes suggests continuing studies of employee moral duty and organizational citizenship behavior.

Jackall (1983) studied 'moral mazes' (i.e. difficult and concealed choices) in organizations. He reported that success and failure tended, once past early stages of career development, not to depend on personal accomplishments. Success becomes socially defined and distributed, because managerial competence can be taken for granted. (This finding corresponds to a modeling assumption of perceived equal quality of competitors in promotion tournaments, discussed below.) Loyalty to authority and organizational ethos are key social factors (Jackall, 1983: 122). Jackall (1983: 126–127) reported a situation in which the new CEO of a large conglomerate found a way to move unwanted and costly capital accounts to operating expenses. Reorganization placed the operating expenses under a new vice-president's division, the earnings of which suffered, illustrating distant effects (or repercussions). The vice-president eventually resigned. More critically, we do not have systematic theory of when specific practices and activities are morally good, bad or suspect.

POLITICS OF RESOURCE ALLOCATION PROCESSES

An important political dimension of organizational life concerns distributional conflict (Inderst et al., 2007) and thus resource allocation, broadly defined to include personnel as well as funding. With respect to personnel, Cai and Feng (2007) model the hiring of new members, upon retirement of incumbents, into a fixed head-count 'club' (i.e. organization) by voting of remaining incumbents. (Candidates differ in a single quality valued equally by all organizational members.) The majority distribute rent distribution among themselves. The authors conclude that there may be an optimum politics level (too little versus too much) relative to long-run organization welfare. The relationship affects whether majority or unanimity voting is better. More critically, businesses are rarely directly clubs meeting the model's conditions. (There are organizations where present members strongly influence selection of new members.) How organization members indirectly 'vote' (i.e. influence decisions and outcomes) requires further investigation. Such highly abstract models – insightful and suggestive of research options – may be too distant from reality and complexity to yield specific testable hypotheses.

Bower (1986) modeled corporate resource allocation processes in terms of three nested spheres. This process model begins with technical and economic aspects of a project. Project evaluation is embedded within a sphere of political support based on individual or unit estimate of self-interest benefits and costs. This political process occurs within and is shaped by the broader organizational context (e.g. strategy, structure, culture, environment, and so forth). Noda and Bower (1996) developed a theory of strategy making as iterated processes of resource allocation, now associated with the Burgelman–Bower RAP approach noted above. More critically, we need to integrate models and theory with detailed study of practices and activities.

A CEO's job history may influence capital allocation decisions within M-form firms (Xuan, 2009). Divisions not previously affiliated with a new CEO receive more capital funds. This reverse-favoritism depends on the CEO's relative authority and divisional bargaining power. Specialist CEOs negatively affect investment efficiency in using the capital budget to obtain cooperation from powerful managers in previously unaffiliated divisions. These findings are revealing. But interpretation of motivation is more difficult. The implication is that CEOs are garnering internal political support. CEOs may be trying to count on support from their area of the company while obtaining support elsewhere by providing resources in exchange for cooperation. What are the efficiency effects; and do they really matter strategically?

Cremers et al. (2010) examined the internal capital market of a large retail-banking group. The authors obtained internal managerial accounting data for internal capital transfers, investments and cash flows for local member banks. They find that internal corporate politics does affect internal capital allocation. Interestingly, they report that member-bank 'power' is not abused but rather operates through self-restraint to overcome asymmetric information problems between member banks and group headquarters concerning deposit volatility.

Management accountants have long studied the game of budget control (Hofstede, 1968). In recent years there has been a movement to introduce budget-less management process. Such budgeting process attempts to focus on strategic alignment rather than meeting predetermined targets (Hope and Fraser, 2003; Jensen, 2001). Budgeting absorbs time, attention, energy and other valuable resources. But we do not have either a formal theory of optimal budgeting process or an understanding of how political practices and activities will influence design, operation and evaluation of such a process.

POLITICS OF PROMOTION TOURNAMENT COMPETITION

'Turf' and 'promotion' are examples of competitive politics within organizations. Who becomes CEO and how is important (Khurana, 2002). Some literature has proposed multiple rules for successful self-advancement to CEO and laws of power within organization. The ethical implications of such rules and the group welfare outcomes have received insufficient attention. Economists have begun to apply the concept of a rank-order 'tournament' to office politics and resource allocation decisions with particular attention to personnel promotions (i.e. selection tournaments) and internal capital market allocation outcomes (i.e. capital rationing and budgeting). A tournament is any contest composed of a series of elimination games or trials.

Contestants have incentives to sabotage rivals, who could be the most productive employees (Münster, 2007). Better candidates may tend to avoid such contests. Some contestants may be easier to sabotage than others. Research should develop this theory, testable hypotheses and evidence from different situations, and alternative institutional designs for countering the tendency. Multiple tournament designs might increase the probability of the most productive contestant being promoted. Research includes budget constraints and adaptive learning models (Stein and Rapoport, 2005). It has proven difficult to isolate key considerations (Carpenter et al., 2010). Tournaments may improve work effort in the absence of sabotage. Evidence on incentive effect is thin because of difficulties in separating effort, ability and output. Sabotage may be subtle versions of subjective peer evaluation or office politics.

Researchers have applied the promotion concept to internal capital rationing. Han et al. (2009) model capital allocation in a conglomerate (i.e. a diversified portfolio firm) in which divisional managers with uncertain (i.e. unobservable) abilities compete for promotion to CEO. A conglomerate is typically understood as a problem in allocating capital among non-comparable business units. The authors propose certain specific implications of the tournament. A divisional manager can sometimes advance towards CEO by secretly increasing the variance of divisional performance. The presumed role of corporate capital rationing is to limit this unobservable distortion, increase conglomerate efficiency and allow a principal to make more accurate promotion decisions. Firms for which CEO talent is more important for firm performance are thus more likely to ration capital. The authors consider the conditions under which incentive wage or capital rationing is the more efficient tournament incentive. The larger the incentive, the more important capital rationing becomes. More critically, we need testable hypotheses and empirical data against which to assess such models.

Sayre et al. (1998) designed an experiment to study investment project selection under conditions of tournament incentive contracts. In this experiment, a principal prefers projects with lower systematic risk and thus highest risk-adjusted rates of return. The authors report that managers may under some conditions maximize their own expected compensation, resulting in lower risk-adjusted return for the principal. The results indicated that subjects recognized the strategic implications of alternative promotion scenarios and responded opportunistically. Experimental studies have an important place in research, but experimental conditions can vary significantly from real field conditions.

A variant concerns views of earnings targets versus rates of return. Graham et al. (2005) surveyed several hundred financial executives. Because of severe market reaction to missing an earnings target, firms tend to sacrifice economic value to meet a short-run earnings target. Over three-quarters of the financial executives would trade economic value to obtain smooth earnings. Over half would avoid initiating a very positive net present value project in order to meet quarterly earnings. More critically, it is important to emphasize that there is a trade-off consideration: Chief Financial Officers (CFOs), like CEOs, must hold their jobs; investor reaction may not be strictly rational. Such findings help illustrate that political considerations are at work.

SOME SUGGESTED RESEARCH OPPORTUNITIES

There are multiple opportunities for research into the rich complexity of the politics of strategy process. These opportunities arise in part because strategy process is vitally important to understand, the political dimension cuts across content and process as well as organizational levels, and present research efforts are fragmented across several disciplines. This section identifies some of the research opportunities that may stimulate scholarly interest. Theory development, empirical testing, case studies and prescription of ethics and tactics are all open for research. Some of the studies reported earlier help indicate possibilities. In addition, organizational (i.e. micro) politics would benefit from development of some overarching conception or framework for how political practices and activities interact with organizational processes, strategy outcomes and environment–organization interactions.

The 'black box' of organizational process is still not fully mapped and understood. Allison and Zelikow (1999) identified three different models of a government behaving as if (1) a unitary rational actor; (2) a bureaucracy of partly competing and partly cooperating subunits headed by imperfectly rational actors engaged in negotiations, tournaments and persuasion; and (3) a set of evolving organizational routines partly subdivided into those subunits. Hart (2010) explains that there are three competing theories of the firm as organization that have not even now been fully developed or organized in working relationship to one another. As Hart notes, the predominant approach in social science literature has been to treat the firm as if a corporate person, a unitary rational actor. This rational assumption draws on economic insights and models the firm as, in effect, its CEO, making all the key decisions and using authority to allocate resources and direct subordinates. A second alternative is to view the firm as a complex nexus of contracts among multiple actors who are self-interested agents possessing asymmetric information. (This nexus of contracts view can be extended to include external as well as internal stakeholders, but the recent tendency has been to characterize stakeholders as a complex locus of relationships.) A third alternative is to view the firm as a set of organizational routines enacted and carried out by individual actors playing various roles within the firm. The second and third views comport well with the micro study of practices and activities in strategy process research.

Considerable research effort addresses corporate political activity, understood as how businesses influence governments. (Hillman et al., 2004, provide the best overall review of that literature.) Extra-organizational (i.e. macro) politics is itself a broad topic, as it involves not simply how domestic and multinational enterprises influence governments in very different contexts across the globe, but also how managers interact with multiple kinds of stakeholders (Jensen, 2002). Activist nongovernmental organizations have arisen for the specific purpose of influencing both businesses and governments. Fruitful research opportunities concern how all the internal considerations identified in this paper as aspects of strategy process affect policy choices and resource allocations affecting corporate political activity, corporate social responsibility, stakeholder management and related matters. This set of topics should be of particular interest to strategy, organizational, stakeholder and political science scholars.

A major conceptual and empirical difficulty concerns the working definitions, interrelationships and contingent illustrations of authority, influence, power and resources. The macro study of strategic management is now strongly shaped by the RBV and theories of dynamic capabilities (i.e. integrated combinations of resources, practices and activities that change both internally as organizational phenomena and in response to external pressures of various kinds). Conceptually, it is still not clear what the notion of power is intended to define. One school of thought tends to conflate power with the authority and influence of executives and managers over subordinates. Another school of thought tends to regard power as individual or organizational capability to affect outcomes. One can speak of power resources, including authority, influence and skills. The working definition of resources is quite broad and thus arguably amorphous, as virtually anything as potential or actual value can be regarded as a resource for actors on the one hand and for organizations on the other hand. There is ample opportunity for research concerning definition, accumulation, exercise and consequences of authority and influence. There is much to uncover about sources, structure, channels and tactics of authority exercise and influence through qualitative case studies and quantitative testing. What are the pertinent differences between influence and manipulation?

Economic reasoning, prominent in strategy content research, has advantages and disadvantages. A key advantage is that it emphasizes logical analysis aimed at generating testable hypotheses about behaviors and outcomes. A key disadvantage is that economic models are dependent on initial assumptions, and perhaps researcher expectations about behaviors and outcomes, in developing logical propositions and testable hypotheses. Behavioral economics, drawing partly on psychological and sociological insights, is helping now to enrich what was previously a purely logical theory not well linked to human motivation, cognition and emotion. The interaction among economic, psychological–sociological and political dimensions may promote both rigorous and relevant research into a broad range of managerial and organizational phenomena. There is ample scope for an economic approach, and economists, in the study of compensation arrangements (there is reason to think that an administered market may be at work), organizational architecture, strategic choices, corporate governance mechanisms, capital allocation processes, promotion tournaments and other intra-organizational matters. Economic analysis may help with identifying optimal mechanisms. As with designing auctions (where the issue concerns how to maximize final price while assuring process integrity), what is the optimal design for promotion tournaments? What is the optimal design for capital budgeting processes?

Corporate governance has been largely the province of legal and economic analyses. Part of economic inquiry has been directed at improving the market rationality of legal doctrines. A new literature is emerging aimed at developing a more behavioral theory of boards of directors and corporate governance arrangements. Van Ees et al. (2009) draw on political bargaining, decision-making routines, satisficing theory and problemistic search to direct greater attention to personal interactions and intra-board processes, coalition building and the interaction of conflict and cooperation within boards. The senior executives of firms are typically board members. How do internal and external directors interact? The importance of understanding behavior and politics in corporate governance is underscored by the recent spate of corporate frauds and scandals (e.g. Enron, Long-Term Capital Management, Parmalat, Royal Ahold, Tyco and WorldCom), apparent industry failures (savings and loans earlier, investment banking and mortgage lending most recently) and regional financial crises (e.g. Asia, Japan, Latin America, Russia and Sweden). Relationships among executives, directors, advisors, rating services, regulators and auditors are not well understood, and appear to be subject to various forces.

The ethics of management choices and behaviors should receive expanded scope of inquiry. There is ample opportunity here for both philosophers and social scientists. The emphasis has rested on developing cases for and against corporate social responsibility and standards for business ethics in varying situations. As Jackall (1983) and other researchers have pointed out, virtually all choices and behaviors might be infused with ethical considerations. Yet we have relatively little attention paid to the ethical dimension of office politics and intra-organizational politics. There is evidence emerging in the literature on promotion tournaments that certain designs may tend to foster backstabbing and other forms of misconduct that could result in better qualified (and honest) candidates exiting or being forced out while less qualified (dishonest and dishonorable) candidates advance. If so, the literature rediscovers Machiavelli's thesis that bad princes ascend to power more rapidly while good princes hold power more easily. It is conceivable that such designs, in combination with the behavioral aspects of corporate governance arrangements, may result in the wrong CEOs being selected. What is the empirical distribution of these choices; and how should the choices be evaluated? More broadly, how do desirable CEOs control and regulate misconduct (including bribery) within the organization? A difficult aspect of intra-organizational ethics concerns whether we can develop and test a useful theory of distributive justice. The large bonuses received by managers in investment banks in recent years, now the subject of governmental scrutiny, raise profound questions concerning whether merit and contribution, extortion or organizational routines and executive misunderstanding are at work.

A fruitful opportunity for scholarship lies in efforts to develop some overarching conceptualization – theories, frameworks and models – for integrating various research strands into a more coherent view of the politics of strategy process. While a key barrier has been a negative view of politics (i.e. internal resource allocation should be market efficient rather than politically influenced), the literature is changing in emphasis to a more positive view of politics, conflict and leadership. We now understand that conflict may be functional (and constructive) or dysfunctional (and destructive), depending on the organization, the actors, the timing and the decision situation. Intel has tried to develop a process (and a culture of supporting beliefs and commitment) of constructive confrontation. Such a contingent view of practices and activities should be placed within some broader understanding of what we characterize as politics.

As an aid in that conceptual development and for suggesting the rich variety of research opportunities arising in a political view of strategy process, Table 3.1 (pp. 45–6) provides a relatively simple listing of antecedents, consequences and opportunities. It is not realistic to provide much more than the preliminary structuring afforded by the table, because the set of considerations arising in the ubiquity of strategy politics is quite rich and complex and also we actually know relatively little as yet about the various research topics. The table does not include a precise mapping from a particular antecedent to a particular consequence, as it is likely that multiple antecedents affect a particular consequence and have multiple consequences (and some consequences in Table 3.1 may themselves be antecedents and vice versa). The likelihood of complex relationships is what generates rich research opportunities for economists, organizational specialists, philosophers, political scientists, psychologists, sociologists and other specialists. At the same time, specialist examination of specific topics may have a tendency not to consider the bigger picture of strategy content and strategy process.

For example, to take micromanagement as a topic, the conventional wisdom is that micromanaging of subordinates is generally a bad idea and tends to foster negative politics. The practice arguably discourages subordinates, risks misallocation of effort and attention by superiors and has other disadvantages. However, the literature also recognizes that there are circumstances in which micromanagement, despite all these defects, is necessary and thus, if not strictly desirable, nevertheless unavoidable. Beyond this general formulation, some evidence that on the whole micromanagement tends to be bad practice and some case illustrations of bad and good instances, we have nothing approaching a formalized and tested contingent theory. Who defines when micromanagement is unavoidable? Is micromanaging behavior a psychological defect or a rational calculation of necessity? There is no well-developed theory of micromanagement, including the antecedents and consequences of office politics and intra-organizational politics. Bernabè, mentioned earlier, is a prime example of a micromanager. Under the conditions prevailing at Eni when he suddenly took over control of the firm, such micromanagement may have been desirable as well as necessary. Is his conduct in that situation by proclivity or by calculation? The strategic situation at Eni (then a state-owned enterprise) involved widespread corruption, managerial inexperience, lack of strategic planning, non-rationalization of a diverse conglomerate built up over time and other conditions.

SUMMARY AND CONCLUSION

This paper identifies, organizes and assesses several disparate literatures that bear on the increasing study of organizational (micro) politics of strategy process. The purpose is to help identify potential future research opportunities and contributions to strategy process theory and practice. A key matter is how to integrate this diversity and combine it with strategic management theory and practice. An executive's job is as much intra-organizational and office politics as leadership, conflict management, resource allocation and strategic choice. Politics is a process activity of great practical importance. Perceptions of intra-organizational and office politics separate into positive and negative theories of politics and partici-pation. The paper first addresses the micro strategy perspective and then the differences between positive and negative politics. The paper identifies four key dimensions of internal politics for research: politics of strategy formulation, implementation and evaluation; moral issues in organiz-ational and office politics; politics of resource allocation processes; and politics of promotion tournament competition (and similar phenomena) within organizations.

The paper provides several value-added contributions to the existing literature. One contribution is to identify multiple strands of research across several disciplines that can be appropriately grouped under politics of strategy process. This grouping helps emphasize the vital importance of the political dimension of strategy content and strategy process. Another contribution is to offer some critical assessments of aspects of those various strands of research. Much of the available research is basically isolated and not integrated into any overarching conception or framework for understanding the role of the specific models and findings in strategic management. Another contribution is to provide a first-cut structuring in Table 3.1 of antecedents, consequences and research opportunities in strategy policies. Another contribution is the paper's discussion of those research opportunities.

REFERENCES

Allison, G. and P. Zelikow (1999), *Essence of Decision: Explaining the Cuban Missile Crisis*, New York: Longman, 2nd edn, Boston, MA: Little, Brown, 1971 (G. T. Allison).

Argyris, C. (1998), 'Empowerment: The emperor's new clothes', *Harvard Business Review*, **76**(3): 98–105.

Atkinson, S. and D. Butcher (2003), 'Trust in managerial relationships', *Journal of Managerial Psychology*, **18**(4): 282–304.

Banfield, E. C. (2003), *Political Influence*, Piscataway, NJ: Transaction Publishers; Glencoe, IL: Free Press (1st edn 1961).

Behnam, M. and A. Rasche (2009), 'Are strategists from Mars and ethicists from Venus? – Strategizing as ethical reflection', *Journal of Business Ethics*, **84**(1) January: 79–88.

Blazejewski, S. and W. Dorow (2003), 'Managing organizational politics for radical change: The case of Beiersdorf-Lechia S.A., Poznan', *Journal of World Business*, **38**(3): 204–223.

Bouquet, C. and J. Birkinshaw (2008), 'Managing power in the multinational corporation: How low-power actors gain influence', *Journal of Management*, **34**(3) June: 477–508.

Bower, J. L. (1986), *Managing the Resource Allocation Process: A Study of Corporate Planning and Investment*, Boston, MA: Harvard Business School Press, rev. edn, Boston, MA: Division of Research, Graduate School of Business Administration, Harvard University, 1970.

Bower, J. L. and Y. Doz (1979), 'Strategy formulation: A social and political process', in D. E. Schendel and C. W. Hofer (eds), *Strategic Management*, Boston, MA: Little, Brown, pp. 152–166.

Bower, J. L. and C. G. Gilbert (eds) (2005), *From Resource Allocation to Strategy*, Oxford, UK: Oxford University Press.

Bower, J. L. and M. W. Weinberg (1988), 'Statecraft, strategy, and corporate leadership', *California Management Review*, **30**(2) Winter: 39–56.

Buchanan, D. A. (2008), 'You stab my back, I'll stab yours: Management experience and perceptions of organization political behaviour', *British Journal of Management*, **19**(1) March: 49–64.

Burgelman, R. A. (1996), 'A process model of strategic business exit: Implications for an evolutionary perspective on strategy', *Strategic Management Journal*, **17**(Special Issue) Summer: 193–214.

Burgelman, R. A. (2002), *Strategy is Destiny: How Strategy-Making Shapes a Company's Destiny*, New York: Free Press (foreword by Andy Grove).

Burns, J. M. (1978), *Leadership*, New York: Harper & Row.

Buskirk, R. H. (1974), *Modern Management and Machiavelli*, Boston, MA: Cahners Books.

Cai, H. and H. A. Feng (2007), 'A theory of organizational dynamics: Internal politics and efficiency', http://ssrn.com/abstract=943608.

Campbell, A. and M. Alexander (1997), 'What's wrong with strategy?', *Harvard Business Review*, **75**(6) November–December: 42–44, 46, 48–51.

Carpenter, J. P., P. H. Matthews and J. Schirm (2010), 'Tournaments and office politics: Evidence from a real effort experiment', *American Economic Review*, **100**(1): 504–517.

Cavanagh, G. F., D. J. Moberg and M. Velasquez (1981), 'The ethics of organizational politics', *Academy of Management Review*, **6**(3) July: 363–374.

Chang, C.-H., C. C. Rosen and P. E. Levy (2009), 'The relationship between perceptions of organizational politics and employee attitudes, strain, and behavior: A meta-analytic examination', *Academy of Management Journal*, **52**(4) August: 779–801.

Cohen, A. R. and D. L. Bradford (2005), *Influence without Authority*, Hoboken, NJ: Wiley, 2nd edn.

Collier, N., F. Fishwick and S. W. Floyd (2004), 'Managerial involvement and perceptions of strategy process', *Long Range Planning*, **37**(1) February: 67–83.

Cremers, M., R. Huang and Z. Sautner (2010), 'Understanding internal capital markets and corporate politics in a banking group', http://ssrn.com/abstract=1183802.

Crozier, M. (1964), *The Bureaucratic Phenomenon*, Chicago, IL: University of Chicago Press.

Cyert, R. M. and J. G. March (1963), *A Behavioral Theory of the Firm*, Englewood Cliffs, NJ: Prentice-Hall.

Danneels, E. (2008), 'Organizational antecedents of second-order competences', *Strategic Management Journal*, **29**(5): 519–543.

Darr, W. and G. Johns (2004), 'Political decision-making climates: Theoretical processes and multi-level antecedents', *Human Relations*, **57**(2) February: 169–200.

Eisenhardt, K. M. and L. J. Bourgeois (1988), 'Politics of strategic decision in high-velocity environments: Toward a midrange theory', *Academy of Management Journal*, **31**(4) December: 737–770.

Engel, C. and E. U. Weber (2007), 'The impact of institutions on the decision of how to decide', *Journal of Institutional Economics*, **3**: 323–349.

Ferris, G. R., R. Zinko, R. L. Brouer, M. R. Buckley and M. G. Harvey (2007), 'Strategic bullying as a supplementary, balanced perspective on destructive leadership', *Leadership Quarterly*, **18**(3) June: 195–206.

Friedrich, C. J. (1963), 'Influence and the rule of anticipated reactions', in *Man and His Government: An Empirical Theory of Politics*, New York: McGraw-Hill, pp. 199–215.

Gary, L. (1996), 'Power: How its meaning in corporate life is changing', *Harvard Management Update Article*, U9610A.

Gary, L. (2002), 'Fighting the enemy within', *Harvard Management Update Article*, U0202B.

Graham, J. R., C. R. Harvey and S. A. Rajgopal (2005), 'The economic implications of corporate financial reporting', *Journal of Accounting and Economics*, **40**: 3–73.

Hamel, G. (2000), 'Waking up IBM: How a gang of unlikely rebels transformed Big Blue', *Harvard Business Review*, **78**(4) July–August: 137–146.

Han, B., D. A. Hirshleifer and J. C. Persons (2009), 'Promotion tournaments and capital rationing', *Review of Financial Studies*, **22**(1): 219–255.

Hart, D. M. (2010), 'The political theory of the firm', in D. Coen, W. Grant and G. K. Wilson (eds), *Oxford Handbook of Business and Government*, Oxford, UK: Oxford University Press, pp. 173–190.

Hayes, J. (1984), 'The politically competent manager', *Journal of General Management*, **10**: 24–33.

Hill, L. and S. Wetlaufer (1998), 'Leadership when there is no one to ask: An interview with Eni's Franco Bernabè', *Harvard Business Review*, **76**(4) July–August: 81–94.

Hillman, A. J., G. Keim and D. Schuler (2004), 'Corporate political activity: A review and research agenda', *Journal of Management*, **30**(6): 837–854.

Hofstede, G. H. (1968), *The Game of Budget Control*, London: Tavistock; Assen, The Netherlands: Van Gorcum; New York: Garland, 1984.

Hope, J. and R. Fraser (2003), 'Who needs budgets?', *Harvard Business Review*, **81**(2) February: 108–115.

Inderst, R., H. M. Müller and K. Wärneryd (2007), 'Distributional conflict in organizations', *European Economic Review*, **51**(2) February: 385–402.

Jackall, R. (1983), 'Moral mazes: Bureaucracy and managerial work', *Harvard Business Review*, **61**(5), September–October: 118–130.

Jarzabkowski, P. and R. Whittington (2008), 'A strategy-as-practice approach to strategy research and education', *Journal of Management Inquiry*, **17**(4) December: 282–286.

Jay, A. (1968), *Management and Machiavelli*, New York: Holt, Rinehart & Winston.

Jensen, M. C. (2001), 'Corporate budgeting is broken – let's fix it', *Harvard Business Review*, **79**(11) November: 94–101.

Jensen, M. C. (2002), 'Value maximization, stakeholder theory, and the corporate objective function', in J. Andriof, S. Waddock, B. Husted and S. S. Rahman (eds), *Unfolding Stakeholder Thinking*, Sheffield, UK: Greenleaf, pp. 65–84.

Johnson, G., L. Melin and R. Whittington (2003), 'Micro strategy and strategizing: Towards an activity-based view', *Journal of Management Studies*, **40**(1) January: 3–22.

Karnani, A. G. (2008), 'Controversy: The essence of strategy', *Business Strategy Review*, **19**(4) Winter: 28–34.

Kellerman, B. (2004), *Bad Leadership*, Boston, MA: Harvard Business School Press.

Khurana, R. (2002), *Searching for a Corporate Savior*, Princeton, NJ: Princeton University Press.

Klein, J. I. (1988), 'The myth of the corporate political jungle: Politicization as a political strategy', *Journal of Management Studies*, **25**(1): 1–12.

Kobayashi, H. (2007), 'Folk theorems for infinitely repeated games played by organizations with short-lived members', *International Economic Review*, **48**(2) May: 517–549.

Kotter, J. P. (1985), *Power and Influence*, New York: Free Press.

Krackhardt, D. and J. R. Hanson (1993), 'Informal networks: The company behind the chart', *Harvard Business Review*, **71**(4) July–August: 104–111.

Lee, B. (1998), *The Power Principle: Influence with Honor*, New York: Simon & Schuster.

Lewis, D. (2002), 'The place of organizational politics in strategic change', *Strategic Change*, **11**(1) January–February: 25–34.

Lord, C. (2003), *The Modern Prince*, New Haven, CT: Yale University Press.

Luehrman, T. A. (1998), 'Strategy as a portfolio of real options', *Harvard Business Review*, **76**(5) September–October: 89–99.

MacMillan, I. C. (1978), *Strategy Formulation: Political Concepts*, St. Paul, MN: West Publishing Co.

Maslyn, J. M. and D. B. Fedor (1998), 'Perceptions of politics: Does measuring different foci matter?', *Journal of Applied Psychology*, **83**(4) August: 645–653.

McAlpine, A. (2000), 'Renaissance realpolitik for modern management', in P. Harris, A. Lock and P. Rees (eds), *Machiavelli, Marketing and Management*, London: Routledge, pp. 95–107.

McFarland, J. (2001), 'Four bulletproof strategies for handling office politics', *Harvard Management Update Article*, U0105B.

McFarland, J. (2004), 'The inside sales job', *Harvard Management Update Article*, U0408F.

Miller, B. K., M. A. Rutherford and R. W. Kolodinsky (2008), 'Perceptions of organizational politics: A meta-analysis of outcomes', *Journal of Business and Psychology*, **22**(3): 209–222.

Mintzberg, H. (1985), 'The organization as political arena', *Journal of Management Studies*, **22**(2) March: 133–154.

Münster, J. (2007), 'Selection tournaments, sabotage, and participation', *Journal of Economics and Management Strategy*, **16**(4) Winter: 943–970.

Narayanan, V. K. and L. Fahey (1982), 'The micro-politics of strategy formulation', *Academy of Management Review*, **7**(1) January: 25–34.

Noda, T. and J. L. Bower (1996), 'Strategy making as iterated processes of resource allocation', *Strategic Management Journal*, **17**(Summer) (Special Issue): 159–192.

Paroutis, S. and A. Pettigrew (2007), 'Strategizing in the multi-business firm: Strategy teams at multiple levels and over time', *Human Relations*, **60**(1) January: 99–135.

Pettigrew, A. M. (1973), *The Politics of Organizational Decision-Making*, London: Tavistock.

Pettigrew, A. M. (1975), 'Towards a political theory of organizational intervention', *Human Relations*, **28**(3): 191–208.

Pettigrew, A. M. (1977), 'Strategy formulation as a political process', *International Studies of Management and Organization*, **7**(2) Summer: 78–87.

Pettigrew, A. M. (1992), 'The character and significance of strategy process research', *Strategic Management Journal*, **13**(Winter) (Special Issue): 5–16.

Pfeffer, J. (1992), *Managing with Power: Politics and Influence in Organizations*, Boston, MA: Harvard Business School Press.

Phillips, D. T. (1992), *Lincoln on Leadership: Executive Strategies for Tough Times*, New York: Warner Books.

Reardon, K. K. (2001), *The Secret Handshake: Mastering the Politics of the Business Inner Circle*, New York: Currency.

Rodrigues, S. B. and J. Child (2008), 'The development of corporate identity: A political perspective', *Journal of Management Studies*, **45**(5) July: 885–911.

Sayre, T. L., F. W. Rankin and N. L. Fargher (1998), 'The effects of promotion incentives on delegated investment decisions', *Journal of Management Accounting Research*, **10**: 313–324.

Stein, W. E. and A. Rapoport (2005), 'Symmetric two-stage contests with budget constraints', *Public Choice*, **124**: 309–328.

Sussman, L., A. J. Adams, F. E. Kuzmits and L. E. Raho (2002), 'Organizational politics: Tactics, channels, and hierarchical roles', *Journal of Business Ethics*, **40**(4): 313–329.

Tivey, L. (1978), *The Politics of the Firm*, New York: St. Martin's.

Van Ees, H., J. Gabrielsson and M. Huse (2009), 'Toward a behavioral theory of boards and corporate governance', *Corporate Governance: An International Review*, **17**(3): 307–319.

Vigoda, E. and A. Cohen (2002), 'Influence tactics and perceptions of organizational politics: A longitudinal study', *Journal of Business Research*, **55**(4) April: 311–324.

Vigoda-Gadot, E. and A. Drory (eds) (2006), *Handbook of Organizational Politics*, Cheltenham, UK and Northampton, MA: Edward Elgar.

Xuan, Y. (2009), 'Empire-building or bridge-building? Evidence from new CEOs' internal capital allocation decisions', *Review of Financial Studies*, **22**(12): 4919–4948.

4 The strategic arena approach to strategy process research*

Anders Melander, Leif Melin and Mattias Nordqvist

INTRODUCTION

Strategy process research has made significant contributions to the field of strategy since the mid 1970s. It opened up the black box of the organization and showed that strategy is a multi-level phenomenon with social, cultural and political influences at both micro and macro levels (Johnson et al., 2003; Hutzschenreuter and Kleindienst, 2006). Researchers subscribing to a process research view have demonstrated that strategy is made by human beings, where forces and activities driving or counteracting change emerge from human actions. Populating the arena of strategy making with human beings has paved the way for new theoretical contributions (Johnson et al., 2007). Another contribution of strategy process research is to legitimate in-depth case studies (Johnson et al., 2003), from single case studies (e.g. Pettigrew, 1985) to comparative case studies (e.g. Eisenhardt, 1989). In-depth case studies allow researchers to develop holistic and contextual understanding of strategy processes through studying complex forces that may drive both strategic change and stability (Melin, 1986, 1989; Johnson et al., 2003). However, the strategy process tradition has also met some criticism. Johnson et al. (2003), for instance, have identified six limitations and the approach presented in this paper considers directly four of these limitations:

- Much strategy process research is based on second-hand and retrospective reports. We need more ethnographic and real-time studies to increase our understanding of the micro activities that construct strategy processes.
- Much strategy process research takes for granted that the top managers are the only actors or, at least, the most central in strategy making. This means that the importance of the CEO and top management team is exaggerated while the importance of actors and activities in the peripheries is downplayed (Regnér, 2003).
- Most strategy process research separates process from content,

reinforced by defining the process tradition as opposite to content (e.g. Chakravarthy and White, 2002). We need to dismantle 'the content–process dichotomy where content instead is regarded as an inherent and dissoluble part of ongoing processes' (Johnson et al., 2003:12).

- Much strategy process research has only resulted in rich descriptions, implying poor development of process theory. Process research should contribute to the building of theory on both strategy processes and related strategic outcomes.

Moreover, we concur with Hambrick (2004: 94) in his claim that to renew research on strategy process we need 'to reintroduce the human element to our research'. We posit that the dynamic context of most industries demands strategy processes to be studied and understood as a continuous process of strategizing, in order to give the emergent and not always hierarchical type of strategy formation more attention (Ericson et al., 2001; Whittington and Melin, 2003; Pettigrew et al., 2003). Strategy processes need to be understood in a way that focuses more on the capacity of strategic leaders on different levels to deal with strategic uncertainty, flexibility and foresight (Floyd and Lane, 2000; Doz and Kosonen, 2008).

The strategy as practice perspective is emphasizing the need for more studies of ongoing micro activities of strategizing. In doing so strategy as practice research strives to overcome limitations of the strategy process tradition. This chapter is positioned within the growing strategy as practice perspective (Johnson et al., 2007; Whittington, 2006), and it aims to contribute to strategy process research by describing an approach for increased understanding of the internal dynamics of strategic change and how strategy processes are organized. This approach addresses the aforementioned limitations through focusing on real-time studies; involving all actors that influence the strategy process; combining process activities with an emphasis on the actual strategic issues that are in focus at each time; and contributing with a conceptualization of strategy processes that has potential for further theorizing.

More specifically, our purpose is to develop and discuss an approach, constituted by five coherent concepts that describe ongoing strategy processes – the *strategic arena* approach. This approach visualizes the strategy as practice perspective on how to understand and study strategy processes and how to support new strategic initiatives. The approach has a theoretical value, showing how the formation of new strategies takes place, as well as why and how strategic change may be supported or counteracted. The approach includes all possible actors in the strategy process. Furthermore, it may have a normative value through its advice to practitioners in strategy processes to reframe their view on strategizing through focusing on the strategic arena. The strategic arena provides a fundamental notion of the strategy process in organizations. This notion implies that strategic change is generated through dialogues on a number of possible and arising strategic issues, between the actors that populate the strategic arena. Strategic action is the outcome of such an arena process. Successful arena management may support both the identification of new and crucial strategic issues, and the necessary development and transfer of knowledge in the strategy process, as well as innovative strategic actions.

The proposed strategic arena approach is based on more than 20 years of theoretical and empirical research on strategic change and strategizing in different types of organizational contexts. The research base consists of a large number of longitudinal, in-depth case studies of strategic change in both big multinationals and medium-sized family firms, as well as in public sector organizations. The research is reported in a series of doctoral dissertations (e.g. Lindell, 1992; Ljung, 1993; Holmström, 1995; Hellqvist, 1997; Melander, 1997; Ericson, 1998; Wigren, 2003; Hall, 2003; Brunninge, 2005; Nordqvist, 2005). The periods studied in these organizations differ from 5 years to 25 years and cover change processes that were taking place during the period 1945–2005. The strategic arena approach discussed in this chapter has found both empirical and theoretical inspiration from these studies. We use one illustration from our case research to illustrate the strategic arena approach (Hellqvist, 1997; Ericson, 1998; Melander and Nordqvist, 2008).

The chapter is organized as follows. First we specify the meaning of our strategic arena approach in relation to strategy process research. Second we present in more detail the set of concepts that constitute the strategic arena approach. In particular, we discuss the concepts of actors, issues, dialogues and actions, as well as different types of arenas. Then the case is presented with the purpose to illustrate the different concepts in the strategic arena approach. In the last section we discuss the implications for future research of this approach to strategy process.

STRATEGIC CHANGE PROCESSES

There are several meanings of strategy present in both the academic literature and in practice. We are particularly interested in change, which means we need to clarify the strategic dimension, i.e. the *strategic* type of change. According to Hickson et al. (1986), top leaders see not only changes in the strategic product/market orientation, and changed boundaries (through mergers and acquisitions) as strategic. Changed organization, changed technology and changed control systems were also defined as strategic. Strategic changes impact an organization in a broader way than just single departments/functions/plants – they are both integrative and boundary spanning in their orientation. The meaning of 'strategic' is situational and dependent on the perspective taken (Pettigrew, 1992). This calls for researchers to develop perspectives to understand strategy processes that are flexible, adaptable and transferable between different organizational contexts.

The interest in the process dimension of strategic change has triggered strategy scholars to conduct studies of long cycles of change (e.g. Pettigrew, 1990; Melin, 1992; Van de Ven and Poole, 1995). The process dimension emphasizes that strategy processes often are without a distinct beginning and end, and that a holistic approach to change often is preferable (Pettigrew, 1997). The process perspective includes the dynamic character of strategic change with forces and counter-forces working for and against change (Melin, 1989). The dynamic process view on strategic change shed light on the often ambiguous and contradictory characteristics of change. An obvious consequence of this is that theories have to overcome the dominating idea of strategic change as divided in two phases: formulation and implementation (Johnson et al., 2003; Hutzschenreuter and Kleindienst, 2006). We argue that the division between formulation and implementation counteracts a deeper understanding of the nature of strategic change (Johnson et al., 2007: 207ff.). We need frameworks that are less hierarchical in their nature, and that abandon the old metaphor of top management as the organizational brain, figuring out what needs to be done and then implementing the message to the rest of the body (Morgan, 1997).

The change dimension represents both the degree and pace of change. For example, change processes may be both evolutionary and revolutionary, where change may take place both incrementally and in more 'qualitative/ big jumps' (Tushman and Romanelli, 1985). Change may be proactive or reactive (Hellgren and Melin, 1993), and change may be sequential or more circular (Mintzberg and Westley, 1992). Strategic change may be planned, i.e. deliberate, or change is evolving more gradually, e.g. imposed by sudden events in the environment (Mintzberg and Waters, 1985). Strategy process research frameworks need to be designed in a way that allows them to capture these wide differences in change characteristics.

Our argument is that a more holistic understanding of the strategic change process will be enhanced if the complex and often political process that precedes the identification of the actual topic of the strategic change is included in strategy process research. Moreover, we have to be open for aspects of negotiation, i.e. recognizing sub-processes in which the selling of issues and the possible reformulation of the change topic over time is an outcome.

THE STRATEGIC ARENA APPROACH

Above we outlined what we regard as the main criteria for an approach able to capture vital dimensions of strategic change processes. We presented also motives for a set of concepts aimed to describe and understand strategic change processes. Our contribution is an approach to strategic change developed around the notion of the strategic arena. In this approach, strategic change is seen as a continuous process, and where the degree of change differs between being continuous and incremental or occasional and radical. We rely on the definition of strategy formation and change as a pattern in a stream of actions over time (Mintzberg and Quinn, 1991). Strategic change is shaped by strategic actions that typically are linked to dialogues taking place on the strategic arena between key actors about strategic issues, defined by these actors. The strategic arena approach includes the politics of strategy formation, i.e. the recognition that formation and implementation of new strategies involve actors representing different interests and with different views on what is happening (Ocasio, 1997). The strategic arena approach also embraces the ongoing sensemaking by the actors involved (Weick, 1995; Gioia and Chittipeddi, 1991). This sensemaking is important for what strategic issues are emerging and treated on the arena. The dialogue on these strategic issues eventually leads to new strategic decisions/actions.

The strategic arena approach has dimensions in common with, and to a certain extent builds upon, the attention-based view of the firm (Ocasio, 1997; Ocasio and Joseph, 2005). Ocasio shares our recognition of an overall need for a more practice-based perspective on process research and he highlights the role of actors and issues in a similar way to us. A main difference, however, is our focus on the arena, referring to the social setting and venue in which strategy process work is communicated. The attention-based view suggests that firm behavior is the result of how firms generally channel and distribute the attention of decision-makers (Ocasio, 1997). The strategic arena approach proposes that strategic action is the result of activities that are performed as a result of the dialogue between actors on the strategic arena. While the basis for Ocasio's view is the limited attentional capability (and bounded rationality) of individuals, the basis of our approach is the circumstances and characteristics of social interaction between a set of individuals. Another difference is that the attention-based view studies strategy as a pattern of organizational attention (Ocasio, 1997: 188), while we see strategy as a pattern in a stream of actions (Mintzberg and Quinn, 1991).

Now we continue with a more elaborated discussion on the concepts of actors, issues, dialogues, actions and arenas that jointly constitute our strategic arena approach.

Actors on the Strategic Arena

The strategic arena approach rests on the basic assumption of the action frame of reference (Silverman, 1970). Action takes place in social interaction between different actors. These social actors act in a purposeful way, and their actions have meanings, shared or individual, among the actors involved (Weick, 1995). The ongoing social construction of reality focuses on one hand on the acting subject – the self, i.e. the actor with her own subjectively perceived environment – and on the other hand on how actions of individual actors are determined by surrounding and institutionalized norms and structures (Berger and Luckmann, 1966). Actors, both as individuals and as coalitions, shape society at the same time as society is shaping them and their actions (Berger and Luckmann, 1966; Denis et al., 2001). This means that our position is grounded in a duality between the view of a subjectively constructed reality with the view of an institutionalized and objectified reality (Giddens, 1984).

Since the strategic arena is defined through social interaction and activities, such as issue recognition and issue dialogue, it is impossible to imagine an arena without actors. Accordingly, with actors we mean human beings that are enacting their own environments of self (Weick, 1995) but at the same time are involved in interactive strategic processes. The arena approach directs attention to actors who are sources for activities on the strategic arena of an organization. Actors populating the arena may come from different hierarchical levels in the organization, as well as from outside the formal organization (Ocasio, 1997). The formal position of actors in relation to an organization is important, but not the only factor that determines their involvement. In other words, influential actors are involved in a dialogue on a strategic issue sometimes based on their formal position or their membership of a formal group or meeting place, such as an executive committee or a board meeting. But also more informal characteristics make individuals become potential actors on the arena, e.g. possessing knowledge on strategic issues or having social relationships with key actors (Ocasio, 1997; Nordqvist and Melin, 2008).

At any given point in time, the actors who can be identified to be on the arena are those involved in the strategic activities on the arena (Ericson et al., 2001). These are activities such as recognition of what becomes a strategic issue, dialogue on present issues and on possible strategic solutions and subsequent strategic actions. Some actors are involved only in small fragments of the arena process, others may have a dominating role in most parts of the process (Ericson et al., 2001).

From cognitive research we know that human beings use automatic processes as they strive to cope with all the information that overflows us (Simon, 1947; Cyert and March, 1963). Through social interaction organizational members conform, and eventually share a set of 'facts', which becomes their objectified organizational reality (Berger and Luckmann, 1966). From this it follows that organizational members develop a taken-for-granted attitude towards many aspects of their organizational life. The taken for grantedness is closely associated with organizational culture, and has important impact with regard to the issues at which their attention is directed (Ocasio, 1997). Furthermore, actors populating the strategic arena make assumptions about the social reality and view these assumptions as 'facts', a part of the actor's objectified world. This means that actors may take a specific strategic position of the firm for granted when they reflect strategically. From a voluntaristic perspective the actor has freedom to act as each individual's perceived organizational reality is at least partly unique (Silverman, 1970). The profession, the organizational belonging, the history, the personality and the life experience of each actor influence to what degree actors reflect on and the issues to which they direct their attention (Ocasio and Joseph, 2005).

Some actors have a high capacity to reflect and to break the path of determinism by taking new actions, while others view their position as restricted and externally determined and therefore are more passive (Giddens, 1984). In the strategic arena approach, the actor is not always an individual. At many occasions *coalitions* are formed to enhance actions (cf. Cyert and March, 1963; Narayanan and Fahey, 1982; Laine and Vaara, 2006). The formation of a coalition is sometimes an intended outcome of a deliberate step taken by a group of individuals; at other times a coalition emerges more unintentionally.

Strategic Issues on the Strategic Arena

Strategic issues refer to questions, subjects and points of strategic debate, such as different problems, threats and opportunities that are given priority in the strategic process of the organization (e.g. Dutton et al., 1983; Dutton, 1986; Dutton and Jackson, 1987). The traditional stream of literature on strategic issues has its roots in strategic decision-making research where emphasis is on the planned and sequential features of the process, which starts with a scanning phase, continues with a negotiation phase and then a decision-taking phase, and finally the implementation of the decision taken. Another literature emphasizes some more chaotic and anarchistic features of decision making, illustrated by March and Olsen's (1972) metaphor of the garbage can. Decisions just happen, when occasions, solutions, problems, people and timing are right. In this later stream of literature the traditional sequential phases are questioned. Instead solutions may exist and find their problems rather than vice versa. In situations where the traditional sequences can be identified, the manager may have constructed such an order to motivate the logic of a decision already made (Brunsson, 1985).

Even if the strategic issues perspective generally is neutral to these two contrasting views, an issue seldom follows a sequential stage process (Dutton and Ashford, 1993; Dutton et al., 2001). Incremental, iterative and disordered types of processes have a better descriptive value regarding how issues are identified, introduced, discussed and transformed into decisions and/or actions. This is also related to the fact that strategic issues may lead to decisions with a complex, controversial and political character and featured by a high level of uncertainty (Hickson et al., 1986). Furthermore, when considering how strategic issues are introduced, processed and transformed into action, there is a major difference compared with the garbage can view – the presence of actors is a necessary condition for the existence of strategic issues in our approach.

In the strategic arena approach, the strategic issue delimits what is important and critical to focus on in the process of creating the future of the organization. This means that the actual set of issues both shapes the strategic dialogue and at the same time restricts the scope for strategic direction and action. Shared attention is given to a strategic issue, meaning that there is some consensus about the existence of a strategic issue (Ocasio, 1997). When a strategic issue is on the arena, time and resources are allocated to the issue and subsequent dialogues. Strategic issues can be distinguished from issues that are not seen as affecting the future conditions for the organization, i.e. issues without an obvious strategic interest. These more operational issues are part of the daily activities of the organization, such as how to handle complaints from an average customer. But such issues can sometimes be redefined as strategic, for example if there are many complaints from customers, which implies that there is a customer relationship problem (Dutton and Ashford, 1993).

Strategic issues may have many different origins. Some issues are created and introduced to the strategic dialogue by the top managers. Some emerge from inside the organization, initiated by actors other than the dominating coalition. Some are even imposed from outside, by external stakeholders or because of external events (Ocasio, 1997). As noted by Dutton et al. (2001) issues may be processed differently according to their origin and sometimes we can discuss specific processing routes and routines according to the origin of the issue.

Dialogues on the Strategic Arena

The social interaction between actors regarding strategic issues forms the *strategic dialogue*. The strategic arena is defined through such dialogues on issues that are defined as strategic. The arena unfolds in all possible situations where a strategic dialogue takes place. All members of the organization, as well as actors outside the formal organization that may become involved in interaction on a strategic issue, are potential actors on the strategic arena. The strategic dialogue refers to communication, discussion and debate on strategic issues, and the arena is the venue for such activities (Hall et al., 2006). The term 'dialogue' may mean that what is taking place in this interaction is 'a sustained collective inquiry into the processes, assumptions, and certainties that structure everyday experience' (Isaacs, 1993: 24). The dialogue gives actors the possibility to influence the course of events (Shotter, 1993). The dialogue can be a trustful talk between two or more actors but it can also be a tense discussion between coalitions of actors with different opinions, views and ideas regarding the strategic development (Jacobs and Heracleous, 2005). The strategic dialogue may eventually reproduce or change the organizational reality depending on the content of the strategic issues, the set of actors involved in the strategic dialogue and the actions that the dialogue results in.

The strategic dialogue takes place in different episodes and in different social contexts – in formal meetings, such as a board meeting, and in informal meetings, both inside the organization (e.g. in the hallway) and outside the organization (e.g. at a lunch or dinner) (Hendry and Seidl, 2003). The strategic dialogue concept is generic in the sense that both issues and actors associated with the dialogue may change over time. The strategic arena becomes concrete and visible through the dialogue on specific issues, at the same time as the strategic arena is used to refer to the context of every meeting place where a strategic dialogue is occurring.

A strategic dialogue involves processes of sensemaking. This means that in order to understand strategy processes from the arena approach, we need to consider how and why certain meanings are created by individuals (Weick, 1995; Balogun and Johnson, 2004). Sensemaking implies that actors continuously construct and deconstruct meaning in change processes. This construction and deconstruction of meaning is going on in the dialogues between actors on the strategic arena. But a strategic dialogue is not only a matter of shared meanings, it is likewise a matter of self-interest. The strategic dialogue can sometimes be understood in terms of a struggle between different interpretations, or a negotiation between different individual standpoints (Gioia and Chittipeddi, 1991). Then we can understand how and why a certain interpretation and construction of meaning can become dominant in a certain group or organization, where meaning comes to coincide when members of the group begin to favor one subjective interpretation over others. When the strategic dialogue features mutual understanding subsequent action is supported. Generally the strategic dialogue connects talk to action. By definition, when a strategic dialogue takes place on a strategic arena there is always a potential strategic action to follow. Moreover, a strategic dialogue on one issue may precede and result in another issue. This means that some issues can be parts of a common theme, while other issues may be more isolated in terms of content.

Actions on the Strategic Arena

Rumelt (1979) pointed out that what is defined as strategic is highly dependent on the actors' organizational position and agenda. Further Mintzberg and Waters (1985) stressed that some actions are viewed as strategic when planned. In retrospect it could be other (streams of) actions that are identified as strategic. In the strategic arena approach strategic actions are closely connected to the ongoing dialogues on the strategic arena. A frequent topic in the dialogue on issues is what actions, in the meaning change of organizational behavior, should/must the organization undertake? Hence, the organizational importance (the mobilization of actors that participate in the dialogue on a specific issue) indicates that the following action is strategic for the organization.

Whether a strategic issue eventually will result in action is dependent on the dialogue on the arena. At one extreme, the issue will disappear from the arena without any other action. But more often, the dialogue transforms strategic issues into some kind of organizational action. However, an issue resulting in action will not necessarily leave the arena. The dialogue on that issue may continue even if strategic action occurs. A new strategic issue can also be born as a result of a strategic action (Dutton and Ashford, 1993). Hence, when the dialogue on strategic issues is transformed into action, this action may be the source of new dialogues on the arena. Issues, dialogues and actions can be seen as tools describing the ongoing construction of an organizational reality (cf. Dutton and Dukerich, 1991).

Issues could be connected to actions in several ways. Issues may be more or less action-oriented. Some strategic issues transform directly into actions without much of a dialogue and/or formal decision, perhaps as the result of a crisis situation (Dutton, 1986) and some issues result in formal decisions without any subsequent action (more symbolic decisions). Some strategic issues can be directed towards a specific type of decision/action, while others have a more multi-final character. Other kinds of issues are seasonal in character, i.e. they appear with a certain regularity on the strategic arena. Furthermore, some issues are introduced on the arena and processed in the dialogue but are never connected to a specific action – these issues may stay 'for ever' on the arena or they perhaps just vanish from the agenda (Ericson et al., 2001).

Besides the strategic actions emerging from dialogues on strategic issues, there is also another type of action related to the strategic arena, and that is the *arena action*. This type of action is partly procedural but establishes also the framework in which strategic issues are discussed. An illustration of how the formation of strategies is affected by the rules applied in the process is the argumentation by Bourgeois and Brodwin (1984) that managers focusing on the formulation of the strategy downplay the critical transformation from articulation of a strategy to the implementation of the action. Arena actions are of decisive importance within the strategic arena approach. These are the actions that decide the level of informality and openness in the strategy process. As argued in the introduction, in order to reach a holistic understanding of the strategy process we must balance our attention on content and process aspects (Johnson et al., 2003: 12). We must also add that arena actions by no means are reserved for top management, even though the power to decide what issues are included on the agenda of a meeting is of obvious importance (cf. Lukes, 1974).

To sum up, a strategic action affects the organization as a whole. It is discernible as something that explicitly intervenes into or amplifies existing behavior. This means that a strategic action, in turn, may change an affected routine. At the same time, a strategic arena is just encompassing some of the activities in the organization, while a lot of activities, decisions and routines within the organization are not taking place on the strategic arena. Arena actions finally are related to the arena process itself, rather than to certain issues. Some arena actions are taken to formalize the dialogue on the arena. Others are related to the entry and exit of actors on the arena.

DIFFERENT STRATEGIC ARENA TYPES

The strategic arena approach implies viewing the arena as a process that unfolds in different kinds of representations, where the arena is a multiple and changing meeting ground for dialogues between actors on strategic issues. The strategic arena metaphor does not take its point of departure in the formal organizational structure and hierarchy, but in the situations, settings and venues where strategizing actually occurs. The notion of the strategic arena is thus a conception of the actual social context for strategy process activities. In many private firms, especially small and medium-sized firms, a limited number of actors often form a dominant coalition. Often these actors are owner-managers, trusted employees and/ or close family members. This can also create a blurry organizational structure in which it is not always explicit where, when and by whom different strategic activities are performed. For instance, even if a family firm has top management team meetings and/or an active board with external members, it is not given that the strategic dialogue always occurs on these firm-connected arenas. The private ownership context also gives room for other relevant meeting grounds, such as a gathering with members of an owner-family interacting on strategic issues. The following dimensions have emerged as particularly relevant in our research on strategic arenas (cf. Nordqvist, 2005; Hall et al., 2006).

The arena can be described as either *formal* or *informal*, depending on the characteristics of the social situation where the arena emerges. A typical example of an activity at a more formal situation is a board meeting where strategic issues are discussed and settled. A typical example of a more informal situation is when actors talk about a strategic issue during a coffee break, in small talk in the hallway or on the golf course. Our research has also revealed the importance of what is labeled the 'hybrid arena' (Nordqvist, 2005). The hybrid arena is characterized by social situations where both formal and informal elements are present. A typical example is a strategy away day, which often is organized in order to leave the formalities of the regular meetings, such as top management team meetings or board meetings. But even if increased informality is a part of the purpose of the away day, it also has formal features such as clear time limits with a decided beginning and end, as well as predefined strategy issues on the agenda.

The arena can also be characterized as *front-stage* or *back-stage*, depending on the characteristics of the social situation where the arena emerges. Following Goffman (1959), the front-stage is when one or several actors perform some type of strategic activity with a specific audience in mind. An archetypical example of this is a CEO holding a speech explaining the firm's new strategy to employees, or addressing a specific and new strategic issue. The back-stage emerges when and if the CEO after the speech continues the dialogue with some actors, addressing issues and using information that was not brought up in the official and communicated version.

The arena can be characterized as *current* or *historical.* This includes a time dimension and refers to whether a specific representation of the strategic arena is previously, presently or will in future be important. History and tradition are often important in firms, with actors referring to 'how we used to strategize' (Brunninge, 2008).

The strategic arena can be characterized as *closed* or *open.* Closed means, for example, that the arena is controlled by the 'power center' of a dominant actor/coalition, while an open arena is more fragmented, where many actors are given the possibility to participate and influence the outcome of arena dialogues (Hall et al., 2006). A typical example of a closed arena may occur in the small company dominated by the founding owner-manager. In the extreme it could be argued that this arena is restricted to the thoughts and actions of one man/woman.

ILLUSTRATION OF THE STRATEGIC ARENA APPROACH

In order to illustrate how the arena approach adds insights in the research process, we include a brief illustration extracted from one of our longitudinal case studies – a ten year investigation of strategic and organizational change in a big Swedish hospital (Hellqvist, 1997; Ericson, 1998; Ericson et al., 2008).

A New Vision Initiates Several Strategic Issues

The demand for change at the Big Hospital was mounting. The governing county council had been initiating actions to increase productivity and reduce costs, but the results were not overwhelming. Recently appointed, the new Managing Director (MD) of the hospital was under pressure to show some results, preferably in the form of a promising change process. He began, somewhat trembling, with an attempt to formulate a broad strategic plan. His aim was that this document should initiate a dialogue about the problems facing the organization, but this plan never played any important role in the change process.

The pressure to take further and more visible actions in order to initiate some fundamental changes in the Big Hospital was the background to a three day 'visionary meeting', in which the leading administrative managers and chief physicians of the hospital participated. The composition of the group of people that attended his meeting was the consequence of the intention of the MD to form a top management team.

This meeting turned out to be the start of a rather new way of defining the strategic issues for the hospital. When the participating actors in a very open atmosphere presented their ideas on how to solve present or anticipated problems, these ideas implied the introduction of some new strategic issues. Some ideas were eventually dropped as a result of the ongoing dialogue while others survived and became a crucial part of the input in the change process, and thus did constitute the issues for the following dialogue. In this process some individuals supported each other in a more or less coordinated way, i.e. they formed coalitions.

As the entire hospital system in Sweden was being questioned in the societal debate it was time to question old truths and the MD was in search of a more fundamental idea or vision for the future. In the process, he found a coalition in two of the most influential representatives for the medical profession within the hospital. Both were highly recognized by the professional community and had been appointed some years ago to manage the two largest clinics at the hospital (surgery and medicine). However, to date they had not been pursuing a new strategic direction for the hospital – it seems they saw a window of opportunity opening with the new MD.

As a result of the strategic dialogue at this visionary meeting these three formed a coalition in the definition of a new, still rather vague vision for the Big Hospital. Three issues were connected to the initial vision: (1) the need to reorganize – the MD had a control span of over 50 clinical departments, (2) the need to focus on the chain of patient curing and caring, and (3) the 'organ-based' principle for how to organize all hospital activities in a more patient centered way rather than the traditional medical specialty way.

Efforts to Broaden the Strategic Arena

After the visionary meeting the MD had in mind a more open process, inviting a larger group to take part in the strategy process and thus widen the arena for the initiated strategic dialogue. One attempt to open up the arena was the strategic seminar that the MD arranged a year after the three day visionary meeting. Over a hundred hospital managers, with a majority representing the medical professions, were invited and participated in the seminar. However, the intention of the MD was not really fulfilled as the seminar did not include much of a dialogue in itself and many actors were very passive in the strategic dialogue after the meeting.

Divisonalizing the Hospital – the Issue of Centers

The MD invited all top and middle managers (mainly physicians) to an extra strategy meeting. At this meeting the basic rules for the new organization were presented. They included three basic principles: the clinics had to unite into centers, the centers were to be led by a center manager recruited from the medical profession, and a center would by definition include more than one clinic. However, the MD left the formation of centers open, as those attending this meeting were only presented with two possible centers. Both these center ideas were constructed bottom-up by two different groups of clinical departments, i.e. these proposed centers were not planned by the MD.

Instead of presenting a final solution, a series of 'network meetings' were initiated. The first round of network meetings was used to present the overall changes in the hospital sector and reflections on how these changes could be handled within the Big Hospital. An exercise in small groups was also used to encourage the silent majority to speak up. Those attending, mainly top and middle managers (physicians), were well aware of the next step, which meant negotiations and lobbying in the process of forming new centers.

At the second round of network meetings the results of these lateral negotiation processes were presented. Very few actors questioned the logic behind the need to merge clinics into larger centers. Those attending went home well aware of the difficulty in finding one simple solution and to some degree confident in the MD's attempt to make the best out of the situation.

The next step in the organizing process was when the final structure was presented by the MD, mainly based on this process. It was a structure of 12 new centers, with 3–4 clinics each. But some clinics were still not part of any center, and were placed on a so-called 'waiting list'.

Positive and Negative Issues

About eight months later the quality issue suddenly emerged as an important strategic issue in the Big Hospital, initiated by the MD. Quality had been given a strong positive value in society related to the view in the private sector that it was an extremely important subject. The private sector was highly valued in the health care sector at the time and the quality issue was translated into this hospital context. Most members of the hospital organization therefore viewed the strong emphasis on the quality issue as something positive and proactive, that could give the hospital a competitive advantage.

On the other extreme, the potential cost reduction issue was seen as a threat to the whole change process, by the MD and his top management group. The fear was that organizational members would connect the initiated organizational changes with cost reductions that threatened to increase the inertia towards change. Top management therefore deliberately avoided cost reduction as a strategic issue for a long time. However, when cost reductions became unavoidable because of budget cuts initiated by the politicians, the trick was to argue that this was the moment to test the new organizational leadership, the center managers that had been appointed for the new centers through the change process.

Managing the Strategic Arena

This process is both an example of how the strategic arena was managed and how strategic issues were transformed into action. The easy way to proceed, after the long discussion in the top management group during the first year, would have been to use the first strategy meeting to present a plan of how to organize the hospital. If so, most physicians would have accepted the idea, even though they probably would have continued their daily operations as before. The three month long process with several meetings was thus a way to engage many in the strategic dialogue around the basic ideas introduced by the vision, and at the same time to convince them about the need to rethink their current ways of organizing. The management of the strategic arena aimed to increase engagement within the organization. Moreover, the arena management – about inclusion and exclusion of individuals in the strategic dialogue – aimed to show the included participants that it was the identification with the new organizing principle within the hospital that was crucial.

External Actors are Invited

The strategic arena in the hospital also included external actors. For example, a close dialogue between the MD and an influential politician of the county council was a way to internalize the political pressure into the strategic arena of the hospital. Further, the introduction of an issue about a joint collaborative strategy for all four hospitals within the county council's remit was a deliberate attempt from the MD of the Big Hospital to enlarge the strategic arena. He invited the MDs from the three other hospitals to this new strategic dialogue and at the same time challenged the political leadership of the county council with his proposal.

The Meaning of Strategic Issues

The arena can be seen as a meeting ground for different cultures or ideologies rather than an expression of one dominating organizational culture (Martin, 2002). The actors on the arena are individuals with their own subjective thoughts but they are also members of and socialized in different subcultures as well as professions. The actors represent partly different organizational frames of reference, which means that there are not one but several collective cognitive structures that constrain the members' way to interpret information about the hospital organization. It is important to note that this cognitive dimension exists beyond the fact that some actors are defending their vested interests within the organization's political process.

The issue of center composition divided the organization into two major camps, where the administrators focused on managerial and control problems while the group of physicians focused on the practical medical work, patients and research. The dialogues at the network meetings expressed the cognitive differences at the same time as they showed that conversations between different actors resulted in the construction of an embryo of a collective view regarding the meaning of the proposed center units in this hospital organization.

When the new centers were formed, the newly appointed center managers had the responsibility to implement the center idea. At this stage they treated the communicated vision – to develop and implement a more patient-oriented and efficient organization – as taken for granted. Instead, the dialogue in the center management team concerned issues about a further elaboration and realization of the vision.

It is important to note that the strategic arena now appears at new locations in the organization in comparison with the concentration around the MD and the upper echelon of the hospital in the early stages of the change process. Now the strategic arena is in action also at the center management level. The strategic dialogue, defining the strategic arena, not only appeared at the top of the organization but also elsewhere in the organization, in this case at the center level and especially in the center management team.

In most centers the strategic dialogue came to a great extent to circle around what was going to happen to the clinical departments that each center was based on. Should the traditional clinical departments become fully integrated or should they continue to be relatively autonomous? This was the dominant issue for the center management teams. There were several other strategic issues that had to be dealt with. However, most other issues were strongly related to and dependent on how the autonomy of the clinical departments should be treated. Therefore, the dominant strategic dialogue took place around the issue of integration versus autonomy for the clinical departments.

Due to the fact that it became obvious that a further development of the new organization was directly dependent on an increased integration of the clinical departments in each center, the continuation of the change process became controversial to many actors. Many physicians showed strong negative reactions to becoming incorporated and integrated in a larger organizational unit.

Different ways of thinking were in action within the hospital organization, which implies several different perspectives on organizational change, perhaps with two major perspectives dominating. The administrative perspective leads to new solutions that are developed from an administrative way of thinking. On the other hand, the medical perspective has its foundation in the medical professions' way of thinking about how to organize health care. Within the medical profession there is a rather coherent way of thinking about how to structure and organize the operations of a big hospital, as there is within the administrative group.

Diversity in Strategic Dialogues

Since the arena can appear at different locations in an organization it implies that several strategic dialogues may be taking place on different arenas at the same time. This was the case with the strategic dialogue in one center management team and the dialogue in the advisory board of this center. The advisory board had an ongoing dialogue concerning several strategic issues that were not discussed at all in the management team, for instance the issue of how to get the management team of the center to work as a successful team. Consequently, the two main representations of the strategic arena at the center level of the hospital did not carry a dialogue on the same issues. Such a diversity in dialogues on the strategic arena illustrates the need for some interlocking mechanisms between different appearances of the arena.

IMPLICATIONS AND CONCLUSION

The strategic arena is an approach for understanding the situations and meeting grounds where strategic processes take place. It is composed of a set of concepts for understanding the dynamics of change processes in organizations. The strategic arena is defined through the dialogues on issues that are strategic for the focal organization. Actors at all different levels of the organizational hierarchy are potential actors on the strategic arena, as well as actors outside the formal organization that may be involved in the interaction around a strategic issue. The strategic arena is a generic approach to strategy process research, which provides a way of understanding the important phenomenon on which we are focusing:

strategic change processes in organizations. The concepts that jointly constitute the strategic arena approach are actors, issues, dialogues and strategic actions.

The arena is in itself a process. It unfolds in different kinds of 'representations', or 'locations', of the arena. The arena is a continuously changing meeting ground for strategic dialogues between actors. The more comprehensive the dialogue is, the greater the amount of locations, and the more visible the arena would be. The strategic arena comprises many or few dimensions of a strategic dialogue as well as many or few actors. In which forms the arena will appear depends on the process itself, the degree and type of management of the arena and on the organizational context.

The strategic arena is defined and given meaning through its present strategic issues, its actors that enter, populate and leave the arena, and its current strategic dialogue. This means that the strategic arena is continuously shaped and reshaped by both informal and formal activities, where actors are engaged in dialogues about possible future change of the organization. The most obvious appearance of the strategic arena is perhaps a formal and scheduled top management meeting. However, this appearance is not necessarily the most important as the arena is activated in many other ways, with other compositions of actors, as well. The strategic arena is politically loaded, as the actors that at a given time have access to the arena often represent different interests. The strategic arena is given 'boundaries' through the type of activities that define it, i.e. the dialogue that is going on regarding different strategic issues. These boundaries are both rather fluid and most often invisible. The strategic arena is an abstract description of the relevant social context for strategic dialogues between actors participating in strategic change processes.

The strategic arena approach contributes to strategy process research, and in particular to the strategy as practice perspective in at least four ways. First, the notion of the strategic arena allows process researchers to focus on real-time studies. The concepts of arena, actor, issue, dialogue and action are useful to track strategic changes and understand how they unfold over time. The strategic arena approach can thus assist in attempts to catch reality in flight (Pettigrew, 1997), which is the aim of much strategy process research. Second, the strategic arena approach addresses the need observed by both strategy process and strategy as practice researchers to generate theories and frameworks that direct more attention to the role of the actual actors who influence the strategy process at micro level (Whittington, 2006; Nordqvist and Melin, 2008). The strategic arena approach thus helps to uncover the 'human element' (Hambrick, 2004), which has been surprisingly invisible in much traditional strategy process research (Johnson et al., 2003). Third, the notion of the strategic arena and the concepts that constitute it offers a way to combine process activities with an emphasis on the actual strategic issues that are in focus at each time. This has been an aim of strategy process research for a long time, and the strategic arena approach supplements the existing body of literature on this topic (cf. Ocasio, 1997; Ocasio and Joseph, 2005; Hutzschenreuter and Kleindienst, 2006; Johnson et al., 2007). Finally, the strategic arena approach offers a conceptualization of how strategic work unfolds within organizations in practice. Conceptual approaches can be powerful tools to make sense of and understand what is going on in practical processes of strategic change.

It should be admitted that the descriptive nature of our approach to strategy process research also represents a limitation. More empirical and theoretical work is needed to further develop the notion of the strategic arena into an explanatory research model. We hope, however, that this chapter will inspire further theorizing and empirical research into the micro-processes of strategic work. Other limitations with the strategic arena approach as described in this chapter include our lack of attention to more macro influences on strategy processes. Future research could, for instance, use institutional theory to address important macro dimensions of how strategic work unfolds over time in organizations. Another limitation is that we have touched upon but not been able to investigate in further depth the rhetorical and political aspects of the processes and practical work that take place on the strategic arena. We encourage strategy process scholars to design studies that focus on these aspects more directly in the future.

NOTE

*   Thomas Ericson, PhD and Anders Hellqvist, PhD have made important contributions to a previous version of this chapter.

REFERENCES

Balogun, J. and G. Johnson (2004), 'Organizational restructuring and middle manager sense-making', *Academy of Management Journal*, **47**(4): 523–49.
Berger, P. and T. Luckmann (1966), *The Social Construction of Reality*, New York: Doubleday & Company Inc.
Bourgeois, L. J. and D. R. Brodwin (1984), 'Strategic implementation: Five approaches to an elusive phenomenon', *Strategic Management Journal*, **5**: 241–64.
Brunninge, O. (2005), 'Organisational self-understanding and the strategy process: Strategy dynamics in Scania and Handelsbanken', *JIBS Dissertation Series*, No. 027. Jönköping International Business School, Sweden.

Brunninge, O. (2008), 'Organisationers självförståelse i strategiprocessen', in M. Nordqvist and A. Melander (eds), *Att förstå Strategi – process och kontext*, Lund: Studentlitteratur.

Brunsson, N. (1982), 'The irrationality of action and action rationality: Decision, ideologies and organizational actions', *Journal of Management Studies*, **19**: 29–44.

Brunsson, N. (1985), *The Irrational Organization: Irrationality as a Basis for Organizational Action and Change*, New York: John Wiley & Sons Ltd.

Chakravarthy, S. B. and E. R. White (2002), 'Strategy process: Forming, implementing and changing strategies', in A. M. Pettigrew, H. Thomas and R. Whittington (eds), *Handbook of Strategy and Management*, London: Sage.

Cyert, R. M. and J.G. March (1963), *A Behavioural Theory of the Firm*, Cambridge, MA: Blackwell Publishers.

Denis, J.-L., L. Lamothe and A. Langley (2001), 'The dynamics of collective leadership and strategic change in pluralistic organizations', *Academy of Management Journal*, **44**(4): 809–37.

Doz, Y. and M. Kosonen (2008), *Fast Strategy: How Strategic Agility Will Help You Stay Ahead of the Game*, Harlow, England: Wharton School Publishing.

Dutton, J. E. (1986), 'The processing of crisis and non-crisis strategic issues', *Journal of Management Studies*, **23**(5): 501–17.

Dutton, J. E. and S. J. Ashford (1993), 'Selling issues to top management', *Academy of Management Review*, **18**: 397–428.

Dutton, J. E. and J. M. Dukerich (1991), 'Keeping an eye on the mirror: Image and identity in organizational adaptation', *Academy of Management Journal*, **34**(3): 517–54.

Dutton, J. E. and S. E. Jackson (1987), 'Categorizing strategic issues: Links to organizational action', *Academy of Management Review*, **12**(1): 76–90.

Dutton, J. E., L. Fahey and V. K. Narayanan (1983), 'Toward understanding strategic issue diagnosis', *Strategic Management Journal*, **4**: 307.

Dutton, J. E., S. Ashford, R. O'Neill and K. Lawrence (2001), 'Moves that matter: Issue selling and organizational change', *Academy of Management Journal*, **44**(4): 713–36.

Eisenhardt, K. (1989), 'Building theory from case study research', *Academy of Management Review*, **14**(4): 532–50.

Ericson, T. (1998), 'Förändringsidéer och meningsskapande – en studie av strategiskt förändringsarbete'. Linköping Studies in Management and Economics, Dissertations No. 37.

Ericson. T., A. Melander and L. Melin (2001), 'The role of the strategist', in H. W. Volberda and T. Elfring (eds), *Rethinking Strategy*, London: Sage Publications.

Ericson, T., A. Hellqvist and A. Melander (2008), 'Den strategiska arenan – Ett sätt att förstå och leda strategisk förändring', in A. Melander and M. Nordqvist (eds), *Att förstå strategi*, Lund: Studentlitteratur.

Floyd, S. W. and P. J. Lane (2000), 'Strategizing throughout the organization: Managing role conflict in strategic renewal', *Academy of Management Journal*, **25**(1): 154–77.

Giddens, A. (1984), *The Constitution of Society*, Berkeley, CA: University of California Press.

Gioia, D. A. and K. Chittipeddi (1991), 'Sensemaking and sensegiving in strategic change initiation', *Strategic Management Journal*, **12**: 433–48.

Goffman, E. (1959), *The Presentation of Self in Everyday Life*, Harmondsworth: Penguin Books.

Hall, A. (2003), 'Strategising in the context of genuine relations: An interpretative study of strategic renewal through family interaction', *JIBS Dissertations Series*, No. 018. Jönköping International Business School, Sweden.

Hall, A., L. Melin, and M. Nordqvist (2006), 'Understanding strategizing in the family business context', in P. Poutziouris, K. Smyrnios and S. Klein (eds), *Family Business Research Handbook*, Cheltenham, UK and Northampton, USA: Edward Elgar.

Hambrick, D. C. (2004), 'The disintegration of strategic management: It's time to consolidate our gains', *Strategic Organization*, **2**(1): 91–8.

Hellgren, B. and L. Melin (1993), 'The role of strategists' ways-of-thinking in strategic change processes', in J. Hendry and G. Johnson (eds), *Strategic Thinking: Leadership and the Management of Change*, Chichester: John Wiley & Sons Ltd.

Hellqvist, A. (1997), 'Praktik och idéer: Om organisationsrutiners betydelse i förändringssammanhang'. Linköping Studies in Management and Economics, Dissertations No. 35.
Hendry, J. and D. Seidl (2003), 'The structure and significance of strategic episodes: Social systems theory and the routine practices of strategic change', *Journal of Management Studies*, **40**(1): 175–96.
Hickson, D. J., R. J. Butler, D. J. Cray, G. R. Malloy and D. C. Wilson (1986), *Top Decisions: Strategic Decision-Making in Organizations*, Oxford: Basil Blackwell.
Holmström, M. (1995), 'Styrning i storföretag – En studie av styrningens utformning och omfattning i tre Svenska koncerner'. Linköping Studies in Management and Economics, Dissertations No. 29.
Hutzschenreuter, T. and I. Kleindienst (2006), 'Strategy process research: What have we learned and what is still to be explored', *Journal of Management*, **32**(5): 673–720.
Isaacs, W. (1993), 'Taking flight: Dialogue, collective thinking and organizational learning', *Organizational Dynamics*, **22**(2): 24–40.
Jacobs, C. D. and L. T. Heracleous (2005), 'Answers for questions to come: Reflective dialogue as an enabler of strategic innovation', *Journal of Organizational Change Management*, **18**(4): 338–52.
Johnson, G., L. Melin and R. Whittington (2003), 'Guest editors' introduction: Micro strategy and strategizing: Towards an activity-based view', *Journal of Management Studies*, **40**(1): 3–22.
Johnson, G., A. Langley, L. Melin and R. Whittington (2007), *Strategy as Practice: Research Directions and Resources*, Cambridge: Cambridge University Press.
Lainc, P. M. and E. Vaara (2006), 'Struggling over subjectivity: A discursive analysis of strategic development in an engineering group', *Human Relations*, **59**(5): 611–36.
Langley, A., G. Johnson L. Melin and R. Whittington (2007), 'Reflections', in G. Johnson, A. Langley, L. Melin and R. Whittington (eds), *Strategy as Practice*, Cambridge: Cambridge University Press.
Lindell, P. (1992), 'Strategisk styrning och förändring – En begreppsutredning baserad på en studie av Swedish Match 1960–1987'. Linköping Studies in Management and Economics, Dissertations No. 22.
Lindell, P., L. Melin, H. Gahmberg, A. Hellqvist and A. Melander (1998), 'A strategic manager's perspective on organizational change', in C. Eden and J.-C. Spender (eds), *Managerial and Organizational Cognition*, London: Sage.
Ljung, L. (1993), 'Idébaserad verksamhet – En studie av frikyrkan som organisation'. Linköping Studies in Management and Economics, Dissertations No. 26.
Lukes, S. (1974), *Power: A Radical View*, London: Macmillan Press, Ltd.
March, J. G. and J. P. Olsen (1972), *Ambiguity and Choice in Organizations*, 2nd edn, Bergen: Universitetsforlaget.
Martin, J. (2002), *Organizational Culture: Mapping the Terrain*, Thousand Oaks, CA: Sage.
Melander, A. (1997), 'Industrial Wisdom and Strategic Change – The Swedish Pulp and Paper Industry 1945–1990', *JIBS Dissertation Series*, No. 001. Jönköping International Business School, Sweden.
Melander, A. and Nordqvist, M. (2008), *Att förstå strategi*, Lund: Studentlitteratur.
Melin, L. (1986), 'The field-of-force metaphor: A study in industrial change', *International Studies of Management and Organization*, **17**(1): 24–33.
Melin, L. (1989), 'The field-of-force metaphor', *Advances in International Marketing*, **3**: 161–79.
Melin, L. (1992), 'Internationalization as a strategy process', *Strategic Management Journal*, **13**: 99–118.
Mintzberg, H. and J. B. Quinn (1991), *The Strategy Process: Concepts, Contexts, Cases*, 2nd edn, Englewood Cliffs, NJ: Prentice Hall.
Mintzberg, H. and J. Waters (1985), 'Of strategies, deliberate and emergent', *Strategic Management Journal*, **6**: 257–72.
Mintzberg, H. and F. Westley (1992), 'Cycles of organizational change', *Strategic Management Journal*, **13**: 39–59.
Morgan, G. (1997), *Images of Organizations*, London: Sage.

Narayanan, V. K. and L. Fahey (1982), 'The micro-politics of strategy formulation', *Academy of Management Review*, **7**(1): 25–34.

Nordqvist, M. (2005), 'Understanding the Role of Ownership in Strategizing: a Study of Family Firms', *JIBS Dissertation Series*, No. 029. Jönköping International Business School, Sweden.

Nordqvist, M. and L. Melin (2008), 'Strategic planning champions: Social craftspersons, artful interpreters and known strangers', *Long Range Planning*, **41**(3): 326–44.

Ocasio, W. (1997), 'Towards an attention-based view of the firm', *Strategic Management Journal*, **18**: 187–206.

Ocasio, W. and J. Joseph (2005), 'Cultural adaptation and institutional change: The evolution of vocabularies of corporate governance, 1972–2003', *Poetics*, **33**(3–4): 163–78.

Pettigrew, A. M. (1985), *The Awakening Giant: Continuity and Change in Imperical Chemical Industries*, Oxford, UK and New York, USA: Blackwell.

Pettigrew, A. M. (1990), 'Longitudinal field research on change: Theory and practice', *Organization Science*, **1**(3): 267–92.

Pettigrew, A. M. (1992), 'The character and significance of strategy process research', *Strategic Management Journal*, **13**: 5–16.

Pettigrew, A. M. (1997), 'What is a processual analysis?', *Scandinavian Journal of Management*, **13**: 337–48.

Pettigrew, A. M. and E. M. Fenton (2000), *The Innovative Organization*, London: Sage.

Pettigrew, A. M., R. Whittington L. Melin and Associates (eds) (2003), *Innovative Forms of Organizing: An International Perspective*, London: Sage.

Regnér, P. (2003), 'Strategy creation in the periphery: Inductive versus deductive strategy making', *Journal of Management Studies*, **40**: 57–82.

Rumelt, R. P. (1979), 'Evaluation of strategies: Theories and models', in D. E. Schendel and C. W. Hofer (eds), *Strategic Management: A New View on Business Policy and Planning*, Boston, MA: Little Brown, pp. 196–212.

Shotter, J. (1993), *Conversational Realities. Constructing through Language*, London: Sage.

Silverman, D. (1970), *The Theory of Organizations*, New York: Basic Books.

Simon, H. A. (1947), *Administrative Behaviour: A Study of Decision Making Processes in Administrative Organistions*, New York: Macmillan.

Tushman, M. L. and E. Romanelli (1985), 'Organizational evolution: A metamorphosis model of convergence and reorientation', in L. L. Cummings and B. M. Staw (eds), *Research in Organizational Behavior*, Greenwich, CT: JAI Press, pp. 171–222.

Van de Ven, A. H. and S. M. Poole (1995), 'Explaining development and change in organizations', *Academy of Management Review*, **20**: 510–40.

Weick, K. (1995), *Sensemaking in Organizations*, Thousand Oaks, CA: Sage.

Whittington, R. (2006), 'Completing the practice turn in strategy research', *Organization Studies*, **27**(5): 613–34.

Whittington, R. and L. Melin (2003), 'The challenge of organizing/strategizing', in A. M. Pettigrew, R. Whittington, L. Melin, C. Sanchez-Runde, F. A. J. van den Bosch, W. Ruigrok and T. Numagami (eds), *Innovative Forms of Organizing: International Perspectives*, London: Sage, pp. 35–48.

Whittington, R., A. M. Pettigrew and H. Thomas (2002), 'Conclusion: Doing more in strategy research', in A. M. Pettigrew, H. Thomas and R. Whittington (eds), *Handbook of Strategy and Management*, London: Sage Publications.

Wigren, Caroline (2003), 'The spirit of Gnosjö: The grand narrative and beyond', *JIBS Dissertation Series*, No. 017 Jönköping International Business School, Sweden.

Wooldridge, B., T. Schmid and S. W. Floyd (2008), 'The middle management perspective on strategy process: Contributions, synthesis and future research', *Journal of Management*, **34**: 1453–1480.

5 Strategy process research and the RBV: social barriers to imitation
Patrick Regnér

INTRODUCTION

The primary mission of strategy process research has been to analyse how strategies develop. While the approach taken has varied between diverse research efforts, conclusions have confirmed that strategy making is much more complex than top management strategy design and choice, as often explicitly or implicitly assumed in strategy content research (e.g. Rumelt et al., 1994). At the most fundamental level it has been concluded that contexts matter for strategy development and change (e.g. socio-cultural, cognitive, political influences). Unfortunately the consequences of this for strategy outcome and content have often not been spelled out (Chakravarty and White, 2002), and if they have been analysed it has frequently been through the lens of flawed and biased processes where various contextual influences distort strategy making. The focus has been on how social contexts and interests disturb economic interests rather than on how they can shape economic outcomes.

While strategy process studies have provided much valuable contributions to strategic management research it would benefit from relating more explicitly to strategy content and outcome (Chakravarty and White, 2002). The division between strategy process and content research is artificial and process examinations may complement and inform strategy content research in many ways. This essay proposes that there are important synergies between strategy process research and resource and capabilities views, which have dominated much of strategy content research during the last decade. The basic argument follows other scholars that have pointed towards a potential fertile combination between the two research strands, as suggested in strategy process and practice research (Floyd and Wooldridge, 2000; Johnson et al., 2003; Kellermanns and Floyd, 2005; Regnér, 2008) as well as in strategy content research (Helfat et al., 2007; Peteraf, 2005).

Strategy process research can specifically assist resource-based and organizational capabilities views concerning imitation barriers. This essay proposes that social interests and interactions that underlie many

contextual influences on strategy making (cultural, cognitive, normative, political, etc.) may be of importance for imitation possibilities with
subsequent economic consequences. It draws attention to the potential
strategic importance and opportunities that may lie in diverse types of
social contexts and that may influence resource and capability imitation.
Besides strategy process research, recent work on strategy-as-practice
has emphasized the significance of socially shared views of practices or
routines that organizational members draw on and the consequences for
strategy making and outcome (Jarzabkowski et al., 2007; Johnson et al.,
2007; Whittington, 2006).

Consequently this chapter examines diverse strategy contexts and their
underlying social interests that may influence imitation behavior. From
a strategy process perspective the chapter contributes by showing how
strategy process research not only may assist in describing and explaining
how strategies develop generally, but that it may be of great value when
describing and explaining the specifics of how imitation behavior and firm
heterogeneity develop. From a resource and capabilities perspective the
chapter attempts to expand imitation impediment explanations by providing details of imitation barriers that involve social complexity (Barney,
1991), including cognitive, normative, motivational and political contexts
and processes.

The chapter is divided into four sections. First, the resource-based view
(RBV) and diverse forms of barriers to imitation are discussed. Second, it is
asserted that imitation barriers may be rooted in social contexts and interests besides in technical complexities and that there are several avenues of
strategy process research that may assist in explaining these. Third, four
fundamental characteristics of behavioral imitation barriers are discussed:
cognitive, normative, motivational and political. Their impediments to
imitation and their foundations in strategy process research are analysed.
Finally, conclusions are drawn and future research is discussed.

THE RBV AND BARRIERS TO IMITATION

Limiting imitation has historically been central to strategy (Porter, 1980,
1985; Ghemawat, 1991) and imperfect and costly imitation of resources
and capabilities is core to contemporary strategic management theories
(Barney, 1986a, 1991, 2001; Lippman and Rumelt, 1982). In fact, imitability received most attention in the groundwork of the RBV and has been
described as what was most new in this view (Barney, 2001). The basic
argument is that sustained competitive advantage stems from resources
and capabilities that are rare, valuable, not substitutable and imperfectly

imitable (Barney, 1991). This implies that resources and capabilities may be heterogeneously distributed across competitors and that these differences may be long term and sustainable. A central tenet is that resources and capabilities must be imperfectly imitable besides being rare and valuable. There are several explanations to this imperfect imitability (Barney, 1986a, 1991). A primary reason why resources may be costly to imitate may be their specialization, sophistication and/or complexity (Kogut and Zander, 1992, Rivkin, 2000; Rumelt, 1984; Winter, 1987). Related to these physical and technological barriers to imitation, others have suggested historical conditions (Barney, 1991; Dierickx and Cool, 1989; Lippman and Rumelt, 1982) and causal ambiguity (Barney, 1986a, 1991; Dierickx and Cool, 1989; Lippman and Rumelt, 1982; Reed and DeFillippi, 1990; Rumelt, 1984) as principal grounds for imperfect imitation. Unique historical conditions and events of time and place may put a firm on a path-dependent trajectory that followers cannot later attain (Barney, 1991; Dierickx and Cool, 1989). Causal ambiguity has received widespread attention in the literature and implies that the relationship between a firm's resources and capabilities and sustained competitive advantage is imperfectly understood by the focal firm itself and by its competitors (Barney, 1986a; Lippman and Rumelt, 1982; Reed and DeFillippi, 1990; Rumelt, 1984; Szulanski, 1996). It is simply not clear to competitors how to develop the desired resources and capabilities in the short to medium term. Still another foundation for imitation impediments is social complexity (Barney, 1991). It implies that resources and capabilities may involve extremely complex social phenomena, including organizational culture, social interrelationships, traditions, trust, reputation, etc., which firms are unable to systematically manage. Even though organizational climate or culture (Barney, 1986b) have been discussed as possible sources of social complexity, little knowledge has been accumulated around the specific details and forms of social complexity.

The border between social complexity and causal ambiguity is not always clear and sharp in the literature. Socially complex resources and capabilities may be causally ambiguous since it may be imperfectly understood exactly how social interrelationships, organizational culture, values, etc. are interrelated with them (cf. King and Zeithaml, 2001; Mosakowski, 1997). Likewise a socially complex resource and capability may of course be uniquely linked to historical conditions and events. While recognizing interaction effects between different forms of imperfect imitability and that this may further increase imitation barriers, this chapter is broadly focused on social complexity and does not analyse these interactions in detail.

In sum, although the essential link between resources and capabilities and social complexity or social contexts has been previously recognized, its particulars have often been overlooked and little attention has been paid to the processes and mechanisms involved. There is little research and analysis on the characteristics of social complexity, what diverse types of social complexity there may be and how it may influence strategy outcome. In particular, little knowledge has been accumulated around the social interests that underlie social complexity and contexts and how these may influence imitation behavior and barriers. In contrast, the focus here is specifically on imitation barriers that relate to strategy process research and thus include an analysis of social contexts and potential consequences for imitation possibilities and outcome.

SOCIAL BARRIERS TO IMITATION

Although social complexity may provide for imperfect imitation it can be argued that some firms and managers may have insights into socially complex beliefs and values that other competitors cannot apply as easily and quickly (cf. Bromiley and Papenhausen, 2003; Jonsson and Regnér, 2009). Hence, managers and organizations could possibly be proactive in influencing some aspects of these elements, even though under normal circumstances it is extremely difficult for them to be fully aware of, let alone manipulate them. In other words, while these elements are not easily managed and manipulated (as some technical capabilities may be) they involve processes that are extremely complex, which suggests that they may include aspects of pure chance, opportunities that serendipitously present themselves over time, but also strains of deliberate strategic action. Hence, while Barney's (1991) assertion about the inability to strategize around social complexity may be correct it may be so only at a specific point of time and for certain actors. Strategy process research has taught us that strategies develop incrementally over time and that diverse contextual elements influence strategy and that managers at different organizational levels may play a role. This implies that strategies may be initiated by chance without complete insight, only to take the shape of strategic opportunities that at a later point serendipitously present themselves as capabilities, and the meanings of them develop over time in the periphery of the firm with deliberate top management action entering at a later point (cf. Regnér, 2003). Hence, in the same way as resources and capabilities accumulate gradually over time, the understanding and application of them develop and change due to social interactions and behavior. This conception of strategy making as a combination of an unsystematic and messy process on the one hand combined with some preparation and planning on the other not only follows fundamental findings in strategy process research, but organizational capabilities views (Dosi et al., 2000).

Recently it has been suggested that an imitation process includes two additional steps besides the technical ability to imitate: the *identification* of what to imitate and the *willingness* to do so (Jonsson and Regnér, 2009). These two additional steps indicate that cognitive and normative contexts of imitation may matter for imitation outcome. Similarly, it may be suggested that the *motivation* to imitate is yet another required step in the imitation process. It seems that if cognitions, norms, motives and, thus, culture (which include aspects of cognitions, norms and motives) may influence imitation behavior, strategy process research provides a rich tradition to build on when investigating imitation impediments. Moreover, since these aspects may differ along the organizational hierarchy, *power and politics*, which is another important aspect of strategy process research, is likely to influence imitation behavior and impediments as well. Much of strategy process research provides descriptions of how strategy making involves these non-economic elements that sometimes depart from pure central economic interests and instead take social interests into consideration, and thus depends on structural, cognitive, cultural, motivational or political elements, but that in the end could have economic consequences. It may thus be helpful to consult this research if we want to understand imitation behavior and impediments and how firms can base their strategies on these elements to create competitive advantage.

Since all firms are not subject to the same cognitions, norms or motivations, strategies may, by chance and/or by choice, be developed around them and provide for social barriers to imitation. On the one hand these elements may make a firm understand certain resources and capabilities in a different way compared with competitors, and this can make the firm exploit them to provide for imitation impediments. On the other hand it is important to realize that such differences in understanding may also provide for lock-in and inertia into a certain view of resources and capabilities that competitors instead can exploit to their advantage.

A careful analysis and understanding of social barriers to imitation is essential not only for understanding how to imitate competitors, but for comprehending how own imitation barriers can be developed and, not least, in determining and exploiting competitors' imitation barriers. The latter involves competitor inertia, which so far has been undervalued in strategy making, even though it may be as important as overcoming competitors' imitation barriers and innovatively shaping own imitation barriers versus competitors (cp. Rumelt, 1995). All three of these levers are critical to strategy making and strategizing around imitation barriers: imitating others and thus overcoming own imitation barriers, raising own

Table 5.1   Strategizing and social complexity

Imitation barrier policy	Focus	Process	Strategizing example
Overcome competitors' imitation barriers	Defeat constraints	Imitating competitors	Copying competitors' resources and capabilities (and products or services) and the social complexity they are based on
Raise new own imitation barriers vs. competitors	Creating constraints for competitor	Innovating	Creating entirely new resources and capabilities (and products or services) based on social complexity that differs from competitors
Exploit competitors' imitation barriers	Identify opportunities around competitors' constraints	Exploiting competitor inertia	Taking advantage of competitor socially complex resources and capabilities by focusing on or introducing resources and capabilities (and products or services) that challenge them

imitation barriers versus competitors, and to take advantage of competitors' imitation barriers and inertia. An overview of these is presented in Table 5.1. While the first two have been extensively discussed by strategy scholars the last one has received considerably less attention. However, it is perhaps of most importance in the context of socially complex resources and capabilities since imitation barriers related to social contexts and interests are extremely difficult to manipulate if at all.

STRATEGY PROCESS RESEARCH AND SOCIALLY COMPLEX RESOURCES AND CAPABILITIES

Below four categories of imitation foundations (cognitive, normative, motivational and political) are discussed and analysed. First is imitation barriers based on *cognition* or a certain world view. If a resource or capability is not spotted and understood in the first place imitation will naturally not occur. Second, *norms* can play an essential role as an imitation barrier. Firms and their managers may be ensnared in norms that go against adapting and imitating the resources and capabilities in question. Hence, even though the resources or capabilities to be imitated have been identified there may be unwillingness to imitate due to institutionalized norms. A third impediment to imitation is lack of *motivation*. Managers in charge may have vested interest in the current resource structure and thus promote the status quo rather than make the organization adjust and/or imitate new resources, and/or there may be initial resource change costs that make them hesitate. Thus, while resources have been identified and norms may be in accordance with imitation, firms may still resist imitation due to lack of motivation. Finally, since cognitions, norms and motives along the organizational hierarchy may be in conflict with those at the top and these conflicts may be difficult or impossible to solve, *politics* and political gridlock may be another important imitation barrier. In brief, even though cognitive, normative and motivational hurdles have been overcome on the top management level they may still play a role and hinder imitation on other organizational levels. In conclusion, four categories of imitation barriers with implications for strategy process research are proposed besides resource and capability specialization and complexity: normative, cognitive, motivational and political imitation barriers. What they all have in common is that they emerge from social interests and interactions between individuals when embedded in an organization.

These social barriers to imitation and their respective basis, means and ways of imitation management are described and categorized in Table 5.2. While this chapter analyses these diverse imitation barriers separately they are in reality often interdependent and manifest themselves in combination. In fact, it is particularly their intertwined character that potentially can provide for sustainable competitive advantage. The first category in Table 5.2 is familiar from the groundwork of the RBV and is included merely as a basis for comparison. It focuses on resource- and routine-based inimitability involving their specialization, sophistication and complexity and has been extensively discussed previously (Barney, 1986a; Kogut and Zander, 1992; Ghemawat, 1991; Porter, 1985; Rivkin, 2000; Rumelt, 1984; Winter, 1987).

Cognitive Barriers to Imitation

The first category of imitation foundations is perhaps most familiar to strategy scholars: cognitive barriers to imitation. It refers to how the organization and its managers view the world and it is intimately linked to beliefs and values. Even though an organization may have the ability to imitate and would be willing to do so it may be unaware of the necessity to imitate or the organization does not realize how to imitate. The organization and its managers may simply not understand the resource,

Table 5.2   Diverse categories of social complexity and imitation: social barriers to imitation

Foundation	Barriers	Means	Management
Resources and capabilities (physical, technological, bundled routines)	Physical/ technological/ bundle uniqueness, specialization, complexity, interdependence, etc. – Historical conditions – Causal ambiguity – Social complexity: related to categories below	Ability and skill	Build and combine resources and capabilities
Cognitive	Cognitive barriers: – Myopic cognitive/ knowledge structures	Identification and understanding	Include alternative knowledge structures (organizational periphery and external actors)
Normative	Normative barriers: – Myopic norm structures	Willingness and compliance	Include alternative normative structures (organizational periphery and external actors)
Motivational	Motivational barriers: – Vested interest in current resources – Upfront resource change costs	Motivation and incentives	Rewards and appraisals focused on firm long-term prosperity
Political	Political barriers: – Incommensurable views grounded in the three categories above: political gridlock	Conflict settlement and resolution	Inclusion of alternative knowledge and normative structures and other means of mixing views (external recruitment, job rotation, etc.)

technology or routine to be imitated since they are locked into another view of the world.

The notion of consensus on a purpose and mission and of a core set of values and beliefs in organizations is referred to throughout the history of organizational theory (Barnard, 1938; Cyert and March, 1963; Thompson, 1967), economics (Axelrod, 1976; Selten, 1967) and sociology (Janis, 1972). Similarly, this type of imitation barrier and inertia has attracted a lot of attention in strategic management either in itself or as a subpart of organizational culture (cf. Johnson, 1987). Collective cognitive or knowledge structures on various levels of analysis (industry, group, individual) and of different forms have been extensively discussed (e.g. Huff, 1982; Johnson, 1988; Porac et al., 1989; Prahalad and Bettis, 1986; Smircich and Stubbart, 1985; Walsh, 1995). In addition, diverse cognitive simplification processes and biases have been specified (Hogarth and Makridakis, 1981; Schwenk, 1984). Knowledge accumulated from prior experiences with existing resources and capabilities risks impeding managers and organizations from understanding new ones or accurately assessing their importance by creating competency traps (Levitt and March, 1988). While there have been some examinations and discussions of how managers' understanding of the world relates to cognitive imperfections and the accumulation of organizational capabilities (e.g. Amit and Schoemaker, 1993; Gavetti, 2005; Gavetti and Levinthal, 2000; Zajac and Bazerman, 1991), little knowledge has been generated around the detailed imitation behavior and processes involved and how they can be exploited in strategy making.

A classical example is how the Swedish corporation Facit – the global leader in mechanical calculators during the 1960s and early 1970s – did not perceive and understand what dramatic impact electronics would have on its industry and products despite an electronics joint venture with Toshiba (Starbuck, 1983; Starbuck and Hedberg, 1977). While the corporation identified electronics as one technology development among several others, it failed to perceive and understand electronics' impact due to its lock-in into its mechanical centered world view. While strategy process research has described and examined the importance of cognitions for strategy making generally and specific cognitive biases have been identified, less knowledge has been accumulated around imitation behavior and barriers specifically. This research has, however, the potential to provide details and explanations regarding the specifics of cognitive imitation patterns and the mechanisms involved. For example, detailed process studies of how managers shape and construct their organizations' conception of specific resources and capabilities over time would be highly beneficial. Examinations of how meanings of resources and capabilities change over time through positive feedback in adaptive processes would be particularly valuable. Resources and capabilities that at one point are not conceived as particularly valuable may over time become regarded as valuable due to environmental changes and changes in meanings tied to cognitive feedback resulting from social interactions among managers. Other studies that would be helpful are examinations of how divergent cognitive views of resources and capabilities across organizations may generate opportunities and possibilities to exploit these cognition differences as a basis for differentiation. These kinds of studies would be of value not only to strategy process research, but to strategy content and strategic management research more generally.

Normative Barriers to Imitation

Another type of social context and underlying social interest and interaction that may bring about imitation barriers involves managers' and firms' adherence to certain norms: normative barriers to imitation. Groups of managers and organizations may be embedded in institutionalized norms and values that can make them unwilling to imitate even though they have identified the resource to be imitated and have the ability to imitate. Besides technical and cognitive abilities the resources and competences to be imitated need to be normatively and socially acceptable for imitation to take place. However, the understanding of how institutionalized norms influence strategy making and imitation barriers and of how managers and firms possibly can exploit institutions strategically remains limited.

Neo-institutional theory emphasizes the general prevalence of norms and how they may have important consequences for firm activities and practices (DiMaggio and Powell, 1983). It is thus reasonable to expect that higher-order institutional logics (Davis and Greve, 1997; Friedland and Alford, 1991) include distinct characteristics that may be significant for resource and capability imitation. Accordingly, potential synergies between strategic management and institutional theory have been explored (Baum and Dutton, 1996; Ingram and Silverman, 2002). Since all firms are not subject to identical sources of institutionalization, norms may partially vary between firms in the same industry (Oliver, 1991) and an analysis of the institutional context thus becomes essential in an analysis of sustainable competitive advantage (Oliver, 1997).

A recent empirical study of the Swedish mutual fund industry demonstrates how the unwillingness to imitate due to institutionalized professional norms regarding certain product categories made some firms enter these profitable products with significantly longer time lags (Jonsson and Regnér, 2009). Product inimitability differed between firms depending on how embedded they were in the institutionalized norms and some firms exploited the differential normative barriers to imitation to their advantage. However, how these imitation barriers develop and if and how they may be managed are questions that largely remain unanswered. This implies we have only started to understand the influence of institutionalized norms on strategy making and we need to know more about the intersection of economic and institutional forces and, in particular, the specific role institutionalized norms and practices might have for imitation and competitive advantage. Work to date in strategic management has often been conceptual and has emphasized a dualist logic (economics vs. social) and institutional forces merely as constraining and isomorphic rather than including institutions as an integral part of strategy, as a strategic opportunity and a basis for differentiation. Strategy process research has the potential to contribute significantly here by determining the prevalence of normative barriers to imitation, to what extent institutions are possible to strategize around, and if managerial mindfulness and capacity may play a role in that process and, if so, how. While there has been strategy process research on institutionalized norms, the progress in neo-institutional theory with an increased focus on organizational and institutional change (Baum and Dutton, 1996) and recent research that brings institutions and strategy more closely together (Jonsson and Regnér, 2009; Oliver, 1991, 1997) have the potential to provide more detailed answers to questions about resource and capability imitation.

Motivational Barriers to Imitation

Individual and organizational motivational structures are still other elements that may generate motivational barriers to imitation. Due to lack of motivation and personal interests, individuals or groups of managers may be unwilling to imitate even though the resources and/or capabilities have been identified, they are in line with prevailing norms and the firm has the ability to imitate. This is because individuals or groups may have vested interest in current resource and capability structures and may thus promote the status quo rather than imitating any new resources and/or there may be initial personal or organizational change costs that make them resist change. Hence, there might be a lack of leadership in terms of formulating a direction or vision, in providing power, information and incentives etc. for imitation. In addition, the necessity to imitate the resources and capabilities may be so threatening and frightening that management simply refuses to take it in. Although this is a kind of fear-based denial that relates to cognitive impediments it is grounded in a lack of motivation to accept the resources and capabilities. In sum, even though all other requirements are in place it may be doubtful if it pays to be a first mover and that might hold back imitation and change.

That interests, goals and information may differ between actors in organizations lies at the very foundation of organizational theory (Barnard, 1938; Chandler, 1962; Galbraith, 1973; March and Simon, 1958; Lawrence and Lorsch, 1967; Thompson, 1967), and the field of agency theory has specifically addressed this dilemma (Eisenhardt, 1989). In strategic management this type of imitation barrier and inertia has attracted less specific attention, but has nonetheless been part of several strategy process studies and discussions that emphasize the role of dissimilar interests, politics and culture in strategy development (Johnson, 1987; Pettigrew, 1979). In addition, strategy process research has demonstrated that managers at different levels of the organizational hierarchy may have different information, interests and incentives and play diverse roles in strategy development (Bower, 1970; Burgelman, 1983; Floyd and Wooldridge, 2000; Regnér, 2003).

An example of how motivational structures may be of importance for strategy development and resource imitation is Swedish-American Autoliv's imitation of airbag technologies. It showed how interests in historical resources and capabilities and immediate change costs made corporate management resist imitation and made business unit-level management extremely hesitant. This was despite identification of the necessary resources and capabilities, that they were in line with prevailing norms and values, and that the firm conceivably would have the ability to imitate. Although there are many diverse elements that come into play in imitation individual and group interests, motivation and incentives can be significant. The specifics of how individual and organizational motivational structures influence imitation behavior and barriers nevertheless remain unclear. While organizational theory and behavior research have examined details of social motives and conflicting interests in organizational change, many questions are unanswered regarding the particular influence on strategy making and imitation behavior. By examining the details of different groups and individuals along the organizational hierarchy with an influence on strategy, strategy process research could possibly determine what specific role vested interests, initial change costs and other indicators of motivational structures may play for imitation behavior and to what extent they could be exploited.

Political Barriers to Imitation

Last, but not least, social interests that result in power games and politics between individuals and groups of individuals within a firm may be critical in the analysis of imitation behaviour and barriers. This category, political barriers to imitation, builds on the previous categories as far as cognitions, norms and motives may differ along the organizational hierarchy with power struggles and politics as a consequence. Although the firm has the ability to imitate and top management has identified the resources to be imitated and may be willing and motivated to imitate, other parts along the organizational hierarchy may not. The consequence may very well be power struggles with imitation impediments as end result.

Power and politics have been widely discussed in organizational theory (Perrow, 1986; Pfeffer, 1997; Pfeffer and Salancik, 1978) and political conflicts and gridlocks have been described as significant and natural factors that get in the way of organizational change (Hannan and Freeman, 1977). This category is thus quite familiar to strategy process scholars and several studies have specifically focused on politics as a primary factor influencing strategy making (Johnson, 1987; Pettigrew, 1977, 1985). It has been suggested that power resources of expertise and information and political access lie at the core of politics and that this represents an overlap between political and cultural analysis in organizations since it involves the management of meaning (Pettigrew, 1973, 1985). In addition, this view emphasizes processes through which strategies are legitimized and delegitimized. In brief, diverse aspects of motivation, cognition and norms are combined in this category.

A study of the Swedish telecommunications giant Ericsson's creation of what later became the largest mobile telecommunications systems business in the world showed how social interests, including world views, norms and motivation, were tied to historical resources and capabilities in corporate management and the management of the principal switching division (Regnér, 1999). This made them strongly resist the new venture into mobile telephony when it was first initiated by a small radio technology unit at the periphery of Ericsson with different social interests based on widely divergent world views, norms and motivations (Regnér, 2003). Although Ericsson finally managed to sell the first mobile telephony system in the world through its tiny radio unit, competitors moved into mobile telephony technologies during the years of political struggles. This illustrates that power games can influence the speed of imitation even though it is still uncertain how and to what extent. It may slow down own imitation efforts while accelerating competitors' imitation processes, but the specific mechanisms involved are unclear. Even though power and politics have been examined in organization theory and strategy process research, the specifics of power struggles and politics in relation to imitation behavior remain unknown territory. Several questions need to be answered; for example: Can firms influence industry cognition and norms to promote own imitation efforts and delay others – and if so, how? How do firms support competitors' internal struggles to promote their own agenda? How can imitation efforts best be timed do exploit competitors' power games?

CONCLUSIONS AND IMPLICATIONS

Despite the centrality of imperfect imitability in contemporary strategic management research, the details and processes of its foundation in social complexity remain largely unknown. This essay has displayed the potential of strategy process research to disentangle social complexity as a foundation for imperfectly imitable resources and capabilities. The key point in the account presented is that if firms capitalize on opportunities for sustainable competitive advantage based on social complexity, strategy process research has much to contribute. The arguments presented here have implications both for strategy process and content research and for building bridges between the two. First, since strategy process research has a long tradition of examining strategy development and decision making in diverse organizational and institutional contexts, it has the potential to untangle the development of imitation strategies around cognitions, norms, motivations and politics as demonstrated above. It can assist not only in determining the details of how social contexts may provide for imitation barriers, but how actors that are embedded in particular organizational and institutional contexts operate in them and try to manage them. Besides detailed examinations of how social contexts may be linked to rare, valuable and inimitable resources and capabilities, process research has the potential to describe and explain how they emerge in the first place. It may thus assist in explaining the specifics and micro-foundations of how firm imitation behavior and heterogeneity develop. Moreover, such examinations of social complexity and contexts may provide answers concerning how social contexts can be analysed and influenced by managers even though they may never be fully managed.

Second, from the perspective of resource and capability views, this essay starts to untangle what sub-parts social complexity may involve and how they can influence imitation behavior. Diverse types of social contexts with specific implications for imitation barriers are identified. Since social complexity is a fundamental requirement for imperfect imitation and this in turn has been described as the core of the RBV (Barney, 2001) it is essential to understand what it is and how it develops. A careful analysis of social complexity is particularly important since it seems even more difficult for managers to gain insight into or understand, let alone manage, other requirements for imperfect imitation such as historical conditions and causal ambiguity (Barney, 1991; Lippman and Rumelt, 1982; Rumelt, 1984). This missing link is imperative if we want to understand how imitation barriers based on social contexts work and how they may provide for sustainable competitive advantage. Even though resources and capabilities in themselves may be idiosyncratic and complex enough, it seems often to be their foundation in certain cognitive or normative meanings that really provides for inimitability. The importance of unique managerial perspectives and perceptions of resources and markets is something that Penrose (1959) emphasized in her analysis of the growth and direction of the firm. In addition, personal motivation and interests linked to resources and capabilities together with politics may further explain imperfect imitation. The mutual reinforcement between and among resources and capabilities and social complexity elements can thus provide for competitive advantage. Additional research of these interconnections and how they bring about imitation barriers is certainly warranted.

Finally, the approach to imperfect imitation behavior presented here has implications for building a bridge between strategy process and content research. There have been many calls for the provision of such a link (e.g. Pettigrew, 1992; Rumelt et al., 1994; Schendel, 1992), but little progress in practice. In contrast to general calls and discussions a focused research effort on explaining imitation behavior and barriers based on social complexity may be a fruitful start. It takes a core feature of current strategy content research, imperfectly imitable resources and capabilities, and adds the experiences and knowledge in strategy process research on organizational and institutional contexts in disentangling imitation behavior and barriers. Such a research endeavor would benefit strategic management research in general and the two research strands individually. For strategy process research it can provide a specification of how social contexts influence strategy making and for strategy content research it can provide explanations of imitation barrier mechanisms. In addressing this common research question the two research streams could possibly in concert explain the micro-foundations of imperfectly imitable resources and capabilities.

Strategy process examinations can in future research determine the existence of social barriers to imitation and to what degree diverse sources and forms of them (e.g. cognitive, normative, motivational and political) influence strategy development and outcomes (cf. Jonsson and Regnér, 2009). This would also contribute to research on micro-foundations that underlie organizational capabilities. More precise definitions and assessments of social barriers to imitation in this respect would be highly beneficial. Comparative studies of how incumbents and new entrants differ in relation to social barriers to imitation may prove to be especially fruitful. Another promising research avenue may be careful examinations of how different forms of strategic decision-making processes handle and possibly resolve different types of social complexity and related causal ambiguity. For example, it has been suggested that calculative experimentation may be superior compared with random trial and error processes and planning processes in response to causal ambiguity, but that experimentation may decrease over time while planning increases as causal ambiguity dissolves (Mosakowski, 1997). Hence, studies that link diverse types of strategic decision processes to social barriers to imitation are clearly warranted (e.g. more creative and experimental processes vs. traditional planning processes; Regnér, 2005a). However, to capture different forms of strategic decision making over time and related social barriers to imitation, longitudinal examinations that do not neglect the pre-history of strategy processes and outcomes are required (Regnér, 2005b). Further study of these and related issues will contribute to our understanding of social barriers to imitation and the relationship between strategy process and content.

REFERENCES

Adner, R. and C. E. Helfat (2003), 'Corporate effects and dynamic managerial capabilities', *Strategic Management Journal*, 2003, **24**: 997–1010.

Amit, R. and P. J. Schoemaker (1993), 'Strategic assets and organizational rent', *Strategic Management Journal*, **14**: 33–46.

Arrow, K. J. (1994), 'Methodological individualism and social knowledge', *American Economic Review*, **84**(2): 1–9.

Axelrod, R. (1976), *Structure of Decision: The Cognitive Maps of Political Beliefs*, Princeton, NJ: Princeton University Press.

Barnard, C. I. (1938), *The Functions of the Executive*, Cambridge, MA: Harvard University Press.

Barney, J. B. (1986a), 'Strategic factor markets: Expectations, luck, and business strategy', *Management Science*, **32**(10): 1231–1241.

Barney, J. B. (1986b), 'Organizational culture: Can it be a source of sustained competitive advantage?', *Academy of Management Review*, **11**(3): 656–665.

Barney, J. B. (1991), 'Firm resources and sustained competitive advantage', *Journal of Management*, **17**: 99–120.

Barney, J. B. (2001), 'Resource-based theories of competitive advantage: A ten-year retrospective on the resource-based view', *Journal of Management*, **27**(6): 643–650.

Baum, J. A. C. and J. E. Dutton (eds) (1996), *The Embeddedness of Strategy*, Stamford, CT: JAI Press.

Blau, P. M. (1977), *Inequality and Heterogeneity*, New York: Free Press.

Bower, J. L. (1970), *Managing the Resource Allocation Process: A Study of Corporate Planning and Investment*, Boston, MA: Harvard Business School Press.

Bromiley, P. and C. Papenhausen (2003), 'Assumptions of rationality and equilibrium in strategy research: The limits of traditional economic analysis', *Strategic Organization*, **1**(4): 413–438.

Burgelman, R. A. (1983), 'A process model of internal corporate venturing in the diversified major firm', *Administrative Science Quarterly*, **28**: 223–244.

Chakravarty, B. and R. E. White (2002), 'Strategy process: Forming, implementing and changing strategies', in A. Pettigrew, H. Thomas and R. Whittington (eds), *Handbook of Strategy and Management*, London: Sage, pp. 182–205.

Chakravarty, B., G. Mueller-Stewens, P. Lorange and C. Lechner (2003), *Strategy Process: Shaping the Contours of the Field*, Oxford: Blackwell.

Chandler, A. D. (1962), *Strategy and Structure: Chapters in the History of the American Industrial Enterprise*, Cambridge, MA: MIT Press.

Cyert, R. and J. G. March (1963), *A Behavioral Theory of the Firm*, Englewood Cliffs, NJ: Prentice-Hall.

Davis, G. F. and H. R. Greve (1997), 'Corporate elite networks and governance changes in the 1980s', *American Journal of Sociology*, **103**(1): 1–37.

Dierickx, I. and K. Cool (1989), 'Asset stock accumulation and sustainability of competitive advantage', *Management Science*, **35**: 1504–1511.

DiMaggio, P. J. and W. W. Powell (1983), 'The iron cage revisited: Institutional isomorphism and collective rationality in organizational fields', *American Sociological Review*, **48**: 147–60.

Dosi, G., R. Nelson and S. Winter (2000), *The Nature of Dynamics and Organizational Capabilities*, London: Oxford University Press.

Eisenhardt, K. M. (1989), 'Agency theory: An assessment and review', *Academy of Management Review*, **14**(1): 57–74.

Floyd, S. W. and B. Wooldridge (2000), *Building Strategy from the Middle: Reconceptualizing Strategy Process*, London: Sage.

Friedland, R. and R. R. Alford (1991), 'Bringing society back in: Symbols, practices, and institutional contradictions', in W. Powell and P. J. DiMaggio (eds), *The New Institutionalism in Organizational Analysis*, Chicago: University of Chicago Press, pp. 232–266.

Galbraith, J. R. (1973), *Designing Complex Organizations*, Boston, MA: Addison-Wesley Longman Publishing Co.

Gavetti, G. (2005), 'Cognition and hierarchy: Rethinking microfoundations of capabilities development', *Organization Science*, **16**: 599–617.

Gavetti, G. and D. Levinthal (2000), 'Looking forward and looking backward: Cognitive and experiential search', *Administrative Science Quarterly*, **45**: 113–137.

Ghemawat, P. (1991), *Commitment – The Dynamic of Strategy*, New York: The Free Press.

Hannan, M. T. and J. H. Freeman (1977), 'The population ecology of firms', *American Journal of Sociology*, **82** : 929–964.

Helfat, C., S. Finkelstein, W. Mitchell, M. Peteraf, H. Singh and S. Winter (2007), *Dynamic Capabilities: Understanding Strategic Change in Organizations*, London: Blackwell.

Hogarth, R. M. and S. Makridakis (1981), 'Forecasting and planning: An evaluation', *Management Science*, **27**: 115–138.

Huff, A. S. (1982), 'Industry influences on strategy reformulation', *Strategic Management Journal*, **3**(2): 119–131.

Ingram, P. and B. S. Silverman (2002), *The New Institutionalism in Strategic Management*, Boston, MA: JAI.

Janis, I. L. (1972), *Victims of Groupthink*, Boston: Houghton-Mifflin.

Jarzabkowski, P., J. Balogun and D. Seidl (2007), 'Strategizing: The challenges of a practice perspective', *Human Relations*, **60b**(1): 5–27.

Johnson, G. (1987), *Strategic Change and the Management Process*, Oxford: Basil Blackwell.

Johnson, G. (1988), 'Rethinking incrementalism', *Strategic Management Journal*, **9**: 75–91.

Johnson, G., L. Melin and R. Whittington (2003), 'Micro strategy and strategizing: Towards an activity-based view', *Journal of Management Studies*, **40**(1): 3–22.

Johnson, G., A. Langley, L. Melin and R. Whittington (2007), *The Practice of Strategy: Research Directions and Resources*, Cambridge, UK: Cambridge University Press.

Jonsson, S. and P. Regnér (2009), 'Normative barriers to imitation: Social complexity of core competences in a mutual fund industry', *Strategic Management Journal*, **30**(5): 517–536.

Kellermans, F. and S. Floyd (2005), 'Strategic consensus and constructive confrontation: Unifying forces in the resource accumulation process', in S. Floyd, J. Roos, F. Kellermanns and C. Jacobs (eds), *Innovating Strategy Process*, Strategic Management Society, London: Blackwell, pp. 149–162.

King, A. W. and C. P. Zeithaml (2001), 'Competencies and firm performance: Examining the causal ambiguity paradox', *Strategic Management Journal*, **22**(1): 75–99.

Kogut, B. and U. Zander (1992), 'Knowledge of the firm, combinative capabilities, and the replication of technology', *Organization Science*, **3**(3): 383–397.

Lawrence, P. R. and J. W. Lorsch (1967), *Organization and Environment,* Cambridge, MA: Harvard Graduate School of Business Administration.

Levitt, B. and J. G. March (1988), 'Organizational learning', *Annual Review of Sociology*, **14**: 319–340.

Lippman, S. A. and R. P. Rumelt (1982), 'Uncertain imitability: an analysis of interfirm differences in efficiency under competition', *Bell Journal of Economics*, **13**: 418–438.

March, J. G. and H. A. Simon (1958), *Organizations*, New York: John Wiley.

Mosakowski, E. (1997), 'Strategy making under causal ambiguity: Conceptual issues and empirical evidence', *Organization Science*, **8**(4): 414–442.

Oliver, C. (1991), 'Strategic responses to institutional processes', *Academy of Management Review*, **16**(1): 145–179.

Oliver, C. (1997), 'Sustainable competitive advantage: Combining institutional and resource based views', *Strategic Management Journal*, **18**(9): 697–713.

Penrose, E. T. (1959), *The Theory of the Growth of the Firm*, New York: John Wiley & Sons.

Perrow, C. (1986), *Complex Organizations – A Critical Essay*, New York: McGraw Hill, 3rd edn.

Peteraf, M. (2005), 'Research complementarities: A resource-based view of the resource allocation process model (and vice versa)', in J. L. Bower and C. G. Gilbert (eds), *From Resource Allocation to Strategy*, Oxford: Oxford University Press.

Pettigrew, A. M. (1973), *Politics of Organizational Decision-Making*, London: Tavistock.

Pettigrew, A. M. (1977), 'Strategy formulation as a political process', *International Studies of Management and Organization*, Summer: 78–87.

Pettigrew, A. M. (1979), 'On studying organizational cultures', *Administrative Science Quarterly*, **24**(4): 570–581.

Pettigrew, A. M. (1985), *The Awakening Giant: Continuity and Change in Imperial Chemical Industries*, Oxford: Basil Blackwell.

Pettigrew, A. M. (1992), 'The character and significance of strategy process research', *Strategic Management Journal*, **13**: 5–16.

Pfeffer, J. (1997), *New Directions for Organization Theory, Problems and Prospects*, New York: Oxford University Press.

Pfeffer, J. and G. R. Salancik (1978), *The External Control of Organizations: A Resource Dependence Perspective*, New York: Harper & Row.

Porac, J. F. and H. Thomas (1990), 'Taxonomic mental models in competitor definition', *Academy of Management Review*, **15**: 224–240.

Porac, J. F., H. Thomas and C. Bador-Fuller (1989), 'Competitive groups as cognitive communities: The case of Scottish knitwear manufacturers', *Journal of Management Studies*, **26**: 397–416.

Porter, M. E. (1980), *Competitive Strategy*, New York: The Free Press.

Porter, M. E. (1985), *Competitive Advantage: Creating and Sustaining Superior Performance*, New York: The Free Press.

Prahalad, C. K. and R. A. Bettis (1986), 'The dominant logic: A new linkage between diversity and performance', *Strategic Management Journal*, **7**(6): 485–501.

Reed, R. and R. J. DeFillippi (1990), 'Causal ambiguity, barriers to imitation and sustainable compatitive advantage', *Academy of Management Review*, **15**(1): 88–102.

Regnér, P. (1999), *Strategy Creation and Change in Complexity – Adaptive and Creative Learning Dynamics in the Firm*, Published doctoral dissertation, Institute of International Business, Stockholm School of Economics: Stockholm, Sweden.

Regnér, P. (2003), 'Strategy creation in the periphery: Inductive versus deductive strategy making', *Journal of Management Studies*, **40**(1): 57–82.
Regnér, P. (2005a), 'Adaptive and creative strategy logics in strategy processes', *Advances in Strategic Management*, **22**: 189–211.
Regnér, P. (2005b), 'The pre-history of strategy processes', in S., Floyd, J. Roos, F. Kellermanns and C. Jacobs (eds), *Innovating Strategy Process*, Strategic Management Society, London: Blackwell, pp. 21–32.
Regnér, P. (2008), 'Strategy-as-practice and dynamic capabilities – steps towards a more dynamic view of strategy', *Human Relations*, **61**(4): 565–588.
Rivkin, J. W. (2000), 'Imitation of complex strategies', *Management Science*, **46**(6): 824–844.
Rumelt, R. P. (1984), 'Towards a strategic theory of the firm', in R. B. Lamb (ed.), *Competitive Strategic Management*, Englewood Cliffs, NJ: Prentice-Hall Inc.
Rumelt, R. P. (1995), 'Inertia and transformation', in C. Montgomery (ed.), *Resources in an Evolutionary Perspective: Towards a Synthesis of Evolutionary and Resource-Based Approaches to Strategy*, Norwell, MA: Kluwer Academic Publishers, pp. 101–132.
Rumelt, R. P., D. Schendel and D. J. Teece (1994), *Fundamental Issues in Strategy*, Boston, MA: Harvard Business School Press.
Schendel, D. (1992), 'Fundamental themes in strategy process research', *Strategic Management Journal*, **13**: 1–3.
Schwenk, C. R. (1984), 'Cognitive simplification processes in strategic decision-making', *Strategic Management Journal*, **5**: 111–128.
Selten, R. (1967), 'Invetitionsverhalten im Oligopolexperiment', in H. Sauermann (ed.), *Reiträge zureperimentellen Wirtschaftsforschung*, **1**, Tubingen: Mohr, pp. 60–102.
Smircich, L. and C. Stubbart (1985), 'Strategic management in an enacted world', *Academy of Management Review*, **10**(4): 724–736.
Starbuck, W. (1983), 'Organizations as action generators', *American Sociological Review*, **48**(1): 91–102.
Starbuck, W. and B. Hedberg (1977), 'Saving an organization from a stagnating environment', in H Thorelli (ed.), *Strategy + Structure = Performance*, Bloomington, IN: Indiana University Press, pp. 249–258.
Szulanski, G. (1986), 'Exploring internal stickiness: impediments to the transfer of best practice within the firm', *Strategic Management Journal*, **17**: 27–43.
Thompson, J. D. (1967), *Organizations in Action,* New York: McGraw-Hill.
Walsh, J. (1995), 'Managerial and organizational cognition: Notes from a trip down memory lane', *Organizational Science*, **6**(3): 280–321.
Whittington, R. (2006), 'Completing the practice turn in strategy research', *Organization Studies*, **27**: 613–634.
Winter, S. G. (1987), 'Knowledge and competence as strategic assets', in D. J. Teece, (ed.), *The Competitive Advantage – Strategies for Industrial Innovation and Renewal*, New York: Harper & Row, pp. 159–184.
Zajac, E. J. and M. H. Bazerman (1991), 'Blind spots in industry and competitor analysis: implications of interfirm (mis)perceptions for strategic decisions', *Strategic Management Journal*, **16**(1): 37–57.

6 The feedback structure of the strategy process and top management's role in shaping emerging strategic behavior
*Vittorio Coda and Edoardo Mollona**

INTRODUCTION

The focus of this essay is the nature of a company strategy process and the role played by top managers. Three themes are at the core of studies on strategy process: the interpretation of the process as a purely analytical-rational or as a learning-by-doing one; the top-down or bottom-up nature of the process; and the interpretation of the role of top management in governing the process. The three themes, however, are often ambiguously interwoven. In this chapter, we propose a qualitative feedback model to elicit the connections among the three issues.

In our theoretical speculation we propose a number of constructs to support the analysis of the nature of the strategy process and to understand the role of top managers in governing a company strategy process. In particular, the construct of the Strategy in Progress helps to deal with the emergent component of strategic behavior while the construct that we label Strategic Gap supports the analysis of top managers' capability in governing the strategy process. In addition, a number of feedback structures capture different strategic sub-processes and facilitate the investigation of the connections between top-down and bottom-up elements in the strategy process.

As for the conceptual approach adopted, in the strategic management literature, a number of scholars have tried to explain strategic and organizational change adopting the concept of feedback (Burgelman, 1983b; Van de Ven and Poole, 1995).[1] A problem that characterizes managerial applications of feedback theory concerns the recurring focus on either the concept of positive feedback or on that of negative feedback.

In this work, however, we adopt the System Dynamics approach (Forrester, 1961; Sterman, 2000; Morecroft, 2007). This approach overcomes the dichotomy between positive and negative feedback loops and focuses on the analysis of aggregated structures in which positive and negative feedbacks work in combination.

The essay is organized as follows. The next section contains a literature review focused on the strategy process literature. We then discuss potential areas of contribution in describing the strategy process. A qualitative model that articulates the strategy process into a number of strategic sub-processes, each captured in a feedback structure, is then presented. The next section discusses findings and the final section presents a number of conclusions.

THE STRATEGY PROCESS IN LITERATURE

Literature on firms' strategy process has investigated how a company's realized and intentional strategies are defined and what the relevant activities are in strategy-making behavior. In particular, theoretical contributions on strategy process have assumed different positions with respect to the following problems:

1. interpretation of the strategy process as a purely analytical-rational or as a learning-by-doing one;
2. interpretation of the strategy process as a top-down or a bottom-up one;
3. interpretation of the role of top management in governing the strategy process.

In the Harvard tradition, which gave rise to the schools which Mintzberg (1990a, b) re-christened Design School (Andrews, 1971) and Planning School (Ansoff, 1965, 1979, 1984, 1991), strategy process is an analytic-rational one in its formulation phase and also in its implementation phase (this latter essentially intended as the design and implementation of an organizational structure, in the broad sense, logically descending from the content of strategic choices). This set-up is decidedly top-down and is based on the hypothesis that decisions are totally rational and implementation logically consequential.

On the other hand, Normann (1977) emphasizes the learning-by-doing process that underpins the development of successful business ideas. On similar lines, Mintzberg (1978, 1979, 1985) advocates the need to remove the distinction between thought and action to look at strategy making as a longitudinal learning process which proceeds by integrating two elements: a top-down rational analysis and an emergent trial-and-error learning mechanism, this latter characterized by a strong bottom-up component.

On the lines of the seminal contribution of Bower (1970), Burgelman (1983a,b,c, 1991, 1994) and Noda and Bower (1996) developed an approach in which the strategy process has a strong bottom-up component and CEOs limit themselves to designing a firm's behavioral context and 'adjust' company strategy a posteriori, responding to the pressures of those strategic initiatives that have survived selective pressures operating in a company's strategic and organizational context. In this approach, the role of top management is not downsized; rather, it changes from one of directly designing corporate strategy to one of planning and building a company's strategic and organizational context, in which the strategy takes shape.

Recently, Burgelman and Grove (2007) proposed a more active role for top managers that, rather than simply amending official strategy ex-post, matches unfolding strategic behavior to environmental dynamics by orchestrating the balance between top-down and bottom-up strategic processes, emphasizing or de-emphasizing one or the other in turn.

Within this group of contributions, which intend strategy as the result of a continuous learning process, rather than as the result of an a priori analytical process, we may also position the contribution of Quinn (1980, 1981), who advocated a view of strategy as a logical incremental process in which company leaders channel flows of activity and events into conscious strategies.[2]

Lastly, another contribution to the analysis of firms' strategy making derives from evolutionary economists Nelson and Winter (1982). According to their theoretical position, environmental changes impose learning processes in which inefficient organizational routines are replaced by efficient ones. A firm's top management has the task of guiding the learning process by facilitating the elimination of inefficient routines, removing the difficulties in transmitting change within the organization and stimulating the update of routines by means of innovation and imitation (Mintzberg et al., 1998). However, the real agents of the evolution of company strategy are the subsystems where organizational routines are localized.

Because of the emphasis assigned to learning processes in forming company strategy, the contributions we have listed – from Normann to Mintzberg, Bower, Burgelman and Noda and possibly Quinn – can be traced back to a line of thought which Mintzberg et al. (1998) have called the Learning School.

THE NATURE AND STRUCTURE OF THE STRATEGY PROCESS

Addressing the nature and structure of firms' strategy process, Normann and Mintzberg stressed the crucial role played by learning. Within the same cultural milieu, Bower (1970) and Burgelman (1983a) highlighted the spontaneous, bottom-up, component of a company's strategic activity. In these contributions, the role of a company's leaders is re-interpreted and lightened from its 'heroic' content. Top manager, rather than an enlightened guide, in perfect control of the situation, plays the no less important role of a meta-manager that acts as a designer, or architect, of complex social systems in which learning is facilitated and knowledge accumulated.[3]

In the line of thought that we are exploring, the analysis of strategy process is closely related to the investigation of firms' adaptation capability to environmental changes. Mintzberg (1991) and Ansoff (1991), for example, debated whether a planned strategy process a learning-by-doing one was better suited to facing dynamic environments, whereas Burgelman (1991), for example, suggested that radical strategic renewal is possible only by means of bottom-up strategic processes that develop autonomously from a company's strategic context.

In the above-mentioned literature, the morphology of a firm's strategy process explains the firm's adaptation performances. In particular, the features of a firm's strategy process affect adaptation behavior by defining a specific trade-off between top-down and bottom-up processes in shaping the direction of change.

Top-down driven adaptation behavior has the advantage of relying on global information and of taking advantage of full control of resources whereas bottom-up driven adaptation relies on local information and incentives (Sull, 2005) – for example, at the level of a single department – and may dissipate resources on projects not aligned with a firm's core competencies. However, bottom-up adaptation may be more effective when radical change is required. In these cases, cognitive and structural inertia (Hannan and Freeman, 1984) is an impending menace and self-referential attitudes are dangerous.

Yet, in the literature mentioned, the discourse on the emergent or planned nature of the strategy process is ambiguously intertwined with the theme concerning its top-down or bottom-up nature. The first theme speaks to a cognitive approach, and requires the analysis of the locus where structural and cognitive inertia reside; the second one pertains to the organizational analysis of the multi-layered structure of decision-making processes. We will articulate further this matter in the following.

The Locus of Learning in Strategy Making

Although Normann, Mintzberg, Bower and Burgelman clearly highlighted the spontaneous, emergent component of strategy, based on learning-by-doing processes, the nature and protagonists of these processes need to be further clarified. Indeed, the analysis of the nature of strategy process is interlaced with the scrutiny of the place where strategic thinking originates within firms.

In Mintzberg, the adjective *emergent* juxtaposed to the word *strategy* has the aim to capture the cognitive structure of strategy thinking as a learning-by-doing process. The focus is not the analysis of who generates the amendment to the strategy being deliberated, thereby giving rise to an emergent strategy, or where such modification takes place within a firm. The crucial aim is to counter the description of strategic thinking as an intellectual exercise leading to the design of a strategy conceived of as an ordered structure of ends and means that is articulated before, and independently of, its implementation.

On the other hand, in the Bower–Burgelman model, the focus is on the different places in an organization where learning takes place. The fragmentation of the strategy process into sub-processes, each enacted by different actors that are located at different hierarchical positions, underpins a definition of strategic thinking as a collective effort that is the emergent aggregation of a variety of contributions that spring in different places within an organization and are associated with different actors.

Along this line, to say that a CEO learns, and accordingly refines strategy, because he, or she, observes the result of his, or her, enacted strategic action is different from proposing that a CEO monitors, approves and includes a posteriori into a company's strategy the results of emergent strategic initiatives, these latter generated by front-line managers or other collaborators like researchers or people close to customers and the market, who are not necessarily members of the top management team.

In the first case, we shall not distance ourselves greatly from the existence of a unique actor as the motor of strategic behavior; the learning process is an individual one: the leading player is the CEO who, by observing ongoing results of past strategy implementation, re-examines his or her strategic intents, or, at least, learns to be more effective in the implementation phase.

This situation, in which the top manager is personally involved in an entrepreneurial-like, strategic innovation activity, reminds us of typical situations of small–medium sized companies in which the articulation of the hierarchical levels and degree of complexity to be managed are of a low level.

The process is substantially different if we consider large, complex companies with an articulated organizational structure. In this case, the CEO manipulates strategic and organizational contexts in order to induce,[4] rather than to develop personally, emergent strategic initiatives that are enacted by other members of the organization and that may be more or less coherent with an 'umbrella strategy'. Here, the CEO decides to what extent to approve or discourage strategic behavior which does not come under the company's umbrella strategy.[5] If he or she decides to allow strategic initiatives of this type to germinate, the CEO necessarily will have to adjust the umbrella strategy a posteriori in order to incorporate the content of these emergent strategic innovations. In this case, realized strategy will influence the content of future intended strategy.

In this interpretation, agents who contribute to learning are distributed throughout the organization and strategic behavior emerges as the result of a choral effort. Front-line managers, bottom upwards gradually enrich the realized strategy with new contents, both within the boundaries established by the company management and in new directions. On the other hand, top management makes its contribution including innovations into intended strategy, thereby creating the premises for further learning and emergent strategies. Ex-post, these latter initiatives may appear to be valid and promising, although they were not originally included under the firm's umbrella strategy.

A sort of 'specialization' is then established according to which the role of top management is to design the company's strategic and organizational contexts, for example by outlining the company business portfolio strategy. On the other hand, middle and front-line managers are engaged in developing specific strategic initiatives like, for example, the development of new products. In this case, learning is articulated within the whole company and strategy evolves as a result of the aggregation of contributions received from various areas and different hierarchical levels in an organization.

A further interpretation of the strategic learning process, which could be configured as an extreme case of 'specialization', is the one described by Burgelman (1991) for the Intel case. Intel gradually shifted its production from semiconductors to microprocessors. What is peculiar about the history of Intel, however, is that apparently top managers let sponsors of alternative strategic initiatives (semiconductors or microprocessors) compete within the organization to finally amend corporate strategy to incorporate outcomes of such competition.

Here, the idea of specialization in the strategy process is pushed to its extreme consequences and the nature of learning processes may be described by saying that company top management governs the relationship between realized and intended strategy and middle or front-line management address the relationship between realized strategy and emergent strategy.

The foregoing discourse suggests that at least two different learning mechanisms need to be illuminated in the strategy process. A first mechanism is the one illustrated in Mintzberg's model of strategy making (1978). In the model, learning is embodied into the emergent strategy. More specifically, information deriving from realized strategy stimulates emergent strategies not originally included in the strategy deliberated.

However, realized strategy, which also incorporates the results of emergent strategy, may also influence intended strategy. Thus, a second learning mechanism works when realized strategy necessarily influences mental models and key beliefs of top managers, that is, future intended strategy. In this latter case, learning unfolds as a cycle of reciprocal influence not only between realized and emergent strategy but also between realized and intended strategy.

It is likely that in the companies, these learning mechanisms co-exist. However, with a view to understanding and governing the mechanisms at the base of strategy dynamics, a distinction should be drawn between processes of a different nature and grounded upon different actors. In his contribution, Mintzberg focuses on the cognitive structure of an individual learning process. On the other hand, Burgelman is interested in the multi-actor and multi-layered nature of the strategy process. In this light, he hints at the feedback nature of the strategy formation process and captures the self-organizing component of the strategy process by looking at the interaction among a network of players that contribute in different ways to the formation of a company strategy.

Strategy Making as a History-Dependent Process

The process of strategy making unfolds longitudinally over time and, as Noda and Bower (1996) have convincingly suggested, its observable results are history dependent. That is, facts and events occurring in the early history of the process mold its successive emerging pattern. To capture the structure of a history-dependent process it is necessary to describe how the process' outcomes influence its forthcoming unfolding. In other words, it is necessary to conceptually distinguish a process from its product and to describe how the two influence reciprocally. Despite this evidence, studies on strategy process have often been reticent regarding the distinction between the products of a process and the process itself.[6]

Returning to Mintzberg's model of strategy making (1978), we note that some of the concepts included refer to processes while others appear to be more specifically the observable results of processes themselves. For example, considering intended strategy, this appears to be an observable result of such processes as planning or environmental analysis. As far as deliberate strategy, we might consider it as a construct encapsulating a number of implementation processes leading to the realization of intended strategy. On the other hand, we might also consider deliberate strategy as a further stock variable in which intended strategy flows when it is translated into an official list of objectives and projects explicitly communicated to, for example, shareholders. In this case, we ought to elicit the processes that transform intentions into deliberate strategies and those latter into implemented strategic actions.

Concerning realized strategy, it is the product of implementation processes and it is observable, for example, in a company's physical-technical, organizational and cultural endowment. But how should we consider emergent strategy? Is this a concept embodying a number of processes that modify realized strategy bottom-up or is it the ongoing outcome of the individual learning of managers?

The distinction between processes and outcomes of processes is a necessary starting point for an accurate description of the dynamics that underpin firms' strategic behavior. If we consider emergent strategy as a product, it is interesting to understand where and how we observe this product. For example, we could identify emergent strategies with the various initiatives enacted without official support from top management, with the ongoing R&D projects or with experiments and trials that top management encourages in order to adjust strategy 'along the way'. If, on the contrary, we consider emergent strategies as processes, we must understand the morphology of these processes and identify the relevant sub-processes.

We need conceptual tools to rigorously distinguish, and clear up the interplay between, processes and products of processes; the former observed over periods of time and the latter in different points in time. For example, intended strategy, as well as being the product of certain processes (strategic planning, visioning, etc.), defines a desirable situation that guides managerial actions. Realized strategy, besides being the product of top-down and bottom-up implementation processes, defines a specific context in which idiosyncratic learning processes take place. Thus, to conceptualize strategy making, we adopt the concepts of stock variables and flow variables.

A FEEDBACK MODEL OF STRATEGY MAKING

Grounding on the distinction between stock and flow variables, in this section we propose a model of the dynamics underpinning strategy process as a system of interconnected feedback loops. The description of the model proceeds in three phases.

The first phase highlights stock variables, which represent the state of a system at a certain point in time as the result of one or more processes. In this first phase, the question that inspired our speculation was the following: if we imagine framing strategic management as a dynamic system, in which various types of processes are intertwined, what are the observable products of these processes? In other words, if we imagine that we can freeze the company strategic management in a certain moment in time, what are the stock variables that will crystallize its state?

The second phase in building our model is the description of the processes, the flow variables, which both are influenced by information concerning the state of the system, the stock variables, and affect the state of the same. In the third phase, we draw cause–effect connections among the elicited stock and flow variables.

Stock Variables

Our model focuses on five concepts that have the property of stock variables and describe, in specific moments in time, the state of a company strategy process: mental models of top management, intentional strategy of top management, strategy in progress, realized strategy and the portfolio of entrepreneurial initiatives.

Deep-rooted mental models of top management are captured in a stock variable that encompasses key strategic orientations (Coda, 1988). By mental models, we refer to key beliefs and cognitive frameworks that inform decision making. For example, Porac and Thomas (1990), investigating how decision-makers simplify their competitive environments, discussed a cognitive approach to competitors' analysis by delineating a mental model of competitive groups. In addition, inspired by the work of Hodgkinson and Johnson (1994), who reported considerable variation in the nature of cognitive categories adopted by decision-makers, both within and between the organizations, we decided to specifically focus on top managers' mental models since these latter do not necessarily coincide with mental models of managers located at different hierarchical layers within an organization. The stock of mental models is the product of previous strategic experiments and learning concerning the causes of past success or failures (Burgelman, 1991: 243).

Although not tangible, the stock of top management's mental models is the pillar upon which hinges a company's strategy dynamics. All the formulation and implementation processes of strategic intentions, and the interpretation and control of results, are permeated by interpretative patterns which have been consolidated over time (Argyris, 1982; Argyris and Schon, 1978).

The second stock variable is a firm's intentional strategy, which is made up of the actual strategic intents pursued by the CEO. This variable includes both the strategic goals and the possible plans for achieving them. The concept also includes the strategic intent as proposed by Hamel and Prahalad (1989), which evokes a desired market leader position and the criteria for monitoring the approach to this position. Strategic intents can be drawn, for example, from official documents like the report to shareholders or the statements issued by top management during interviews, press conferences, meetings with collaborators and other events in communication.

The third stock variable we shall deal with is the stock of strategy in progress. This stock captures the preliminary outcomes of plans, investments and the projects that have been launched to implement intentional strategy. These outcomes are not the definitive planned results, and thus cannot be considered as part of realized strategy. However, they are observable consequences of implementation processes and, thus, they provide information and suggestions to decision-makers in order to eventually adjust along the way the trajectory of a firm's strategic behavior.

What we stress here is the fact that the activities that add up to make up a process of strategy implementation crystallize into intermediate observable products which are, nevertheless, stimuli for further learning. It is the distinction between the concepts of realized strategy and the one of strategy in progress, both observable as stock variables, that helps to elucidate the role of learning-by-doing in molding a firm's strategic behavior.

The fourth stock is realized strategy. This variable defines the strategy that underpins a company's operations, in a given environmental context as a result of past strategy implementation processes. It includes, for example, accumulated investments that are functional to a specific strategic positioning, a specific organizational set-up, and a company's entrenched culture and values. In addition, realized strategy contains historical accumulated economic, financial, competitive and social performances. These latter are observable results when accumulated into stock variables. For example, monthly profit or loss, average production rates, average monthly billing rates or average level of customer satisfaction and staff motivation.

The last stock variable that we highlight is the portfolio of entrepreneurial strategic initiatives; it embraces projects and business ideas in the experimentation and development phase.

Flow Variables

Having described the stock variables, we now describe the concepts that capture processes. These concepts have the property of flow variables that work, over a certain interval of time, to modify the state of stock variables.

We consider five flow variables which modify the state of stock variables: mental model learning processes; intentional strategy formation processes; intentional strategy realization processes, innovation generation processes and innovation selection processes.

The first group includes top management learning processes that enrich or modify the content of top management's mental models. By observing the results of past decisions incorporated into the realized strategy or the information conveyed by strategy in progress, the members of the top management team learn and adapt their mental models. For example, they adjust their ambitions according to whether these latter appeared unachievable or not very challenging and they, a posteriori, include retroactively within a company's official strategy results from bottom-up strategic initiatives (Burgelman, 1991). In addition, top management adapts mental models in response to the interpretation of environmental trends.

The second group includes all the processes that contribute to shape the content of the official strategy of a firm. These include processes of environmental analysis; processes of visioning, by which the top management's ambition takes shape into challenging goals; processes of competitors' benchmarking; and analytic-rational processes of strategic planning. These processes are present with different levels of importance. Dissimilarities are explained by different degrees of organizational formality/informality, by different level of top management's ambition, by more or less participatory leadership style, by different top management's ability to conduct in-depth analysis of problems, and by top management's interpretation of its leadership.

A third flow variable represents intentional strategy implementation processes, which are the managerial processes aimed at closing the gap between strategic intentions and realized strategy.

These processes can be ascribed to the following classes: processes of communication and sharing the intentional strategy; processes for structuring a company's business portfolio; processes that set up, or adjust, organizational structures and operating mechanisms; processes that encapsulate the launching of company challenges and the projects into which these latter translate; and processes that crystallize managerial decision making, such as planning, budgeting, controlling and staff management.

The fourth group includes processes leading to the generation of innovations, these latter including both operational innovations and internal entrepreneurship processes which generate strategic innovations. The innovation generation processes are, in various ways, stimulated by environmental opportunities and by cultural and morphological characteristics of a company's strategic and organizational contexts. By morphology of organizational context, we intend, for example, the characteristics of the mechanisms, formal or informal, by which internal entrepreneurship is stimulated, disciplined or discouraged. As far as informal mechanisms are concerned, culture, history and folklore, which permeate the life of an organization, add up to create a deposit of accumulated information that reveals widespread attitudes towards innovation.

On the other hand, these attitudes are frequently formalized into programs or routines, systems of reward and promotion. Suffice it to think, for example, of the 'melting-pot of ideas' created by General Electric at the end of 1988. The initiative involved the creation of periodic meetings where employees presented their ideas and proposals on how to make their business more effective and received immediate feedback. On the other hand, at 3M, official mechanisms provided stimuli to innovative behavior. For example, the '15 percent rule' enabled employees to allocate 15 percent of their time to work on ideas which they believe to have some development potential. In addition, the evaluation system imposed to divisions the goal of having at least 30 percent of turnover originating from products introduced in the last four years.

The last flow variable that we consider regulates the selection of emergent strategic initiatives. These processes may be officially incorporated into formalized routines. In this case, they assume the form, for example, of periodic assessments of economic-financial, commercial and strategic potentials of single emergent strategic initiatives. These processes are usually linked to resource allocation mechanisms which enable the initiatives to survive, grow stronger and eventually consolidate within an organization.

On the other hand, there are also informal mechanisms that stimulate or discourage emergent strategic initiatives. For example, as Burgelman (1983a, 1991) reported, autonomous strategic initiatives, which lead to the conception of products outside a firm's core strategy, may develop outside official evaluation and selection mechanisms unofficially supported by management located in superior hierarchical positions.

Map of Cause–Effect Relationships

The described flow and stock variables are connected by causal relationships. By reporting these relationships, we elicit a number of feedback loops. We show four fundamental loops: the strategic control loop, the strategic intent formation loop, the entrepreneurial loop and the learning loop of mental models.

Strategic control loop

The first feedback mechanism is loop 1 that controls the implementation of a firm's intentional strategy. Once intentional strategy is generated and articulated into action plans, a phase of implementation starts off that is aimed at closing what we call the Strategic Gap. The Strategic Gap is the observed discrepancy between intentional strategy and realized strategy (Figure 6.1). The construct is an auxiliary variable (Forrester, 1961) that crystallizes information stemming from two stock variables – intentional strategy and realized strategy – and shares the same characteristics of stock variables. Thus, it is a reservoir of information that adapts gradually. Not only should the size of such a reservoir, but also its quality be considered.

In order to govern the dynamics of the system, the management gauges the distance between goals and results and accordingly activates implementation processes. Loop 1 is a mechanism which performs a strategic control activity and therefore behaves as a thermostat: it aims at preserving the homeostasis of a company's strategy when this latter does not require adjustment, or to place strategy on a new trajectory of evolution

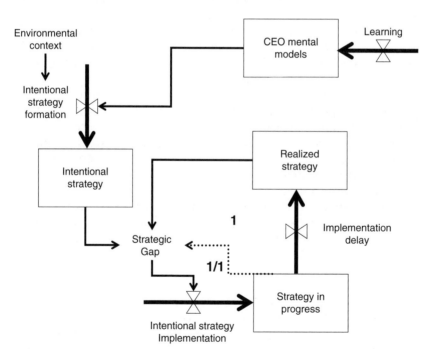

Figure 6.1   Strategic control loop

if the company management intends to modify corporate or business strategy. We may liken this loop to the first-order learning loop of Argyris (1982).

The strategic control loop describes a company's ability to execute a certain strategy promptly and efficaciously. For example, on his arrival as a CEO at IBM in 1993, Gerstner showed concern about the dangerous weakness that he unveiled in the firm's strategy implementation capability. According to Gerstner, at IBM strategic plans were left on the shelves and never realized, and one of his early interventions was to introduce the concept of *execution* and to reward into management performance assessment the ability to execute strategic plans rapidly and effectively.[7]

In this respect, in the diagram of Figure 6.1, implementation processes accumulate into the stock strategy in progress and, after an implementation delay, they modify the state of the company's realized strategy. Longer or shorter delays suggest different execution capabilities.

The stock that captures strategy in progress, however, also advises on the fact that intermediate products of implementation processes are observable outcomes that may stimulate learning. Thus, in Figure 6.1, we can elicit loop 1/1 that connects the stock strategy in progress to the gap. Loop 1/1 signals the ability of managers to make use of sensors to monitor the outcomes of an implementation process along the way and to accordingly calibrate the direction of strategy execution. In other words, the loop 1/1 is a further mechanism to collect information on the gap between strategic intentions and implementations.

On the one hand, we expect that loop 1 tends to play its role in closing the Strategic Gap. On the other hand, however, it may be a fact that the gap is never totally eliminated when intentional strategy is continuously adapted. The idea here is that if top management frequently modifies content and levels of the goals captured in strategic intentions, it may be difficult to close the difference between goals and results, and a question emerges concerning the desirability of such a gap.

Thus, the Strategic Gap is a fundamental construct in order to analyse the dynamics of the strategy, and executives ought to be interested in the quality of this gap. This latter depends above all on the depth of the strategic analysis that underpins the design of intentional strategy and on the values and ambitions crystallized in top managers' mental models. An excessive amount of ambition and the desire for individual prestige and power associated with superficial analysis, or in-depth analyses not supported by an ethical conception of the company (warped by the interests of the controlling group), lead the top management team to create Strategic Gaps that have a noxious nature because they emanate destructive tensions in the organization.

Inversely, as an example of a gap producing creative tension, we may look at the one generated by Hayek when, in 1984, he assumed the leadership of SMH. The quality of this gap is marked, on the one hand, by an in-depth analysis of the competitive problems and the situation of Swiss watchmaking companies and, on the other, by sound values and beliefs.

In the case of turnaround, with the intent to transform radically large organizations, top managers may intentionally leverage an existing gap by communicating to stakeholders the severity of a particular situation in order to produce tensions and creative destruction leading to the legitimization of dramatic turnaround processes. For example, in the case of General Electric, the strategic intent of being the number one or two in its businesses and the analysis of the actual competitive situation led to decisions regarding the company's portfolio (disinvestment of 200 businesses and 370 acquisitions); the goal of being a 'lean and flexible' business, compared with the high degree of bureaucracy previously existing in the company, led to dramatic interventions in the firm's organizational structure, the thinning out of jobs with the cutting of 50 percent of the strategic planning group's employees, and the reduction of hierarchical levels from nine to four.

At IBM, in 1994, well ahead of other companies in the industry, Gerstner's strategic intent of winning the leadership in the Internet business or, more generally, in the business of the services dealing with connectivity technologies, resulted in the decision to shift 25 percent of R&D budget to Internet related projects and to create a study group to draw out the discrepancy between the needs of consumers in the emergent industry and the state of product portfolio offered by IBM. After about a year's work, in September 1995, the study group presented its conclusions and in October the fundamental decision was taken to allocate three hundred million dollars for the creation of the Internet Division.

A final remark concerns implementation delay. To capture the dynamics of loops 1 and 1/1, the role played by the time needed for a strategy to be realized is crucial. However, how can we exactly measure this delay? In other words, when can we say that a strategy implementation process is completed? In this respect, Coda suggests that companies perceive a strategy to be realized when costs and revenues connected to new strategic initiatives give rise to recurring operations that materialize into a recognizable dynamics of working capital (Coda, 2008). For example, when sporadic acquisition of factors of production become stable procurement processes and generate accounts with suppliers, we may say that a strategy has been realized that, for example, consisted in the launch of a new product.

Strategic intent formation loop

This loop represents the mechanism through which top managers draw indications from the realized strategy in order to re-examine and adjust intentional strategy (Figure 6.2). In our model, we keep the two processes of the formation of strategic intents and adaptation of mental patterns distinct.

The fact that intentional strategy changes according to the observation of the results of past actions does not necessarily imply that the basic beliefs and values of top management must also change. Many incremental adjustments to intentional strategy may simply derive from the need to refine a realized strategy without any change in the fundamental supporting ideas. For example, a company can re-dimension its goals in terms of market share when it has seen that it was unable to achieve these goals. Re-examining the goals in the delineation of intentional strategy may have the aim of not 'stressing' the organization at a given point in time and granting it the time to reorganize its forces, to then re-attempt to achieve the most challenging goal. Nevertheless, all this may take place without challenging the deep belief that the ambitious market share goal can sooner or later be achieved.

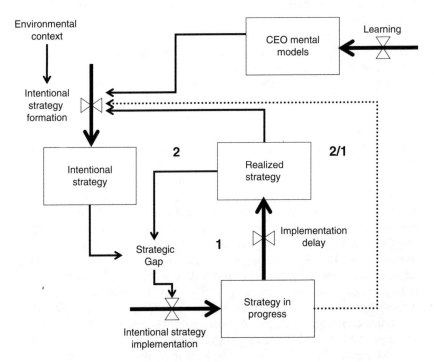

Figure 6.2   Strategic intent formation loop

Thus, we use the term 'learning' where there is a real adjustment of mental patterns and we use the expression 'intentional strategy formation' to refer to changes in intentional strategy. These changes are not necessarily a result of updating mental models but, rather, may be the consequence of a gradual elucidation and awareness of mental models underpinning strategic intentions or of a tactical need for managing the gap. A concrete example of how this motor works is provided by an interview which Jack Welch, General Electric's CEO, released in the late 1980s when GE's restructuring process had already been under way for a number of years. In the interview, Welch observed that, in the mid-1980s, the hardware part, or the organizational structure, was more or less at a satisfactory stage and the time had come to tackle the software. In this interview, it emerges how the observation of what had been achieved led to the gradual enrichment of the content of the intentional strategy without, however, changing long-term plans and basic goals.

Whereas through the strategic control loop top managers monitor and intervene on the state of advancement of strategic goals, through the strategic intent formation loop, observation of the realized strategy is preparatory to the adjustment of the goals themselves. In this light, since time delays may disconnect the beginning of a strategy implementation process from its completion, a desirable property of the strategy process is the possibility to link incremental adjustment of intended strategy to the assessment of intermediate results of implementation processes, as reported in the strategy in progress stock (loop 2/1).

Entrepreneurial loop

The third loop describes the bottom-up innovation processes that are an expression of internal entrepreneurship. In the diagram shown in Figure 6.3, loop 3 consists of a series of elements. The process hinges on the stock variable that accumulates entrepreneurial initiatives; these latter describe the results of the sub-processes which, positioned upstream and downstream of the stock, modify its level.

The stock variable that describes entrepreneurial strategic initiatives captures the energies, tensions and resources that are operating to renovate the strategy of a company in a given moment in time. For example, the patents owned by a company are tangible results of innovative initiatives after these latter have been selected and funded and have become part of the realized strategy. These crystallized results of previous innovation activity contribute to the richness and cultural fertility of a certain organizational context.

On the other hand, ideas and projects in support of which resources and energies have been officially allocated represent the ongoing official

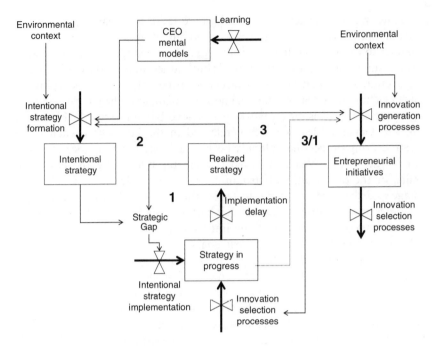

Figure 6.3   Entrepreneurial loop

innovation activity, which is captured in the strategy in progress stock variable.

By representing the stock variable of entrepreneurial initiatives, an attempt is made to take a picture of the intermediate moment in time in which stimuli and incentives existing in an organizational context have taken shape and combined into initiatives that have not been officially sponsored by the top management and that are still in the development phase. The stock of entrepreneurial initiatives is accumulated and depleted by two flow variables. Upstream are the 'innovation generation processes' that are rooted into a firm's strategic and organizational context. Downstream are the 'innovation selection processes', by means of which single initiatives exit from the stock of entrepreneurial initiatives.

The selection process may bring about a negative outcome and thus lead to the dismantling of an initiative, or it may entail the funding of the initiative. In case of favorable selection, the funded initiative begins to contribute to the molding of the strategy in progress. Thus, realized initiatives define the cultural environment in which the subsequent initiatives will be conceived. This description is coherent, for example, with the contribution of Burgelman (1983a,b,c, 1991). The latter highlights how the strategic initiatives generated inside a company, which are fundamental elements of both incremental and revolutionary strategic innovation, are at the same time products of certain strategic and organizational contexts and triggers for changing these contexts.

Loop 3 describes the potential of large organizations for renewal. The behavior of companies, and in particular the ability to generate strategic innovations, may remain confined to trajectories defined by the company's past history, with obvious problems of inertia, or they may emerge as self-organized phenomena, totally new and unpredicted, in the sense that they originated not in a top-down fashion, or as the product of top management's rationality alone, but as a result of the repeated interaction of a strategic and organizational context with individual and local behavior.

An example of how the mechanism of loop 3 functions is provided by the well-known case that describes the conquest of the US motorcycle market by Honda in the late 1950s–early 1960s (Pascale, 1984). The intentional strategy in 1958, when Honda was the domestic market leader, was to embark on a process of internationalization, starting from the California coast of the United States. This strategic intent resulted in decisions and actions leading to the setting up in Los Angeles of a tiny bridgehead made up of just a few men, with very few financial resources and a modest stock of motorcycles of all capacities, headed by a director in whose ability to get by with the few resources placed at his disposal, Mr Honda and his partner, Takeo Fujisawa, placed their complete trust.

On the field, this small group of managers was able to develop a radically innovative learning process which soon led to the discovery of the existence of a market for low capacity motorcycles in the USA, about which no one had previously even thought. Ex-post, such a previously ignored market segment proved to be the appropriate way to penetrate the US market, thereby moving to widen the outlet for medium and large capacity motorcycles and open new channels and build new commercial relationships.

In conclusion, the bottom-up working of loop 3 provided the stimulus to explore a segment that was previously ignored and that originated from a new function assigned to the motorbike as a means of healthy amusement. This market segment, so far neglected, was rather more extensive than the one in which both European manufacturers and Harley Davidson had been positioned for years.

In the case of Honda, the managers who were sent to the USA were able to exploit the resources placed at their disposal within the sphere of the realized strategy, by means of a learning process, by trial and error, behaving as entrepreneurs in the true sense of the word. The reported case of Honda suggests that entrepreneurial behavior diffused within an organization may illuminate new avenues for strategy making.

More generally, there are situations in which, both because the strategic intents are only generally outlined – for example, in situations of environmental uncertainty – or because top management is not able to foresee new opportunities that arise, internal entrepreneurship diffused inside a company becomes a key intangible asset.

In the description of the bottom-up process, it is also important to elicit the role played by the stock variable labeled strategy in progress. For example, the positive selection of a strategic initiative implies the allocation of funds for a pilot study or a study of feasibility. This small investment does not modify realized strategy but only implants a seed that may blossom only if preliminary results are encouraging and, thus, persuade original promoters and sponsors that it is worth further supporting the initiative.

The introduction of the stock variable strategy in progress is important to capture an intermediate accumulation of resources that is not necessarily going to be conveyed into realized strategy. For example, Burgelman's field study on Intel (1991, 1994, 2002; Burgelman and Grove, 2007) reports how strategic initiatives disconnected from a company's core competence and official strategy – or, in Burgelman's words, autonomous from the firm's existent corporate strategy – are funded by slack resources that middle managers sneakily convey to support specific experiments or by funds that top management subtracts from the official resource allocation mechanism to support specific strategic challenges.

In addition, accounts from field studies confirm that, to be successful, a bottom-up initiative needs to produce, at the level of strategy in progress, some preliminary results that encourage supporters to further invest time and money into the endeavor (Noda and Bower, 1996).

Thus, in the diagram of Figure 6.3, we highlight the feedback loop 3/1 that portrays the causal link between preliminary emergent strategic consequences of bottom-up initiatives and further push at the level of innovation generation process.

Learning loop of mental models

The process represented in loop 4 of Figure 6.4 highlights the impact of analysis of past strategic action on top management learning. Compared with the mechanism described in loop 2, the learning process shown in loop 4 goes to greater depth because it changes management's mental patterns and describes a mechanism which is very similar to the second-order learning of Argyris (1982).

Here, however, it is important to distinguish between two different

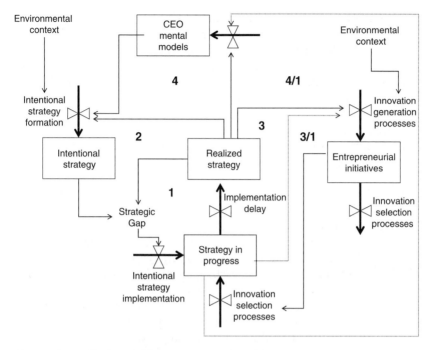

Figure 6.4   The loop of learning mental model

mechanisms through which top managers adapt their mental models. The fact that people learn from the results of past actions is a well-accepted tenet in social sciences. More generally, the idea that decision-makers tend to repeat actions that produced good results and abandon actions that generated bad results is rooted in the early studies of micro-sociology (Homans, 1961), in the behavioral decision theory, according to which decision-makers change a decision-making rule and search for another one when motivated by unsatisfying results (March and Simon, 1958; Cyert and March, 1963; Ginsberg and Baum, 1994), and in the prospect theory (Tversky and Kahneman, 1979).

Thus, it appears fairly obvious that top managers, by looking at the results of previously implemented strategies, adjust their mental models. In this light, strategic behavior seems to unfold as a series of segments, each encompassing a sequence of strategy definition, strategy implementation and ex-post learning from results of strategy implementation; this latter step being the trigger for further strategy definition.

What we want to stress here, however, is that the adaptation of top management's mental models is a continuous, ongoing process. For this reason, the diagram of Figure 6.4 suggests that mental models' adaptation is often the consequence of information that is contained into the stock variable that we labeled strategy in progress (loop 4/1). For example, during the IBM restructuring process, which began in 1993, Gerstner constantly refined the basic beliefs concerning IBM's field of activities and its role in the competitive arenas in which it operated. Concerning the field of activity in particular, Gerstner realized that the information technology sector was evolving profoundly and that the value for the customer was created not so much in production as in assembling services. This audacious reconsideration of the corporate field of activity was the consequence of an in-depth analysis of IBM's distinctive competencies and of competitive arenas in which the company was operating.

However, while implementing the idea of transforming IBM into a service company, Gerstner both interpreted the evolution of the competitive environment and recognized emerging capabilities within the company. As for the environmental analysis, Gerstner captured the trend of the ICT industry towards network-centric computing (i.e. the possibility of communicating and exchanging various types of digitalized information like video, high resolution images, voice and music by means of interconnected networks of computers). Following his analysis of environmental evolution, Gerstner further refined IBM's field of activity and, around 1995, the idea that IBM was essentially a service company became even clearer and developed into the strategy of making IBM not only an important company in information technology sector but also, and above all, the biggest service company in network-centric computing. Further on, Gerstner became conscious that network-centric computing and the tool which is its prime motor, the Internet, would lead to a profound revolution in world culture and way of life and, therefore, in the business strategies of client companies. So IBM's mission gradually became one of guiding companies in this technological and cultural transition. In this example, we observe a continuous refinement of top management interpretation of unfolding trends in the IT sector that stimulate a connected update of the firm's strategic intentions.

GOVERNING FIRMS' STRATEGIC BEHAVIOR: A FEEDBACK APPROACH

In the foregoing, we presented a qualitative feedback model. The model suggests that in order to manage strategy as a continuous transformation process, top management must acknowledge the existence of the feedbacks described. More importantly, in the following, we address how, in order to successfully manage a company's strategic behavior, it is necessary to orchestrate the simultaneous operation of the four feedback loops controlling two delicate areas. The first area concerns the calibration of the Strategic Gap between realized and intentional strategy within the top-down strategy process, while the second area is the harmonization of the top-down process, which works through feedback loops 1, 2 and 4, with the bottom-up process, which operates through feedback loop 3.

The Calibration of the Strategic Gap in the Top-Down Strategic Process

As far as the first area is concerned, each of the three feedback processes (1, 2 and 4) has a specific role in the calibration of the gap. The feedback loop of strategic control, loop 1, is a mechanism of homeostasis. If we assume to be in a state of equilibrium, in which realized strategy is coherent with intentional strategy and the gap is equal to zero, and we imagine that suddenly the content of intentional strategy changes, then the gap would widen. If this was the case, an increased gap would lead to a greater implementation effort that would result in a change, in the same direction, of the strategy in progress and, with an implementation delay, in the realized strategy as well.

The modification of the realized strategy is in the direction indicated by the behavior of the intentional strategy. Such a modification would entail the reduction of the gap and the return to the original equilibrium. Due to its tendency to balance exogenous stimuli that a system receives, the feedback mechanism described by loop 1 has the typical balancing, or gap-closing, properties that characterize a negative feedback. This balancing feedback, or gap-closing loop, embodies the capability of a firm to implement processes of strategic change. Jack Welch of General Electric and Lou Gerstner of IBM are examples of leaders able to achieve strategic intentions effectively and to reduce the implementation delay by rapidly shifting resources within the organization, redesigning operational mechanisms and creating the necessary motivation for pursuing the new goals with determination.

The strategic intent formation loop, governed by feedback 2, regulates incremental adjustments of the gap by influencing a firm's intentional strategy. The company management must be able to adjust strategic intentions in order to govern the gap. A persistent and significant gap between intentional strategy and its achievement can be the result of shallow analysis and excessively high ambitions which lead to the definition of unachievable goals or to inconsistent plans and managerial actions. When an organization experiences a persistent gap, stress and negative tensions arise. On the other hand, the existence of a comfortable situation of well-being, with no gap, can be a symptom of a dangerous state of equilibrium, featuring no positive tension. In such a situation, the company may be drawn towards a state of inertia which is detrimental to its very survival. Feedback loop 2 may show both the properties of a balancing loop and those of a reinforcing, or positive, feedback loop.

In the first case, the feedback works to counteract a change emerging in the realized strategy. For example, let's assume that a company includes in its intentional strategy the objective of differentiating one of its products by increasing the quality of this latter. Had realized strategy to incorporate an increase in the accumulated investments for the differentiation of a product and a connected reported advance in its quality, the company would perceive that the objective has been obtained. If this information is used to amend intentional strategy in the direction of reducing the desired level of investment in product differentiation, loop 2 would function as a balancing loop.

On the other hand, the loop would manifest the properties of a positive, or reinforcing, loop if it used the information concerning the increase of the accumulated investments to modify strategic intentions in the direction of requiring additional escalation in the level of investments in product differentiation. This positive link between objectives, which in our model are embodied in the intentional strategy, and the actual state of the world, or the realized strategy, has been previously described as 'superstitious learning' (Levitt and March, 1988). Superstitious learning occurs, for example, when performance objectives are based upon past performance. If performance goes up, performance objectives go up as well, thereby maintaining performance discrepancy and fostering corrective actions. On the other hand, the same connection can work as a vicious circuit in the opposite direction. It is the well known 'ratchet effect' according to which decreasing performances lead to the erosion of targets (Milgrom and Roberts, 1992, 14–15, 233–236).

Finally, feedback loop 4 captures top management learning. Top management's learning illuminates new potential fields of interest and leads to the re-opening of the gap between realized strategy and intentional strategy. The widening of the gap may create constructive tension which pushes towards new challenging goals. Relying on a metaphorical usage of complexity theory, we refer to McKelvey's (2000) idea of 'adaptive tension' as resulting from energy differentials within an organization. Along similar lines, we expect that the existence of a difference between desired and reported state of key variables, as a consequence of learning, may create a useful tension within organizations.

The mechanism described by loop 4, however, also conveys a warning on possible pathological outcomes of top management's learning that occurs when a firm has accumulated a long series of previous successes. As mentioned before, typically, decision-makers repeat courses of action that brought successful outcomes; along similar lines, top managers' learning from past success may lead to a reckless reinforcement of previously realized strategy.

In this light, Burgelman described co-evolutionary lock-in in the induced process where positive feedbacks emerge that increasingly bind a company's previous success to the existing product-market environment (2002: 326). On the other hand, feedback loop 4 may also assume a negative, or balancing, polarity and induce a sway in the content of the intentional strategy. In this case, learning from realized strategy, or from strategy in progress, brings about a dramatic swing in the mental models of top management that may decide to completely redirect the corporate strategy.

Concluding, assuming that the calibration of the Strategic Gap is a fundamental locus where top managers intervene to mold a firm's strategic behavior, we suggest that top managers' capability to dynamically govern the strategy process is connected to:

1. The ability to exploit gap-closing, or balancing, properties of the loop labeled 1 (and 1/1) that highlights top management's effectiveness in creating managerial actions aimed at achieving the contents of the intentional strategy.
2. The ability to maintain equilibrium between reinforcing and balancing properties of loops 2 (and 2/1) and 4 (and 4/1) in order to appropriately calibrate the Strategic Gap. This latter needs to be small enough not to infuse in the organization a sense of frustration and impotence and large enough not to quench necessary stimuli that arise from organizational challenges.

Harmonizing Top-Down and Bottom-Up Strategic Processes

The second area to which attention must be paid concerns the harmonization of loops 1, 2 and 4, on the one hand, and loop 3 on the other. In fact the first group of feedback mechanisms is driven by the top management that plays a key role in their calibration. By means of loop 1, top management governs the achievement of strategic intents; via loop 2 it adjusts intentional strategy and finally, by means of loop 4, top management reviews and updates his or her mental models and, as a consequence, the intentional strategy. On the other hand, loop 3 is only indirectly governed by a company's top management.

The actors that potentially play a role in feedback loop 3 are distributed more or less throughout the organization and are all those who are able to develop new ideas and initiatives, stimulated by the knowledge that develops in everyday operations and dwells in a specific strategic and organizational context. The company's top management influences this loop only indirectly as an architect, or engineer, who designs and shapes the strategic and organizational context, creating an appropriate 'behavioral environment' (Bartlett and Ghoshal, 1995) which is more or less favorable to the generation of strategic innovations.

In this vein, the organizational context of a firm can be shaped in order to leave more or less freedom in exploring new business areas outside the official strategy and the core competencies of a company. In addition, a company's resource allocation mechanisms and reward systems may be more or less prone to allocate resources to experiments and initiatives that cannot assure tangible results in the short term.

The greater the freedom of action assigned to loop 3, the stronger stimulus will be given to creative energies and entrepreneurial behavior but, on the other hand, the greater the disorder and dissipation of resources and energies might be in non-correlated directions, and the more difficult it will be to exploit synergies.

Here, the concept of feedback loops and of polarity of a feedback loop helps to delineate hypotheses concerning emergent pressures on a company's aggregate strategic behavior as they stem from the bottom-up strategic processes. Going back to the diagram in Figure 6.3, we first address the polarity of feedback 3. What is the meaning of assigning a positive or negative polarity to this feedback?

Loop 3 may counteract the content of corporate strategy. In other words, the innovation generation process may carry projects and initiatives that diverge, or contrast, with the official corporate strategy. In this case, the feedback loop is balancing, or negative. On the other hand, the content of initiatives developed within the bottom-up process may be coherent and reinforce corporate strategy; in this latter case, loop 3 is a positive feedback with a reinforcing behavior.

The polarity of loop 3/1 is also important. When loop 3/1 takes on a negative, or balancing, polarity, it implies that preliminary results of a strategic initiative discourage further investments in the initiative while a positive polarity entails that preliminary results reinforce and legitimize further investments in the initiative.

In this respect, the emergence of positive feedback is often a necessary condition to create a critical mass of financial and human resources to leverage bottom-up strategic initiatives. Along these lines, Noda and Bower referred to escalating commitment to a new business and success-bred-success patterns (1996) in the bottom-up strategic process. They report how at BellSouth early operational results of emergent wireless business justified iterated cycles of resource allocation by top managers that gave rise to an escalating commitment to the new business.

Here, we suggest that top managers' capability to dynamically govern the strategy process is connected to the ability to orchestrate the top-down and the bottom-up components of the strategy process by intervening on the reinforcing or balancing properties of the four loops described in the model. The combined management of top-down and bottom-up strategic processes is vital to preserve a firm's attitude to balance exploration and exploitation capabilities in strategy making (March, 1991). In this respect,

1. Since reinforcing loops are typically path dependent and irreversible, or hardly reversible, processes, if loop 3 tends to reinforce behavior of loops 1, 2 and 4, the strategic behavior is at risk of remaining entrapped into inertial trajectories that once triggered cannot easily be reversed or stopped. In this case, the potential for strategic innovation is clearly threatened since for a firm it becomes hard to explore new territories and to walk over unfamiliar avenues. Thus, to maintain a firm's exploration capabilities top managers need to the restrain reinforcing properties of loop 3.
2. Since balancing loops typically counteract stimuli received, if loop 3 is always characterized by balancing properties the risk for a firm is to dissipate resources without exploiting current realized strategy. In this case, top managers need to facilitate strategic initiatives that are aligned to the current realized strategy and, thus, reinforce these latter.
3. To manage the bottom-up process, top managers may need to govern different polarities of loops 3 and 3/1. To escape self-referential strategic behavior, top managers may tolerate, or encourage, negative polarity in loop 3. Negative polarity is connected to bottom-up strategic initiatives that break away from previously realized strategy. On the other hand, however, for these initiatives to survive within an organization, it may be needed that loop 3/1 acquires a reinforcing polarity. In this case, preliminary results are observable results of the strategy in progress that legitimate further investments.

CONCLUSIONS

The main contribution of our work deals with the analysis of the role of top managers in the strategy process of large firms. In a feedback perspective, top management action deals with the interpretation of the relation between the feedback structure underpinning key strategy processes and emerging strategic behavior.

Indeed, dynamic complexity produced by the interplay of the described feedback processes suggests that chances for managerial leadership may be reduced (Lant and Mezias, 1992). However, strategic behavior can be interpreted as a 'guided evolution' (Lovas and Ghoshal, 2000) or 'path creation' (Garud and Karnøe, 2000: 6–9) and managers maintain some discretion in governing change by mindfully deviating and molding emergent strategic behavior. According to such a perspective, successful managers are endowed with a 'system perspective' and recognize points in time in which it is possible to intervene and points in time in which strategic behavior emerges as the necessary result of underlying pressures.

In this respect, as Carroll and Harrison (1994) noted, a large number of organizational studies rely on the assumption of historical efficiency. Historical efficiency implies that observed social behaviors in any point of time reflect the unique outcome of underlying systematic processes, independently of historical path. In our framework, strategic behavior is a historically inefficient process and the pattern of unfolding behavior is decided in windows of time and the emerging trajectory is path dependent. In these windows of time, we suggest that managers can intervene on the properties of feedbacks by calibrating the relative strength, and the dominating polarity.

More precisely, top managers can govern a firm's strategic behavior by maneuvering two levers. First, they need to monitor and tune the dimension and the quality of the gap between intended strategy and realized strategy. Second, top management needs to harmonize top-down and bottom-up strategy processes in order to regulate the balance between the strengthening of existing competencies, with connected increase in inertia and core rigidities following from the tendency of positive feedbacks to produce undesired irreversible patterns of behavior, and competence base renewal, with connected risk of resource dissipation among diverse strategic initiatives.

More generally, the chapter provides a platform for organizing and interpreting literature on the strategic process by using the symbolic language of feedback loops and the logic of analysis crystallized into these latter. In this respect, the presented work proposes an example of how feedback loops can be used to represent and communicate theories of the strategic behavior of companies. In fact, strategic management literature increasingly dedicates attention to research approaches that are influenced by studies on dynamic systems and complexity, and are therefore characterized by non-mechanistic, interpretative logics in which increasing attention is paid to relations of the circular type, rather than one way, among variables. However, the circular nature of conceived causal models frequently remains implicit, concealed in the web of narrative theories and not represented and communicated in an explicit way (Farjoun, 2002). Interestingly, however, a rich repertoire of concepts and tools exists within feedback theory that could appropriately contribute to theory development in management studies. Richardson (1991), for example, suggests, and thoroughly demonstrates that feedback thought has a long tradition in social sciences. In the strategic management literature, a number of scholars have tried to explain the emergence of order and disorder by looking at the feedback structure of change mechanisms.

However, a problem that characterizes managerial applications of feedback theory concerns the recurring focus on either the concept of positive feedback or on that of negative feedback. Managerial literature seems divided in two fields as far as the approach to feedback theory is concerned.

A first group of contributions has been interested mainly in positive feedback, or self-reinforcing mechanisms, to explain emerging and self-amplifying differences in competitive behaviors. For example, in Noda and Bower (1996), positive feedbacks are at the base of the description of how strategic initiatives gain momentum and become established in organizations.

A second group of contributions has focused on the properties of negative feedbacks as gap-closing, homeostatic processes (Sanchez and Heene, 1997; Sanchez et al., 1996). Beer (1966, 1972, 1975, 1979), for example, has pioneered the study of negative feedbacks as control mechanisms in organizations, thereby looking at firms as cybernetic systems and exploring how managers design and control such systems. In this line of enquiry, authors have stressed the features of negative feedbacks as manifest expressions of goal-oriented behavior in organizations.

In this work, however, we adopt the System Dynamics approach (Forrester, 1961; Sterman, 2000; Morecroft, 2007; Coda and Mollona, 2010) and use the concept of feedback to explain firms' behavior. This approach overcomes the dichotomy between positive and negative feedback loops and focuses on the analysis of aggregated structures in which positive and negative feedbacks work in combination.

In this respect, we suggest that further studies may go in the direction of formalizing and further articulating the theory through computer simulation, thereby testing its internal coherency and honing hypotheses for empirical testing. Along these lines, we hope the chapter will provide a theoretical reference to guide modeling.

NOTES

* The author acknowledges the contribution from the Italian Ministry of the University and Scientific Research funding project 'TOCAI.IT: Knowledge-oriented technologies for enterprise aggregation in Internet' (RBNE05BFRK).
1. In general, we define a positive feedback loop as a mechanism that tends to push a system away from its original state and negative feedback loops as mechanisms that work to keep a system close to its state of equilibrium. Thus, assuming that a system that is in equilibrium receives an exogenous disturbance that pushes the system away from its original state, a positive feedback tends to amplify the disturbance whereas a negative feedback counterbalances the disturbance. More precisely, we can define positive and negative feedback as processes in which, respectively, $sign(d\dot{x}/dx) > 0$ and $sign(d\dot{x}/dx) < 0$ (Richardson, 1995), where $\dot{x}$ is the derivative of x with respect to time; that is, $dx/dt = \dot{x}$.
2. As Mintzberg et al. (1998: 180–182) point out, Quinn can be considered as an exponent of the Learning School because of the emphasis placed on the incremental component of strategy. However, the authors highlight a dose of ambiguity that could position the author half way between the Learning School and the Design School. In fact, in certain contributions, Quinn describes the shaping of strategy as a process in which the CEO has a very clear idea, a priori, of a company strategy; incrementalism seems to be more the fruit of the pressures faced by top managers in the implementation effort, which has to pass through the gradual creation of the necessary political conditions for the strategy to be accepted. In this light, incrementalism could be thought of as the product not so much of a learning process in the strategy definition process, as the outcome of the difficulty in controlling political coalitions within companies.
3. We do not explore here the dynamics of learning processes within organizations. The vast body of literature on organizational learning provides a useful support for understanding the problems relating to the control and design of learning processes. Yet, it is useful to mention a number of contributions that addressed the connection between organizational learning and the processes of strategic and organizational change of a company. For example, Nonaka dealt with the issue of balancing order and chaos in organizational learning (Nonaka, 1988). March (1991) tackled the problem of how to balance the exploitation of existing knowledge with the exploration of new terrain. Nonaka and Takeuchi (1995) analysed the link between the production of knowledge inside an organization and the generation of innovation by the organization itself, while Spender (1996) laid the foundations for a dynamic theory of the firm based on knowledge creation.
4. For this type of emergent strategic initiative, Burgelman uses the concept of induced strategic initiatives (Burgelman, 1991).
5. For this type of emergent strategic initiative, Burgelman uses the term 'autonomous strategic initiatives' (Burgelman, 1991).
6. In the Resource-Based View of the firm, the contribution of Dierickx and Cool (1989) appears as an encouraging exception to this evasiveness. Addressing the origin of strategic assets within firms, they use a bathtub metaphor and describe a resource accumulation process as a flow that conveys liquid into an asset-stock. The asset-stock, which plays the role of a container, is the result of the resource accumulation process. The structural properties of this history-dependent process are teased out by illuminating the causal relationship between the resource accumulation process (a flow) and the result of the process (the accumulated asset).
7. In 2001 we interviewed Lucio Stanca, who was until 2000 Chairman and General Manager of IBM EMEA. When we interviewed him, he reported to us the atmosphere of those years: 'Gerstner told us "You should not create strategy. I, myself, and the BRAND managers will create strategy. You carry out".' Then, Stanca adds, 'Previously, we all created strategy. We had bands of planners! In IBM Italy alone we had 300–400 planners. Gerstner forced us to emphasize execution.'

REFERENCES

Andrews, K. R. (1971), *The Concept of Corporate Strategy*, Homewood, IL: Irwin.

Ansoff, H. I. (1965), *Corporate Strategy*, New York: McGraw-Hill.

Ansoff, H. I. (1979), *Strategic Management*, London and Basingstoke: Macmillan Press, Ltd.

Ansoff, H. I. (1984), *Implanting Strategic Management*, Englewood Cliffs, NJ: Prentice-Hall International.

Ansoff, H. I. (1991), 'Critique of Henry Mintzberg's "The Design School: Reconsidering the basic premises of strategic management"', *Strategic Management Journal*, **12**(6): 449–461.

Argyris, C. (1982), *Reasoning, Learning, and Action: Individual and Organizational*, San Francisco: Jossey-Bass Inc.

Argyris, C. and D. A. Schon (1978), *Organizational Learning: A Theory of Action Perspective*, Reading, MA: Addison-Wesley Publishing Co.

Bartlett, C. A. and S. Ghoshal (1995), 'Rebuilding behavioral context: Turn process reengineering into people rejuvenation', *Sloan Management Review*, **37**(1): 23–36.

Beer, S. (1966), *Decisions and Control: The Meaning of Operational Research and Management Cybernetics*, London: John Wiley & Sons.

Beer, S. (1972), *Brain of the Firm: The Managerial Cybernetics of Organization*, London: Allen Lane, The Penguin Pres.

Beer, S. (1975), *Platform for Change*, London: John Wiley & Sons.

Beer, S. (1979), *The Heart of the Enterprise: The Managerial Cybernetics of Enterprise*, Chichester: John Wiley & Sons.

Bower, J. L. (1970), *Managing the Resource Allocation Process: A Study of Corporate Planning and Investment*, Boston, MA: Harvard University Press.

Brown, S. L. and K. Eisenhardt (1998), *Competing on the Edge: Strategy as Structured Chaos*, Boston, MA: Harvard Business School Press.

Burgelman, R. A. (1983a), 'A process model of internal corporate venturing in the diversified major firms', *Administrative Science Quarterly*, **28**: 223–244.

Burgelman, R. A. (1983b), 'Corporate entrepreneurship and strategic management: Insights from a process study', *Management Science*, **29**(12): 1349–1364.

Burgelman, R. A. (1983c), 'A model of interaction of strategic behavior, corporate context, and the concept of strategy', *Academy of Management Review*, **8**(1): 61–70.

Burgelman, R. A. (1991), 'Intraorganizational ecology of strategy making and organizational adaptation: Theory and field research', *Organization Science*, **2**(3): 239–262.

Burgelman, R. A. (1994), 'Fading memories: A process theory of strategic business exit in dynamic environments', *Administrative Science Quarterly*, **39**: 24–56.

Burgelman, R. A. (2002), 'Strategy as vector and the inertia of coevolutionary lock-in', *Administrative Science Quarterly*, **47**(2): 325–357.

Burgelman, R. A. and A. S. Grove (2007), 'Let chaos reign, then rein in chaos – repeatedly: Managing strategic dynamics for corporate longevity', *Strategic Management Journal*, **28**(10): 965–979.

Carroll, G. R. and J. R. Harrison (1994), 'On the historical efficiency of competition between organizational populations', *American Sociological Review*, **100**: 720–749.

Coda, V. (1988), *L'Orientamento Strategico dell' Impresa*, Torino: UTET.

Coda, V. (2008), 'Gestire l'Azienda', in S. Cherubini (ed.), *Scritti in Onore di Giorgio Eminente*, Milan: FrancoAngeli.

Coda, V. and E. Mollona (2006), 'Dynamics of strategy: A feedback approach to corporate strategy-making', in G. Minati, E. Pessa and M. Abram (eds), *Systemics of Emergence*, New York: Springer.

Coda, V. and E. Mollona (2010), 'Governing Strategy Dynamics', in Coda, V. (ed.), *Entrepreneurial Values and Strategic Management*, Palgrave-Macmillan: Houndmills, Basingstoke, UK.

Cyert, R. M. and J. M. March (1963), *A Behavioral Theory of the Firm*, Englewood Cliffs, NJ: Prentice-Hall.

Dierickx, I. and K. Cool (1989), 'Asset stock accumulation and sustainability of competitive advantage', *Management Science*, **35**(12): 1504–1511.

Elderkin, K. W. and C. A. Bartlett (1991), *General Electric: Jack Welch's Second Wave (A)*, Boston, MA: Harvard Business School Press.

Farjoun, M. (2002), 'Towards an organic perspective on strategy', *Strategic Management Journal*, **23**(7): 561–594.

Forrester, J. W. (1961), *Industrial Dynamics*, Cambridge, MA: Productivity Press.

Garud, R. and P. Karnøe (2001), 'Path creation as a process of mindful deviation', in R. Garud and P. Karnøe (eds), *Path Dependence and Creation*, Mahwah, NJ: Lawrence Erlbaum Associates, Publishers.

Ginsberg, A. and J. A. C. Baum (1994), 'Evolutionary processes and patterns of core business change', in J. A. C Baum and J. V. Singh (eds), *Evolutionary Dynamics of Organizations*, New York: Oxford University Press.

Hamel, G. and C. K. Prahalad (1989), 'Strategic intent', *Harvard Business Review*, **67**(3): 63–76.

Hannan, M. T. and J. Freeman (1984), 'Structural inertia and organizational change', *American Sociological Review*, **49**: 149–164.

Hodgkinson, G. P. and G. Johnson (1994), 'Exploring the mental models of competitive strategists: The case for a processual approach', *Journal of Management Studies*, **31**(4): 525–552.

Homans, G. C. (1961), *Social Behavior: Its Elementary Forms*, New York: Harcourt, Brace and World.

Lant, T. K. and S. J. Mezias (1992), 'An organizational learning model of convergence and reorientation', *Organization Science*, **3**: 47–71.

Levitt, B. and J. G. March (1988), 'Organizational learning', *Annual Review of Sociology*, **14**: 319–340.

Lovas, B. and S. Ghoshal (2000), 'Strategy as guided evolution', *Strategic Management Journal*, **21**: 875–896.

March, J. G. (1991), 'Exploration and exploitation in organizational learning', *Organization Science*, **2**(1) (Special issue): 71–87.

March, J. G. and H. A. Simon (1958), *Organizations*, New York: Wiley.

McKelvey, B. (2000), 'Dynamics of new science leadership: Strategy, microevolution, distributed intelligence, complexity', in A. Y. Lewin and H. Volberda (eds), *Mobilizing the Self-renewing Organization*, Thousand Oaks, CA: Sage.

Milgrom, P. and J. Roberts (1992), *Economics, Organization and Management*, Englewood Cliffs, NJ: Prentice-Hall.

Mintzberg, H. (1967), 'Crafting strategy', *Harvard Business Review*, **65**(4): 66–75.

Mintzberg, H. (1978), 'Patterns in strategy formation', *Management Science*, **24**: 935–948.

Mintzberg, H. (1979), *The Structuring of Organizations*, Englewoods Cliffs, NJ: Prentice-Hall.

Mintzberg, H. (1985), 'Of strategies, deliberate and emergent', *Strategic Management Journal*, **6**: 934–948.

Mintzberg, H. (1990a), 'The design school: reconsidering the basic premises of strategic management', *Strategic Management Journal*, **11**(3): 121–195.

Mintzberg, H. (1990b), 'Strategy formation: ten schools of thought', in J. Fredrickson (ed.), *Perspectives on Strategic Management*, New York: Ballinger.

Mintzberg, H. (1991), 'Learning 1, planning 0: reply to Igor Ansoff', *Strategic Management Journal*, **12**(6): 463–466.

Mintzberg, H., B. Ahlstrand and J. Lampel (1998), *Strategy Safari*, New York: Free Press.

Morecroft, J. D. W. (2007), *Strategic Modelling and Business Dynamics. A Feedback Systems Approach*, Chichester: John Wiley & Sons.

Nelson, R. R. and S. Winter (1982), *An Evolutionary Theory of Economic Change*, Cambridge: Belknap Press.

Noda, T. and J. L. Bower (1996), 'Strategy making as iterated processes of resource allocation', *Strategic Management Journal*, Summer Special Issue, **17**: 159–192.

Nonaka, I. (1988), 'Creating organizational order out of chaos: Self-renewal in Japanese firms', *California Management Review*, **30**: 57–73.

Nonaka, I. and H. Takeuchi (1995), *The Knowledge-Creating Company: How Japanese Companies Create the Dynamics of Innovation*, New York: Oxford University Press.

Normann, R. (1977), *Management for Growth*, New York: Wiley.

Pascale, T. R. (1984), 'Perspective on strategy: The real story behind Honda's success', *California Management Review*, **26**(3): 47–72.

Porac, J. F. and H. Thomas (1990), 'Taxonomic mental models in competitor definition', *Academy of Management Review*, **15**(2): 224–240.

Quinn, J. B. (1980), *Strategic Change: Logical Incrementalism*, Englewood Cliffs, NJ: Prentice-Hall.

Quinn, J. B. (1981), 'Formulating strategy one step at a time', *Journal of Business Strategy*, **1**(3): 42–63.

Richardson, G. P. (1991), *Feedback Thought in Social Science and System Theory*, Philadelphia, PA: University of Pennsylvania Press.

Richardson, G. P. (1995), 'Loop polarity, loop dominance, and the concept of dominant polarity', (1984), *System Dynamics Review*, **11**(1): 67–88.

Sanchez, R. and A. Heene (1997), 'A competence perspective on strategic learning and knowledge management', in R. Sanchez and A. Heene (eds), *Strategic Learning and Knowledge Management*, Chichester: John Wiley & Sons.

Sanchez, R., A. Heene and H. Thomas (eds), (1996), 'Introduction: Towards the theory and practice of competence-based competition', in *Dynamics of Competence-Based Competition Theory and Practice in the New Strategic Management*, Oxford: Elsevier Science.

Spender, J. C. (1996), 'Making knowledge the basis of a dynamic theory of the firm', *Strategic Management Journal*, **17** (Special Issue: Knowledge and the Firm): 45–62.

Sterman, J. D. (2000), *Business Dynamics. System Thinking and Modeling for a Complex World*, Boston, Irwin MA: McGraw-Hill.

Sull, D. N. (2005), 'No exit: The failure of bottom-up strategic processes and the role of top-down disinvestment', in J. L. Bower and C. G. Gilbert (eds), *From Resource Allocation to Strategy*, Oxford: Oxford University Press.

Tversky, A. and D. Kahneman (1979), 'Prospect theory: An analysis of decision under risk', *Econometrica*, **47**(2): 263–292.

Van de Ven, A. H. and M. Scott Poole (1995), 'Explaining development and changes in organizations', *Academy of Management Review*, **20**(3): 510–540.

7 Putting the manager back into the picture: the value of a strategy process perspective

*Torsten Schmid, Steven W. Floyd and
Bill Wooldridge*

INTRODUCTION

This essay argues that strategy process literature can and should inform recently emerging theoretical and empirical research on the micro-foundations of strategic management. We start with the observation that the individual manager as focal point of inquiry currently experiences a renaissance. Scholars interested in established theories, such as institutional theory or the resource-based view, and well-known empirical topics, such as diversification or organizational structure, are in search of micro-foundations (Johnson et al., 2003). Interest in strategic decision-making and cognition has also re-entered the mainstream. In addition, distinctly micro approaches provide impetus to fields such as strategy-as-practice (Johnson et al., 2003) and entrepreneurial learning (Cope, 2005).

The re-consideration of individuals as a fundamental level of analysis springs from several motivations. First, it provides an opportunity to operationalize more aggregated concepts such as strategy, corporate entrepreneurship and dynamic capability. In doing so, it has the potential to illuminate the individual-level origins and micro-foundations of these collective entities as well as their theoretical and empirical status. Second, a focus that begins with the individual advances the potential to link micro- and macro-level outcomes. Micro approaches re-consider heterogeneity in individual dispositions and behaviors as a 'basic factor' (Barnard, 1938) in explaining organizational effectiveness, for example. Third, micro approaches provide a better understanding of subjectivity, intent and managerial agency in today's complex, dynamic settings. Finally, micro-level research informs management education and practice and speaks to the conditions necessary for competent behavior at work.

A more comprehensive incorporation of individual-level phenomena in strategy research represents a demanding intellectual endeavor. The elaboration of micro-foundations requires management scholars to traverse paradigmatic, theoretical and methodical frontiers. While promoting a strong form of methodological individualism, micro scholars must avoid an atomistic, overly individualistic approach. In line with its core theme, the ultimate goal and challenge of this form of strategy research are micro-level explanations of organizational-level phenomena. Stated differently, micro-level strategy studies aim for integrated, theoretical and empirical accounts of important micro–macro linkages. Although there have been multiple calls for such multi-level research, efforts to explore micro–macro linkages remain relatively scarce and suffer from a deficiency of integrative theory.

This essay hopes to encourage and support high-quality micro-level research by leveraging lessons learned in the more well-established strategy process literature. In our view, strategy process research represents an essential and robust launching point for present and future micro-level studies. Rooted in a critique of the classical overemphasis on extraordinary individuals, a process perspective informs research on how to avoid the perils of the 'great man' theories of the past. Process scholars, in turn, will gain from a fuller incorporation of the effects of individuals involved in the strategy process (Hutzschenreuter and Kleindienst, 2006).

More specifically, our purpose here is to support progress in micro-level research by capitalizing on prior strategy process research conducted from a middle management perspective. While it represents only one of several possible approaches relevant to the study of the micro-foundations of strategy, middle management research has a long history of investigating strategy processes from the perspective of specific (middle-level) actors (Wooldridge et al., 2008). We define middle managers as those actors who combine access to top management with knowledge of operations. This includes a broad variety of mid-level professionals such as general and functional line managers, and team- and project-based executives. Due to their intermediate position in the organization, middle managers have been found to serve as important interfaces that link otherwise disconnected actors and domains in the strategy process.

Thus, in our view, a middle management perspective has great potential for putting the individual manager back into the strategy process equation. It offers general guidelines for micro-level scholars and provides specific suggestions for micro-level strategy research conducted from the middle management perspective. Finally, while our essay is primarily concerned with strategy process research, we also assert the value of a process perspective within the more general strategic management research domain.

The remainder of this essay will be structured as follows: First, based on a brief review of the historical evolution of process perspectives, we identify what we consider two basic imperatives in micro research: (1) the need for grounding in an explicit and consistent theory of process, and (2) the need for realistic assumptions about human nature and managerial agency. Second, drawing from the extant middle management literature, we identify three theoretical building blocks necessary for responding to these imperatives: (1) a more nuanced elaboration of the social embeddedness of human behavior; (2) a more comprehensive anthropology that acknowledges the multifaceted character of human nature; and (3) a more complex understanding of performance–outcome linkages. We close with a discussion of two methodical aspects of high-quality micro-level research, again illustrating our argumentation on the basis of middle management research.

IMPERATIVES OF A PROCESS PERSPECTIVE: PROCESS AND AGENCY

From its beginnings, strategy process research has focused on the black box of the firm and 'humanized' the strategic management field by exploring individual and collective behavior in strategic choice and change processes (Chakravarthy and Doz, 1992; Huff and Reger, 1987). Thus, while primarily focused on overarching organizational patterns, process research has forged a path to studying micro-level phenomena. The orientation of strategy process research suggests two important imperatives for micro-level scholars. First, it emphasizes the need for an explicit discussion of the underlying processes (Van de Ven, 1992) associated with micro-level phenomena in order to address potential incommensurabilities that arise between individualistic and collectivist research models. Second, it suggests situational models of managerial agency and strategic choice, encouraging micro-level scholars to make 'realistic' assumptions about human agency that balance the role of individual and organizational origins in explaining differences in firm performance.

The Need for a Theory of Process

Recent micro-level perspectives represent a renaissance of the concern for the individual expressed in the early strategy literature. Strategy process research grew out of a critique of classic rational unitary actor models derived from neo-classical economics. Contrasting early prescriptive models of strategy with descriptive views induced from practice, a process perspective therefore can sensitize micro scholars to the potential theoretical conflicts between individualistic and collectivistic conceptualizations of process. Indeed, the tension between viewing firms as unitary actors versus collectivities has carried over into process research itself. In the next section, we summarize this duality as the choice (or upper echelons)

Table 7.1   *Differentiating choice and social learning perspectives of strategy process (adapted from Wooldridge et al., 2008)*

	Choice perspective	**Social learning perspective**
Intellectual roots	Chandler (1962); Child (1972); Ansoff (1965); Andrews (1971); Porter (1980); Hambrick and Mason (1984)	Mintzberg (1978); Bower (1970); Kanter (1982); Schilit (1987); Burgelman (1983a, b)
Process model	Decision-making (rooted in models of individual choice)	Social learning process (rooted in models of complex, adaptive systems)
Key actors	Top management team as key decision-maker (based on strategic vision and hierarchical power)	Multiple actors with middle management as important mediator (based on intermediate position in organization)
Core processes	Sequence of top management analysis and choice (formulation), followed by implementation and control (separation of thinking from acting)	Evolution of idea generation, initiative development, execution/ re-integration (continuous interplay of thinking and acting)
Context	Complexity manageable by one central actor	Complexity beyond single actor's ability to integrate fragmented power and knowledge base

perspective and the social learning (or middle management) perspective. Table 7.1 displays key differences.

Research in strategy started with an interest in the 'extraordinary individual' – focusing on the characteristics and choices of top managers. Classical writings in the general management tradition of the Harvard Business School elaborated the role of senior executives in shaping firms (Andrews, 1971; Chandler, 1962). What later became known as the design school depicted strategy-making as a sequential, rational and individualized process. Strategy was assumed to be a decision-making process involving the CEO or a relatively small group of upper-level actors, followed by subsequent implementation. Categorized here as the choice perspective, central questions from this vantage point revolved around how characteristics of the CEO and top management team impacted their influence on firm strategy, organizational design and financial performance. The unitary actor model later informed the upper echelons perspective (Hambrick and Mason, 1984; Hambrick, 2007) as well as the rational-mechanistic perspective of strategy process (Hutzschenreuter and Kleindienst, 2006). Paralleling these developments, strategy content domains introduced industrial economics frameworks (Porter, 1980, 1985) to explain firm strategy as a function of its industry environment. This orientation again favored an individualized view of top managers' choosing profitable industries and successful competitive positions based on calculated rationality.

While process research proliferated into a diverse field, its founding concern was to confront the rational actor model, or choice perspective, with a more collective and socialized view of strategy-making. Clinical studies in the 1970s contrasted the prescriptive approach to strategy with detailed descriptions of a messier, partly emergent process (Bower, 1970; Mintzberg, 1978). Over time strategy-making came to be seen as a complex social learning process involving managers at multiple levels with different, but interrelated strategic roles (Burgelman, 1983a,b; Floyd and Lane, 2000). The dichotomy differentiating strategy formulation from implementation inherent in the choice perspective became increasingly challenged as a false division of work between top managers as thinkers and other organizational actors as doers (Mintzberg, 1978).

As a consequence, the focus of strategy process research shifted from strategic choice to strategic change. While strategic choice models assumed that new strategies were derived from top management intent, strategic change now came to be seen as emanating from autonomous initiatives triggered by problem-solving and experimentation at operating levels (Burgelman, 1983c). Strategy-making, from this perspective, was less a process of choice and more a social learning process that occurrs over time as managers and others in the organization discover how to adapt to an evolving environment. Due to their intermediate position in the organization, middle managers were identified as important interfaces influencing social learning and thus how strategy developed (Wooldridge et al., 2008). Strategy-making as social learning also gained impetus as a result of the shift from industrial organization to the resource-based view in explaining competitive advantage. In particular, the extension of the resource-based view into dynamic capability theory posits path-dependent knowledge creation and learning processes as sources of enduring competitive advantage (Teece et al., 1997). From this perspective, processes once construed as strategy-making were re-conceptualized as dynamic capabilities.

In contrasting the choice and social learning perspectives, our intention is to encourage micro-level scholars to think through their underlying model of process. Otherwise, they may risk the development of theoretically incommensurable models of strategy. Researchers pursuing micro-level studies need to be aware of the limits of individualistic views of strategy to explain organizational dynamics, and, in turn, understand that a micro-level view can inform collectivist views of strategy by re-incorporating intentionality and subjectivity. Thus, for example, a study of CEO personality effects on organizational outcomes (Chatterjee and Hambrick, 2007) has more explanatory power to the extent it is grounded in a theory of decision-making and strategic change. A careful consideration of potential incommensurabilities and commonalities across micro and macro views provides the basis for both a better understanding of micro-level influences and a more dynamic theory of strategy process (Porter, 1991). Process scholars have pointed to several meta-theories that may permit consistent theoretical grounding across micro and macro levels of analysis, including evolutionary theory (Chakravarthy and White, 2002), resource-based views (Barney, 1991) and learning perspectives (Crossan et al., 1999).

The Need for Realistic, Nontrivial Models of Human Agency

An explicit understanding of individual human nature, choices, abilities and motivations is critical to micro approaches to strategy (Felin and Foss, 2002). Strategy process scholars have always shared a preoccupation for developing 'realistic' conceptualizations of managers' roles in the complex social processes of strategic change and corporate entrepreneurship (Burgelman, 1983c; Lovas and Ghoshal, 2000). Elaborations on human agency in strategy process research may therefore inform micro-level foundations.

In addition to the unitary actor and agency theory assumptions associated with micro-economic perspectives, micro-level scholars may benefit from considering the view of human agency associated with the middle management perspective. Middle management research acknowledges that complex, geographically dispersed organizations cannot be managed by single actors or even small teams, but require distributed and interactive leadership throughout the organization. This view problematizes simple reliance on hierarchical authority as the primary source of influence on organizational outcomes (Hambrick, 1989). Middle management research is focused on actors in the middle of the management hierarchy and evaluates their potential for strategic influence. However, rather than studying these actors per se, as in managerial work studies (Dopson and Stewart, 1990), or granting her/him primacy in strategy decision-making, as in CEO research, the focus is on understanding interactions among multiple actors across multiple levels.

Bartlett and Ghoshal (1993), for example, in their sketch of a 'managerial theory of the firm' develop an alternative to agency theory as an underlying model of human behavior. They aim for theory that derives from an interpretive understanding of practicing managers (Weber, 1964), while at the same time avoiding exaggerating the importance of managers and other professionals. They call for complementing views of dysfunctional strategic management, emphasized in neo-institutional and evolutionary economics, by a constructive view of managerial behavior. However, rather than relying on a premise of altruism as a consistent human disposition, they propose a relativist view of personal attributes and a situational perspective of human behavior (Kenrick and Funder, 1988). Thus, organizational actors 'are capable of both initiative and shirking, they are given to both collaboration and opportunism, they are constrained by inertia, but also capable of learning. Within a firm, actual behavior is determined in part by the prior disposition of actors . . . and in part by the situation the face' (Bartlett and Ghoshal, 1993: 45). While conceptualizations of human agency will vary across different studies, micro-level scholars would therefore do well to build on the 'middle ground' view of strategy process scholars, balancing an emphasis on individual heterogeneity with a recognition of organizations as 'strong situations' that are essentially involved in the production of the nature, choices, abilities and motivations of organizational actors.

THEORETICAL BUILDING BLOCKS OF A PROCESS PERSPECTIVE: EMBEDDEDNESS, ANTHROPOLOGY, STRATEGIC OUTCOMES

While a process perspective calls for an elaborate theory of process and agency in micro-level research, an overview of theory and research from a middle management perspective serves to identify and elaborate three theoretical building blocks important for responding to these imperatives: (1) the need to understand and further elaborate the embedded nature of micro-level managerial action; (2) the challenge of developing a comprehensive micro-level anthropology that integrates cognitive, affective and behavioral perspectives; and (3) the search for linkages between micro-level action and organizational outcomes. The goal is to show how the agenda of scholars pursuing the micro-foundations of strategy coincides with that of strategy process researchers, especially those interested in a point of observation beyond the upper echelons. Thus, the discussion will draw on both existing literature and gaps in strategy process theory to motivate future micro-level research. Table 7.2 summarizes the three streams of research that have developed around these themes and suggests future research avenues for micro-level studies.

Table 7.2   Micro-level research from a middle management perspective

Research streams and core findings	High-priority research areas
Strategic roles and their antecedents • Middle managers' multiple and varied strategic roles extend from traditional administrative to entrepreneurial activities • Role conflict complicates enactment of a broader role-set • Organizational conditions enabling middle managers' strategic behavior and mediating role conflict ('bottom-up' effects)	The embeddedness of managerial behavior • Individual-level antecedents of middle management strategic behavior • (Individual) strategic roles within the context of group and organizational-level processes • Agency and ethical problems in middle-level entrepreneurial behavior • Transformation of individual dispositions and behaviors into organizational outcomes ('top-down' effects) • Evolution of middle managers' strategic influence in changing contexts
Managerial cognition and involvement • Broader definition of strategic consensus to elaborate performance effects of shared cognitions about strategic priorities across top and middle levels (intra-organizational alignment) • Involvement of middle management as important mechanism to improve managers' knowledge, understanding and support of strategy • Middle managers' key role in managing emotions during strategic change	Toward a comprehensive anthropology • Middle managers' cognitions of environmental events • Links between cognition and action, e.g. cognitive capabilities underlying middle managers' strategic behaviors • Multi-level investigation of mental model similarities/differences and their effects on middle management behaviors and outcomes • The role of affect, e.g. affective and physiological antecedents of middle managers', emotion management
Managerial activity and organizational outcomes • Relationships between middle management activity and economic performance, and between middle management activity and emergent and realized strategy • Positive effects of middle management vs. traditional views of middle management inertia	Outcomes between managerial action and organizational performance • Complex middle management–performance linkages, incorporating individual-level heterogeneity and part–whole conflicts between individual and collective interests • Micro-dynamics of emergent strategy • Micro-level balancing mechanisms, e.g. middle managers' role in ambidexterity

Elaborate the Embeddedness of Human Behavior

Strategy process scholars stress that organizational processes and managerial action are deeply embedded in their contexts (Pettigrew, 1992). The recognition of the embedded nature of human action is critical for micro-level scholars if they are to avoid an overemphasis on individual-level factors. It implies two analytical building blocks. The first is that strategic management needs to be conceptualized as a multi-level sequence of interlocking processes and activities that are embedded in multiple internal and external contexts (Bower, 1970). The second guiding principle is that scholars may begin with linear or singular micro-level explanations, but ultimately must strive for holistic theory that captures dynamic, reciprocal relationships between micro- and macro-level phenomena.

Within the middle management research domain, one major stream investigates middle managers' strategic roles and organizational antecedents, putting relationships between micro-level managerial action and macro-level organizational contexts center stage. Studies have identified middle managers as corporate entrepreneurs, for example, who engage in roles such as championing and facilitating divergent ideas and initiatives, selling strategic issues to top management, and communicating strategic change to external constituencies or peers. This literature focuses not only on the roles themselves, however, but also reveals important organizational factors that support middle-level entrepreneurship, that is, appropriate rewards, top management support, available resources, a supportive administrative structure and a tolerance for risk-taking (Hornsby et al., 2002). In addition, role conflict has been found an overarching factor that complicates the enactment of roles (Floyd and Lane, 2000). Differing interpretations of external environmental cues and internally defined job demands create a context of uncertainty about which role to enact and how to reconcile administrative with entrepreneurial functions. The literature points to organizational and leadership contextual factors that may minimize role conflict, for example alignment of control systems to environmental conditions (Floyd and Lane, 2000), distinct job assignments in administrative controls (Marginson, 2002), and two-way communication between top and middle management to develop reciprocal and consistent expectations across levels (Mantere, 2008). In addition to organizational and leadership factors surrounding how middle managers perceive their strategic roles, other studies demonstrate that middle managers' social network position influences role enactment and participation in strategy process, for example boundary-spanning positions and different forms of network centrality have been found to enable middle managers' strategic influencing activities (Floyd and Wooldridge, 1997; Pappas and Wooldridge, 2007).

In short, efforts to describe and account for middle management strategic roles have led to theory that connects micro-level action to the internal and external organizational contexts. There are, however, numerous avenues for future research to further elaborate the interplay of individual managerial actions and contexts. For example, while organizational-level antecedents have to date been the primary focus, future micro-level research needs to further explore individual-level and group-level contingencies to obtain a fuller understanding of various sources of strategic influence. Individual abilities and dispositions that enable middle managers to become effective strategists or corporate entrepreneurs remain largely unexplored. The traits and abilities of top managers have received attention in upper echelons research, but the individual characteristics of strategic middle managers await systematic investigation. This topic represents another way in which the agenda of micro-level scholars connects with strategy process research from a middle management perspective.

In a similar vein, it is important for individual managerial roles to be examined within the context of organizational and group-level dynamics. Existing role theory tended to isolate managerial behavior and favored micro-level explanations over group and organizational-level processes. This focus has obfuscated links between individual managerial activity and broader strategy processes and, in particular, underemphasized the social interactions that are known to be important in strategic change. Future micro-level research, therefore, would be well served to use established process models to re-ground and integrate dispersed micro-level research into a more holistic theory of context. For example, research might begin conceptualizing strategic roles in the context of Teece's (2007) framework of three organizational processes underlying a firm's dynamic capability, that is sensing new opportunities, seizing these opportunities, and later the management of thread and recombination. This more holistic process perspective organizes the plethora of roles identified in prior studies into a more comprehensive theory and establishes linkages between managerial action and well-established process categories. It reveals, for instance, that prior research, despite the interest in middle managers' role in innovation, has primarily investigated how middle managers seize opportunities, while the recognition or creation of new opportunities as well as later resource re-configuration have received less research attention.

Future research should investigate how individual managerial behaviors relate to group-level activity (e.g. project teams pursuing entrepreneurial initiatives) and, in turn, how these individual behaviors affect organizational outcomes through the group. Meso-level processes, such as team learning or inter-group conflict, could provide a bridge between micro and macro phenomena, but this remains fairly unexplored within the strategy literature. Along these lines, and consistent with emerging strategy-as-practice studies (Whittington, 2006), future micro-level research may leverage sociological perspectives to explore nuanced conversation and interaction patterns in strategy processes and link these micro processes to macro institutional settings, such as strategic discourses or strategic planning routines (Samra-Fredericks, 2003; Westley, 1990).

Taking a middle management perspective also raises under-explored questions of managerial agency and the legitimacy of hierarchical structures for micro-level scholars. Middle managers often gain strategic influence without or even against formal authority (Burgelman, 1994). Future research therefore needs to explore the psychological dynamics that underlie firm inefficiencies or the agency problems that arise in such circumstances. For example, how do firms manage the personal and organizational risks of behavior that diverges from official strategy (Dutton and Ashford, 1993)? In a similar vein, Kuratko and Goldsby (2004) describe ethical challenges faced by middle management in contexts that create tendencies for uncontrolled risk-taking such as entrepreneurial ventures or corporate venturing programs. Their discussion highlights the field's need to learn more about the personal traits and organizational contexts that help companies ensure ethical behavior.

A primary consequence that derives from the assumption of contextual embeddedness is the search for more holistic theory. Still, for most process scholars, 'holistic theorizing is barely an ambition, and rarely an accomplishment' (Pettigrew, 1992: 9). Future micro-level research therefore needs to further elaborate dynamic, reciprocal micro–macro influences. More specifically, extant research has often focused on 'top-down' effects of organizational antecedents on individual managerial action (Hitt et al., 2007). Future studies should put more emphasis on 'bottom-up' effects to demonstrate middle managers' agency in mobilizing aspects of context as they seek strategic outcomes. Overall, more fine-grained insights into the question of how individual dispositions and behaviors transform into organizational capabilities and processes represent one of the key potential contributions of a micro-level approach (Felin and Foss, 2002).

Rather than static organizational contexts, a process perspective acknowledges evolving and shifting contexts, but has often failed to establish dynamic explanations of strategic influence. For instance, we do not yet have a good understanding of how and why mid-level leaders emerge. Prior research (Floyd and Wooldridge, 1997) indicates that, in high-performing organizations, different managers influence strategy in different ways at different points in time. For example, the conflicting requirements in new venture creation often force managers to focus on single performance criteria to secure immediate survival, which, in turn, often implies the replacement of leaders between start-up phase and venture management (Burgelman, 1983a). Future micro-level research should therefore undertake longitudinal studies that illuminate key patterns in the dynamics of middle-level influence over time.

Develop a Comprehensive Anthropology

Although the emphasis on contextual factors and dynamics motivates much important research, micro-level researchers also face the challenge of developing a broad understanding of what goes on in the hearts and minds of strategic actors. In the past, scholars often borrowed concepts from psychology and applied them to the collective or organizational level, for example the aforementioned extension of models of individual decision-making to classic strategy frameworks. Micro-level scholars therefore need to be aware of the limits and problems of importing theories and concepts across levels (Markoczy and Deeds, 2009). In addition, they may profit from cross-disciplinary teams of scholars who investigate complex organizational phenomena from multiple theoretical perspectives (Hitt et al., 2007). The true potential lies in multi-disciplinary explanations that integrate theory and empirical work from several, related social science disciplines (e.g. exploring the psychological foundations of economic concepts such as organizational routines).

Turning again to process research from a middle management perspective, a second stream has focused on middle management cognition and involvement in strategy processes. The key contribution micro-level scholars can make to this sub-stream is a more comprehensive understanding of the multifaceted nature of human behavior, integrating behavioral, cognitive and affective approaches. The original focus on individual rationality still imprints contemporary middle management cognition research. We see three high-priority research areas: First, extant research has primarily focused on strategic consensus and the alignment of managerial cognition around strategic priorities across organizational levels. This suggests the need for investigations into other cognitive processes, in particular middle managers' perceiving and processing of external events. Second, research to date suffers from a separation between cognitive and behavioral approaches, with most work focusing on one or the other but rarely integrating the two. Future micro research that examines links between cognition and action is therefore needed. Third, and perhaps most challenging, prior research has focused almost exclusively on emotion-free mental perceptions, leaving out the role of affect in strategy formation and strategic change. Fortunately, there are recent threads in middle management research that focus on affect, and this provides a springboard for important future research.

Research on middle management consensus emanates from the tension created by managers' tendency to view organizational issues from functional and sub-unit perspectives and the need to adopt a wider organizational perspective when contributing to strategy. Research in this area expanded the concept of strategic consensus from top team agreement to shared cognitions among a broader group of managers, including middle managers (Kellermanns et al., 2005). Earlier studies maintain an upper echelons perspective, asserting, for instance, that middle management consensus on top managers' goals is positively related to efficient strategy implementation (Wooldridge and Floyd, 1989). Later studies build on the social learning perspective and highlight the role of middle management as important catalysts in the development and exploitation of organizational capabilities (Floyd and Wooldridge, 1999; King and Zeithaml, 2000).

Although research has not demonstrated a consistent relationship between strategic consensus and organizational performance, there is considerable evidence suggesting that middle managers' involvement in the strategy process enhances consensus, that is managers' shared understanding, knowledge and support of strategy. Several studies have investigated how middle management involvement can improve the alignment of managerial activities with top management intent, for example via participation and communication in strategic planning (Ketokivi and Castaner, 2004; Mangaliso, 1995) or via middle management sense-making and lateral interactions in the implementation of top-down change (Balogun and Johnson, 2004).

Due to its focus on building consensus inside the organization, research on middle management cognition has been fairly introspective. Although prior research indicates that middle managers attend to environmental conditions, for example as boundary-spanners, future research needs to illuminate the micro-specifics of how external cues influence middle managers' behavior in isolation or in combination with internal conditions. Studies on middle managers' noticing and sense-making of environmental events may, for instance, investigate how middle managers develop practices to avoid cognitive biases, such as framing bias or attribution errors (Hutzschenreuter and Kleindienst, 2006).

Although the middle management perspective was launched in opposition to the separation of thinking and acting in strategy, overtones of this distinction continue to be replicated in the research. For instance, research on strategic consensus focused on exploring associations between shared understandings and performance. This approach followed the logic of contemporaneous research focused on top management but ignored the rather obvious mediating effects of action on the cognition–performance relationship. More generally, micro-level research in strategy-making has repeatedly been criticized for its inability to explain how individual cognitive schemata and personal traits translate into actual behavior.

Future research therefore will profit from creating bridges between cognitive and behavioral approaches. Some of these linkages are rather obvious, such as the need to explore how cognitive dispositions are associated with the enactment of strategic behavior. For instance, it would be interesting to confirm that middle managers who champion entrepreneurial initiatives actually have a divergent mind-set (Floyd and Wooldridge, 1992) and to investigate whether these activities are positively and monotonically related to divergence; that is, whether more disagreement or questioning of official strategy results in more championing behavior. Also interesting would be research highlighting interactions between cognition and affect in role enactment. For instance, to what extent are cognitive and affective characteristics complementary, compensatory or mutually exclusive in supporting or hindering the enactment of strategic roles? Another rich area for future micro-level research would be to highlight varieties of mental models across individual, team and organizational levels. To investigate the tensions between shared cognition and divergent thinking, for example, researchers could observe mental model similarity within strategic initiatives: How do mental model similarities and differences between individuals within a team as well as similarities and differences between the team and other units (e.g. top management) influence the enactment of roles and subsequent success or failure of an initiative? How do organizations maintain shared understandings of strategy among organizational actors without eliminating divergent thinking and entrepreneurial activities? What contexts require shared thinking at middle levels, how are these mental models maintained over time, and how does middle management thinking complement and/or conflict with managerial perceptions and cognitions at other levels?

Beyond cognitive perspectives, affect has been identified only recently as a major topic in entrepreneurship and strategy research. The factors that influence middle managers' motivation to implement top-down change, for instance, have been a founding topic of middle management research (Guth and MacMillan, 1986). Yet, prior studies have focused on factors that inhibited middle managers' contribution to top management intent (e.g. resistance and negative affect toward goals). Future studies may focus on factors that enable middle management motivation (e.g. cooperation and positive affect toward goals). For instance, middle managers' feelings have been found to be sensitive to fairness concerns (Hornsby et al., 1993), implying that firms may increase middle management motivation via resource allocation processes that are perceived as fair (Lechner and Floyd, 2007). Other scholars highlight middle managers' role in managing emotions in radical strategic change (Huy, 2001, 2002) and the need to cope with pervasive social conflict in entrepreneurial ventures (Cope and Watts, 2000). Future research needs to provide further insight into the cognitive, affective and physiological resources that enable middle managers to manage emotions in the face of the negativity, stress and fear often associated with some forms of strategic change (e.g. downsizing) and corporate venturing.

Problematize Performance

Micro-level scholars have emphasized difficulties in establishing linkages from micro-level phenomena to distant organizational outcomes (Johnson et al., 2003). Strategy process scholarship, already aiming for explicit and robust links between process and content, suggests two main solutions. One is focusing on organizational outcomes that content research has established as critical, such as diversification or resource formation, and working 'backwards', empirically tracing associated processes and activities to micro-level phenomena (Chakravarthy and White, 2002). Another option is to investigate more immediate, group-level or individual outcomes, as a means of linking micro phenomena to organizational outcomes; for example, the performance of strategic initiatives, as in strategic renewal studies (Lechner and Floyd, 2007), may be a bridge between individual and organizational levels.

Again, middle management research offers both guidelines and gaps for future research opportunities. For example, future studies of middle manager strategic roles need to establish fine-grained performance linkages that recognize individual heterogeneity and both individual and collective aspirations. Several large-scale, cross-sectional studies show positive relationships between middle management behaviors and economic performance, both at firm (Floyd and Wooldridge, 1997) and business unit levels (Mair, 2005). As Floyd and Wooldridge (1997) indicate, however, individual middle managers significantly differ in their authorization and competence to perform strategic roles. In their study, high firm performance was associated with variation in entrepreneurial role performance across a cohort of managers. Thus, effective participation in the strategy process may be limited to a small group of managers. Complicating the connection between role and organization performance further, the pursuit of self- (and sub-unit) interests may not always be compatible with support of organizational goals and strategies. Actors' motivations are difficult to discern. What seems like middle management resistance, for example, may actually represent middle managers' honest appraisals of what is feasible or in the best interest of the organization. Future micro-level research would do well to examine these dynamics, and extend work that identifies 'part–whole conflicts' between individual and sub-unit aspirations and those of the larger organization.

It must also be recognized that the outcome of middle managers' activity differs in different types of strategy process (Burgelman, 1983c). In particular, extant research indicates that middle management can play an important role in emergent strategies, championing and facilitating divergent ideas and initiatives (Burgelman, 1983a). However, there is still limited or no empirical inquiry into micro-dynamics of emergent strategy and middle managers' contribution to it. Moreover, prior research on generic tensions in dynamic capability and organizational learning, including exploration vs. exploitation and opportunity vs. risk-framing, focuses primarily on the firm-level and top management leadership. Middle management research has begun to identify individual-level role conflicts between exploration and exploitation activity (Floyd and Lane, 2000; Taylor and Helfat, 2009), and much more could be done to illuminate the micro-specifics and contingencies in balancing the two forms of organizational learning.

METHODICAL IMPLICATIONS OF A PROCESS PERSPECTIVE: MULTI-LEVEL DESIGN AND PLURALISTIC METHODS

While a micro approach to strategy-making takes the individual as the focal level of analysis, it aims for micro-level explanations of broader organizational phenomena and, thus, for multi-level theory. In this part of the chapter, we discuss some important methodical challenges that micro-level scholars need to address in designing and executing multi-level, multi-method research. As before, we make particular reference to research from a middle management perspective as a way to suggest what these challenges mean for future micro-level scholarship.

Multi-level Designs

If micro-level scholars measure individual-level phenomena to theorize on broader organizational outcomes, the problems of level-related confounds or so-called 'fallacies of the wrong level' (including problems of causality and endogeneity) are readily apparent. To avoid this at the level of theory development, scholars should aim for a clear and consistent definition of focal units as well as the recognition of reciprocal influences across and within levels. The definition of focal units can be more difficult than one might suspect. It may be relatively easy to make the distinction between individuals and collectives, but it can become more challenging if boundaries of collectives have to be established. Indeed, how does one differentiate middle management from other levels of management in a way that is theoretically and empirically consistent across studies? Inconsistent definitions of middle management have blurred findings and hindered cumulative progress in prior research, and micro-level scholars will therefore profit from systematic, context-sensitive and theory-driven sampling of focal actors, combined with methods that triangulate their identification (e.g. formal designation, respondent judgment and a priori classification of generic sub-types).

We have already emphasized that micro-level scholars may start with establishing linear or singular relationships, but must be sensitive to the complex, dynamic realities of the strategic setting. Macro and micro phenomena are not likely to be linked in simple linear or causal fashion. Scholars therefore may use more complex, non-linear compilations where higher-level entities are not reduced to simple aggregations of lower-level entities, but are conceptualized and measured as different gestalts (Kozlowski and Klein, 2000). For instance, models of team or organizational competencies may consider that characteristics of some members (e.g. middle managers in a central, boundary-spanning position) may have greater influence on collective abilities than characteristics of other (e.g. more peripheral actors) members (Floyd and Lane, 2000). It may also be necessary to collect data at multiple managerial levels. Measuring dependent and independent variables at different hierarchical levels avoids potential mono-method bias, permits, in the case of perceptual data, triangulation of managerial self-reports with assessments from peers and supervisors, and the assessment of differences in individual characteristics across levels (e.g. distinct effects of top vs. middle managers).

Multi-method Approaches

Thanks to prominent strategy process studies, longitudinal case-based research has entered the mainstream of strategy research. Micro-level scholars can build on this legacy as case studies are particularly well suited to capture the nuances of micro-level dynamics (Langley, 1999) and the complex, dynamic relationships across multiple levels (Yin, 2009). At the same time, micro-level scholars have repeatedly called for multi-method approaches (Johnson et al., 2003). The inquiry of individual and inter-subjective phenomena can and should therefore also be conducted on the basis of established non-experimental survey designs. In addition, scholars should also consider integrated multi-method research approaches developed in other disciplines with long-standing experience in investigating micro-level phenomena, such as psychological methodologies that combine observation of naturally occurring phenomena with experimental designs (Chatman and Flynn, 2005).

CONCLUSION

This essay has elaborated the value of a strategy process perspective for recent efforts to study the micro-foundations of strategy-making. Building on an overview of the challenges of process research from a middle management perspective, we identified and discussed issues that may be confronted by micro-level scholars and suggested fruitful areas of inquiry. While we view the middle management perspective as a useful vehicle for articulating requirements of high-quality micro-level research, we offer this view more as an orienting device than as a basis for strict guidelines or as a preferred paradigm. A middle management perspective represents only one of several approaches relevant for research on the micro-foundations of strategy. As we hope to have demonstrated, however, this perspective has much to offer future micro-level scholarship in the way of lessons learned, and it suggests even more about the open questions that should inspire future research.

REFERENCES

Andrews, K. R. (1971), *The Concept of Corporate Strategy*, Homewood, IL: Dow Jones-Irwin.

Ansoff, H. I. (1965), *Corporate Strategy*, New York: McGraw-Hill.

Balogun, J. and G. Johnson (2004), 'Organizational restructuring and middle manager sensemaking', *Academy of Management Journal*, **47**: 523–549.

Barnard, C. I. (1938), *The Functions of the Executive*, Cambridge, MA: Cambridge University Press.

Barney, J. B. (1991), 'Firm resources and sustained competitive advantage', *Journal of Management*, **17**: 99–120.

Bartlett, C. A. and S. Ghoshal (1993), 'Beyond the M-form: Toward a managerial theory of the firm', *Strategic Management Journal*, **14**: 23–46.

Bower, J. L. (1970), *Managing the Resource Allocation Process*, Boston, MA: Harvard University Press.

Burgelman, R. A. (1983a), 'A process model of internal corporate venturing in the diversified major firm', *Administrative Science Quarterly*, **28**(2): 223–244.

Burgelman, R. A. (1983b), 'Corporate entrepreneurship and strategic management: Insights from a process study', *Management Science*, **29**(12): 1349–1364.

Burgelman, R. A. (1983c), 'A model of the interaction of strategic behavior, corporate context, and the concept of strategy', *Academy of Management Review*, **8**: 61–70.

Burgelman, R. A. (1994), 'Fading memories: A strategic process theory of strategic business exit in dynamic environments', *Administrative Science Quarterly*, **39**: 24–56.

Chakravarthy, B. S. and Y. Doz, (1992), 'Strategy process research: focusing on corporate self-renewal', *Strategic Management Journal*, **13**(S1): 5–14.

Chakravarthy, B. S. and R. E. White (2002), 'Strategy process: Forming, implementing and changing strategy', in A. Pettigrew, H. Thomas and R. Whittington (eds), *Handbook of Strategy and Management*: 182-205. London: Sage.

Chandler, A. D. (1962), *Strategy and Structure*, Cambridge, MA: MIT Press.

Chatman, J. A. and F. J. Flynn (2005), 'Full-cycle micro-organizational behavior research', *Organization Science*, **16**(4): 434–447.

Chatterjee, A. and D. C. Hambrick (2007), 'It's all about me: Narcisstic CEOs and their effects on company strategy and performance', *Administrative Science Quarterly*, **52**: 351–386.

Child, J. (1972), 'Organizational structure, environment, and performance', *Sociology*, **6**: 1–22.

Cope, J. (2005), 'Toward a dynamic learning perspective of entrepreneurship', *Entrepreneurship Theory and Practice*, **29**(4): 373–397.

Cope, J. and G. Watts (2000), 'Learning by doing: An exploration of experience, critical incidents and reflection in entrepreneurial learning', *International Journal of Entrepreneurial Behavior and Research*, **6**(3): 104–124.

Crossan, M. M., H. W. Lane and R. E. White (1999), 'An organizational framework: From intuition to institution', *Academy of Management Review*, **24**(3): 522–537.

Dopson, S. and R. Stewart (1990), 'What *is* happening to middle management?', *British Journal of Management*, **1**: 3–16.

Dutton, J. E. and S. J. Ashford (1993), 'Selling issues to top management', *Academy of Management Review*, **18**: 397–428.

Felin, T. and N. J. Foss (2002), 'Strategic organization: A field in search of micro-foundations', *Strategic Organization*, **3**(4): 441–455.

Floyd, S. W. and P. M. Lane (2000), 'Strategizing throughout the organization: Managing role conflict in strategic renewal', *Academy of Management Review*, **25**: 154–177.

Floyd, S. W. and B. Wooldridge (1992), 'Middle management involvement in strategy and its association with strategic type: A research note', *Strategic Management Journal*, **13**: 153–167.

Floyd, S. W. and B. Wooldridge (1997), 'Middle management's strategic influence and organizational performance', *Journal of Management Studies*, **34**: 465–485.

Floyd, S. W. and B. Wooldridge (1999), 'Knowledge creation and social networks in corporate entrepreneurship: the renewal of organizational capability', *Entrepreneurship Theory and Practice*, **Spring**: 123–143.

Guth, W. D. and I. C. MacMillan (1986), 'Strategy implementation versus middle manager self-interest', *Strategic Management Journal*, **7**: 313–327.

Hambrick, D. C. (1989), 'Guest editor's introduction: Putting top managers back in the strategy picture', *Strategic Management Journal*, **10**(Summer Special Issue): 5–15.

Hambrick, D. C. (2007), 'Upper echelons theory: An update', *Academy of Management Review*, **32**(2): 334–343.

Hambrick, D. C. and P. A. Mason (1984), 'Upper echelons: The organization as a reflection of its top managers', *Academy of Management Review*, **9**: 193.

Hitt, M. A., P. W. Beamish, S. E. Jackson and J. E. Mathieu (2007), 'Building theoretical and empirical bridges across levels: Multilevel research in management', *Academy of Management Journal*, **50**(6): 1385–1399.

Hornsby, J. S., D. F. Kuratko and S. A. Zahra (2002), 'Middle managers' perception of the internal environment for corporate entrepreneurship: Assessing a measurement scale', *Journal of Business Venturing*, **17**: 253–273.

Hornsby, J. S., D. W. Naffziger, D. E. Kuratko and R. V. Montagno (1993), 'An interactive model of the corporate entrepreneurship process', *Entrepreneurship Theory and Practice*, **Winter**: 29–37.

Huff, A. S. and R. K. Reger (1987), 'A review of strategy process research', *Journal of Management*, **13**(2): 211–236.

Hutzschenreuter, T. and I. Kleindienst (2006), 'Strategy-process research: What have we learned and what is still to be explored', *Journal of Management*, **32**(5): 673–720.

Huy, Q. (2001), 'In praise of middle managers', *Harvard Business Review*, **79**(8): 72–79.

Huy, Q. (2002), 'Emotional balancing of organizational continuity and radical change: The contributions of middle managers', *Administrative Science Quarterly*, **37**: 634–665.

Johnson, G., L. Melin and R. Whittington (2003), 'Guest editors' introduction: Micro strategy and strategizing: Towards an activity-based view', *Journal of Management Studies*, **40**(1): 1–22.

Kanter, R. M. (1982), 'The middle manager as innovator', *Harvard Business Review*, July–August: 95–106.

Kellermanns, F. W., J. Walter, C. Lechner and S. W. Floyd (2005), 'The lack of consensus about strategic consensus: Advancing theory and research', *Journal of Management*, **31**(5): 719–737.

Kenrick, D. T. and D. C. Funder (1988), 'Profiting from controversy: Lessons from the person–situation debate', *American Psychologist*, **43**(1): 23–34.

Ketokivi, M. and X. Castaner (2004), 'Strategic planning as an integrative device', *Administrative Science Quarterly*, **49**: 337–365.

King, A. W. and C. P. Zeithaml (2000), 'Competencies and the causal ambiguity paradox', *Strategic Management Journal*, **22**: 75–99.

Kozlowski, S. W. J. and K. J. Klein (2000), 'A multi-level approach to theory and research in organizations: Contextual, temporal and emergent processes', in K. J. Klein and S. W. J. Kozlowski (eds), *Multilevel Theory, Research, and Methods in Organizations: Foundations, Extensions, and New Directions*: 3-90. San Francisco: Jossey-Bass.

Kuratko, D. E. and M. G. Goldsby (2004), 'Corporate entrepreneurs or rogue middle managers? A framework for ethical corporate entrepreneurship', *Journal of Business Ethics*, **55**: 13–33.

Langley, A. (1999), 'Strategies for theorizing from process data', *Academy of Management Review*, **24**(4): 691–710.

Lechner, C. and S. W. Floyd (2007), 'Searching, processing, codifying and practicing: Key learning activities in exploratory initiatives', *Long Range Planning*, **40**(1): 9–29.

Lovas, B. and S. Ghoshal (2000), 'Strategy as guided evolution', *Strategic Management Journal*, **21**: 875–896.

Mair, J. (2005), 'Exploring the determinants of unit performance: The role of middle managers in stimulating profit growth', *Group and Organization Management*, **30**: 263–288.

Mangaliso, M. P. (1995), 'The strategic usefulness of management information as perceived by middle managers', *Journal of Management*, **21**(2): 231–250.

Mantere, S. (2008), 'Role expectations and middle manager strategic agency', *Journal of Management Studies*, **45**(2): 294–316.

Marginson, D. E. W. (2002), 'Management control systems and their effects on strategy formation at middle-management levels: Evidence from a UK organization', *Strategic Management Journal*, **23**: 1019–1031.

Markoczy, L. and D. L. Deeds (2009), 'Theory building at the intersection: Recipe for impact or road to nowhere?', *Journal of Management Studies*, **16**(6): 1076–1088.

Mintzberg, H. (1978), 'Patterns in strategy formation', *Management Science*, **24**(9): 934–948.

Pappas, J. M. and B. Wooldridge (2007), 'Middle managers' divergent strategic activity: An investigation of multiple measures of network centrality', *Journal of Management Studies*, **44**(3): 323–341.

Pettigrew, A. M. (1992), 'The character and significance of strategy process research', *Strategic Management Journal*, **13**: 5–16.

Porter, M. E. (1980), *Competitive Strategy: Techniques for Analysing Industries and Competitors*, New York: Free Press.

Porter, M. E. (1985), *Competitive Advantage: Creating and Sustaining Superior Performance*, New York: Free Press.

Porter, M. E. (1991), 'Towards a dynamic theory of strategy', *Strategic Management Journal*, **12**: 95–117.
Samra-Fredericks, D. (2003), 'Strategizing as lived experience and strategists' everyday efforts to shape strategic direction', *Journal of Management Studies*, **40**(1): 141–174.
Schilit, W. K. (1987), 'An examination of the influence of middle-level managers in formulating and implementing strategic decisions', *Journal of Management Studies*, **24**: 271–293.
Taylor, A. and C. E. Helfat (2009), 'Organizational linkages for surviving technological change: Complementary assets, middle management, and ambidexterity', *Organization Science*, **20**(4): 718–739.
Teece, D. J. (2007), 'Explicating dynamic capabilities: The nature and microfoundations of (sustainable) enterprise performance', *Strategic Management Journal*, **28**: 1319–1350.
Teece, D. J., G. Pisano and A. Shuen (1997), 'Dynamic capability and strategic management', *Strategic Management Journal*, **18**(7): 509–533.
Van de Ven, A. H. (1992), 'Suggestions for studying strategy process: A research note', *Strategic Management Journal*, **13**: 169–188.
Weber, M. (1964), *Basic Concepts in Sociology*, New York: Citadel Press.
Westley, F. R. (1990), 'Middle managers and strategy: The micro-dynamics of inclusion', *Strategic Management Journal*, **11**: 337–352.
Whittington, R. (2006), 'Completing the practice turn in strategy research', *Organizations Studies*, **27**(5): 613–634.
Wooldridge, B. and S. W. Floyd (1989), 'Strategic process effects on consensus', *Strategic Management Journal*, **10**: 295–302.
Wooldridge, B., T. Schmid and S. W. Floyd (2008), 'The middle management perspective on strategy process: Contributions, synthesis, and future research', *Journal of Management*, **34**(6): 1190–1221.
Yin, R. K. (2009), *Case Study Research: Design and Methods*, Thousand Oaks, CA: Sage

PART II

DELIBERATE
STRATEGIES

8 Making strategy work: a literature review on the factors influencing strategy implementation*

Li Yang, Guo-hui Sun and Martin J. Eppler

INTRODUCTION

Although formulating a consistent strategy is a difficult task for any management team, making that strategy work – implementing it throughout the organization – is even more challenging (Hrebiniak, 2006). Strategy implementation has received less systematic attention than one could expect, and it has been under-investigated in comparison with strategy formulation. As a dynamic, iterative and complex process, strategy implementation comprises a series of decisions and activities by managers and employees – affected by a number of interrelated internal and external factors – to turn strategic plans into reality in order to achieve strategic objectives. There are many factors that influence the success of strategy implementation, ranging from the people who communicate or implement the strategy to the systems or mechanisms in place for coordination and control. How can we better understand these issues and their importance for successful strategy implementation? In this article, we try to respond to this question by conducting an analysis in the most widely used literature databases to identify key factors influencing the process of strategy implementation, to surface current areas of agreement and disagreement, as well as missing evidence and resulting future research needs. Our study also examines the ways in which strategy implementation has been researched, in terms of the applied research methods and the examined strategy contexts. It will consequently also reveal under-exploited methods or contexts.

The structure of this paper is as follows: First, we describe the methodology that we have used to conduct our literature review and define its scope. The next section contains the review of literature, focusing on the theoretical bases and research methods used as well as the main results of prior studies. In that section, we present a discussion of nine major factors that affect strategy implementation and a review of existing models and frameworks. In the following section, we discuss the implications of our findings and present a conceptual framework that organizes current research findings. In the final section, we discuss directions for future research and how they may be pursued.

METHODOLOGY

To identify the factors that enable or impede effective strategy implementation, we have analysed relevant academic, peer reviewed journals, using the literature databases of EBSCOhost, ProQuest ABI, ScienceDirect, JSTOR and Wiley Interscience.

We have used the following criteria to choose articles for our analysis: We have selected articles which contain the keywords 'strategy implementation' or 'strategy execution' or where the title includes one of these compound terms. From this, we have continued to identify further articles using the references sections of the previously retrieved articles. Consequently, we have also included articles which treat strategy implementation as one of the major subjects even if their title or keywords did not include the terms 'strategy implementation' or 'strategy execution'. As a final selection criterion we have checked whether the articles explicitly discuss factors impeding or enabling strategy implementation success.

Based on the above criteria, we have selected 63 articles for inclusion in our review. Almost all of these are long research papers, published in top journals in the fields of strategic management, organization studies, marketing (with regard to the implementation of marketing strategy) or management.[1] In terms of time span, we have focused on articles from 1984 to 2008. More specifically, there are 14 papers from the 1980s, 22 papers from the 1990s, and 27 papers from 2000 to 2008.

LITERATURE REVIEW

In this section, we will review the 63 identified studies and analyse their theoretical bases, research methods used as well as the main results.

Theoretical Bases

In order to analyse and better understand strategy implementation, the researchers reviewed below make use of a variety of theoretical perspectives. Govindarajan and Fisher (1990) try to integrate an organizational control framework with agency theory and modify Ouchi's model by incorporating a key variable from agency theory, namely the observability of behavior. Kim and Mauborgne (1991, 1993) examine the importance of procedural justice judgments, a psychological phenomenon, in a global strategy setting. Govindarajan (1988) refers to internal and external control of reinforcement – which evolved out of social learning theory – as a key variable of influencing strategy implementation. Guth and MacMillan (1986) point out that the individual manager's commitment to a strategy as a construct is derived from the expectancy theory of motivation. It thus seems that strategy implementation lends itself to a multitude of theoretical perspectives that could also be employed in an interdisciplinary manner, mutually enriching our understanding of this complex phenomenon. In our review of the literature we have not found such explicitly interdisciplinary studies of strategy implementation (although Govindarajan and Fisher (1990) combine two theories elegantly).

Research Methods

Regarding research methods used to explore strategy implementation, we distinguish among the following frequently used methods: questionnaire and/or interviews, conceptual analysis, case analysis, field investigation and other methods (such as hypothetical scenario, literature review, laboratory experiment, intervention methods comprising a set of meetings, archival and records analysis).

Questionnaire is a method which is frequently used by researchers in this domain (25 articles) followed by case studies (11 articles). The most rarely used methods, by contrast, are hypothetical scenario (1 article), literature review (3 articles), laboratory experiment (1 article) and an intervention method (1 article).

Research Results

In our review of existing studies, we have found two types of strategy implementation studies: those highlighting the importance of individual factors for strategy implementation and those that emphasize the 'big picture' of how such factors interrelate. In the first stream of research we have identified nine recurring, individual factors that influence strategy implementation. The researchers in this group shed light on single factors, such as strategy formulation (as it relates to implementation), relationships among different units or departments and different strategy levels, executors, communication, and so on, and investigate the relationship between strategy implementation and those factors individually. The second stream of research analyses multiple factors together within a single (arguably comprehensive) framework. Some researchers try to draw a 'big picture' of strategy implementation, including many factors in order to describe a comprehensive strategy implementation process.

Below, we first summarize the nine individual factors and their impact on strategy implementation and then discuss the identified strategy implementation frameworks.

Studies focusing on single factors
The nine factors we have found in existing studies can be divided into soft, hard and mixed factors. Soft factors (or people-oriented factors) include the people or executors of the strategy, the communication activities as well as the closely related implementation tactics, the consensus about and commitment to the strategy, while the hard (or institutional) factors include the organizational structure and administrative systems. The way in which the strategy was developed and articulated (strategy formulation) contains hard and soft factors alike and is thus considered a mixed factor. Relationships among different units/departments and different strategy levels are also treated as mixed factors. Below, we first discuss the mixed factors, then the soft factors, and finally the hard factors affecting strategy implementation.

Strategy formulation   Good execution cannot overcome the shortcomings of a bad strategy or a poor strategic planning effort (Hrebiniak, 2006). Several studies mention the importance of a consistent and fitting strategy (Alexander, 1985; Allio, 2005). Alexander (1985) states that the need to start with a formulated strategy that involves a good idea or concept is mentioned most often in helping promote successful implementation. As Allio (2005) notes, good implementation naturally starts with good strategic input: the soup is only as good as the ingredients.

Whether a strategy itself is consistent and fitting or not is a key question for successful strategy implementation, but even a consistent strategy cannot be all things to all people. Synergies between strategy types and implementation capabilities exist (Bantel, 1997), the procedural justice of the strategy formulation process (Kim and Mauborgne, 1991, 1993), as well as the specific cognitive requirements of the strategy implementation process (Singh, 1998) also influence implementation outcome.

Relationships among different units/departments and different strategy levels   Several studies treat institutional relationships among different units/departments and different strategy levels as a significant factor that affects the outcome of strategy implementation. Some researchers suggest that corporate–business unit relationships can either facilitate or inhibit the implementation of a strategic business unit's (SBU's) intended strategy

(Walker and Ruekert, 1987; Gupta, 1987; Golden, 1992). According to Noble's (1999a) summary, cross-functional issues are frequently examined from the perspective of the marketing unit, especially marketing and R&D or marketing and manufacturing. Other cross-functional pairings or the overall network of relationships needed for successful implementation receive little attention. Chimhanzi (2004) also suggests that cross-unit working relationships have a key role to play in the successful implementation of marketing decisions and points out that the marketing and R&D interface remains the most extensively researched dyad within the specific context of the new product development process. Chimhanzi and Morgan's (2005) findings indicate that firms devoting attention to the alignment of marketing and human resources are able to realize significantly greater successes in their strategy implementation.

The relationships between different strategy levels also reflect the effect of relationships among different cross-organizational levels on strategy implementation. Slater and Olson (2001) observe that superior performance at the firm or SBU level was achieved when specific marketing strategy types (i.e., aggressive marketers, mass marketers, marketing minimizers, value marketers) were matched with business strategy types (i.e., prospectors, analysers, low cost defenders and differentiated defenders).

Executors　The effectiveness of strategy implementation is affected by the quality of people involved in the process (Govindarajan, 1989), who comprise top management (CEO, CFO, Chief Operating Officer, etc.), middle management, lower management and non-management, playing different roles in strategy implementation and receiving varying degrees of attention in the respective literature.

Several authors have emphasized the important figurehead role of top management in the process of strategy implementation, but they tend to have a somewhat weak empirical base for their advice (Smith and Kofron, 1996). Hrebiniak and Snow (1982), for example, find that the process of interaction and participation among the top management team leads to greater commitment to the firm's goals and strategies. This serves to ensure the successful implementation of the firm's chosen strategy (cited in Dess and Priem, 1995). Schmidt and Brauer (2006) take the board as one of the key subjects of strategy implementation and discuss how to assess board effectiveness in guiding strategy execution. Schaap (2006) has tested the following hypothesis: effective senior-level leadership behaviors will be directly related to successful strategy implementation. This hypothesis, however, has resulted in mixed support; those senior-level leaders who have been trained in or studied strategic planning and implementation are more likely to meet the performance targets set for the company. This hypothesis was not strongly supported. More empirical research is needed to clarify the role of top management for strategy implementation.

We can divide the viewpoints and approaches regarding middle management's effect on strategy implementation into three categories. The first emphasizes the match of strategy and middle managers' leadership style (Gupta and Govindarajan, 1984; Guth and MacMillan, 1986; Govindarajan, 1989; Judge and Stahl, 1995; Heracleous, 2000). This viewpoint assumes that personality is the primary determinant of strategy implementation actions. The second perspective considers the effect of context on behavior and emphasizes the managers' flexibility to master different strategic situations (Waldersee and Sheather, 1996). The third analyses the impact of relationships between top management and middle management on strategy implementation (Floyd and Wooldridge, 1990, 1992b, 1997; Qi, 2005).

Unfortunately, few authors have studied the impact of lower management and non-management on strategy implementation. Gronroos (1985) believes that an organization must first persuade its employees about the importance of the strategy before turning to customers (cited in: Rapert et al., 1996). If lower-level management and non-management personnel are not aware of the same information, or if information must pass through several (management) layers in the organization, consensus regarding that information may never come about (Nutt, 1986). Thus, the lack of shared knowledge with lower-level management and non-management employees creates a barrier to successful strategy implementation (Noble, 1999b). There clearly is a lack of theory development and empirical testing regarding the roles of lower-level management and non-management in the strategy implementation process.

Communication   Forman and Argenti (2005: 245) rightly note that 'although an entire discipline is devoted to the study of organizational strategy, including strategy implementation; little attention has been given to the links between communication and strategy'. However, numerous researchers have at least emphasized the importance of communication for the process of strategy implementation (Alexander, 1985; Rapert and Wren, 1998; Peng and Litteljohn, 2001; Heide et al., 2002; Rapert et al., 2002; Forman and Argenti, 2005; Schaap, 2006). For example, Rapert and Wren (1998) find that organizations where employees have easy access to management through open and supportive communication climates tend to outperform those with more restrictive communication environments (cited in Rapert et al., 2002).

Also the findings of Peng and Litteljohn (2001) show that effective communication is a key requirement for effective strategy implementation.

Organizational communication plays an important role in training, knowledge dissemination and learning during the process of strategy implementation. Communication barriers are reported more frequently than any other type of barrier, such as organizational structure barriers, learning barriers, personnel management barriers or cultural barriers (Heide et al., 2002).

Implementation tactics   Nutt (1986, 1987, 1989), Bourgeois and Brodwin (1984), Prasa (1999), Lehner (2004), Sashittal and Wilemon (1996), and Akan et al. (2006) research the effects of implementation tactics on strategy implementation. Nutt (1986, 1987) describes the success rates and conditions surrounding the use of four archetypical tactics (i.e., intervention, participation, persuasion and edict) and sets up a useful contingency framework to identify conditions under which these tactics could be used (Nutt, 1989).

Bourgeois and Brodwin (1984) examine five process approaches used to advance strategy implementation: the commander model, change model, collaborative model, cultural model, crescive model. The first three models assume implementation as after-the-fact. This implies that the number of strategy developers is few and that the rest of the organization is somehow manipulated or cajoled into implementation. For the latter two models, most of the energy is used for strategy formulation and the strategy requires relatively little effort in its implementation.

Lehner (2004) views the study of Bourgeois and Brodwin (1984) as the first attempt to explicitly link behavioral patterns to the context of strategic management and adapts the five implementation tactics to command, change/politics, culture, collaboration and crescive/market. Command and politics/change are both somewhat autocratic. In contrast, both collaboration and the market approach to implementation utilize participation to a high degree and in a way that gives subordinate groups a strong voice. It also gives them the possibility to influence the selected courses of action. Only culture remains as a single category.

Sashittal and Wilemon (1996) take marketing implementation as their research focus and point out that marketing professionals often use a variety of tactics to gain the cooperation of other functional groups: persuasion, teamwork, negotiation, commonality of goals and total quality management methods.

Consensus   Kellermanns et al. (2005) draw the conclusion that there is no sufficient consensus about strategic consensus after an in-depth and elaborate literature review. The differences of construct definition, research methodology, model specification (antecedents, outcome relationships and moderators) may have led to inconsistent findings (supportive, partially supportive and not supportive) on the relationship between consensus and performance (Kellermanns et al., 2005). As far as construct definition is concerned, Floyd and Wooldridge (1992a) define strategic consensus as the agreement among top-, middle-, and operating-level managers on the fundamental priorities of the organization. Dess and Priem (1995) define consensus as the level of agreement among the top management team members or dominant coalition on factors such as goals, competitive methods and perceptions of the environment.

Many studies emphasize TMT and/or middle managers' consensus during strategy formulation; just a few, however, notice the important role of consensus in the process of strategy implementation (Nielsen, 1983; Floyd and Wooldridge, 1992a; Dess and Priem, 1995; Rapert et al., 1996; Noble, 1999b; Dooley et al., 2000). For example, Floyd and Wooldridge (1992a) classify consensus into four levels (according to the dimensions of consensus, shared understanding and commitment): strong consensus, blind devotion, informed skepticism and weak consensus. They label the gulf bctween strategies conceived by top management and the awareness at lower levels as an 'implementation gap' which can be closed by improving understanding and commitment (Floyd and Wooldrige, 1992a). The relationship between decision consensus and implementation speed and success is mediated by decision commitment in the study of Dooley et al. (2000).

Commitment   There are various inconsistent viewpoints regarding the definitions of commitment and consensus. While some scholars treat commitment as one of the dimensions of consensus (Floyd and Wooldridge, 1992a; Noble, 1999a), or the outcome of consensus (Dooley et al., 2000), some authors think that strategic commitment involves a deeper intimacy with the strategy, paralleling the concept of strategic consensus (Rapert et al., 1996).

Strategy implementation efforts may fail if the strategy does not enjoy support and commitment by the majority of employees and middle management. This may be the case if they were not consulted during the development phase (Heracleous, 2000). Alexander (1985) thinks obtaining employee commitment and involvement can promote successful strategy implementation. Guth and MacMillan (1986) suggest that there are three fundamentally different sources of low to negative individual manager commitment to implementing a particular strategy: low perceived ability to perform successfully in implementing that strategy; low perceived probability that the proposed outcomes will result, even if individual performance is successful; and low capacity of the outcome to satisfy individual goals/needs. Middle managers with low or negative commitment to the strategies formulated by senior management obviously create significant obstacles to effective implementation.

Noble and Mokwa (1999) put forward three dimensions of commitment that emerged as central factors which directly influence strategic outcomes: organizational commitment, strategy commitment and role commitment. Their findings suggest that an individual manager's implementation role performance will influence the overall success of the implementation effort. Both strategy commitment and role commitment were shown to influence role performance. However, the most commonly studied dimension, organizational commitment, showed no relationship to role performance in either of their samples! Their results highlight the complexity of the commitment construct and stress that the study of commitment to an organization alone does not explain this complicated variable fully.

Organizational structure   Factors relating to the organizational structure are the second most important implementation barrier according to Heide et al.'s (2002) study. Drazin and Howard (1984) see a proper strategy–structure alignment as a necessary precursor to the successful implementation of new business strategies (cited in Noble, 1999b). They point out that changes in the competitive environment require adjustments to the organizational structure. If a firm lags in making this realignment, it may exhibit poor performance and be at a serious competitive disadvantage. Gupta (1987) examines the relationships between SBUs' strategies, aspects of the corporate–SBU relationship and implementation, and finds that structures that are more decentralized produce higher levels of SBU effectiveness, regardless of the strategic context. Schaap (2006) also suggests that adjusting the organizational structure to the pursued strategy can ensure successful strategy implementation. But different strategy types have different requirements regarding an adequate organizational structure (e.g., White, 1986; Olson et al., 2005). Olson et al. (2005) develop a classification comprising four different combinations of structure/behavior types, which they label as: management dominant, customer-centric innovators, customer-centric cost controllers and middle ground. These alternative structure/behavior types are then matched with specific business strategies (i.e., prospectors, analysers, low cost defenders, differentiated defenders) in order to identify which combination(s) of structures and behaviors best serve to facilitate the process of implementing a specific strategy.

Administrative systems   Govindarajan (1988) suggests that there are three key administrative mechanisms that firms can use to cope with uncertainty, which is the fundamental problem in implementing strategies effectively: design of organizational structure (decentralization), design of control systems (budget evaluative style) and selection of managers (locus of control). Based on these distinctions, Govindarajan identifies the following constellations: high managerial internal locus of control and low emphasis on meeting a budget are associated with high performance in SBUs employing a strategy of differentiation. Bivariate results nevertheless did not provide support for the interaction between SBU strategy, decentralization and effectiveness. But when these three mechanisms were aligned appropriately to meet the requirements of SBU strategy, superior performance occurred. This systems fit was quite strong among SBUs with a differentiation approach but not so strong among low cost units. On the basis of the above research, Govindarajan and Fisher (1990) believe that relationships among control systems, resource sharing and competitive strategies contribute differentially to the effectiveness of SBUs practicing differentiation and low cost strategies; namely, output control and high resource sharing are associated with higher effectiveness for a low cost strategy, and behavior control and high resource sharing are associated with higher effectiveness for a differentiation strategy.

Roth et al. (1991) have different explanations regarding the content of administrative systems. Their study suggests that business units utilize three administrative mechanisms – formalization, integrating mechanisms and centralization – to create operational capabilities of configuration, coordination and managerial philosophy – to support the international strategy implementation. The fit achieved among international strategy, operational capabilities and administrative mechanisms will be associated with superior business unit performance.

There are also studies focusing on control systems as an ingredient of administrative systems (Drazin and Howard, 1984; Nilsson and Rapp, 1999; Peljhan, 2007). Drazin and Howard (1984) discuss the role of formal control systems in the process of strategy implementation and suggest that the fluidity or flexibility of a control system contributes to strategy implementation (Noble, 1999b). Nilsson and Rapp (1999) found that control systems at management and operational levels are based on different logics and should have a different design. Regarding Simons' (1990, 1995, 2000) four levers of control (diagnostic control systems, interactive control systems, beliefs systems and boundary systems), Peljhan (2007) examines the relationship between the use of management control systems (MCS) and the implementation of organizational strategy, and suggests that MCS influence the implementation and monitoring of strategies, providing feedback for learning and information to be used interactively to formulate strategy further.

We have discussed nine key factors that can determine the success of strategy implementation. This list cannot be comprehensive, as many other issues potentially affect strategy implementation. These other factors, however, are mentioned less or not analysed in depth, as many of them are also much harder to control or modify. These important other factors include culture, firm size, the external environment, the implementation stages, internal guidelines, the power structure, material resources, and so on.

Studies focusing on multiple related factors

The studies reviewed in this section approach the factors that influence strategy implementation from a holistic or 'big picture' perspective. They do so in two distinct ways: either through the simple categorization of various factors into groups or categories (such as the studies of Skivington and Daft, 1991; Noble, 1999b; Noble and Mokwa, 1999; Okumus, 2001), or by relating them in an (often graphic) framework (as in Hambrick and Cannella, 1989; Noble, 1999a; Beer and Eisenstat, 2000; Higgins, 2005; Brenes et al., 2007).

Both Skivington and Daft (1991) and Noble (1999b) classify implementation variables into two dimensions: framework and process, but with different content in their categories. Skivington and Daft (1991) stipulate two generic types of strategic decisions – low cost and differentiation – that need to be implemented through two organizational modalities, namely framework (i.e., rules and resources) and process (i.e., interactions, meanings and sanctions). Their findings indicate that low cost and differentiation strategy implementation employ different variables, and that a specific pattern (or gestalt) of variables may exist for each type of strategy.

Based on the study of Skivington and Daft (1991), Noble (1999b) reviews strategy implementation research from a structural view (emphasizing organizational structure and control mechanisms) and an interpersonal process view (emphasizing strategic consensus, autonomous strategic behaviors, diffusion perspectives, leadership and implementation style, communication and interaction processes). Noble and Mokwa (1999) add a third view – the individual-level processes view (emphasizing cognition, organizational roles and commitment) – besides the structural and interpersonal process view.

Earlier studies led by Pettigrew (e.g., Pettigrew, 1985; Pettigrew et al., 1992) group implementation variables into a larger number of categories. These categories are: strategic content, context (consisting of organizational context: organizational structure, organizational culture; and environmental context: uncertainty in the general and uncertainty in the task environment), process (operational planning, resources, people, communication, control and feedback) and outcome (cited in Okumus, 2001).

Okumus (2001) also adopts the above framework, but adds three new variables: multiple project implementation, organizational learning, and external partners. It appears that any problem or inconsistency with one variable influences other variables and subsequently the success of the implementation process. As we have seen now in several other studies, it is the combination of all variables working together which makes a successful implementation process possible. One emergent consensus thus clearly is that there is no silver bullet in implementing strategies.

Studies in the second group compile multiple factors in a framework or model, thus not only grouping implementation variables but organizing them in a web of causal or temporal relations (Hambrick and Cannella, 1989; Noble, 1999a; Beer and Eisenstat, 2000; Higgins, 2005; Brenes et al., 2007). Noble's (1999a) strategy implementation framework is organized around four major stages of the implementation effort – pre-implementation, organizing the implementation effort, managing the implementation process and maximizing cross-functional performance. There are five managerial levers for these implementation phases: goals, organizational structure, leadership, communications and incentives. According to Noble, the management of these factors changes through the implementation stages (although they are all important in every single phase). Considering these factors in combination with each major stage provides a useful heuristic to improve strategy implementation.

Beer and Eisenstat (2000: 31) propose six silent killers of strategy implementation that are 'rarely publicly acknowledged or explicitly addressed', namely: top-down or laissez-faire senior management style; unclear strategy and conflicting priorities; an ineffective senior management team; poor vertical communication; poor coordination across functions, businesses or borders; and inadequate down-the-line leadership skills and development. Poor vertical communication is treated as a core barrier which not only hinders strategy implementation but also impedes discussion of the barriers themselves. The six killers are grouped into three categories: quality of direction, quality of learning and quality of implementation.

Higgins (2005) sets up an '8 S's' framework of strategy implementation, including strategy and purposes, structure, resources, shared values, style, staff, systems and processes, and strategic performance. The '8 S's' of strategy execution' are a revision of the original McKinsey 7 S model.

Brenes et al. (2007) point out five key dimensions of successful implementation of business strategy. These five dimensions are the strategy formulation process; systematic execution, implementation control and follow-up; CEO's leadership; suitable, motivated management and employees; and, finally, corporate governance (board and shareholders) leading the change. All five dimensions must be managed together to align them with the firm's strategic choices. Their framework arranges these factors in a simple value chain model.

As a preliminary conclusion, we thus see that both the categorizations and the frameworks are extremely heterogeneous in terms of their overall logic. All, however, include soft as well as hard factors in their elaborations.

DISCUSSION

Having reviewed the 63 articles, we can now generalize regarding their main contributions.

Above all, the articles we have reviewed emphasize various issues of strategy implementation which have practical significance but have received less attention compared with strategy formation. Our review shows that there is no silver bullet or magic recipe to get strategy implementation right, but rather that one needs to be aware of the intricate inter-play of various soft and hard factors that affect the implementation process. Unfortunately, these factors have not yet been described systematically and the field has been correctly described as fragmented and eclectic (Noble, 1999a). Our review has looked at these factors and highlighted recurring themes and issues that seem to be of greater importance than others. This can be a first solid step towards a more controlled and fully understood strategy implementation process.

In terms of results, the articles we have reviewed mainly discuss single factors that affect strategy implementation success, while some authors also make an attempt to test relationships among different factors empirically. Another group of researchers also synthesize their findings in elaborate (e.g., phase-based) frameworks and models, though with less rigor regarding the employed methods than the studies focusing on individual factors. Although their findings on a detail level do not always match, they nevertheless converge regarding the key issues that managers have to keep in mind during the implementation process. The diagram below (Figure 8.1) summarizes these key issues raised in our review and organizes them in a conceptual framework or map of the domain of strategy implementation. The main message of our framework is that strategy implementation has to be understood as a process that already needs to be considered during strategy formulation and that is affected by multiple hard (institutional), soft (people-oriented) and mixed factors (that interact in multiple ways).

As a mixed factor, strategy formulation is both an institutional and

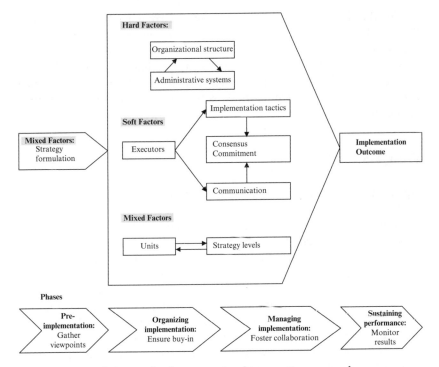

Figure 8.1   A framework of strategy implementation research

an interpersonal process in which data are gathered and viewpoints are exchanged. It ultimately results in strategic decisions. These strategic decisions and how they have been reached have a major impact on strategy implementation success. Hard, institutional factors (organizational structure, administrative systems) and soft, people-oriented factors (executors, communication, implementation tactics, consensus and commitment) influence implementation outcomes dialectically. Consensus and commitment can be achieved with the help of proper implementation tactics and targeted communication activities. There are complex relationships among the mixed factors (relationships among different units/departments and different strategy levels), soft factors and hard factors. These factors are influenced by four generic phases of strategy implementation: pre-implementation, organizing implementation, managing implementation and sustaining performance. This sequence is based on Noble's (1999a) framework. We have allocated key success factors mentioned in several studies to the respective steps.

LIMITATIONS AND FUTURE RESEARCH AVENUES

As mentioned at different points in this chapter, several implications for further research arise from our literature review.

First, most of the existing studies that examine the functional level of strategy implementation focus on marketing strategy. Other areas, however, seem equally crucial and should receive more attention in the future (such as human resources, production or finance strategy implementation).

Second, we find that many studies focus on the influence of executors (such as middle or upper managers) on strategy implementation. Most of the studies focus on top management and point out the important figurehead role of executives in the process of strategy implementation, but there tends to be a somewhat weak empirical base for their advice. There is no extensive research relating to lower management and non-management, even if several authors state that it is important to consider their effect on strategy implementation. None of them analyse the different ways in which employees enable or interfere with strategy implementation and why.

Another major research challenge consists of better understanding the relationships among several of the nine reviewed factors. There are, for example, major disagreements in relation to the exact meanings, content, relationships and influence on strategy implementation regarding the variables of communication, commitment and consensus.

Fourth, there are several studies that examine how the relationships of different organizational units influence strategy implementation, but more studies should focus on the real dialogues among different strategy levels.

The fifth point regards models and frameworks. Although there is a trend towards holistic frameworks of strategy implementation, most of the frameworks which we have reviewed do not add a lot of value to the current debate. Several authors call their frameworks 'models' although they cannot be tested empirically. Future research should thus focus on further developing both focused models examining key relationships, as well as comprehensive strategy implementation frameworks that provide guidance to practitioners on different levels.

Sixth, strategy implementation involves many theories, including agency theory, social system theory, social learning theory and expectancy theory. Future research on strategy implementation could move beyond these approaches and consider the use of communication theory, innovation diffusion theory, actor network theory or the strategy-as-practice paradigm, to name but a few of the possible alternative paradigms for the study of implementation processes (not to mention their careful combinations). Similarly, there is a trend in implementation research to combine different research methods together in order to achieve more robust and triangulated results (interviews, surveys, experiments, field observations).

In the 63 articles we have collected, there have only been two relatively old papers (Walker and Ruekert, 1987; Noble, 1999b) that have provided a review of the field of strategy implementation. Consequently, in our study we have summarized the research results, theoretical bases and research methods used in this field to provide an overview, synthesis and future directions for this crucial field of management research. We hope that our framework can provide guidance to practitioners and act as a checklist of factors to consider before and during the implementation process, and we anticipate that many of the open research questions we have mentioned will be addressed in future research.

NOTES

*   The China Scholarship Council provided financial support for this study.
1.   Among the 63 articles, there were 11 articles on strategy implementation in the *Strategic Management Journal*, 6 articles in the *Academy of Management Journal*, 4 in the *Journal of Management Studies*, 3 in the *Journal of Business Research*, 2 in the *Journal of Management*, 2 in the *Sloan Management Review*, 2 in the *Journal of Marketing* and 1 in the *Harvard Business Review*.

REFERENCES

Akan, O., R.S. Allen, M.M. Helms and S.A. Spralls III (2006), 'Critical tactics for implementing Porter's generic strategies', *Journal of Business Strategy*, **27**: 43–53.
Alexander, L. D. (1985), 'Successfully implementing strategic decisions', *Long Range Planning*, **18**: 91–97.
Allio, M. K. (2005), 'A short, practical guide to implementing strategy', *Journal of Business Strategy*, **26**: 12–21.
Bantel, K. A. (1997), Performance in adolescent, technology-based firms: Product strategy, implementation, and synergy', *The Journal of High Technology Management Research*, **8**: 243–262.
Beer, M. and R. A. Eisenstat (2000), 'The silent killers of strategy implementation and learning', *Sloan Management Review*, **41**: 29–42.
Bourgeois III, L. J. and D. R. Brodwin (1984), 'Strategic implementation: Five approaches to an elusive phenomenon', *Strategic Management Journal*, **5**: 241–264.
Brenes, E. R., M. Mena and G. E. Molina (2007), 'Key success factors for strategy implementation in Latin America', *Journal of Business Research*, **61**: 1–9.
Chimhanzi, J. (2004), 'The impact of marketing/HR interactions on marketing strategy implementation', *European Journal of Marketing*, **38**: 73–98.
Chimhanzi, J. and R. E. Morgan (2005), 'Explanations from the marketing/human resources dyad for marketing strategy implementation effectiveness in service firms', *Journal of Business Research*, **58**: 787–796.
Dess, G. G. and R. L. Priem (1995), 'Consensus-performance research: Theoretical and empirical extensions', *Journal of Management Studies*, **32**: 401–417.

Dooley, R. S., G. E. Fryxell and W. Q. Judge (2000), 'Belaboring the not-so-obvious: consensus, commitment, and strategy implementation speed and success', *Journal of Management*, **26**: 1237–1257.

Drazin, Robert and Peter Howard (1984), 'Strategy implementation: A technique for organizational design. Columbia Design', *Columbia Journal of World Business*, **19**: 40–46.

Floyd, S. W. and B. Wooldridge (1992a), 'Managing strategic consensus: the foundation of effective implementation', *Academy of Management Executive*, **6**: 27–39.

Floyd, S. W. and B. Wooldridge (1992b), 'Middle management involvement in strategy and its association with strategic type: A research note', *Strategic Management Journal*, **13**: 153–167.

Floyd, S. W. and B. Wooldridge (1997), 'Middle managements strategic influence and organizational performance', *Journal of Management Studies*, **34**: 465–485.

Forman, J. and P. A. Argenti (2005), 'How corporate communication influences strategy implementation, reputation and the corporate brand: An exploratory qualitative study', *Corporate Reputation Review*, **8**: 245–264.

Golden, B. R. (1992), 'SBU strategy and performance: The moderating effects of the corporate–SBU relationship', *Strategic Management Journal*, **13**: 145–158.

Govindarajan, V. (1988), 'A contingency approach to strategy implementation at the business-unit level integrating administrative mechanisms with strategy', *Academy of Management Journal*, **31**: 828–853.

Govindarajan, V. (1989), 'Implementing competitive strategies at the business unit level: Implications of matching managers to strategies', *Strategic Management Journal*, **10**: 251–269.

Govindarajan, V. and J. Fisher (1990), 'Strategy, control systems, and resource sharing: effects on business-unit performance', *Academy of Management Journal*, **33**: 259–285.

Gronroos, C. (1985), 'Internal marketing-theory and practice', in T. M. Bloch, G. D. Upah and V. A. Zeithaml (eds), *Services Marketing in a Changing Environment*, Chicago, IL: American Marketing Association, 41–47.

Gupta, A. K. (1987), 'SBU strategies, corporate–SBU relations, and SBU effectiveness in strategy implementation', *Academy of Management Journal*, **30**: 477–500.

Gupta, A. K. and V. Govindarajan (1984), 'Business unit strategy, managerial characteristics and business unit effectiveness at strategy implementation', *Academy of Management Journal*, **27**: 25–41.

Guth, W. D. and I. C. Macmillan (1986), 'Strategy implementation versus middle management self-interest', *Strategic Management Journal*, **7**: 313–327.

Hambrick, D. C. and A. A. Cannella, Jr. (1989), 'Strategy implementation as substance and selling', *Academy of Management Executive*, **3**: 278–285.

Hantang Qi (2005), 'Strategy implementation: The impact of demographic characteristics on the level of support received by middle managers', *Management International Review*, **45**: 45–70.

Harrington, R. J. (2006), 'The moderating effects of size, manager tactics and involvement on strategy implementation in food service', *Hospitality Management*, **25**: 373–397.

Heide, M., K. Grønhaug and S. Johannessen (2002), 'Exploring barriers to the successful implementation of a formulated strategy', *Scandinavian Journal of Management*, **18**: 217–231.

Heracleous, L. (2000), 'The role of strategy implementation in organization development', *Organization Development Journal*, **18**: 75–86.

Higgins, J. M. (2005), 'The eight 'S's of successful strategy execution', *Journal of Change Management*, **5**: 3–13.

Homburg, C., H. Krohmer and J. P. Workman (2004), 'A strategy implementation perspective of market orientation', *Journal of Business Research*, **57**: 1331–1340.

Hrebiniak, L. G. (2006), 'Obstacles to effective strategy implementation', *Organizational Dynamics*, **35**: 12–31.

Hrebiniak, L. G. and C. Snow (1982), 'Top management agreement and organizational performance', *Human Relations*, **38**: 1139–1158.

Judge, W. Q. and M. J. Stahl (1995), 'Middle-manager effort in strategy implementation: A multinational perspective', *International Business Review*, **4**: 91–111.

Kellermanns, F. W., J. Walter, C. Lechner and S. W. Floyd (2005), 'The lack of consensus about strategic consensus: Advancing theory and research', *Journal of Management*, **31**: 719–737.

Kim, W. C. and R. A. Mauborgne (1991), 'Implementing global strategies: the role of procedural justice', *Strategic Management Journal*, **12**: 125–143.

Kim, W. C. and R. A. Mauborgne (1993), 'Making global strategies work', *Sloan Management Review*, **34**: 11–27.

Lehner, J. (2004), 'Strategy implementation tactics as response to organizational, strategic, and environmental imperatives', *Management Revue*, **15**: 460–480.

Neilson, G. L., K. L. Martin and E. Powers (2008), 'The secrets to successful strategy execution', *Harvard Business Review*, **86**: 61–70.

Nielsen, R. P. (1983), 'Strategic planning and consensus building for external relations – five cases', *Long Range Planning*, **16**: 74–81.

Nilsson, F. and B. Rapp (1999), 'Implementing business unit strategies: The role of management control systems', *Scandinavian Journal of Management*, **15**: 65–88.

Noble, C. H. (1999a), 'Building the strategy implementation network', *Business Horizons*, **42**: 19–27.

Noble, C. H. (1999b), 'The eclectic roots of strategy implementation research', *Journal of Business Research*, **45**: 119–134.

Noble, C. H. and M. P. Mokwa (1999), 'Implementing marketing strategies: Developing and testing a managerial theory', *Journal of Marketing*, **63**: 57–73.

Nutt, P. C. (1986), 'Tactics of implementation', *Academy of Management Journal*, **29**: 230–261.

Nutt, P. C. (1987), 'Identifying and appraising how managers install strategy', *Strategic Management Journal*, **8**: 1–14.

Nutt, P. C. (1989), 'Selecting tactics to implement strategic plans', *Strategic Management Journal*, **10**: 145–161.

Okumus, F. (2001), 'Towards a strategy implementation framework', *International Journal of Contemporary Hospitality Management*, **13**: 327–338.

Olson, E. M., S. F. Slater and G. T. Hult (2005), 'The importance of structure and process to strategy implementation', *Business Horizons*, **48**: 47–54.

Peljhan, Darja (2007), 'The role of management control systems in strategy implementation: The case of a Slovenian company', *Economic and Business Review*, **9**: 257–280.

Peng, W. and D. Litteljohn (2001), 'Organisational communication and strategy implementation – a primary inquiry', *International Journal of Contemporary Hospitality*, **13**: 360–363.

Pettigrew, A., E. Ferlie and L. McKee (1992), *Shaping Strategic Change*, London: Sage.

Pettigrew, A. M. (1985), 'Examining change in the long-term context of culture and politics', in J. M. Pennings and associates (eds), *Organisational Strategy and Change: New Views on Formulating and Implementing Strategies*, San Francisco: Jossey-Bass, pp. 269–318.

Prasa, H. G. (1999), 'Interaction of strategy implementation and power perceptions in franchise systems: An empirical investigation', *Journal of Business Research*, **45**: 173–185.

Qi, H. (2005), 'Strategy implementation: the impact of demographic characteristics on the level of support received by middle managers', *Management International Review*, **45**: 45–70.

Rapert, M. I., D. Lynch and T. Suter (1996), 'Enhancing functional and organizational performance via strategic consensus and commitment', *Journal of Strategic Marketing*, **4**: 193–205.

Rapert, M. I. and B. M. Wren (1998), 'Reconsidering organizational structure: A dual perspective of frameworks and processes', *Journal of Managerial Issues*, **10**: 287–302.

Rapert, M. I., A. Velliquette and J. A. Garretson (2002), 'The strategic implementation process evoking strategic consensus through communication', *Journal of Business Research*, **55**: 301–310.

Roth, K., D. M. Schweiger and A. J. Morrison (1991), 'Global strategy implementation at the business unit level: Operational capabilities and administrative mechanisms', *Journal of International Business Studies*, **22**: 369–402.

Sashittal, H. C. and D. Wilemon (1996), 'Marketing implementation in small and midsized industrial firms: An exploratory study', *Industrial Marketing Management*, **25**: 67–78.

Schaap, J. I. (2006), 'Toward strategy implementation success: An empirical study of the role of senior-level leaders in the Nevada gaming industry', *UNLV Gaming Research & Review Journal*, **10**: 13–37.

Schmidt, S. L. and M. Brauer (2006), 'Strategic governance: How to assess board effectiveness in guiding strategy execution', *Strategic Governance*, **14**: 13–22.

Simons, R. (1990), 'The role of management control systems in creating competitive advantage: New perspectives', *Accounting, Organizations and Society*, **15**: 127–143.

Simons, R. (1995), *Levers of Control: How Managers Use Innovative Control Systems to Drive Strategic Renewal*, Boston: Harvard Business School Press.

Simons, R. (2000), *Performance Measurement and Control Systems for Implementing Strategy*, Upper Saddle River: Prentice Hall.

Singh, D. T. (1998), 'Incorporating cognitive aids into decision support systems: The case of the strategy execution process', *Decision Support Systems*, **24**: 145–163.

Skivington, J. E. and R. L. Daft (1991), 'A study of organizational "Framework" and "Process" modalities for the implementation of business-level strategic decisions', *Journal of Management Studies*, **28**: 46–68.

Slater, S. F. and E. M. Olson (2001), 'Marketing's contribution to the implementation of business strategy: An empirical analysis', *Strategic Management Journal*, **22**: 1055–1067.

Smith, K. A. and E. A. Kofron (1996), 'Toward a research agenda on top management teams and strategy implementation', *Irish Business and Administrative Research*, **17**: 135–152.

Viseras, E. M., T. Baines and M. Sweeney (2005), 'Key success factors when implementing strategic manufacturing initiatives', *International Journal of Operations & Production Management*, **25**: 151–179.

Waldersee, R. and S. Sheather (1996), 'The effects of strategy type on strategy implementation actions', *Human Relations*, **49**: 105–122.

Walker, Jr. O. C. and R. W. Ruekert (1987), 'Marketing's role in the implementation of business strategies: A critical review and conceptual framework', *Journal of Marketing*, **51**: 15–33.

Wernham, R. (1985), 'Obstacles to strategy implementation in a nationalized industry', *Journal of Management Studies*, **22**: 632–648.

White, R. E. (1986), 'Generic business strategies, organizational context and performance: An empirical investigation', *Strategic Management Journal*, **7**: 217–231.

Wooldridge, B. and S. W. Floyd (1990), 'The strategy process, middle management involvement, and organizational performance', *Strategic Management Journal*, **11**: 231–241.

9 Five alternative approaches to the strategic reorientation process

Robert Chapman Wood and Osvald M. Bjelland

The strategy process subfield recognizes the importance of strategic reorientation (Tushman and Romanelli, 1985) and strategic renewal (Floyd and Lane, 2000), events that redefine the nature of organizations and dramatically alter strategies and strategy processes. However, the theory of this kind of change is by no means complete. There is a tendency for literature on strategic reorientation, strategic renewal and related kinds of change to assume implicitly that there is one single process of reorientation and renewal. There is relatively little effort to draw on literature from outside the strategy field for a more complete theory. Where ideas are imported from other research streams, moreover, there is almost no effort to leverage streams that suggest an array of radically different approaches might be possible.

The literature of organizational change and development offers important potential extensions to our understanding of strategic reorientation and renewal processes. Scholars studying organizational change often articulate the process of strategic reorientation as a series of discrete steps, often summarized in three stages derived from the work of Lewin (1951): unfreeze, change, refreeze. (See Weick and Quinn (1999) for a review.) Such a well-defined understanding of how managers can overcome inertia to introduce and effectively implement radically new strategies could obviously contribute to our comprehension of the strategy process.

However, two problems exist. First, careful studies show that the standard sets of steps are radical oversimplifications (Pettigrew, 1985; Johnson, 1987). Second, studies have shown that transformation sometimes departs from the standard script completely (Orlikowski, 1996; Feldman, 2004), and analysts have documented other processes through which deliberate reorientation has sometimes been achieved (Collins, 2001; O'Reilly and Tushman, 2004; Larsson et al., 2004).

The traditional, essentially three-step, model of organizational change remains dominant in organizational change research and prescription (Kotter, 1996; Nadler, 1998; Burke, 2007) and little systematic comparison of the different processes has been carried out. This creates obvious difficulties for the analysis of the strategy process and for practice. Much strategic management theory is based on the idea that managers can exercise control over what their organization does. Yet it is well established that institutional inertia severely constrains organizations even when they appear to have sufficient resources for the pursuit of potentially effective strategies (Hannan and Freeman, 1989; Henderson and Clark, 1990). The current state of research on organizational change, strategic reorientation and strategic renewal makes it difficult to analyse what kind of changes managers can actually carry out in organizations, what processes would bring those changes about, and how those processes should be managed. Thus an adequate understanding of the strategy process demands broader analyses of managed organizational change and how managed change processes relate to reorientation and renewal.

This article reports on a study in progress that takes a broad approach to understanding managed organizational change, reorientation and renewal. We will argue that there is considerable value in existing analyses of organizational change processes. However, we will suggest that the value is best tapped by acknowledging the enormous diversity of those processes while recognizing that diversity is not unlimited. Just as medical doctors study poorly understood phenomena by looking for 'syndromes' – groups of symptoms that run together – perhaps there are elements that often go together in effectively managed organizational change processes. Perhaps understanding these configurations of related elements can help us understand the alternative ways that strategic reorientation and strategic renewal can occur.

We suggest that with due modification based on the vast literature of organizational change, the conventional process whose established descriptions partially derive from Lewin's work in the 1940s is one such process that can effectively produce strategic reorientation. We also describe four other processes whose ability to produce strategic reorientation has been documented to a significant degree. These are:

- Reorientation by changing firm boundaries – acquisition of other firms that materially change the firm's resource portfolio, or spinning off of units so the firm will focus more narrowly.
- Reorientation through the ambidextrous organizational form – creation of new units that enter new businesses and may grow to radically change the firm's nature.
- Reorientation through Collins' (2001) 'Good to Great' process – re-working the management team and then struggling with the new team to confront the 'brutal facts' of an existing business and gradually developing a simple, powerful concept that can be implemented over many years.
- A recently documented way of reorientation we call 'improvisational

transformation', which involves improvisation of new strategies during a crisis and the emergence or innovation routines that can support repeated reorientation.

As will be discussed below, additional processes have been plausibly argued to create change that might amount to strategic reorientation. However, we focus on those above because our research has shown that there is a significant degree of empirical evidence that they can work.

The paper begins with a summary of our core concepts and data. Then we describe the five managed organizational change processes that seem to have been shown capable of producing strategic reorientation. For each, we describe empirical reports of how managers have made the process work. Next, we analyse key differences among the five reorientation processes described: what elements distinguish them and how differences between the standard model and the other documented processes may suggest rethinking some assertions commonly made about change. The next section discusses under what circumstances managers might appropriately choose the different processes. Next, we examine the contribution that this analysis makes to strategy process research and the need for further examination of alternative strategic reorientation processes. A final section summarizes our argument, discusses limitations and summarizes the need for further research.

KEY CONCEPTS AND DATA SOURCES

The concepts of strategic reorientation and strategic renewal seem to overlap considerably. Both designate processes that change the organization fundamentally. There seem to be two main differences. First, strategic reorientation is traditionally understood to be a rapid process, while this is not necessarily assumed about strategic renewal. Second, strategic reorientation is defined as being complete when certain changes have occurred in the organization (even if they do not result in improved performance), while strategic renewal seems by definition to involve the overcoming of strategic problems and would not be considered complete unless success ('renewal') had been achieved.

Tushman and Romanelli's standard definition of strategic reorientation (1985: 179) seems simpler and clearer than any definition of strategic renewal that we encountered ('simultaneous and discontinuous shifts in strategy [defined by products, markets and/or technology], the distribution of power, the firm's core structure, and the nature and pervasiveness of control systems'). We decided to focus on events that met this definition with the exception that (1) we did not limit ourselves to cases where the changes were simultaneous, and (2) we did limit our examination to cases where there was evidence of good performance resulting from the changes. We thus seek to report on cases that can be called both strategic reorientation and strategic renewal, with the exception that we include some cases where the changes that occurred were not simultaneous and thus might not be called 'strategic reorientation' under the traditional definition. These criteria for case selection mean we are examining cases with evidence of substantial deliberate institutional change inside the organizations. For convenience, we will consistently refer to these change processes as 'reorientation'.

To gain insight into the diversity of processes capable of producing strategic reorientation and renewal, we first sought literature that asserted particular processes could produce this kind of change. In other words, we sought process models (Mohr, 1982) of dramatic, positive organizational change. As the study is ongoing, we should not be assumed to have generated a comprehensive list. However, we have so far identified at least ten processes that have been plausibly argued to create change that might amount to strategic reorientation: the standard organizational change model; boundary-changing (Larsson et al., 2004); 'ambidextrous' management (O'Reilly and Tushman, 2004); Good-to-Great (Collins, 2001); improvisational transformation (Wood, 2007); socio-technical systems (Burns and Stalker, 1966); total quality management (Deming, 1986); appreciative inquiry (Cooperrider and Srivastva, 1987); interactive management (Ackoff, 1994); and several strands of learning theory (Argyris and Schon, 1996; Senge, 1990). As processes argued to produce strategic reorientation have been identified, we have sought published case material that documents these processes actually working. In order to maximize the variety of change processes examined, cases are utilized not only from academic sources but also from books written for non-academic purposes.

Descriptions are used only when they provided data credibly (1) describing the organization before the reorientation, (2) describing the process of reorientation, and (3) documenting success with relevant indicators, generally for a period of at least two years after the reorientation. These criteria suggest that while not all cases meet desirable academic standards of rigor, and reports in some of the cases are undoubtedly affected by hindsight biases and other defects, it is possible to draw from the multiple cases for each type of change evidence suggestive that these reorientation processes really do exist and of how they work. (We did not find studies of the rigor of such academic works as Pettigrew (1985) and Johnson (1987) for any of the alternatives to the standard model of transformation.) Where at least two cases document that a process has provided strategic reorientation at the corporate level, we conclude that there is some empirical evidence that a particular change process can be said to generate real strategic reorientation.

The work so far is preliminary and an exploratory study. We included cases we had studied ourselves, case studies we were aware of that documented major reorientation processes appropriately, and cases found in a review of all books found with the keywords 'corporate transformation' (41 books) in a major combined academic and public library.

We limited the cases to business organizations because we believed we would gain best understanding of the differences in strategic effects of the different kinds of reorientation if we focused on organizations with comparable goals. This review produced 46 cases of strategic reorientation that contained adequate credible data. (Twelve from our own research, 23 from publications we were already familiar with, and 11 cases that met our criteria for data adequacy from our library review.) The cases examined so far appear in the appendix. For each of the five strategic reorientation processes, the appendix lists at least three cases for which supporting data met our criteria. For each case, it provides the date of the reorientation process and the data source or sources.

Many additional descriptions providing adequate data on actual transformation processes no doubt exist, for instance in books catalogued under other keywords in the library (e.g., 'organizational change'). However, the cases were sufficient to illustrate a range of well-documented change processes, including both cases where the change followed something like the standard theory and also cases that did not follow it. Thus the sample seemed appropriate for a preliminary report aimed at identifying opportunities for strategy process research and creating a clearer understanding of the strategic change processes available to managers.

THE STANDARD MODEL AND OTHER REORIENTATION PROCESSES IN EXISTING RESEARCH

While a majority of the reports on organizational change that we studied seem to either presume or document cases of reorientation that roughly follow the standard model, four other reorientation processes are also well documented. So far, we have not found adequately documented examples of the other processes argued to create change that might amount to strategic reorientation.

The standard model and the four other documented approaches are summarized in Table 9.1, which briefly describes each of the processes, provides a citation to a scholarly description of each, and lists one example

Table 9.1 Documented ways to achieve strategic reorientation

Change process	Description	Descriptive work	Example
The standard model	A crisis unfreezes the organization, then the leaders decide how it should change, plan and manage the process of change, and change systems to ensure that the new ways are supported	See review by Weick and Quinn (1999)	Xerox refocusing on quality in the 1980s
Ambidextrous form	Managers recognize new opportunities and create separate business units to pursue them while the existing business continues to exploit old opportunities. Often the new businesses grow far larger than the old, transforming the nature of the firm	O'Reilly and Tushman (2004)	Hewlett-Packard creating its printer business
Acquisition/ restructuring	Leaders seek alterations in the firm through buying new elements from others or separating out existing elements. After purchases and other legal restructurings, leaders nurse a new and different kind of organization into existence in the often-chaotic process of integration and re-launch	Haspeslagh and Jemison (1991)	Managers of Asea and Brown Boveri & Cie. creating Asea Brown Boveri as an integrated leader in engineering
Good to Great	Leaders seeking dramatically better organizations spend years developing a group of managers to work with and determining how to focus their efforts, finally focusing on doing a core group of things really well	Collins (2001)	Walgreen's developing the modern drug store
Improvisational transformation	In a crisis, leaders promote a strong but vague strategic intent and encourage improvisation to move the organization toward it. After initial successes, people in the organization seek to learn from them and the largely improvised innovation processes evolve into innovation routines	Wood (2007)	Monsanto learning to produce marketable innovations from its biotechnology

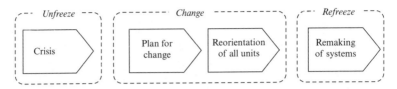

Figure 9.1   A standard model of organizational transformation

of each. The processes and the evidence suggesting that they can be effective ways of reorientation are described in more detail below.

The Standard Model

The standard model of transformational change processes is usually understood to have evolved from the work of Kurt Lewin (1951) on managed change in human groups during World War II. During the 1950s a clear and simple summary of this approach to change evolved: unfreeze, change, refreeze. The change process involved leaders clearly defining what they want the organization to become, then using the loosening of structure caused by a crisis to make the 'picture of the future' (Kotter, 1996) a reality. Figure 9.1 presents a simple summary of this process.

For better or worse, this has been an extremely influential and durable model. Hendry (1996: 624) comments: 'Scratch any account of creating and managing change and the idea that change is a three-step process which begins with unfreezing will not be far below the surface. Indeed, it has been said that the whole theory of change is reducible to this one idea of Kurt Lewin's.' For a comprehensive account of this research tradition, see Pettigrew (1985). Many authors have expressed concern about the lack of advance. Kahn's (1974: 487) comment is widely repeated: 'A few theoretical propositions are repeated without additional data or development; a few bits of homey advice are repeated without proof or disproof; and a few sturdy empirical observations are quoted with reverence but without refinement or explication' (Pettigrew, 1985; Macy and Izumi, 1993; Weick and Quinn, 1999).

Though Kahn's comment is memorable and captures the slow pace of change in organizational change theory, it clearly exaggerates, however. The last few decades have seen progress in the understanding of the kind of change that the theory describes. In particular, careful studies such as Pettigrew (1985) and Johnson (1987) have shown that the image of a heroic change coalition deciding what the organization should become at the start of a transformation can be very misleading. Pettigrew and Johnson both found new strategic ideas were constantly under development in the firms they studied. Ideas under development then received impetus at the time of crisis, rather than being introduced through interventions in the crisis period.

However, recent research leaves the basic ideas of the standard model of transformational change intact. Crises unfreeze organizations, change happens rapidly and in considerable accord with a senior management plan, and new systems then limit change for a long time. Many studies as well as non-academic books demonstrate that this process occurs in real businesses. In addition to Pettigrew's study (on the chemical company ICI) and Johnson's (on the apparel retailer Foster Bros.), this process is documented at Xerox by Kearns and Nadler (1992), at National Semiconductor by Miles (1997) and at Continental Airlines by Bethune (1998).

For the analysis of strategic management, however, the dominance of this one model in change theory is perplexing. The undoubted existence of transformations that follow the model does not mean it is the only way to change. Other change processes have also been documented.

Reorientation by Changing the Boundaries of the Firm

It is widely recognized that leaders can also deliberately launch a reorientation by acquiring other companies that materially change the firm's resource portfolio or by spinning off units so a newly created firm will focus on a single business. Such change is sometimes treated within the standard model (as, for example, by Burke (2007)). A dramatic acquisition or a spin-off creates a crisis and thus unfreezes things; the transition to a new way of working can be presented as similar to the process of defining and bringing into existence a new way of working in a standard model transformation.

However, for the purpose of understanding alternatives in strategic change it is helpful to think of reorientation by acquisition or spin-off as a different kind of metamorphosis. The decision to restructure involves a different kind of break with the past than the changes analysed in most standard organizational transformation analysis – more final and precise. The planning for change and reorientation of the units in the new organization is to a significant extent forced by the existence of new resources in the organization whose relationship to other resources in the organization is not clear (or by the absence of units that the organization had in the past depended on).

Most acquisitions do not involve strategic reorientation. However, a large literature on acquisitions and restructuring clearly shows that these techniques can be used to reorient organizations in a way quite distinct

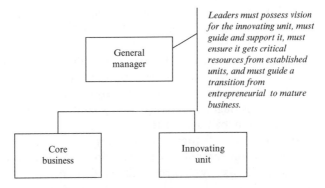

Figure 9.2   The ambidextrous form

from that described in conventional transformation literature (Haspeslagh and Jemison, 1991; Hitt et al., 2001; Pablo and Javidan, 2004). Both extended case examples within works on acquisitions and restructuring (e.g., the Esmark case within Gaughan (1999)) and popular books (Barham and Helmer, 1998) document how acquisitions and restructuring can reorient a firm.

The Ambidextrous Organizational Form

While reorientations spawned by acquisitions and spin-offs can be studied within the framework of the standard model of transformation, other well-documented processes that can result in strategic reorientation of a firm cannot. Probably the clearest example of this is the use of the ambidextrous organizational form (O'Reilly and Tushman, 2004).

An ambidextrous organizational form involves two different kinds of units – one of them capable of exploiting a well-established business, the other capable of exploring something radically new (Figure 9.2). But it requires much more than just the division of the firm into distinct exploiting and innovating units. The construction of innovating units is complex. It always requires dealing with ambiguity, and progress is far harder to evaluate than the progress of established businesses (for which sales and profitability are usually good measures). If leaders simply create distinct units, one exploiting an established business and others seeking to introduce something new, the established business will almost always seize far more than the appropriate share of the firm's resources simply because it's in a position to explain its need for resources in a more 'business-like' way than the innovators. Thus an ambidextrous organizational form cannot be said to exist unless the firm has senior leaders with a vision for what the innovating units can accomplish and ability to guide and support them as they advance (and judge fairly if they are failing to do so). The form requires leaders who will identify the critical few resources the innovating business needs from established units and make sure they are supplied. And it requires leaders to guide the complex transition of the innovating unit from entrepreneurial organization to stable, profitable business.

Most organizations that attempt to create ambidextrous organizational forms are not aiming at reorientation. The form is appropriate for any kind of innovation that does not fit neatly in an established business. Moreover, when organizations do transform themselves using the ambidextrous organizational form, it is often unclear whether their leaders deliberately sought reorientation or understood that reorientation was a likely result. For example, Hewlett-Packard used the ambidextrous organizational form to create its printer and personal computer units, and these transformed the firm by becoming far larger than the measurement equipment business that had previously been its heart. However, there is not much published evidence on the extent to which Hewlett-Packard leaders understood and deliberately sought this possibility.

At least a few reorientations seem to have been deliberately managed through the ambidextrous form, however, and the possibility clearly exists for more. One example is the transition of IBM from punched-card sorting machines to electronic computers (Watson, 1990).

'Good to Great'

The 'Good to Great' process documented by Collins (2001) is less widely discussed in academic literature than the ambidextrous form. However, there is reason to believe the process does deserve to be considered as another alternative way of reorienting organizations.

Collins' work is from a popular publisher, and it contains numerous cute phrases that mark the author's style as non-academic. However, it also contains a clear appendix describing the methodology used to develop the theories presented. The names of the companies studied are disclosed, and Collins and his research team have followed the solid research practice of studying a comparison company that did not succeed for each company that did. Collins' work has been faulted for implying that it has an approach that leaders should copy. Walker (2006) notes that Collins 'sampled on the dependent variable' – choosing to study firms because they were successful – and therefore we cannot know how many unsuccessful firms followed the same process. However, Walker's analysis is consistent with Collins' claim that Collins has described a kind of change

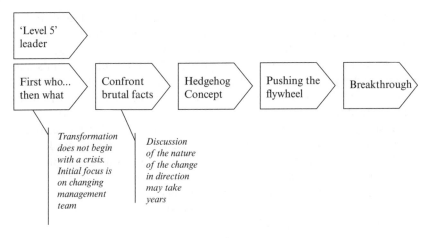

Figure 9.3   The 'Good-to-Great' transformation

process different from what theory, including the standard model of organizational transformation, had led him to expect.

Collins describes a process by which organizations in relatively slow-moving industries such as steel, retailing, banking and consumer products manufacturing discovered and implemented clear, simple concepts of their businesses. These enabled them to produce returns to shareholders at least three times the stock market average for at least 15 years. Unlike the standard model, Collins' process does not begin with a crisis and does not involve deciding what the organization will become early in the transformation process. To aid in comparison between the Collins process and others, Figure 9.3 summarizes the Collins process in six steps. Collins first suggests that an approach he calls 'Level 5 Leadership' is a precondition for transformation. It is a non-charismatic approach to leading. Level 5 leaders 'blend extreme personal humility with intense professional will' (Walker, 2006).

The process of change begins with re-working the management team. Collins suggests that leaders can begin working on transformation deliberately through a focus on personnel change without having a defined direction. Moreover, in his approach transformation can start regardless of whether or not any crisis exists. He says leaders in the process he studied

> did not first figure out where to drive the bus and then get people to take it there. No, they first got the right people on the bus (and the wrong people off the bus) and then figured out where to drive it. They said, in essence, 'Look, I don't really know where we should take this bus. But I know this much: if we get the right people on the bus . . . we'll figure out how to take it someplace great'. (Collins, 2001: 21)

Once they have the right people on the bus (and also while they're putting them there), the leader and the team 'confront the brutal facts'. The team thinks together with the leaders, often over a period of many years.

Through this process, the well-developed management team develops a simple driving idea. Collins calls this the 'Hedgehog Concept' after the spiny mammal that is successful because it knows one important thing: that it can protect itself by rolling into a spiky ball. Like the hedgehog, the company seeking transformation develops an extremely simple idea about what it needs to do very well. For example, Walgreen's settled on the idea of learning to manage big drugstores that would get the customer to buy more mass-market products than just drugs. The development of this kind of idea is the third step.

The Hedgehog Concept must be implemented – a long, slow process. Collins summarizes it with the image of pushing on a flywheel with continual small changes that make the company better and better. The final stage of his transformation process is what Collins calls 'breakthrough'. The hard work finally makes the firm clearly better than its competitors. Sales and profits increase, and outsiders notice how great the company has become.

Examples in Collins' published research include Kimberly Clark's carefully thought through transition from a commodity paper maker to a consumer products giant, Wells Fargo's development of a focused approach to consumer banking, and Walgreen's invention of the modern US drug store.

Improvisational Transformation

While scholars such as Pettigrew and Johnson have helped us understand that the portrayal of senior managers in the standard model as heroically developing a 'picture of the future' (Kotter, 1996: 68) overstates top management's power and role, executive leaders' strategic decision-making (Eisenhardt and Zbaracki, 1992) launches each of the reorientation processes discussed above. However, recent evidence suggests that not all reorientation begins with decision-making. In recent years, scholars have shown interest in improvisation (Weick, 1998; Miner et al., 2001), that is, behavior whose design and enactment are so 'fused' that they cannot be separated (Miner, et al., 2001: 313).

Recent data indicate that there exist managed organizational change processes in which improvisation plays a key role. These processes do not seem to have strategic decision-making at the beginning in any of the senses discussed by Eisenhardt and Zbaracki. The research (Wood, 2007; Wood et al., 2007; Bjelland, 2008) suggests that improvisational transformation can be summarized in the five steps diagrammed in Figure 9.4.

Figure 9.4   Improvisational transformation

Like reorientation through the standard model, these more improvisational reorientations begin with a crisis. Organizations go through periods when an improved ability to innovate seems necessary for survival, and this unfreezing makes further developments possible. However, while the opening of the improvisational transformation process closely parallels the opening of transformation in the standard model, the rest of the process differs.

In the traditional model, the second element as summarized in Figure 9.1 is for leaders to respond to the crisis by creating a plan for change – a clear 'blueprint'. By contrast, leaders in companies that carried out improvisational transformation began by articulating goals that were notably vague (though emotionally appealing). Companies found to have gone through these processes include Monsanto, General Electric, the US utility firm NiSource and SSB Bank in Scandinavia. At Monsanto, for instance, the stated goal in the agricultural unit during the time of crisis in the early 1990s was 'abundant food and a healthy environment'. There was never any comprehensive map indicating how the firm would deliver on this goal.

Once the blueprint has been drawn, the standard model calls for carefully reorienting people in each part of the organization to the new way of working. By contrast, the improvisational transformation organizations plunged into experiments in innovation. For example, after Jack Welch created a crisis at GE Capital by insisting on dramatic performance improvement, the first big innovations came in response to an accidental stimulus. First, GE Capital moved aggressively to take advantage of Reagan-era tax breaks that allowed highly profitable leasing deals. In itself, that was a minor innovation whose value would soon have disappeared as Congress cut back on tax-leasing benefits. However, in response to the cutbacks, GE Capital managers launched into an aggressive examination of opportunities in leasing that did not depend on tax rules. They discovered that by combining secured finance with special services for individual industries, they could leverage GE's excellent operational discipline to produce reliable sources of profitable growth. Similarly, improvisational efforts were important steps in getting innovation started in each of the other organizations.

The next step was learning from the largely improvisational processes that had produced success. At GE Capital, that meant setting up mechanisms – business development units and changes in the organization's planning process – designed to replicate the successes in leasing.

Finally, the improvised processes and the efforts to learn from them evolve into new innovation routines. The routines that emerge involve combinations of deliberately created elements and ways of innovating that have evolved in a largely unplanned way from the improvisational processes that produced the initial successful major innovations.

Improvisational transformation seems connected to the emergence of capability for repeated strategic innovation. The standard model and the Good-to-Great process each are associated with the creation of new, stable positions. Changing boundaries and the ambidextrous organizational form may be used to create innovation systems. (See, for example, Harreld, et al., 2007.) Improvisational transformation, however, seems to come inherently from efforts to increase innovativeness. It inevitably seems to embed routines based on processes that have created innovations that impressed people in the organization.

Hybrid Reorientation Processes

Many organizations reorient themselves through two or more of the ways of change outlined above. For example, NiSource used an improvisational transformation process to enable senior management to begin innovating, carried out a transformation that followed the standard model to reinvent its core business, and used the ambidextrous form and small-scale acquisitions to explore ideas that were emerging in its industry. As managers became confident in a new vision of the industry, it remade the entire business through large-scale acquisition.

Other Change Processes in the Literature

As indicated above, we have not so far found documented examples of strategic reorientation through socio-technical systems, total quality management, appreciative inquiry, interactive management and learning theory. We reviewed literature on these processes. However, for some of these we could not extract a step-by-step summary of the transformation process comparable to those above from the literature. For none of them could we find documented case examples that met our data standards. Review of additional cases may well result in the discovery of examples of transformation that showed some of these processes could be considered well-defined ways that actually are utilizable for reorientation.

The diversity of the innovation and change literatures suggests that additional ways of managing organizational change to produce strategic reorientation are likely to exist. However, the above analysis does suggest that the five ways of transformation described above are all among the best-documented means of managing organizational transformation to achieve strategic reorientation in the literature today. They are thus perhaps the most reliable known means of achieving strategic reorientation and renewal.

COMPARING THE REORIENTATION PROCESSES

The first conclusion to be drawn from this review is that the diversity of reorientation processes suggests prescriptions about the management of change drawn from the study of any single transformation process may mislead scholars and managers. This is important in a world where the study of 'organizational change' is often equated with the study of processes following the standard model.

Two kinds of differences among the processes capable of producing reorientation are most striking. First, some of the reorientation processes require that leaders develop a well-defined understanding of where the organization is going at the beginning of the transformation process; some do not. Proponents of transformation through the standard model or through acquisitions argue strongly that leaders employing those strategies need a clear vision of what they are trying to do.

In fact, organizations using the 'Good-to-Great' process and the improvisational transformation process did not define where they were going at the beginning of transformations and yet achieved good results. Use of the ambidextrous form, moreover, allows leaders to experiment with multiple approaches that could be transforming without deciding at the beginning which is really most important or most likely to succeed.

The second striking difference among the types of reorientation is their differing impacts on the ability to keep innovating after an initial transformation. The standard model was not originally constructed with a view to promoting ongoing innovation after the transformation. Nadler (1998) argued that an approach that followed the standard model could create organizations capable of continual innovation. However, several of the firms whose efforts to create a capability for continual change he celebrated (ATand T, Lucent Technologies, Xerox and Sun Microsystems) subsequently had difficulties in maintaining leadership in their industries through innovation. Similarly, as noted above, the 'Good to Great' process produces simple, stable systems that work effectively in relatively slow-moving industries but may not achieve ongoing strategic innovation.

By contrast, the improvisational transformation process and the ambidextrous form can lead to capabilities for repeated innovation. The improvisational transformation process was found to lead to routines for innovation peculiar to individual firms. The ambidextrous form is a process for innovating that can be used continually after it has transformed an organization.

THE PROCESSES AS STRATEGIC CHOICES FOR LEADERS

The different characteristics of reorientation processes described above make clear that the process of strategic management of firms that need reorientation and renewal is even more complex than might be imagined. It cannot be understood simply as the management of the organization down a well-documented path of organizational change. Leaders must choose what kind of path to take. The choice of which transformation process to use depends on the organization's situation.

Perhaps the most basic question is whether leaders can define the goal they are seeking. If not, they have three choices: the simplest is not to pursue reorientation at all until they can make the goal clear. But that is not the only option. It may be that the challenges facing the organization are simply too complex or subtle to allow a leadership team to develop a clear picture of the future quickly.

Alternatively, leaders can begin the 'Good to Great' process by working on improving the management team and starting an inevitably long discussion of how the organization should change. On the other hand, they can also choose to begin an improvisational transformation by focusing on a big, vague, emotional goal. The Good to Great process is appropriate in a slow-moving industry, where the simple, stable systems it produces will be effective. The improvisational transformation process is appropriate in a faster-moving industry.

If managers can define the goal they seek, or at least a large part of it, they can use the standard model, pursue reorientation by changing the borders of the firm, or use the ambidextrous form.

CONTRIBUTIONS TO THE THEORY OF STRATEGY PROCESS

An understanding of the strategic management process requires understanding of what kinds of strategic changes firms can actually make and what they have to do to make them. Much literature that attempts to give insight on this is based on small samples of firms (often analyses of single firms) or on the repetition of venerable theories whose generality has not been much tested. The existing prescriptive literature is valuable for many purposes. However, the analysis presented here suggests that it is time to go beyond it, to review with care the literature that offers alternatives to mainstream approaches, and to evaluate what ways of reorienting and renewing firms can be said to have been documented empirically.

With the argument above, we believe we begin to contribute to two important tasks. First, as outlined above, data on alternative approaches to strategic reorientation can serve as a guide to scholars, consultants and managers facing particular management problems. It can enable them to analyse what approaches to strategic change are real alternatives in particular situations.

Second, such data can contribute to a more general analysis of the strategic reorientation and renewal process. Today, analyses such as Tushman and Romanelli (1985), Floyd and Lane (2000) and Crossan et al. (1999) provide partial pictures of the strategic reorientation/renewal process. However, it is often unclear whether the processes discussed by these authors are supposed to exist in all companies that successfully renew themselves or only in some subset of such companies. It is probably impossible to say today to what extent statements about renewal processes are true of most or all firms going through renewal. Proper analysis of alternative approaches and of empirical literature that documents how some of them work can put us in a far better position to analyse what statements about reorientation and renewal are consistently true and what statements are likely to apply to narrower ranges of cases.

Thus, the task of examining alternative approaches to strategic reorientation and renewal, while only partially completed in this paper, is an important one.

CONCLUSION

This review and analysis of strategic reorientation processes has shown that reorientation and renewal can be achieved through a variety of very different paths. We identified a range of processes that had been proposed in the literature and then reviewed empirical reports seeking evidence of which processes had been shown to be able to produce strategic reorientation. We analysed key differences among the processes and discussed some differing situations in which strategic managers may wisely choose different alternatives. The purpose of this analysis has been to illuminate a crucial aspect of the strategic management process – the alternative ways that strategic managers can approach strategic reorientation. To do this, we have summarized five managed organizational change processes and noted striking differences in their requirements and their impacts on ongoing innovative capacity. Through this, we have sought to provide the basics of a theory of the process choices managers face when inertia radically limits their ability to make use of their resources.

The analysis reported here is preliminary and based on a limited share of the literature. Much additional study of non-standard approaches to strategic reorientation is needed. In future research we hope to survey a broad sample of change case studies to learn whether additional processes of managed organizational change can produce strategic reorientation. In particular, it is important to examine whether empirical documentation exists to demonstrate that other proposed organizational change processes can create strategic reorientation.

Managers and scholars both need a better understanding of alternative approaches to overcoming inertia and implementing radically new strategies. A more comprehensive theory of this should be a central component of the analysis of strategy process.

REFERENCES

Ackoff, R. L. (1994), 'Systems thinking and thinking systems', *System Dynamics Review*, Summer–Fall: 175–188.

Argyris, C. and D. A. Schon (1996), *Organizational Learning II: Theory, Method and Practice*, Reading, MA: Addison-Wesley.

Barham, K. and C. Helmer (1998), *ABB: The Dancing Giant*, London: Financial Times/Prentice Hall.

Bethune, G. (1998), *From Worst to First*, New York: John Wiley & Sons, Inc.

Bjelland, O. M. (2008), *The role of leadership in transforming information intensive corporations through the application of information and communication technologies.* Doctoral dissertation, University of Leeds.

Burke, W. W. (2007), *Organization Change: Theory and Practice*, Thousand Oaks, CA: Sage.

Burns, T. and G. Stalker (1966), *The Management of Innovation*, London: Social Science Paperbacks (original work published 1961).

Carlzon, J. (1987), *Moments of Truth: New Strategies for Today's Customer-Driven Economy*, New York: Harper & Row.

Collier, P. and D. Horowitz (1987), *The Fords: An American Epic*, New York: Summit.

Collins, J. C. (2001), *Good to Great*, New York: HarperBusiness.

Cooperrider, D. L. and S. Srivastva (1987), 'Appreciative inquiry in organizational life', *Research in Organizational Change and Development*, **1**: 129–169.

Crossan, Mary and Iris Berdrow (2005), ' Organizational learning and strategic renewal', *Strategic Management Journal*, **24**(11): 1087–1105.

Crossan, M., H. Lane and R. E. White (1999), 'An organizational learning framework: From intuition to institution', *Academy of Management Review*, **24**(3): 522–537.

Cruikshank, J. and D. B. Sicilia (1997), *The Engine that Could: 75 Years of Values-Driven Change at Cummins Engine Company*, Boston, MA: Harvard Business School Press.

Dannemiller Tyson Assoc. (2000), *Whole-Scale Change*, San Francisco, CA: Berrett-Kohler.

Deming, W. E. (1986), *Out of the Crisis*, Cambridge, MA: MIT Center for Advanced Engineering Study.

Doornik, K. and J. Roberts (2001), *Nokia Corporation: Innovation and Efficiency in a High-Growth Global Firm*, Stanford University Graduate School of Business Case No. S-IB-23.

Eisenhardt, K. M. and M. J. Zbaracki (1992), 'Strategic decision-making', *Strategic Management Journal*, **13**: 17–37.

Feldman, M. S. (2004), 'Resources in emerging structures and processes of change', *Organization Science*, **15**(3): 295–309.

Floyd, S. W. and P. J. Lane (2000), 'Strategizing throughout the organization: managing role conflict in strategic renewal', *Academy of Management Review*, **25**(1): 154–177.

Fox, J. (2000). 'Nokia's secret code', *Fortune*, 1 May.

Gaughan, P. A. (1999), *Mergers, Acquisitions, and Corporate Restructuring*, New York: John Wiley.

Grove, A. S. (1996), *Only the Paranoid Survive*, New York: Doubleday Currency.

Hannan, M. T. and J. Freeman (1989), *Organizational Ecology*, Cambridge, MA: Harvard University Press.

Harreld, J. B., M. L. Tushman and C. A. I. O'Reilly (2007), 'Dynamic capabilities at IBM: Driving strategy into action', *California Management Review*, **49**(4): 21–43.

Haspeslagh, P. C. and D. B. Jemison (1991), *Managing Acquisitions: Creating Value through Corporate Renewal*, New York: Free Press.

Henderson, R. M. and K. B. Clark (1990), 'Architectural innovation: The reconfiguration of existing product technologies and the failure of established firms', *Administrative Science Quarterly*, **35**: 9–30.

Hendry, C. (1996), 'Understanding and creating whole organizational change through learning theory', *Human Relations*, **49**: 621–641.

Hitt, M. A., J. S. Harrison and R. D. Ireland (2001), *Mergers and Acquisitions: A Guide to Creating Value for Stakeholders*, Oxford: Oxford University Press.

Johnson, G. (1987), *Strategic Change and the Management Process*, Oxford: Basil Blackwell.

Kahn, R. (1974), 'Organizational development: Some problems and proposals', *Journal of Applied Behavioral Science*, **10**: 485–502.

Kearns, D. T. and D. A. Nadler (1992), *Prophets in the Dark: How Xerox Reinvented Itself and Beat Back the Japanese*, New York: HarperBusiness.

Kotter, J. P. (1996), *Leading Change*, Boston: Harvard Business School Press.

Larsson, R., K. R. Brousseau, M. J. Driver and P. L. Sweet (2004), 'The secrets of merger and acquisition success: A co-competence and motivational approach to synergy realization', in A. L. Pablo and M. Javidan (eds), *Mergers and Acquisitions: Creating Integrative Knowledge*, Malden, MA: Blackwell.

Lee, T. H., S. Shiba and R. C. Wood (1999), *Integrated Management Systems: A Practical Approach to Transforming Organizations*, Wiley Operations Management Series for Professionals, New York: John Wiley & Sons, Inc.

Levin, D. P. (1995), *Behind the Wheel at Chrysler: The Iacocca Legacy*, New York: Harcourt Brace.

Lewin, K. (1951), *Field Theory in Social Science*, New York: Harper & Brothers.

Macy, B. and H. Izumi (1993), 'Organizational change, design, and work innovation: A meta-analysis of 131 North American field studies – 1961–1991', *Research in Organizational Change and Development*, **7**: 235–313.

Martinez, A. (2001), *The Hard Road to the Softer Side*, New York: Crown.

Miles, R. H. (1997), *Corporate Comeback: The Story of Renewal and Transformation at National Semiconductor* (Gil Amelio, Foreword), San Francisco, CA: Jossey-Bass.

Miner, A. S., P. Bassoff and C. Moorman (2001), 'Organizational improvisation and learning: A field study', *Administrative Science Quarterly*, **46**: 304–337.

Mohr, L. (1982), *Explaining Organizational Behavior*, San Francisco, CA: Jossey-Bass.

Moore, G. A. (2005), *Dealing with Darwin: How Great Companies Innovate at Every Phase of Their Evolution*, New York: Portfolio.

Nadler, D. A. (1998), *Champions of Change: How CEOs and their Companies are Mastering the Skills of Radical Change* (Mark B. Nadler, Writer), San Francisco, CA: Jossey-Bass.

Nadler, D. A. and M. L. Tushman (1997), *Competing by Design: The Power of Organizational Architecture*, New York: Oxford University Press.

O'Reilly, C. A., III, and M. L. Tushman (2004), 'The ambidextrous organization', *Harvard Business Review*, **82**(4): 74–82.

O'Reilly, M. (1983), *The Goodyear Story*, Elmsford, NY: Benjamin.

Orlikowski, Wanda J. (1983), 'Improvising organizational transformation over time: A situated change perspective', *Information Systems Research*, **34**(1): 63–92.

Pablo, A. L. and M. Javidan (eds) (2004), *Mergers and Acquisitions: Creating Integrative Knowledge*, Malden, MA: Blackwell.

Pettigrew, A. M. (1985), *Awakening Giant: Continuity and Change in ICI*, Oxford: Basil Blackwell.

Senge, P. M. (1990), *The Fifth Discipline: The Art and Practice of the Learning Organization*, New York: Doubleday Currency.

Snyder, N. T. and D. L. Duarte (2003), *Strategic Innovation: Embedding Innovation as a Core Competency in your Organization*, San Francisco, CA: Jossey-Bass.

Tichy, N. M. and S. Sherman (1994), *Control your Destiny or Someone Else Will: Lessons in Mastering Change — the Principles Jack Welch is Using to Revolutionize General Electric*, New York: HarperBusiness.

Tushman, M. L. and E. Romanelli (1985), 'Organizational evolution: A metamorphosis model of convergence and reorientation', in L. Cummings and B. Staw (eds), *Research in Organizational Behavior* (Vol. 7), Greenwich, CT: JAI Press.

Tushman, M., W. K. Smith, R. C. Wood, G. Westerman and C. O'Reilly (2010), 'Organizational designs and innovation streams', *Industrial and Corporate Change*, pp. 1–36 (doi: 10.1093/icc/deq040).

Walker, G. (2006), 'Good to great: Why some companies make the leap – and others don't'; (book review), *Academy of Management Perspectives*, **20**(1): 120–122.

Watson, T., Jr (1990), '*Father, Son & Co.: My Life at IBM and Beyond*, New York: Bantam.

Weick, K. (1998), 'Improvisation as a mindset for organizational analysis', *Organization Science*, **9**(5): 543–621.

Weick, Karl E. and Robert E. Quinn (1999), 'Organizational change and development', *Annual Review of Psychology*, **50**: 361–386.

Wood, R. C. (2007), 'How strategic innovation really gets started', *Strategy and Leadership*, **35**(1), 21–29.

Wood, R. C., K. J. Hatten and P. Williamson (2007), *Improvisation and Large-Scale Organizational Change: Unfreeze, Improvise, Learn, Institutionalize*, San Jose State University Department of Organization and Management Working Paper No. 051G.

APPENDIX: COMPANY CASE EXAMPLES

	Date of reorientation	Change processes	Sources
BOC Industrial Gases	Early 1990s	Standard model	Nadler and Tushman 1997
Continental Airlines	1990s	Standard model	Bethune 1998
Cummins Engine	Several cycles	Standard model	Cruikshank and Sicilia 1997
Ford	1940s	Standard model	Collier and Horowitz 1987
Goodyear	1970s	Standard model	O'Reilly 1983
HP Medical Products Group	Late 1980s/ early 1990s	Standard model	Lee et al. 1999
Imperial Chemical Industries	1970s, 1980–83	Standard model, but author documents that change was supported by building of political and intellectual positions over time	Pettigrew 1985
Intel	1990s	Standard model	Grove 1996
K Bank	2000s	Standard model	Co-author unpublished research
Kaiser Permanente	1990s	Standard model	Nadler 1998
National Semiconductor	Early 1990s	Standard model	Miles 1997
Richmond Savings (Canada's third largest credit union)	1990s	Standard model	Dannemiller Tyson Assoc. 2000
Scandanavian Airlines Sys	1980s	Standard model	Carlzon 1987
Sears	Mid 1990s	Standard model	Martinez 2001
Teradyne	Late 1980s– early 1990s	Standard model	Lee et al. 1999
Xerox	1980s	Standard model	Kearns and Nadler 1992

	Date of reorientation	Change processes	Sources
ABB	1990s	Changing firm boundaries	Barham and Helmer 1998
Cisco	1990s, renewed in 2000s	Changing firm boundaries	Moore 2005
Esmark	1970s–1980s	Changing firm boundaries	Gaughan 1999
IBM Global Services	Late 1990s–2000s	Changing firm boundaries	Author unpublished research
EDB	2000s	Ambidextrous structure	Co-author unpublished research
HP	Early–mid 1990s	Ambidextrous structure	Tushman et al. 2010
IBM	1960s	Ambidextrous structure	Watson 1990
Abbot Labs	1970s	Good to Great	Collins 2001
Circuit City	1970s–1980s	Good to Great	Collins 2001
Gillette	1970s–1980s	Good to Great	Collins 2001
IBM	Mid–late 1990s	Good to Great	Author and co-author unpublished research
Ikea	2000s	Good to Great	Author unpublished research
Kimberly-Clark	1970s	Good to Great	Collins 2001
Nokia	1990s	Good to Great	Fox 2000; Doornik and Roberts 2001
Nucor	1970s	Good to Great	Collins 2001
Philip Morris	1960s	Good to Great	Collins 2001
Walgreen's	1970s	Good to Great	Collins 2001
Wells Fargo	1980s	Good to Great	Collins 2001
Apple	2000s	Improvisational transformation	Dossier of published research compiled by author and associate
General Electric	1980s	Improvisational transformation	Tichy and Sherman 1994; Wood 2007
Monsanto	Late 1990s	Improvisational transformation	Wood 2007
NiSource	1990s–2000s	Improvisational transformation	Wood 2007
SSB Bank	1990s, 2000s	Improvisational transformation	Bjelland 2008

	Date of reorientation	Change processes	Sources
Hybrid and sequential change processes			
Chrysler	Late 1970s–1980s	Several episodes of standard model transformation; some boundary-changing	Levin 1995
Foster Brothers	1970s–early 1980s	Standard model, some boundary-changing	Johnson 1987
Intel	1980s	Ambidextrous structure, holism	Grove 1996
Telenor	1990s, 2000s	Changing firm boundaries, improvisational transformation	Author, co-author unpublished research
Varian Medical	1990s	Changing firm boundaries followed by Good to Great	Author unpublished research
Whirlpool	1999–2003	Standard model and improvisational transformation	Snyder and Duarte 2003
Wilhelmsen Lines	2000s	Standard model, changing firm boundaries	Author unpublished research

10 Managerial interplay: linking intent to realized strategy

Bill Wooldridge and J. Ignacio Canales

In various ways previous theory and research have noted the importance of managerial interactions in the development, implementation and legitimization of organizational strategy (Balogun and Johnson, 2004; Burgelman, 1991; Floyd and Wooldridge, 1997; Labianca et al., 2000). These interactions occur to varying degrees at different stages of the strategy-making process and have an important effect on how strategy proceeds from a set of intentions to realized strategy (Mintzberg and Waters, 1985). We investigate the process that links the intent with the realized strategy. Throughout this process, managerial interactions facilitate organizational learning about strategy, providing a forum for managers to understand, 'buy in' and develop strategic intentions. At the most fundamental level, research demonstrates that managers who feel excluded from strategic conversations become de-energized and strategy formation becomes unnecessarily inefficient (Westley, 1990).

A primary distinction in the way managerial interactions about strategy have been conceptualized has to do with whether interactions are vertical or lateral. Vertical interactions focus on alignment between higher and lower levels of the organization (Dutton et al., 2001; Floyd and Wooldridge, 1992, 1997; Hart, 1992; Huy, 2002; Ketokivi and Castañer, 2004). From this perspective, top managers' roles range from commander through facilitator to sponsor. In turn, middle managers' roles range from champions to implementers as they interact with managers both above and below in the organizational hierarchy. Alternatively, lateral interactions influence how the organization comes to understand operational implications of strategy and advance the organizational learning necessary to realize strategic intent. From a sense-making perspective, lateral interactions influence how middle and lower level managers interpret change initiatives (Balogun and Johnson, 2004; Bartuneck and Moch, 1987; Gioia and Chittipeddi, 1991; Gioia et al., 1994; Isabella, 1990; Labianca et al., 2000). From a social learning perspective, lateral interactions among managers are central to the process of developing new ideas into strategic initiatives (Floyd and Wooldridge, 2000).

The purpose of this paper is to develop theory on how vertical and lateral interactions affect strategic outcomes. We fulfill this purpose through a multiple case study, comparing patterns of managerial interactions across six firms to inductively derive theory on how managerial interactions affect the content of realized strategy. Hence, our outcome variable is the consistency between intended and realized strategy. The research can best be described as inductive theory-building that elaborates theoretical linkages not addressed in the current literature (Eisenhardt, 1989; Yin, 1994). Existing theory recognizes vertical interactions between top and mid level managers (Dutton et al., 2001; Floyd and Wooldridge, 1992, 1997; Hart, 1992; Huy, 2002; Ketokivi and Castañer, 2004) and lateral interactions across the organization (Balogun and Johnson, 2004; Bartuneck and Moch, 1987; Gioia and Chittipeddi, 1991; Gioia et al., 1994; Isabella, 1990; Labianca et al., 2000). To date, however, existing theory has failed to both systematically describe vertical and lateral interactions and consider how they combine to influence strategy. Focusing on these combinations, the present study attempts to shed light on processes that influence the formation of strategy, but that have not been previously considered (Berg, 2004).

The concept of *managerial interplay* emerged from the case data as an important factor influencing how strategy becomes accepted and realized consistently within organizations. Our use of the term 'interplay' reflects insights derived from the data concerning how interactions at one level influence subsequent interactions and how the overall pattern of interactions determines strategic outcomes. Thus, as used here, managerial interplay is defined as the entire set of social interactions (both vertical and lateral) regarding strategy that generate reciprocal actions and reactions between and across managerial levels. It was through these interactions that the mutual validation and legitimization of strategy, by top and lower level managers, occurred.

By considering both vertical and lateral interactions we move beyond previous work focused on issues of implementation (Dobni and Luffman, 2003; Hickson et al., 2003; Nutt, 1999), offering a novel conceptualization that has the potential to add new insights into the strategy process (Chakravarthy and Doz, 1992). The concept of managerial interplay comprises previous notions as strategic initiatives or change initiatives as it focuses on all interactions among managers. More specifically, we examine how managerial interactions influence the perceived legitimacy of top management intentions, and thus the degree to which strategy unfolds in ways consistent with intentions. Our intended contribution is to present an inductively derived model that considers content and process elements to explain consistency between intended and realized strategy.

PREVIEW OF THE MODEL

Although this model is the outcome of the analysis of the multiple case study we have inverted the analytical approach used during the research process. This inversion has been used for presentation purposes only, providing the reader with a summary of the outcome at the outset using a suspense structure (Yin, 1994). This summary is presented here as an overview of its main elements (see Figure 10.1).

First, strategic intent is represented as an intended 'product-market configuration' (Miles and Snow, 1978). Second, vertical and lateral interactions (managerial interplay) produce legitimacy of strategy, which represents a necessary intermediate condition leading to consistency between intended and realized strategy. As described here, legitimacy of strategy comprises two elements or dimensions: cognitive and normative (Scott, 1995). The cognitive basis for legitimacy stems from organizational members 'buying in' to a common conceptualization of strategy, while the normative basis comes through concept development, where organizational members come to understand operational implications of strategy and their specific roles and responsibilities to it. The extent to which these conditions are met determines the degree to which intended strategy is understood and viewed as legitimate. The third element, the consistency between intended and realized strategy, represents the outcome variable that results from the pattern of managerial interactions and the degree of strategic legitimacy achieved.

The model assumes that such intent is stable over relatively long periods of time. As described here, therefore, strategic intent defines the boundaries of managerial discretion and the 'umbrella' under which strategy is developed through managerial interplay (Mintzberg and Waters, 1985). The quality and nature of vertical interactions affect the degree to which the strategy achieves a cognitive basis of legitimacy within the organization, while the quality and nature of lateral interactions affect its normative basis of legitimacy. Said differently, vertical interactions

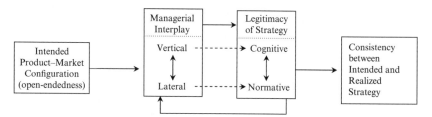

Figure 10.1   Consistency between intended and realized strategies

mostly transfer knowledge either from the bottom up or the top down, and constitute the process by which members of the organization come to understand and accept a shared underlying strategic logic (Prahalad and Bettis, 1986). Conversely, lateral interactions primarily involve knowledge creation where initiatives supporting the broad intent are designed, developed and tested for feasibility. Through this 'proof of concept' process strategy achieves a normative basis of legitimacy in the minds not only of top management but throughout the organization.

The remainder of the paper is organized as follows. The next section describes the research method and provides an overview of the case studies. We then draw from the case data and strategy process literature to develop our model of managerial interplay in detail and to explicate theoretical linkages with intended strategy and the external environment. Finally, in the last section we discuss the limitations of our approach and highlight implications of the model for future strategy process research.

METHODS

The research was conducted in two phases. During the first phase, we examined the strategy process of six Spanish-based organizations, where interactions between managers were an outstanding trait. We chose to use a qualitative method as the best way to develop insight into what determines the realization of strategic intent. In the second phase we drew from existing theories in strategy and institutional theory to inform the development of a theoretical model of managerial interplay.

Research Setting: The Six Case Studies

The multiple case design used in this research supports a 'replication logic' where a set of cases is treated as experiments, each serving to confirm or disconfirm a set of observations (Yin, 1994). The rationale is to analyse each case independently and sequentially to learn how the theoretical interpretation changes with new data. The unit of analysis used is the strategy-making process, both formal and informal, of each organization. In particular, we examined whether, within each strategy-making process type, strategic legitimacy was replicated as a result of managerial interplay.

By considering a range of organizations, the design aims at external validity typical of multiple cases (Yin, 1994). Table 10.1a describes the basic elements of the six organizations studied. Each organization's strategy process is concisely described in Table 10.1b. All studied firms are

Table 10.1a   Description of the six organizations studied

Organization	Main Industry	Self-reported measure of performance in 2003	Synthetic name for their strategy process	Strategy process participants (% total managers)
Inssubanc	Insurance	16% profit increase over last decade	MEETING POINT	50 (86.0%)
Engconsult	Consulting and engineering	Sustained growth for last five years	SPREAD OUT	80 (87.5%)
Techno	Technology IT (subsidiary)	Growth over the last three years	CASCADE	80 (60.0%)
Prosteel	Steel manufacturing	Stable and sustained growth	SIMON SAYS	120 (50.0%)
Refoil	Oil refinery (subsidiary)	Stable and sustained growth	NESTED	30 (66.7%)
Mobility	Mobility-related services	25% turnover increase for the last five years	CLOSE KNITTED	100 (80.0%)

similar in that they operate in Spain and reported a positive performance up to 2003. Yet, each is different in its approach to strategy-making and, in particular, its degree of managerial participation in the strategy process. These differences are reflected in the name given to each organization shown in Table 10.1a. Due to the sensitivity of the issues involved, the names of the organizations have been disguised.

Theoretical selection of the cases (Glaser and Strauss, 1967) attempted to include variation in vertical and lateral interactions associated with a range of strategy-making types (Hart, 1992) and was based on two criteria. First, to ensure the phenomenon we wanted to study (participation in strategy-making) was present, we only considered firms that included a relatively broad number of managers in their strategy process. Second, to ensure a range of strategy-making types each of the selected firms was somewhat different in their approach to strategy-making. To achieve these goals, a preliminary list of 35 organizations was contacted, through a 15- to 30-minute telephone interview. Each organization was asked for both the extent to which they encouraged interactions among managers and a description of their strategy process. Interview transcripts were then coded against Hart's strategy-making types (e.g. command, symbolic, rational, transactive and generative) and the six selected cases were chosen as the best available for study. The main modes used by each case appear in Table 10.1b.

Data Collection

Data were collected from three main sources: semi-structured interviews, archival and public documents, and a five-hour focus group (interactive discussion) session. All interviews were carried out between 2003 and 2004. The interactive discussion group was held in November 2003, and archival data continued to be gathered until 2004. Table 10.2 summarizes these sources.

Interviews
Of a total of 30 interviews, 24 were in-depth semi-structured interviews with senior and middle level executives in the six cases studied. An interview protocol ensured that the same steps and themes were covered in each interview, aiming at reliability (Yin, 1994). The themes concerned the frequency, outputs and improvements made and difficulties encountered regarding the strategy process, how revisions to strategy were achieved when needed, and organizational factors such as satisfaction, agreement, coordination, autonomy and delegation. Across these themes, we asked about managerial interactions. Early in the research process, interviews helped develop an understanding of the strategy process in each organization. To consolidate this understanding a narrative profile, based on initial interviews and archival data, was developed for each case (Miles and Huberman, 1994; Pentland, 1999; Silverman, 2001). Interviewees and at least one other executive in each company were then asked to independently read, revise and validate these profiles. Contrasting our account with those of research subjects in focal firms increased accuracy and minimized interpretation errors (Yin, 1994). The outcome was a set of strategy process profiles that were regarded as accurate descriptions by the organizations studied. In subsequent interviews emerging insights and conclusions were iterated back to respondents for refinement and validity. Throughout the process, we used multiple informants and checked archival data to avoid possible interview bias. To ensure data integrity, most interviews were recorded, transcribed immediately and stored in a secure database.

Table 10.1b   Synthetic description of the strategy process for each case

---

Inssubanc (Meeting point):   **Main Mode: Transactive**
They structured their strategy process to foster middle and lower levels of
the organization to share the company's strategy. Once the six top managers
have decided a broad strategic intent, synthesized in 20 corporate goals, all 43
managers have to prepare the argument of how they can contribute from their
responsibilities. Then, within the group of each manager's unit and through
deliberation they have to come up with objectives and projects that converge
to top management's corporate strategy. Then, top management invites each
member of the middle management to propose his/her unit's goals and projects
to top management. Through discussion and negotiation an agreement is reached
between top management and each unit. This formal interaction between top
and middle level management forced middle managers to look cross-functionally
instead of only at their unit. The results of this practice have been that the
owners of goals and projects are middle managers and they drive subsequent
action.

Engconsult (Spread out):   **Main Mode: Generative**
The process is scarcely formalized and the bulk of the strategy is developed
on a need-to-know basis. Born as an engineering firm formed by freelance
professionals, this company favors the spirit of 'free association' and rejects
hierarchical levels to push the organization to stay a network of professionals.
A managerial base of 80 sets every five years the broad but challenging
organizational purpose together with breaking objectives for the future. The CEO
with the management team would annually tour the offices worldwide addressing
the key challenges the company faces. Habitually, middle level managers, mainly
project managers and office managers, in close contact with the customers, offer,
sell and develop ad hoc projects. For instance, should a new capability be needed
to serve a customer, the company would either learn or buy such capability.
Strategy then emerges from lower levels closely coupled with market needs.
Strategy-making is linked to the development projects, which result from middle
managers' decisions, inspired by a challenging strategic intent.

Techno (Cascade):   **Main Mode: Rational**
Organized into four main business groups, this subsidiary has evolved from a
highly structured planning process into a more result-oriented system. Strategic
reflection is carried out by the business group top management team, which then
incorporates the guidelines from headquarters, adapting them to local needs.
This turns out to be the strategic intent within which each department and finally
each person states his or her objectives on a participative basis. The strategy
to go to market is devised on the basis of the local needs and the requirements
from headquarters at each business. Once locally defined to go to market, the
requirements in products and distribution channels are allocated. Results are
tracked every four months by the top management team of each business.

Table 10.1b   (continued)

Prosteel (Simon says):   **Main Mode: Command**

Their strategy process is hierarchical and yearly based. In a one-day retreat, the
CEO marks the future strategic intent of the group and each business specifies
its proposals of individual strategic lines. About 120 managers participate in this
retreat. Each business must present a coherent and agreed upon set of lines to be
approved by the CEO. Rather than imposing the CEO's views it is sought after
that executives are convinced of their proposals. Once proposals turn into official
strategy, they are tracked monthly. Nevertheless, the CEO would regularly
challenge managers to take ambitious projects on board. The CEO, as the
founder of the group, is the main change driver. Each business is to get approval
from the CEO for any investment they anticipate. Any emergence would have to
go up the hierarchy for approval as well.

Refoil (Nested):   **Main Mode: Symbolic**

Vertical interactions translate headquarters goals into goals that are property of
the subsidiary. Top management receives annual guidelines in key performance
areas from headquarters (HQ). Aiming at matching these guidelines with
local goals and needs, the five top managers generate a preliminary document
containing potential strategic intent. This document is then discussed in
working groups, which include these 5 top managers and 25 middle and lower
level managers. Their task is to generate via brainstorming a set of initiatives
within a performance contract that is subsequently sent to HQ for approval.
Once approved, this contract becomes the strategic intent, whose achievement
is tracked by the group that proposed it. In parallel, there are five strategic
integration groups (SIGs) in operation, which cut across the functional areas
including members from all functions, who are renewed each year. Their tasks
are to develop enhancement projects in the key areas outlined in the performance
contract, and lateral interactions tend to happen within these SIGs

Mobility (Close knitted):   **Main Mode: Transactive**

The process sets off by collecting feedback from the previous strategic exercise.
Next, about 100 persons, in working groups coordinated by the planning
department, take part in raising issues on the external analysis. The key premise
at this stage of analysis is to consider no internal restrictions. The internal analysis
follows, carried out in a similar fashion and it incorporates internal restriction to
the whole scrutiny. The results from these analyses are the main input for the six
top managers to produce the strategic intent. This purpose takes the form of a set
of strategic lines that serve as an umbrella to develop each business' strategy. Each
business would collectively construct a set of objectives tied with specific projects
to contribute to the organizational purposes. The contribution is tested out in an
oral presentation in front of the six top managers. Through deliberation, projects
are included or not included in the strategy. Every month top management tracks
the evolution of projects and annually objective achievement is assessed.

Table 10.2 Sources of data

Case	Interviews and profiles[a]					Archival documents		Interactive discussion group[b]	
	Total [c]	Top Man.	Line Man.	Infor-mants	Profile reviewers	Number	Examples	Participants	Position
Inssubanc	4 (1)	2 (1)	2	2	2	7	Strategic alignment (50 slide ppt), annual reports and newspaper segments	2	– Human resources manager – Organizational development manager
Engconsult	5 (1)	3 (1)	2	3	3	7	Projects reports, company's history, internal bulletins	2	– Director of innovation and technology – Branch manager
Techno	4 (1)	2 (1)	2	2	2	8	Description of objective-setting process presentation, strategic plan	1	– Director of strategic development
Prosteel	3 (1)	1 (1)	2	2	2	5	Company history, expansion business plan	2	– Director of human resources – General manager

215

Table 10.2 (continued)

Case	Interviews and profiles[a]					Archival documents		Interactive discussion group[b]	
	Total[c]	Top Man.	Line Man.	Infor-mants	Profile reviewers	Number	Examples	Participants	Position
Refoil	3 (1)	2 (1)	1	2	2	16	Strategy overview (85 slide ppt) and target definition, objective-setting report	1	– Director of human resources
Mobility	5 (1)	2 (1)	3	4	3	20	Strategic plans, strategy process presentations, objective-setting systems	3	– Director of strategic planning – 2 strategic planning analysts
Total	24 (6)	12 (6)	12	15		63		11	

Notes:

a Data collection included 24 in-depth one- to two-hour semi-structured, in-person interviews with personnel from the studied organizations. All interviews were carried out during 2003 and 2004. To enforce construct validity, the content of the first interview was written down in narrative format as a profile of the strategy process for each organization. Each organization's profile provides a detailed description of their strategy process. Subsequently, at least two different persons from each organization independently reviewed and validated their respective profiles as the true reflection of their strategy process.

b The interactive discussion group or focus group was carried out in November 2003 during five hours throughout one whole afternoon.

c Six telephone interviews, lasting about 30 minutes, were carried out for initial exploration of the strategy process characteristics for each case study. These telephone interviews are shown in parentheses.

Archival documents

The 63 internal archival documents included strategy overview presentations, descriptions of objective setting, strategy process presentations,
participants' list activities and responsibilities, strategic plans, business
plans, organizational charts, corporate bulletins and annual reports.
These documents constituted a valuable primary data source and also
aided the cross-checking process. In total, 1196 document pages were filed
into a database for accessible retrieval (Miles and Snow, 1978).

Interactive discussion group

Following the interviews, each organization was invited to participate
in an 'interactive discussion group' (Balogun et al., 2003) or focus group
(Berg, 2004). In total, 11 participants representing all six organizations
attended a five-hour afternoon session in November 2003. The session
focused on individuals' opinions, attitudes, beliefs and memories about
the phenomenon of interest, i.e. interactions occurring during the development of strategy (Balogun et al., 2003). Through this process, we were
able to actively compare approaches across and within organizations.
To facilitate the session, we used a set of questions that helped guide the
dialogue. The questions, along with all six organizations' strategy profiles,
were given to participants ahead of time. This encouraged comparative
discussion and resulted in rich insights into the variability of interactions
among managers. Researchers acted only as moderators (Berg, 2004),
allowing attendees to shape how the issues were addressed (Krueger,
1999). The session was recorded and transcribed immediately into a 41-
page document.

Data Analysis

Data were analysed via content analysis. Iterating between the data and
existing theories, the analysis unfolded transformed data segments into
theoretical elaboration (Berg, 2004). Transcriptions of the interviews, the
focus group and the process profiles, along with the archival data, were
reviewed, making side notes and comments in thematic coding fashion
(Glaser and Strauss, 1967). During this process, whenever a statement by
an interviewee seemed dubious, it was verified with another interviewee
and/or with archival data. It was during this phase that we started identifying the distinct use of recurrent phrases and words that challenged
the premise of strategy-making being either top down or bottom up.
While interviewees acknowledged that no initiatives took root without
top management's consent, they also noted that strategies without broad
managerial acceptance did not take root either. In order to eliminate

redundancies and contrasting previous theory with data, we grouped all emerging categories into the main constructs presented in Figure 10.1. This step, apart from achieving data reduction, produced the theoretical model.

A MODEL OF MANAGERIAL INTERPLAY IN STRATEGY-MAKING

Building on the description in the introductory section, the model can be summarized as follows. The firm's product-market configuration determines the open-endedness of strategic intent, which in turn triggers interactions between managers (managerial interplay). These interactions then determine the degree to which a strategy is viewed as legitimate within the organization. Legitimacy of strategy then influences the consistency between the originally intended strategy and realized strategy.

Legitimacy of Strategy

A primary focus among scholars of institutional theory is how institutions at societal, organizational and sub-organizational levels achieve legitimacy. That is, how do formalized rules, social mores, norms, etc. that define social roles and constrain individual behavior become justified, and supported by necessary constituents? In the present study, legitimacy of strategy refers to the extent to which organizational actors accept, support and are willing to put forth effort towards an organizational strategy.

Institutions are seen as comprising regulative, normative and cognitive elements and each of these provides a basis for legitimacy (Scott, 1995). The early strategy literature, for example, took a regulatory perspective, stressing authority associated with hierarchy and strategic controls in its development of the formulation–implementation dichotomy (Schendel and Hofer, 1979). More recent literature assumes strategy-making to be a social learning process where strategies evolve through complex social interactions (Floyd and Wooldridge, 2000; Mintzberg, 1990). Consistent with this latter view, data from the present study suggest that interactions among managers both between and across organizational levels provide cognitive and normative bases for legitimizing organizational strategy.

The concept of legitimacy emerged in the present study from the unanimous view, among the cases studied, that consensus was either too costly to achieve or was not achievable at all. Among the study's informants, pursuing consensus or agreement was perceived as 'the way to never reach a decision'. In contrast, the common view among the managers in the study was that achieving 'buy in' coupled with knowledge development more accurately described the mechanism by which strategies were coordinated and executed. While the notion of consensus or agreement was perceived as involving compromise, legitimacy of strategy as derived from the case data can more accurately be described in terms of knowledge transfer and creation where strategy, grounded in a set intent, emerges as an appropriate course of action.

The conception of consensus has evolved from an 'agreement of all parties to a group decision' (Dess and Origer, 1987: 313) through a general agreement of the top management team (Dess and Priem, 1995) to an agreement on priorities among managers (Floyd and Wooldridge, 1992). Yet limited agreement on the nature and measurement of the consensus construct exists, and to accommodate recent thinking strategic consensus is defined as 'the shared understanding of strategic priorities among managers at the top, middle, and/or operating levels of the organization' (Kellermanns et al., 2005: 721). In sum, consensus hinges on reaching a common ground to achieve coordination. Conversely, strategic legitimacy centers on shaping a higher order principle to then develop knowledge on how to achieve it.

Institutional theory holds that organizational legitimacy is acquired either by conforming to the social system in which organizations are embedded, by altering the social system itself, or by a combination of both (Dowling and Pfeffer, 1975; Suchman, 1995; Zucker, 1989). Analogously, organizational members in the cases studied constructed strategic legitimacy by conforming, by changing the strategy or through a hybrid that combined conformance and change. As can be seen in Table 10.3, legitimacy by conformity occurred when top management communicated strategy downward and organizational members carried out the strategy. This form of legitimacy is represented in the study by the case of Prosteel. In contrast, Engconsult represents an opposite extreme form of legitimacy, where line (middle) managers engaged in lateral interactions to develop specific operational projects. In the remaining cases the patterns of interactions generated a more multi-faceted form of legitimacy with both cognitive and normative bases.

The Intended Product-Market Configuration

Strategic intention, characterized by the firm's product-market configuration, serves as a starting point for managerial interplay. Established by top management, it varies from rather broad, open-ended guidelines to narrowly bounded, constrained direction. Broadly articulated, open-ended intentions as in Engconsult provide leeway for and encourage managerial

Table 10.3 Legitimacy of strategy and its components[a]

Case	Legitimacy of strategy		Cognitive basis		Normative basis	
	Legitimacy description	Examples (sources of data)	Cognitive description	Examples (sources of data)	Normative description	Examples (sources of data)
Inssubanc	*Legitimacy based on both elements.* Ownership of strategy comes from involvement and alignment with the product–market configuration	'The basis of the process is that each middle manager becomes fully responsible of their business unit, but at the same time they have to be integrated with the corporate objectives' **(Profile p1)**	The strength achieved by giving and taking strategic knowledge	'Once we have issued targets within our unit, at almost the same time we are asking ourselves what action plan will make the targets work. One thing goes next to the other; actually don't ask me which one comes first' **(Int. 2 p2)**	Each part of operations has to be integrated with the total	'We are all in the same ship, even if individually each one is in a part we all have to get to the same port' **(Int. 2 p5)**

Engconsult	*Legitimacy based mainly on Normative.* To produce new business ideas is the driver within an ambiguous framework	'First the framework is set, each unit elaborates their particular strategy by themselves with maximum participation, then alignment with the framework is assessed' (**ID Group, p7**)	It is the set of boundaries of the organization, which could be altered should new businesses emerge	'In fact we've got a general vision of us as a group of professionals and accordingly share a set of values, and then new businesses emerge naturally aligned with those values' (**ID Group p31**)	The key driver to allow generation of projects and knowledge creation	'Debate and discussion among (line) managers aim at generating new ideas that can become strategic and at the same time coordinate knowledge across geographical, technical and functional units' (**Profile p6**)
Techno	*Legitimacy based on both elements* Acceptance of strategy relies on owning a portion of the general objectives combined with incorporation of local knowledge	'Deployment of objectives from the business plan down to the individual level is standard at Techno. We aim at aligning the objectives at different levels and each one has specific metrics' (**Profile p3**)	Is an integrative configuration that encourages common effort	'At the general level, well we must achieve a certain market share, then what do we do to achieve it, what marketing, production, distribution, from there we go down deploying objectives and involving people' (**ID Group p4**)	The formal strategy process builds in knowledge on how to go to market	'Specifically the 'go to market' decision describes how resources are allocated, marketing, administration and process management and it is a result of group deliberation within each unit' (**Profile p3**)

Table 10.3 (continued)

Case	Legitimacy of strategy		Cognitive basis		Normative basis	
	Legitimacy description	Examples (sources of data)	Cognitive description	Examples (sources of data)	Normative description	Examples (sources of data)
Prosteel	*Legitimacy based only on cognitive* Acceptance of strategy relies on the leader's authority and capacity-knowledge	'In our case I think that the key is leadership. One leader may generate enthusiasm while others can't' **(ID group p25)**	It is the respect granted to the strategy based on the CEO's expertise	'At the end of the day, I'd rather be told and be told in detail what to do, and then I can manage from then onwards' **(ID Group p6)**	Limited to requesting explanation from top management	'When we speak of how to execute, then people would like to have a say on the decision, a bit more freedom should be given, their opinions could be heard, even if only as opinions' **(ID Group p13)**
Refoil	*Legitimacy based on both elements* Acceptance of strategy relies on ownership of the company objectives and transversal execution	'The process of involvement of people with the objectives of the company has allowed the generation of sense of ownership amongst employees,' **(Profile p2)**	Is a set of rules to take on board and adapted to local needs	'Top management proposes a strategy, based on the regional strategy, to be taken on board by the people' **(Profile p2)**	To articulate executable tactics by understanding courses of action and their consequences	'If I want a team to assess something, I just have to get them together and make them work towards where they want to go, which may not coincide with where top management wants them to go.' **(ID Group p25)**

	Legitimacy based on both elements			
Mobility	Acceptance of strategy relies on shared knowledge and participation to generate meaning	'We have developed alignment amongst the people who define what are we going to do in a top down fashion and the ones who design how we'll go about it, across the company' (ID Group p9)	Is a shared and accepted framework that provides boundaries for courses of action	'This is the framework, and we can move within it. To get where we want we are going step by step, next year we might attempt to go further. It is key to connect short, medium and long range' (ID Group p38)

Producing and assessing initiatives to attempt fulfilling the strategic intent	'There is no other better way to define how, in terms of actionable ideas, than promoting participation amongst middle managers, since this generates acceptance' (ID Group p10)

Note: ª These categories have been developed using as evidence interviews, profiles and the ID group iterating between data and theory. Each example shows the sources of data in parentheses.

interplay, while more tightly defined direction as in Prosteel constrains and discourages broad-based discussion of strategy. In between, however, managerial interplay is allowed to happen, albeit controlled, as happened in the rest of the cases.

Managerial Interplay

Managerial interplay represents the entire set of social interactions, both vertical (between managerial levels) and lateral (across managerial levels), regarding strategy. By encompassing both types of interaction, managerial interplay characterizes the extent to which these interactions are linked together. As data in Table 10.4 show, vertical interactions appeared balanced with lateral interactions in the case of Inssubanc and Mobility. For the rest of the cases one type of interaction predominates. In all cases, however, both types of interactions are linked in such a way that managerial roles match. While this is largely the result of case selection, it seems reasonable to speculate that decoupled vertical and lateral interactions would hinder the legitimating process.

In distinguishing managerial interplay from previous descriptions of how managers interact during strategy-making it is important to note the process by which the concept was inductively derived from the data. Our original lens was to examine firm processes through the conventional bottom-up top-down framework common in the strategy process literature (Dutton et al., 2001; Floyd and Wooldridge, 2000; Hutzschenreuter and Kleindienst, 2006; Ketokivi and Castañer, 2004; Lovas and Ghoshal, 2000; Mintzberg and Lampel, 1999). Yet, as our inquiry began to examine how bottom-up projects were generated, it was evident that a distinctive process that included a mix of vertical and lateral interactions was taking place. In Mobility, for example, a middle manager described the bottom-up process as follows,

> Daniel look, something has occurred to me. What do you reckon? Can we do it? What do you think? Shall we look into it? . . . Then we work out an approach and kick off the analysis, see if it fits our strategy and we begin digging . . . only when we had gone through this phase we took it up [to top management].

Recurrent descriptions of this type led us to realize that an important process was being overlooked, namely lateral interactions. The generation of bottom-up projects was linked to lateral interactions. Moreover, top-down processes also generated a variety of lateral interactions. Table 10.4 illustrates how vertical and lateral interactions occurred across the cases and how they configured to shape realized strategy.

Table 10.4 Managerial Interplay[a]

Case	Managerial interplay description	Examples (sources of data)	Vertical interactions (VI)	Examples of VI (sources of data)	Lateral interactions (LI)	Examples of LI (sources of data)
Insubanc	Balanced vertical and lateral interactions Matching roles: Top management encourages bottom-up initiatives and middle managers take part in generating them	'Middle managers' goals must be argued in such a way that they convince top management of how they contribute to organizational goals' **(Profile pg2 par 1)**	VI: General guidelines come from the top and specific goals come from the bottom	'After learning the basic guidelines from top management each middle manager must in turn present their unit's objectives to top management' **(Profile, pg1, par 2)** 'The planning process acts as an element to transfer knowledge between the different departments, making coordination and decision-making easier' **(Arch data, A. Report 2002 pg35)**	LI: Projects are developed within units to attempt realizing intended product-market configuration	'You are much better prepared if you gather ideas from people besides you who know much more on specific areas' **(ID group. pg14)** 'The objectives of each unit are integrated, by exchange of ideas, no unit can ignore the others by running their own show' **(Int. 2 pg 5)**

Table 10.4 (continued)

Case	Managerial interplay description	Examples (sources of data)	Vertical interactions (VI)	Examples of VI (sources of data)	Lateral interactions (LI)	Examples of LI (sources of data)
Engconsult	Mainly lateral interactions Matching roles: Top management sponsors and endorses bottom-up initiatives, while middle management generates initiatives and takes risks	'We have encouraged all initiatives aiming at creating and transmitting knowledge, facilitating internal communication and fostering interactions among units' (**Arch data, A. Report 2002 pg48**)	VI: Largely vast communication of the broad boundaries of the product-market configuration	'Any new business opportunity is always taken on board. Even if we do not have the capability, we will develop it' (**Int. 2 pg 2**) 'Our company uses a bidirectional flow. Once general guidelines and boundaries are set, it is different heads boiling innovative ideas what opens new possible futures, maybe different from anticipated' (**ID group pg1**)	LI: Ad hoc projects that define the product offering by generating any needed knowledge	'We have intentionally built-in a participation-reflection component so every one designs strategy and aligns it, align the strategy of different groups, areas, business units, and technical and geographical'(**ID group pg2**) 'Most times these ad hoc plans are negotiated and carried out between business units and offices' (**Profile pg6 par 2**)

Techno	Vertical interactions are relatively stronger than lateral interactions. Matching roles: Top management evaluates and controls while middle managers tend to follow the system	VI: Broad goals from HQ are deployed to the subsidiary and then in turn to each department and then to each employee. 'Goals and objectives are deployed down the hierarchy to the individual level so that each objective has an owner' (**Profile pg3 par 4**)	'Participation is about the lower levels believing and trusting the TMT and the TMT generating fruitful discussion and debate' (**ID group pg21**) 'Cascading of objectives from the top and then bottom up achieves aligning' (**ID Group p7**)	LI: Involvement of middle and line managers is continuous in formulating plans or developing needed capabilities	'If we receive a specific strategy and the current organization does not allow us to achieve it, then we can re-skill managers to attempt achieving it later' (**ID group pg10**) 'Involvement of line managers in designing plans is essential in them buying in ' (**Profile pg2 par 2**)
Prosteel	Mainly vertical interactions. Matching roles: Top management plays a command role while the remaining managers conform	VI: The CEO announces the product market configuration in detail while the remaining managers may propose tactics. 'From broad strategic lines, each business sets their strategy which is translated into budgets that are controlled monthly' (**Profile pg3 par 3**)	'Bottom up initiatives must fit the corporate mandate, if not initiatives must be reformulated' (**Profile p2**) 'Look, this is the strategy we have decided, for such and such reasons, yet what really matters is that you have to explain it clearly down the ranks' (**ID group pg11**)	LI: Mostly for implementation tactics, which are developed by line managers rather disjoined from top managers	'It is worth to become involved if you have a say, if not as in our case it is better to be told what to do' (**ID group pg6**) 'Now if I wanted to involve middle managers in making strategy, it would take three, four, I don't know how many months. We simply cannot afford it' (**ID group pg13**)

Table 10.4 (continued)

Case	Managerial interplay description	Examples (sources of data)	Vertical interactions (VI)	Examples of VI (sources of data)	Lateral interactions (LI)	Examples of LI (sources of data)
Refoil	Vertical interactions are relatively stronger than lateral interactions Matching roles: Top management acts as facilitator while middle managers agree to participate	'HQ sends goals that are adapted by TM and proposed to MM. Middle managers then negotiate to include and exclude elements' (**Profile pg3 par 2**)	VI: TM negotiates feasibility of specific plans while MM incorporate, specifics of the business	'Promoting participation has created a feeling of ownership of strategy in employees' (**Profile p2**) 'Involvement can cause contradictions that require adaptation of the strategy proposed by top management' (**ID Group p9**)	LI: Is encouraged for relevant issues and coordination is sought through creation of know-how	'Overlapping the functional structure we created strategic integration groups to favor coordination across units' (**Profile pg3 par 2**) 'Participation is effective when it is something important and when an answer will be given back to lower levels' (**ID group pg36**)

Mobility	Balanced vertical and lateral interactions Matching roles: Top management enables participation while middle and lower levels learn and improve by making strategy workable	'Based on the framework of corporate strategy, each business collectively develops objectives and projects to contribute to the corporate strategy' **(Profile pg2 par 4)**	VI: TM gives guidelines that MM uses to design projects to fulfill the intended product-market configuration. It's a two way street.	'Top management gathers data on external and internal analysis from middle managers to come up in turn with the corporate strategy, but it is dual since middle managers then develop the projects to attempt achieving corp. strategy' **(Profile p2)** 'Enhancing credibility by discussing facts rather than advocating individual interests favors the relationship between top and middle' **(ID Group p27)**	LI: Is instrumental in generating knowledge to define how to achieve the strategic intent	'Involvement is essential in defining how to achieve a strategy and in generating commitment. Contacting colleagues develops the know-how and commitment' **(ID group pg10)** 'The creation of meaning by group deliberation connects business strategy and implementation tactics' **(ID group pg1)**

Note: ª These categories have been developed using as evidence interviews and profiles, the ID group as well as arch. data. Each example shows the sources of data in parentheses.

229

Vertical interactions (and knowledge transfer)
Overall, the data suggest that vertical interactions facilitate knowledge transfer between managerial levels. From the top down, vertical interactions communicate intentions to middle managers and operational levels. From the bottom up, vertical interactions channel information about project proposals from operational and middle levels to top management. As shown in Table 10.4, vertical interactions tend to be formal and episodic, characterized by presentations, specific retreats and workshops. The key outcome of vertical interactions is a multi-level understanding and acceptance of strategy, i.e. a cognitive basis of legitimacy.

Lateral interactions (and knowledge creation)
As shown in Table 10.4, lateral interactions often generate new strategic knowledge by developing and evaluating concepts that can be translated into strategic initiatives. In so doing, lateral interactions establish links and coordination among different units within an organization. Although they tend to be continuous and informal, lateral interactions are importantly influenced by formal administrative systems, e.g. planning departments and reward systems. Lateral interactions can be seen as 'costly' as they distract line personnel from day to day, operational, activities. In the cases studied, lateral interactions varied from basic assessment of conceptually simple strategies demanding a small number of interactions to the creation of more complicated strategies demanding more participants and a greater number of interactions. In all cases, however, the outcome of lateral interactions was to some degree the development of a feasible strategy and recognition of the roles and responsibilities of various parts of the organization to its execution, i.e. a normative basis of legitimacy.

Consistency between Intended and Realized Strategy

Mintzberg and Waters (1985) suggest two basic reasons why realized strategies may differ from intentions. First, internal factors, including existing capabilities, commitments, etc., can result in unrealized intentions. Second, unanticipated challenges and opportunities presented by the external environment can cause strategy to emerge differently than planned. To the extent possible, in this study we attempted to control for major unanticipated environmental contingencies. This provided an increased focus on the model's core constructs, specifically connections between managerial interplay and strategic legitimacy.

As shown in Table 10.5, realized strategy, as judged by archival and public sources, was highly consistent with stated intentions in three of the six cases. For these firms, the data suggest that no major environmental

Table 10.5 Strategic legitimacy determines consistency between intended and realized strategy

Case	Strategic legitimacy		Consistency	Examples Strategic legitimacy (source of data)	Examples Consistency (source of data)
	Cognitive basis[a]	Normative basis[a]	Intended vs. realized		
Inssubanc	Present	Present	High	'The basis of the process is that middle managers are responsible of their unit's objectives, but at the same time these objectives must be integrated with Inssubanc's objective' (**Profile p2**)	'We have consistently achieved what we were created for, ten years ago. Depending on the measurement you get, we are first or second in the fragmented Spanish insurance market' (**Int. 1 p1**)
Engconsult	Limited	Present	Intermediate	'I ask the newcomers to read and then read again the documents in the Welcome Manual. There you will find answers to such fundamental questions as what is our mission? Which objectives we have? and how we intend to achieve them . . . We need to reinforce mutual trust to face the future challenges' (**Arch data Annual Report 2003**)	'What happens is that we work by projects. Independently of the structure each project has one person who is responsible and you may even find the CEO subordinated temporarily to this person. Our structure is quite flat' (**ID Group p30**)
Techno	Present	Present	High	'When there are too many discrepancies someone must assume the responsibility and say this is the way we go forward' (**ID Group 36**)	'The main thing we do well is to integrate higher order objectives into lower order and then into actions in the marketplace, which is simpler said than done' (**Int. 2 p1**)

Table 10.5 (continued)

Case	Strategic legitimacy		Consistency Intended vs. realized	Examples Strategic legitimacy (source of data)	Examples Consistency (source of data)
	Cognitive basis[a]	Normative basis[a]			
Prosteel	Present	Not present	Low	'We are severely dependent on top management, maybe if opinions were heard more this would help' **(ID group p15)**	'We need guidelines, push from above, but building it into systems, we lack coordination. We have problems inside if we double production with the same scheme, here the mandate is tons, which we do but what about all the rest?' **(Int. 1 p2)**
Refoil	Present	Present	Intermediate	'The main benefit of our process is that department goals are brought together and the scope is broadened to look for the general interest. The main difficulty is to convince the proponent that it is not the right moment, when a proposal does not match the strategy' **(Int. 2 p2)**	'We have a ten-year long-term plan, that most probably is too ambitious and does not pass a reality check, but it serves as a guideline for decision in the shorter term' **(ID group p39)**

| Mobility | Present | Present | High | 'While preparing to make a decision there is participation and creation of ideas, when it comes to the decision itself it is not democracy or consensus but somebody must make it taking into account the global strategy' (**ID group p6**) | 'We bounced ideas back and forth, then I spent a weekend writing a proposal I passed on to my peers, who made comments, then we got together to discuss it. Then the final document was what we presented to top management' (**Int. 2 p15**) |

Note: [a] See Table 10.3.

change occurred during the period studied. In a fourth case (Engconsult), although no unanticipated environmental changes were evident, results were not as intended in two geographical areas. In a fifth case (Refoil), a sudden and unexpected rise in oil prices resulted in incremental strategic adjustments. In the sixth case (Prosteel), although no external change was apparent, top management began to embark on an acquisition strategy without any internal deliberations. As a result the company struggled with internal challenges that resulted in a set of unrealized intentions. Thus, for different reasons Refoil, Prosteel and Engconsult represent examples where realized strategy began to depart from intentions.

Strategic Legitimacy and Consistency between Intended and Realized Strategy

Table 10.5 reveals apparent relationships between strategic legitimacy and consistency between realized and intended strategy. As observed in these cases, the presence of both a normative and cognitive basis for strategic legitimacy is associated with a high level of consistency. The only exception to this pattern is the case of Refoil, where unexpected environmental change necessitated a shift in strategy. In each of the other cases, where both a cognitive and normative basis for legitimacy existed, there was a high degree of consistency between strategic intentions and realized strategy.

In addition, the cases of Engconsult and Prosteel suggest that when either basis of strategic legitimacy is not present the consistency between intentions and realized strategy is diminished. In the case of Engconsult, for example, a lack of vertical interactions limited development of a common validation of strategy, i.e. a cognitive basis. As a result, realized strategy resulted from the emergence of multiple disconnected strategic initiatives. At Prosteel, the opposite seemed to occur. Communication of closed-ended intentions through vertical interactions drove out lateral interactions, initiative development and a normative basis for legitimizing strategy. As illustrated in Table 10.5, the resulting difficulty in realizing intentions was evident in interview data calling for increased coordination among managers.

DISCUSSION

Our purpose in this paper has been to build theory to explain the effect of management interactions on the realization of strategy. In doing so, the paper moves beyond issues of implementation described in the existing literature (Dobni and Luffman, 2003; Hickson et al., 2003; Nutt, 1999). Our emphasis on managerial interplay is consistent with previously described managerial roles (Floyd and Wooldridge, 1992, 1997) but provides an alternative focal point for strategic process research. Patterns among the two dimensions of managerial interplay have the potential to reveal issues of alignment among higher and lower managerial levels (Hart, 1992), and the mechanisms by which lower and mid level managers influence strategy (Dutton et al., 2001).

Of particular note, the importance of lateral interactions in channeling middle management's contribution to strategy-making entails constructing knowledge, and in turn producing the cognitive element necessary to the process of strategic legitimacy. Balogun and Johnson (2004) studied the critical importance of lateral interactions among middle managers for change processes in the absence of senior management. Our findings differ from theirs in that lateral interactions actively shape strategy, but seem most effective when coupled with vertical interaction. The suggestion from our findings is that decoupling of vertical and lateral interactions results in either orphan initiatives or a 'sterile' intent that fails to take root in the organization. Conflict across lateral units, as presented by Balogun and Johnson (2004), can also be explained by decoupled vertical and lateral interactions. The absence of this link obstructs effective communication of strategic intent causing divergence among lateral units. The importance of managerial interplay is that it links lateral and vertical interactions, thus allowing top and middle level managers to create and share the strategic knowledge necessary to develop the process of strategic legitimacy.

In this regard, the notion of managerial interplay relates closely to the work of Labianca et al. (2000). These authors argue that negotiation of a shared organizational schema produces its replacement. Consistent with this thinking, managerial interplay adds the notion of strategic legitimacy as a resolution mechanism for these negotiations and offers an original approach that unlocks theorizing on consensus or agreement (Dess and Priem, 1995; Iaquinto and Fredrickson, 1997; Priem et al., 1995; Wooldridge and Floyd, 1989). Past research suggests that the process of achieving consensus can overrule its benefits (Bourgeois, 1985), cause group homogeneity (Hambrick, 1998) and drive out healthy skepticism about strategy (Wooldridge and Floyd, 1990). As described here, strategic legitimacy unfolds from interactive discussions of strategy that allow for revision, concept development and organizational learning. The emphasis is less on achieving a shared understanding (Kellermanns et al., 2005) and more with developing organizational knowledge necessary to the realization of strategic intent. Thus, whereas the process of strategic legitimacy offers the opportunity for discussion and involvement, which are the benefits of consensus-building, it neither obstructs decision-making nor causes blind agreement. It does this because strategic legitimacy is based on developing higher order principles followed by developing a logic of appropriateness for what managers should do.

Implications for Future Research

Although known precautions to strengthen the study's validity and reliability were taken, limitations of exploratory, qualitative research must be considered in interpreting its results. While multiple case studies are considered more robust (Yin, 1994) than studies based on a single organization, the present study was carried out entirely within a Spanish context. Thus cultural elements may in part explain the findings. In addition, given its multiple case study design, a replication as opposed to a sampling logic was used, thus only allowing for theoretical generalization. Finally, while we attempted to eliminate potential sources of systematic bias, as in all qualitative studies, a certain amount of subjective interpretation of the data was necessary. While this approach is highly powerful for developing theory, it does not provide unequivocal results.

The above limitations notwithstanding, the constructs and relationships presented here have the potential to add new insight into the formation of organizational strategy. Although recognized in institutional theory, cognitive and normative bases of legitimacy have not been integrated previously into explanations of how strategy forms. As asserted here, each bases of legitimacy is achieved through a particular type of managerial interaction and both are necessary to the effective realization of strategic intent. By unpacking the types of understanding necessary to achieve legitimacy within organizations and linking these to managerial interactions the paper suggests new focal constructs for strategy process research.

Future research should refine and sharpen the field's understanding of these by focusing on specific relationships between patterns of managerial interplay, other process variables and outcomes of the strategic process. For example, while the observations from the cases studied can be interpreted as managerial interactions converging into a view of strategy that is both valuable and worth pursuing, future research might examine how regulatory bases of legitimacy, including rewards and incentives, influence strategic outcomes. In addition, the construct of managerial interplay proposed in this paper could be tested in a quantitative way. By using the number of vertical and lateral interactions one could measure the density of managerial interplay and by investigating the nature of these interactions one could measure the effect they have on the final strategy realized. Regarding the nature of interactions, this paper suggests that vertical interactions mostly transfer knowledge while lateral interactions mostly create knowledge. The extent to which vertical interactions transfer knowledge both ways will have an effect on the acceptance of strategy while the extent to which lateral interactions create knowledge will have an effect on how strategy translates into concrete measures. In addition to individual vertical and lateral interactions, the extent to which vertical and lateral interactions are connected will determine the consistency between intent and realized strategy.

CONCLUSIONS

The main contribution of this paper is to explain how vertical and lateral interactions taken together account for the realization of the strategic intent. All in all, this paper has shown one possible way to produce strategy through managerial interplay. In doing so, we have inductively derived a construct with the potential to overcome the difficulties associated with previous concepts such as consensus or agreement. Proposing the process of strategic legitimacy we present a feasible tool for managers and a robust concept for future research. The concept of strategic legitimacy complements existing theory and research that has looked into what makes strategy take root in middle and lower managerial levels (Balogun and Johnson, 2004; Floyd and Lane, 2000; Labianca et al., 2000). By looking at this process through managerial interplay, we have extended the conceptualization of a collaborative endeavor instead of a disjoint relationship. We have described this construct as the mechanism that resolves middle and top management interplay in such a way that goals and means are mutually accepted. Additionally, using notions of institutional theory, we have extended the use of the concept of legitimacy, turning it towards the inside of the organization and applying it to strategy formation.

REFERENCES

Balogun, J. and G. Johnson (2004), 'Organizational restructuring and middle manager sensemaking', *Academy of Management Journal*, **47**: 523–549.

Balogun, J., A. Huff and P. Johnson (2003), 'Three responses to the methodological challenge of studying strategizing', *Journal of Management Studies*, **40**: 197–224.

Bartuneck, J. M. and M. K. Moch (1987), 'First-order, second-order, and third-order change and organizational development interventions: A cognitive approach', *Journal of Applied Behavioral Sciences*, **23**: 483–500.

Berg, B. L. (2004), *Qualitative Research Methods for the Social Sciences*, Toronto: Allyn and Bacon.

Bourgeois, L. J. (1985), 'Strategic goals, perceived uncertainty and economic performance', *Academy of Management Journal*, **28**: 548–573.

Burgelman, R. A. (1991), 'Intraorganizational ecology of strategy making and organizational adaptation: Theory and field research', *Organization Science*, **2**: 239–262.

Chakravarthy, B. and Y. Doz (1992), 'Strategy process research: Focusing on corporate self renewal', *Strategic Management Journal*, **13**: 5–14.

Dess, G. G. and N. K. Origer (1987), 'Environment, structure, and consensus in strategy formulation: A conceptual integration', *Academy of Management Review*, 12: 313–330.

Dess, G. G. and R. Priem (1995), 'Consensus-performance research: Theoretical and empirical extensions', *Journal of Management Studies*, **32**: 401–417.

Dobni, C. B. and G. Luffman (2003), 'Determining the scope and impact of market orientation profiles on strategy implementation and performance', *Strategic Management Journal*, **24**: 577–585.

Dowling, J. and J. Pfeffer (1975), 'Organizational legitimacy: Social values and organizational behavior', *Pacific Sociological Review*, **18**: 122–136.

Dutton, J. E., S. J. Ashford, R. M. O'Neill and K. A. Lawrence (2001), 'Moves that matter: Issue selling and organizational change', *Academy of Management Journal*, **44**: 716–736.

Eisenhardt, K. M. (1989), 'Building theories from case study research', *Academy of Management Review*, **14**(4): 532–550.

Floyd, S. W. and P. J. Lane (2000), 'Strategizing throughout the organization: Managing role conflict in strategic renewal', *Academy of Management Review*, 25: 154–178.

Floyd, S. W. and B. Wooldridge (1992), 'Managing strategic consensus: The foundation of effective implementation', *Academy of Management Executive*, **6**: 27–40.

Floyd, S. W. and B. Wooldridge (1997), 'Middle management's strategic influence and organizational performance', *Journal of Management Studies*, **34**: 465–485.

Floyd, S. W. and B. Wooldridge (2000), *Building Strategy from the Middle: Reconceptualizing Strategy Process*, London: Sage Publications.

Gioia, D. A. and K. Chittipeddi (1991), 'Sensemaking and sensegiving in strategic change initiation', *Strategic Management Journal*, **12**: 433–448.

Gioia, D. A., J. B. Thomas, S. M. Clarck and K. Chittipeddi (1994), 'Symbolism and strategic change in academia: The dynamics of sensemaking and influence', *Organization Science*, **5**: 363–383.

Glaser, B. and A. Strauss (1967), *The Discovery of Grounded Theory: Strategies for Qualitative Research*, Hawthorne, NY: Aldine de Gruyter.

Hambrick, D. C. (1998), 'Corporate coherence and top management team', in M. Tushman (ed.), *Navigating Change: How CEOs Top Teams and Boards Steer Transformation*: 123–140. Boston, MA: Harvard University Press.

Hart, S. L. (1992) 'An integrative framework for strategy-making process', *Academy of Management Review*, **17**: 327–351.

Hickson, D. J., S. J. Miller and D. C. Wilson (2003), 'Planned or prioritized? Two options in managing the implementation of strategic decisions', *Journal of Management Studies*, **40**: 1803–1837.

Hutzschenreuter, T. and I. Kleindienst (2006), 'Strategy-process research: What have we learned and what is still to be explored', *Journal of Management*, **32**: 673–720.

Huy, Q. N. (2002), 'Emotional balancing of organizational continuity and radical change: The contribution of middle managers', *Administrative Science Quarterly*, **47**: 31–69.

Iaquinto, A. L. and J. W. Fredrickson (1997), 'Top management team agreement about the strategic decision process: A test of some of its determinants and consequences', *Strategic Management Journal*, **18**: 63–75.

Isabella, L. A. (1990), 'Evolving interpretations as change unfolds: How managers construe key organizational events', *Academy of Management Journal*, **33**: 27–41.

Kellermanns, F. W., J. Walter, C. Lechner and S. W. Floyd (2005), 'The lack of consensus about strategic consensus: Advancing theory and research', *Journal of Management*, **31**: 719–737.

Ketokivi, M. and X. Castañer (2004), 'Strategic planning as an integrative device', *Administrative Science Quarterly*, **49**: 337–365.

Krueger, R. (1999), *Analysing and Reporting Focus Group Results*, London: Sage.

Labianca, G., B. Gray and D. J. Brass (2000) 'A grounded model of organizational schema change during empowerment', *Organization Science*, **11**: 235–257.

Lovas, B. and S. Ghoshal (2000), 'Strategy as guided evolution', *Strategic Management Journal*, **21**: 875–896.

Miles, M. B. and A. M. Huberman (1994), *Qualitative Data Analysis: An Expanded Sourcebook* (second edn), Thousand Oaks, CA: Sage.

Miles, R. E. and C. C. Snow (1978), *Organizational Strategy, Structure, and Process*, New York: McGraw-Hill Book Co.

Mintzberg, H. (1990), 'The design school: Reconsidering the basic premises on strategic management', *Strategic Management Journal*, **11**: 171–195.

Mintzberg, H. and J. Lampel (1999), 'Reflecting on the strategy process', *Sloan Management Review*, **40**: 21–30.

Mintzberg, H. and J. Waters (1985), 'Of strategies, deliberate and emergent', *Strategic Management Journal*, **6**: 257–272.

Nutt, P. (1999), 'Surprising but true: Half the decisions in organizations fail', *Academy of Management Executive*, **13**: 75–90.

Pentland, B. (1999), 'Building process theory with narrative: From description to explanation', *Academy of Management Review*, **24**: 711–724.

Prahalad, C. K. and R. Bettis (1986), 'The dominant logic: A new linkage between diversity and performance', *Strategic Management Journal*, **7**: 485–502.

Priem, R. L., D. A. Harrison and N. K. Muir (1995), 'Structured conflict and consensus outcomes in group decision making', *Journal of Management*, **21**: 691–711.

Schendel, D. E. and C. W. Hofer (eds) (1979), *Strategic Management: A New View of Business Policy and Planning*, Boston, MA: Little, Brown and Co.

Scott, W. R. (1995), *Institutions and Organizations*, Thousand Oaks, CA: Sage.

Silverman, D. (2001), *Interpreting Qualitative Data: Methods for Analysing Talk, Text and Interaction* (second edn), London: Sage.

Suchman, M. C. (1995), 'Managing legitimacy: Strategic institutional approaches', *Academy of Management Review*, **20**: 571–610.

Westley, F. R. (1990), 'Middle managers and strategy: Microdynamics of inclusion', *Strategic Management Journal*, **11**: 337–351.

Wooldridge, B. and S. W. Floyd (1989), 'Strategic process effects on consensus. Research notes and communications', *Strategic Management Journal*, **10**: 295–302.

Wooldridge, B. and S. W. Floyd (1990), 'The strategy process, middle management involvement, and organizational performance', *Strategic Management Journal*, **11**: 231–241.

Yin, R. K. (1994), *Case Study Research: Design and Methods* (second edn), London: Sage.

Zucker, L. (1989), 'Combining institutional theory and population ecology: No legitimacy no history', *American Sociological Review*, **54**: 524–545.

11 Banking on ambidexterity: a longitudinal study of ambidexterity, volatility and performance

Amir Sasson and Mario Minoja

While exploration and exploitation are necessary for enhancing an organization's performance, the simultaneous pursuit of exploration and exploitation has long been considered a major organizational challenge (see further: March, 1991; Tushman and O'Reilly, 1996). Research has identified a variety of organizational arrangements, including structural, task and temporal separations, and an organizational context, that enable organizations to exploit current resources and capabilities and simultaneously explore new territories (Benner and Tushman, 2003; Gibson and Birkinshaw, 2004; Tushman and O'Reilly, 1996). Some researchers, however, doubt whether ambidexterity, the simultaneous pursuit of exploration and exploitation activities, enhances performance, arguing that organizations should primarily concentrate on their resources, management routines and knowledge flows in only one direction so as to avoid running the risk of being mediocre at both (for further discussion see: Lubatkin et al., 2006; Raisch and Birkinshaw, 2008).

The uncertainty surrounding the actual value of ambidexterity stems from both theoretical and empirical issues. A theory that explicates the emergence of ambidexterity is absent (Alder et al., 1999; Gibson and Birkinshaw, 2004). While the key research question is '[H]ow does a business unit become ambidextrous?' (Gibson and Birkinshaw, 2004: 212), previous studies have advanced conditions, such as temporal, task and structure segregations and empowerment initiatives (see: Gibson and Birkinshaw, 2004), under which ambidexterity may materialize. There is a need to further specify the factors that directly impact ambidexterity in the first place prior to examining its actual value as well as consider mediators that may affect the ambidexterity–performance relationship (Raisch et al., 2009). The lack of knowledge of such factors distorts the evaluation of the viability of the investment required, prevents the appreciation of the cost and time involved, and prevents a constructive debate on the costs and benefits of embarking on the journey to ambidexterity.

From a methodological point of view, the current research can be improved on four important points. First, the scant empirical work that directly addresses the ambidexterity hypothesis is cross-sectional in nature (Gibson and Birkinshaw, 2004; He and Wong, 2004; Lubatkin et al., 2006). Research has been advanced elucidating anecdotal evidence (Tushman and O'Reilly, 1996, 1997), simulation studies (e.g., Rivkin and Siggelkow, 2003) and cross-sectional surveys (e.g., Gibson and Birkinshaw, 2004; He and Wong, 2004; Jansen et al., 2009) in studying organizational ambidexterity. Second, research relies on perceptual ambidexterity as well as on self-reported perceptual performance. Third, it utilizes very heterogeneous samples but assumes that the dissimilar organizations studied should all strive to use the same, identical, levels of exploration and exploitation. Finally, the empirical work directly addressing the viability of the ambidexterity hypothesis discounts the dimension of time, which is so central to the materialization of the effects of exploration and exploitation on performance (March, 1991). Studies that take a longitudinal perspective of organizational ambidexterity are scarce (Raisch et al., 2009: 693). Uncertainty with regard to how ambidexterity can be achieved and to the value of ambidexterity presents a challenge for organizations in deciding whether to either focus on one direction only or explore and exploit simultaneously (Lubatkin et al., 2006).

In this paper, we directly address the issue of underspecified antecedents of organizational ambidexterity by theorizing how volatility in organizational behavior with respect to exploration and exploitation affects the attainment of ambidexterity and firm performance. Volatility refers to the instability of a firm's utilization of exploration and exploitation. We argue that high volatility injects uncertainty into the organization and that this hinders learning how to simultaneously explore and exploit. High variation in terms of the organizational utilization of exploration and exploitation prevents the internalization of experiences and increases organizational uncertainty, which renders the organization less effective in the simultaneous execution of those activities.

In addition, we examine the demand-side market/customer dimension of organizational activities. The literature on ambidextrous organizations has primarily focused on supply-side, technological and product innovations (e.g., He and Wong, 2004; Katila and Ahuja, 2002; Lubatkin et al., 2006; Tushman and O'Reilly, 1996). Exploration and exploitation are, however, conceptualized as having both supply-side technology/product and demand-side market/customer dimensions (Benner and Tushman, 2003). The literature that examines demand-side ambidexterity is in its infancy (for one notable exception see: Sidhu et al., 2007).

We provide an empirical contribution to the literature on ambidextrous organizations by testing the ambidexterity hypothesis through the use of a methodology that utilizes time-series panel data and objective measures of exploration, exploitation, organizational performance and ambidexterity. We address some of the methodological issues, including heterogeneity, cross-sectional designs and perception-based measurement, evident in previous research into the ambidexterity hypothesis, by testing our hypotheses that link volatility, ambidexterity and performance on a large sample of banks operating in Norway between 1995 and 2003.

The banking industry is especially conducive for the longitudinal empirical examination of demand-side ambidexterity-based hypotheses. Fundamental exploration and exploitation activities in banking are demand-side activities that are aligned with the *raison d'être* of banks, i.e., the amelioration of information asymmetries (Bhattacharya and Thakor, 1993). Furthermore, due to the role of banks in the economy, banks are highly regulated. These characteristics result in standardized and reliable information about the banking industry.

We find that organizational volatility impairs organizational performance, but that these effects are indirect. Organizational volatility affects a firm's ability to become ambidextrous. Ambidexterity is found not only to affect organizational performance but also to mediate the relationship between organizational volatility and performance.

The strong empirical support for the ambidexterity hypothesis and the explication of the factors that affect ambidexterity are important steps toward reconciling the proponents of ambidexterity and those who focus on only one direction. By developing a theory that explicates the antecedents of ambidexterity and empirically testing it, we here begin to address the call for the development of a theory on the attainment of ambidexterity over time (Alder et al., 1999; Gibson and Birkinshaw, 2004).

THEORY

The concepts of exploration and exploitation have been employed in multiple contexts, including organizational learning, technical innovation, post-merger integration, organizational adaptation, organizational survival and competitive advantage (Benner and Tushman, 2003; Katila and Ahuja, 2002; Levinthal and March, 1993; March, 1991). Exploration involves radical innovation, risk-taking, broad searching and increased internal variation, change and experimentation. It allows an organization to develop new capabilities and to adapt to a changing environment (Gilbert, 2006). Exploitation involves incremental innovation, efficiency, coordination, implementation and local searching (e.g., Beckman, 2006; March, 1991). It is necessary to extract rents from existing capabilities through economies of scale, coordination and cost reduction. Exploitation is necessary to achieve or reinforce the fit between strategy, structure, people and processes (Tushman and O'Reilly, 1996: 18), and is realized through incremental and continuous improvements.

The simultaneous execution of exploration and exploitation is crucial for organizational survival and prosperity (March, 1991; Tushman and O'Reilly, 1996). While exploitation positively affects short-term performance, exploration is a must for organizational survival and prosperity in the long run (Gibson and Birkinshaw, 2004; March, 1991). 'An organization that engages exclusively in exploration will ordinarily suffer from the fact that it never gains the returns of its knowledge', while 'an organization that engages exclusively in exploitation will ordinarily suffer from obsolescence' (Levinthal and March, 1993: 105). At the same time, purely explorative organizations are vulnerable to efficiency-oriented competitors; those that are merely exploitative gain returns that could be unsustainable in the long run (Lubatkin et al., 2006).

The attainment of the ability to simultaneously explore and exploit has remained rather illusory for organizations as well as for organizational scholars. While some authors cast doubt on the performance benefits of ambidexterity (e.g., Van Looy et al., 2005), others extend initial cross-sectional empirical support to take in the benefits of ambidexterity (e.g., Gibson and Birkinshaw, 2004; He and Wong, 2004). Nonetheless, a causal relationship between ambidexterity and performance has not yet been empirically established or fully grounded theoretically (Lubatkin et al., 2006).

Exploration and exploitation activities require contradictory knowledge-processing capabilities (Floyd and Lane, 2000), routines, structures (Tushman and O'Reilly, 1996) and context (Gibson and Birkinshaw, 2004). Exploitation routines may crowd out exploration routines (Benner and Tushman, 2003; Gilbert, 2006). While the combination of exploitation and exploration is imperative (Levinthal and March, 1993), their simultaneous execution remains a major challenge for organizations (Levinthal and March, 1993; Tushman and O'Reilly, 1997).

Hence, organization scholars have suggested that organizations need to become ambidextrous, i.e., to develop the ability to execute both exploration and exploitation activities simultaneously, in order to remain successful over long periods (e.g., Gibson and Birkinshaw, 2004; Tushman and O'Reilly, 1996). Early conceptualizations of ambidexterity have emphasized the configuration of activities that exhibit tradeoffs in executing cost leadership and differentiation strategies (Porter, 1980), global integration and local responsiveness (Bartlett and Ghoshal, 1989), or flexibility and efficiency in manufacturing (Alder et al., 1999). Current literature re-emphasizes the focus on activities by highlighting the ability to execute explorative and exploitative activities simultaneously. Lubatkin et al. (2006) succinctly argued that organizational ambidexterity involves those activities that underpin the exploitation of existing competencies as well as the exploration of new opportunities. Similarly, while arguing for the importance of attaining ambidexterity, Benner and Tushman (2003), He and Wong (2004) and Jansen et al. (2006) all maintained that organizations must learn how to conduct exploration and exploitation activities concurrently. Hence, we define organizational ambidexterity as the simultaneous execution of both explorative activities and exploitative activities.

The phenomenon whereby the achievement of advantages inherent in the simultaneous pursuit of exploration and exploitation is also coupled with organizational paradoxes is receiving increasing levels of attention from organizational scholars. Scholars have argued that organizations should develop autonomous businesses in order to reap the benefits of ambidexterity (Duncan, 1976; Tushman and O'Reilly, 1996). Organizational ambidexterity can also be achieved through structural separation, by locating new business development in a separate unit or by creating autonomous business units (Tushman and O'Reilly, 1996), so that innovation and exploration needs are not undermined by inertial and conservative logics. Another perspective advances the notion that, while structural separation is not a necessity, task partitioning or temporal separations are required (see further: Gibson and Birkinshaw, 2004). Finally, contemporary theory argues that ambidexterity is best achieved through the empowerment of employees to make their own judgments on how best to divide their time between conflicting demands (Gibson and Birkinshaw, 2004). The benefits of implementing the systems and processes needed to achieve ambidexterity seem in general to outweigh the costs, so long as ambidexterity takes a contextual rather than a structural form, which entails lower costs in the controlling and supervision of employees (Gibson and Birkinshaw, 2004).

Demand-Side Ambidexterity and Performance

The literature on ambidextrous organizations has primarily focused on supply-side, technological and product innovations as the context in which organizations can become ambidextrous (He and Wong, 2004; Katila and Ahuja, 2002; Lubatkin et al., 2006; Tushman and O'Reilly, 1996). Exploration and exploitation are, however, conceptualized as having both supply-side technology/product and demand-side market/customer dimensions (Benner and Tushman, 2003). An organization can 'resist the threat of obsolescence of its competences not only by developing new products and services . . . but also by entering new markets and finding new customers' (Jansen et al., 2006: 1670). The marketing literature has drawn on the concept of demand-side exploration and exploitation for many years (e.g., Kohli and Jaworski, 1990; Levitt, 1960). Demand-side exploration includes the identification and targeting of new customer groups, innovative segmentation, improved product use and substitution patterns (see further: Sidhu et al., 2007). Innovations that emerge from customers or markets are exploratory, since they require new knowledge or departures from existing skills (Benner and Tushman, 2003).

The recruitment and management of new-to-the-market customers entail organizational engagement in explorative activities. First, specific structures and routines are often needed to identify, analyse and finally capture significant and stable flows of new customers. The 'newness' of these customers to the economy often makes them unknown and unexplored within an industry environment, which leads organizations to adopt specific organizational arrangements to deal with them. Second, these customers are a source of growth and profits for companies that learn how to serve them, since they can be lead-users of emerging technologies and new and fast-growing market segments (Lilien et al., 2002). Third, they encourage product, distribution and organizational innovation that may spill over to existing customers. Finally, they can help an organization to understand and anticipate future market and demand trends.

At the same time, organizations gain significant returns from exploiting old demand-side certainties. Serving retained customers avoids search and recruitment costs, capitalizes on trust-driven relationships (Uzzi and Lancaster, 2003) and takes advantage of lower information asymmetry (Petersen and Rajan, 1994). This is not to say, however, that innovation can be overlooked. Rather, it is incremental innovation, consisting of continuous improvements and refinements of existing services, that is required to both retain customers and increase the margins that can be extracted from them through cross-selling and by exploiting opportunities to enlarge the gap between the value delivered to them and the production costs (Besanko et al., 1999).

By simultaneously managing explorative and exploitative strategies, an organization avoids the risk of sustaining experimentation costs and investments without gaining adequate returns – which would occur if there were an imbalance in favor of exploration – and the risk of losing its adaptability to environmental changes – which arises when exploration is overlooked (March, 1991). Hence, organizations that manage simultaneously to explore and exploit crucial demand-side factors obtain returns from the pursuit of old certainties while also exploring new opportunities that infuse the necessary level of variation to ensure organizational survival.

Hypothesis 1. The higher the level of demand-side organizational ambidexterity, the higher the level of organizational performance.

Volatility and Ambidexterity

How does an organization become ambidextrous? Previous research has established that the underlying ability to engage simultaneously in explorative and exploitative activities develops over a long period of time (Alder et al., 1999; Ghoshal and Bartlett, 1994; Gibson and Birkinshaw, 2004). Nevertheless, a theory that explicates the emergence of ambidexterity has yet to be developed (Alder et al., 1999). Scholars have argued that structural separation tied with a common culture and vision (Tushman and O'Reilly, 1996), shared vision tied with clear managerial career paths (Bartlett and Ghoshal, 1989), or, more generally, the organizational context, systems, processes and beliefs that shape individual-level behavior in an organization (Gibson and Birkinshaw, 2004), as well as top-management integration (Lubatkin et al., 2006) create the conditions under which ambidexterity may materialize. Further insights on how organizations attain ambidexterity can stem from examining how their engagement in exploitation and exploration evolves over time.

Regardless of the level of ambidexterity an organization has achieved at a given point in time, its engagement in explorative and exploitative activities may continuously change. An organization can increase both its exploration and its exploitation, decrease both, or increase its involvement in exploration while reducing exploitation or vice versa. We argue that volatility in organizational behavior with respect to exploration and exploitation affects the attainment of ambidexterity. Volatility refers to the instability of a firm's utilization of exploration and exploitation (Carson et al., 2006). Low levels of volatility imply that an organization has the required time to develop routines that manage internal paradoxes through experiencing the emerging levels of exploration and exploitation, and enough time to encode inferences with which to guide its future behavior. The process is gradual and incremental (Feldman, 2000). High levels of volatility entail the continuous modification of organizational routines, roles, positions and control. This continuous change renders inadequate the time needed for an organization to experience, observe, reflect and learn how to cope with the conflicting demands imposed upon it. This lack of time to encode inferences from history into routines that would guide its behavior thus negatively affects skill-building (Argote, 1999; Zollo and Winter, 2002).

High volatility may also signal that an organization is trying to exploit short-term opportunities to exploit/explore rather than to choose a strategy and craft organizational context accordingly. This shows a reactive rather than proactive approach, while the attainment of ambidexterity would require the development of specific routines, incentives and specific functions for the process to be learned (Zollo and Winter, 2002). High volatility may also signal inconsistent management (Gibson and Birkinshaw, 2004). This includes using the practices only for a short while, which generates confusion, reduces the motivation to learn, and triggers an internal struggle and resistance to change in the workforce (Barley, 1986).

Rapid and continuous change in terms of organizational exploration and exploitation requires corresponding changes in existing routines and structures in order to align organizational resource allocation, remuneration, incentive systems, hiring, training and budgeting routines with the new organizational objectives. For example, an organization that substantially alters the intensity of its engagement in explorative activities from one period to another will need to build specialized networks or other structures specifically aimed at recruiting new-to-the-market customers or exploring new technologies. Nonetheless, once built, these structures will either be dismantled or remain unexploited in the next time period through a rapid reduction in the firm's engagement in exploration.

Furthermore, the organization must adopt new, more search-oriented routines in times of organizational focus on exploration. This entails the adoption of corresponding performance evaluation systems that provide incentives for activities relating to innovation, technological breakthroughs and new customer recruitment, including new, less standardized criteria and procedures for customer evaluation. The focus on rewarding innovations and risk-taking will be short lived as the organizations will in the next period substantially amend their exploration focus. Similar effects occur in relation to resource allocation and especially hiring. Opposing organizational requirements happen when large changes take place from one period to another in terms of organizational focus on exploitation. The adoption and subsequent abandonment of organizational resource allocation, remuneration, incentive systems, hiring focus, training and budgeting routines entails the loss of learning investments (Zollo and Winter, 2002), costs (Ocasio, 1997) and risks, that lead to not being skillful at the simultaneous execution of exploration and exploitation activities.

Non-tradable assets such as ambidexterity need to be built up over a long period of time (Dierickx and Cool, 1989: 1506). Dierickx and Cool argue that a strategic asset is the cumulative result of adhering to a set of consistent policies over a period of time. Strategic assets are accumulated through a time path of flows. Supporting our arguments for a consistent pattern of investment in exploration and exploitation, Dierickx and Cool (1989: 1506) argue that a consistent pattern of resource flows is required in order to achieve a desired change in strategic asset stocks.

Taking into consideration the temporal nature of the development of capacities for action, we argue that ambidexterity is dependent on variability in the demands imposed on an organization. Capacities for successful exploration and exploitation and their ultimate combination are developed through a gradual introduction of complexities to an organization. Hence, high variability in terms of exploration and exploitation is expected to hinder the development of the underlying ability to explore and exploit simultaneously.

Hypothesis 2. The higher the volatility in engaging in exploration and exploitation, the lower the organizational ambidexterity.

The Mediation Effect of Ambidexterity

As a final point in our framework of volatility, ambidexterity and organizational performance, we propose that ambidexterity acts as a vehicle through which volatility affects organizational performance. We concur with previous research in viewing ambidexterity as a meta-capacity for action (Gibson and Birkinshaw, 2004), which is developed gradually over time (Alder et al., 1999; Ghoshal and Bartlett, 1994). The pattern of evolution of exploration and exploitation over time impacts performance by affecting the learning process through which an organization builds its ambidextrous capacity. The organizational learning gained from a gradual experimentation with exploration and exploitation activities influences the firm's performance positively. As argued above, rapid and drastic changes in the organizational utilization of exploration and exploitation hinder the attainment of ambidexterity.

The process by which an organization becomes ambidextrous tends to be conceptualized as being lengthy, bumpy, partially obstructed, complex, uncertain and hazardous (e.g., Benner and Tushman, 2003; Gibson and Birkinshaw, 2004; Tushman O'Reilly, 1996). Managers may be tempted to leapfrog the learning and gradual adaptation process that an organization is required to go through in order to become ambidextrous. They may dramatically and frequently change the organization's objectives, structures and processes in order to explore and exploit simultaneously and become ambidextrous instantaneously. Furthermore, they may exploit profit-making opportunities arising from environmental evolution without focusing on building any specific capacity. We have argued above, however, that time-compression diseconomies (Dierickx and Cool, 1989) prevent managerial leapfrogging over the accumulative learning process. Such a leap will negatively affect ambidexterity and hence also organizational performance. Similarly, the initiation of incremental changes in the organizational configuration of exploration and exploitation cannot be expected to lead automatically to improved performance. Volatility influences performance only through the lengthy and uncertain development of ambidexterity.

The cumulative nature of ambidexterity as a non-tradable strategic asset requires an adherence to a set of consistent organizational policies over a period of time. The flow or input of organizational policies by themselves is unlikely to directly produce performance effects (Dierickx and Cool, 1989). It is the gradual accumulation of these policies that is required in order to achieve a desired change in the organizational capacity to explore and exploit simultaneously and hence also in organizational performance. One method by which an organization can smooth the transition from one level of exploration and exploitation to another is to gradually introduce initiatives that address the new challenges. The abrupt change in organizational routines is likely to create struggle and resistance, which will hinder the learning that underpins ambidexterity and, in turn, negatively affecting organizational performance.

Hypothesis 3. Ambidexterity mediates the relationship between volatility and organizational performance.

DATA AND METHODS

This research employs a longitudinal design to explicate the relationship between ambidexterity, volatility and performance. Such a design has four clear advantages over previous studies. First, the incorporation of longitudinal elements augments existing literature on organizational ambidexterity. Somewhat surprisingly, the available empirical work that directly addresses the viability of the ambidexterity hypothesis discounts the time dimension when considering underlying exploration and exploitation activities. The time dimension, however, is pivotal for the materialization of the effects of exploration and exploitation. As March (1991) has argued, exploration focuses on current actions that may yield future returns, while exploitation encompasses current behavior pertaining to limited search and risk-taking that improves present returns. Cross-sectional designs are not optimal to test exploration- and exploitation-based hypotheses. The second advantage is that longitudinal construct measurement coupled with objective measures avoid common methods, retrospective recall and manager bias as well as concerns about respondents' actual knowledge (Venkatraman and Grant, 1986). Third, longitudinal research incorporates into the analysis change in organizational behavior. Fourth, longitudinal research improves the understanding of causal inferences by directly addressing the time-order criteria for the identification of causal relationships.

The dataset employed in this study is truly unique in its continuity over time and of the actors, as well as in its comprehensiveness and richness. The data were collected from multiple longitudinal sources. The dataset encompasses firm–bank relationships for 98 percent of organizations operating in Norway over the period from 1995 to 2003. The dataset provides detailed information at the firm level regarding the type and strength of firms' relationships with banks. It averages over half a million entries per year, and is not limited to listed firms, but encompasses nearly all firms in the economy irrespective of their size, age, etc. On annual bases, all financial institutions are required to disclose data encompassing the existence and nature of their relationships with firms.

We tested our hypotheses on a sample of 467 bank-year observations. We focused on banks that have built commercial customer portfolios, and hence we excluded small savings banks that primarily serve consumers. The banking industry is especially conducive for the longitudinal empirical examination of demand-side ambidexterity. Customers, which are distributed in time and space, are the main source of uncertainty, thus constituting the largest impediment to the operation of organizational technology in banking (Thompson, 1967). Exploration is attained by experimenting with new customers, which represent banks' entry into new geographical locations, new industries, new technologies and new markets. Exploitation entails committing to existing customers embedded in already explored locations and industries. For a bank, exploitation involves developing and consolidating relationships with existing customers, since long-term credit relationships with affiliated customers help banks solve problems of informational asymmetry when compiling information about organizations for use in credit decisions (Boot, 2000). Long-term credit relationships may also enhance banks' profits through more aligned financial services to customer needs and a better distribution of search and information acquisition costs over time. Not surprisingly, then, customer loyalty is a major challenge for banks (e.g., Sharpe, 1990).

Furthermore, mandatory disclosure of standardized banking data allows the comparisons made across banks to be reliable and complete, which circumvents any issue around missing or imputed values. The banking industry provides a rich empirical context for the examination of multiple organizational phenomena, including knowledge transfer and embeddedness (Uzzi and Gillespie, 2002), and director interlocks (Davis and Mizruchi, 1999). Extensive organizational research into banking has resulted in consistent and robust measures.

Measures

Bank performance

Bank returns on assets is a widely used measure of bank performance. It is utilized by both bank regulators and numerous organizational researchers (e.g., Barnett et al., 1994; Deephouse, 1999). Previous empirical research on ambidexterity has focused on self-reported performance (Gibson and Birkinshaw, 2004; He and Wong, 2004; Lubatkin et al., 2006). Gibson and Birkinshaw (2004) relied upon how senior and middle management perceived a business unit's performance over five years. Testing the ambidexterity hypothesis using objective performance data eliminates the biases inherent in the use of self-reported performance, including common-method bias, respondents' actual knowledge, retrospective recall and manager biases.

Exploration and exploitation

To verify whether bank ambidexterity is associated with bank perform-ance, we first constructed detailed measures of exploration and exploitation for each calendar year between 1995 and 2003. Previous research has suggested a wide range of operationalizations primarily based on supply-side technological exploration and exploitation, including patent search scope and depth (Katila and Ahuja, 2002), attention division and resource allocation in innovation projects (He and Wong, 2004), technical innovation (Beckman, 2006), project newness (McGrath, 2001) and product innovation (Jansen et al., 2006). Our focus on demand-side uncertainties and on actual organizational behavior, as opposed to perceived self-behavior, calls for novel operationalizations of those activities on the customer side.

Exploration in a given year was operationalized as the number of new customers divided by the total size of the customer base in the previous year. In other words, exploration is the percentage of new customers (new in the economy and for the bank, not merely for the bank) that each bank acquired in a given year out of the total number of customers that the bank had immediately prior to the acquisition of the new customers. The acquisition of such customers is explorative since it entails bank-wide searches, increased internal variation, discovery and risk-taking (March, 1991). Learning occurs within the bank–firm relationship (Uzzi and Gillespie, 2002) because newly established organizations have neither a track record nor audited accounts. Furthermore, newly established organizations are often agents of change in the economy, experimenting with new technologies, new markets and new distribution channels. Hence, the information asymmetry between banks and these customers is the most severe (Berger and Udell, 1998).

Such customers are conducive for exploratory learning for banks, since they are a source of information about new markets, new industries, new technologies and new demand trends, and hence can foster bank product innovation. As the percentage of new customers relative to the number of customers increases, banks enhance the variation in their customer sets, are involved in wide organizational search behavior, have to invest in reducing information asymmetry and are exposed to a larger amount of new information about technologies and markets.

Exploitation involves the pursuit of old certainties involving refinement, efficiency, selection, implementation and execution activities (March, 1991). Banks utilize existing knowledge of markets, technologies, distribution channels and organization-specific knowledge in refining their offerings. The banking literature emphasizes that returns to bank–firm relationships are increasing but at a decreasing rate (e.g., Petersen and Rajan, 1994). The persistence of bank–firm relationships allows banks to be more efficient in providing financial services. Banks provide firms with already developed financial services or further refine them. Continuous relationships therefore involve refinement of the knowledge acquired and the implementation and execution of services based on the initial investment in learning. In our research, exploitation in a given year was thus operationalized as the number of retained customers divided by the total customer base. Exploitation is the percentage of a bank's current customers that were also customers of that bank in the previous year. This directly controls for variations associated solely with bank size.

Ambidexterity
Our measure of ambidexterity uses the multiplicative method of exploration and exploitation (e.g., Gibson and Birkinshaw, 2004). This measure addresses two fundamental issues in empirically testing the ambidexterity hypothesis. First, in line with the literature that emphasizes that ambidexterity manifests itself in an organization's actual behavior (He and Wong, 2004; Lubatkin et al., 2006; Smith and Tushman, 2005; Tushman and O'Reilly, 1996), we examine actual observed ambidextrous behavior. Previous studies of the ambidexterity hypothesis (Gibson and Birkinshaw, 2004; He and Wong, 2004; Lubatkin et al., 2006) have relied solely upon participants' perceptions of what their organizations were doing as opposed to measuring what the organizations actually did. The second issue is that previous research that has used the multiplicative method has assumed an equality of importance between exploration and exploitation activities across a large number of industries, which were examined jointly. We focus on one relatively homogeneous industry and hence do not need

to assume that the balance between exploration and exploitation is the same across industries.

Volatility
Volatility refers to the instability of a firm's utilization of exploration and exploitation (Carson et al., 2006). When the utilization of exploration and exploitation varies rapidly and abruptly, an organization will continuously change its demands. Building on previous research (Carson et al., 2006), we operationalized volatility by measuring for each bank the average of the standard deviations of exploration and exploitation. The standard deviations are calculated from the first year for which data are available up until the year in question. The lower the standard deviations, the more the organization maintains its levels of investment in exploration and exploitation. The change in organizational activities and the corresponding demands on the organization are gradual and incremental. By contrast, high levels indicate that an organization changes its *modus operandi* frequently, i.e., it modifies frequently and/or intensively its emphasis on exploration and exploitation.

We controlled for a number of alternative explanations for bank performance:

Bank size. An increasing number of findings suggest that bank size is negatively related to bank performance (e.g., Barnett et al., 1994; Deephouse, 1999). Hence, we measured bank size as the lagged natural logarithm of bank assets.

Bank loss. We also controlled for the lagged loan loss per bank measured in terms of the percentage of actual loss of a bank's total assets. The nature of the customer set serviced can be argued to affect bank performance.

Customer-set performance. The average returns on assets of all customers affiliated with each bank controls for the current quality of the customer set. When bank customers perform well, their higher average returns on assets are expected to negatively impact bank loss.

Customer-set performance variability. Similarly, the level of variability in customers' return on assets – measured by its standard deviation – indicates the risk associated with serving particular groups of customers. Riskier customer sets will make it harder to predict returns.

Customer-set intangible assets. Banks find it more difficult to evaluate organizations that have a high percentage of intangible assets on their balance sheets. For example, organizations that invest heavily in R&D are riskier than manufacturing organizations that can pledge collaterals with high resalable values. The value of intangible assets is not only uncertain but also subject to low market value owing to its specificity. We measured customer-set intangible assets as the percentage of intangible assets of total assets averaged across each bank's customers.

RESULTS

To analyse the relationships between exploration, exploitation, ambidexterity, volatility and bank performance, we used random-effects time-series regression analysis. Similar results were found when we utilized Prais–Winsten regression models. Two preliminary tests establish the appropriateness of random effect modeling and the inclusion of year dummies. A Hausman test indicated that a random-effect model is more suitable than a fixed-effect model ($\chi = 10.22$, $d.f. = 12$, $p = 0.59$). We also examined whether year dummies should be included in the model. Taking into consideration the macro-economic effects on firms' financial behavior, bank earnings are expected to be sensitive to macro-economic conditions. A specific test indicated that it is clearly more appropriate to include year dummies in the models ($\chi = 118.62$, $d.f. = 6$, $p < 0.001$). Means, standard deviations and correlations among the variables are shown in Table 11.1.

Model 1 of Table 11.2 presents the base model including only control variables of factors affecting bank performance. As expected from the sensitivity of bank performance to macro-economic conditions, a number of the year dummies are significant. Furthermore, bank size and bank loss are negatively and significantly related to bank performance. Models 2 and 3 of Table 11.2 respectively examine the impact of exploitation and exploration on bank performance. Consistent with March's (1991) predictions, bank exploitation is positively and significantly associated with current bank performance (Model 2 of Table 11.2) and current exploration activities have a negative but insignificant effect on current bank performance (Model 3 of Table 11.2).

To evaluate hypothesis 1, which states that bank ambidexterity is positively associated with performance, we mean-centered the underlying factors before calculating their multiplicative term (Cohen et al., 2003). Thereafter, we inputted the multiplicative variable, ambidexterity, into Model 4 of Table 11.2. The coefficient for ambidexterity in Model 4 of Table 11.2 is positive and significant ($\beta = 26.90$, s.e. $= 5.36$, $p < 0.01$), hence supporting hypothesis 1. The Wald statistic reported at the bottom of Model 4 establishes the significant improvement of Model 4 in

Table 11.1 Means, standard deviations and correlations

Variable	Mean	s.d.	1	2	3	4	5	6	7	8	9
1. Bank performance	1.13	.71									
2. Exploitation	.81	.07	.22								
3. Exploration	.05	.03	.02	–.11							
4. Ambidexterity	–.00	.00	.19	.22	.50						
5. Bank size	8.30	1.41	–.23	.00	–.23	.00					
6. Bank loss	.27	.46	–.32	–.22	–.19	.06	.00				
7. Customer performance	.01	.23	.19	–.01	.09	–.06	–.13	–.28			
8. Customer performance (std)	.26	.03	.09	–.05	–.97	–.02	.30	.06	–.26		
9. Customer intangible assets	.01	.00	–.20	–.17	–.30	–.12	.15	.19	–.19	.16	
10. Volatility	.00	1.00	–.18	–.54	–.06	–.40	–.06	.26	.10	.00	.10

N = 467.

Table 11.2 Panel time-series GLS regression model of bank performance and ambidexterity

	Model 1 Bank performance	Model 2 Bank performance	Model 3 Bank performance	Model 4 Bank performance	Model 5 Ambidexterity	Model 6 Bank performance	Model 7 Bank performance
2002	−.44**	−.56**	−.46**	−.45**	−.29**	−.45**	−.44*
	(.09)	(.09)	(.13)	(.13)	(.05)	(.08)	(.13)
2001	−.07*	−.23*	−.13	−.15	−.88**	−.10	−.15
	(.10)	(.10)	(.14)	(.14)	(.09)	(.10)	(.14)
2000	.45**	.31**	.43**	.36**	.82**	.41**	.36*
	(.10)	(.10)	(.15)	(.15)	(.09)	(.10)	(.15)
1999	.44*	.29*	.37*	.36*	.69**	.39**	.36*
	(.13)	(.13)	(.15)	(.15)	(.11)	(.13)	(.15)
1998	−.04	−.12	−.00	−.09	.87**	−.03	−.10
	(.14)	(.14)	(.18)	(.18)	(.11)	(.14)	(.16)
1997	.26	.12	.24	.14	.78**	.18	.13
	(.14)	(.14)	(.18)	(.18)	(.11)	(.14)	(.18)
Bank size	−.10**	−.10**	−.11**	−.10**	−.02	−.10**	−.10**
	(.03)	(.03)	(.03)	(.03)	(.02)	(.03)	(.03)
Bank loss	−.21**	−.20**	−.20**	−.25**	.12	−.17*	−.26**
	(.06)	(.06)	(.06)	(.06)	(.07)	(.06)	(.07)
Performance	1.00	1.57	1.58	1.53	1.07	1.65	1.36
	(1.59)	(1.55)	(1.55)	(1.53)	(1.18)	(1.59)	(1.54)
Performance (std)	.53	.49	.54	.29	1.43	.40	−.08
	(1.10)	(1.07)	(1.07)	(1.05)	(.84)	(1.14)	(1.10)
Intangible assets	−2.16	−2.38	2.28	.25	−5.78	1.18	−.53
	(6.08)	(5.96)	(5.96)	(5.77)	(4.68)	(6.05)	(5.80)

	Bank performance					
Exploitation	1.63** (.42)	1.33** (.51)	1.00* (.50)	-.07 (.05)		.98 (.57)
Exploration		-1.55 (1.48)	1.50 (1.56)			1.56 (1.60)
Ambidexterity			26.90** (5.36)			28.88** (5.79)
Volatility				-.29** (.02)	-.10** (.03)	-.02 (.04)
Wald	178.96**	199.38**	240.73***	200.06**	188.79**	241.36**
R^2 within	.32	.32	.36	.16	.32	.37
R^2 between	.36	.43	.43	.78	.42	.44
R^2 overall	.29	.32	.36	.31	.30	.36

* $p < 0.05$, ** $p < 0.01$, $N = 467$, number of groups = 71, observation per group = 6.6.

comparison to Model 3, hence providing further support for the significant effect of organizational ambidexterity on performance. Table 11.1 reports that ambidexterity is correlated with exploitation and exploration (0.22 and 0.50 respectively). In order to ensure that multicollinearity between exploitation, exploration and ambidexterity does not affect our findings, we omitted both exploration and exploitation variables from the analysis. The results were unchanged. Ambidexterity remained a highly significant predictor of bank performance ($t = 6.12, p < 0.001$).

Hypothesis 2 predicts that volatility is negatively associated with organizational ambidexterity. As reported in Model 5 of Table 11.2, which has ambidexterity as its dependent variable, volatility negatively and significantly affects ambidexterity ($\beta = -0.29, p < 0.01$), thus supporting hypothesis 2.

Hypothesis 3 predicts that ambidexterity mediates the relationship between volatility and bank performance. The analysis of mediation effects involved four steps (Baron and Kenny, 1986), the first of which was to establish that volatility significantly affects the mediating variables, namely ambidexterity. We found support for this association in Model 5 of Table 11.2, discussed above in relation to hypothesis 2. The second step required the establishment of an association between volatility – the independent variable – and bank performance – the dependent variable. Model 6 of Table 11.2 examines the effects of volatility on bank performance. It provides strong support for the argument that, as organizations increase their pace in changing their *modus operandi*, their performance deteriorates ($\beta = -0.10$, s.e. $= 0.03, p < 0.01$), thus supporting the second step. The third step of mediation requires a demonstration that the mediator variable (ambidexterity) significantly impacts the dependent variable (performance) when the independent variable (volatility) is controlled for, and that the latter, volatility, is no longer significant in the model that contains the mediating variable.

Model 4 of Table 11.2, as reported above in discussing hypothesis 1, establishes that ambidexterity positively and significantly affects bank performance. As reported in Model 7 of Table 11.2, ambidexterity positively and significantly affects bank performance also when volatility is controlled for. Furthermore, with the presence of ambidexterity in the model, the coefficient of volatility is no longer significant ($\beta = -0.02$, *n.s.*). The fourth step requires the establishment of the significance of the mediated effect. We calculated the significance of the mediated effect by dividing it by the computed standard errors of the coefficient responsible for the effect. The obtained z score is highly significant ($z = -4.42$). Thus, the above tests provide support for hypothesis 3, which states that ambidexterity mediates the relationship between volatility and performance.

DISCUSSION

The objectives of this paper were to enhance our understanding of the antecedents and consequences of ambidexterity with the specific emphasis on the effects of volatility of organizational behavior with respect to ambidexterity and organizational performance. We examined the impact of exploration, exploitation, volatility and ambidexterity on organizational performance in the context of the banking industry. In doing so, we found support for the argument that ambidexterity positively and significantly impacts organizational performance. We then incorporated the concept of volatility and found that the degree of volatility in the organizational utilization of exploration and exploitation over time negatively impacts organizational ambidexterity. We also established that ambidexterity acts as a mediator between volatility and organizational performance as the effects of volatility on organizational performance are transmitted through ambidexterity.

This paper contributes to the literature on organizational ambidexterity in a number of ways. First, it provides a conceptual model that sheds light on the factors that impact the achievement of ambidexterity involved in becoming ambidextrous as well as on the value of ambidexterity to organizations. We provided a longitudinal test of the effects that volatility has on ambidexterity and organizational performance. We addressed the call for the development of a theory regarding the attainment of ambidexterity over time (Alder et al., 1999; Gibson and Birkinshaw, 2004) by introducing, elucidating and testing the effects of volatility. The lack of a consistent strategy regarding exploration and exploitation creates organizational unrest and uncertainty, which hinder the development of ambidexterity. Our findings also suggest that ambidexterity needs to be built through a gradual and systematic process of learning. A relatively stable pattern of explorative and exploitative activities over time seems to be required both for an organization to learn how to manage them simultaneously and to internally communicate a consistent set of signals. Explorative and exploitative activities *per se* are conducive for learning through experience accumulation. A gradual and controlled process of evolution along the two dimensions of organizational learning makes it viable for an organization to build and capitalize on specific sets of structures and routines aimed at developing ambidexterity. The effective use of such structures and routines, in turn, requires a process of learning. Future research should explore the processes underlying the achievement of ambidexterity. Many questions fall into this research stream: What conditions can lead an organization unbalanced toward either exploration or exploitation to change its pattern of activities in search of ambidexterity? Which kinds of inertial forces can hamper organizational efforts toward a consistent and gradual attainment of ambidexterity? Which intra-organizational mechanisms and processes (e.g., reward systems) are the most effective for the attainment of ambidexterity? Furthermore, how can environmental variables – like stability vs. dynamism – affect the process leading to ambidexterity?

The second contribution made by this paper is that it augments the existing cross-sectional empirical literature. First, we provided a longitudinal design that is more in line with the underlying time-dependent effects of exploration and exploitation postulated by March (1991). Second, we employed objective measures of exploration, exploitation, ambidexterity and organizational performance. Third, we did not combine various industries in one study and hence did not assume that the balance between exploration and exploitation is equal across industries. We tested our hypothesis in the context of the banking industry that may represent a case similar to traditional manufacturing industries whereby organizations are engaged in exploitative activities and only to a lesser extent in explorative activities. Future research should extend this work to other industries with different features. The biotechnology industry, for example, may represent a rather different case in which organizations are much more concerned with exploration than with exploitation activities. Building on the argument advanced in this paper that the desired level of exploration and exploitation activities is industry-dependent, future research should therefore examine whether the ambidexterity hypothesis applies equally across industries that require a rather different distribution of exploration and exploitation activities.

We are aware that our operationalization of exploration and exploitation, and hence ambidexterity, presents some limitations, that could be addressed through further research. In particular, relying upon the importance of information asymmetry as established by the economics of banking literature, we focused on customer newness for a bank and for the economy to capture a bank's exploration and exploitation. Hence, we provided a dichotomous assignment of organizational activities. Valuable extensions to the operationalization of exploration/exploitation may explore refinements of the measure that include a number of dimensions of organizational activities underlying exploration and exploitation. Such refinements in terms of the multi-dimensionality of ambidexterity have the potential to further advance the contingency approach to ambidexterity (e.g., Gibson and Birkinshaw, 2004; Jansen et al., 2009) by identifying moderating and mediating variables that impact the ambidexterity–organizational performance relationship (see also Raisch et al., 2009).

Finally, we extend the literature on ambidextrous organization to include demand-side ambidexterity. While Benner and Tushman (2003) conceptualized exploration and exploitation as having both supply and demand dimensions, the conceptualization prevailing in the literature primarily emphasizes technology or supply-side effects (see: Sidhu et al., 2007). Future research should explore the effects of dual ability on firm performance. Dual ability refers to the ability of an organization to develop both supply- and demand-side ambidexterity simultaneously. Can organizations develop simultaneous abilities to explore and exploit technologies as well as customers and markets? While this dual capacity is hypothesized to be extremely rare, it may also be very valuable.

In conclusion, the current study contributes to our understanding of the antecedents of and the benefits that flow from investing in ambidexterity. 'The basic problem confronting an organization is to engage in sufficient exploitation to ensure its current viability and, at the same time, to devote enough energy to exploration to ensure its future viability' (Levinthal and March, 1993: 105). While it is challenging to explore and exploit simultaneously (Gibson and Birkinshaw, 2004; March, 1991; Tushman and O'Reilly, 1996), this study establishes that ambidexterity is valuable, but that its accomplishment requires patience and steadiness.

REFERENCES

Alder, P., B. Goldoftas and D. I. Levine (1999), 'Flexibility versus efficiency? A case study of model changeovers in the Toyota production system', *Organization Science*, **10**(1): 43–68.

Argote, L. (1999), *Organizational Learning: Creating, Retaining and Transferring Knowledge*, Boston, MA: Kluwer Academic Publishers.

Barley, S. R. (1986), 'Technology as an occasion for structuring: Evidence from observations of CT scanners and the social order of radiology departments', *Administrative Science Quarterly*, **31**(1): 78–108.

Barnett, W. P., H. R. Greve and D. Y. Park (1994), 'An evolutionary model of organizational performance', *Strategic Management Journal*, **15**(special issue): 11–28.

Baron, R. M. and D. A. Kenny (1986), 'The moderator-mediator variable distinction in social psychological research: Conceptual, strategic and statistical considerations', *Journal of Personality and Social Psychology*, **57**: 1173–1182.

Bartlett, C. A. and S. Ghoshal (1989), *Managing Across Borders: The Transnational Solution*, Boston, MA: Harvard Business School Press.

Beckman, C. M. (2006), 'The influence of founding team company affiliation on firm behavior', *Academy of Management Journal*, **49**(4): 741–758.

Benner, M. J. and M. L. Tushman (2003), 'Exploitation, exploration, and process management: The productivity dilemma revisited', *Academy of Management Review*, **28**(2): 238–256.

Berger, A. N. and G. F. Udell (1998), 'The economics of small business finance: The roles of private equity and debt markets in the financial growth cycle', *Journal of Banking and Finance*, **22**(6–8): 613–673.

Besanko, D., D. Dranove and M. Shanley (1999), *Economics of Strategy*, New York: Wiley.

Bhattacharya, S. and A. Y. Thakor (1993), 'Contemporary banking theory', *Journal of Financial Economics*, **3**(1): 2–50.

Boot, A. W. A. (2000), 'Relationship banking: What do we know?', *Journal of Financial Intermediation*, **9**(1): 3–25.

Carson, S. J., A. Madhok and T. Wu (2006), 'Uncertainty, opportunism and governance: The effects of volatility and ambiguity on formal and relational contracting', *Academy of Management Journal*, **49**(5): 1058–1077.

Cohen, J., P. Cohen, S. G. West and L. S. Aiken (2003), *Applied Multiple Regression/ Correlation Analysis for the Behavioral Sciences*, Mahwah, NJ: Lawrence Erlbaum.

Davis, G. F. and M. S. Mizruchi (1999), 'The money center cannot hold: Commercial banks in the U.S. system of corporate governance', *Administrative Science Quarterly*, **44**(2): 215–239.

Deephouse, D. L. (1999), 'To be different, or to be the same? It's a question (and theory) of strategic balance', *Strategic Management Journal*, **20**(2): 147–166.

Dierickx, I. and K. Cool (1989), 'Asset stock accumulation and sustainability of competitive advantage', *Management Science*, **35**(12): 1504–1513.

Duncan, R. B. (1976), 'The ambidextrous organization: Designing dual structures for innovation', in Ralph H. Kilmann, Louis R. Pondy and Dennis P. Slevin (eds), *The Management of Organization Design*, New York: Elsevier, pp. 167–188.

Feldman, M. S. (2000), 'Organizational routines as a source of continuous change', *Organization Science*, **11**(6): 611–629.

Floyd, S. W. and P. J. Lane (2000), 'Strategizing throughout the organization: Managing role conflict in strategic renewal', *Academy of Management Review*, **25**(1): 154–177.

Ghoshal, S. and C. A. Bartlett (1994), 'Linking organizational context and managerial action: The dimensions of quality of management', *Strategic Management Journal*, **15**(S2): 91–112.

Gibson, C. B. and J. Birkinshaw (2004), 'The antecedents, consequences, and mediating role of organizational ambidexterity', *Academy of Management Journal*, **47**(2): 209–226.

Gilbert, C. G. (2006), 'Change in the presence of residual fit: Can competing frames coexist?', *Organization Science*, **17**(1): 150–167.

He, Z.-L. and P.-K. Wong (2004), 'Exploration vs. exploitation: An empirical test of the ambidexterity hypothesis', *Organization Science*, **15**(4): 481–494.

Jansen, J. J. P., F. A. J. Van den Bosch and H. W. Volberda (2006), 'Exploratory innovation, exploitative innovation and performance: Effects of organizational antecedents and environmental moderators', *Management Science*, **52**(11): 1661–1674.

Jansen, J. J. P., M. P. Tempelaar, F. A. J. Van den Bosch and H. W. Volberda (2009), 'Structural differentiation and ambidexterity: The mediating role of integration mechanisms', *Organization Science*, **20**(4): 797–811.

Katila, R. and G. Ahuja (2002), 'Something old, something new: A longitudinal study of search behavior and new product introduction', *Academy of Management Journal*, **45**(6): 1183–1194.

Kohli, A. and B. Jaworski (1990), 'Market orientation: The construct, research propositions, and managerial implications', *Journal of Marketing*, **54**(2): 1–18.

Levinthal, D. A. and J. G. March (1993), 'The myopia of learning', *Strategic Management Journal*, **14**(Special issue): 95–112.

Levitt, T. (1960), 'Marketing myopia', *Harvard Business Review*, **38**(July–August): 45–56.

Lilien, G. L., P. D. Morrison, K. Searls, M. Sonnack and E. von Hippel (2002), 'Performance assessment of the lead user idea-generation process for new products development', *Management Science*, **48**(8): 1042–1059.

Lubatkin, M. H., Z. Simsek, Y. Ling and J. F. Veiga (2006), 'Ambidexterity and performance in small- to medium-sized firms: The pivotal role of top management team behavioral integration', *Journal of Management*, **32**(5): 646–672.

March, J. G. (1991), 'Exploration and exploitation', *Organization Science*, **2**(1): 71–87.

McGrath, R. G. (2001), 'Exploratory learning, innovative capacity, and managerial oversight', *Academy of Management Journal*, **44**(1): 118–131.

Ocasio, W. (1997), 'Towards an attention-based view of the firm', *Strategic Management Journal*, **18**(S1): 187–206.

Petersen, M. A. and R. G. Rajan (1994), 'The benefits of lending relationships: Evidence from small business lending', *Journal of Finance*, **49**(1): 3–37.

Porter, M. E. (1980), *Competitive Strategy: Techniques for Analysing Industries and Competitors*, New York: The Free Press.

Raisch, S. and J. Birkinshaw (2008), 'Organizational ambidexterity: Antecedents, outcomes and moderators', *Journal of Management*, **34**(3): 375–409.

Raisch, S., J. Birkinshaw, G. Probst and M. L. Tushman (2009), 'Organizational ambidexterity: balancing exploitation and exploration for sustained performance', *Organization Science*, **20**(4): 685–695.

Rivkin, J. W. and N. Siggelkow (2003), 'Balancing search and stability: Interdependence among elements of organizational evolution', *Management Science*, **49**(3): 290–311.

Sharpe, S. A. (1990), 'Asymmetric information, bank lending and implicit contracts: A stylized model of customer relationships', *Journal of Finance*, **45**(4): 1069–1087.

Sidhu, J. S., H. R. Commandeur and H. W. Volberda (2007), 'The multifaceted nature of exploration and exploitation: Value of supply, demand, and spatial search for innovation', *Organization Science*, **18**(1): 20–38.

Smith, W. K. and M. T. Tushman (2005), 'Managing strategic contradictions: A top management model for managing innovation streams', *Organization Science*, **16**(5): 522–536.

Thompson, J. D. (1967), *Organizations in Action*, New York: McGraw-Hill.

Tushman, M. T. and C. A. O'Reilly III (1996), 'Ambidextrous organizations: Managing evolutionary and revolutionary change', *California Management Review*, **38**(4): 8–30.

Tushman, M. T. and C. A. O'Reilly III (1997), *Winning through Innovation: A Practical Guide to Leading Organizational Change and Renewal*, Boston, MA: Harvard Business School Publishing.

Uzzi, B. and J. J. Gillespie (2002), 'Knowledge spillover in corporate financing networks: Embeddedness and the firm's debt performance', *Strategic Management Journal*, **23**(7): 595–618.

Uzzi, B. and R. Lancaster (2003), 'Relational embeddedness and learning: The case of bank loan managers and their clients', *Management Science*, **49**(4): 383–399.

Van Looy, B., T. Martens and K. Debackere (2005), 'Organizing for continuous innovation: On the sustainability of ambidextrous organizations', *Creativity and Innovation Management*, **14**(3): 208–221.

Venkatraman, N. and J. J. Grant (1986), 'Construct measurement in organizational strategy research: A critique and proposal', *Academy of Management Review*, **11**(1): 71–87.

Zollo, M. and S. G. Winter (2002), 'Deliberate learning and the evolution of dynamic capabilities', *Organization Science*, **13**(3): 339–351.

12 From theory to action: the story of one strategy
Paul N. Friga

INTRODUCTION

The professor gazed out of his windowless office and thought carefully about the task at hand. Develop a three year strategy for the consulting function at a top 20 business school. Rather than study or teach strategy, the time had come to actually craft a strategy. OK, now where to start?

The purpose of this chapter is to give you a firsthand account of a strategy professor charged with putting strategy theory to work. This is intended to be a contribution to the growing literature on the process or practice of strategy. In essence, a micro based perspective of what is actually done during the strategizing within an organization. As I began my research and outlining for this paper, it dawned on me that a reasonable approach could be to adopt my teaching philosophy of experiential learning. In my mind, experiential learning begins with the identification of relevant theory, moves to application to an actual phenomenon, and then concludes with a reflection upon the process. So that is just what I decided to do for this chapter; what follows is my 'experiential' story of strategy development for a function within the business school.

It all started when I was asked if I would be interested in coming back to the University of North Carolina (UNC) as the academic lead of the consulting programs. I was excited about the opportunity to return to my alma mater and especially about the chance to positively impact the consulting function of which I care so deeply. During the interview process, the Dean and Associate Deans asked what my strategy would be for the program; more specifically, how I would take it from 'good to great'. I certainly had familiarity with the topic of strategy given my experience in consulting (with PricewaterhouseCoopers and McKinsey) and my PhD in strategy, and here was my chance to put some of my espoused ideas to work.

The rest of the paper documents my journey of bridging strategy theory to action. I present the ideas in the general progression of the steps I took in crafting the strategy for the consulting function at UNC: internal analysis, external analysis and the actual strategy creation. I will discuss the theories I considered as well as the applied steps I took. I pay particular attention to the 'artifacts' I created along the way and share those as well. In general, I will keep the theoretical discussion to a minimum, as the primary goal is to explore the ideas in action. The final section of the paper is a discussion on key takeaways from the experience and ideas for future research.

Theory

My underlying theoretical assumption is that strategy (and 'strategizing') is alive and well (Whittington and Cailluet, 2008). In fact, crafting strategy is one of the most prominent management tools in use today (Rigby, 2005). Of course, there are theories that posit much more of an 'emergent' versus 'deliberate' philosophy (Mintzberg, 1987), but for this essay, the goal is to explore strategy formulation, realizing of course that changes and iterations will occur as the strategy is implemented (Sull, 2007).

So what is strategy? A good starting point for a definition is from one of the top selling strategy textbooks in the country, *Strategic Management – Concepts and Cases*. The goal of strategic competitiveness is for a firm to 'successfully formulate and implement a value creating strategy; and a strategy is an integrated and coordinated set of commitments and actions designed to exploit core competencies and gain a competitive advantage' (Hitt et al., 2009, p. 4). My interpretation of this guidance is that I need to do the right activities that will result in an advantage over competitors. Strategy rules also apply to non-profit entities, with an obvious difference in performance metrics (e.g. more about behaviors, satisfaction assessments and efficiency measures).

The focus on the set of activities, not only of the employees in the organization, but also of the strategist, has increasingly become a priority topic for strategy researchers. This is operationalized as 'strategy process' or 'strategy as practice'. Strategy process literature recognizes that strategy is a dynamic process and best realized by studying the actions of employees with the organization and in particular the activities of strategy actors at the functional, business unit and corporate levels (Chakravarthy et al., 2003). Strategy as practice, which in my mind may be a subset of strategy process, also focuses on the activities of strategy actors, rather than an 'organizational property': examining what is done, how and by whom (Whittington and Cailluet, 2008). As both the process and practice literature seem to agree that the 'strategy process' is best focused on decisions and actions, I will attempt to describe these in detail in the application sections of this essay. The literature also warns against excessive rigidity in strategy research and suggests an open mind to context specific actions and the benefits of reviewing strategy 'artifacts' used in the strategy process (Giraudeau, 2008). It is recommended to consider the 'laughter, frustration, anger, excitement, repetition and other detailed observations during the process (Jarzabkowski and Whittington, 2008, p. 283). In general, we have to be wary of the strategy 'straight-jacket' when it comes to strategy research and writings (Bettis, 1991), so I will attempt to be creative in the strategy process and documentation thereof.

The research also suggests a focus on the actual strategy tools used, and researchers are encouraged to employ much more of an ethnographic approach to observing and learning from practitioners. Both process and practice literature seem to understand that strategy involves a careful look within the organization, as well as outside, by referring to the direction of 'macropraxis' and 'extra-organizational actors' (Jarzabkowski and Spee, 2009).

The final introductory theoretical concept on my radar screen for this exercise is 'strategic communication'. I was particularly inspired by the recent piece in *Harvard Business Review* entitled 'Can you say what your company's strategy is?' (Collis and Rukstad, 2008). The premise is that a goal of good strategy is to ensure that the majority of employees are able to articulate the essence of the business strategy in a few, easy to remember and easy to share statements. The only way for this to happen is for it to be carefully developed and strategically communicated, over and over, and using no more than 35 words. I find that this concept strikes an initial chord of enthusiasm with executives I teach during strategy sessions but then gets lost as more and more people get involved with the strategy process. Eventually, the priority of strategy communication seems to become subjugated to other objectives and I truly believe this to be one of the most significant contributors to failed strategy efforts.

Application

So what does all of that mean for me as I approach this strategy project?

After reflection on the guidance above, I have decided to implement three guiding principles as I go through this process. *First, I will use the key concepts of strategy taught during a basic strategy class.* For me, that means that the strategy process involves three distinct steps: (i) external analysis, (ii) internal analysis and (iii) strategy creation. While strategy is usually taught in this sequence, I found that my particular experience actually started with the internal analysis, rather than the external analysis. I felt that I had to get a sense of the current state of affairs related to the consulting program before venturing out to a competitive survey and customer analysis. And I had to get my arms around both the internal and external analysis before crafting my strategy.

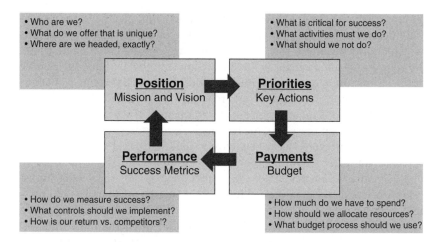

- Who are we?
- What do we offer that is unique?
- Where are we headed, exactly?

- What is critical for success?
- What activities must we do?
- What should we not do?

Position
Mission and Vision

Priorities
Key Actions

Performance
Success Metrics

Payments
Budget

- How do we measure success?
- What controls should we implement?
- How is our return vs. competitors'?

- How much do we have to spend?
- How should we allocate resources?
- What budget process should we use?

Figure 12.1   Paul's 4 Ps of Strategy

Second, I will pay particular attention to the activities of strategy during the process. As activities seem to be the focus of some recent strategy research, I will document the activities I undertake to compare with what researchers are finding elsewhere. Since commitments and actions are essentially the tools of strategy, I will also think carefully about the activities that will be needed to support the stated strategy I am creating. The emphasis on decision making is one of the key tenets I use in all of my strategy sessions to students and executives: 'The whole goal of strategy is to ensure that the daily decision making of employees within an organization is consistent with the agreed-upon positioning and priorities.'

Third, in terms of application of the strategic communication advice, I will create a strategy captured in a clear, concise manner and ensure that I use no more than 35 words for the high level strategy statements. Toward that end, I will utilize a framework that I created for my strategy students that I refer to as 'Paul's 4 Ps of Strategy', which is shown in Figure 12.1 (Friga, 2009). I will also implement and recommend guidance that all strategies should be documentable on one page.

The first 'P' is *Position*. In my mind, this is the starting point for any strategy – the mission and vision for the organization. The mission answers the question 'Why are we here?' and the vision addresses the question of 'Where are we going?' Both statements must be clear and concise so that they can be understood by everyone in the organization, so as to be helpful to drive daily decision making. In my case, the positioning statements must be clearly understood by the students in the program, recruiters, and fellow faculty and staff with whom I interact. Two other constituent groups who may be interested in these statements include alumni, who may donate money to support the program, and other business schools which indirectly affect the school's rankings through the reputational surveys. I also realize that my statements must go beyond just the generic propositions often adopted in mission and/or vision statements – such as 'excel at teaching, service and research and be the leader'. Effective positioning statements must capture some uniqueness of the entity. I will also work hard to keep these statements concise and understandable at a high level, following Peter Drucker's advice to make sure that they can fit on a 'T-Shirt' (Drucker, 1990).

Next come *Priorities*. Once the positioning is set, the leaders must establish scope and priorities. What is most important to assist the entity in achieving the vision? What must be done differently and what should be continued? The most critical decisions (and often the most difficult) are related to the elimination of activities that are not essential to the core mission and vision. What should we *not* do?

The *Payments* portion of my model is where the 'rubber hits the road'. The way that strategy is really implemented is through resource allocations and incentive programs. Many organizations are overly reliant on what my wife refers to as 'SALY' – same as last year (plus or minus a few percentage points). This is not strategic. I will be sure to carefully spend my allocated budget on the kinds of activities that are necessary to move the consulting program in a new direction.

Finally, there is *Performance*. I will need to construct a *few* (no more than three) overall performance metrics to track how well the strategy is working. It is important to consider the long term perspective as an over-focus on short term performance metrics can have devastating results (perhaps a contributor to our current economic woes). In my case, I will set a strategy with a three year performance window. Now that I have introduced the theoretical underpinnings, definitions and objectives for the strategy process I plan to follow, it is time to move to action. The starting point is the internal analysis.

INTERNAL ANALYSIS

Theory

One of the dominant theoretical perspectives related to the internal analysis related to strategy is the resource-based view or RBV (Barney, 1991). The RBV theory posits that organizations can work toward competitive advantage through strategic management of resources and capabilities, by ensuring that certain competencies are valuable, rare, inimitable and non-substitutable.

Another relevant strategy theory comes from the infamous SWOT analysis – Strengths, Weaknesses, Opportunities and Threats (Andrews, 1971). The strengths and weaknesses components are intended to be a careful and candid review of the current state of affairs within the organization vis-à-vis the best in the industry (and sometimes beyond). What are the elements of the company's value chain that are performed to a world class level and ultimately translate to competitive advantage? In the event that there are internal deficiencies that would impede the progress toward the stated vision, what corrective steps could be taken to improve the internal capabilities or should we consider outsourcing the function?

Finally, from a theoretical perspective, strategy occurs at multiple levels in an organization. Generally, this is viewed at three levels – corporate, business unit and function. One of the areas of the strategy literature currently under investigation in the strategy process literature pertains to how these different levels of strategy interrelate. It is logical that they should adhere to a common corporate mission and vision, as well as a set of values that guides behaviors. Each business unit and function will also have its own mission, vision and priorities, but these statements should reconcile very cleanly with the higher level corporate strategy statements. In essence, they articulate the particular role of the unit or function in accomplishing the higher level objectives and should not be in conflict in any way. Next, I will move to how these ideas informed me as I began to design related strategy actions.

Application

I sensed that the starting point was to spend some time understanding the current and historical situation. I certainly had a few hypotheses as to what types of activities may help but I still needed some more basic information to solidify the ideas. My intuition as to the strategic actions was based upon my experience leading the consulting program at Indiana University, where I found that bringing more consulting alumni on campus and institutionalizing more formal case interview preparation programs were very productive actions. The challenge was to understand the informal and formal context in the new environment, in order to determine the strategic priorities and the strategic communication mechanisms at UNC. This is the basis for my internal analysis.

In retrospect, the strategy formulation process actually began before I had the new leadership position. During my interview process, I asked many questions about the current state of affairs. I knew that I would be asked about initial ideas for strategic changes, so I needed information from the leadership team as well as students and staff to get a broader perspective. I quickly learned some of the most important strengths and weaknesses of the program which directly impact the strategy formulation.

From a strength perspective, the business school maintained a top 20 reputation, counted many alumni in consulting, and had a committed leadership team that believed consulting to be a priority. On the negative side, current interest in consulting courses and the concentration had dwindled, the consulting program was isolated from the core courses and faculty, and alumni were not extensively engaged in helping students prepare for and land jobs in the consulting field. Ironically, what some key constituents were concerned about was the lack of a coherent, consistent and exciting strategy for the program.

So, my first 'official' activities related to strategy creation took place prior to assuming the new position. I interviewed many different people to get a sense of the strengths and weaknesses of the program as it existed. I also floated hypotheses as to what might help the program and paid particular attention to the reaction I received as the ideas were discussed. The hypothesis-driven approach was ingrained in me during my time at McKinsey and a methodology I research and teach to students in my consulting classes (Friga, 2009). My first 'artifact' was created during this process and is shown below (Figure 12.2). It represented my 'draft' ideas as to the mission and priorities for the consulting and related programs over the next three years. I also included some key performance metrics that would give me focus as to what we were trying to achieve with the program.

Note that the documented strategy was shaped greatly by conversations during the interview process and is only intended to be a guide. I did feel it would be helpful (to me and others) to actually take a stand and document at least the preliminary plan for future reference.

EXTERNAL ANALYSIS

Theory

After completing the internal analysis, I moved to Step 2, the external analysis. The external components of the aforementioned SWOT analysis are threats and opportunities. When I teach these concepts, I stress that the threats are potential negative external issues related to our organization's performance and achievement of competitive advantage.

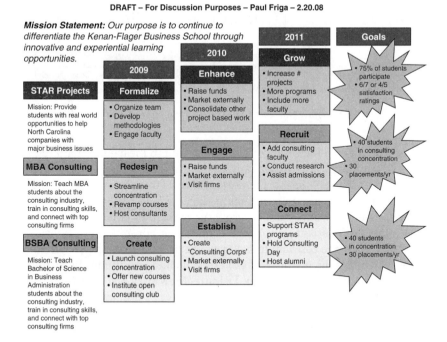

Figure 12.2   Star program and consulting strategies at Kenan-Flagler

The opportunities represent all of the potential priorities and actions we could undertake and once we identify the right shortlist – it becomes our strategy.

The threats may come from three general sources – the macro/general environment, competitors (industry level) and from customers (in terms of negative shifts). One of the most common frameworks used to capture the macro/general environment issues is STEEP: Social, Technological, Environmental, Economic and Political/Legal (Fleisher and Bensoussan, 2003). The goal is to create a shortlist of the most important issues that may affect us after carefully considering the impact of the issue as well as the implications for strategy. Next, I will describe how I moved to actions related to the external analysis.

Application

One of the tenets of my strategy teaching is how important it is to truly prioritize. A SWOT analysis that results in 8 weaknesses and 10 strengths, in my opinion, has not truly been completed as each of the 8–10 items

Figure 12.3   External Analysis Consulting Program at UNC KFBS

cannot be of equal importance. The rule of thumb I teach is to require the identification of the top three of any type of list. In this case, I am required, therefore, to identify the most important threats from an external perspective, as shown and discussed in Figure 12.3.

By far the most important macro issue is the *overall economic decline*. The impact of this issue is that the demand for consulting positions has decreased (in some cases up to a 40 percent decline) from the six primary firms which hire the majority of our students into consulting (Bain, Booz Allen, Boston Consulting Group, Deloitte, McKinsey and ScottMadden). The implication for strategy is that we will have to dramatically shift our target market to include many more firms, including small to medium sized firms with whom we have historically had little or no contact.

The next important macro issue is a political issue and social movement toward more *nationalism*. In this context, companies in the United States are increasingly scrutinized for the hiring of international students for positions in the US. Historically, consulting was one of the few industries where hiring international students on H1 Visas was a bit more common. The impact of this is a drop in the number of openings for international students, which was a major draw for a number of these students to come to a US business school in the first place. The implication of this issue from a strategy perspective is the need to seek relationships and placements in other countries. It also requires an increased effort in education to match the students' expectations with the reality of the changes.

The final macro issue comes from a *competitive perspective*. An increasing number of business schools are bringing in ex-consultants to assist in creating consulting programs and the schools have also become much more adept at utilizing alumni in consulting firms to prepare students for the interviews. The implication is that to effectively compete against some programs with even more relationships than we have, we will need to devise more innovative and outstanding activities than ever before.

And speaking of activities . . . I almost forgot to share the key activities I undertook during this phase of the strategy journey. On an ongoing basis, I subscribe to the key consulting industry journals and book lists (including Kennedy Information). I also periodically review the websites of the other top 20 business schools to see what they are up to in terms of programs and activities. Finally, I engaged in a dialogue (via email and in person/phone) with many of the over 900 UNC KFBS alumni who are currently working in consulting. I found the consulting alumni to be very informative and candid in their responses! After completing the internal and external analysis, it is time to move to the final step – creating the strategy.

STRATEGY FORMULATION

Theory

So what is necessary for me to conclude that I have a good strategy? From an analysis perspective, it is important to conduct a thorough internal and external review as described above. I know that I will be filling in the 4 Ps of Strategy as shown in the first section of this chapter (Position, Priorities, Payments and Performance), and I know that my ultimate goal for this program is competitive advantage.

From an organizational perspective, strategies of corporate, business units and functions must be aligned and consistent. They obviously increase in level of specificity as they go downward and the sets of questions and activities will naturally vary. I will keep this in mind as I move toward application in the strategy formulation stage as described below.

Application

So my first task was to secure an understanding of the corporate and business unit strategies. In my case, the corporate level strategy was the university as a whole and the business unit was the UNC Kenan-Flagler School of Business. In terms of the University of North Carolina's strategy statements (Figure 12.4), I thought through how my strategy would need to align with the priorities of attracting/inspiring, recruiting/supporting and serving/elevating. In my case, 'attracting and inspiring' ties to my objectives to raise money for the program related to attracting and inspiring both students and faculty. The 'recruiting and supporting' priority directly ties to my intentions to use funds for innovative programming and active involvement of graduate students in the planning and execution of consulting strategies. Finally, the 'serve and elevate' priority corresponds to my plans to use experiential learning as a key part of the curriculum, and I decided to add a component that includes service to the

```
                              ┌─────────────────────┐
                              │       Mission       │
                              └─────────────────────┘
```

To serve all the people of the state,
and indeed the nation, as a center for
scholarship and creative endeavor

Attract and Inspire	Recruit and Support	Serve and Elevate
Raise funds for merit and need based aid to make Carolina even more financially attractive. Inspire students by looking carefully with the faculty at our academic programs to make them more attractive to students' interests while enhancing their academic rigor	We need to support our gifted teacher-scholars and attract their *new* colleagues to inspire our students. We must do *more* – with professorships, funds for research and support for graduate students	We must serve and elevate our region, state and beyond. Work with our colleagues in local governments to support our local community. Work closely with President Bowles, update our Academic Plan, and we will partner more with our UNC sister institutions

Source: UNC Undergraduate Bulletin; Chancellor Holon Thorpe, Installation Address.

Figure 12.4   UNC mission and priorities

UNC campus operationalized as one action learning project a year for the UNC system.

Next, I set out to understand the strategy of the UNC KFBS, my direct business unit. I met with the Dean several times, as he was in the process of crafting the strategy for the business school at the same time, as this was his first year in the leadership position. I learned quite a bit from his experiences, especially with regard to the importance of connecting with all relevant constituents (for ideas and buy-in), taking it slow (offering bits of the strategy over the course to gauge reactions) and the need for strategic communication (simple and repetitive). One interesting footnote was that over the course of the year, the Dean referred to the vision statement as 'his' vision statement for the school, which was normally followed up with, 'and I hope you can make it yours as well'. This may have been strategic communication or his humility or both.

Figures 12.5 and 12.6 show the Dean's vision statement and strategy summary presented to the faculty over the course of the year. The priorities were announced early and he assigned taskforces to each of them. The vision statement violates the aforementioned guidance of 35 words (over twice that at 73 words); so while it seemed to successfully guide the activities of key lieutenants in the process it is unlikely that the majority of faculty could recite it (it is a busy T-shirt). There are also four priorities, rather than the 'rule of thumb maximum' of three, but I still found it very

'We will be a leading global professional school of business. Our research will influence business leaders, academics and policy makers. Our graduates will be known for their effective and principled leadership as well as their technical and managerial skills. We will be a workplace of choice for faculty, staff and students, a valued member of the UNC community, and a contributor to the welfare of North Carolina and the world beyond its borders.'

– James Dean, Jr. Dean, KFBS

Source: Dean Jim Dean's presentation to faculty, March 17, 2009.

Figure 12.5   Dean's Vision for the Kenan-Flagler Business School

helpful as I began shaping my strategy for consulting, which needed to be aligned of course.

In terms of 'leadership', I will continue to align the efforts of the consulting program with the school's leadership initiative, in particular through the STAR Program (Student Teams Achieving Results), where we provide consulting training and methodology development for the students. We will try to find ways to align with the 'globalization and research impact' priorities through our support of the STAR global projects as well as participating in global conferences on education, experiential learning and consulting. Finally, I plan to find ways to incorporate 'technology' in our projects, with an emphasis on using Skype and video conferencing during global coordination efforts.

CRAFT THE STRATEGY

Now, with the background work and context done, it was time to craft the strategy for the consulting program. I worked to incorporate the internal and external analysis as I went about the process.

My first step was to draft some ideas and begin my 'constituent conversations'. I documented some initial ideas as to the mission and vision and met with the deans, faculty, staff (in particular, the Career Management Center or CMC), alumni, recruiters and students. The most important meetings proved to be a series of strategy sessions with the CMC and the student officers of the consulting club. We reviewed the internal and external analysis results and iterated on the potential positioning and priorities

- **Drivers** are organizational attributes needed to reach the goals
- **Initiatives** provide focus for action to reach the goals

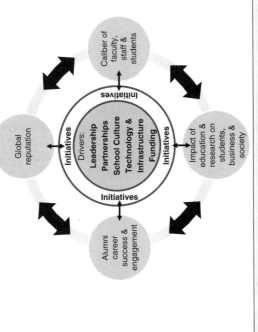

Strategic Initiatives			
Leadership Development: Develop students as exceptional global leaders in all career areas	**Globalization:** Conduct research, education and engagement programs that reflect the global economy	**Research Impact:** Increase the mpact of our research and thought leadership on business executives, policy makers and the academy	**Technology in Research and Education:** Utilize technology strategically to enhance research and the teaching and learning experience

Source: Dean Jim Dean's presentation to faculty, March 17, 2009

Figure 12.6   Dean's strategic roadmap

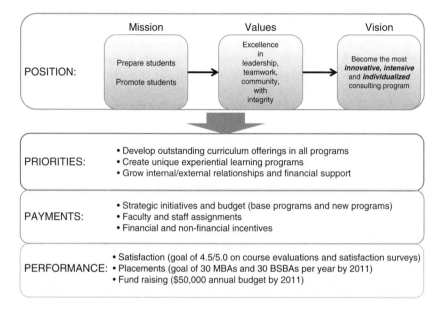

Figure 12.7   UNC KFBS consulting program strategy

of the consulting program. The results are shown in our strategy 'one pager' organized around the aforementioned 4 Ps (Figure 12.7). Note that the mission is particularly concise and the vision is meant to be a bit differentiating. The priorities and payments help explain how we will achieve the desired positioning and the performance is how we will measure success (with stated goals in each area).

The strategic communication was the next critical step as we needed to make others aware of the new strategy. In addition to many in-person meetings and presentations with staff and students, we put significant effort into documenting the strategy as clearly and concisely as possible. We put together flashy brochures, updated the website, and used the mission and vision as much as possible as talking points whenever the consulting program was mentioned. Another key tool for getting the word out was an alumni magazine article written about the new consulting program that included a discussion of the new strategy. In essence, we viewed this effort just as we would an advertising campaign for a new product. Feedback from students and other key constituents has been very positive and we are making progress in our performance measures as the first year of roll-out concludes.

DISCUSSION

The goal of this paper was to discuss the strategy process of theory to action through the lens of one strategy's formulation. Since the strategy process is a micro based phenomenon, examining the actions of one actor offers a unique perspective on what truly takes place and the insights that result therein. As I reflect upon the writing of this paper and the creation of this strategy, the following insights surfaced.

First, strategy is not as complicated as many would make it out to be. Essentially, there are only three steps – internal analysis, external analysis and crafting the strategy. That being said, the devil is in the detail, as the exact actions one takes in each bucket of activity are not as clear cut. Many strategy frameworks are helpful for external analysis (e.g. STEEP and Porter's 5 Forces for external analysis) and internal analysis (RBV and Value Chain) but less guidance exists for the crafting and presentation of the strategy. I offered a few new ideas here related to the 4 Ps as an organizing framework and the desire to keep strategy to one page for strategic communication, but this is an area that could be further examined for tool creation.

The second insight is that strategic communication is undervalued as a critical step in the strategy process. Designing the proper communication mechanisms and devoting the proper resources to delivering the messages took much more time than I imagined but proved to be one of the most important steps to successful strategy roll-out. I am realizing more and more how this should be viewed as a marketing challenge, just as with the introduction of a new product or company launch. In my case, I was able to leverage our marketing and communication staff as well as the unique talents of my student research assistants, but the importance and effort should not be underestimated.

My third insight centers on the iterative process of strategy. I employed the scientific method and anticipated iterations, but I quickly realized that the strategy process mandates minor changes as you go, especially to manage buy-in from all constituent groups. At one point, however, you need to take a stake in the ground and issue strategic communication, but then it is necessary to continue to monitor the results and feedback for the next 'major' iteration.

Finally, as I think about how this paper surfaces ideas for future research, I make the following humble observations. I think we should continue the micro based research stream to learn more about the individual level actions and decisions for the strategy process. Particularly useful efforts may be multiple person examinations within one organization and/or comparisons of similar actors in multiple organizations. The goal would be to begin to identify taxonomies and patterns that could actually inform practice, rather than just observe. Perhaps as this research stream moves forward, 'strategy process audits' by academics could be developed that parallel clinical checkups in the medical field, but that may be the subject for another paper.

REFERENCES

Andrews, K. (1971), *The Concept of Corporate Strategy*, Homewood, IL: R.D. Irwin.

Barney, J. (1991), 'Firm resources and sustained competitive advantage', *Journal of Management*, **17**(1): 99–120.

Bettis, R. (1991), 'Strategic management and the straightjacket: An editorial essay', *Organization Science*, **2**(3): 315–319.

Chakravarthy, B., G. Mueller-Stewens, P. Lorange and C. Lechner (2003), 'Defining the contours of the strategy process field', *Strategy Process – Shaping the Contours of the Field*, Malden, MA: Blackwell Publishing Ltd, pp. 1–18.

Chia, R. and R. Holt (2006), 'Strategy as practical coping: A Heideggarian perspective', *Organization Studies*, **25**(4): 529–532.

Collis, D. and M. Rukstad (2008), 'Can you say what your company's strategy is?', *Harvard Business Review*, **86**(4): 82–89.

Drucker, P. (1990), *Managing the Non-Profit Organization – Principles and Practices*, New York, NY: Harper Collins Publishers.

Fleisher, C. and B. Bensoussan (2003), 'Macroenvironmental (STEEP) analysis', *Strategic and Competitive Analysis – Methods and Techniques for Analysing Business Competition*, Upper Saddle River, NJ: Pearson Education Inc, pp. 269–283.

Friga, P. (2009), 'The McKinsey Engagement: A powerful toolkit for more efficient and effective team problem solving', New York, US: The McGraw-Hill Companies.

Giraudeau, M. (2008), 'The drafts of strategy: Opening up strategic plans and their uses', *Long Range Planning*, **41**(3): 291–308.

Hitt, M.A., R.D. Ireland, and R.E. Hoskisson (2009), *Strategic Management – Concepts and Cases*, 8th edition, Mason, OH: South-Western Cengage Learning.

Jarzabkowski, P. and A. P. Spee (2009), 'Strategy-as-practice: A review and future directions for the field', *International Journal of Management Reviews*, **11**(1): 69–95.

Jarzabkowski, P. and R. Whittington (2008), 'A strategy-as-practice approach to strategy research and education', *Journal of Management Inquiry*, **17**(4): 282–286.

Knott, P. (2008), 'Strategy tools: Who really uses them?', *Journal of Business Strategy*, **29**(5): 26–31.

Mintzberg, H. (1987), 'Crafting strategy', *Harvard Business Review*, **65**: 66–75.

Rigby, D. (2005), 'The Bain 2005 management tool survey', *Strategy & Leadership*, **33**(4): 4–12.

Sull, D. (2007), 'Closing the gap between strategy and execution', *MIT Sloan Management Review*, **Summer**: 30–38.

Whittington, R. and L. Cailluet (2008), 'The crafts of strategy: Special issue introduction by the guest editors', *Long Range Planning*, **41**(3): 241–247.

PART III

EMERGING STRATEGIES

13 Strategic initiatives: past, present and future

Christoph Lechner and Markus Kreutzer

INTRODUCTION

The significance of strategic initiatives was aptly demonstrated in Nag et al.'s (2007) article, 'What is strategic management, really?' Based upon an inductive consensus analysis, they defined the field of strategic management as consisting of (a) major intended and emergent initiatives (b) taken by general managers on behalf of owners (c) that utilize resources (d) to enhance the performance (e) of firms (f) in their external environments. Thus, they recognized strategic initiatives as a core element of our discipline by encompassing a broad range of strategic moves under the umbrella of strategic initiatives, including new product development, corporate ventures, acquisitions, strategic renewal efforts, and so on.

Parallel to the academic world, the concept of strategic initiatives has proliferated in managerial practice, with corporations such as GE, Intel, Siemens, Helvetia and Deutsche Bank pursuing major strategic moves. Unfortunately, despite this increasing popularity, research suggests that strategic initiatives often do not achieve expected or desired benefits. Estimates of failure rates range from 50 to 70 percent (e.g., Beer and Nohria, 2000; Miller, 2002; Saunders et al., 2008). As this can hardly be considered as a positive, evidence-based insights are needed to improve practices.

In this chapter, we examine current disciplinary knowledge on strategic initiatives and outline future research areas. We begin by defining the concept and its various types and classifications, then describe several relevant research streams. We propose an organizing framework for elaborating research on strategic initiatives, discuss in detail its single elements and close by outlining future research opportunities.

INITIATIVE DEFINITIONS

Over time, a wide variety of definitions of strategic initiatives has been proposed (for an overview, see Table 13.1). Comparing these definitions,

Table 13.1   Definitions of strategic initiatives

Definition	Author(s)
'A discrete, proactive undertaking that advances a new way for the corporation to use or expand its resource. [. . .] An initiative is essentially an entrepreneurial process, beginning with the identification of an opportunity and culminating in the commitment of resources to that opportunity.'	Birkinshaw, 1997: 207
'An integrated set of programs and/or projects managed in a coordinated way and aimed at building core or differentiating business capability.'	Brown and Gill, 2006: 4
'Entrepreneurial opportunities within large organizations that fall outside the current concept of corporate strategy' [referring to autonomous initiatives]	Burgelman, 1983c: 241
'Autonomous efforts within a group to effect significant change in organizational capability.'	Floyd and Wooldridge, 2000: 117
'An initiative is a project of finite duration that supports a strategic objective.'	Katz and Manzione, 2008: 3
'An initiative is any project or program outside of an organization's day-to-day operational activities that is meant to help the organization achieve its strategy.'	LaCasse and Manzione, 2007: 3
'Coordinated undertakings (formal or informal) to develop or renew the capabilities associated with competitive advantage.'	Lechner and Floyd, 2007: 10
'A deliberate effort by a firm at creating or appropriating economic value from the environment, which is organized as an independent project with its own profit and loss responsibility.' 'They represent the means by which the firm expects to justify its existence and create and appropriate economic value from the environment.'	Lovas and Ghoshal, 2000: 881, 883
'Discrete proactive undertakings that are launched by ideas, composed of groups, and reinforce or alter the current strategy of the firm.'	Marx and Lechner, 2005: 136
'New ideas that lead to the creation of new capabilities and competitive advantage.'	McGrath, 2001: 121 McGrath et al., 1995: 258
'Strategic initiatives are strategy focused and often emerge and evolve over time, while projects have a task-oriented view and are time-bound.'	Saunders et al., 2008: 1096
'A specific form of entrepreneurship that starts with the recognition of an opportunity and ends with a form	Wielemaker et al., 2003: 165

Table 13.1   (continued)

Definition	Author(s)
of approval. During the process, the initiative seeks to acquire resources (capital and assets) and create knowledge.'	
'A process by which individuals inside organizations identify and pursue an opportunity to create future goods and services without regard to the resources they currently control, culminating in the approval of that opportunity.'	Wielemaker, 2003: 4

we find, as one might expect, areas of disagreement as well as consensus. With regard to the former, previous definitions deviate in respect to the life cycle of initiatives. While some authors consider initiatives as ending upon approval (e.g., Birkinshaw, 1997), most extend their life span until they deliver results or are stopped and eliminated (e.g., McGrath, 2001). Another perspective considers initiatives as formal independent projects with their own profit and loss responsibility that are approved by top management (e.g., Lovas and Ghoshal, 2000). Other researchers emphasize their often 'rebellious' and anarchic tendencies and include autonomous, informal initiatives that evolve in more subtle ways, often triggered at middle and lower managerial levels (e.g., Burgelman, 1983c).

With regard to consensus, most definitions share five elements that characterize the essence of strategic initiatives. First, initiatives represent only a *temporary* organizational undertaking. They are designed to last only until they fulfill their purpose or are stopped due to failure or changing priorities. Eventually, an initiative might become part of the organization's base (e.g., if established as a new business unit), but this is not considered a defining element. Second, initiatives require a *coordinated* effort, ranging from a loosely coupled group to a closely interconnected team or task force. Who these actors are and which hierarchical positions they hold are less relevant and more empirical questions. Initiatives can be pursued by top-, middle- or lower-level managers or combinations thereof. As they unfold within organizations over time, initiatives are often cross-level phenomena. Numerous researchers have examined the interplay of managerial levels and the various roles of managers (e.g., Floyd and Lane, 2000; Floyd and Wooldridge, 2000). Third, initiatives do not repeat actions the organization is already undertaking. They chart new territory and *renew or expand* established structures, practices and routines. Fourth, initiatives require the alteration of an organization's resource base (i.e., leveraging existing resources, creating new resources, accessing external resources and releasing resources) in order to *refresh existing capabilities* or add *new capabilities.* The question of whether or not firms officially allocate those resources openly or appropriate them to clandestine 'skunk-work' projects is less relevant to this research. Fifth, initiatives are not minor projects. They possess characteristics such as substantial risk-taking, major investment needs, partial nonreversibility, and exposure to a high degree of internal as well as external risk and uncertainty. Initiatives require the allocation of a substantial amount of corporate resources to existing or new capabilities, be it in terms of time commitments of managers and employees or financial or technical in nature (Lovas and Ghoshal, 2000). The effects of minor projects that do not reach their objectives are negligible. However, if major initiatives fail, there is a significant impact on the *evolution and performance* of a firm.

Based on these five characteristic elements, we define strategic initiatives as temporary, coordinated undertakings for renewing or expanding the capabilities of an organization that have the potential to substantially impact its evolution and performance.

INITIATIVE TYPES

Nag et al. (2007) emphasize that strategic initiatives come in various shapes and sizes. As initiatives encompass a wide array of topics, several proposals have been made for their classification and application to empirical studies. Most classifications result in dichotomies along a continuum, such as deliberate versus emergent (Mintzberg and Waters, 1985), induced versus autonomous (Burgelman, 1983b, 1991), exploratory versus exploitive (McGrath, 2001), product versus process (Wielemaker, 2003; Wielemaker et al., 2003) and formal versus informal (Zahra et al., 1999). Similar differentiations include deployment, modification and development (Floyd and Lane, 2000), as well as internal, local, global and global–internal (Birkinshaw, 1997). For a list of classifications, see Table 13.2.

Burgelman's distinction between induced and autonomous initiatives has been influential. While the former signifies initiatives in congruence with the current strategy of a corporation, the latter explores uncharted territory. Burgelman argues that autonomous initiatives develop around experimental ideas and emerge mostly from the bottom up, usually with little or no direction from top management, while induced strategic initiatives are more deliberately steered and supported by top management. A company's relentless and successful pursuit of a narrow business strategy through induced initiatives may produce coevolutionary lock-in and

Table 13.2   Typologies of strategic initiatives

Criterion	Classification of initiative	Author(s)
Alignment (with existing capabilities)	• Very high alignment • Very low alignment	Leonard-Barton, 1992
Fit (with current concept of corporate strategy)	• Induced • Autonomous	Burgelman, 1983b, 1991, 2002
Focus	• Product • Process	Wielemaker, 2003; Wielemaker et al., 2003
Formality	• Formal • informal	Zahra et al., 1999
Impact (on existing or new businesses)	Subsidiary initiatives • Renewal (affecting a subsidiary's existing businesses) • Venturing (creating new business ventures)	Verbeke et al., 2007
Internal impact	Subsidiary initiatives • Domain developing (including internal, local, and global) • Domain consolidating • Domain defending	Delany, 2000
Learning	• Exploratory • Exploitative	Hansen etal., 2001; McGrath, 2001
Locus (of subsidiary initiatives)	Subsidiary initiatives • Internal market • Local market • Global market • Global–internal hybrid	Birkinshaw, 1997
Managerial challenge (related to ROIC)	• Growth (in the core, outside the core) • Cost (efficiency, quality) • Capital (net working, fixed)	Kreutzer, 2008; Kreutzer and Lechner, 2010
Organizational level	• Intraorganizational • Interorganizational (alliances)	Bryson and Bromiley, 1993
Origin	• Deliberate • Emergent	Mintzberg and Waters, 1985
Product innovativeness	• Brand-new products • Incremental products	Song and Montoya-Weiss, 1998
Structural level	• Corporate/headquarter • Subsidiary	Darragh and Campbell, 2001; Harvey and Novicevic, 2002

Table 13.2   (continued)

Criterion	Classification of initiative	Author(s)
Technological and market knowledge newness	• No exploration of knowledge (product improvement) • Exploration of market knowledge • Exploration of technological knowledge • Exploration of both technological and market knowledge	Burgers et al., 2008
Trigger for search activity	• Slack •· Problemistic • Institutional	Greve, 2003

reduce the effectiveness of autonomous initiatives, thereby weakening long-term adaptation. In sum, he argues for a balance between autonomous and induced initiatives in order to achieve renewal and adaptation.

The distinction between exploration and exploitation (March, 1991) that has arisen from learning theory has also been widely applied to research on initiatives. Exploratory initiatives are defined as innovative projects whose goals and methods are incompatible with the organization's existing knowledge base and capability. They are characterized by 'search, variation, risk taking, experimentation, play, flexibility, discovery, innovation' (March, 1991: 71) and are intended to create or develop new capabilities. Exploitative initiatives encompass 'refinement, choice, production, efficiency, selection, implementation, execution' (March, 1991: 71) and focus on the improvement of existing capabilities. Some studies have focused exclusively on exploratory initiatives, while others have used initiative degree of exploration as a key contingency factor (McGrath, 2001).

Because most distinctions are built on a single continuum, the complexities of such undertakings in the empirical world are captured only to a certain degree. Further, managers generally are not concerned with initiative classification, but with connecting them to specific business objectives they are trying to achieve. Therefore, another distinction was recently proposed that connects theoretical considerations with managerial concerns by applying the financial metric of ROIC (return on invested capital) as a starting base (Kreutzer and Lechner, 2010). By splitting this metric into its constituent parts, one can derive a set of initiatives, each focusing on a particular managerial issue. Growth initiatives enlarge the revenue (top-line) of the organization by generating additional sales on the existing capital base. Cost initiatives, which improve the margins of an organization, include efficiency- and quality-enhancing initiatives. Capital initiatives reduce the capital employed in a business by optimizing fixed assets or net working capital. These types of initiatives are expected to differ theoretically as well as in terms of their practical application (Berlien et al., 2006).

RESEARCH STREAMS

Several research streams examine the concept of strategic initiatives. *Corporate entrepreneurship* (also, internal corporate venturing or intrapreneurship) traditionally fosters and shapes entrepreneurial processes in large, established organizations, with initiatives considered as entrepreneurial opportunities to create new business ventures (Birkinshaw, 1997; Wielemaker et al., 2003). The majority of researchers in this domain consider initiatives to be successful if corporate resources and top management attention are committed to them (Birkinshaw, 1997; e.g., Bower, 1970; Burgelman, 1983a, c). The explicit or implicit internal approval or rejection by top management marks the end of the initiative process. Consequently, research has mainly dealt with topics such as opportunity-seeking, recognizing, evaluating or developing initiatives, while excluding the ongoing management of established business activities.

Strategy process (Bromiley et al., 2007) and *innovation research* (Leonard-Barton, 1992) have broadened this scope to include the whole developmental process of initiatives. Both literature streams use a 'strategic renewal' lens to focus on tensions between inertia and stress and corresponding challenges (Huff et al., 1992; Crossan and Berdrow, 2003). Initiatives encompass the transformation of existing businesses and all 'activities a firm undertakes to alter its path dependency' (Volberda et al., 2001: 160); that is, their scope is extended from creating new ventures to those undertakings affecting existing businesses (Verbeke et al., 2007). Along with questioning, revising and reshaping the key ideas and capabilities on which a business is built (Floyd and Lane, 2000), initiatives extend abstract descriptions of how organizations renew their capabilities (Crossan and Berdrow, 2003; Zahra and George, 2002). This broadens the dominant approach to theory development in this area to include not only forces in the intraorganizational selection environment (organizational context) but also the activities of individuals and groups and the mechanisms of adaptation.

Some strategy process scholars distinguish between ideas, issues and the actual formation of an initiative (Floyd and Wooldridge, 1999, 2000; Lovas and Ghoshal, 2000). Ideas are 'thought experiments' involving one or a few people. If they attract managerial attention as opportunities or threats, middle managers might be motivated to consider the idea as a strategic issue (Dutton and Ashford, 1993). For an issue to evolve into an initiative, a coordinated course of action is required, supported by a group of people that responds to these issues and invests organizational resources. Thus, strategy process scholars, as opposed to entrepreneurship scholars, perceive the sensing of an entrepreneurial opportunity as necessary but insufficient without purposeful, coordinated action (McGrath, 2001).

In the realm of *international strategy*, strategic initiatives have been analysed in the context of large multinational corporations (MNCs). In the past, MNCs were viewed as centralized and hierarchically run, in which headquarters initiatives predominated (Verbeke et al., 2007). The modern MNC, however, is considered as a differentiated network (Rugman and Verbeke, 2003), in which subsidiaries can be the source and thus the locus of initiatives (Birkinshaw, 1997; Delany et al., 2007). These initiatives are not restricted to the identification and pursuit of a new local product market opportunity, but are considered as having the potential to enhance worldwide learning and global integration, a much broader role than previously envisioned (Birkinshaw, 1997).

Research on *corporate strategy* has also examined the development of corporate initiatives (Darragh and Campbell, 2001). Scholars interpret the possession of a portfolio of value-adding corporate initiatives and their subsequent execution as a main reason that corporate centers ('parents') achieve advantages and justify their existence (e.g., Collis et al., 2007).

Finally, project management has recently been examined as an essential method of strategizing in the *strategy-as-practice* stream (Hoon, 2007; Whittington et al., 2006). Scholars stress the importance of mastering the tools and processes of project management and investing in practical crafting skills.

ORGANIZING FRAMEWORK FOR RESEARCH ON STRATEGIC INITIATIVES

In this chapter, we propose an organizing framework for illustrating research on strategic initiatives (see Figure 13.1) based on four components. The first is related to all factors of the organizational context in which initiatives emerge and develop. Depending on initiative type, these

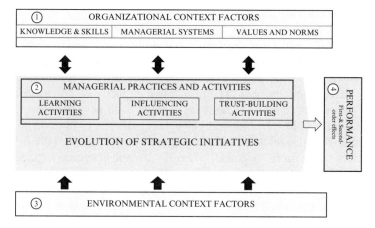

Figure 13.1   Organizing framework for research on strategic initiatives

factors might support or impede their evolution. The second component deals with all managerial practices and activities of organizational actors pursuing these initiatives. The third component consists of environmental context factors; the fourth, which covers performance implications, will be discussed together with the other components.

Organizational Context Factors

Prior research has shown that organizational context influences both the chances for strategic initiatives to emerge as well as their development and final outcome. The underlying rationale is that initiatives are not conducted in isolation but are subject to internal and external circumstances, which either facilitate or impede their development. Research on strategic renewal from an evolutionary theory perspective has focused on how corporations deal with rigidities caused by their organizational context. Variation (emergence of new initiatives) is shaped by organizational context, which acts as an internal selection mechanism. It consists of both formal management systems, including administrative networks and processes that steer resource allocation (Bower, 1970; Lovas and Ghoshal, 2000), and informal, sociocultural forces such as values and norms, culture and leadership style (Chakravarthy et al., 2003; Chakravarthy and White, 2002). In addition, employee knowledge and skill sets form an important part of organizational context (Leonard-Barton, 1992). Such forces determine whether an initiative acquires financial and other resources needed to sustain its development and to be retained. Next, we concentrate on these three dimensions of organizational context.

Established knowledge and skills

An organization's knowledge base impacts what it can learn in the future. Since strategic initiatives are forward-looking, they require an ongoing accumulation of knowledge. This learning challenge is shaped by the established knowledge and skill set of the organization as well as its capacity to absorb new insights. The absorptive capacity of an organization limits as well as enables the learning path of each new initiative (Zahra and Hayton, 2008).

Studies reveal interesting insights. Bryson and Bromiley (1993) found initiatives to be more successful when the organization has experienced, skilled and sufficient planning staff and there is an understanding among the potentially affected groups of cause–effect relations in the substantive area that prompts the initiative. Similarly, McGrath and colleagues (1995) found a positive relationship between comprehensiveness of the management team (i.e., a precise understanding of the resource combinations required to achieve objectives) and achievement of goals.

To activate the existing skills and knowledge base, organizations must assure that potentially affected groups are aware of and concerned about the issues that the initiatives will address and will give them high priority. Empirical evidence of corporate initiatives reveals that this is not necessarily the case. The main reason for corporate initiatives to stall is disagreements between business units and corporate managers on the existence of an issue (Darragh and Campbell, 2001). Thus, clearly communicating the need, content and scope of initiatives has been shown to increase the chances of a successful outcome (Bryson and Bromiley, 1993).

While sufficient knowledge and skills are a basic precondition for initiatives, they might fall prey to certain traps stemming from structural inertia. For example, local search behavior might reveal information that is too close to existing knowledge in order to solve the learning challenge. An organization might be overconfident in its skills and underestimate the demands of new initiatives; it might neglect feedback and input from external stakeholders and pursue a suboptimal learning trajectory. It is well known that an organization's core capabilities can degenerate into core rigidities that impede the development of new initiatives (Leonard-Barton, 1992).

Established managerial systems

Such systems, which represent one of the most intensively researched context variables, encompass administrative networks and organizational processes, such as planning, budgeting and control (Noda and Bower, 1996). Top management can set these systems directly in place and use them to steer the subsequent selection of new initiatives. Because these systems are constructed in line with the officially espoused strategy of a firm, all selected initiatives are tightly coupled to this strategy. Therefore, a strict and rigid selection mechanism picks only those initiatives that fit predefined requirements. New initiatives are less likely to be successful in acquiring resources because of their unfamiliarity within the organization.

Formal management control systems (MCS) have received predominant research attention. Bower (1970) and Burgelman (1983c) note that new initiatives have a higher chance of survival if they are not exposed too early in their development to the demands of formal control systems. Protecting the initiative initially by maintaining a low profile may be important for nurturing nascent incompatible initiatives. Mintzberg and Westley (1992) describe this as 'enclaving', where secluded areas in an organization are deliberately created to test and improve deviant ideas before they are exposed to a broader and more critical formal arena.

In line with this finding that isolation from the formal organizational structure enhances the initial development of strategic initiatives, other studies have identified the positive role of autonomy from supervisory relationships. Focusing on exploratory new business development projects, McGrath (2001) finds the two autonomy constructs (goal and supervisory) to positively influence initiative performance. Support for this argument was found by a study of new business development projects (Burgers et al., 2008). Burgers et al. show that aligning project autonomy with the degree of required exploration of technological versus market knowledge is essential for successfully managing new business development projects. When exploration of both knowledge types is high, high degrees of autonomy benefit the initiative and vice versa.

Other researchers have differentiated three specific types of MCS: belief, boundary and performance (including its diagnostic and interactive use), and have studied their effect on the emergence, development and implementation of strategic initiatives. Simons (1991) argues that by interactively using control systems and applying belief and boundary systems, top managers can influence the development of new ideas and strategic initiatives. Marginson (2002) finds support for belief and boundary systems to be used as mechanisms for strategic change. While belief systems influence and enable managers' 'triggering' decisions for new ideas, boundary systems motivate a search for new ideas within the prescribed acceptable domain. Thus, they 'influence which ideas and initiatives managers will champion and, more importantly perhaps, given problems of information asymmetry, which are discarded at the outset' (Marginson, 2002: 1024).

In a study of ten newly appointed top managers, Simons (1994) finds that belief and boundary systems are initially used as important levers for strategic renewal by managers attempting strategic turnaround. The interactive use of control systems is highlighted later in the process. He concludes, contrary to accepted wisdom, that MCS can, depending on the context, act not only as agents of intended change, but also of autonomous, emergent strategic initiatives.

Established values, norms and interests
The third component of the organizational context that influences initiative development deals with social relations, norms, values and beliefs as well as established coalitions and micropolitical interests. This social context represents a normative rigidity impeding the development of exploratory initiatives mainly due to its negative effect on their legitimacy and subsequent institutionalization in the capability set of the organization (Burgelman, 1991; Leonard-Barton, 1992).

McGrath et al. (1995) found support for the importance of *deftness*, that is, the creation of intensive working relationships, for effective initiative task execution and the achievement of goals. Lechner et al. (2010) studied the social context of strategic renewal; more specifically, the impact of three dimensions of social networks. Their empirical evidence supports curvilinear relationships between initiative performance and relational and structural variables; however, the relationship of performance to cognitive variables remains positive across all levels. In addition, the degree of exploration moderates relationships between all dimensions of social networks and initiative performance. Units engaged in strategic initiatives may suffer from an abundance of social capital, both in terms of occupying a central position and in forming strong ties with other organizational units. Contrary to Hansen et al. (2001), who found that in teams whose task was more exploratory (exploitative), a network structure characterized by many strong and non-redundant ties (weak and moderately connected) resulted in significantly lower project completion time. Lechner et al. (2010) find that at certain thresholds, relational and structural forms of social networks become a group liability irrespective of the degree of exploration inherent in the initiative's task.

Managerial Practices and Activities

Individuals and groups pursuing initiatives rely on a set of managerial practices to accomplish their goals, including opportunity-sensing, learning, influencing and role-related activities.

Opportunity sensing and envisioning
Sensing and recognizing opportunities is both a major challenge for established companies and a central domain of entrepreneurship

research. Researchers have commonly distinguished between two paths of identifying entrepreneurial opportunities: systematic search and discovery process (Shane, 2000). Disproving a previously assumed contradiction, recent research finds variance in the characteristics of an opportunity that affects these paths and their effectiveness. First, relatively codified (tacit) opportunities are more likely to be discovered through systematic search (discovery) (Smith et al., 2009). Second, the effectiveness of the identification process depends on the degree of problem complexity involved in an opportunity. As complexity levels rise, theorizing becomes more useful and consensus-based hierarchical governance forms are seen as more beneficial than market-oriented forms (Hsieh et al., 2007).

Major factors that influence opportunity recognition were analysed at the individual level of a single entrepreneur, focusing on prior knowledge and personality traits such as optimism, self-efficacy, motivation, alertness, risk propensity and creativity (e.g., Corbett, 2007). Recent multilevel models (e.g., creativity) have extended this original focus from the individual to the initiative group and organizational levels (Drazin et al., 1999). The concept of entrepreneurial orientation, with its three core ingredients of innovativeness, proactiveness and risk-taking, describes an organization's ability to recognize and respond to new opportunities (Miller, 1983). This construct, used extensively in existing research, has been found to positively influence the performance of strategic initiatives (e.g., Li et al., 2006). Consequently, researchers have analysed how organizations can spur innovative, proactive behavior and embrace risk-taking; for example, by providing employees with the necessary freedom, time and incentives to explore new ideas.

Learning
Several learning activities are considered essential to master the challenges necessary for new initiatives to overcome skill- and technology-related deficiencies (Crossan and Berdrow, 2003; Lechner and Floyd, 2007): searching (acquiring new information both internally and externally); processing (assimilating information through analysis and discussion of issues, considering alternatives and reaching decisions about particular courses of action); codifying (putting concepts and procedures into written form to serve as guidelines in the development of new routines); and practicing (experimenting with new behavior, typically in the form of prototypes, pilot projects and other experimental trials). Thus, the more time and energy groups expend on these activities, using feedback from one learning activity to improve the others, the better their subsequent performance.

Influencing

To overcome challenges related to established managerial systems as well as micropolitical coalitions, a variety of influencing activities are applied in organizations. They range from the official use of hierarchical power, building of coalitions, and persuasion and negotiation, to the more unpleasant behavioral acts of pressuring and spreading biased information. In an empirical study, Lechner and Floyd (2006) examined three influencing activities, namely formal authority, coalition-building (building informal relationships between the initiative and other individuals and groups) and rational justification (the use of rational appeals, data, analysis or arguments to demonstrate the benefits of an initiative). Results indicate that formal authority and coalition-building activities are more important in exploratory initiatives while there is no significant interaction effect for rational justification. Bryson and Bromiley (1993) studied the role of other micropolitical behaviors, namely forcing (in contrast to problem-solving) and compromise (affected groups attempting to compromise) as conflict resolution strategies. While compromise does not appear to increase the chances of a successful outcome, problem-solving (rather than forcing) was positively related to initiative success.

Role behavior

Another research stream deals primarily with the roles of managers in strategic initiatives. Originally, research focused on the role top management plays in the initiative process. While some authors attributed to top managers only a limited role as shapers of a supportive organizational context (Ghoshal and Bartlett, 1994: 108), others attributed a much more active role. Along with setting the context, top managers provide impetus and guide the progress of an initiative throughout its development (Lovas and Ghoshal, 2000). Subsequent research has extended this focus to other managerial levels and explored the interplay among them. Floyd and Lane (2000) note that for initiatives to be successful in the corporate context, managers at all operating levels need to understand and embrace various roles. Inconsistent expectations based on the need to deploy existing competencies or develop new ones may lead to strategic role conflict. Floyd and Wooldridge (2000), who stress the important roles middle managers play in the initiative process as links between lower and top management, highlight the importance of formal and informal social relations to gain top management's ratification of strategic initiatives. Considering the interplay among top, middle and frontline management, Volberda et al. (2001) describe four renewal processes to manage strategic initiatives: emergent, directed, facilitated and transformational. Similarly, Lechner and Kreutzer (2010) propose a framework that differentiates among four coordination modes through which multiunit firms pursue growth initiatives based on the degree of top management involvement: agenda-setting, context-setting, directing and self-organizing.

Environmental Context Factors

Only a few studies propose environmental context as an important factor for the evolution of strategic initiatives (e.g., Bryson and Bromiley, 1993; Dvir and Lechler, 2004). For example, Bryson and Bromiley found empirical support for a contingency model in which organizational and environmental context variables influence the planning and implementation process directly and influence the outcomes of major change initiatives indirectly. More specifically, they found greater initiative success and learning to be associated with an environment that requires little change to existing technology and offers stability on the general economic and political levels.

AREAS FOR FUTURE RESEARCH

We see six major areas as warranting attention for future research. First, there is high potential in examining differences between various types of strategic initiatives (e.g., comparing M&A with alliance initiatives, or cost-cutting to growth initiatives). This line of thought can be extended to compare managerial activities and practices used to pursue these initiatives. For example, control activities in cost-cutting initiatives may require a different composition of levers than in growth initiatives. The same might hold for managerial behavior related to target-setting, consensus formation, providing feedback, and so on. These differences have not yet been carefully examined; however, such an understanding is necessary before we can derive empirically grounded managerial recommendations.

Second, future research might extend and explore beyond the traditional intra-firm locus of initiatives. Increasingly, strategic initiatives cut across firm boundaries and are no longer confined to the activity system of a single organization (Bryson and Bromiley, 1993; Wielemaker, 2003). For example, manufacturers pursuing initiatives involving electrically powered vehicles are in close contact with electricity firms, battery producers, chemical corporations and governmental agencies, each of which shapes the developmental path and outcome of these initiatives. If the traditional boundaries of firm activities are blurring, researchers need to consider the various links and interconnections in their research designs (e.g., Child, 2001; Teng, 2007).

Third, although we have made progress in studying the interplay between top, middle and lower managerial levels in the pursuit of strategic initiatives, many open questions remain. For example, our knowledge about the optimal mix of the roles and activities across these levels depending on contextual factors and initiative types is limited. Also, as most corporations operate in the M-Form, we need to know more about the interactions between corporate centers and their business units, or between global headquarters, regional headquarters and local units. While existing research has predominantly focused on initiatives at the business-unit level, we know much less about corporate initiatives or the delicate interplay between horizontal and vertical units of major organizations. Such research designs (Hitt et al., 2007) are needed to deepen our understanding of these relationships.

Fourth, albeit demanding in their execution, quantitative longitudinal research designs might substantially advance our understanding of initiatives. Interestingly, early work was dominated by rich, single case studies; however, they lacked clear performance indicators and control of involved variables was weak. While enriching our understanding, only recently have cross-sectional studies abandoned this descriptive nature, clarified causal relationships between constructs and allowed for statistical generalization. Using cross-sectional data, however, does not allow us to directly observe changes in the independent variables over time. One fruitful direction for future research, therefore, would be to track the development of process variables across the life cycle of initiatives (or at least across two periods of time), since the significance of process variables might vary. For example, theory suggests that early-stage initiatives perform better when allowed 'breathing space' and are more sheltered from organizational scrutiny (Mintzberg and Westley, 1992). At later stages, however, closer relationships and more direct control seem to be crucial in order to gain political support within the organization. Such details and temporal nuances cannot be detected with cross-sectional research designs.

A fifth avenue for future initiative research might be that of a configurational approach (e.g., Meyer et al., 1993; Miller, 1986). As shown, much of the empirical research on strategic initiatives has emphasized the contingencies between organizational context, initiative-related activities and performance, pointing out optimal combinations across these three elements. We think that extending this to consider sets of configurations might be a promising next step, in both research and practice, to demonstrate internally consistent fits between process variables and initiative types. Researchers might also incorporate external context factors, as these variables have often been neglected in initiative studies. In addition to variables such as dynamism, complexity or munificence that have been frequently identified as moderators of the relationship between strategy process and organizational outcomes (e.g., Dess and Beard, 1984), one might consider the competitive dynamics between strategic initiatives of firms in a particular industry. Therefore, future research could explore the impact of such environmental factors as moderators of the configuration–initiative relationship.

Finally, research might move from the study of single initiatives to that of portfolios of initiatives. At present, most major corporations pursue many strategic initiatives at each point in time. Some exist as 'corporate programs' while others flourish beside each other, sometimes with contradictory impacts. Our knowledge about corporate programs and the pursuit of sets of initiatives, however, is quite limited. We do not know, for example, if it is useful to coordinate at the program level or reduce potential discrepancies. Thus far, research has called for balancing different types of strategic initiatives (e.g., exploratory and exploitative) (Burgelman, 1991, 2002; Crossan and Berdrow, 2003; Volberda et al., 2001), known as organizational ambidexterity (Raisch and Birkinshaw, 2008), and has cautioned against pursuing too many initiatives of one type. However, we lack a clear understanding of an 'adequate' balance, and questions regarding how to steer these portfolios and promote an adequate context remain unanswered. We have seen, for example, that a single structural context cannot facilitate all types of initiatives. It may also be important to examine complementarities across strategic initiatives in a portfolio. Current knowledge of the consequences of such situations, based only on a few practitioner-oriented articles, is limited (e.g., Katz and Manzione, 2008; LaCasse, 2008; LaCasse and Manzione, 2007). It remains an open question whether it is possible to spatially and temporally separate such initiatives within firms. Are managers capable of simultaneously employing and differentiating, per initiative, diverging process configurations and corresponding management styles? These and other questions offer interesting future research opportunities for studying sets of strategic initiatives.

Overall, it seems that research on strategic initiatives offers promise both theoretically and empirically, as many important issues are still unresolved. For corporations, which may be perceived as 'ecologies of strategic initiatives', an understanding of these phenomena and their performance impact is highly relevant.

REFERENCES

Beer, M. and N. Nohria (2000), 'Cracking the code of change', *Harvard Business Review*, **78**(3): 133–141.
Berlien, O., A. S. Kirsten, J. Oelert and R. Schutt (2006), 'Wertsteigerungen Durch

Das Konzernprogramm *Best* Bei Thyssen Krupp', in N. Schweickart and A. Töpfer (eds), *Wertorientiertes Management. Werterhaltung – Wertsteuerung – Wertsteigerung Ganzheitlich Gestalten*: 597–608, Berlin and Heidelberg: Springer.

Birkinshaw, J. (1997), 'Entrepreneurship in multinational corporations: The characteristics of subsidiary initiatives', *Strategic Management Journal*, **18**(3): 207–229.

Bower, J. L. (1970), *Managing the Resource Allocation Process*, Boston, MA: Harvard University.

Bromiley, P., M. De Rond, S. Floyd, M. Kriger, C. Lechner, A. M. Pettigrew, A. Ranft and H. W. Volberda (2007), 'Strategy Process Interest Group Domain Statement', http:// strategicmanagement.net/ig/Strategy_process.php.

Brown, T. S. and M. R. Gill (2006), 'Charting new horizons with initiative management', *Balanced Scorecard Report* (September–October): 3–6.

Bryson, J. M. and P. Bromiley (1993), 'Critical factors affecting the planning and implementation of major projects', *Strategic Management Journal*, **14**(5): 319–337.

Burgelman, R. A. (1983a), 'Corporate entrepreneurship and strategic management – insights from a process study', *Management Science*, **29**(12): 1349–1364.

Burgelman, R. A. (1983b), 'A model of the interaction of strategic behavior, corporate context, and the concept of strategy', *Academy of Management Review*, **8**(1): 61–70.

Burgelman, R. A. (1983c), 'A process model of internal corporate venturing in the diversified major firm', *Administrative Science Quarterly*, **28**(2): 223–244.

Burgelman, R. A. (1991), 'Intraorganizational ecology of strategy making and organizational adaptation: theory and field research', *Organization Science*, **2**(3): 239–262.

Burgelman, R. A. (1994), 'Fading memories – a process theory of strategic business exit in dynamic environments', *Administrative Science Quarterly*, **39**(1): 24–56.

Burgelman, R. A. (2002), 'Strategy as vector and the inertia of coevolutionary lock-in', *Administrative Science Quarterly*, **47**(2): 325–357.

Burgers, J. H., F. A. J. Van Den Bosch and H. W. Volberda (2008), 'Why new business development projects fail: Coping with the differences of technological versus market knowledge', *Long Range Planning*, **41**(1): 55–73.

Chakravarthy, B. S. and R. E. White (2002), 'Strategy process: Forming, implementing and changing strategies', in A. M. Pettigrew, H. Thomas and R. Whittington (eds), *Handbook of Strategy and Management*: 182–205, London, New Delhi and Thousand Oaks: Sage.

Chakravarthy, B. S., G. Müller-Stevens, P. Lorange and C. Lechner (2003), 'Defining the contours of the strategy process field', in B. S. Chakravarthy, G. Müller-Stevens, P. Lorange and C. Lechner (eds), *Strategy Process. Shaping the Contours of the Field*: 1–17, Malden: Blackwell Publishing.

Child, J. (2001), 'Learning through strategic alliances', in M. Dierkes, A. B. Antal, J. Child and I. Nonaka (eds), *Handbook of Organizational Learning and Knowledge*: 657–680, Oxford: Oxford University Press.

Collis, D., D. Young and M. Goold (2007), 'The size, structure, and performance of corporate headquarters', *Strategic Management Journal*, **28**(4): 383–405.

Corbett, A. C. (2007), 'Learning asymmetries and the discovery of entrepreneurial opportunities', Babson-Kauffman Entrepreneurship Research Conference: 97–118. Boulder, CO: Elsevier Science Bv.

Crossan, M. M. and I. Berdrow (2003), 'Organizational learning and strategic renewal', *Strategic Management Journal*, **24**(11): 1087–1105.

Darragh, J. and A. Campbell (2001), 'Why corporate initiatives get stuck?', *Long Range Planning*, **34**(1): 33–52.

Delany, E. (2000), 'Strategic development of the multinational subsidiary through subsidiary initiative-taking', *Long Range Planning*, **33**(2): 220–244.

Dess, G. G. and D. W. Beard (1984), 'Dimensions of organizational task environments', *Administrative Science Quarterly*, **29**(1): 52–73.

Drazin, R., M. A. Glynn and R. K. Kazanjian (1999), 'Multilevel theorizing about creativity in organizations: A sensemaking perspective', *Academy of Management Review*, **24**(2): 286–307.

Dutton, J. E. and S. J. Ashford (1993), 'Selling issues to top management', *Academy of Management Review*, **18**(3): 397–428.

Dvir, D. and T. Lechler (2004), 'Plans are nothing, changing plans is everything: The impact of changes on project success', *Research Policy*, **33**(1): 1–15.

Floyd, S. W. and P. J. Lane (2000), 'Strategizing throughout the organization: Managing role conflict in strategic renewal', *Academy of Management Review*, **25**(1): 154–177.

Floyd, S. W. and B. Wooldridge (1999), 'Knowledge creation and social networks in corporate entrepreneurship: The renewal of organizational capability', *Entrepreneurship Theory and Practice* (Spring): 123–143.

Floyd, S. W. and B. Wooldridge (2000), *Building Strategy from the Middle: Reconceptualizing Strategy Process*, Thousand Oaks, CA: Sage.

Ghoshal, S. and C. A. Bartlett (1994), 'Linking organizational context and managerial action – the dimensions of quality of management', *Strategic Management Journal*, **15**: 91–112.

Gray, B. (1990), 'The enactment of management control-systems – a critique of Simons', *Accounting Organizations and Society*, **15**(1–2): 145–148.

Greve, H. R. (2003), *Organizational Learning from Performance Feedback: A Behavioral Perspective on Innovation and Change*, Cambridge: Cambridge University Press.

Hagedoorn, J. (1993), 'Understanding the rationale of strategic technology partnering – interorganizational modes of cooperation and sectoral differences', *Strategic Management Journal*, **14**(5): 371–385.

Hambrick, D. C., T. S. Cho and M. J. Chen (1996), 'The influence of top management team heterogeneity on firms' competitive moves', *Administrative Science Quarterly*, **41**(4): 659–684.

Hansen, M. H., J. M. Podolny and J. Pfeffer (2001), 'So many ties, so little time: A task contingency perspective on corporate social capital', in S. M. Gabbay, and R. T. A. J. Leenders (eds), *Social Capital of Organizations*: 21–57, New York, NY: JAI Press.

Harvey, M. and M. M. Novicevic (2002), 'The co-ordination of strategic initiatives within global organizations: The role of global teams', *International Journal of Human Resource Management*, **13**(4): 660–676.

Hitt, M. A., P. W. Beamish, S. E. Jackson and J. E. Mathieu (2007), 'Building theoretical and empirical bridges across levels: Multilevel research in management', *Academy of Management Journal*, **50**(6): 1385–1399.

Hoon, C. (2007), 'Committees as strategic practice: The role of strategic conversation in a public administration', *Human Relations*, **60**(6): 921–952.

Hsieh, C., J. A. Nickerson and T. R. Zenger (2007), 'Opportunity discovery, problem solving and a theory of the entrepreneurial firm', *Journal of Management Studies*, **44**(7): 1255–1277.

Huff, J. O., A. S. Huff and H. Thomas (1992), 'Strategic renewal and the interaction of cumulative stress and inertia', *Strategic Management Journal*, **13**(Special Issue): 55–75.

Hutzschenreuter, T. and I. Kleindienst (2006), 'Strategy-process research: What have we learned and what is still to be explored', *Journal of Management*, **32**(5): 673–720.

Katz, K. and T. Manzione (2008), 'Maximize your "return on initiatives" with the initiative portfolio review process', *Balanced Scorecard Report* (May–June): 3–5.

Kreutzer, M. (2008), 'Controlling strategic initiatives: A contribution to corporate entrepreneurship', unpublished dissertation, St. Gallen, University of St. Gallen.

Kreutzer, M. and C. Lechner (2010), 'Control configurations and strategic initiatives', in S. B. Sitkin, L. Cardinal and K. Bijlsma-Frankema (eds), *Organisational Control*, Chapter 15, pp. 463–503, Cambridge: Cambridge University Press.

LaCasse, P. (2008), 'Rebalance your initiative portfolio to manage risk and maximize performance', *Balanced Scorecard Report* (September–October): 3–5.

LaCasse, P. and T. Manzione (2007), 'Intiative management: Putting strategy into action', *Balanced Scorecard Report* (November–December): 3–7.

Lechner, C. and S. W. Floyd (2006), 'The role of authority, justification and coalition-building in the development of exploratory initiatives', Winner of the Best Paper Award, Strategic Management Society (Conference 2006).

Lechner, C. and S. W. Floyd (2007), 'Searching, processing, codifying and practicing – key learning activities in exploratory initiatives', *Long Range Planning*, **40**(1): 9–29.

Lechner, C. and M. Kreutzer (2010), 'Coordinating growth initiatives in multi-unit firms', *Long Range Planning*, **43**(1): 6–32.

Lechner, C., K. Frankenberger and S. Floyd (2010), 'Task contingencies in the curvilinear relationships between inter-group networks and initiative performance', *Academy Management Journal*, **53**(4): 865–889.

Leonard-Barton, D. (1992), 'Core capabilities and core rigidities – a paradox in managing new product development', *Strategic Management Journal*, **13**(Special Issue S1): 111–125.

Li, Y., Y. Liu and Y. B. Zhao (2006), 'The role of market and entrepreneurship orientation and internal control in the new product development activities of Chinese firms', *Industrial Marketing Management*, **35**(3): 336–347.

Lovas, B. and S. Ghoshal (2000), 'Strategy as guided evolution', *Strategic Management Journal*, **21**(9): 875–896.

March, J. G. (1991), 'Exploration and exploitation in organizational learning', *Organization Science*, **2**(1): 71–87.

Marginson, D. E. W. (2002), 'Management control systems and their effects on strategy formation at middle-management levels: Evidence from a UK organization', *Strategic Management Journal*, **23**(11): 1019–1031.

Maritan, C. A. (2001), 'Capital investment as investing in organizational capabilities: An empirically grounded process model', *Academy of Management Journal*, **44**(3): 513–531.

Marx, K. and C. Lechner (2005), 'The role of the social context for strategy making: examining the impact of embeddedness on the performance of strategic initiatives', in S. W. Floyd, J. Roos, C. D. Jacobs and F. W. Kellerman (eds), *Innovating Strategy Process*: 135–148, Oxford: Blackwell Publishing.

McGrath, R. G. (1995), 'Advantage from adversity – learning from disappointment in internal corporate ventures', *Journal of Business Venturing*, **10**(2): 121–142.

McGrath, R. G. (2001), 'Exploratory learning, innovative capacity, and managerial oversight', *Academy of Management Journal*, **44**(1): 118–131.

McGrath, R. G., I. C. MacMillan and S. Venkataraman (1995), 'Defining and developing competence – a strategic process paradigm', *Strategic Management Journal*, **16**(4): 251–275.

Meyer, A. D., A. S. Tsui and C. R. Hinings (1993), 'Configurational approaches to organizational analysis', *Academy of Management Journal*, **36**(6): 1175–1195.

Miller, D. (1983), 'The correlates of entrepreneurship in 3 types of firms', *Management Science*, **29**(7): 770–791.

Miller, D. (1986), 'Configurations of strategy and structure – towards a synthesis', *Strategic Management Journal*, **7**(3): 233–249.

Miller, D. (2002), 'Successful change leaders: What makes them? What do they do that is different?', *Journal of Change Management*, **2**(4): 359–368.

Mintzberg, H. and J. A. Waters (1985), 'Of strategies, deliberate and emergent', *Strategic Management Journal*, **6**(3): 257–272.

Mintzberg, H. and F. Westley (1992), 'Cycles of organizational-change', *Strategic Management Journal*, **13**: 39–59.

Nag, R., D. C. Hambrick and M. J. Chen (2007), 'What is strategic management, really? Inductive derivation of a consensus definition of the field', *Strategic Management Journal*, **28**(9): 935–955.

Noda, T. and J. L. Bower (1996), 'Strategy making as iterated processes of resource allocation', *Strategic Management Journal*, **17**(Special Issue S1): 159–192.

Raisch, S. and J. Birkinshaw (2008), 'Organizational ambidexterity: Antecedents, outcomes, and moderators', *Journal of Management*, **34**(3): 375–409.

Rugman, A. M. and A. Verbeke (2003), 'Extending the theory of the multinational enterprise: Internalization and strategic management perspectives', *Journal of International Business Studies*, **34**(2): 125–137.

Saunders, M., R. Mann and R. Smith (2008), 'Implementing strategic initiatives: A framework of leading practices', *International Journal of Operations & Production Management*, **28**(11–12): 1095–1123.

Shane, S. (2000), 'Prior knowledge and the discovery of entrepreneurial opportunities', *Organization Science*, **11**(4): 448–469.

Simons, R. (1991), 'Strategic orientation and top management attention to control-systems', *Strategic Management Journal*, **12**(1): 49–62.

Simons, R. (1994), 'How new top managers use control-systems as levers of strategic renewal', *Strategic Management Journal*, **15**(3): 169–189.

Simons, R. (1995), *Levers of Control. How Managers Use Innovative Control Systems to Drive Strategic Renewal*, Boston, MA: Harvard Business School Press.

Smith, B. R., C. H. Matthews and M. T. Schenkel (2009), 'Differences in entrepreneurial opportunities: The role of tacitness and codification in opportunity identification', *Journal of Small Business Management*, **47**(1): 38–57.

Song, X. M. and M. M. Montoya-Weiss (1998), 'Critical development activities for really new versus incremental products', *Journal of Product Innovation Management*, **15**(2): 124–135.

Teng, B. S. (2007), 'Corporate entrepreneurship activities through strategic alliances: A resource-based approach toward competitive advantage', *Journal of Management Studies*, **44**(1): 119–142.

Verbeke, A., J. J. Chrisman and W. L. Yuan (2007), 'A note on strategic renewal and corporate venturing in the subsidiaries of multinational enterprises', *Entrepreneurship Theory and Practice*, **31**(4): 585–600.

Volberda, H. W., C. Baden-Fuller and F. A. J. van den Bosch (2001), 'Mastering strategic renewal – mobilising renewal journeys in multi-unit firms', *Long Range Planning*, **34**(2): 159–178.

Whittington, R., E. Molloy, M. Mayer and A. Smith (2006), 'Practices of strategising/organising – broadening strategy work and skills', *Long Range Planning*, **39**(6): 615–629.

Wielemaker, M. W. (2003), *Managing Initiatives. A Synthesis of the Conditioning and Knowledge-Creating View*, Rotterdam: Erasmus University Rotterdam.

Wielemaker, M. W., H. W. Volberda, T. Elfring and C. Baden-Fuller (2003), 'The conditioning and knowledge-creating view: Managing strategic initiatives in large firms', in A. M. Pettigrew, H. Thomas and R. Whittington (eds), *Handbook of Strategy and Management*: 164–190, London, New Delhi and Thousand Oaks, CA: Sage.

Zahra, S. A. and G. George (2002), 'Absorptive capacity: A review, reconceptualization, and extension', *Academy of Management Review*, **27**(2): 185–203.

Zahra, S. A. and J. C. Hayton (2008), 'The effect of international venturing on firm performance: The moderating influence of absorptive capacity', *Journal of Business Venturing*, **23**(2): 195–220.

Zahra, S. A., A. P. Nielsen and W. C. Bogner (1999), 'Corporate entrepreneurship, knowledge, and competence development', *Entrepreneurship Theory and Practice*, **23**(3): 169–189.

14 The risky prospects of entrepreneurial initiatives: bias duality and bias reversal in established firms*

James J. Chrisman, Alain Verbeke and Erick P. C. Chang

INTRODUCTION

In their landmark study on the differences between entrepreneurs (founders of companies) and managers in established organizations, Busenitz and Barney (1997) use prospect theory (e.g., Tversky and Kahneman, 1974) to argue that entrepreneurs are much more likely than managers to exhibit biases of overconfidence and over-generalization on the basis of limited information, leading them to select simple decision rules or heuristics. In contrast Busenitz and Barney view managers in established firms as driven by company routines and organizational structures that reduce uncertainty and complexity, thereby allowing them to be more analytical in their decision-making practices. The implication of their work is that entrepreneurs differ from managers in their willingness to take risks in making resource allocation decisions based upon partial and uncertain information on the likely outcomes of entrepreneurial opportunities.

Although Busenitz and Barney's (1997) comparison of the traits that differentiate independent entrepreneurs from corporate managers may be valid as a general rule, the literature on corporate entrepreneurship is devoted to the exceptions, in the sense of managerial behavior that goes beyond implementing prevailing routines or relying on existing organizational structure in large established firms (e.g., Burgelman, 1991, 1994). Furthermore, some managers and some established companies are more entrepreneurial than others (e.g., Covin and Slevin, 1991).

In this chapter we use the precepts of prospect theory to help explain how the frames of reference of managers at different levels in an established company will create stable or shifting biases for or against entrepreneurial initiatives depending upon the type and source of the initiative. We argue that managers' biases toward entrepreneurial initiatives may vary according to their roles in the entrepreneurial process and these variations will affect initiative evaluation and implementation challenges.

Understanding the causes of these biases represents a first step toward the design of corporate policies to minimize their potentially adverse consequences to firm performance.

We therefore contribute to both theory and practice by explaining the bases for the differences in the decision-making biases of managers in established organizations toward different entrepreneurial initiatives. We refer to these differences as bias duality, which is the tendency of corporate managers to perceive the risk of entrepreneurial initiatives as desirable or undesirable according to the role that they assume in the entrepreneurial process. We argue that managers may play different roles in different entrepreneurial initiatives (strategic renewal versus corporate venturing) depending on both their level in the organization (top versus middle or lower) and the source of the initiative (autonomous versus induced). In turn, the roles that managers play determine the frame for their mental accounting of the risk of entrepreneurship. We further contribute to the literature by explaining how and why there might sometimes be a reversal of initial biases of managers as an entrepreneurial initiative unfolds. Bias reversal refers to the tendency of managers to alter their mental accounting of the risk associated with an entrepreneurial initiative in accordance with changes that occur in their roles.

Achieving a better understanding of the conditions that influence the propensity of managers in established firms to behave entrepreneurially is important: such organizations face strong competitive pressures and consequently need entrepreneurial initiatives as much as newly established firms (Birkinshaw, 2000). Managers in established organizations therefore often need to take on entrepreneurial roles and adopt patterns of risk taking, including making decisions based on limited information in the face of high uncertainty, very similar to the entrepreneurial role of a company's founder as described by Busenitz and Barney (1997).

However, unlike company founders, managers in established organizations must deal with a broader and more complex organizational context when making or implementing entrepreneurial decisions. This organizational context typically means that the managers who conceive entrepreneurial initiatives may be different from those who approve and implement them. This by itself helps explain bias duality in established firms, with some managers acting in a risk-seeking manner and others in a risk-averting fashion. In addition the more complex organizational context prevailing in established companies also suggests that the same managers may perform different roles in different entrepreneurial processes within the same company, and that their roles may change over time, even within a single entrepreneurial process. As a result, bias reversal may occur. Bias duality and bias reversal imply that a manager may frame all of the entrepreneurial initiatives that he or she initiates based on one mental account (typically associated with risk seeking), whereas the framing for the same manager may be based on a second mental account (typically associated with risk averting) when acting as the evaluator and funder, as opposed to the implementer, of entrepreneurial initiatives that are initiated by others.

A mental account is a frame for evaluating a class of activities that is distinct in an individual's mind (Thaler, 1999). The mental account is linked to the individual's past experiences, and is associated with specific heuristics affecting subsequent decisions and actions regarding the activity class. Individuals operate a number of mental accounts, each associated with specific routines (and biases) to evaluate and act upon new information. This cognitive segmentation explains why the same manager can sometimes adopt radically different decision-rules and engage in radically different behavior when faced with entrepreneurial initiatives, which substantively may be similar, depending on his or her role in the process.

In the following section we distinguish among four distinct corporate entrepreneurial processes based on their type (corporate venturing versus strategic renewal) and their source (autonomous versus induced entrepreneurial initiatives). After laying this foundation we use prospect theory to explain the biases that can be expected from managers at different hierarchical levels and how in certain cases these biases can be subject to reversal as the entrepreneurial process unfolds. We conclude by discussing implications for research and practice.

DEFINITIONS AND SCOPE

Managers sometimes do engage in risk-seeking behavior similar to that expected from the company founders in Busenitz and Barney's (1997) study. However, managerial biases toward risk seeking or risk aversion do not simply result from entrepreneurial proclivities: these biases also depend upon the specific roles managers play in the entrepreneurial process, a point well understood in the literature on strategic decision making in established firms (Bower, 1970; Burgelman, 1983a, b).

However, before explaining how managerial roles influence risk biases, we need to make a distinction between the two basic types of entrepreneurial initiatives: corporate venturing and strategic renewal (e.g., Birkinshaw, 1999, 2000; Burgelman, 1983a, b; Covin and Miles, 1999; Zahra, 1993). Guth and Ginsberg (1990: 5) refer to corporate venturing as 'the birth of new businesses within existing organizations' and to strategic renewal as the 'transformation of organizations through renewal of the key ideas on which they are built'. Sharma and Chrisman (1999) further clarify the above distinction when they suggest that corporate venturing leads to the creation of completely new businesses within a company and strategic renewal involves the reconfiguration of the strategies and/or structures of existing businesses.

Both corporate venturing and strategic renewal initiatives can arise in two ways: through autonomous or induced processes (Sharma and Chrisman, 1999). Autonomous initiatives arise from the bottom-up. They are created by middle and/or lower level managers, who do so without the prior mandate or approval of top management. By contrast, top managers drive induced initiatives and then assign middle and lower level managers to implement those initiatives. Where an entrepreneurial initiative originates determines which manager(s) assume the role of entrepreneur, and influences other managers' attitudes toward the initiative.

AUTONOMOUS CORPORATE VENTURING AND INDUCED STRATEGIC RENEWAL

In this section we discuss internal corporate venture creation efforts (i.e., the creation of new businesses inside the firm) that occur through the autonomous activities of managers and employees at middle and lower levels in an organization, and strategic renewal activities that are induced by top management (Birkinshaw, 1999, 2000; Sharma and Chrisman, 1999). We focus on these types of initiatives first because the biases of managers toward risk seeking or risk aversion are expected to remain stable as the entrepreneurial process unfolds.

In a later section we will discuss the initiatives where corporate venturing is induced by top managers (Sharma and Chrisman, 1999) and those whereby strategic renewal reflects autonomous initiatives of middle to lower level managers (e.g., Burgelman, 1991). We suggest that in these initiatives the individuals who perform the roles of entrepreneur and non-entrepreneur may change as the entrepreneurial process unfolds, causing bias reversal to occur. Here the process of evaluation and implementation will be more complex, as the biases of managers at different hierarchical levels will switch back and forth from those of risk-seeking entrepreneurs to risk averse non-entrepreneurs, or vice versa. Figure 14.1 presents a simple classification of the four types of internal entrepreneurial initiatives.

Autonomous corporate venturing reflects strategic behavior characterized by lower and middle level managers' attempts to respond to opportunities for the creation of new businesses within a company and to gain top management support for them (Burgelman, 1983b). Autonomous

Initiative Source

	Induced	Autonomous
Strategic Renewal	Induced Strategic Renewal	Autonomous Strategic Renewal
Initiative Type		
Corporate Venturing	Induced Corporate Venturing	Autonomous Corporate Venturing

Figure 14.1   Unbundling internal entrepreneurial initiatives in established firms

corporate venturing is therefore a bottom-up process. In contrast, induced strategic renewal at the business level addresses changes to a company's business strategy in response to emerging opportunities, environmental change (Meyer et al., 1990) or a gap between an organization's perform-ance and its present or future aspirations (Cyert and March, 1963). It is a top-down process instigated by top management, which selects and enacts different initiatives to promote changes in a particular business or set of businesses.

These stylized distinctions are mirrored by differences in the specific location of the entrepreneurs who formulate and promote these two types of initiatives in the firm. Since autonomous corporate venturing emerges through processes originating at lower managerial levels (Burgelman and Sayles, 1986), the actual entrepreneurs for a specific initiative are the indi-viduals or teams at lower and middle managerial levels who will create and implement the ventures, provided they are able to gain approval and funding from top management. In contrast, induced strategic renewal occurs when top management prescribes major changes in the strategy or structure of an existing business to create or sustain competitive advan-tages (Covin and Miles, 1999; Floyd and Lane, 2000). In that case, top managers are the actual entrepreneurs. However, in contrast to the case of autonomous corporate venturing, induced strategic renewal initiatives are not implemented by the entrepreneurs (top managers) themselves but rather by managers and employees at middle and lower levels in the organ-ization who may have had little if anything to do with the entrepreneurial idea. Put differently, unlike the case of autonomous corporate venturing, induced strategic renewal implies an entrepreneurial process that distances the entrepreneurs who identify, define and initially act upon the entrepreneurial opportunity, from the managers who are responsible for carrying out this predefined initiative.

The distinction between the location of manager-entrepreneurs and non-entrepreneurs in the firm's hierarchy, as well as the respective roles of each in the entrepreneurial process, is important because they help identify the different biases and resulting tensions that occur in autonomous corporate venturing versus induced strategic renewal. For example, in the former, dysfunctional selection pressures to achieve immediate results may lead to strategic forcing efforts, whereby the manager-entrepreneur attempts to implement plans for product development or market penetration quickly so top management does not become discouraged or lose interest and withdraw its support (Burgelman and Sayles, 1986). Unfortunately such forcing often occurs at the expense of the development of an administrative infrastructure, with potentially deleterious consequences for the venture (Burgelman and Sayles, 1986).

By contrast, induced strategic renewal initiatives may experience different dysfunctional effects, most notably organizational resistance (Crossan and Berdrow, 2003) or inertia (Hannan and Freeman, 1989). Resistance or inertia occurs when the managers who did not contribute to the original idea but are responsible for its implementation do not fully share the vision, commitment and understanding of the need for the change, or otherwise experience difficulties in adjusting to their new roles and tasks (Floyd and Lane, 2000). Such dysfunctions could diminish the probability of the success of the renewal initiative (Hannan and Freeman, 1989).

The problems facing entrepreneurial initiatives in established firms are well documented in the literature (Christensen, 1997). In the next section we go a step further and use prospect theory to analyse the unfolding of the corporate entrepreneurial process.

THE CONTRIBUTION OF PROSPECT THEORY

Kahneman (2003) explains that people's observed tendency to switch from risk averse to risk-seeking behavior, depending on the circumstances, does not correspond at all with Bernoulli's theory of expected utility. Bernoulli's decision rule for choice under risk is to maximize the expected utility of wealth, but this appears incorrect as a descriptive model of risky choices. In contrast, prospect theory (Kahneman and Tversky, 1979, 2000; Tversky and Kahneman, 1986, 1992) proposes that individuals normally exhibit the bias of risk aversion for two reasons. First, they systematically prefer alternatives that appear more certain to alternatives that seem less certain (i.e., that involve gambles) even if such preferences conflict with the choice of alternatives that offer the highest expected value. This bias is the certainty effect. Second, when faced with gambles, possible losses are systematically given higher weights than possible gains. This bias is the loss aversion effect, which favors avoiding risks. However, there are two important exceptions to this observation of risk aversion. The opposite bias of risk seeking may occur if the possibility exists of very high gains, even if associated with a low probability of occurrence, as with the purchase of a lottery ticket. In addition the bias of risk seeking is also likely if it permits losses to be avoided that otherwise would be certain, even if by doing so it creates the possibility of even higher losses.

APPLICATION TO ENTREPRENEURIAL INITIATIVES

Entrepreneurial initiatives typically both require and stimulate risk-seeking bias on the part of entrepreneurs, because most initiatives embody a possibility of high return (at least as compared with the return of the present, mainstream activities of the firm), even if associated with a high risk of failure or significant losses. These initiatives may also be viewed in terms of avoiding losses that would be certain if no action were undertaken: if an entrepreneur truly believes in an initiative, he/she will view inaction as handing the opportunity over to a competitor, thus leading to a certain opportunity loss.

However, the question then arises why manager-entrepreneurs would view an entrepreneurial initiative differently from other managers or, in other words, why entrepreneurs are more likely to adopt the biases of overconfidence and over-generalization in favor of new initiatives than non-entrepreneurs (Busenitz and Barney, 1997; Palich and Bagby, 1995)? A primary reason is the framing effect, which has two components. First, manager-entrepreneurs usually conceive initiatives from information received directly from the external environment. This information is typically framed in the form of very broad opportunities (new customer demands, supplier suggestions, macro-economic trends, etc.). Here manager-entrepreneurs are typically subject to positive framing forces from the outside or, as Kirzner (1973) has suggested, they are alert to opportunities. Second, manager-entrepreneurs then engage in their own framing efforts: they reconstruct the outside information in the form of demand-forecasts, growth scenarios, and so on. Such reconstruction leads to the creation of an 'inside view' (Kahneman and Lovallo, 1993). The inside view typically leads to an overestimation of both the probability of gain and the 'certain' losses associated with the status quo (cf., Palich and Bagby, 1995). The drivers of this excessive optimism include three parameters: the self as the source of success, the probable state of future environmental parameters, and the ability to control events (Taylor and Brown, 1988). As a result, scenarios of the future often tend to be divorced from the analysis of past performance and events, which, if taken into account, would lead to a more conservative view (Kahneman and Lovallo, 1993). From a cognitive perspective, the entrepreneurial initiative is driven by risk-seeking heuristics prevailing in the mental account of the manager-entrepreneur, which is relevant to the entire class of self-initiated entrepreneurial initiatives.

In contrast, managers (non-entrepreneurs) who have not been involved in the entrepreneurial framing process tend to frame the entrepreneurial initiative using a mental account that involves the more conventional risk aversion bias (e.g., Alvarez and Barney, 2005). For non-entrepreneurs who act as decision makers on resource allocation, or as managers implementing the decisions of others, the entrepreneurial initiative is presented to them as a gamble, which they compare with the status quo. The status quo means the continuation and further implementation of initiatives entailing well-known activity bundles and relatively certain outcomes. In the absence of a major crisis situation, and assuming a generally favorable context, non-entrepreneurial managers will show a bias favoring the present situation and reject the gamble (Kahneman et al., 1991). Put differently, managers tend to use a very different mental account when assessing the initiatives of others as compared with the mental account that would prevail for self-initiated entrepreneurial efforts.

Interestingly, even though the stakes involved in autonomous corporate venturing are usually relatively small vis-à-vis mainstream activities (Kanter et al., 1991), and there is a possibility of portfolio effects from the pursuit of multiple, small entrepreneurial ventures, managerial risk aversion will typically not be moderated by these factors. Here the isolation effect prevails (Kahneman and Lovallo, 1993), meaning that managers (non-entrepreneurs) will tend to frame their decision as if they were assessing a stand-alone venture, without relating it to the organization's other activities (thus neglecting portfolio benefits) or to the organization's future development path (thus neglecting real options for the future). Empirical results provide support for the isolation bias effect. For example, it has been reported that subjects tend to overestimate the probability of loss on a gamble even though that probability decreases when the number of gambles is repeated (Klos et al., 2005).

Even when moving away from a narrow frame of reference, individuals will tend to base their decisions on entrepreneurial initiatives according to strategic reference points such as perceived internal capabilities, external conditions and time (Fiegenbaum et al., 1996), within the context of the specific mental account considered relevant; that is, for managers (non-entrepreneurs) one that does not include self-initiated initiatives. Here reference points such as outcome history and domain familiarity can affect the risk behavior of decision makers (Sitkin and Pablo, 1992). Interestingly, when managers (non-entrepreneurs) evaluate an entrepreneurial initiative, their attempt to broaden the framing will typically include a comparison with the performance of past initiatives within the class of non-self-initiated efforts, but still discarding the portfolio effects of the present set of new entrepreneurial initiatives. This last bias has been termed myopic loss aversion (Thaler, 1999).

Thus, because individuals do not adopt a comprehensive view of consequences (Whyte, 1986), a single initiative can be subject to risk-seeking or risk aversion biases, depending upon whether the initiative is viewed from the perspective of the entrepreneur who uses one mental account, or from the perspective of the non-entrepreneurial manager who uses a different mental account, when evaluating or implementing this same initiative (Tversky and Kahneman, 1992).

Although both the entrepreneur and the non-entrepreneur have in principle the same information, different aspects of the information become more relevant to each. For example, the entrepreneur will realize that not executing the initiative will lead to losses with certainty far quicker than they will realize that the initiative might have a high probability of leading to even more severe losses; the initiative has been framed in terms of an opportunity for high gains and avoidance of certain (sure) losses. Absent careful scrutiny by an outside voice, this bias leads to the systematic presence of 'optimistic errors' in project implementation (Kahneman and Lovallo, 1993). Perceptions lead to intuitive judgments far quicker than rational choices, which are based on reasoning, a slower process.

AUTONOMOUS CORPORATE VENTURING AND INDUCED STRATEGIC RENEWAL REVISITED

Prospect theory thus suggests that individuals will normally evaluate possible outcomes as gains or losses relative to some frame of reference rather than evaluating them according to the expected values of the alternatives (Kahneman and Tversky, 1979, 2000; Tversky and Kahneman, 1986, 1992). Since autonomous corporate venturing and induced strategic renewal are different with regard to the reference points of managers at different organizational levels, the biases from which top managers and managers at middle and lower levels approach these initiatives will also be different.

In the case of induced strategic renewal, top managers, acting as entrepreneurs, will pursue an initiative when they perceive the failure to do so will lead to a certain loss. Again the perceived loss may be tangible or may reflect the loss of an opportunity. Being the creator and promoter of the initiative, top managers will operate within the mental account of self-initiated initiatives, and will therefore be biased in favor of risk seeking, that is, perceiving that the organization will certainly lose (i.e., aspiration levels will not be achieved) if the initiative is not implemented. Top managers will also focus on the possibility of a high return as compared with the status quo (i.e., aspiration levels will be achieved or surpassed).

In contrast, in the case of autonomous corporate venturing, biases may lead top managers to perceive entrepreneurial opportunities brought from lower or middle levels of the organization as risky chances of gain enhancement relative to the certain gain of the status quo. Here the mental account of non-self-initiated efforts prevails. As a result, top managers will tend to be risk averse in their evaluation of corporate venturing efforts. Thus:

Proposition 1: A bias duality will be observed at the level of top managers, who are likely to evaluate induced strategic renewal initiatives more positively than autonomous corporate venturing initiatives.

Owing to differences in their proximity to the initial stages of autonomous corporate venturing and induced strategic renewal initiatives, the entrepreneurial managers at lower and middle organizational levels are likely to operate according to different mental accounts with opposite reference points and, therefore, opposite risk biases. Thus, similar to the argument stated above, entrepreneurs at middle and lower levels in an organization who promote a venturing initiative are likely to perceive a certain loss of opportunity if the initiative is not implemented, and will consequently focus on the high possible gain associated with the self-initiated entrepreneurial initiative. These entrepreneurs will therefore tend to operate on the basis of a mental account favoring risk seeking, in keeping with their commitment to making the initiative a success.

In contrast, non-entrepreneurs at middle and lower organizational levels will tend to be biased toward risk aversion when asked to implement strategic renewal initiatives induced by top management. Relative to top management, a different mental account will prevail, namely the one for non-self-initiated efforts that is a consequence of their lack of ownership of the idea, lack of understanding the need for change and perhaps even the potential loss to their status or security brought about by the change. Consequently, non-entrepreneurs at middle and lower organizational levels are likely to contrast the risky gain of renewal with, in their minds, the more certain gain of the status quo. Thus, the commitment to strategic renewal among those responsible for implementing the changes, when those managers are not the entrepreneurs, is expected to be lower than the commitment of these same managers, when initiating autonomous initiatives themselves. The commitment will also be lower than that of the entrepreneurs (top managers) who proposed the renewal initiative. As a result, we propose:

> *Proposition 2: A bias duality will be observed at the level of middle and lower level management, who are more likely to show a higher commitment to the autonomous corporate venturing initiatives they have conceived than to the induced strategic renewal initiatives they must implement.*

INDUCED CORPORATE VENTURING AND AUTONOMOUS STRATEGIC RENEWAL

Now that we have dealt with autonomous corporate venturing and induced strategic renewal where risk biases are likely to remain stable, we turn our attention to induced corporate venturing and autonomous strategic renewal where risk biases are likely to shift as the initiative unfolds. We consider induced corporate venturing first.

Induced corporate venturing involves efforts mandated by top management to create new businesses within an existing company (Sharma and Chrisman, 1999). As a consequence of similarities in where the initiative originates, induced corporate venturing efforts should have some of the same problems inherent in induced strategic renewal during its initial stages. However, as explained below, owing to the nature of the venturing process, induced venturing efforts may begin to resemble autonomous venturing efforts as time progresses.

Induced corporate venturing will share, at least initially, the characteristic of the location of the entrepreneur in the firm's hierarchy with induced strategic renewal, implying that the top managers who instigate such initiatives will frame them from a risk-seeking perspective and that the middle and lower level managers who are assigned the task of actually creating the ventures will adopt a risk aversion bias. This risk aversion bias of middle and lower level managers responsible for actually setting up the venture suggests that their commitment to the venture might initially be low. Unlike strategic renewal, however, venturing initiatives involve, by definition, discrete businesses. Thus, the middle and lower level managers assigned the responsibility of championing the initiatives can be expected to have greater discretion in decision making than those involved in strategic renewal efforts. The discretion in decision-making authority, combined with the accumulation of new knowledge as the venture development process unfolds, increase the probability that the perceived ownership and commitment of the middle and lower level managers assigned to the venture will increase, thereby changing their framing bias from risk aversion to risk seeking. Simply put, as the entrepreneurial process unfolds, induced venturing efforts may come to resemble induced strategic renewal efforts less and autonomous venturing efforts more in regard to the mental accounts in which they are framed.

However, such bias reversal comes at a price: top management's risk perceptions may also shift toward those described for ventures of the autonomous variety, corresponding to the shift in entrepreneurial 'ownership' of the initiative, as well as the changes that occur to the venture strategy in its natural process of development. Furthermore, corporate venturing, which usually involves a smaller investment, is likely to command a smaller proportion of top management's attention than strategic renewal (Guth and Ginsberg, 1990; Kanter et al., 1991). Put differently, owing to the nature of the corporate venturing process, top managers may come to view induced ventures from a bias of risk aversion, in contrast to their initial risk-seeking bias. Such bias reversal is particularly likely when only the *concept* of corporate venturing is institutionalized by top managers, as in the case of the creation of a new venture division designed to promote entrepreneurship among employees (cf. Kanter et al., 1991).

Unfortunately, entrepreneurship by fiat is less likely to produce a venture champion than entrepreneurship by choice, especially if potential champions believe that the problems inherent in autonomous ventures will also materialize for the induced variety (as we propose they will): in this case, the intended, and hoped-for, bias reversal may not materialize. The difficulties in producing a champion are exacerbated by the role ambiguities middle level managers might experience as they are called upon to switch from being facilitators and implementers at early stages in the venturing process to synthesizers and champions during later stages of venture development (Floyd and Lane, 2000). In summary, for induced internal ventures, not only will bias duality occur, but also the framing of risk, being dependent on a more complex and less stable set of factors, may cause bias reversals over time. Thus:

Proposition 3: The perception of top managers of induced corporate venturing is subject to bias reversal: the risk-seeking bias during the early stages of a venture's development is likely to be replaced by a risk-averting bias during its later stages of development.

Proposition 4: The commitment of middle and lower level managers involved in induced corporate venturing is subject to bias reversal: the risk-averting bias during the early stages of a venture's development is likely to be replaced by a risk-seeking bias during its later stages of development.

As was the case for induced corporate venturing, the location of the primary entrepreneur is also expected to shift over time, with a corresponding bias reversal, in the case of autonomous strategic renewal. However, the reversal will be in the opposite direction. Furthermore, the initial problems with evaluation, as well as those of commitment inherent in the bias reversals, are expected to be more severe, owing to the need for widespread involvement of managers throughout the organization (Floyd and Lane, 2000). Thus, in the initial stages of autonomous strategic renewal, the entrepreneurs at middle and lower levels of an organization who are responding to stimuli from the external environment face the uphill battle of convincing top management of the need for change. Even in situations where the organizational environment is such that approval and support are more readily forthcoming, this can be a difficult and tedious task (Burgelman, 1991, 1994).

The initial difficulties of obtaining positive evaluations from top management are further complicated in autonomous strategic renewal because the middle and lower level managers who initiate the renewal effort may need to convince at least some of the middle and lower level managers in other parts of the organization that renewal is required. For example, it could become necessary to elicit their support in presenting formal proposals to top management (Floyd and Lane, 2000). However, managers who are not directly involved in the initiative are likely to adopt a non-entrepreneurial mental accounting frame and thus exhibit risk aversion bias. The risk aversion biases of these managers might be even stronger than those of top management if their orientations, organizational sub-cultures or functional expertise are substantially different from the entrepreneurial managers who initiated the renewal effort (Floyd and Lane, 2000).

Assuming that the evaluation by top management of the autonomous strategic renewal effort is positive (if it is not, of course, the initiative will not be pursued further), their biases concerning the risk of the initiative should reverse from risk aversion toward risk seeking in accordance with their shift toward an entrepreneurial perspective when assuming control of the initiative. At this point the problems of autonomous strategic renewal efforts are expected to resemble those of induced strategic renewal efforts:

middle and lower level managers who were not involved in the initiative from the outset and/or who did not 'buy into' the idea when it was presented to top management (and this is likely to be the majority of such managers) will tend to adopt a risk aversion bias. Changing such biases can be slow and difficult (Burgelman, 1991; Crossan and Berdrow, 2003). Unlike induced corporate venturing, perceptions of entrepreneurial ownership are less likely to develop owing to the fact that strategic renewal entails changes throughout the organization, obligating greater top management involvement and correspondingly diminishing the roles and potential rewards of prospective champions. As Kahneman and Lovallo (1993) suggest, in general blame for failure is likely to be more quickly bestowed and more pronounced than the credit for success; anything that exacerbates such asymmetries will likely bode ill for the risk assessments of middle and lower level managers involved in implementation. Furthermore, if, as is likely, non-entrepreneurial middle and lower level managers are emotionally attached to the old strategy or view the renewal effort as a threat to their power positions (Burgelman, 1994), their risk aversion bias will be even greater. Thus, if top management approves an autonomous strategic renewal initiative, the situation may evolve into one similar to that described for induced strategic renewal and we have:

Proposition 5: The perception of top managers of autonomous strategic renewal initiatives is subject to bias reversal: the risk averse bias during the early stages of the renewal's development is likely to be replaced by a risk-seeking bias during its later stages.

Proposition 6: Middle and lower level managers who were not responsible for starting autonomous strategic renewal initiatives are likely to exhibit a risk aversion bias, with a concomitant low commitment to the initiative.

To summarize, the risk assessments of managers for autonomous strategic renewal and induced corporate venturing will be less stable compared with their risk assessments for induced strategic renewal and autonomous corporate venturing (see Figure 14.2). As the entrepreneurial process unfolds, evaluations of risk averse top managers are expected to cause induced corporate venturing to take on characteristics that resemble autonomous corporate venturing. Likewise with the passage of time, the commitment of risk averse middle and lower level managers to autonomous strategic renewal is expected to become the central issue, just as it is for induced strategic renewal. Both shifts involve reversals in the risk biases of top and middle/lower managers, vis-à-vis the situations at the time when the initiative is proposed and launched.

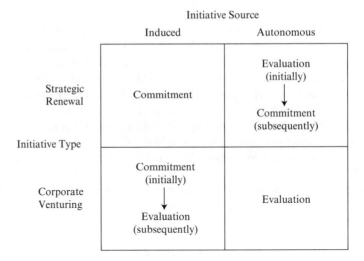

Figure 14.2 Main problems associated with strategic renewal and corporate venturing

DISCUSSION AND CONCLUSION

We have argued that managers' risk assessments of entrepreneurial initiatives are likely to be biased and this bias will depend upon both the type (strategic renewal versus corporate venturing) and source (autonomous versus induced) of initiative undertaken. A primary source of the distinction lies in the difference in the specific mental account by which manager-entrepreneurs (the 'initiators') and non-entrepreneurs frame the initiatives. This difference in the mental accounts adopted is critical to explain the existence of bias duality in established firms, and to determine which specific actors involved will adopt a risk seeking- versus a risk-averting bias. The key point is that the occurrence of risk-seeking versus risk-averting behavior depends on the manager's role in the evolving autonomous or induced initiative process.

Thus, this chapter contributes to theory and practice by explaining the sources of bias toward entrepreneurial initiatives held by managers in established companies and how these biases might influence the evaluation, funding and implementation of such initiatives. A further contribution of this chapter is the identification of the situations where the initial biases of managers might reverse as the entrepreneurial process unfolds. These contributions are important because understanding managerial biases helps in predicting when sub-optimal decision making with regard to entrepreneurial initiatives might occur as well as in designing corporate policies that might reduce the likelihood and impact of such biases. We address these issues below and thereby expand upon the contributions of this chapter by discussing the performance implications of bias duality and bias reversal, how biases in decision making might be reduced and the more complex decision-making contexts facing multidivisional and multinational corporations. We also briefly discuss how the propositions developed in this chapter might be tested.

Performance of Corporate Venturing Initiatives

It should be apparent from our discussion that there are structural, built-in biases in the way top managers will evaluate the prospects for different types and sources of entrepreneurial initiatives. All things being equal, we have suggested that top managers are more likely to favor induced strategic renewal and less likely to support autonomous internal corporate venturing. Because these biases in evaluation result from different mental accounts, which are likely to be relatively stable, autonomous ventures that do make it through the corporate evaluation process are likely to be subject to perverse selection pressures, which may diminish their ability to meet performance expectations (Burgelman and Sayles, 1986). In other words, when top managers do approve autonomous corporate venturing initiatives, they will tend to be biased in favor of ventures that are less innovative because these will be seen to entail lower risk. Unfortunately, if our arguments are correct, induced corporate venturing efforts will not long escape the problems inherent in autonomous corporate venturing because of the possible bias reversal of top managers from risk seeking to risk aversion as the venture develops. Thus, it is not surprising that past research has shown that many corporate ventures fail to meet expectations and, in general, experience performance outcomes that are lower or no better than independent ventures (Shrader and Simon, 1997).

Second, such unfavorable performance outcomes may heighten the risk aversion biases of managers in established organizations. Specifically, the narrow framing by managers who were not involved in formulating a new entrepreneurial initiative will typically include information on how earlier initiatives have fared when assessing a new initiative. Such tightened scrutiny may negatively affect the risk-seeking biases of the would-be manager-entrepreneurs themselves, and these actors may become increasingly reluctant to take responsibility for any future losses (Kahneman and Lovallo, 1993). As regards to framing, it should also be remembered that autonomous initiatives are always at a disadvantage vis-à-vis all other initiatives in terms of the evaluations of top management. There is an inherent bias in human decision making that favors the default option; meaning in this case induced initiatives, which are, by definition, consistent with top management's conception of strategy (Burgelman, 1983a, b). Because of the mental account prevailing for the assessment of existing operations and induced initiatives, top managers will tend to view the expected gains and risks from existing operations and/or induced initiatives more favorably, whether a more objective assessment would warrant that view or not. In contrast, the mental account operated for autonomous initiatives will foster the rejection of autonomous initiatives, even if those initiatives could potentially raise a firm's gains substantially (Thaler, 1999). Here the concept of target earnings within a short-term time frame prevails over a longer-term perspective.

Interestingly, the above problem can likely be somewhat attenuated if induced and autonomous initiatives are assessed as part of the same capital budgeting effort. With a single capital budgeting process, diversification bias involving the simultaneous assessment of many different initiatives should incite individuals not to put all their eggs in one basket, but rather to achieve some, perhaps naive, level of distributive equity (Kahneman and Lovallo, 1993; Thaler, 1999). The objective, of course, is not to achieve distributive equity per se, but rather to ensure that all initiatives are assessed, using a single mental account. In particular, autonomous initiatives should not be assessed on a stand-alone basis or in a sequential fashion, as this could lead to the systematic rejection of each of these independent 'gambles' in favor of the status quo. Simultaneity in entrepreneurial initiative evaluation could potentially foster broader framing and more favorable risk assessments (e.g., Klos et al., 2005).

Further Problems with Strategic Renewal

Bias in evaluation is perhaps more troubling with respect to induced strategic renewal efforts. Because these generally put more of an organization's resources at risk than corporate venturing efforts (Guth and Ginsberg, 1990; Kanter et al., 1991), corporations cannot afford to make the wrong choices. Yet our theoretical discussion suggests that firms will make such mistakes, more often than not. Making matters worse, because the middle and lower level managers responsible for implementing the new strategy and/or structure are likely to possess different frames of reference and make different assessments of the probabilities of success, as compared with the higher-ranked corporate entrepreneurs, the commitment of the former to the initiative can be expected to be lower. As we have explained, lower commitment might engender resistance or inertia, slowing down the process of implementation and further reducing the probabilities of success. Thus, at any given level of entrepreneurial orientation induced strategic renewal efforts are more likely to be pursued and less likely to succeed than corporate venturing efforts (cf., Wiseman and Bromiley, 1996). Unfortunately, though autonomous strategic renewal efforts that successfully overcome the obstacles placed in their way by risk averse top managers are perhaps more likely to be well conceived as a consequence, they will still ultimately face the same problems of commitment that can plague induced strategic renewal efforts owing to the need to elicit broad support from middle and lower level managers across the organization. The prospects of a broad group of managers admitting to ownership of such an initiative are more remote than in corporate venturing efforts where responsibility and rewards are more focused. Consequently, risk aversion may limit the willingness of middle and lower level managers to make the commitment necessary for the success of an autonomous strategic renewal initiative.

Thus, strategic renewal efforts are likely to exhibit lower average performance, yet potentially even wider performance variations (more spectacular successes and failures), than corporate venturing efforts. Whether empirical analysis proves this to be the case or not, we feel rather confident that a more complete understanding of risk frames and risk perceptions, through the use of prospect theory, will yield better answers to the problems we have enumerated than have been available heretofore.

Multidivisional and Multinational Contexts

Before closing, we turn to a brief discussion of the implications of the situation of companies that have multiple product divisions, multiple groups, or compete internationally using global or multi-domestic structures. Here the situation becomes even more complex and potentially more interesting due to the presence of additional layers of management, each with different frames of reference and assessments of risk probabilities. One might expect, for instance, that even allowing for advantages in experience, the challenge of strategic renewal efforts in multidivisional or multinational corporations would be at least different, if not greater, than in single-business corporations since corporate strategic renewal efforts would require the collaboration of managers at all levels of the organization (Burgelman, 1991, 1994). Thus, divisional managers, recognizing the need to engage in strategic renewal efforts, would not only need to rally their subordinate managers to the cause but also need to gain the support of managers at corporate headquarters. This latter group of managers would be likely to view those efforts from the bias of risk aversion rather than risk seeking. Although this might put a brake on ill-conceived efforts, it might also stop ones that were more carefully thought out. Likewise corporate venturing efforts might be less common in companies where approval depends upon the assessments of corporate as well as divisional management. In such cases favorable entrepreneurial orientations in the firm become more important for any initiative to have a chance (Covin and Slevin, 1991).

There is a wide scope for investigating entrepreneurial initiatives from a risk orientation in multidivisional and multinational companies, and such investigations may yield important insights. For example, the potential impediments to entrepreneurship may be especially great in situations where strategic coordination across business units needs to be high, such as when a multinational firm follows a global strategy, but where a high level of cultural, administrative, geographic and economic distance separates corporate level managers and entrepreneurs in foreign subsidiaries. Such impediments to entrepreneurship may help to explain Rugman's (2005) observation that most large multinational enterprises are home-region based, and lack a strong position in host regions, especially at the downstream end of the value chain. In cases of high distance, even top managers in the home country with strong entrepreneurial orientations may become risk averse to autonomous subsidiary initiatives (Verbeke and Yuan, 2005).

Empirical Testing

The propositions developed in this chapter can be tested directly or indirectly. Direct tests may require qualitative methods owing to the need to assess biases in decision making at different managerial levels, how biases vary for different entrepreneurial initiatives and whether such biases change as initiatives unfold. However, indirect tests are also possible. For example, archival data might be used to assess the frequency with which different kinds of initiatives are implemented and survey methodologies might assist in determining the levels of funding and commitment for the initiatives that were approved. As suggested above, a comparison of the survival and performance of different types of initiatives would constitute another indirect test of our propositions. Finally, conjoint analyses offer another fruitful opportunity to test the biases of managers toward different kinds of entrepreneurial initiatives.

CONCLUSION

In conclusion, using the precepts of prospect theory we have introduced the concepts of bias duality and bias reversal to explain the differences in the risk perceptions of top and middle level managers concerning different types of entrepreneurial initiatives in established companies. By doing so, we have offered a more nuanced explanation of the tendency for risk aversion among corporate managers noted by Busenitz and Barney (1997). We have also explained when this general rule does not apply, owing to the framing of entrepreneurial initiatives from a mental account that promotes risk-seeking behavior. Furthermore, we have discussed situations where the framing of corporate managers may be reversed as an entrepreneurial initiative unfolds.

The organizational context of specific entrepreneurial initiative categories related to initiative type and initiative source will influence which managers will wear an entrepreneurial hat and which managers will not, irrespective of their intrinsic entrepreneurial traits. Importantly, established firms face the constant duality of the contradictory biases of risk seeking and risk aversion, which may help explain the recurrent observation that these firms have trouble innovating (Christensen, 1997). Our chapter contributes to the literature on corporate entrepreneurship by showing how this structural bias duality unfolds in autonomous corporate venturing and induced strategic renewal initiatives, and also how bias reversal is likely to play out in the less stable cases of induced corporate venturing and autonomous strategic renewal.

More importantly, our application of prospect theory suggests that the potential benefits corporate entrepreneurship can bring to established organizations may be less likely to occur if differences in dominant mental accounts and related risk perceptions among managers, depending on their role in the entrepreneurial process, are not addressed. We therefore encourage researchers and managers to use these insights in particular, and the precepts of prospect theory in general, in future studies of strategic renewal and corporate venturing initiatives.

NOTE

* The authors thank LaKami Baker, Frances Bowen, Lowell Busenitz, Jim Dewald, Nathan Greidanus, Franz Kellermanns, Ayesha Malhotra and Pietro Mazzola for their comments on earlier drafts of this manuscript.

REFERENCES

Alvarez, S. A., and J. B. Barney (2005), 'How do entrepreneurs organize firms under conditions of uncertainty?', *Journal of Management*, **31**(5): 776–793.
Birkinshaw, J. (1999), 'The determinants and consequences of subsidiary initiative in multinational corporations', *Entrepreneurship Theory and Practice*, **24**(1): 9–36.

Birkinshaw, J. (2000), *Entrepreneurship in the Global Firm*, London: Sage.
Bower, J. L. (1970), *Managing the Resource Allocation Process: A Study of Corporate Planning and Investment*, Boston, MA: HBS Division of Research.
Burgelman, R. A. (1983a), 'Corporate entrepreneurship and strategic management: Insights from a process study', *Management Science*, **29**: 1349–1364.
Burgelman, R. A. (1983b), 'A model of interaction of strategic behavior, corporate context, and the concept of strategy', *Academy of Management Review*, **8**: 61–70.
Burgelman, R. A. (1991), 'Intraorganizational ecology of strategy making and organizational adaptation: Theory and field research', *Organization Science*, **2**: 239–262.
Burgelman, R. A. (1994), 'Fading memories: A process theory of strategic business exit in dynamic environments', *Administrative Science Quarterly*, **39**(1): 24–56.
Burgelman, R. A. and L. R. Sayles (1986), *Inside Corporate Innovation: Strategy, Structure, and Management Skills*, New York: Free Press.
Busenitz, L. W. and J. B. Barney (1997), 'Differences between entrepreneurs and managers in large organizations: Biases and heuristics in strategic decision making', *Journal of Business Venturing*, **12**(1): 9–30.
Christensen, C. M. (1997), *The Innovator's Dilemma: When New Technologies Cause Great Firms to Fail*, Cambridge, MA: Harvard Business School Press.
Covin, J. G. and M. P. Miles (1999), 'Corporate entrepreneurship and the pursuit of competitive advantage', *Entrepreneurship Theory and Practice*, **23**(3): 47–65.
Covin, J. G. and D. P. Slevin (1991), 'A conceptual model of entrepreneurship as firm behavior', *Entrepreneurship Theory and Practice*, **16**(1): 7–25.
Crossan, M. M. and I. Berdrow (2003), 'Organizational learning and strategic renewal', *Strategic Management Journal*, **24**: 1087–1105.
Cyert, R. M. and J. G. March (1963), *A Behavioral Theory of the Firm*, Englewood Cliffs, NJ: Prentice Hall.
Fiegenbaum, A., S. Hart and D. Schendel (1996), 'Strategic reference point theory', *Strategic Management Journal*, **17**: 219–235.
Floyd, S. W. and P. J. Lane (2000), 'Strategizing throughout the organization: Managing strategic renewal and strategic role conflict', *Academy of Management Review*, **25**: 154–177.
Guth, W. D. and A. Ginsberg (1990), 'Guest editor's introduction: Corporate entrepreneurship', *Strategic Management Journal*, **11**(Summer): 5–16.
Hannan, M. T. and J. Freeman (1989), *Organizational Ecology*, Cambridge, MA: Harvard University Press.
Kahneman, D. (1992), 'Reference points, anchors, norms, and mixed feelings', *Organizational Behavior and Human Decision Processes*, **51**: 296–312.
Kahneman, D. (2003), 'Maps of bounded rationality: Psychology for behavioral economics', *American Economic Review*, **93**: 1449–1475.
Kahneman, D and D. Lovallo (1993), 'Timid choices and bold forecasts: A cognitive perspective on risk taking', *Management Science*, **39**: 17–31.
Kahneman, D. and A. Tversky (1979), 'Prospect theory: An analysis of decision under risk', *Econometrica*, **47**: 263–291.
Kahneman, D. and A. Tversky (2000), *Choices, Values and Frames*, Cambridge, UK: Cambridge University Press.
Kahneman, D., J. Knetsch and R. Thaler (1991), 'The endowment effect, loss aversion and status quo bias anomalies', *Journal of Economic Perspectives*, **5**: 193–206.
Kanter, R. M., L. Richardson, J. North and E. Morgan (1991), 'Engines of progress: Designing and running vehicles in established companies; the new venture process at Eastman Kodak, 1983–1989', *Journal of Business Venturing*, **6**: 63–82.
Kirzner, I. M. (1973), *Competition and Entrepreneurship*, Chicago, IL: University of Chicago Press.
Klos, A., E. Weber and M. Weber (2005), 'Investment decisions and time horizon: Risk perception and risk behavior in repeated gambles', *Management Science*, **51**(12): 1777–1790.
Meyer, A. D., G. R. Brooks and J. B. Goes (1990), 'Environmental jolts and industry

revolutions: Organizational responses to discontinuous change', *Strategic Management Journal*, **11**(Summer): 93–110.

Palich, L. E. and D. R. Bagby (1995), 'Using cognitive theory to explain entrepreneurial risk-taking: Challenging conventional wisdom', *Journal of Business Venturing*, **10**: 425–438.

Rugman, A. M. (2005), *The Regional Multinationals: MNEs and 'Global' Strategic Management*, Cambridge, UK: Cambridge University Press.

Sharma, P. and J. J. Chrisman (1999), 'Toward a reconciliation of the definitional issues in the field of corporate entrepreneurship', *Entrepreneurship Theory and Practice*, **23**(3): 11–28.

Shrader, R. C. and M. Simon (1997), 'Corporate versus independent new ventures: Resource, strategy, and performance differences', *Journal of Business Venturing*, **12**(1): 47–66.

Sitkin, S. B. and A. L. Pablo (1992), 'Reconceptualizing the determinants of risk behavior', *Academy of Management Review*, **17**(1): 9–38.

Taylor, S. E. and J. D. Brown (1988), 'Illusion and well-being: A social and psychological perspective on mental health', *Psychological Bulletin*, **103**: 193–210.

Thaler, R. (1999), 'Mental accounting matters', *Journal of Behavioral Decision Making*, **12**: 183–206.

Tversky, A. and D. Kahneman (1974), 'Judgment under uncertainty: Heuristics and biases', *Science*, **185**: 1124–1131.

Tversky, A. and D. Kahneman (1986), 'Rational choice and the framing of decisions', *Journal of Business*, **59**: S251–S278.

Tversky, A. and D. Kahneman (1992), 'Loss aversion in riskless choice: A reference-dependent model', *Quarterly Journal of Economics*, **107**: 1039–1061.

Verbeke, A. and W. Yuan (2005), 'Subsidiary autonomous activities in multinational enterprises: A transaction cost perspective', *Management International Review*, **45**(S.I. 2): 31–52.

Whyte, G. (1986), 'Escalating commitment to a course of action: A reinterpretation', *Academy of Management Review*, **11**: 311–321.

Wiseman, R. M. and P. Bromiley (1996), 'Toward a model of risk in declining organizations: An empirical examination of risk, performance and decline', *Organization Science*, **7**: 524–543.

Zahra, S. A. (1993), 'Environment, corporate entrepreneurship, and financial performance: A taxonomic approach', *Journal of Business Venturing*, **8**: 319–340.

15 Entrepreneurial orientation: the driving force for corporate entrepreneurship
Esra Memili, G. T. Lumpkin and Gregory G. Dess

INTRODUCTION

Corporate entrepreneurship (CE) and entrepreneurial orientation (EO) have received considerable research interest as they are crucial to organizational survival, profitability, growth, and renewal (Zahra, 1996). Whereas CE serves the purpose of creation and pursuit of new venture opportunities and strategic renewal (Dess and Lumpkin, 2005), EO is the driving force for CE. Indeed, firms with a strong EO – involving the processes, practices, and decision-making styles that help firms identify and capture entrepreneurial opportunities – tend to have competitive advantages in pursuing CE activities that can take the form of internal or external corporate venturing, innovation, and/or strategic renewal (Covin and Slevin, 1991; Kuratko, 2005; Lumpkin and Dess, 1996; Sharma and Chrisman, 1999; Zahra, 1995). Hence, firms that want to successfully pursue CE need to have an EO (Dess and Lumpkin, 2005).

Despite general agreement on the positive contribution of EO and CE, the field of entrepreneurship still lacks agreement on the definitions of terms and the distinctive characteristics of CE and EO (Sharma and Chrisman, 1999). The term 'entrepreneurship' is often used without differentiating between individual, group, and organizational entrepreneurship. In addition to ambiguity regarding the level of analysis, the difference between corporate entrepreneurship and entrepreneurial orientation seems to be conceptually unclear. Such a lack of theoretical clarity inhibits the specification of the domain of the constructs and the development of appropriate measures in empirical entrepreneurship studies, consequently preventing researchers' scientific understanding, explanation, and prediction as well as limiting guidance available for practitioners through research findings (Churchill, 1979; Sharma and Chrisman, 1999).

This review contributes to the entrepreneurship literature in several ways. First, it guides readers toward universally acceptable definitions concerning entrepreneurship and entrepreneurial activities. Clearly stated definitions help researchers to build on each others' work and advance the theory of entrepreneurship (Sharma and Chrisman, 1999). Second, this review highlights the differentiation between EO and CE and explores EO as a key antecedent of CE. By so doing, this review contributes to a better understanding of the differences and the relationship between EO and CE. On the one hand, the review of explanations of CE types and distinctive dimensions of EO supports the notion that EO differs from CE. On the other hand, this review provides further insights into how EO and CE are related.

We begin with the definitions for CE and EO and related terms (see Appendices A and B). By focusing on the clarification of terminologies, we provide a review of the CE and EO literature that addresses Dess and Lumpkin's (2005) call for the enhancement of 'the descriptive and prescriptive EO theory', and also provide an extended review of CE and EO. We conclude by presenting future research directions and implications for practice.

CORPORATE ENTREPRENEURSHIP

Entrepreneurship is defined as 'new entry' in a broad sense (Lumpkin and Dess, 1996: 136). Lumpkin and Dess (1996) suggest that new entry is the act of starting a new venture either by launching a start-up firm or through internal corporate venturing processes by an existing firm. Sharma and Chrisman (1999) extend this definition by adding renewal and innovation to the organizational creation act within or outside an existing organization.

The level of analysis in entrepreneurship research has focused primarily at individual, group, and firm levels. At the individual level, Schumpeter (1934) defines entrepreneurs as individuals who carry out new combinations. Entrepreneurs are not only independent business people, but also may be the dependent employees of companies such as managers and members of boards of directors. In both cases, it is the act of bringing about new value-adding combinations that determines who is considered an entrepreneur. Schumpeter (1934) describes economic life from the standpoint of a circular flow of economic periods. In the Schumpeterian perspective, the entrepreneur breaks away from the routine, destroys existing structures, and moves the system away from the circular flow of equilibrium in the long run. By contrast, Kirzner (1973) argues that the entrepreneurs create equilibrium, enabling the market process to work with the possibility of development.

In line with neoclassical economic thinking wherein the individual entrepreneur is considered as the firm and new ventures are often seen as an extension of an individual entrepreneur, organizational studies address entrepreneurship as a firm-level behavior (Covin and Slevin, 1991; Lumpkin and Dess, 1996). Covin and Slevin (1991) argue that firm-level entrepreneurial behavior is influenced by, and thereby can be managed through, organizational strategies, structures, systems, and cultures. Consistent with Covin and Slevin's (1991) argument, an empirical study by Zahra (1996) found that corporate governance and ownership are important variables affecting CE in firms. Corporate governance is the system regulating the relationship between executives and shareholders. Zahra's (1996) study also found that executive stock ownership and long-term ownership are positively related to CE; by contrast, a high ratio of outside directors and short-term ownership have been found to be negatively associated with CE. In addition, technological opportunities in an industry have been shown to moderate the relationships between governance and ownership variables and CE.

Within the context of CE, Sharma and Chrisman (1999) distinguish among three types of phenomena: (1) the creation of new businesses within an existing corporation, (2) strategic renewal of existing organizations, and (3) innovation. Entrepreneurship studies refer to the first type as 'internal corporate venturing, intrapreneurship, corporate new venture division, internal innovation, and internal venturing' (Sharma and Chrisman, 1999: 19). The framework outlined by Sharma and Chrisman (1999: 20) suggests that there is a 'hierarchy of terminology in corporate entrepreneurship', in which corporate venturing exhibits subdivisions that include 'internal corporate venturing' and 'external corporate venturing' involving joint ventures, spin-offs, and venture capital initiatives.

Strategic renewal, the second type of CE, has been referred to as 'strategic change, revival, transformation, strategic departure, new product development, reorganization, redefinition, and organizational renewal' (Sharma and Chrisman, 1999: 19). The primary purpose of strategic renewal is to align the organization's strategy with the changing environment (Floyd and Lane, 2000). Hence, strategic renewal is an evolutionary process involving the acquisition of new knowledge to modify an organization's core competencies and/or a change in its strategic position. Floyd and Lane (2000) draw attention to management's critical role in strategic renewal through their involvement in recognizing the need for change, deploying resources, and encouraging exploration. Thereby, strategic renewal may involve intense social processes depending on executive characteristics. Indeed, not all top management team members are open to organizational renewal (Hambrick et al., 1993). For example, Hambrick et al. (1993) found that an executive's organizational tenure, tenure in an industry, and the organization's current performance were positively associated with top management's commitment to the status quo.

Innovation is the third CE category identified by Sharma and Chrisman (1999), but not all CE activities involve innovation. Schumpeter has defined entrepreneurship as innovation that disrupts the circular flow of economic life by creating new things and new ways of doing things, opening up new markets, and revolutionizing economic structure by creating economic disequilibrium out of equilibrium (Schumpeter, 1934; Kirzner, 1973). This entrepreneurial process has been referred to as the process of creative destruction. By contrast, a more contemporary and broader view of entrepreneurship does not require the existence of innovation. 'Doing something even a little different from what is currently being done' and short-run market adjustments exercised by the imitators as much as long-run developmental changes can also be entrepreneurial activities (Kirzner, 1973: 129). Thus, this suggests that entrepreneurship is not limited to the efforts of innovators but can also be exercised by the imitators. Consistent with Kirzner's (1973) broader view of entrepreneurship, Sharma and Chrisman (1999) point out that organizational creation or renewal can occur without innovation. These authors also argue that innovation may be sufficient for corporate entrepreneurship, but it is not a necessary condition and not the only act that makes entrepreneurship possible.

In an attempt to define innovation, Van de Ven (1986) drew attention to the difference between technical innovations (new technologies, products, and services) and administrative innovations (new procedures, policies, and organizational forms). He points out that not all good ideas get developed and implemented (i.e., creation of new businesses, strategic renewal, and innovation). Indeed, little is known about how and why certain new ideas get attention and are developed by organizations, while some others are not. Prior research suggests an organization's strategic leaders and its culture together tend to play an important role igniting innovation, risk taking, and aggressive pursuit of new venture opportunities (Dess and Lumpkin, 2005). Although the CE concept is useful for describing certain categories of organizational activity, it does not set for the range of behaviors that determine whether an organization is acting entrepreneurially. For that, we need to consider entrepreneurial orientation, which encompasses the elements that are critical for corporate entrepreneurship. Hence, in the next section, we turn our attention to EO as a key force in turning new ideas into practice.

ENTREPRENEURIAL ORIENTATION (EO)

Effective corporate entrepreneurship requires firms to have an entrepreneurial orientation (Dess and Lumpkin, 2005). Entrepreneurial orientation involves 'the processes, practices, and decision-making activities that lead to new entry' (Lumpkin and Dess, 1996: 136). Hence, EO sets the stage for CE by providing the entrepreneurial mindset and organizational impetus to achieve CE outcomes.

EO is a multidimensional phenomenon including autonomy, innovativeness, risk taking, proactiveness, and competitive aggressiveness (Covin and Slevin, 1989; Knight, 1997; Lumpkin and Dess, 1996; Miller, 1983; Wiklund, 1999). Each dimension is important but they may not all be important to the same degree. That is, the dimensions of EO are expected to vary independently based on a range of possible environmental and organizational factors (Kreiser et al., 2002). In some studies, a few of these dimensions (e.g., competitive aggressiveness and proactiveness) have been confounded with similar effects on performance (Knight, 1997; Antoncic and Hisrich, 2001). However, in general empirical studies show that the five dimensions of EO are distinct in how they are associated with each other, how they are linked to performance, and how their effects on performance may vary given different contingencies (Knight, 1997; Kreiser et al., 2002; Lumpkin and Dess, 1996, 2001; Lyon et al., 2002).

Autonomy

Autonomy is 'the independent action of an individual or a team in bringing forth an idea or a vision and carrying it through to completion' and 'the ability and will to be self-directed in the pursuit of alternatives' (Lumpkin and Dess, 1996: 140). Thus, autonomy requires the individuals' or groups' freedom to act independently in the decision-making process to pursue entrepreneurial activities and achieve strategic advantages (Lumpkin et al., 2009).

Within the framework of EO, autonomy refers primarily to strategic autonomy (i.e., the extent to which an individual or a group has control over its goals), which is critical in entrepreneurial value creation (Lumpkin et al., 2009). The extent of organizational actors' freedom depends on the firm size, management style, and ownership (Lumpkin and Dess, 1996). Firms promoting CE tend to have flatter hierarchies and more delegation in operational activities. In addition, champions play a critical role in promoting entrepreneurial projects carried out by autonomous firm members. Dutton et al. define the actions of champions as 'issue selling'; that is, 'the voluntary and discretionary behaviors organizational members use to influence the organizational agenda by getting those above them to pay attention to an issue' (2002: 355). An issue becomes a strategic interest when top management believes that it has relevance to organizational performance (Dutton and Ashford, 1993). However, given that time and attention of top management are limited, not all projects developed by the autonomous firm members can be considered by top management. Hence, champions' 'issue selling' role is important in guiding top management's attention toward the projects of autonomous firm members and enhancing top management's understanding of such issues. Accordingly, the champion role involves deliberate and elaborate behaviors such as the naming of an issue, collection of issue relevant information, conversations about the issue, and the creation of roles or task forces.

Organizational studies highlight the role of middle managers in selling issues to top managers as well as in downward influence through affecting the congruence of organizational arrangements with the strategy of the firm (Floyd and Wooldridge, 1992; Dutton and Ashford, 1993; Dutton et al., 1997; Huy, 2002). Floyd and Wooldridge (1992) state that upward strategic involvement of middle managers includes championing alternatives and synthesizing information, whereas downward involvement includes facilitating adaptability and implementing deliberate strategy. In championing alternatives, middle managers select the projects, influence their resource allocation, and perform issue selling based on feasibility through 'persistent and persuasive communication of strategic options to upper management' (Floyd and Wooldridge, 1992: 155). To synthesize information, middle managers interpret and evaluate information and subsequently influence perceptions of top management. Through facilitating adaptability, middle managers promote flexible organizational arrangements. To implement deliberate strategy, middle managers manifest interventions aligning organizational actions with strategic goals. Hence, middle managers can provide or even conceal information about issues, portray issues in particular ways, and affect the allocation of resources to direct top management's attention toward autonomous team members' projects (Dutton and Ashford, 1993).

Innovativeness

Innovativeness represents a firm's tendency to pursue 'creative and novel solutions to challenges confronting the firm, including the development and enhancement of products and services, as well as new administrative techniques and technologies for performing organizational functions (e.g., production, marketing, sales, and distribution)' (Knight, 1997: 214). Hence, firms use innovativeness to pursue new opportunities, which can keep them ahead of competitors and help gain competitive advantages, consequently leading to higher financial performance (Wiklund, 1999; Wiklund and Shepherd, 2003, 2005).

In a study of multiple-product innovation in firms in the computer industry, Brown and Eisenhardt (1997) examined continuously changing organizations and found that the successfully innovative firms tended to exhibit 'semistructures' with 'clear responsibilities and priorities with extensive communication and freedom' (1997: 25, 28). Therefore, semi-structure balances rigidity and freedom in innovativeness. Organizations manifesting successful innovativeness also tended to have 'links in time' with a vision of the future while managing current projects (Brown and Eisenhardt, 1997: 29). These transitions enhance innovative firms' moving from the past to the present and into the future.

Hult et al. (2004) highlight the salience of innovativeness in enabling managers to devise solutions to business problems and challenges, and providing a basis for the survival and success of the firm. The authors also suggest that innovativeness is one of the factors over which management has considerable control. The managers are responsible for the initiation and design of much of the controlled change in organizations. Management's openness to innovativeness is also crucial in recognizing the need for new ideas and actions (Hult et al., 2004). Moreover, a study by Richard et al. (2004) shows that a combination of an innovative strategic posture and relatively high levels of diversity in management has a highly positive impact on firm performance.

Nevertheless, exploiting existing competencies for profitability and exploring new possibilities for innovativeness may create a dilemma in many firms since they are equally useful (Chakravarty, 2005; March, 1991). Indeed, exploitation and exploration are strategic activities that may be in opposition because they often compete for scarce resources. On one hand, a firm focusing its efforts on exploration may never gain returns since there are relatively more uncertainties in returns from exploration and the returns tend to incur in the long run (March, 1991). Accordingly, high levels of exploration have been associated with variance-seeking rather than mean-seeking strategies (McGrath, 2001). On the other hand, a firm primarily engaged in exploitation may become obsolete (Levinthal and March, 1993). Further, exploration and exploitation tend to be inter-dependent such that what is currently exploited must have been explored at some earlier time (Rothaermel and Deeds, 2004). Therefore, mastering ambidexterity, that is, a balance of exploitation and exploration, is the key to innovativeness and can help to ensure present and future viability (Gibson and Birkinshaw, 2004; Lubatkin et al., 2006).

Risk Taking

Risk is perceived as exhibiting 'variation in the distribution of outcomes, their likelihoods, and their subjective values' and 'measured either by nonlineari-ties in the revealed utility for money or by the variance of the probability dis-tribution of possible gains and losses associated with a particular alternative'

(March and Shapira, 1987: 1404). Hence, as Shapira (1995: 126) argues, risk taking should not be perceived as 'playing the odds' or 'gambling'. Accordingly, organizational studies draw attention to risk bearing as an integral entrepreneurial function that can lead to success (Brockhaus, 1980; Shapira, 1995). The strategic types of risk are business risk deriving from venturing in uncertainty, financial risk due to commitment of large amounts of assets and/or heavy borrowing, and personal risk related to the individual behavior of executives (Brockhaus, 1980; Lumpkin and Dess, 1996).

Entrepreneurial risk preferences can be low, intermediate (or moderate), and high (Brockhaus, 1980). Traditional economic theory assumes that many organizations tend to be risk averse and will not undertake high risk unless a high return is expected (Singh, 1986). Interestingly, organizational research has identified a risk–return paradox where poor performance is related to high risk taking and good performance is associated with low risk taking (Singh, 1986). Studies show other determinants of risk taking as industry performance, performance expectations and aspirations, and slack (Bromiley, 1991).

Nevertheless, March and Shapira (1987: 1415) suggest that risk is manageable and controllable through 'engineering of risk taking' and 'risk management' rather than through simply accepting a degree of risk. Indeed, management can modify risks rather than simply accepting them within the context of corporate entrepreneurship. As Dess and Lumpkin (2005) suggest, companies can research and evaluate risk factors in order to reduce uncertainty and apply useful techniques and practices utilized in other domains. Accordingly, Shapira (1995) highlights the role of managers in defining risk, risk attitudes they hold, and how they manage risk. Stevenson (1988) suggests that risk management involves managing a firm's revenues in such a way that they can be rapidly allocated or withdrawn from new projects. In addition, Shapira (1995) draws attention to the influence of reward systems to minimize the tendency toward risk aversion. However, managerial behavior is also shaped by various perceptions, cognitive biases, and shared understandings that can play an important role in managerial risk-taking behaviors. Consequently, successful risk management can lead to outperforming competitors, whereas failure can lead to financial and personal losses in organizations (Dess and Lumpkin, 2005).

Proactiveness

Proactiveness encompasses not only alertness to unnoticed opportunities, but also efforts to capture these opportunities through monitoring and influencing trends, forward-looking activities, and assertively acting on future needs or changes (Kirzner, 1973; McMullen and Shepherd,

2006; Lumpkin and Dess, 1996). Entrepreneurial action, affected by the degree of uncertainty, is critical in seizing opportunities (McMullen and Shepherd, 2006). McMullen and Shepherd (2006) argue that high levels of uncertainty can be detrimental to entrepreneurial action by generating hesitancy, indecisiveness, and procrastination.

Three types of uncertainty that can affect proactiveness negatively are state, effect, and response uncertainties (Milliken, 1987). State uncertainty exists when the strategic decision makers of an organization perceive the organization's external environment as unpredictable and cannot foresee how components of the environment might change. Hence, the nature of the environment is unclear to management. Effect uncertainty occurs when management cannot predict the effects of environmental events or changes on the organization. In organizations with response uncertainty, management lacks knowledge of response options and what the consequences of those response choices may be.

Proactiveness is an appropriate strategy in dynamic environments with rapid change during early stages of the industry life cycle (Lumpkin and Dess, 2001). Proactive firms strive for not only improving processes and products but also shaping and changing their environments via industry leadership and first mover advantages (Barrett and Weinstein, 1998; Dess and Lumpkin, 2005). Accordingly, Bhuian et al. (2005: 10) view entrepreneurship primarily as 'a dynamic capability, which allows organizations to reconfigure internal and external competencies to address rapidly changing environments' via proactiveness.

Richard et al. (2004) suggest that the combination of high proactiveness and high levels of diversity in management is likely to have the most negative impact on firm performance since diverse decision-making groups are slower to reach an agreement than homogeneous groups, subsequently impeding the decision-making speed and ability to implement strategic change. Hence, a moderate level of diversity in management is ideal for a proactive strategic posture.

Competitive Aggressiveness

Competitive aggressiveness represents 'a firm's propensity to directly and intensely challenge its competitors to achieve entry or improve position to outperform industry rivals in the marketplace' (Lumpkin and Dess, 1996). Hence, 'competitive aggressiveness is a response to threats' in hostile business environments where competition is intense and resources are constrained, whereas 'proactiveness is a response to opportunities' (Lumpkin and Dess, 2001: 430, 434).

Competitively aggressive firms direct their efforts toward outperforming rivals (Covin and Covin, 1990a). According to Covin and Covin (1990a), competitive aggressiveness is a managerial disposition reflected in a firm's willingness to take on and intention to dominate competitors. Competitively aggressive firms are characterized by initiating actions to which competitors then respond, introducing new products, administrative techniques and operating technologies, and adopting a very competitive posture. Ferrier et al. (1999) argue that the greater the number of new competitive actions, the greater the competitive aggressiveness. Additionally, competitively aggressive firms tend to outperform rivals quickly and forcefully (Ferrier et al., 2002). As a result, firms remaining competitively aggressive can maintain or improve their market share and become capable of undertaking more moves (Ferrier et al., 1999). However, since extreme levels of competitiveness can damage a firm's reputation, firms rigorously applying this strategy may not always attain competitive advantages (Dess and Lumpkin, 2005). Hence, competitive aggressiveness in strategy making requires moderation.

A study by Ferrier (2001) shows that top management team heterogeneity, past performance, slack, and industry characteristics (i.e., barriers to entry, industry growth, and industry concentration) can influence a firm's competitive aggressiveness. Heterogeneous top management teams tend to carry out complex strategies and competitive moves because of their cognitive and experiential diversity. Slack can also facilitate competitive aggressiveness through the availability of resources. However, good past performance can lead to complacency and limit competitive aggressiveness. Industry characteristics such as high levels of growth, industry concentration, and barriers to entry can also reduce competitive aggressiveness. On the other hand, in hypercompetitive industries, firms may exhibit higher levels of competitive aggressiveness since the sustainability of competitive advantages depends on the speed of entrepreneurial action and the degree of competitiveness (D'Aveni, 1994; Young et al., 1996). Competitive advantages can generally only be sustained short term in industries with high levels of competitive action. Hence, a series of competitive actions are necessary to continuously regenerate competitive advantage. Consequently, firms that are more competitively aggressive can have superior performance in the long run in hypercompetitive industries.

FUTURE RESEARCH DIRECTIONS AND IMPLICATIONS FOR PRACTICE

In this chapter, we have differentiated between CE and EO, explained CE types and the distinctive dimensions of EO, and addressed the role of EO dimensions in CE activities. As a result of the impetus provided by EO, CE plays an important role in the creation of new businesses within an existing business, or strategic renewal of an existing business, or innovation (Sharma and Chrisman, 1999). EO is a crucial antecedent of CE (Dess and Lumpkin, 2005); however, future research is needed to understand how particular combinations or configurations of EO contribute to CE outcomes.

The dimensions of EO include autonomy, innovativeness, risk taking, proactiveness, and competitive aggressiveness (Lumpkin and Dess, 1996). Prior research indicates a firm with entrepreneurial orientation can have high levels of proactiveness but lower levels of competitive aggressiveness (Lumpkin and Dess, 2001). We suspect that other configurations of the dimensions of EO, including both high and low levels of the dimensions, may be evident as antecedents of various types of CE activity. As Churchill (1979: 67) suggests, 'definitions of constructs are means rather than ends in themselves'. Hence, future research can provide further clarification in CE and EO terminologies and investigate how and why these five dimensions of EO may vary independently and shape CE that can influence performance and/or growth as a result. Further, the identification of organizational and environmental factors can shed light on this variation that can have impact on firm-level outcomes. For example, organizations vary in their business and industry life cycles that can affect their performance (Covin and Slevin, 1991; Lumpkin and Dess, 2001). Longitudinal studies can capture variations in dimensions of EO at different stages of organizational and industry life cycles, the effects on CE, and consequently the impact on performance or growth.

Another organizational factor that can affect the variation in dimensions of EO is a firm's strategic orientations such as prospector, defender, analyser, or reactor (Miles and Snow, 1978). A firm with a prospector strategy emphasizing growth may exhibit higher levels of EO compared with a firm with a reactor strategy and no consistent and clear strategy (Snow and Hrebiniak, 1980; Hambrick, 1983; Smith et al., 1989; Shortell and Zajac, 1990). Hence, future studies could explore the moderation effects of different strategies on the relationships between antecedents of EO and CE.

Top management team (TMT) characteristics such as TMT expertise, tenure, and cognitive diversity can also influence CE in firms (Srivasta and Lee, 2005). Accordingly, Miller and Shamsie (2001) show an inverse U-shaped relationship between top managers' tenure and organizational performance, suggesting that top managers who experiment intensively during the early years of their career can increase performance up to an optimum level, but tend to reduce experimentation later on, leading to a decline in the organizational performance in the later years of their tenure. Additionally, Lumpkin et al. (2005) suggest that TMTs' potency (i.e., the collective belief that the team can be effective) (Lester et al., 2002) is positively associated with risk taking, proactiveness, and competitive aggressiveness, whereas potency is negatively associated with innovativeness. The authors also suggest that TMTs with relatively higher levels of cohesion may be unwilling to take risks and exhibit lower levels of innovativeness, proactiveness, and competitive aggressiveness. Shared vision is expected to increase risk-taking propensities, innovativeness, proactiveness, and competitive aggressiveness (Lumpkin et al., 2005). However, as Srivasta and Lee (2005) empirically show, TMT characteristics have limited effects on CE. Future research, therefore, might investigate how different components of TMT potency are likely to influence CE outcomes given the presence of strong or weak levels of EO.

Organization structure and culture are also expected to influence CE (Pettigrew, 1979; Covin and Slevin, 1988; Gordon and DiTomaso, 1992; Dess et al., 1999; Lumpkin et al., 2005). Accordingly, Jennings and Lumpkin (1989) found that entrepreneurial firms tend to be more decentralized than other firms. Interestingly, Miller (1987) found that formalization was not negatively correlated with risk taking and proactiveness. Furthermore, a balanced individualism and collectivism as firm culture is expected to foster entrepreneurial behavior (Morris et al., 1993). Hence, future research is needed to understand the extent of TMTs' influence on EO that can be investigated within the context of various organization structures and cultures.

The personality factors and leadership styles of middle management as well as TMTs can also shape the EO and CE in firms (Miller, 1983; Howell and Higgins, 1990). A recent meta-analysis of entrepreneurial founders that used the Five Factor Model of personality (Costa and McCrae, 1992) to classify a broad range of personality scales, indicates that personality plays an important role in the emergence and success of entrepreneurs (Zhao et al., forthcoming). The Five Factor Model of personality, often termed the Big Five Traits, involves neuroticism, extraversion, openness to experience, agreeableness, and conscientiousness (Goldberg, 1990). Openness to experience and conscientiousness personality dimensions have the strongest association with entrepreneurial intentions and entrepreneurial performance. However, agreeableness is found to be unrelated to either outcome (Zhao et al., forthcoming). Future research might consider how the Five Factor Model personality indicators could be used to assess the influence of the entrepreneurial personalities of executives and TMTs in a CE setting. Consistent with transformational leaders' risk taking, experimentation, and innovation propensities highlighted by Bass (1998), Howell and Higgins (1990) argue that transformational leadership is associated with champions' issue-selling role in organizations. Therefore, future studies could investigate the effects of various leadership styles of middle management and TMTs on EO and CE.

This chapter also has implications for other lines of research, in particular the theory of the family firm, since transgenerational survival and success require an enduring 'entrepreneurial orientation across generations' (Chrisman et al., 2003b: 443). Nevertheless, family firms' EO tends to decrease at later stages of business life cycles owing to established traditions (Hall et al., 2001; Ward, 1997). Other family firm studies also suggest that CE can contribute to family firm survival, profitability, and growth (Rogoff and Heck, 2003; Salvato, 2004) and a family-related business culture can affect EO (Nordqvist, 2008). However, little is known about family firm-specific determinants of EO and CE. Future research could extend this line of inquiry to assess how levels of EO affect the entrepreneurial performance of family businesses. For a better understanding of CE within the framework of family firms, future studies could explore other idiosyncratic family firm antecedents of EO and CE as well as the outcomes. Studies concerning the interrelatedness between CE and family business could help explain why family businesses are so prevalent in world economies (Aldrich and Cliff, 2003).

Furthermore, EO and CE could be studied within the framework of transaction cost theory, which is concerned with governance decisions that involve defining the efficient boundaries of a firm (Williamson, 1975, 1981, 1985). The primary governance choices (i.e., hierarchical governance and market contracting, with a third, hybrid possibility in the form of strategic alliances) may affect EO and CE differently. Whether key transaction cost factors – such as asset specificity, opportunism, behavioral uncertainty, risk aversion, and bargaining power – affecting governance decisions facilitate or hinder EO and CE suggest applications of transaction cost theory to the study of EO and CE.

In conclusion, this review of the literature could help both researchers and practitioners better understand the distinctive EO and CE phenomena and how they relate to each other, through the clarification of definitions and terminology. Organizations with better understanding and capability to utilize dimensions of EO can attain CE leading to growth and competitive advantages.

REFERENCES

Aldrich, H. and J. Cliff (2003), 'The pervasive effects of family on entrepreneurship: Toward a family embeddedness perspective', *Journal of Business Venturing*, **18**(5): 573–596.

Antoncic, B. and R. D. Hisrich (2001), 'Intrapreneurship construct refinement and cross cultural validation', *Journal of Business Venturing*, **16**(5): 495–527.

Barrett, H. and A. Weinstein (1998), 'The effect of market orientation and organizational flexibility on corporate entrepreneurship', *Entrepreneurship Theory and Practice*, **23**(1): 57–70.

Barringer, B. R. and A. C. Bluedorn (1999), 'The relationship between corporate entrepreneurship and strategic management', *Strategic Management Journal*, **20**(5): 421–444.

Bass, B. M. (1998), *Transformational Leadership: Industrial, Military, and Educational Impact*, Mahwah, NJ: Lawrence Erlbaum Associates, Inc.

Begg, D. K. H., S. Fischer and R. Dornbusch (1991), *Economics*, London: McGraw Hill.

Bhuian, S. N., B. Menguc and S. J. Bell (2005), 'Just entrepreneurial enough: The moderating effect of entrepreneurship on the relationship between market orientation and performance', *Journal of Business Research*, **58**(1): 9–17.

Block, Z. and I. C. MacMillan (1993), *Creating new Businesses within the Firm*, Cambridge, MA: Harvard Business School Press.

Brockhaus, R. H. (1980), 'Risk taking propensity of entrepreneurs', *Academy of Management Journal*, **23**(3): 509–520.

Bromiley, P. (1991), 'Testing a causal model of corporate risk taking and performance', *Academy of Management Journal*, **34**(1): 37–59.

Brown, S. L. and K. M. Eisenhardt (1997), 'The art of continuous change: Linking complexity theory and time-paced evolution in relentlessly shifting organizations', *Administrative Science Quarterly*, **42**(1): 1–34.

Burgelman, R. A. (1983), 'A process model of internal corporate venturing in the diversified major firm', *Administrative Science Quarterly*, **28**(2): 223–244.

Chakravarty, B. (2005), 'Regaining relevance lost', in S. W. Floyd, J. Ross, C. Jacobs and F. W. Kellermanns (eds), *Innovating Strategy Process*, 247–251, Malden, MA: Blackwell Publishing.

Chrisman, J. J., J. H. Chua and R. Litz (2003a), 'A unified systems perspective of family firm performance: An extension and integration', *Journal of Business Venturing*, **18**(4), 467–472.

Chrisman, J. J., J. H. Chua and L. P. Steier (2003b), 'An introduction to theories of family business', *Journal of Business Venturing*, **18**(4): 441–448.

Churchill, G. A. (1979), 'A paradigm for developing better measures of marketing constructs', *Journal of Marketing Research*, **16**(1): 64–73.

Costa, P. T. Jr and R. R. McCrae (1992), *Revised NEO Personality Inventory (NEO-PI-R) and NEO Five Factor Inventory (NEO-FFI) Professional Manual*, Odessa, FL: PAR.

Covin, J. G. and T. Covin (1990a), 'Competitive aggressiveness, environmental context, and small firm performance', *Entrepreneurship Theory and Practice*, **14**(4): 35–50.

Covin, J. G. and T. Covin (1990b), 'New venture posture, structure, and performance: An industry life cycle analysis', *Journal of Business Venturing*, **5**(2): 123–135.

Covin, J. G. and M. P. Miles (1999), 'Corporate entrepreneurship and the pursuit of competitive advantage', *Entrepreneurship Theory and Practice*, **23**(3): 47–63.

Covin, J. G. and D. P. Slevin (1988), 'The influence of organization structure on the utility of an entrepreneurial top management style', *Journal of Management Studies*, **25**(3): 217–234.

Covin, J. G. and D. P. Slevin (1989), 'Strategic management of small firms in hostile and benign environments', *Strategic Management Journal*, **10**: 75–87.

Covin, J. G. and D. P. Slevin (1991), 'A conceptual model of entrepreneurship as firm behavior', *Entrepreneurship Theory and Practice*, **16**(1): 7–24.

D'Aveni, R. A. (1994), *Hypercompetition: Managing the Dynamics of Strategic Maneuvering*, New York: Free Press.

Dess, G. G. and G. T. Lumpkin (2005), 'The role of entrepreneurial orientation in stimulating effective corporate entrepreneurship', *Academy of Management Executive*, **19**(1): 147–156.

Dess, G. G., G. T. Lumpkin and J. E. McGee (1999), 'Linking corporate entrepreneurship to strategy, structure, and process: Suggested research directions', *Entrepreneurship Theory and Practice*, **23**(3): 85–102.

Dutton, J. E. and S. J. Ashford (1993), 'Selling issues to top management', *Academy of Management Review*, **18**(3): 397–428.

Dutton, J. E., S. J. Ashford, R. M. O'Neill, E. Hayes and E. E. Wierba (1997), 'Reading the wind: How middle managers assess the context for selling issues to top managers', *Strategic Management Journal*, **18**(5): 407–425.

Dutton, J. E., S. J. Ashford, R. M. O'Neill and K. A. Lawrence (2001), 'Moves that matter: Issue selling and organizational change', *Academy of Management Journal*, **44**(4): 716–736.

Dutton, J. E., S. J. Ashford, K. A. Lawrence and K. Miner-Rubino (2002), 'Red light, green light: Making sense of the organizational context for issue selling', *Organization Science*, **13**(4): 355–369.

Ferrier, W. J. (2001), 'Navigating the competitive landscape: The drivers and consequences of competitive aggressiveness', *Academy of Management Journal*, **44**(4): 858–877.

Ferrier, W. J., K. G. Smith and C. M. Grimm (1999), 'The role of competitive action in market share erosion and industry dethronement: A study of industry leaders and challengers', *Academy of Management Journal*, **42**(4): 372–388.

Ferrier, W. J., C. M. Fhionnlaoich, K. G. Smith and C. M. Grimm (2002), 'The impact of performance distress on aggressive competitive behavior: A reconciliation of conflicting views', *Managerial and Decision Economics*, **23**: 301–316.

Floyd, S. W. and P. J. Lane (2000), 'Strategizing throughout the organization: Managing role conflict in strategic renewal', *Academy of Management Review*, **25**(1): 154–177.

Floyd, S. W. and B. Wooldridge (1992), 'Middle management involvement in strategy and its association with strategic type: A research note', *Strategic Management Journal*, **13** (Special Issue): 153–167.

Gibson, C. B. and J. Birkinshaw (2004), 'The antecedents, consequences, and mediating role of organizational ambidexterity', *Academy of Management Journal*, **47**(2): 209–226.

Goldberg, L. R. (1990), 'An alternative "description of personality": The big-five factor structure', *Journal of Personality and Social Psychology*, **59**: 1216–1229.

Gordon, G. G. and N. DiTomaso (1992), 'Predicting corporate performance from organizational culture', *Journal of Management Studies*, **29**(6): 783–798.

Greene, P. G., G. C. Brush and M. M. Hart (1999), 'The corporate venture champion: A resource-based approach to role and process', *Entrepreneurship Theory and Practice*, **23**(3): 103–122.

Guth, W. D. and A. Ginsberg (1990), 'Guest editor's introduction: Corporate entrepreneurship', *Strategic Management Journal*, **11**(4): 5–15.

Habbershon, T. G. and J. Pistrui (2002), 'Enterprising families domain: Family-influenced ownership groups in pursuit of transgenerational wealth', *Family Business Review*, **15**(3): 223–238.

Hall, A., L. Melin and M. Nordqvist (2001), 'Entrepreneurship as radical change in the family business: Exploring the role of cultural patterns', *Family Business Review*, **14**(3): 193–208.

Hambrick, D. C. (1983), 'Some tests of the effectiveness and functional attributes of Miles and Snow's strategic types', *Academy of Management Journal*, **26**(1): 5–26.

Hambrick, D. C., M. A. Geletkanycz and J. W. Fredrickson (1993), 'Top executive commitment to the status quo: Some tests of its determinants', *Strategic Management Journal*, **14**(6): 401–418.

Howell, J. M. and C. A. Higgins (1990), 'Champions of technological innovation', *Administrative Science Quarterly*, **35**(2): 317–341.

Hult, G. T. M., R. F. Huley and G. A. Knight (2004), 'Innovativeness: Its antecedents and impact on business performance', *Industrial Marketing Management*, **33**(5): 429–438.

Huy, Q. N. (2002), 'Emotional balancing of organizational continuity and radical change: The contribution of middle managers', *Administrative Science Quarterly*, **47**(1): 31–69.

Jennings, D. F. and J. R. Lumpkin (1989), 'Functioning modeling corporate entrepreneurship: An empirical integrative analysis', *Journal of Management*, **15**(3): 485–502.

Kirzner, I. M. (1973), *Competition and Entrepreneurship*, Chicago, IL: University of Chicago Press.

Knight, G. A. (1997), 'Cross-cultural reliability and validity of a scale to measure firm entrepreneurial orientation', *Journal of Business Venturing*, **12**(3): 213–225.

Kreiser, P. M., L. D. Marino and K. M. Weaver (2002), 'Assessing the psychometric properties of the entrepreneurial orientation scale: A multi-country analysis', *Entrepreneurship Theory and Practice*, **26**(4): 71–94.

Kuratko, D. F. (2005), 'The emergence of entrepreneurship education: Development, trends, and challenges', *Entrepreneurship Theory and Practice*, **29**(5): 577–597.

Kuratko, D. F., R. D. Ireland, J. G. Covin and J. S. Hornsby (2005), 'A model of middle-level managers' entrepreneurial behavior', *Entrepreneurship Theory and Practice*, **29**(6): 699–716.

Lester, S., B. Meglino and M. A. Korsgaard (2002), 'The antecedents and consequences of group potency: A longitudinal investigation of newly formed work groups', *Academy of Management Review*, **45**(2): 352–368.

Levinthal, D. A. and J. G. March (1993), 'The myopia of learning', *Strategic Management Journal*, **14**(S2): 95–112.

Lubatkin, M. H., Z. Simsek, Y. Ling and J. F. Veiga (2006), 'Ambidexterity and performance in small- to medium-sized firms: The pivotal role of top management team behavioral integration', *Journal of Management*, **32**(5): 646–672.

Lumpkin, G. T. and G. G. Dess (1995), 'Simplicity as strategy-making process: The effects of stage of organizational development and environment on performance', *Academy of Management Journal*, **38**(5): 1386–1407.

Lumpkin, G. T. and G. G. Dess (1996), 'Clarifying the entrepreneurial orientation construct and linking it to performance', *Academy of Management Review*, **21**(1): 135–172.

Lumpkin, G. T. and G. G. Dess (2001), 'Linking two dimensions of entrepreneurial orientation to firm performance: The moderating role of environment and industry life cycle', *Journal of Business Venturing*, **16**(5): 429–451.

Lumpkin, G. T., W. J. Wales and M. D. Ensley (2005), 'Assessing the context for corporate entrepreneurship. The role of entrepreneurial orientation', in T. Habbershon and M. Rice (eds), *Praeger Perspectives on Entrepreneurship*, Vol. 3: 1–43, Westport, CT: Praeger Publishers.

Lumpkin, G. T., C. C. Cogliser and D. R. Schneider (2009), 'Understanding and measuring autonomy: An entrepreneurial orientation perspective', *Entrepreneurship Theory and Practice*, **33**(1): 47–69.

Lyon, D. W., G. T. Lumpkin and G. G. Dess (2000), 'Enhancing entrepreneurial research: Operationalizing and measuring a key strategic decision process', *Journal of Management*, **26**(5): 1055–1085.

March, J. G. (1991), 'Exploration and exploitation in organizational learning', *Organization Science*, **2**(1): 71–87.

March, J. G. and Z. Shapira (1987), 'Managerial perspectives on risk and risk taking', *Management Science*, **33**(11): 1404–1418.

McGrath, R. G. (2001), 'Exploratory learning, innovative capacity, and managerial oversight', *Academy of Management Journal*, **44**(1): 118–131.

McMullen, J. S. and D. A. Shepherd (2006), 'Entrepreneurial action and the role of uncertainty in the theory of the entrepreneur', *Academy of Management Review*, **31**(1): 132–152.

Memili, E., K. A. Eddleston, T. M. Zellweger, F. W. Kellermanns and T. Barnett (2008), *The Importance of Looking Toward the Future and Building the Past: Corporate Entrepreneurship and Reputation Concerns in Family Firms*, Paper submitted for consideration for publication in *Advances in Entrepreneurship, Firm Emergence, and Growth*.

Miles, M. P. and J. G. Covin (2002), 'Exploring the practice of corporate venturing: Some common forms and their organizational implications', *Entrepreneurship Theory and Practice*, **26**(3): 21–40.

Miles, R. and C. Snow (1978), *Organizational Strategy, Structure, and Process*, New York: McGraw-Hill.

Miller, D. (1983), 'The correlates of entrepreneurship in three types of firms', *Management Science*, **29**(7): 770–791.

Miller, D. (1987), 'Strategy making and structure: Analysis and implications for perform-ance', *Academy of Management Journal*, **30**(1): 7–32.

Miller, D. and J. Shamsie (2001), 'Learning across the life cycle: Experimentation and performance among the Hollywood studio heads', *Strategic Management Journal*, **22**(8): 725–745.

Milliken, F. J. (1987), 'Three types of perceived uncertainty about the environment: State, effect, and response uncertainty', *Academy of Management Review*, **12**(1): 133–143.

Morris, M. H., R. A. Avila and J. Allen (1993), 'Individualism and the modern corpor-ation: Implications for innovation and entrepreneurship', *Journal of Management*, **19**(3): 595–612.

Nordqvist, M. (2008), 'Entrepreneurial orientation in family firms', *Zeitschrift für KMU und Entrepreneurship*, **56**(1–2): 1–14.

Pettigrew, A. M. (1979), 'On studying organizational cultures', *Administrative Science Quarterly*, **24**(4): 570–581.

Quinn, R. E. and K. Cameron (1983), 'Organizational life cycles and shifting criteria of effec-tiveness: Some preliminary evidence', *Management Science*, **29**(1): 33–51.

Richard, O. C., T. Barnett, S. Dwyer and K. Chadwick (2004), 'Cultural diversity in manage-ment, firm performance, and the moderating role of entrepreneurial orientation dimen-sions', *Academy of Management Journal*, **47**(2): 255–266.

Rogoff, E. G. and R. K. Z. Heck (2003), 'Evolving research in entrepreneurship and family business: Recognizing family as the oxygen that feeds the fire of entrepreneurship' (Introductory Editorial Note for Special Issue), *Journal of Business Venturing*, **18**(5): 559–566.

Rothaermel, F. T. and D. L. Deeds (2004), 'Exploration and exploitation alliances in bio-technology: A system of new product development', *Strategic Management Journal*, **25**(3): 201–221.

Salvato, C. (2004), 'Predictors of entrepreneurship in family firms', *Journal of Private Equity*, **7**(3): 68–76.

Schumpeter, J. A. (1934), *The Theory of Economic Development*, Cambridge, MA: Harvard University Press.

Shapira, Z. (1995), *Risk Taking: A Managerial Perspective*, New York: Russell Sage Foundation.

Sharma, P. and J. J. Chrisman (1999), 'Toward a reconciliation of the definitional issues in the field of corporate entrepreneurship', *Entrepreneurship Theory and Practice*, **23**(3): 11–27.

Shortell, S. M. and E. J. Zajac (1990), 'Perceptual and archival measures of Miles and Snow's strategic types: A comprehensive assessment of reliability and validity', *Academy of Management Journal*, **33**(4): 817–832.

Singh, J. V. (1986), 'Performance, slack, and risk taking in organizational decision making', *Academy of Management Journal*, **29**(3): 562–585.

Smith, K. G., J. P. Guthrie and M. J. Chen (1989), 'Strategy, size, and performance', *Organization Studies*, **10**(1): 63–81.

Snow, C. C. and L. G. Hrebiniak (1980), 'Strategy, distinctive competence, and organiz-ational performance', *Administrative Science Quarterly*, **25**(2): 317–336.

Srivasta, A. and H. Lee (2005), 'Predicting order and timing of new product moves: The role of top management in corporate entrepreneurship', *Journal of Business Venturing*, **20**(4): 459–481.

Stevenson, H. H. (1988), 'A perspective on entrepreneurship', in W. A. Sahlman, H. H. Stevenson, M. J. Roberts and A. Bhide (eds), *The Practice of Venture*, 7–22, Cambridge, MA: Harvard Business School Press.

Van de Ven, A. H. (1986), 'Central problems in the management of innovation', *Management Science*, **32**(5): 590–607.

Ward, J. L. (1997), 'Growing the family business: Special challenges and best practices', *Family Business Review*, **10**(4): 323–337.

Wiklund, J. (1999), 'The sustainability of the entrepreneurial orientation–performance rel-ationship', *Entrepreneurship Theory and Practice*, **24**(1): 339–350.

Wiklund, J. and D. Shepherd (2003), 'Research notes and commentaries: Knowledge-based resources, entrepreneurial orientation, and the performance of small and medium-sized businesses', *Strategic Management Journal*, **24**(13): 1307–1314.

Wiklund, J. and D. Shepherd (2005), 'Entrepreneurial orientation and small business performance: A configurational approach', *Journal of Business Venturing*, **20**: 71–91.

Wilken, P. H. (1979), *Entrepreneurship: A Comparative and Historical Study*, Norwood, NJ: ABLEX Publishing Corporation.

Williamson, O. E. (1975), *Markets and Hierarchies*, New York: Free Press.

Williamson, O. E. (1979), 'The governance of contractual relations', *Journal of Law and Economics*, **22**: 233–261.

Williamson, O. E. (1981). 'The economics of organization: The transaction cost approach', *American Journal of Sociology*, **87**(3): 548–577.

Williamson, O. E. (1985), *The Economic Institutions of Capitalism*, New York: Macmillan.

Young, G., K. G. Smith and C. M. Grimm (1996), 'Austrian and industrial organization perspectives on firm-level competitive activity and performance', *Organization Science*, **7**(3): 243–254.

Zahra, S. A. (1995), 'Corporate entrepreneurship and financial performance: The case of management leveraged buyouts', *Journal of Business Venturing*, **10**(3): 225–247.

Zahra, S. A. (1996), 'Governance, ownership, and corporate entrepreneurship: The moderating impact of industry technological opportunities', *Academy of Management Journal*, **39**(6): 1713–1735.

Zhao, H., S. E. Seibert and G. T. Lumpkin (forthcoming), 'The relationship of personality to entrepreneurial intentions and performance: A meta-analytic review', *Journal of Management*, **36**(2): 387–404.

APPENDIX A   CORPORATE ENTREPRENEURSHIP

Term	Author	Definition
Entrepreneurship	Schumpeter (1934)	The act of carrying out new combinations (p. 74).
	Kirzner (1973)	Is manifested in short-run movements fully as much as in long-run developmental changes, and is exercised by the imitators (who move in to exploit the opportunities exposed by the activities of the innovators) fully as much as by the innovators themselves (p. 128).
	Lumpkin and Dess (1996)	New entry (p. 136).
	Sharma and Chrisman (1999)	Entrepreneurship encompasses acts of organizational creation, renewal, or innovation that occur within or outside an existing organization (p. 17).
Corporate entrepreneurship	Guth and Ginsberg (1990)	Encompasses the birth of new business within existing organizations, i.e., international innovation (p. 5).
	Barringer and Bluedorn (1999)	An organizational process that contributes to firm survival and performance (p. 421).
	Sharma and Chrisman (1999)	The process whereby an individual or a group of individuals, in association with an existing organization, create a new organization or instigate renewal or innovation within that organization (p. 18).
	Kuratko et al. (2005)	Encompasses new venture creation within existing organizations and the transformation of ongoing organizations through strategic renewal (p. 700).
Corporate venturing	Block and MacMillan (1993)	Involves an activity new to the organization, is initiated or conducted internally, involves significantly higher risk of failure or large losses than the organization's base business, is characterized by greater uncertainty than the base business, will be managed separately at some time during its life, is undertaken for the purpose of increasing sales, profit, productivity or quality (p. 14).

a. Internal corporate venturing	Sharma and Chrisman (1999)	Corporate efforts that lead to the creation of new business organizations within the corporate organization (p. 19).
	Greene et al. (1999)	Approaches new business development through either internal development (exploiting internal resources), acquisition, joint ventures, or minority venture capital positions (p. 104).
	Sharma and Chrisman (1999)	The corporate venturing activities that result in the creation of organizational entities that reside within an existing organizational domain (p. 20).
	Miles and Covin (2002)	In the direct form, new ventures are funded without financial intermediation (directly through the operating or strategic budgets) and developed within the domain of the corporation by corporate employees. In the indirect form, the corporation invests in a venture capital fund designed to encourage corporate employees to develop internal ventures. The venture capital fund typically originates and operates within the corporation and is managed by corporate employees (p. 25).
Or a. Intrapreneurship	Sharma and Chrisman (1999)	The development within a large organization of internal markets and relatively small and independent units designed to create, internally test-market, and expand improved and/or innovative staff services, technologies or methods within the organization (p. 15).
	Antoncic and Hisrich (2001)	Entrepreneurship within existing organizations (p. 496).
b. External corporate venturing	Sharma and Chrisman (1999)	Corporate venturing activities that result in the creation of semi-autonomous or autonomous organizational entities that reside outside the existing organizational domain (p. 19).

Term	Author	Definition
	Miles and Covin (2002)	In the direct form, the corporation, without using a dedicated new venture fund, acquires or takes an equity position in an external venture. In the indirect form, the corporation invests in a venture capital fund that targets external ventures in specific industries or technology sectors. The venture capital fund may originate outside the corporation and be managed by persons who are not corporate employees, or the fund may originate within the corporation and be managed by corporate employees (p. 25).
Innovation	Van de Ven (1986)	A new idea, which may be a recombination of old ideas, a scheme that challenges the present order, a formula, or a unique approach which is perceived as new by the individuals involved (p. 591).
	Zahra (1996)	A company's commitment to creating and introducing products, production processes, and organizational systems (p. 1715).
Strategic renewal	Zahra (1996)	Revitalizing the company's operations by changing the scope of its business, its competitive approach, or both (p. 1715).
	Covin and Miles (1999)	The pursuit of a new strategic direction (p. 57).
	Sharma and Chrisman (1999)	The corporate entrepreneurial efforts that result in significant changes to an organization's business or corporate level strategy or structure (p. 19).

APPENDIX B   ENTREPRENEURIAL ORIENTATION

Term	Author	Definition
Entrepreneurial orientation	Lumpkin and Dess (1996)	The processes, practices, and decision-making activities that lead to new entry (p. 136).
	Wiklund and Shepherd (2003)	Represents how a firm is organized in order to discover and exploit opportunities (p. 1310).
Autonomy	Lyon et al. (2000)	Actions undertaken by individuals or teams intended to establish a new business concept, idea, or vision (p. 1056).
	Lumpkin and Dess (2001)	Independent action by an individual or team aimed at bringing forth a business concept or vision and carrying it through to completion (p. 431).
Championing	Burgelman (1983)	The establishment of contact with top management to keep them informed and enthusiastic about a particular area of development (p. 238).
	Floyd and Wooldridge (1992)	The persistent and persuasive communication of strategic options to upper management (p. 155).
Issue selling	Dutton et al. (1997)	The set of behaviors that middle managers use to direct top management's attention to and understanding of issues (p. 408).
	Dutton et al. (2001)	The process by which individuals affect others' attention to and understanding of the events, developments, and trends that have implications for organizational performance (p. 716).
Innovativeness	Lyon et al. (2000)	Attempts to embrace creativity, experimentation, novelty, and technological leadership in both products and processes (p. 1056).
	Lumpkin and Dess (2001)	A willingness to support creativity and experimentation in introducing new products/services, and novelty, technological leadership, and R&D in developing new processes (p. 431).

Term	Author	Definition
Exploration	March (1991)	Includes search, variation, risk taking, experimentation, play, flexibility, discovery, and innovation (p. 71).
	Levinthal and March (1993)	The pursuit of new knowledge of things that might come to be known (p. 105).
	Lubatkin et al. (2006)	Involves a bottom-up learning process, in which senior managers are persuaded to abandon their old routines and make a commitment to a new course of action (p. 648).
Exploitation	March (1991)	Includes refinement, choice, production, efficiency, selection, implementation, and execution (p. 71).
	Levinthal and March (1993)	The use and development of things already known (p. 105).
	Lubatkin et al. (2006)	Involves learning from a top-down process, in which senior managers move to institutionalized routines and behaviors that are best suited for refining current competencies (p. 648).
Ambidexterity	Gibson and Birkinshaw (2004)	The capability to simultaneously achieve alignment and adaptability at a business-unit level (p. 209).
	Lubatkin et al. (2006)	The capability of exploiting existing competencies as well as exploring new opportunities with equal dexterity (p. 647).
Risk taking	Lyon et al. (2000)	Activities such as borrowing heavily, committing a high percentage of resources to projects with uncertain outcomes, and entering unknown markets (p. 1056).
	Lumpkin and Dess (2001)	A tendency to take bold actions such as venturing into unknown new markets, committing a large portion of resources to ventures with uncertain outcomes, and/or borrowing heavily (p. 431).
Competitive aggressiveness	Lyon et al. (2000)	The tendency of firms to assume a combative posture towards rivals and to employ a high level of competitive intensity in attempts to surpass rivals (p. 1056).

	Lumpkin and Dess (2001)	How firms react to competitive trends and demands that already exist in the marketplace (p. 431).
Proactiveness	Lyon et al. (2000)	Forward looking, first mover advantage-seeking efforts to shape the environment by introducing new products or processes ahead of the competition (p. 1056).
	Lumpkin and Dess (2001)	How firms relate to market opportunities by seizing initiative in the marketplace (p. 431).

16 A complexity perspective on strategic process research
Terry B. Porter

Competitive advantage is proving to be less and less enduring in the high velocity environments facing most industries today. Specifically, conventional strategic models of top-down formulation followed by line-level implementation are cumbersome and unwieldy in the current conditions of most industries, where change is ubiquitous, rapid, and unpredictable. While an important body of knowledge has developed in this traditional lineage, we argue in this chapter that the meta-theoretical paradigm upon which it rests is increasingly awkward and untenable in the face of the radically dynamic marketplaces now commonplace. In contrast to traditional canons of Modernism and positivist inquiry, this chapter asserts that complexity theory and complex adaptive systems (CAS) provide an integrative framework that provides a robust platform for understanding the adaptive responses of firms in the face of the turbulence now common in most industries and environments of business. Still new to the management field, the introduction of complexity theory has garnered great interest, though it has yet to be assimilated into common models of research and practice, and particularly into strategic process knowledge and research (Anderson, 1999).

'Complexity thinking' has arisen as a descriptor for this new vision of organizational phenomena (Richardson, 2008), encompassing a singular framework of ontology, epistemology, and action: 'complexity thinking is a particular attitude towards our ideas about the world and the world itself, not a particular tool/method, or even a particular language . . . [it is] a perspective that is rather more sensitive to the complexities that are inherent in daily experience' (Richardson, 2008: 21–2). Anderson (1999: 229) writes that 'We are not on the verge of a revolution that will render a century of organization theory obsolete, but remarkable new vistas are opening up, thanks to the melding of the science of complexity and organization theory'. The purpose of this chapter is to present the fundamental concepts and dynamics of CAS; to apply a complexity perspective to organizational and strategic process inquiry; to discuss several streams of incipient research and important debates regarding the strategic management of complex adaptive organizations; to introduce several key methodologies; to clarify the early-stage limitations of the complexity perspective; and to invite scholars to include complexity thinking and research questions in their studies of today's increasingly turbulent organizational terrain.

COMPLEXITY THEORY AND COMPLEX ADAPTIVE SYSTEMS

Complexity theory is not a monolithic, fully formed edifice, but rather an emerging amalgam of developments in many fields of study. Space restrictions permit only a brief overview; what follows is a description of its key tenets and dynamics (for more detailed accounts please see: Anderson, 1999; Richardson, 2008; Rihani, 2002; Wulun, 2007). Complex systems are densely populated collections of agents, which may be cells, individuals, organizations, or nations, for example, that act autonomously and in relation to one another. Interaction amongst agents is non-linear, asymmetric, and unpredictable. *Holism* is a key property of complex systems, meaning that the system cannot be reduced to anything less than itself: it is 'incompressible' (Richardson, 2008). Examples of complex systems are the weather, large ecological systems, ant and bee colonies, the internet, and many organizations. A complex system differs from a merely complicated system in that it is 'an interacting network system, and not a reductive simple system' (Wulun, 2007: 399), meaning that the whole cannot be understood by division and analysis of discrete components or subsystems (Sawyer, 2005). In addition, causality is networked rather than singular (Richardson, 2008), a profound shift that calls into question conventional models and methods of linear causality. Other foundational characteristics of complex systems are *self-organization* and *emergence*. Self-organization refers to an inherent process whereby a system's agents and networks interact and recombine to generate new forms and behaviors. Emergence refers to this arising from within and below of new forms and behavior in the system. In this sense complex systems are 'self-transcendent' (Nishiguchi, 2001), meaning that the system continually shifts and shapes itself through the actions and interactions amongst its many different agents.

Amongst the important dynamics of complex systems, *nonlinear feedback* may be the most fundamental (Richardson, 2008). As in more simple systems, feedback may be negative, or change dampening, such as a temperature-regulating thermostat, or positive, change amplifying, like the convection cycle in thunderhead clouds that leads towards dramatic thunderstorms. However, it is neither of these but instead the nonlinearity of feedback in complex systems that makes them unique, as it implies a second-order adaptive capability:

> It is not just the existence of feedback loops that leads to complex behavior. These loops must themselves interact with each other. Once we have three or more *interacting* feedback loops, accurately predicting the resulting behavior via standard analytical methods becomes problematic at best . . . [thus] we say the prediction of overall system behavior from knowledge of its parts is *intractible*. (Richardson, 2008: 14, italics in original).

Closely related to nonlinear feedback, *coevolution* describes the process by which agents and networks continually adapt to each others' adaptations in an ongoing dance of shaping and selecting to improve fitness and survival (Macready and Meyer, 1999). Thus, nonlinear feedback enables thousands and thousands of ongoing micro-interactions to generate a 'copious internal variety' (Rihani, 2002: 8) which, through coevolution, leads to the permanent retaining of some new forms or features that are more adaptive for the larger system (Porter, 2006). This is the meaning of 'bottom up' in complex systems, the quality by which dispersed, micro-level, nonlinear feedback and coevolution can lead to system-wide adaptations irrespective of top-down planning or direction.

An additional characteristic of CAS is *path dependence*, the idea that 'history matters'. Preexisting pathways of development (i.e. feedback and coevolutionary histories) are indelibly stamped into ongoing trajectories of evolution, which means that even identically structured systems do not evolve in the same ways. Related to local histories, the 'edge of chaos' (Langton, 1992) or 'sweet spot' (Clippinger, 1999) describes the tendency for coevolutionary processes to be situated in arising and subsiding vortices of maximum creativity. Palombo (1999) writes that the edge of chaos marks the phase transition between order and chaos, and as such is a precarious, fleeting, and highly fertile site(s) of emergent innovation. There may be many sweet spots in a complex system, similar to local peaks in a fitness landscape in evolutionary biology (Kauffman, 1993). Nishiguchi (2001) compares the edge of chaos with the elusive 'zone' of peak performance for an athlete, that unbidden heightening of simultaneous internal creativity and external opportunity that is the dream of athletes in every sport.

What makes a system both complex and adaptive at the same time? CAS are special kinds of complex systems in that they have the capacity to learn and adapt to their experience (Kauffman, 1993; Longair, 1997; Rihani, 2002). Richardson (2008: 15) notes that complex systems that contain many interconnected parts and types of parts are referred to as complex adaptive systems, where the parts themselves are described as complex systems. Unlike simple complex systems in which the parts are simple, such as the molecules of air and water in a weather system, the parts in a complex adaptive system contain local memories to which they are able to respond; they are capable of learning from their experiences by generating new responses to their local contexts (p. 15). CAS, therefore, have the property *self-similarity*, meaning that all levels – agent, network, and system – may themselves be described as complex adaptive systems. Notably, however, it is important to point out that the adaptive capability of CAS does not necessarily equate with evolutionary success and survival. As McKelvey (1997) explains, emergent anomalous behaviors cannot be assumed to reliably or predictively produce successful adaptive order; they produce only variations in existing order which may or may not equate with success and survival for the agent, the network, or the system.

COMPLEXITY IN CURRENT STRATEGIC PROCESS RESEARCH

The description of complexity theory presented above exposes significant differences between complexity thinking (Richardson, 2008) and conventional Modernist, linear frameworks of organizational research. In turn, these differences profoundly affect the way strategic processes are conceived and studied in a complexity framework. First, we must recognize a paradox: strictly speaking, from the perspective of complex systems there is nothing that is *not* process. By definition, complex systems are systems in process that continually evolve (Arthur et al., 1997). Complexity thus represents an ontological flip flop for the basis of strategy, from organizations as relatively stable, self-evident, equilibrium-seeking entities, to organizations as fluid, ongoing processes to which equilibrium and stability are largely anathema. Conceptions of the organization's surrounding environment have shifted radically as well: change is everywhere; traditional boundaries are breaking down; it is difficult to avoid the commonplace experience of radical upheavals in today's fast-paced, information-intense, hypercompetitive, and rapidly evolving environments (D'Aveni and Gunther, 1994). Given the enormity of these shifts, it is not surprising to find a remarkable breadth of awareness, variability in understanding, and degree of incorporation of complexity thinking into existing literatures of strategy and strategic process research. This section of the chapter presents three exemplars of these differing levels of integration, conceived along a continuum from no integration to full incorporation. Both ends of the spectrum are represented, and a middle ground exemplar represents a partial integration. In addition to illustrating the state of the field at this time, these 'snapshots' will lead to the framing of a complexity-based definition of strategy and strategic processes at the end of the section. One caveat: this 'snapshot' approach does not presume a normative teleology or hierarchical scheme of value; it is strictly for heuristic purposes in reference to the current state of the field.

The first stream of thinking reinforces conventional Modernist approaches through reductionist typological classifications and prescriptions for further refinements in conventional research – effectively positioning complexity thinking as entirely external to the field. A recent example is Hutzschenreuter and Kleindienst's (2006) excellent review of 227 articles published in top journals since 1992. This paper identifies a presumably closed conceptual domain which is then subdivided into a matrix of categories and factors into which existing work is classified. Strategic processes are included in some of the boxes but only secondarily, in service to the primary issues of decision making, strategic positioning, and bottom line performance. Equilibrium is the norm in this view, and process is the temporary transit to a new equilibrium. The methodologies employed in the reviewed studies are 'mostly simple, bivariate, contingency relationships' (Hutzschenreuter and Kleindienst, 2006: 677), and recommendations for new research are neatly defined as the empty boxes in the grid. This oversimplifying description notwithstanding, these and similar studies contribute valuable perspectives through meta-analysis and commentary, but their unexamined assumptions belie no recognition or accommodation of complexity theory and dynamics. Paradoxically, the principal nod to dynamism in Hutzschenreuter and Kleindienst's (2006) paper is that 'current outcomes' are declared identical to 'future antecedents', but the full implications of this assertion – a more central role of process and a serious challenge to linear causality – are not addressed.

A second stream implicitly recognizes and includes complexity concepts, but with little or no explicit reference to a complexity ontology. For example, in the preface to their edited volume on strategy process, Chakravarthy et al. (2003: XV) raise a call to look beyond simple one-way linear causality: 'good strategy process research must be multi-period, multi-level, multi-context, multi-actor, and multi-disciplinary: it has to catch reality in flight . . . we need stronger research paradigms . . . theoretical contributions . . . [and] methodologies'. The introduction goes on to define strategy as 'an emerging pattern of decisions and actions' (p. 2) based on Mintzberg's (1978) early insights. Although incremental rather than transformational, the volume includes examinations of coevolutionary development, collective rather than individualistic causality, and different kinds of feedback, all of which are ideas imported from complexity theory but with only an occasional nod to its ontology.

An example of this second stream from a different source is Rindova and Kotha's (2001) case study of Yahoo and Excite that explores the firms' continual changing in form in order to maintain fit with hypercompetitive (D'Aveni and Gunther, 1994) conditions. The authors interpret their qualitative data and results through the lens of dynamic capability theory, but are careful to distinguish their contribution from previous, received perspectives. Noting that while much of received theory argues that 'dynamic capabilities are structured and persistent in a given organization', they found them to be 'emergent and evolving, resting on open-ended organizing principles' (p. 1274). They coin the term 'continuous morphing' to describe the phenomenon they observed. A complexity reading of this paper would argue that Rindova and Kotha (2001) are pushing the dynamic capability concept to its ontological limits and beyond, to the point where they must differentiate their findings from conventional theory in order to establish their relevance. A complexity framework would parsimoniously explain 'continuous morphing' as 'the passage of an organization through an endless series of organizational microstates that emerge from local interactions among agents trying to improve their local payoffs' (Anderson, 1999: 228). Notably, Rindova and Kotha's (2001) calls for future research on continuous morphing urge the 'blending [of] existing theories with theoretical insights developed inductively' (p. 1278). To a complexity mindset, however, the authors are awkwardly straddling the transition zone between linear, Modernist change and the nonlinear change processes inherent in CAS, to the point where a clean break and adoption of complexity framework might more robustly encompass the observed phenomena. Nonetheless, there is great value in this and similar transitional scholarship in that it seeks to address the new realities of organizing and strategizing in a markedly changed world. The drawback is that by neglecting the full scope of complexity thinking, some of this work may lose punch and explanatory capability in the overstretching of theories beyond their ontological assumptions.

The third stream represented here is that of complexity theory as the primary explanatory framework of an empirical or theoretical study. In this approach, the features and dynamic operations of CAS provide a model for organizations to imitate or otherwise apply, in order to cope and succeed under turbulent conditions. The specifics of strategic processes and managerial guidelines for adopting complexity principles into daily operations are an open question at this stage of early development, as the next section of the chapter will discuss, but what does seem to be consensually agreed upon is that strategic processes must incorporate principles of self-organization, emergence, second-order feedback, coevolution, and so forth in achieving strategic objectives. An empirical example of this third stream is Plowman et al.'s (2007) qualitative study of changing organizational forms, which is nearly the same topic addressed by Rindova and Kotha (2001). Moving a step beyond the dynamic capability lens, these authors argue that 'complexity constructs' provide an elegant alternative to 'the inability of existing theories of radical change to account for the emergent, continuous nature of some radical change' (Plowman et al., 2007: 521). The paper explores several aspects of complexity dynamics they see evident in the data, and notes that although their original approach to understanding the case was *not* complexity, a CAS framework parsimoniously fit their observations. These authors' call for future research differs markedly from conventional prescriptions: they urge scholars to 'move beyond reductionist thinking' in order to explore deeper 'patterns of interaction' in the system – not the more common type of statistical interactions, but nonlinear and dynamic interactions (p. 516).

In summary, these three examples of differing degrees of adoption of complexity principles clearly demonstrate a wide range of viewpoints regarding the value of complexity thinking in strategic process research and practice. Part of this variability is due to varying awareness and interest in complexity in the management academy, but there are other factors that account for the observed differences as well. For one, all systems and organizations are *not* by any means complex. Diffused, less dense, smaller, and simpler systems, where change takes place more slowly, are not complex. They have fewer and/or more dispersed agents that interact less frequently and with less speed and intensity; feedback is not recursive; and coevolution is not in evidence. Thus, such systems may be very complicated but they do not exhibit the key qualities of self-organization and emergence, and therefore do not fall under complexity rubrics or thinking. Similarly, just as all systems are not complex, the purpose of adding complexity-based approaches to current strategic process perspectives is *not* to replace one system with another: trying to do so would only create a new set of problems (Richardson, 2008). Complex and not-complex systems may be analysed concurrently or collectively without hindering analysis, provided the underlying assumptions and ontologies of each are clear and appropriately applied. In particular, conventional analytical methodologies may be part of an analysis of CAS, but linear approaches must be understood to be providing a limited, cross-sectional view of a system that behaves in the aggregate as a nonlinear self-organizing system. Therefore, any results gained in this way have very limited explanatory value.

What is the value, then, of applying complexity thinking and CAS to strategic process research? The chapter argues that complexity adds fresh outlooks and relevance to current strategic process toolboxes in three ways. First, it offers a radically new meta-framework for understanding and explaining emerging phenomena and themes in strategic process research. Current frameworks have progressed incrementally since the inception of the field, but are stretched to the limit of their underlying ontologies by new conditions and new phenomena. Complexity, in contrast, offers a robust theoretical foundation that fully accommodates precisely these issues. Second, it offers a revised definition of the strategic undertaking: under conditions of complexity, 'the aim of organizations' strategy is to evolve temporary advantages more rapidly than competitors can' (Anderson, 1999: 228). In other words, strategy in complex adaptive systems is the rapid evolution of temporary advantages aimed at staying ahead of other firms' adaptations, involving a continual and ongoing search for temporary endstates of competitive advantage that will inevitably erode under hypercompetitive conditions. Strategic processes therefore address all aspects of *how* the organization achieves its strategic objectives within the ontological framework of complexity. As the following section details, complexity is so new to the field that we are far from agreement on these important questions. Third, complexity offers a set of concepts and methodological approaches through which to make tractable the radical changes that have become commonplace in today's complex organizations and environments. The subject of methodologies will be taken up shortly, where it will be argued that a plurality of approaches are evolving and that ongoing plurality is the preferred state of affairs from a complexity perspective, over and above the Modernist urge to blend and homogenize under the rubric of triangulation. First, however, we turn to a core issue for every perspective of organization theory: how shall complex adaptive *organizations* be managed to achieve their strategic objectives?

STRATEGIC PROCESS RESEARCH AND MANAGEMENT IN COMPLEX ADAPTIVE ORGANIZATIONAL SYSTEMS

To this point in the chapter, a descriptive explanation of organizations from a complexity theoretical perspective has been presented, the variability of awareness and inclusion of complexity across the management academy has been illustrated, and the argument has been made that full adoption of a complexity framework offers the analyst unique lenses and approaches to the study of strategic processes. Henceforth in the chapter the full complexity perspective is adopted, so that attention may be turned to important questions regarding management and governance in complex adaptive organizations. This shift is not to dismiss alternate theories of organization, but to facilitate a deeper examination of the crucial issues behind the management role in complex adaptive organizational systems.

Given the early-stage adoption of complexity in organization studies, it is unsurprising to find a plurality of approaches within the complexity paradigm to understanding the strategic processes behind management issues. Specifically, two major streams of inquiry seem to be emerging. Though not unrelated, each stream addresses complexity from a different direction and emphasizes different priorities for research and management practice. The first is termed the emergent, open system approach. Its fundamental premise is that organizations in complex adaptive systems and environments should mimic or adapt complexity principles in their own structure and operations, thereby reinforcing the fundamental strategy process principle that organizations should strive to maximize their fit with the environment. The second stream focuses more on the governance aspect of CAS, and finds that complexity dynamics alone do not offer a full answer to the question of strategic processes and management. It draws from earlier cybernetic systems theories in fashioning what is here termed the closed system, post-cybernetic approach. These two approaches are examined in detail below.

The Emergent, Open System Approach

The emergent, open system approach adopts an assumption of isomorphism in the dynamic properties of many kinds of CAS: 'it is probable that processes of emergence in strategic management have characteristics in common with other CAS. This premise implies that complex *organizations* are at risk in equilibrium, tend to move towards the edge of chaos, and cannot be directed or managed but only disturbed' (French, 2009: 69–70).

The challenge for strategic managers, therefore, is to translate the revolutionary dynamics of emergence and other principles of complexity theory into organizational terms, in order to encourage the emergence of innovative products and services that generate competitive advantage. However, this task is far from a straightforward reductionist exercise: 'the shift from a linear simplistic attitude to a nonlinear complex attitude is significantly more challenging than a simple fad or framework as is so common in our faddish world' (Richardson, 2008: 24). In other words, the research challenge is to go beyond simple Modernist definitions of terms that have a different meaning in complexity theory – such as coevolution (Porter, 2006) – to carefully examine the minute and elusive processes through which complex and adaptive dynamics evolve (Malerba, 2006).

The open system approach emphasizes the permeability of boundaries in organizational systems, the free and open communication between agents at all levels and the entities and ideas around them, and therefore the importance of facilitating bottom- and middle-up exchanges that can lead to new sources of competitive advantage. Bottom-up innovation is equated with emergent adaptation, but the theoretical principle is far easier to recognize than to operationalize. Since strategic processes cannot be understood by being divided into or reduced to their elements (Wulun, 2007), the concepts of holism, self-organization, emergence, nonlinear feedback, coevolution, the edge of chaos, path dependence, bottom-up change, and non-causal determinism (Wulun, 2007) have to be somehow interpolated into meaningful practice terms.

Progress towards these ends is advancing in two general directions. First, microprocess research has explored and traced the mechanisms of complexity as they are successfully applied in organizational practice. Exacting descriptions of the minutiae of the emergent moment, the tiny but earthshattering shift at the edge of chaos, or the adoption company-wide of a bottom-up innovation, for example, are exciting and crucial to our developing understanding of what leads to the adaptiveness of complex organizations. Exemplar studies on coevolution (Inkpen and Currall, 2004), path dependency and emergence (Colbert, 2004), and bottom-up change (Rihani, 2002) illustrate the value of this microprocess approach. Second, a complementary macro-level approach involves applying the entire 'gestalt' of complexity thinking (Richardson, 2008) to current topics in organizational adaptation, strategy, and strategic processes. Strategic management (Cunha and Cunha, 2006), knowledge creation (Nonaka and Nishiguchi, 2001), innovation (Carlisle and McMillan, 2006), sustainability (Espinosa et al., 2008), and social entrepreneurship (Goldstein and Hazy, 2008) have been explored in this way, revealing the tip of a very promising iceberg that invites further examination.

Based upon such research, recommendations for strategic managers in the open system emergent view include two main levers: altering incentive systems and reconfiguring organizational architecture. Both are indirect; managers may shape the context within which adaptive patterns emerge (Anderson, 1999: 229) but not command a process that is intrinsically unpredictable and uncontrollable. Leverage points include managing the composition of departments, teams, or other internal groups; payoff schedules; information provided to local networks; resource availability and the slack needed to use them; and the provision of a compelling mission and goals. Mechanisms include highlighting different goals and measures at different times, offering several different performance measurement systems and adjusting their overlap or importance to each unit, and altering the distribution of agents in each network (Anderson, 1999). Below are several examples of managerial guidelines from this view of strategic processes. The subjects are managers, but the objects and content are focused on a particular complexity mechanism in bottom-up practice:

- To facilitate bottom-up innovation, top managers establish a common culture that reflects the mission and values of the organization and respects the autonomy of all members and stakeholders (Howard-Grenville and Hoffman, 2003).
- Managers create and empower diffused local networks in order to facilitate bottom-up innovation in CAS (Hayes, 2002; Wood, 1999).
- Managers design incentive and reward systems that support new ideas and initiative development, and these systems should reward both quantity and quality of ideas.
- Top management institutes structural and personnel network changes when necessary to increase the organization's responsiveness to shifting adaptive challenges.
- Middle managers nurture initiative development and champion promising ideas upward (Floyd and Wooldridge, 2000).

Recommendations of this type reflect the assumption that mirroring CAS dynamics in organizations' strategic processes will lead to more adaptive organizations. Yet, as the citations indicate, the origin of many of these recommendations is 'bridging research' or scholarship that leans towards complexity but does not take up its letter. Does this mean that the complexity approach adds no new value to what we already know and do? Quite to the contrary, and for two reasons. First and most important, donning the complexity lens reveals a new, more robust theoretical underpinning to familiar guidelines, in contrast to conventional theory which is stretched to the breaking point to accommodate them. Second, the overlap reflects the point made earlier, that we are in the midst of a blurring of Modernist and complexity 'paradigms' today, in the slow, incremental, and uneven complexity revolution in organization studies. Time and further exploration will eventually lead to clearer operational differences, but as Tait and Richardson (2008) remind us, we are beginning a new journey where our trusted toolbox is inadequate and our attempts at inroads are still disconnected and unclear.

While the open system, emergent approach to complexity management is beginning to flesh out the operational dynamics of complex adaptive organizations, its chief limitation is that there seems to be little concrete direction provided for managers. The closed system, post-cybernetic approach offers a novel source of answers to these questions.

The Closed System, Post-cybernetic Approach

Mintzberg (1978) long ago intuited the complexity principle of emergence with the idea that realized strategy is a blend of top-down intention with bottom-up experience and spontaneous adaptation. The open system, emergent approach described above is beginning to give substance to the second half of his prescient intuition, through operationalizing the principles of self-organization and bottom-up innovation. But to date a complementary understanding of what top-down intention actually means in complex adaptive systems has not been clear. This section of the chapter presents a closed system, post-cybernetic approach that provides an intriguing perspective and promising directions for the first half of Mintzberg's intuition.

Building on earlier ideas of Bateson (1973), the closed system, post-cybernetic approach also draws heavily from the work of Beer (1981, 1985) and associates (see: Espejo, 1999; Espinosa et al., 2008; Stacey, 1997), to develop an alternative, complexity-based view of organizational systems and subsystems that elegantly addresses the management function. Building from the metaphor of living neurological systems, a revised reading of cybernetics describes the way the human nervous system is understood to control and coordinate the myriad functions that enable a person to deal flexibly and proactively with the social and physical world which they both exist within and actively constitute through their own activities. This 'second-order cybernetics' (Espinosa et al., 2008: 638) diverges from traditional or 'first order' cybernetics, which is a mechanistic approach that leaves 'no room for learning, cognition, synergy, and emergence' (French, 2009: 53), in that it emphasizes the importance of organizational boundaries that protect the coherence, identity, and integrity of the system. Unlike the rigid, impermeable boundaries of past organization theory, however, the boundaries of what Beer and colleagues call the Viable System Model (VSM) function to maintain the integrity of an entity or organization in symbolic, interpretive, and structural terms, all the while permitting an open flow of exchange between the entity and its environment. Formally: 'A viable system is a system or complex entity capable of maintaining an independent existence – not an existence totally separate from an environment, but one where structural changes take place without loss of identity and without severance from a niche' (Espinosa et al., 2008: 640). A viable system cannot be analysed apart from the 'niche' or environment with which it continually co-constitutes itself. Emphasis is placed on the recursive process through which the organization is able to maintain its internal coherence and viability in the midst of ongoing, unpredictable change. The VSM thus proposes that for organizations to be both complex and adaptive they must maintain their symbolic or physical boundaries while being selectively open to the external environment. This is the meaning of 'holism' in the VSM: the balancing of organizational autonomy and cohesion with the adaptive demands of an ever-changing environment.

The managerial role in the VSM is occupied by a meta-system, metaphorically a brain, that occupies a distinct vantage point and possesses a capacity for reflection on systemic operations. Its object is to provide services to the many nested subsystems of the organization to allow maximal local autonomy and adaptability while also ensuring cohesion between the diverse operations of the larger system as well as a common identity. The meta-system does not dictate, but rather enables through resource provision, recursive intra-system communication structures, and the holding and protection of its consensually shared identity. A number of management principles emerge from this 'closed system' epistemology that can in turn be applied and tested as propositions for practitioners and managers. The management function, or meta-system:

- Uses its broader perspective to provide a 'meta' understanding of issues that concern system members.
- Ensures the cohesion between the various parties and interests that constitute the organization.
- Protects the shared identity of system components and the wider system itself.
- Makes sure that resources are allocated between the various demands of the system.
- Does not interfere through decree, but works collaboratively to ensure policy is adhered to.
- Exercises authority in the case that an operational unit exceeds the organization's physical, procedural, or symbolic identity and policy.

These propositions, drawn from research by Espinosa and colleagues (2007), provide the basis of a research program on strategic processes in complex organizations that focuses on the governance function.

In summary, the two models of management presented here do not so much contradict one another as they begin to shed light on two possible ways to understand the intended and emergent processes of strategy in the context of CAS. Strategic process research encompasses both the management, or meta-system level and the organizational, or bottom-up aspects of emergence and self-organization. As this section has demonstrated, promising research leads do exist but most of the work remains to be done, thereby offering rich opportunities for scholarship in many modalities.

However, the topic of methodologies is non-trivial in such undertakings, and it is this topic that is addressed in the following section of the chapter.

METHODOLOGIES AND MEASUREMENT

The meta-agenda of a complexity perspective on strategic process research is to apply complexity thinking to understand the processes that contribute to ongoing successful adaptation in complex adaptive organizations. We immediately run into several challenges for this type of research, however, and these must be kept in mind when engaging with a particular methodology or research question. First, complexity research is anti-monolithic in the sense that neither does there exist a consensual body of knowledge based in complexity theory in the management academy, nor is a search for this type of positivist unification warranted: the 'triangulation' that is familiar to conventional research is anathema to the very nature of complex systems. Triangulation is a non sequitur in complexity research; in its place there are calls for a 'critical pluralism' of research methods and representations (Richardson, 2008: 17): 'for complex systems . . . there exists an infinitude of equally valid, non-overlapping, potentially contradictory descriptions'. Second, complexity resists representation, because any attempt to describe it can only ever be partial (Baskin, 2008). It also resists generalization, precisely because it is so complex. Thus, any method (of taking the measure of complexity) that simplifies will fail because it ignores what complexity is (Vesterby, 2008). Finally, we must remember that complexity theory and thinking cannot be deduced from traditional Newtonian systems frameworks of organization studies. It represents a quantum jump into an entirely different ontology and epistemology from Modernist linear positivism (French, 2009). For these reasons, therefore, strategic process research in complex adaptive organizations is neither a straightforward endeavor nor a simple transfer of linear methodologies, but something more challenging and more intriguing: an opportunity to think carefully and apply creative techniques of understanding in an emerging, largely uncharted 'paradigm' of organizational life. Three methodological approaches are introduced below: natural science or computational, interpretive or social constructivist, and a mixed methodological middle ground between the two.

Natural Science, Computational Approaches

Computational or mathematic modeling approaches to complexity processes attempt to simulate the emergence of complex systemic behavior from the micro-processes of autonomous individual agents. The basic assumption is that 'organizations can be understood as symbolic systems, systems of meaning as well as systems of action and choice, all of which can be "reduced" to proclivities to follow certain rules, or, certain rule sets in certain conditions' (Moldoveanu, 2008: 3). The basic operation of agent-based modeling (ABM) is to assemble systems of rule-following agents of multiple types and then to run large-scale computer simulations of these agent-systems. Emergent behavior may thus be simulated in a very short time, which then permits the researcher to adjust rule systems and run further simulations in iterative fashion (North and Macal, 2007). There is a proliferating number of modeling procedures and research streams, most of them imported and adapted from the natural sciences, such as Kauffman's (1993) *NK* model and Bak et al.'s (2009) Forest Fire Model (as cited in Robertson and Caldart, 2008). While the potential for ABM to help us better understand how complex macro-level behavior emerges from thousands of micro-level interactions amongst agents is great, great challenges also exist in that it tends to overly rely on Modernist assumptions of the decomposability of problems, hierarchies of decision making, and rationalism in agents' decision making (Robertson and Caldart, 2008: 66–67). More simply stated, the limitations of this approach are that any set of simple rules cannot capture all sources of nonlinear feedback and coevolution, nor does this 'neo-reductionist approach' fully incorporate the principles of complexity (Richardson, 2008: 19).

Interpretive or Social Constructivist Approaches

In counterpoint to computational methods, Baskin (2008) argues that social CAS differ from non-human CAS by the innate human ability to conceptualize and reflect on experience and to subsequently *act on the basis* of such subjective interpretations of lived experience – in other words, to create and respond to symbolic meanings and double-loop feedback. He describes *human* complex adaptive systems as 'storied spaces' where social networks frame interpretive webs of meaning that are expressed through 'the stories we tell', which in turn reveal to embedded actors what actions should be taken (Baskin, 2008: 3). Because we are able to construct 'reality' through social interaction, Griffin et al. (1998) insist that emergence in CAS is the consequence of a process of creative co-imagination amongst and within interacting networks that themselves are embedded CAS in the organizational system. In addition to the human meaning making processes indelible to this interpretive or social construction perspective, scholars have emphasized the 'soft' aspects of complexity dynamics as key drivers of adaptive change in organizational systems. Arguments have been made, for example, that values, culture, and identity-making processes are the underlying glue and driving force in complex adaptive social systems, both at the personal level and at the organizational level (Baskin, 2008; Frederick, 1998). Similarly, Nonaka and Nishiguchi (2001: 4) argued that knowledge creation could not be managed through top-down control systems and traditional types of incentive systems: rather, it thrives best in 'caring' and 'trustful' environments. The constructivist position challenges the computational assumption that individual behavior can be captured in the form of a set of if–then rules. No matter how detailed the rule systems may become, constructivists counter that they cannot accommodate the interpretive, constructivist position that future behavior and adaptive patterns are actually co-created by the agents themselves in spontaneous unpredictable encounters (Griffin et al., 1998: 319–320). A third methodological position is the both–and argument that computational and constructivist approaches are both necessary to a fuller picture of complexity processes in organizational life.

Mixed Methods

Amongst the many scholars who argue convincingly for the importance of combining 'hard' and 'soft' methods to better understand complexity in organizational processes, McKelvey (1997) provides a compelling vision for a 'quasi-natural organization science' focused on the intersection of intentionally and naturally occurring phenomena. In his view, the 'paradigm wars' regarding the representation of complexity are irresolvable in either framework exclusively, because neither can accommodate both idiosyncracy and objectivist justification logic (p. 356). In McKelvey's (1997) scheme, by contrast, 'firms are composed of numerous structures and processes amenable to natural science methods of inquiry and justification logic, including prediction, generalization, and falsifiability. But they also comprise behaviors directly attributable to human intentionality: behaviors and causes that may not be fruitfully understood in terms of natural science methods' (p. 357). Similarly, Frederick (1998) offers a 'naturological view of the corporation' where organizations are seen as 'energy-transforming operations' that, to be successful, must operate as economically as possible to sustain their own growth and development, by balancing at the edge of chaos between too much and too little adaptive change. Interestingly, though, it is not technological innovation or profit that drives these operations in his view, but the underlying shared values and identity that are expressed socially and culturally in the organization's interpersonal networks (Frederick, 1998). Though it is in its infancy, early explorations of the middle ground position between computational and constructivist epistemologies may represent just the 'tip of the iceberg' (McKelvey, 1997: 359) that has vast potential for further development.

CONCLUSION

This chapter has discussed both the great potential of complexity perspectives for strategic process research today, and cautions and limitations stemming from our early-stage level of knowledge of complex adaptive organizational systems. The fundamental characteristics of complex systems have been described, including the differentiators of complex from complex and adaptive systems; the current state of incorporation of complexity into strategic process research was illustrated through three exemplar positions along a continuum; two streams of complexity research in organizations were presented including empirical propositions for management research that may be applied and tested; and methodologies and epistemological issues were addressed. In a sense, the field of strategic process research may itself be considered a complex adaptive system today. As this volume attests, overlapping, complementary, and competing lines of thinking are continually encountering and coevolving with one another in academic debates. Numerous 'edges of chaos' are in evidence, where simmering controversies are confronted more deeply: it is these diffused but interconnected 'sweet spots' that are also emblematic of self-organizing systems. Surely the intersection of complexity theory and received strategic process research is one such 'sweet spot' of heightened attention at this time. Thus, the way is open for new scholarship to take these preliminary observations much further, where, from a complexity perspective, the aim of debate is neither right and wrong nor a teleological unification of all perspectives into an integrative framework, but acknowledgement of a plurality that is healthy and generative. It is hoped that strategic process researchers will both adopt and question a more sophisticated understanding of complexity theory and thinking in today's new worlds.

REFERENCES

Anderson, P. (1999), 'Complexity theory and organization science', *Organization Science*, **10**(3): 216–232.
Arthur, W. B., S. Durlauf and D. Lane (1997), *The Economy As An Evolving Complex System II* (Santa Fe Institute Studies in the Sciences of Complexity Lecture Notes), New York: Westview Press.
Bak, P., K. Chen and C. Tang (2009), 'A forest-fire model and some thoughts on turbulence', *Physics Letters A*, **147**(5–6): 297–300.

Baskin, K. (2008), 'Storied spaces: The human equivalent of complex adaptive systems', *Emergence*, **10**(2): 1–12.

Bateson, G. (1973), *Steps to an Ecology of Mind*, New York: Ballantine Books.

Beer, S. (1981), *The Brain of the Firm (2E)*, Chichester: John Wiley & Sons.

Beer, S. (1985), *Diagnosing the System for Organizations*, Chichester: John Wiley & Sons.

Carlisle, Y. and E. McMillan (2006), 'Innovation in organizations from a complex adaptive systems perspective', *Emergence: Complexity and Organization*, **8**(1): 2–9.

Chakravarthy, B., G. Mueller-Stewens, P. Lorange and C. Lechner (2003), 'Defining the contours of the strategy process field', in B. Chakravarthy, G. Mueller-Stewens, P. Lorange, and C. Lechner (eds), *Strategy Process: Shaping the Contours of the Field*: 1–17. Malden, MA: Blackwell.

Clippinger, J. (1999), 'Order from the bottom up: Complex adaptive systems and their management', in J. Clippinger (ed.), *The Biology of Business: Decoding the Natural Laws of Enterprise*, 1–30. San Francisco: Jossey-Bass.

Colbert, B. (2004), 'The complex resource-based view: Implications for strategic human resource management', *Academy of Management Review*, **29**(3): 341–358.

Cunha, M. and J. Cunha (2006), 'Towards a complexity theory of strategy', *Management Decision*, **44**(7): 839–850.

D'Aveni, R. and R. Gunther (1994), *Hypercompetition: Managing the Dynamics of Strategic Maneuvering*, New York: The Free Press.

Durie, R. and K. Wyatt (2007), 'New communities, new relations: The impact of community organization on health outcomes': 1–19. Hull University Business School, unpublished manuscript.

Elfring, T. and H. Volberda (2001), 'Multiple futures of strategy synthesis: Shifting boundaries, dynamic capabilities and strategy configurations', in H. Volberda and T. Elfring (eds), *Rethinking Strategy*: 245–285. Thousand Oaks, CA: Sage.

Espejo, R. (1999), 'Aspects of identity, cohesion, citizenship and performance in recursive organizations', *Kybernetes*, **28**(6/7): 535–622.

Espinosa, A., R. Harnden and J. Walker (2007), 'Beyond hierarchy: A complexity management perspective': 1–28. Hull University Business School, unpublished manuscript.

Espinosa, A., R. Harnden and J. Walker (2008), 'A complexity approach to sustainability – Stafford Beer revisited', *European Journal of Operational Research*, **187**: 636–651.

Floyd, S. and B. Wooldridge (2000), *Building Strategy from the Middle: Reconceptualizing Strategy Process*, Thousand Oaks, CA: Sage.

Frederick, W. (1998), 'Creatures, corporations, communities, chaos, complexity: A natural-ological view of the corporate social role', *Business and Society*, **37**(4): 358–374.

French, S. (2009), 'Re-thinking the foundations of the strategic business process', *Journal of Management Development*, **28**(1): 51–76.

Goldstein, J. and J. Hazy (2008), 'Complexity and the generation of social value', *Emergence*, **10**(3): vi–x.

Griffin, D., P. Shaw and R. Stacey (1998), 'Speaking of complexity in management theory and practice', *Organization*, **5**(3): 315–339.

Hayes, R. (2002), 'Challenges posed to operations management by the "New Economy"', *Production and Operations Management*, **11**(1): 21–32.

Howard-Grenville, J. and A. Hoffman (2003), 'The importance of cultural framing to the success of social initiatives in business', *Academy of Management Executive*, **17**(2): 70–84.

Hutzschenreuter, T. and I. Kleindienst (2006), 'Strategy-process research: What have we learned and what is still to be explored?', *Journal of Management*, **32**(5): 673–720.

Inkpen, A. and S. Currall (2004), 'The coevolution of trust, control, and learning in joint ventures', *Organization Science*, **15**(5): 586–599.

Kauffman, S. (1993), *The Origins of Order: Self-organization and Selection in Evolution*, New York: Oxford University Press.

Langton, C. (1992), *Artificial Life*, New York: Addison-Wesley.

Lewin, A. and M. Koza (2001), 'Empirical research in co-evolutionary processes of strategic adaptation and change: The promise and the challenge', *Organization Studies*, **22**(6): 9–15.

Longair, M. (ed.) (1997), *The Large, the Small, and the Human Mind*, Cambridge: Cambridge University Press.

Macready, W. and C. Meyer (1999), 'Adaptive operations: Creating business processes that evolve', in J. Clippinger (ed.), *The Biology of Business: Decoding the Natural Laws of Enterprise*: 181–199. San Francisco, CA: Jossey-Bass

Malerba, F. (2006), 'Innovation and the evolution of industries', *Journal of Evolutionary Economics*, **16**: 3–23.

McKelvey, B. (1997), 'Quasi-natural organization science', *Organization Science*, **8**(4): 352–380.

Mintzberg, H. (1978), 'Patterns in strategy formation', *Management Science*, **24**(9): 934–948.

Mintzberg, H. and J. Waters (1985), 'Of strategies deliberate and emergent', *Strategic Management Journal*, **6**: 257–272.

Moldoveanu, M. (2008), 'Organizations as universal computing machines: Rule systems, computational equivalence, and organizational complexity', *Emergence: Complexity and Organization*, **10**(1): 2–22.

Nishiguchi, T. (2001), 'Coevolution of interorganizational relations', in I. Nonaka, and T. Nishiguchi (eds), *Knowledge Emergence: Social, Technical and Evolutionary Dimensions of Knowledge Creation*: 197–222. Oxford: Oxford University Press.

Nonaka, I. and T. Nishiguchi (eds.) (2001), *Knowledge Emergence: Social, Technical, and Evolutionary Dimensions of Knowledge Creation*, Oxford: Oxford University Press.

North, M. and C. Macal (2007), *Managing business complexity: Discovering Strategic Solutions with Agent-Based Modeling and Simulation*, New York: Oxford University Press.

Palombo, S. (1999), *The Emergent Ego: Complexity and Coevolution in the Psychoanalytic Process*, Madison, CT: International Universities Press.

Plowman, D., L. Baker, T. Beck, M. Kulkarni, S. Solansky and D. Travis (2007), 'Radical change accidentally: The emergence and amplification of small change', *Academy of Management Journal*, **50**(3): 515–543.

Porter, T. (2006), 'Coevolution as a research framework for organizations and the natural environment', *Organization and Environment*, **19**(4): 479–504.

Richardson, K. (2008), 'Managing complex organizations: Complexity thinking and the science and art of management', *Emergence*, **10**(2): 13–26.

Rihani, S. (2002), *Complex Systems Theory and Development Practice*, New York: Zed Books.

Rindova, V. and S. Kotha (2001), 'Continuous "morphing": Competing through dynamic capabilities, form, and function', *Academy of Management Journal*, **44**(6): 1263–1280.

Robertson, D. and A. Caldart (2008), 'Natural science models in management: Opportunities and challenges', *Emergence: Complexity and Organization*, **10**(2): 61–75.

Sawyer, R. (2005), *Social Emergence: Societies as Complex Systems*, Cambridge: Cambridge University Press.

Stacey, R. (1997), *Complexity and Creativity in Organizations*, London: Berrett-Koechler Publishers Inc.

Tait, A. and K. Richardson (2008), 'Confronting complexity', *Emergence: Complexity and Organization*, **10**(2): 27–40.

Vesterby, V. (2008), 'Measuring complexity: Things that go wrong and how to get it right', *Emergence: Complexity and Organization*, **10**(2): 90–102.

Wood, R. (1999), 'The future of strategy: The role of the new sciences', in M. Lissack, and H. Gunz (eds), *Managing Complexity in Organizations: A View in Many Directions*: 118–162. Westport, CT: Quorum Books.

Wulun, J. (2007), 'Understanding complexity, challenging traditional ways of thinking', *Systems Research and Behavioral Science*, **24**: 393–402.

PART IV

SPECIAL TOPICS

17 Strategic decision processes in the realm of strategic alliances*
Jorge Walter

Strategic alliances are voluntary, cooperative agreements between two or more independent firms to exchange, share, jointly develop, and/or commercialize new products, services, or technologies (Gulati, 1995, 1998). Firms increasingly rely on strategic alliances to cope with the rising complexity of learning and building new sources of competitive advantage to compete successfully in the global economy (Ireland et al., 2002; Kale et al., 2002; Teng, 2007). As a result, the number of alliances has increased dramatically over the last two decades (Schilling, 2009), and so has their impact on firms' performance. A study by Dyer et al. (2001), for instance, reports that the top 500 global business companies average 60 major strategic alliances each, and that 80 percent of the top-level executives they surveyed consider strategic alliances to be primary growth vehicles and expect alliances to account for 25 percent of their company's market value in 2005. As a consequence, most firms today find themselves embedded in dense networks of alliances (Gulati et al., 2002).

In spite of the proliferation and increasing importance of strategic alliances, failure rates lie between 50 and 80 percent (Bleeke and Ernst, 1991; Geringer and Hebert, 1991; Park and Ungson, 1997; Yan and Zeng, 1999). Scholars examining strategic alliances have acknowledged that these collaborations present significant managerial challenges to their parent organizations and have identified numerous reasons explaining the failure of alliances, such as substantial coordination costs, opportunism, conflicting strategic objectives, incompatibility in national and corporate cultures, lack of trust, risks of proprietary knowledge leakage, disproportional appropriation of rents, and free-rider problems (Balakrishnan and Koza, 1993; Das and Teng, 1998a, 2000; Kumar and Das, 2007; Kumar and Nti, 1998; Ring and Van de Ven, 1994).

The stark contrast between prevalence and importance on the one hand, and disappointing outcomes on the other hand, has triggered both academic and managerial interest and fueled the quest for factors that affect alliance success. Reflecting the trend in the broader strategy literature (Dess and Lumpkin, 2001; Lechner and Müller-Stewens, 2000), however, previous alliance research has been dominated by studies on

371

content-related issues, such as fit between alliance partners (e.g., Douma et al., 2000), alliance governance structures (e.g., Gulati and Singh, 1998; Oxley and Sampson, 2004), alliance scope (e.g., Khanna, 1998; Oxley and Sampson, 2004), and alliance-based competitive dynamics (e.g., Silverman and Baum, 2002). In contrast, process-related issues addressing *how* alliance-related strategies are formulated and implemented have received significantly less attention.

In his recent critique of the alliance literature, Hennart (2006: 1623) even argues that '[t]he only areas that are solidly under the control of managers are the ex post management of the alliance relationship (for example, the fostering of communication and trust) and the crafting of its initial structure. [. . .] I believe that of the two, crafting the initial structure is both easier and more crucial.' He therefore concludes that 'we do not need detailed accounts of human interactions and of their consequences to predict what will happen to alliances. Often a good analysis of their initial structure suffices' (2006: 1623). This conclusion appears premature, however, as previous research has found that alliance management accounts for 23 percent of variation in alliance success rates, versus 5 percent for alliance experience, and 7 percent for alliance structure (Kale et al., 2001). It therefore seems to be the management of an alliance, and not just the design of the initial structure, that exerts a crucial influence on the performance of that alliance. Similarly, Noorderhaven (2005) points out that while structural conditions intend to influence alliance partners' behaviors in specific ways, partners in their interactions with each other engage in joint sensemaking processes which affect their interpretation of structural conditions (see also Salk and Shenkar, 2001, for an illustration of different meanings alliance partners attach to alliance structures). Noorderhaven (2005: 2) concludes that it is thus 'entirely plausible that alliances with a "bad" structure (not fitting the objective circumstances) can nevertheless be successful if they are managed very effectively. Conversely, alliances with the "right" structure may fail when managed ineffectively.' Moreover, as the management of socially complex and causally ambiguous strategy processes is difficult to comprehend and imitate, those companies that master alliance management processes may achieve a sustainable competitive advantage (Ireland et al., 2002).

It is apparent that alliance partners have to make multiple crucial decisions during the life span of their collaboration. These decisions range from selecting an appropriate partner (Saxton, 1997) to defining alliance scope (Oxley and Sampson, 2004), designing governance and monitoring systems (Das and Teng, 1998a; Gulati and Singh, 1998), allocating resources (Das and Teng, 1998b), or determining dissolution procedures

(Park and Ungson, 1997). Managing an alliance, therefore, is not simply a matter of selecting the right partner and alliance governance, but of designing processes that generate high-quality decisions as the alliance progresses over time.

This chapter constitutes, to the best of my knowledge, the first review of the empirical literature on strategic decision processes in the realm of strategic alliances. I focused my review on those decision processes that are *strategic*, i.e., that deal with the question of how alliance-related strategies are formulated and implemented, and what impact formulation and implementation have on alliance and partner firm performance. By providing a synthesis of empirical findings on decision processes in interfirm collaborations, I intend to make two contributions: (1) outline the substantial body of knowledge that this research stream – in contrast to the fragmented and incoherent body of research on general alliance processes (Bell et al., 2006; Hennart, 2006) – has accumulated, and discuss both its academic and managerial relevance; and (2) based on this review, I suggest a number of promising avenues for future research.

METHOD

To identify relevant empirical studies of strategic decision processes in alliances, I conducted electronic keyword searches of the ten most 'influential' scholarly journals as identified by Podsakoff and colleagues (2005): *Academy of Management Journal, Administrative Science Quarterly, Decision Sciences, Human Relations, Journal of Management, Journal of Management Studies, Journal of Organizational Behavior, Management Science, Organization Science,* and *Strategic Management Journal*.[1] The keywords I used to identify relevant articles were alliance*, interfirm, inter-firm, interorganization*, inter-organization*, relation*, joint venture*, JV*, collaborat*, and cooperat*. The asterisk at the end of a search word allows for different suffixes. By reading through the abstracts first and then the articles in their entirety, I managed to extract 43 articles on strategic decision processes in alliances (see Table 17.1 for details).

To more systematically evaluate the contribution of this body of literature on decision processes in strategic alliances, I employed an analytical review scheme (Ginsberg and Venkatraman, 1985). In particular, I structured this review according to the framework proposed by Rajagopalan et al. (1993), which is outlined in Figure 17.1.

In spite of enduring differences between rational (Andrews, 1971; Ansoff, 1965) and political (Narayanan and Fahey, 1982; Pettigrew, 1973; Tushman, 1977) models, the literature on strategic decision

Table 17.1 Overview of the literature on decision processes in alliances

Study	Sample	Data sources/methods	Link(s)
Sullivan et al. (1981)	48 US and 72 Japanese managers from different industries	Questionnaire on joint venture scenarios	[2–2–4], [4–2–4]
Habib (1987)	38 multinational joint ventures in chemical and petrochemical industries	Interviews, questionnaires	[4–6]
Levinthal and Fichman (1988)	1,884 auditor–client relationships of publicly held US companies	Secondary sources	[5–6]
Seabright et al. (1992)	340 auditor–client relationships of publicly held US companies	Secondary sources	[5–6]
Lyles and Reger (1993)	One international joint venture in the manufacturing industry	Interviews, secondary sources (longitudinal)	[2–4]
Thomas and Trevino (1993)	Three alliances in US healthcare industry	Interviews, observations, secondary sources, questionnaires	[4–6], [4–3–6]
Mohr and Spekman (1994)	124 manufacturer–dealer relationships in US personal computer industry	Questionnaires	[4–6], [5–6]
Rai et al. (1996)	70 international alliances in the information technology industry	Interviews, questionnaires	[4–6]
Nooteboom et al. (1997)	97 buyer–seller relationships in the microelectronics assembly industry in the Netherlands	Questionnaires	[2–4]
Saxton (1997)	98 international alliances in the chemical and allied products industry	Questionnaires (longitudinal)	[4–6], [4–2–6]
Simonin (1997)	151 US partners of international alliances	Questionnaires	[2–5], [5–6]
Monczka et al. (1998)	154 international supplier alliances	Interviews, questionnaires	[4–6], [5–6]

374

Author (year)	Description	Method	Codes
Zaheer et al. (1998)	107 buyer–supplier relationships in the electrical equipment manufacturing industry	Interviews, questionnaires	[1–4], [2–4], [4–4], [4–6]
Young-Ybarra and Wiersema (1999)	91 US firms involved in strategic alliances in the information technology industry	Questionnaires	[2–4], [4–4], [4–5], [4–6], [5–4]
Anand and Khanna (2000)	870 joint ventures in manufacturing industries	Secondary sources	[5–6], [5–2–6]
Kale et al. (2000)	212 alliances in US high-technology industries	Questionnaires, secondary sources	[2–5], [4–4], [4–5], [5–5]
Steensma and Lyles (2000)	121 international service and manufacturing joint ventures in Hungary	Interviews	[2–4], [4–6], [5–6]
Lane et al. (2001)	78 international joint ventures in Hungary	Interviews, questionnaires	[1–5], [2–5], [4–5], [4–6]
Luo (2001)	282 international manufacturing joint ventures in China	Questionnaires, secondary sources	[1–5], [2–5], [5–6]
Pearce (2001)	75 US-based operating joint ventures	Questionnaires, secondary sources	[2–4], [4–4], [4–6]
Yan and Grey (2001)	90 US manufacturing joint ventures in China	Questionnaires, interviews, secondary sources	[4–6]
Fryxell et al. (2002)	129 US-based international manufacturing joint ventures	Questionnaires	[2–4–6], [4–6], [5–6]
Johnson et al. (2002)	51 international manufacturing joint ventures	Questionnaires, secondary sources	[2–5], [4–5], [4–2–5]
Kale et al. (2002)	1,572 alliances in high-technology industries	Questionnaires, secondary sources	[5–6]
Luo (2002a)	255 cross-cultural manufacturing alliances in China	Questionnaires, interviews, secondary sources	[2–4], [4–1–6], [4–2–6], [4–5–6], [5–4], [5–6]
Shenkar and Yan (2002)	One Australian–Chinese hotel joint venture	Interviews, secondary sources	[2–4], [4–4], [4–6]

Table 17.1 (continued)

Study	Sample	Data sources/methods	Link(s)
Subramani and Venkatraman (2003)	211 supplier–retailer relationships in the Canadian consumer products industry	Questionnaires, interviews, secondary sources	[1–4], [2–4], [5–4]
Lui and Ngo (2004)	233 architect–contractor alliances in Hong Kong	Questionnaires	[4–6], [2–4–6]
Li and Hambrick (2005)	71 Sino-foreign joint ventures	Questionnaires	[2–4], [4–6], [5–4], [5–6]
Lui and Ngo (2005)	263 architect–contractor partnerships in Hong Kong	Questionnaires, interviews	[2–4], [4–2–4]
Luo (2005)	124 cross-cultural manufacturing alliances in China	Questionnaires, secondary sources	[4–6], [4–1–6], [4–2–6], [5–6]
White and Lui (2005)	231 architect–contractor partnerships in Hong Kong	Questionnaires	[2–4], [3–4], [4–4]
Krishnan et al. (2006)	126 international alliances in India	Questionnaires, secondary sources	[4–6], [4–1–6], [4–2–6], [5–6]
Luo (2006)	152 international manufacturing joint ventures in China	Questionnaires, secondary sources	[1–4], [1–5], [2–4], [2–4–4], [2–4–5], [2–5], [4–5], [4–6], [5–4], [5–6]
Klein et al. (2007)	91 client–vendor relationships	Interviews, questionnaires	[2–4], [4–5], [5–6]
Luo (2007)	127 international manufacturing alliances in China	Questionnaires, secondary sources	[4–6], [4–2–6], [4–4–6], [5–6]
Faems et al. (2008)	Two exploratory R&D alliances	Interviews, secondary sources	[2–4], [4–4]
Gulati and Nickerson (2008)	222 component-sourcing arrangements of two assemblers in the automotive industry	Questionnaires, interviews	[4–4], [4–6]

376

Luo (2008a)	168 international manufacturing alliances in China	Questionnaires, secondary sources	[4–6], [4-2–6], [5–6]
Luo (2008b)	198 international manufacturing alliances in China	Questionnaires, secondary sources	[4–6], [4-2–6], [5–6]
Patzelt and Shepherd (2008)	2,816 decisions of 88 alliance managers in the software and information technology industries	Questionnaires on alliance scenarios, secondary sources	[4–6], [4-2–6]
Robson et al. (2008)	177 international alliances	Interviews	[2–4], [4–4], [4–6], [4-2–6]
Walter et al. (2008)	106 alliances in European high-technology industries	Questionnaires, secondary sources	[4–6], [4-4–6], [5–6]

377

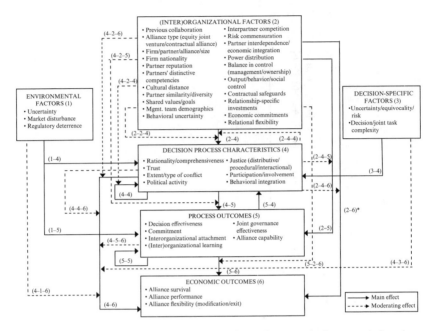

Note: Link 2–6 is excluded from this literature review as it represents the research domain of alliance content and structure.

Figure 17.1　Analytical review scheme for literature on decision processes in alliances

making generally agrees on the main elements of decision processes (see Rajagopalan et al., 1993, for an overview). Adapting this general framework to the context of interfirm collaborations leaves us with six main factors that characterize decision-making processes in strategic alliances. Any strategic decision process is embedded both in the alliance partners' external environment (Box 1), such as environmental uncertainty, and the (inter)organizational environment (Box 2), which comprises previous collaborations, alliance structure, partner diversity, and others. Even within a specific collaboration, however, decision processes may vary according to differences in decision-specific factors (Box 3), such as joint task complexity. These three factors exert an influence on the process by which decisions are made and decision characteristics. The decision process itself can be categorized by decision process characteristics (Box 4), such as procedural rationality, conflict, and justice, which are associated with both process outcomes (Box 5), such as commitment, attachment, and learning, as well as economic outcomes (Box 6), including alliance survival, flexibility, and performance. The empirical studies in the sample have examined links between two or more of these factors. In the following sections, I will review these links and the empirical studies examining them in more detail. Given the focus of my research on decision processes, however, I did not include studies on Link 1–6, which falls into the domain of alliance structure (Contractor, 2005), which has been reviewed elsewhere (e.g., Hennart and Zeng, 2005).

ENVIRONMENTAL FACTORS

Link 1–4: Environmental Factors ➔ Decision Process Characteristics

The three studies examining associations between environmental factors and decision process characteristics have all focused on environmental dynamism or uncertainty – defined as turnover, absence of pattern, and unpredictability (Dess and Beard, 1984) – and, as a whole, have produced mixed results. In theory, higher levels of uncertainty in the alliance's environment demand greater flexibility and adaptability from a collaboration, and may expose the partners to the possibility of opportunistic behavior (Williamson, 1995). While Zaheer et al. (1998) found that uncertainty had a negative influence on joint action between partners, Subramani and Venkatraman (2003) found no significant relationship between uncertainty and joint decision making between partners. Luo (2006) found industry uncertainty to be positively related to interorganizational conflict, but did not find a significant relationship between uncertainty and interpersonal trust between boundary-spanning executives.

Link 1–5: Environmental Factors ➔ Process Outcomes

Three studies examined how industry-level uncertainty influences process outcomes, again with mixed results. Luo (2001) found both market disturbance and regulatory deterrence to have a positive influence on personal attachment between boundary spanners, i.e., the extent to which both partners are bound together through personal relationships, mutual learning, and joint routinization. Uncertain environments not only tend to be viewed as part of the necessary costs and risks of doing business in emerging markets, but may even create market opportunities for the alliance, which emphasizes interdependencies and requires cooperation between partners to exploit them. Faced with *regulatory deterrence* – defined as the extent to which an international joint venture's business operations are hampered by administrative regulations imposed by the host government

– alliance partners are likely to enhance cooperation and attachment to better buffer the joint venture from the impediments of the institutional environment. In a later study by the same author, however, industry uncertainty was negatively associated with interorganizational attachment and decision effectiveness (Luo, 2006). Similarly, Lane et al. (2001) found that demand volatility was not significantly related to joint venture learning.

(INTER)ORGANIZATIONAL FACTORS

Link 2–4: (Inter)organizational Factors → Decision Process Characteristics

A number of studies have examined the link between (inter)organizational factors and decision process characteristics. These studies have focused on four characteristics – trust, conflict, politics, and behavioral integration – which I will review in turn below.

Trust

The literature has defined trust as 'the willingness of a party to be vulnerable to the actions of another party based on the expectation that the other will perform a particular action important to the trustor, irrespective of the ability to monitor or confront that other party' (Mayer et al., 1995: 712). Trust in interfirm collaborations can either refer to the extent of an individual boundary-spanning agent's trust in her counterpart in the partner organization, i.e., *interpersonal trust*, or to the extent of trust placed in the partner organization by the members of a focal organization, i.e., *interorganizational trust* (Zaheer et al., 1998).

Concerning the former, Luo (2006) found previous collaboration between alliance partners to be positively related to interpersonal trust, indicating that 'knowing each other well before forming the joint venture is important to subsequent team decision-making, trust and attachment building and conflict reduction' (Luo, 2006: 1038). In contrast, cultural distance between alliance partners diminished trust between alliance managers (Luo, 2002a, 2006), possibly because shorter cultural distances make cultural blending between partners easier and facilitate open and prompt communication between them.

Concerning the latter, the existence of previous relationships was not significantly related to interorganizational trust between alliance partners (Young-Ybarra and Wiersema, 1999), despite the argument that partners can only be expected to rely on trust if they have successfully completed previous transactions and perceive that the partner has acted equitably

(Ring and Van de Ven, 1992). Besides relying on direct experience and/ or reputation of a partner, trust may also be a function of partners' faith in each other, which is often a result of their shared values and beliefs. Accordingly, partner similarity (Robson et al., 2008) and shared values (Young-Ybarra and Wiersema, 1999) were positively related to interpartner trust, whereas cultural distance between alliance partners had a negative influence on interpartner trust (Luo, 2002a).

In line with social exchange (Blau, 1964) and resource dependence (Pfeffer and Salancik, 1978) theoretic arguments, a unilateral dependence by one partner was negatively related to interpartner trust (Young-Ybarra and Wiersema, 1999), whereas a mutual interdependence among partners had a positive effect (Robson et al., 2008). Somewhat in contrast to these arguments, however, Young-Ybarra and Wiersema (1999) found that the existence of alternatives and the importance of the alliance relationship were not significantly related to trust.

Following the argument of transaction cost theory that economic constraints may serve to decrease partners' opportunistic behavior by increasing reliability and predictability (Williamson, 1995), economic commitments (i.e., balanced asset specificity, hostages) between partners (Young-Ybarra and Wiersema, 1999) and relationship-specific investments (Klein et al., 2007) were all positively related to trust among alliance partners.

Conflict

Jehn and Mannix (2001: 238) defined conflict as 'an awareness on the part of the parties involved of discrepancies, incompatible wishes, or irreconcilable desires'. Previous collaboration between partners (Luo, 2006) and technical support provided by the parent (Steensma and Lyles, 2000) were found to decrease conflict between partners. In contrast, cultural distance between partners (Luo, 2006), as well as an imbalance in the management control structure between partners (Steensma and Lyles, 2000), enhanced interpartner conflict, possibly due to negative perceptions of cultural differences and inequity in partners' relationship. An imbalance in the ownership control structure and managerial support, however, did not affect the level of parental conflict (Steensma and Lyles, 2000). Lastly, Li and Hambrick (2005) found that *factional faultline size*, i.e., when a joint venture management group, in which members are representatives of the two joint venture partners, differ distinctly in their demographic characteristics, was positively related to both *emotional* and *task conflict*, defined, respectively, as disagreements about personal issues and disagreements about the work being performed.

Politics
Politics in strategic decision processes are defined as 'intentional acts of influence to enhance or protect the self-interest of individuals or groups' (Dean and Sharfman, 1996: 374). Three studies have found that (inter) organizational factors could trigger such political behavior. For example, shifts in bargaining power between partners prompted political behavior by the power-losing party, which attempted to restore the power balance (Shenkar and Yan, 2002). Examining more nuanced political influence attempts, Pearce (2001) found that *partner interdependence*, i.e., problem resolution or decision implementation that require both coordination and the open exchange of ideas and information, enhanced rational persuasion, consultation, use of coalitions (marginally), and legitimating. A study by Lui and Ngo (2005), in contrast, found no support for the hypothesized relationship between asymmetric dependence and the political action patterns action acquiescence, simplicity, or reciprocity. Pearce (2001) further found that *factionalism*, i.e., the degree of difference between in-group and out-group sentiment, enhanced the use of hard influence tactics, such as coalitions and legitimating behaviors, while diminishing the use of soft tactics, such as consultation, whereas rational persuasion had no effect.

Behavioral integration
Besides these studies on trust, conflict, and politics, a few studies have examined the influence of (inter)organizational factors on behavioral integration, i.e., the degree to which mutual and collective interaction exists within the group (Hambrick, 1994). Studies have generally found partner differences to decrease behavioral integration, and partner similarity to enhance it. For instance, interpartner diversity in goals, objectives, and operating procedures was correlated with a higher likelihood of more time and effort spent coordinating (White and Lui, 2005), whereas partner similarity was positively related to *action acquiescence*, i.e., level of cooperative behavior as the process unfolds (Lui and Ngo, 2005). Similarly, Li and Hambrick (2005) have examined the influence of joint venture management team demographics on *behavioral disintegration*, i.e., the inverse of the degree to which mutual and collective interaction exists within the group, and found that factional faultline size was positively related to behavioral disintegration while alliance age had no impact.

Supporting the argument that information from previous relationships tends to decrease transaction costs, more prior relationships have been found to decrease the time and effort spent coordinating between partners (White and Lui, 2005). Furthermore, Faems and colleagues (2008) found that a narrow contractual interface structure hampered

joint sensemaking at the operational level as it is likely to limit information exchange on unanticipated technological problems between partners, whereas a broad interface facilitated joint sensemaking, as it tends
to stimulate discussions about emerging technological problems. Since
higher levels of relational flexibility encourage sharing of information
and exploration of opportunities to maximize joint outcomes, relational
flexibility was also positively related to joint decision making (Subramani
and Venkatraman, 2003). Other variables that had a positive effect on
joint decision making were partner size (marginally) and relationship-
specific investments, such as business process specificity (marginally),
domain knowledge specificity, and physical asset specificity, whereas
site specificity was not significant (Subramani and Venkatraman, 2003).
While being beneficial for joint decision making, partner size did
not affect information flow between partners (Klein et al., 2007).
Relationship-specific investments in the form of asset specificity were
further found to have a positive influence on joint action between alliance partners (Zaheer et al., 1998).

Link 2–2–4: (Inter)organizational Factors ➜ Decision Process Characteristics (Moderated by (Inter)organizational Factors)

Sullivan et al.'s (1981) study of Japanese–American alliances uncovered
several examples for the influence of intercultural differences on decision
processes. Contrary to their hypothesis, they found that Japanese managers saw future interpersonal trust as developing better when a joint venture
contract provided for a binding arbitration requirement, instead of mutual
conferral, to resolve disputes, but only when an American was in charge
of operations. While Japanese generally prefer flexibility in responding to
unfolding problems, with an American in charge of operations in Japan,
their preference seems to give way to avoiding conflict before it occurs.
Moreover, while both Japanese and American managers defined the deliberate development of a close personal relationship with the other group as
crucial to the creation of mutual trust, the American managers deemed it
important that future behavior is consistent with past behavior, whereas
the Japanese managers seemed more willing to tolerate ambivalent behavior on the part of the other party (Sullivan et al., 1981).

Link 2–4–4: (Inter)organizational Factors ➜ Decision Process Characteristics (Moderated by Decision Process Characteristics)

Luo (2006) is the only study examining a moderating effect of a decision
process characteristic on the relationship between an (inter)organizational

factor and another decision process characteristic. However, he found no support for his hypothesis that interactional justice between boundary-spanning executives in a cross-cultural joint venture would suppress the negative effects of cultural differences between partners on interpartner trust and conflict, concluding that 'cultural distance and [interactional justice] each affect interpersonal trust in a parallel, rather than interactive fashion (with opposite coefficients)' (Luo, 2006: 1036).

Link 2–5: (Inter)organizational Factors ➔ Process Outcomes

Resonating with both transaction cost and social exchange theoretic arguments, three studies found that the antecedents of attachment or commitment 'encompass individual attributes that affect a boundary spanner's trustworthiness, [and] organizational factors that affect congruence between partners' (Luo, 2001: 181). Johnson et al.'s (2002: 1143) study, for instance, offers marginal support for a positive relationship between decision-making control and *commitment*, defined as 'the belief in and acceptance of organizational goals and values, a willingness to exert effort on behalf of the organization, and a desire to maintain organizational membership'. Two other studies found attachment to be influenced negatively by cultural distance between partners (Luo, 2001, 2006) and marginally negatively by dominant foreign ownership (Luo, 2006), positively by previous collaboration between parties (Luo, 2006), tenure overlap between boundary spanners, and goal congruity between partners (Luo, 2001), whereas educational difference between boundary spanners had no effect (Luo, 2001).

Two other studies examined antecedents of learning, with mixed results. Lane et al. (2001) found that cultural compatibility, prior knowledge from foreign parent, relatedness, flexibility/adaptability, and training by foreign parent were positively related to joint venture learning, whereas size and management support by and specialization of foreign parent were non-significant. Kale et al. (2000), in contrast, found that partner fit, previous alliances, alliance duration, partner nationality, and alliance governance were all non-significant predictors of both learning and protection of proprietary assets.

Luo (2006) further examined antecedents of decision effectiveness, and found that dominant foreign ownership and previous collaboration between parties enhanced decision effectiveness, whereas cultural distance had no effect. Lastly, Simonin (1997) found that firm size was positively related to collaborative experience.

Link 2–4–5: (Inter)organizational Factors ➔ Process Outcomes (Moderated by Decision Process Characteristics)

Luo (2006) found that interactional justice suppressed the negative influence of national cultural differences between partners on interorganizational attachment, possibly because interactional rules such as respect, honesty, and dignity displayed in interactions may reduce cultural friction and induce trust and attachment between alliance managers. He was unable, however, to find support for the hypothesized suppression effect of interactional justice on the negative association between cultural differences and decision effectiveness, suggesting that cultural distance and interactional justice may each influence interparty conflict in their own way.

Link 2–4–6: (Inter)organizational Factors ➔ Economic Performance (Moderated by Decision Process Characteristics)

Das and Teng (1998a) have distinguished two dimensions of trust: *goodwill* or *affect-based trust* refers to the expectation that a partner intends to fulfill its role in the relationship, which captures relational risk, whereas *competence trust* refers to the expectation that partners have the ability to fulfill their roles, which captures performance risk. While this distinction is not yet widely adopted in alliance research, three studies examining the moderating effect of decision process characteristics on relationships between (inter)organizational factors and economic performance provide the exception. Lui and Ngo (2004), for example, found mixed effects of interpersonal trust on alliance performance: the relationships between contractual safeguards and relationship performance (both completion time and performance satisfaction) were more positive when interpersonal goodwill trust was low and interpersonal competence trust was high. This opposite impact may be explained by the fact that goodwill trust and contractual safeguards are substitutes, and thus may offset each other, while competence trust and contractual safeguards have a complementary effect in enhancing partner cooperation (Lui and Ngo, 2004).

Fryxell et al. (2002: 872) further found that social control mechanisms, i.e., *a priori* restrictions on managerial behavior, and joint venture performance were related in a positive way, but only when affect-based trust between partners was high, suggesting that '[t]o be effective, social control mechanisms must be supplemented by affect-based trust [which] promotes the belief that the [international joint venture] partners will not take advantage of the attendant vulnerability resulting from the use of social control mechanisms'.

And lastly, Patzelt and Shepherd (2008) reported evidence of the 'dark side' of interorganizational trust by finding that the relationships between output and behavior control, and the likelihood that alliance managers decide to persist with an underperforming alliance, were more positive when interorganizational competence trust was high. However, they found no significant moderating relationship for social control. Moreover, the relationships between any control mode and the likelihood that alliance managers decide to persist with an underperforming alliance were more positive when interorganizational goodwill trust was high. It appears that in the context of underperforming alliances, a belief in their partner's competence and goodwill provides alliance managers with an enhanced motivation to disregard or reinterpret current information, and therefore magnifies the positive relationship between control and persistence.

DECISION-SPECIFIC FACTORS

Link 3–4: Decision-Specific Factors ➜ Decision Process Characteristics

White and Lui (2005) found a curvilinear relationship between joint task complexity and the likelihood of managers spending substantial time and effort to coordinate with a partner. Specifically, in the case of less complex projects, the firm was less likely to spend a significant amount of time and effort coordinating with the partner. After a certain threshold level, task complexity had a net positive effect on coordination effort.

DECISION PROCESS CHARACTERISTICS

Link 4–4: Decision Process Characteristics ➜ Decision Process Characteristics

A number of studies have examined relationships between decision process characteristics, such as trust, conflict, politics, and behavioral integration, which I will review below.

Trust
Both interactional justice (Luo, 2006) and procedural justice (Luo, 2008a) were found to enhance interpersonal trust, perhaps because 'justice is associated with positive attitudes toward a decision, such as satisfaction, agreement, and commitment, and these attitudes then propel cooperative behaviors, such as harmony, attachment, and trust' (Luo, 2008a: 32).

Interpersonal trust, in turn, may limit the inclination of alliance partners to employ available room for opportunism and was thus found to decrease the perception of relational risk in the form of perceived probability of loss (Nooteboom et al., 1997). Zaheer et al. (1998) further argued that negotiations may be easier due to boundary spanners' willingness to share sensitive information and their confidence that information is not misrepresented by the partner. Contrary to their argument, they found interpersonal trust to increase, rather than decrease, negotiation costs between partners, suggesting a conjunctive effect of interpersonal and interorganizational trust (see below). Other studies, however, were not able to find significant relationships between either interpersonal trust and both time and effort spent coordinating (White and Lui, 2005), or conflict between partners (Zaheer et al., 1998).

Interorganizational trust was positively affected by the level and quality of communication between partners (Young-Ybarra and Wiersema, 1999), joint sensemaking at the operational level (Faems et al., 2008), and integrative conflict management (Kale et al., 2000), all in line with the argument that personal contact allows firms to learn about their alliance partners' idiosyncrasies and develop a better understanding of each other, which are key factors for the development of trust. Interorganizational trust also had a positive effect on both distributive (Robson et al., 2008) and procedural justice (Luo, 2008a). Faems et al. (2008) further found that rigid (flexible) contract application was likely to trigger negative (positive) trust dynamics between partners at both operational and managerial levels, as a rigid application of the contract triggered behaviors, such as searching for technological shortcuts, which, in turn, increased suspicions between partners about each other's intentions.

Interorganizational trust, in turn, had a positive effect on strategic information flows (Klein et al., 2007), action acquiescence, and *action simplicity*, i.e., the degree of specialization of firms towards their partners in terms of actions taken towards them (Lui and Ngo, 2005). Moreover, interorganizational trust had a negative effect on interorganizational conflict (Gulati and Nickerson, 2008; Zaheer et al., 1998) and *action reciprocity*, i.e., the extent to which firms reciprocate the actions of their partners (Lui and Ngo, 2005). As a whole, these findings suggest that trust between partners can lower transaction costs, provide incentives to engage in long-term, value-added initiatives, and make it more likely that partners give each other the benefit of the doubt, which tends to reduce dysfunctional conflict.

Zaheer et al. (1998: 156) further found that interorganizational trust decreased negotiation costs between partners, which, combined with the opposite effect of interpersonal trust, suggests that 'even though the individuals across the dyad may not trust each other, as long as the institutionalized structures accompanying high interorganizational trust are in place, negotiating costs will be kept down'. Lastly, positive (negative) trust dynamics between partners at both operational and managerial levels led to increased flexibility (rigidity) regarding contract application (Faems et al., 2008), which, combined with the causally reverse results discussed above, suggest a co-evolutionary relationship between contract application and trust dynamics.

Conflict

In spite of his argument that interactional justice can help reduce conflict between alliance partners by enhancing confidence and commitment from alliance managers, Luo (2006) did not find such a relationship. Moreover, Li and Hambrick (2005) found that emotional conflict was positively related to behavioral disintegration, whereas there was no significant effect for task conflict. These distinct findings for the two types of conflict suggest that while personal dislike may have driven alliance managers apart in conducting their work, they were either able to surmount any task-related discord in their efforts to operate as a team or adopted constructive norms to deal with conflict.

Politics

On the one hand, Lyles and Reger (1993) showed that joint venture managers – despite a relative power disadvantage – had a variety of techniques at their disposal to successfully influence decision-making processes about the joint venture's future, particularly if several techniques were used at the same time combined with the right timing. For example, joint venture managers used personal interactions with parent firm managers to influence the decisions made, and successfully gained cooperation from those outside the formal authority structure, such as the joint venture's and the parent firms' stakeholders, to create pressures on its parent. In contrast to successful influence attempts via the vertical parent–joint venture relationship, the latter pressures were more likely because outside stakeholders may benefit from an increased independence of the joint venture, and they do not stand to lose control as the parents might.

On the other hand, Shenkar and Yan (2002) found that political behavior in general intensified interpartner conflict. Pearce (2001) further found support for a negative relationship between information exchange among partners and factionalism, suggesting that parental norms endorsing collaborative behavior diminish 'us' versus 'them' attitudes, whereas carefully controlled information exchanges may be interpreted as a signal that it is both legitimate and acceptable to behave similarly, which fosters factionalism. However, both flexibility and shared problem solving had no impact on factionalism (Pearce, 2001).

Behavioral integration

Despite their hypothesis that alliance managers will be more willing to incur cooperation costs if they perceive the relationship between them and their partner to be equitable, perceptions of a lack of mutual adaptation and a lack of cooperative problem solving did not have significant effects on time and effort spent coordinating (White and Lui, 2005). The authors suggest that respondents in a positive atmosphere of equitable collaboration may not perceive these coordination costs to be onerous or requiring effort.

Link 4–2–4: Decision Process Characteristics ➔ Decision Process Characteristics (Moderated by (Inter)organizational Factors)

Sullivan et al. (1981) found that Japanese managers believed in building future interpersonal trust by resolving disputes as they come up through conferral, rather than through binding arbitration, regardless of the nationality of the manager in control. The nationality of the manager, therefore, did not moderate the relationship between conflict resolution and the development of future trust between alliance managers. Moreover, Lui and Ngo (2005) found that the positive relationship between interorganizational trust and action acquiescence was stronger in situations with low asset specificity, and that the positive relationship between interorganizational trust and action simplicity was stronger when the partner had a good reputation. These findings suggest that transaction cost characteristics of a partnership, such as asset specificity and partner reputation, may be able to mitigate opportunistic behavior of the partners.

Link 4–5: Decision Process Characteristics ➔ Process Outcomes

Studies on this link examined the impact of decision process characteristics on decision effectiveness, commitment, and learning, which I will review in turn.

Decision effectiveness

Corroborating his argument that justice fosters information processing – through improved communication and heightened willingness to share information – as well as confidence and commitment, Luo (2006) found that interactional justice between alliance managers was positively associated with these managers' joint decision effectiveness.

Commitment
Johnson et al. (2002) found support for a positive link between procedural justice in joint venture decision process and commitment to the joint venture and both parents. Moreover, higher procedural justice resulted in more similar commitment to all three entities. As the management team's commitment to the joint venture depends least on interactions with the parents, procedural justice has its greatest impact on managers' identification with and commitment to the parents (Johnson et al., 2002).

Learning
Lane et al. (2001) argued that trust functions as an ongoing social control and risk reduction mechanism, which not only enhances the extent but also the efficiency of knowledge exchange due to a positive influence on partners' absorptive capacities. As a result, trust between partners was marginally positively (Lane et al., 2001) and positively (Kale et al., 2000) associated with learning from alliance partners. Moreover, constructive conflict resolution techniques, such as joint problem solving, enhanced organizational learning (Kale et al., 2000).

The flip side of learning *from* the partner in a collaborative relationship would arguably be learning *by* the partner. While the transfer of knowledge and capabilities to the partner may be an explicit part of some collaborations, the unintentional spillover of proprietary knowledge represents a severe threat to a firm's competitive advantage. One study found that integrative conflict management enhanced the protection of proprietary assets, whereas relationship capital did not have a significant influence (Kale et al., 2000).

Link 4–2–5: Decision Process Characteristics ➜ Process Outcomes (Moderated by (Inter)organizational Factors)

Johnson et al. (2002: 1147) found support for their argument that the lower the decision-making control, the higher the impact of procedural justice on commitment to the joint venture and both partners, suggesting that when joint venture managers have little control over decision processes, 'procedural justice assumes greater salience, as a signal of the protection of their interests, the integrity of decision-makers, and their value to the organization'.

Link 4–6: Decision Process Characteristics ➜ Economic Outcomes

A large number of studies have examined the influence of decision process characteristics on economic outcomes. I will review their findings for trust, conflict, politics, justice, behavioral integration, and other decision process characteristics.

Trust

Supporting the notion that trust may complement, or even substitute, control in an interfirm collaboration (Luo, 2002b; Poppo and Zenger, 2002), and therefore benefits its economic outcomes, three studies found a marginally positive association of interpersonal trust with joint venture profitability (Luo, 2006) and the financial outcome of an alliance (Luo, 2008a), and a positive effect of interpersonal goodwill trust and competence trust on alliance performance (Lui and Ngo, 2004). Two studies, however, were not able to find a significant relationship between interpersonal trust and supplier performance (Zaheer et al., 1998), or the operational outcome of an alliance (Luo, 2008a).

Concerning interorganizational trust, a number of studies have found interorganizational trust to have a positive effect on strategic flexibility of an alliance, in terms of modification or exit (Young-Ybarra and Wiersema, 1999); both financial and operational outcomes of an alliance (Luo, 2008a); alliance performance (Gulati and Nickerson, 2008; Krishnan et al., 2006; Lane et al., 2001; Luo, 2008b; Mohr and Spekman, 1994; Monczka et al., 1998; Robson et al., 2008; Zaheer et al., 1998); and alliance stability (Luo, 2008b). One study, however, found no support for interorganizational trust as a critical success factor for strategic alliances (Rai et al., 1996). Yet another study qualified any effect by finding that interorganizational affect-based trust was positively related to joint venture performance as rated by the US, but not as rated by the foreign parent, and that interorganizational cognitive trust had no significant effect on joint venture performance (Fryxell et al., 2002).

Conflict

Studies on interpartner conflict have produced somewhat ambiguous findings. Habib's (1987) study showed that perceived conflict between partners was negatively related to the satisfaction with a partner's performance. This finding was somewhat corroborated by Luo (2006), who found that interorganizational conflict was marginally negatively associated with joint venture profitability, and by Steensma and Lyles (2000), who found that interpartner conflict had a negative impact on joint venture survival. Li and Hambrick (2005) qualified these results by finding that emotional conflict was negatively related to joint venture performance, whereas task conflict had no significant impact. Another set of studies on the impact of conflict in alliances, however, has not been able to support a relationship between interpartner conflict and alliance performance (Rai et al., 1996; Yan and Gray, 2001; Zaheer et al., 1998).

Yet another set of studies has focused on conflict resolution techniques and their impact on alliance outcomes. Constructive conflict resolution techniques, such as joint problem solving, enhanced alliance success (Mohr and Spekman, 1994; Monczka et al., 1998; Pearce, 2001; Thomas and Trevino, 1993). Persuasion, however, was found to have no significant impact (Mohr and Spekman, 1994), and a negative impact on partnership success (Monczka et al., 1998). Conflict avoidance tactics, such as smoothing over problems, were negatively associated with alliance success (Mohr and Spekman, 1994), and not significantly related to partnership success (Monczka et al., 1998). Destructive resolution tactics, such as domination and harsh words (Mohr and Spekman, 1994; Monczka et al., 1998), and outside arbitration (Monczka et al., 1998), were negatively associated with alliance success, although harsh words decreased new product development time (Monczka et al., 1998).

Politics

Evidence for the impact of political activity in alliances on their economic outcomes is mixed. While Thomas and Trevino (1993) found that political activity at the alliance level had a positive impact on alliance success, to the extent it was used for increased information flow, equivocality reduction, and conflict resolution, two other studies found support for a negative association of alliance-level politics and joint venture stability (Shenkar and Yan, 2002), and between firm-level politics and alliance performance (Walter et al., 2008). One study has examined more specific political tactics at the alliance level and found that the use of coalitions was negatively related to partnership success, whereas rational persuasion, consultation, and legitimating were non-significant (Pearce, 2001).

Justice

Luo (2007) has distinguished different types of justice, and found procedural, distributive, and interactional justice to be positively associated with alliance performance. Two other studies have qualified the type of economic outcome, and found that procedural justice was positively related to financial and operational outcomes (Luo, 2008a), as well as to both alliance profitability and alliance stability (Luo, 2008b). The second study found that there was a positive relationship between shared perceptions of procedural justice and alliance profitability (Luo, 2005). This relationship was stronger, however, between shared perceptions and alliance profitability than between unilaterally perceived procedural justice and profitability.

Behavioral integration

Studies on the influence of behavioral integration on economic outcomes have focused on information sharing and joint decision making, with mixed results. While Monczka et al. (1998) found that partnership success was positively associated with information sharing, Mohr and Spekman (1994) – although finding support for the positive impact of communication quality, i.e., accuracy, timeliness, adequacy, and credibility – found a negative influence of information sharing on alliance success. The latter authors speculate that their counter-intuitive finding may be caused by firms sharing more information with their alliance partners – including information about profit margins – which gives the partners the impression that they are entitled to a greater share of the profits from the partnership.

Thomas and Trevino (1993) found support for their argument that a high capacity for information processing, i.e., low formality, high participation, and high interaction, is positively related to alliance success by providing a structure for both the reduction of *uncertainty*, i.e., lack of information, and of *equivocality*, i.e., existence of multiple and conflicting interpretations. They cautioned, however, that a potentially rich information-processing mechanism or communication medium must be saturated, i.e., used to its richness capacity, to effectively manage equivocality during strategic alliance building. For example, the potentially rich medium of a combination of group meetings and a corporate retreat to bring factions together was underutilized when it became a forum to transmit the top management's own vision, thereby preventing reciprocal communication, the synthesis of diverse viewpoints, and equivocality reduction.

The positive influence of participation in the decision process on alliance performance was supported by several studies (Mohr and Spekman, 1994; Monczka et al., 1998; Saxton, 1997). Mohr and Spekman (1994) further found that coordination between partners, i.e., boundary definitions reflecting the set of tasks each party expects the other to perform, enhances alliance success. And lastly, Li and Hambrick (2005) found that behavioral disintegration was negatively related to joint venture performance. A similar line of inquiry was pursued by two other studies that examined the degree to which decision processes are open to inputs from managers. While Thomas and Trevino (1993) found that managing the momentum to prevent premature closure of relevant issues and to allow equivocality reduction was positively related to alliance success, Walter et al. (2008) were unable to find a significant effect of openness on alliance performance.

Other decision process characteristics
Two studies found support for a positive impact of interpartner consensus on alliance performance (Yan and Gray, 2001), but no support for the influence of consensus within one partner organization, mutual agreement on goals and objectives, and shared understanding of risks on alliance performance (Rai et al., 1996). Other studies found no support for the influence of procedural rationality on alliance performance (Walter et al., 2008); a marginally positive effect of decision-making speed on alliance performance (Walter et al., 2008); and a positive effect (Pearce, 2001), no effect (Rai et al., 1996), and a negative effect (Walter et al., 2008) of flexibility on alliance performance.

Link 4–1–6: Decision Process Characteristics ➔ Economic Outcomes (Moderated by Environmental Factors)

Luo (2002a) found that the relationships between interpersonal and interorganizational trust and alliance performance were stronger when the market was more uncertain, whereas Krishnan et al. (2006) found that the relationship between interorganizational trust and alliance performance was stronger under less market uncertainty. Moreover, the relationship between shared perceptions of procedural justice and alliance profitability was stronger when uncertainty was higher (Luo, 2005).

Link 4–2–6: Decision Process Characteristics ➔ Economic Outcomes (Moderated by (Inter)organizational Factors)

Trust–performance relationship
The one study examining interpersonal trust found no moderating effects of cultural distance, risk commensuration, and interpartner dependency on the relationship between interpersonal trust and alliance performance (Luo, 2002a).

Three studies examining interorganizational trust have found that the relationship between interorganizational trust and alliance performance was stronger when the degree of interpartner competition was higher (Krishnan et al., 2006), when partner interdependence was higher (Krishnan et al., 2006; Luo, 2002a), when economic integration, i.e., interdependence between alliance partners with respect to resources pooled and subsequent operations utilizing these resources, was higher (Luo, 2008b), and when risk was more commensurate between partners (Luo, 2002a). However, no moderating effect of cultural distance on the relationship between interorganizational trust and alliance performance could be found, suggesting that while cultural barriers may obstruct initial trust building, once trust is built, alliance partners may be able to cooperate successfully regardless of cultural distance (Luo, 2002a).

One study examined alliance size as a potential moderator, and found that the relationship between interpartner trust and alliance performance was stronger when alliance size decreased, possibly because the positive effect of trust on network connections between alliance managers is mitigated by 'facets of size-driven bureaucracy such as differentiation, formalization, and decentralization [that] establish barriers that disconnect actors' (Robson et al., 2008: 651).

Justice–performance relationship

Empirical support is also accumulating for several moderators of the justice–performance relationship. Two studies by Luo found mixed support for cultural distance as a moderator of the relationship between shared perceptions of procedural justice and alliance profitability. In the first study, the relationship was stronger when cultural distance was greater (Luo, 2005), whereas interpartner cultural distance was not a significant moderator in the second study (Luo, 2008a). Luo explains his non-finding in the latter study by arguing that executives with a rich experience in a foreign country may be able to mitigate the negative effects of cultural distance by amplifying their personal trust with their foreign counterparts.

Furthermore, the relationship between procedural justice and alliance performance was stronger when alliances were equity joint ventures, versus contractual agreements (Luo, 2008a), suggesting that justice contributes more to cooperation when one or both parties view the alliance as more important, which is manifested in its form. Similarly, the relationship between procedural justice and alliance performance was stronger when economic integration was higher (Luo, 2008b). However, economic integration did not significantly moderate the relationship between procedural justice and alliance stability, implying that integration and justice both independently influence alliance stability (Luo, 2008b). Examining a three-way interaction, Luo (2007) found that when goal differences between partners were high, the joint effect of procedural and distributive justice on alliance performance was positive.

Behavioral integration–performance relationship

Saxton (1997) found that the positive relationship between shared decision making and alliance performance was stronger for alliances in which partners had shared equity positions.

Link 4–3–6: Decision Process Characteristics ➔ Economic Outcomes (Moderated by Decision-Specific Factors)

Only one study examined such a moderating relationship, and found that matching the richness of information-processing mechanisms, i.e., formality, participation, interaction, to information-processing needs contributed to alliance success (Thomas and Trevino, 1993).

Link 4–4–6: Decision Process Characteristics ➔ Economic Outcomes (Moderated by Decision Process Characteristics)

Luo (2007) examined interactive influences of different types of justice on alliance performance and found that the positive relationship between procedural justice and alliance performance was stronger when interactional justice was higher. However, he found no significant moderating influence of interactional justice on the relationship between distributive justice and alliance performance, suggesting that distributive and interactional justice 'work separately, not jointly, to influence alliance performance and that unlike procedural justice, distributive justice is not significantly sensitive to social exchanges between alliance members' (Luo, 2007: 656).

Walter et al. (2008) further examined the moderating influence of firm-level politics, and found that in a context of low politics, openness and procedural rationality had a positive influence on alliance performance, whereas recursiveness negatively affected alliance performance. In a context of high politics, however, openness and procedural rationality exerted a negative influence, and the negative impact of recursiveness was aggravated.

Link 4–5–6: Decision Process Characteristics ➔ Economic Outcomes (Moderated by Process Outcomes)

Luo (2002a) found that the relationship between trust and alliance performance was stronger when commitment from each partner to the alliance was higher, suggesting that reciprocal commitment counters opportunism, fosters cooperation, and serves as a stabilizing device mitigating (market) uncertainties and interparty conflict. Moreover, alliance age as an indicator of organizational attachment moderated the relationships between interpersonal and interorganizational trust and alliance performance. In particular, the relationships were stronger when the alliance was younger, and therefore more susceptible to risk and failure (Luo, 2002a).

PROCESS AND ECONOMIC OUTCOMES

Link 5–4: Process Outcomes ➔ Decision Process Characteristics

A number of authors have argued for a trust–attachment effect, but in the opposite direction. In particular, collaboration over time likely fosters institutionalization (i.e., partners' shared norms and values) and habitualization (i.e., partners having established habits, bonds, good communication, and empathy), which then induce perceived trust between alliance partners and alliance managers (Nooteboom et al., 1997). However, results are mixed with respect to the influence of alliance age, as a proxy for attachment between partners, on trust. Contrary to their hypothesis, Young-Ybarra and Wiersema (1999) were unable to find a significant relationship between attachment and interorganizational trust. Moreover, Luo (2002a) failed to find a significant effect of alliance age on interpersonal or interorganizational trust, whereas a later study by the same author found that alliance age was positively associated with interpersonal trust (Luo, 2006). Luo (2006) further found that interactional justice was positively related to interorganizational attachment, and that conflict between partners decreased with an increasing age of the collaboration. However, Subramani and Venkatraman (2003) found no significant relationships between length of association and joint decision making, and Li and Hambrick (2005) found no effect of joint venture age on emotional conflict, task conflict, or behavioral disintegration.

Examining other antecedents of trust, Luo (2002a) found that both interpersonal and interorganizational trust were enhanced by reciprocal commitment from each alliance partner.

Link 5–5: Process Outcomes ➔ Process Outcomes

Only one study examined relationships between process outcomes. Kale et al. (2000) found, however, that alliance duration was not significantly related to either learning from the alliance partner or the protection of proprietary assets.

Link 5–6: Process Outcomes ➔ Economic Outcomes

A first set of studies examined commitment and attachment as predictors of economic outcomes, with mixed results. Two studies support a marginally positive (Luo, 2006) and positive association (Luo, 2001) between interorganizational relational attachment and joint venture profitability. Moreover, Seabright et al. (1992) found that the greater the individual attachment between exchange partners, the lower the likelihood of dissolution of their relationship, but found no effect of structural attachment, i.e., the duration of the relationship. Levinthal and Fichman (1988) further qualified the effects of structural attachment by finding support for their argument that in the initial years of interorganizational attachment, the hazard rate of relationship dissolution increased, whereas for longer durations, the hazard rate for it ending in a given year decreased over time. Other studies examined alliance duration or age as a proxy for attachment. Some found a positive effect of alliance age on alliance performance (Krishnan et al., 2006; Luo, 2001, 2002a, 2005, 2007, 2008a,b; Walter et al., 2008) and stability (Luo, 2008b), while others found no relationship between alliance age and performance (Fryxell et al., 2002; Klein et al., 2007; Li and Hambrick, 2005) or operational outcome (Luo, 2008a). Concerning the influence of commitment, Mohr and Spekman (1994) found a positive impact of partners' willingness to exert effort on behalf of the relationship on alliance success, while Monczka et al. (1998) found no relationship between commitment and partnership success.

A second set of studies examined the influence of information flow, learning, and, more generally, the development of an alliance capability on alliance performance. In particular, strategic information flow was positively associated with relationship-specific performance (Klein et al., 2007; Krishnan et al., 2006), and joint venture learning enhanced the likelihood of joint venture survival (Steensma and Lyles, 2000). Decision effectiveness was marginally positively related to alliance profitability (Luo, 2006), while joint governance effectiveness was positively related to alliance stability (Luo, 2008b). More generally, Simonin (1997) and Anand and Khanna (2000) found evidence for substantial learning effects in managing alliances. The former author, however, qualified the impact of experience by showing that collaborative experience has to be internalized, i.e., translated into collaborative know-how, before it can contribute to future collaborative benefits. Similarly, Kale et al. (2002) found that firms with a dedicated alliance function, with the intent of strategically coordinating alliance activity and capturing/disseminating alliance-related knowledge, achieve greater alliance success.

Link 5–2–6: Process Outcomes ➔ Economic Outcomes (Moderated by (Inter)organizational Factors)

Luo (2008b) found that the positive relationship between joint governance effectiveness and alliance stability was stronger when economic integration was higher. However, he did not find a significant moderating effect for the relationship between joint governance effectiveness and alliance profitability. Moreover, Anand and Khanna (2000) found that the effects of learning on value creation are strongest for research joint ventures, less in production joint ventures, and weakest for marketing joint ventures, which supports their argument that learning matters most for alliances confronted with the greatest ambiguity and uncertainty.

DISCUSSION AND FUTURE RESEARCH

Scholars have often lamented that '[s]trategy process research has to become more normative if it is to be of relevance to the general managers' (Chakravarthy and Doz, 1992: 9). Critics have been particularly vocal with respect to alliance process research (see Bell et al., 2006; Hennart, 2006, for recent examples). This review of the literature on decision-making processes in the realm of strategic alliances, however, demonstrates that prior research has developed a rich, albeit not always conclusive, body of knowledge, with numerous normative implications for alliance practitioners and researchers alike. Moreover, roughly two thirds of the studies reviewed here were published in the year 2000 or later, which suggests a growing scholarly interest in alliance-related decision processes. In contrast to earlier and largely descriptive studies on general alliance processes (e.g., Arino and de la Torre, 1998; de Rond and Bouchiki, 2004; Doz, 1996; Ring and Van de Ven, 1992), the studies reviewed here enhance our knowledge about the management of alliances and have the potential to contribute to a reduction in alliance failures through improved managerial practices (Barringer and Harrison, 2000). In the next section, I will discuss the findings as a whole, before suggesting several avenues for future research.

Environmental Factors

Five studies have examined factors of the environment alliances are embedded in, and found mixed support for the influence of environmental dynamism or uncertainty on decision process characteristics and outcomes (Lane et al., 2001; Luo, 2001, 2006; Subramani and Venkatraman, 2003; Zaheer et al., 1998). Reflecting a tendency in broader decision process research, however, alliance researchers have so far neglected the influence of other environmental aspects, such as *complexity* (i.e., the number of elements and their interconnectedness) and *munificence* (i.e., the resource support provided by the environment) (Dess and Beard, 1984). This is unfortunate as alliance managers facing more environmental complexity likely have higher information-processing requirements, which might affect the relationship between decision process characteristics and process outcomes. Moreover, as alliances can be conceived as means to ensure resource access and obtain a more munificent environment (cf., Hirsch, 1975), environmental munificence is also likely to influence decision process characteristics and outcomes. As Priem et al. (1995: 926) have pointed out, firms are 'less likely to be penalized for suboptimal decisions in munificent than in non-munificent environments. Thus, decision processes suited to munificent environments may be inappropriate for less munificent environments.'

Moreover, some studies have argued that the development of a more comprehensive understanding of the context specificity of the relationships between decision process characteristics and outcomes requires the simultaneous examination of multiple environmental dimensions (Goll and Rasheed, 1997; Priem et al., 1995):

> For example, environmental complexity may require the firm to employ greater rationality in its analysis in order to understand the numerous environmental elements and their interconnectedness. Research on cognitive processes suggests that high environmental complexity may lead to greater use of cognitive simplification processes such as selective perception, heuristics, and analogies, which in turn may affect strategic decision processes by potentially restricting the range of alternatives considered and the information used to evaluate them. Similarly, in munificent environments, organizations may have the resources needed to engage in comprehensive decision processes, but the decision-makers themselves may perceive less need to do so. (Goll and Rasheed, 1997: 584)

Future research might therefore benefit from including complexity and/or munificence as independent or moderating variables in alliance-related decision processes, and from clarifying the impact of environmental uncertainty, a variable that studies in other contexts have deemed a critical contingency variable for decision process research (e.g., Baum and Wally, 2003; Eisenhardt, 1989; Priem et al., 1995).

(Inter)organizational Factors

Despite Noorderhaven's (2005: 103) assertion that '[s]tructure obviously influences the behavior of alliance partners, and hence process, but the specifics of this influence have not yet received much detailed attention', numerous studies have examined the link between (inter)organizational factors and decision process characteristics. The studies reviewed in this section offer some insights with respect to the impact of alliance structure on strategic decision processes. Empirical findings on these relationships corroborate the arguments of Doz (1996), Contractor (2005), and others that alliance structure and processes together and interacting with each other determine alliance success. As a whole, the studies reviewed above provide a rich, albeit fragmented, picture on the interplay between structure and process in alliances. The studies on trust (Klein et al., 2007; Luo, 2002a, 2006; Robson et al., 2008; Young-Ybarra and Wiersema, 1999), conflict (Li and Hambrick, 2005; Luo, 2006; Steensma and Lyles, 2000), politics (Lui and Ngo, 2005; Pearce, 2001; Shenkar and Yan, 2002), and behavioral integration (Faems et al., 2008; Klein et al., 2007; Li and Hambrick, 2005; Lui and Ngo, 2005; Subramani and Venkatraman, 2003; White and Lui, 2005; Zaheer et al., 1998) between alliance partners provide broad consensus on positive and negative structural determinants of these crucial decision process variables (Link 2–4). Explicitly incorporating – or at least controlling for – such (inter)organizational factors not only addresses Hennart and Zeng's (2005: 112) criticism that 'much of the variance in performance attributed to process characteristics may in fact be due to structural conditions', but also provides alliance managers with normative guidelines for the design of alliance structures. In fact, numerous studies found that (inter)organizational factors – such as alliance size (Kale et al., 2002; Klein et al., 2007; Krishnan et al., 2006; Luo, 2001, 2005, 2008a,b; Robson et al., 2008; Walter et al., 2008), alliance type (Luo, 2005, 2007), ownership (Luo, 2008a,b), and asset specificity (Lui and Ngo, 2004; Nooteboom et al., 1997) – were non-significant predictors of alliance performance. Even more striking, though, is the fact that in one study, a marginally significant (inter)organizational predictor of alliance performance, i.e., alliance type, became nonsignificant once alliance process characteristics were added to the model (Krishnan et al., 2006).

In spite of these positive examples, the fact that only a fraction of the studies have addressed structural influences supports the criticism of previous literature reviews that contributions emphasizing structural and processual aspects of alliances have remained largely separate from each other (Contractor, 2005; Noorderhaven, 2005). Given their profound influence, however, an explicit recognition of (inter)organizational factors in future research would serve to better isolate the contributions of decision process characteristics on alliance performance.

Decision Process Characteristics

This section contains the vast majority of studies and, as a whole, these studies provide a rich account of how decision process characteristics relate to each other and how they determine process and economic outcomes in alliances. Not only do these studies answer Salk's (2005) call for research that directly studies process characteristics, instead of inferring them from secondary data, but they further provide ample evidence for the profound influence of decision process characteristics on the success of interfirm collaborations (Links 4–5 and 4–6). This performance impact, together with the abundant interrelationships among decision process characteristics (Link 4–4), demonstrates the complexity of alliance management, but it also outlines numerous levers for managerial intervention into alliance-related decision processes. Any intervention – and particularly any deliberate design of decision processes – has to further account for environmental (Link 4–1–6: Krishnan et al., 2006; Luo, 2002a, 2005), (inter)organizational (Links 4–2–4, 4–2–5, 4–2–6: Johnson et al., 2002; Lui and Ngo, 2005; Luo, 2002a, 2005, 2007, 2008a,b; Robson et al., 2008; Saxton, 1997), and decision-specific factors (Link 4–3–6: Thomas and Trevino, 1993), as well as other decision process characteristics (Link 4–4–6: Walter et al., 2008) and process outcomes (Link 4–5–6: Luo, 2002a) acting as contingency variables.

There are, however, two areas in particular that are in need of future research to consolidate ambiguous findings across studies. Trust between alliance partners can be defined as either goodwill or competence trust with differential effects on alliance outcomes (Das and Teng, 1998a), but only two studies examining decision process characteristics have made this distinction (Fryxell et al., 2002; Lui and Ngo, 2004). Some of the conflicting results, for instance with respect to the moderating effect of environmental uncertainty on the relationship between trust and alliance performance (Krishnan et al., 2006; Luo, 2002a), might therefore be an artifact of differences in the type of trust being examined. Similarly, in spite of Zaheer et al. (1998) introducing the distinction between interpersonal and interorganizational trust in alliances, very few studies make their level of analysis explicit and/or incorporate both levels into their theorizing. This ambiguity is unfortunate as two of the studies comparing both levels of analysis found differential effects of the two levels of trust on other decision process characteristics (Luo, 2006; Zaheer et al., 1998). Future research might clarify some of these inconsistent results by distinguishing between different types of and analytical levels of trust. While none of the studies has attempted this, it may be beneficial to further combine these distinctions and examine, for instance, whether there are any differences between the effects of interpersonal and interorganizational goodwill versus competence trust.

Related to the ambiguities concerning different types of conflict, the prior literature has also distinguished between two types of conflict. Emotional conflicts – also referred to as 'relationship conflicts' (Jehn, 1995) or 'affective conflicts' (Pelled, 1996) – are disagreements and incompatibilities among group members about personal issues, and include affective components, such as feeling tension and friction (Jehn and Mannix,

2001). Task conflicts, on the other hand, are disagreements among group members about the work being performed (Jehn and Mannix, 2001). Although this distinction is well established in other research fields – and despite empirical support for a contingency effect of conflict type on process outcomes (e.g., Jehn, 1995) – only one study has distinguished between different types of conflict and their distinct influences on alliance performance (Li and Hambrick, 2005). Not accounting for the type of conflict may therefore explain the inconsistent results of studies that either found a negative influence of interpartner conflict on alliance performance and survival (Habib, 1987; Luo, 2006; Steensma and Lyles, 2000), or were unable to find any significant relationship between interpartner conflict and alliance performance (Rai et al., 1996; Yan and Gray, 2001; Zaheer et al., 1998). Future research may want to consolidate these inconsistencies by explicitly distinguishing task and emotional conflicts and their differential influences on strategy processes and outcomes.

Conceptual differences between types of trust or conflict are only one reason for ambiguous empirical results. In general, the definitions and empirical conceptualizations of many decision process characteristics are largely inconsistent across studies, making it difficult to directly compare findings and to ensure the reliability and replicability of results. To mitigate these concerns, future research should at least review the relevant prior literature and justify any deviations from previous measures.

Process and Economic Outcomes

Despite the publication of numerous studies on alliance performance (e.g., Arino, 2003; Mohr and Spekman, 1994; Olk, 2002), there is no widespread agreement on how to conceptualize or measure it. Alliance performance has been conceptualized, among others, as satisfaction with the relationship (Gulati and Nickerson, 2008; Krishnan et al., 2006), effectiveness, efficiency, and responsiveness (Robson et al., 2008), financial and operational outcomes (Luo, 2008a), ROI and sales per asset (Luo, 2002a), asset turnover (Luo, 2007), profitability (Luo, 2005), survival (Steensma and Lyles, 2000), or combinations of the above (Luo, 2008b). Measurements of alliance performance have been similarly diverse. Studies have used perceptual assessments of alliance managers (Robson et al., 2008; Walter et al., 2008), accounting measures (Luo, 2007, 2008b), abnormal stock market returns (Anand and Khanna, 2000), or combinations of the above (Gulati and Nickerson, 2008; Kale et al., 2002; Luo, 2008a).

In response to the plethora of measurement approaches, the alliance literature has voiced several criticisms. On the one hand, studies that have outright rejected any subjective performance measures have not prevented numerous studies from employing managerial assessments of alliance performance. These latter studies often invoke Olk's (2002) argument that subjective performance assessments are appropriate when respondents represent top management, and Geringer and Hebert (1991) and Kale et al.'s (2002) empirical findings that subjective and objective measures of alliance performance are highly correlated with each other.

On the other hand, some studies have argued that neither survival nor financial indicators fully capture the extent to which an alliance has achieved its objectives. Survival or termination can hardly be distinguished from planned or unplanned terminations; in particular, an alliance can be successful and discontinued – e.g., because it has served its purpose – or unsuccessful and not (yet) discontinued, e.g., because the partners still hope to improve the relationship (Yan and Zeng, 1999). Moreover, most alliances do not report financial performance, which, in any case, tends to be biased by partners' accounting preferences (Krishnan et al., 2006), and spillovers from the alliance or emergent returns are even more difficult to capture with financial measures (Gulati, 1998). Further questioning financial measures, Reuer (2001) found that some alliance partners' stock prices rose for both alliance creation and termination announcements.

Given the advantages and disadvantages of each alliance performance measure, the best approach for future research would be to employ multiple, complementary measures (see Gulati and Nickerson, 2008; Kale et al., 2002; Luo, 2008a, for recent examples employing combinations of several measures). Moreover, it may be interesting for future research to assess whether previous studies' findings may be contingent on the conceptualization and/or measurement of the dependent variable. For instance, whereas alliance managers' perceptions of justice or conflict may influence their subjective assessments of alliance performance, accounting-based or stock market performance measurements may be unaffected by such perceptions. Such an approach could not only confirm the reliability of findings across performance measurements, but also provide an empirical test of the argument that the appropriateness of measures varies with the context (Yan and Gray, 1995) or the research question (Gulati and Zajac, 2000; Reuer and Koza, 2000).

Other Future Research

Multi- and cross-level research
Whereas prior studies have found distinct effects of decision process characteristics – such as trust (Luo, 2002a, 2006; Zaheer et al., 1998) – at both interpersonal and interorganizational levels, our understanding of how decision processes at the firm and alliance levels interact with each

other is very limited. This stands in contrast to the prevalent argument that the ability of firms to realize alliance benefits critically depends on their interactions with the partner (Doz, 1996). A recent study by Walter et al. (forthcoming), for example, examines the interactive effects of decision process characteristics at the firm and alliance levels on alliance performance. Their results show that high degrees of procedural rationality at both levels enable decision coordination and integration within and between firms and thereby enhance alliance performance, but also suggest that below a certain degree of alliance-level procedural rationality, alliance performance is enhanced when combined with a low degree of firm-level procedural rationality. A reliance on procedural rationality at the firm level likely is detrimental when decision making is based on inadequate or even misleading information resulting from alliance-level decision processes that do not exhibit high degrees of procedural rationality. Moreover, a high degree of politics at the firm level amplifies the negative effect of alliance-level politics. The significant cross-level interaction effects suggest the importance of considering decision processes at the firm and alliance levels simultaneously; examining one without the other risks not fully capturing the complexity of alliance-related decision processes.

Phase-specific decision processes
None of the studies reviewed for this chapter have incorporated the life-cycle stage of the alliance into their investigation of decision processes. The alliance literature, however, recognizes several stages in an alliance's development, such as (1) formation; (2) operation, i.e., growth, reformation, termination; and (3) outcome, i.e., stabilization, reformation, decline, termination (Das and Teng, 2002). Examining these distinctive stages may provide additional insights into alliance-related decision processes. For example, a longitudinal approach examining the impact of environmental factors, (inter)organizational factors, and decision process characteristics on alliance performance in each life-cycle stage – and assessing whether there are differences across the stages of an alliance – could result in a better understanding of whether and how these factors and their effects change over time.

Reverse causality
While the majority of studies have employed cross-sectional designs which prohibit any inferences of causality, several studies openly admitted the possibility of reverse causality. Faems et al. (2008), for instance, suggested a co-evolutionary relationship between contract application and trust dynamics. Lui and Ngo (2005: 1130) found it 'worth noting that the relationship between trust and action acquiescence may be reciprocal'.

Similarly, Lyles and Reger's (1993: 397) analysis showed that relationships between joint venture managers' influence attempts, cooperation from outside stakeholders, and pressures on the joint venture parents, were neither simple nor linear and, '[i]n many cases, long-term effects are quite different from short-term impacts as repeated influence attempts feed into long linked and amplifying loops'. The ambiguous direction of decision process factors in cross-sectional studies therefore offers future research an opportunity to clarify the causality of the previously examined relationships, and thereby enhance our understanding of decision processes in alliances and their impact on alliance performance.

In conclusion, this review provided an outline of the substantial body of knowledge that research on decision processes in strategic alliances has accumulated. Despite its fragmented nature and its small scale compared with research on structural issues in alliances, the patterns of empirical results emerging from this literature stream demonstrate both its academic and managerial relevance, and will hopefully motivate future research on alliance-related decision processes.

NOTES

*   The author is grateful to Kylene Fickenscher and Lisa Peifer for research assistance.
1.   Given the focus of this chapter, I excluded theoretical journals (*Academy of Management Review*), practitioner journals (*Harvard Business Review*), and more micro-oriented journals (*Journal of Applied Psychology*, *Journal of Human Resources*, *Journal of Occupational and Organizational Psychology*, *Journal of Vocational Behavior*, *Industrial and Labor Relations Review*, and *Personnel Psychology*).

REFERENCES

Note: * Empirical studies reviewed for this chapter.
* Anand, B. N. and T. Khanna (2000), 'Do firms learn to create value? The case of alliances', *Strategic Management Journal*, **21**: 295–315.
Andrews, K. R. (1971), *The Concept of Corporate Strategy* (3rd edn), Homewood, IL: Dow Jones-Irwin.
Ansoff, H. I. (1965), *Corporate Strategy: An Analytical Approach to Business Policy for Growth and Expansion*, New York: McGraw-Hill.
Arino, A. (2003), 'Measures of strategic alliance performance: An analysis of construct validity', *Journal of International Business Studies*, **34**(1): 66–79.
Arino, A. and J. de la Torre (1998), 'Learning from failure: Towards an evolutionary model of collaborative ventures', *Organization Science*, **9**(3): 306–325.
Balakrishnan, S. and M. P. Koza (1993), 'Information asymmetry, adverse selection and joint ventures: Theory and evidence', *Journal of Economic Behavior and Organization*, **20**(1): 99–117.
Barringer, B. R. and J. S. Harrison (2000), 'Walking a tightrope: Creating value through interorganizational relationships', *Journal of Management*, **26**(3): 367–403.

Baum, J. R. and S. Wally (2003), 'Strategic decision speed and firm performance', *Strategic Management Journal*, **24**: 1107–1129.

Bell, J., B. den Ouden and G. W. Ziggers (2006), 'Dynamics of cooperation: At the brink of irrelevance', *Journal of Management Studies*, **43**(7): 1607–1619.

Blau, P. M. (1964), *Exchange and Power in Social Life*, New York: Wiley.

Bleeke, J. and D. Ernst (1991), 'The way to win in cross-border alliances', *Harvard Business Review*, **69**(6): 127–135.

Chakravarthy, B. S. and Y. Doz (1992), 'Strategy process research: Focusing on corporate self-renewal', *Strategic Management Journal*, **13**: 5–14.

Contractor, F. J. (2005), 'Alliance structure and process: Will the two research streams ever meet in alliance research?', *European Management Review*, **2**: 123–129.

Das, T. K. and B.-S. Teng (1998a), 'Between trust and control: Developing confidence in partner cooperation in alliances', *Academy of Management Review*, **23**(3): 491–512.

Das, T. K. and B.-S. Teng (1998b), 'Resource and risk management in the strategic alliance making process', *Journal of Management*, **24**(1): 21–42.

Das, T. K. and B.-S. Teng (2000), 'Instabilities of strategic alliances: An internal tensions perspective', *Organization Science*, **11**(1): 77–101.

Das, T. K. and B.-S. Teng (2002), 'The dynamics of alliance conditions in the alliance development process', *Journal of Management Studies*, **39**(5): 725–746.

de Rond, M. and H. Bouchiki (2004), 'On the dialectics of strategic alliances', *Organization Science*, **15**(1): 56–69.

Dean, J. W. J. and M. P. Sharfman (1996), 'Does decision process matter? A study of strategic decision-making effectiveness', *Academy of Management Journal*, **39**(2): 368–396.

Dess, G. G. and D. W. Beard (1984), 'Dimensions of organizational and task environments', *Administrative Science Quarterly*, **29**: 52–73.

Dess, G. G. and G. T. Lumpkin (2001), 'Emerging issues in strategy process research', in M. A. Hitt, E. Freeman and J. S. Harrison (eds), *The Blackwell Handbook of Strategic Management*, Oxford, UK: Blackwell, pp. 3–34.

Douma, M. U., J. Bilderbeek, P. J. Idenburg and J. K. Looise (2000), 'Strategic alliances: Managing the dynamics of fit', *Long Range Planning*, **33**: 579–598.

Doz, Y. L. (1996), 'The evolution of cooperation in strategic alliances: Initial conditions or learning processes?', *Strategic Management Journal*, **17**: 55–83.

Dyer, J. H., P. Kale and H. Singh (2001), 'How to make strategic alliances work', *MIT Sloane Management Review*, **Summer**: 37–43.

Eisenhardt, K. M. (1989), 'Making fast strategic decisions in high-velocity environments', *Academy of Management Journal*, **32**(3): 543–576.

* Faems, D., M. Janssens, A. Madhok and B. van Looy (2008), 'Toward a perspective on alliance governance: Connecting contract design, trust dynamics, and contract application', *Academy of Management Journal*, **51**(6): 1053–1078.

* Fryxell, G. E., R. S. Dooley and M. Vryza (2002), 'After the ink dries: The interaction of trust and control in US-based international joint ventures', *Journal of Management Studies*, **39**(6): 865–886.

Geringer, J. M. and L. Hebert (1991), 'Measuring performance of international joint ventures', *Journal of International Business Studies*, **22**(2): 249–263.

Ginsberg, A. and N. Venkatraman (1985), 'Contingency perspectives of organizational strategy: A critical review of empirical research', *Academy of Management Review*, **10**(3): 421–434.

Goll, I. and A. M. A. Rasheed (1997), 'Rational decision-making and firm performance: The moderating role of environment', *Strategic Management Journal*, **18**: 583–591.

Gulati, R. (1995), 'Does familiarity breed trust? The implications of repeated ties for contractual choices in alliances', *Academy of Management Journal*, **38**(1): 85–112.

Gulati, R. (1998), 'Alliances and networks', *Strategic Management Journal*, **19**: 293–317.

* Gulati, R. and J. A. Nickerson (2008), 'Interorganizational trust, governance choice, and exchange performance', *Organization Science*, **19**(5): 688–708.

Gulati, R. and H. Singh (1998), 'The architecture of cooperation: Managing coordination costs and appropriation concerns in strategic alliances', *Administrative Science Quarterly*, **43**: 781–814.

Gulati, R. and E. J. Zajac (2000), 'Reflections on the study of strategic alliances', in D. Faulkner and M. de Rond (eds), *Cooperative Strategies: Economic Business and Organizational Issues*, Oxford: Oxford University Press, pp. 365–374.

Gulati, R., D. A. Dialdin and L. Wang (2002), 'Organizational networks', in J. A. C. Baum (ed.), *The Blackwell Companion to Organizations*, Oxford: Blackwell Business, pp. 281–303.

* Habib, G. M. (1987), 'Measures of manifest conflict in international joint ventures', *Academy of Management Journal*, **30**(4): 808–816.

Hambrick, D. C. (1994), 'Top management groups: A conceptual integration and reconsideration of the "team" label', in B. M. Shaw and L. L. Cummings (eds), *Research in Organizational Behavior*, Vol. 37, Greenwich, CT: JAI Press, pp. 110–127.

Hennart, J.-F. (2006), 'Alliance research: Less is more', *Journal of Management Studies*, **43**(7): 1621–1628.

Hennart, J.-F. and M. Zeng (2005), 'Structural determinants of joint venture performance', *European Management Review*, **2**: 105–115.

Hirsch, P. (1975), 'Organizational effectiveness and the institutional environment', *Administrative Science Quarterly*, **20**: 327–344.

Ireland, R. D., M. A. Hitt and D. Vaidyanath (2002), 'Alliance management as a source of competitive advantage', *Journal of Management*, **28**(3): 413–446.

Jehn, K. A. (1995), 'A multimethod examination of the benefits and detriments of intragroup conflict', *Administrative Science Quarterly*, **40**: 256–282.

Jehn, K. A. and E. A. Mannix (2001), 'The dynamic nature of conflict: A longitudinal study of intragroup conflict and group performance', *Academy of Management Journal*, **44**(2): 238–251.

* Johnson, J. P., M. A. Korsgaard and H. J. Sapienza (2002), 'Perceived fairness, decision control, and commitment in international joint venture management teams', *Strategic Management Journal*, **23**: 1141–1160.

Kale, P., J. H. Dyer and H. Singh (2001), 'Value creation and success in strategic alliances: Alliancing skills and the role of alliance structure and systems', *European Management Journal*, **19**(5): 463–471.

* Kale, P., J. H. Dyer and H. Singh (2002), 'Alliance capability, stock market response, and long-term alliance success: The role of the alliance function', *Strategic Management Journal*, **23**: 747–767.

* Kale, P., H. Singh and H. Perlmutter (2000), 'Learning and protection of proprietary assets in strategic alliances: Building relational capital', *Strategic Management Journal*, **21**: 217–237.

Khanna, T. (1998), 'The scope of alliances', *Organization Science*, **9**(3): 340–355.

* Klein, R., A. Rai and D. W. Straub (2007), 'Competitive and cooperative positioning in supply chain logistics relationships', *Decision Sciences*, **38**(4): 611–646.

* Krishnan, R., X. Martin and N. G. Noorderhaven (2006), 'When does trust matter to alliance performance?', *Academy of Management Journal*, **49**(5): 894–917.

Kumar, R. and T. K. Das (2007), 'Interpartner legitimacy in the alliance development process', *Journal of Management Studies*, **44**(8): 1425–1453.

Kumar, R. and K. O. Nti (1998), 'Differential learning and interaction in alliance dynamics: A process and outcome discrepancy model', *Organization Science*, **9**(3): 356–367.

* Lane, P. J., J. E. Salk and M. A. Lyles (2001), 'Absorptive capacity, learning, and performance in international joint ventures', *Strategic Management Journal*, **22**: 1139–1161.

Lechner, C. and G. Müller-Stewens (2000), 'Strategy process research: What do we know, what should we know?', in S. B. Dahiya (ed.), *The Current State of Business Disciplines, Management – I*, Vol. 4, Rohtak, India: Spellbound, pp. 1863–1906.

* Levinthal, D. A. and M. Fichman (1988), 'Dynamics of interorganizational attachments: Auditor–client relationships', *Administrative Science Quarterly*, **33**: 345–369.

* Li, J. and D. C. Hambrick (2005), 'Factional groups: A new vantage on demographic

faultlines, conflict, and disintegration in work teams', *Academy of Management Journal*, **48**(5): 794–813.

* Lui, S. S. and H.-y. Ngo (2004), 'The role of trust and contractual safeguards on cooperation in non-equity alliances', *Journal of Management*, **30**(4): 471–485.

* Lui, S. S. and H.-y. Ngo (2005), 'An action pattern model of inter-firm cooperation', *Journal of Management Studies*, **42**(6): 1123–1153.

* Luo, Y. (2001), 'Antecedents and consequences of personal attachment in cross-cultural cooperative ventures', *Administrative Science Quarterly*, **46**: 177–201.

* Luo, Y. (2002a), 'Building trust in cross-cultural collaborations: Towards a contingency perspective', *Journal of Management*, **28**(5): 669–694.

Luo, Y. (2002b), 'Contract, cooperation, and performance in international joint ventures', *Strategic Management Journal*, **23**: 903–919.

* Luo, Y. (2005), 'How important are shared perceptions of procedural justice in cooperative alliances?', *Academy of Management Journal*, **48**(4): 695–709.

* Luo, Y. (2006), 'Toward the micro and macro-level consequences of interactional justice in cross-cultural joint ventures', *Human Relations*, **58**(8): 1019–1047.

* Luo, Y. (2007), 'The independent and interactive roles of procedural, distributive, and interactional justice in strategic alliances', *Academy of Management Journal*, **50**(3): 644–664.

* Luo, Y. (2008a), 'Procedural fairness and interfirm cooperation in strategic alliances', *Strategic Management Journal*, **29**, 27–46.

* Luo, Y. (2008b), 'Structuring interorganizational cooperation: The role of economic integration in strategic alliances', *Strategic Management Journal*, **29**: 617–637.

* Lyles, M. A. and R. K. Reger (1993), 'Managing for autonomy in international joint ventures: A longitudinal study of upward influence', *Journal of Management*, **30**(3): 383–404.

Mayer, R. C., J. H. Davis and F. D. Schoorman (1995), 'An integration model of organizational trust', *Academy of Management Review*, **20**(3): 709–734.

* Mohr, J. and R. Spekman (1994), 'Characteristics of partnership success: Partnership attributes, communication behavior, and conflict resolution techniques', *Strategic Management Journal*, **15**: 135–152.

* Monczka, R. M., K. J. Petersen, R. B. Handfield and G. L. Ragatz (1998), 'Success factors in strategic supplier alliances: The buying company perspective', *Decision Sciences*, **29**(3): 553–577.

Narayanan, V. K. and L. Fahey (1982), 'The micro-politics of strategy formulation', *Academy of Management Review*, **7**(1): 25–34.

Noorderhaven, N. (2005), 'Introduction to the special section on structure and process in alliance research', *European Management Review*, **2**: 103.

* Nooteboom, B., H. Berger and N. G. Noorderhaven (1997), 'Effects of trust and governance on relational risk', *Academy of Management Journal*, **40**(2): 308–338.

Olk, P. (2002), 'Evaluating strategic alliance performance', in F. Contractor and P. Lorange (eds), *Cooperative Strategies and Alliances*, Amsterdam, Netherlands: Pergamon, pp. 119–143.

Oxley, J. E. and R. C. Sampson (2004), 'The scope and governance of international R&D alliances', *Strategic Management Journal*, **24**: 723–749.

Park, S. H. and G. R. Ungson (1997), 'The effect of partner nationality, organizational dissimilarity, and economic motivation on the dissolution of joint ventures', *Academy of Management Journal*, **39**(2): 279–307.

* Patzelt, H. and D. A. Shepherd (2008), 'The decision to persist with underperforming alliances: The role of trust and control', *Journal of Management Studies*, **45**(7): 1217–1243.

* Pearce, R. J. (2001), 'Looking inside the joint venture to help understand the link between inter-parent cooperation and performance', *Journal of Management Studies*, **38**(4): 557–582.

Pelled, L. H. (1996), 'Demographic diversity, conflict, and work group outcomes: An intervening process theory', *Organization Science*, **7**: 615–631.

Pettigrew, A. M. (1973), *The Politics of Organizational Decision Making*, London: Tavistock.

Pfeffer, J. and G. R. Salancik (1978), *The External Control of Organizations*, New York: Harper & Row.

Podsakoff, P. M., S. B. MacKenzie, D. G. Bachrach and N. P. Podsakoff (2005), 'The influence of management journals in the 1980s and 1990s', *Strategic Management Journal*, **26**: 473–488.

Poppo, L. and T. Zenger (2002), 'Do formal contracts and relational governance function as substitutes or complements?', *Strategic Management Journal*, **23**: 707–726.

Priem, R. L., A. M. A. Rasheed and A. G. Kotulic (1995), 'Rationality in strategic decision processes, environmental dynamism and firm performance', *Journal of Management*, **21**(5): 913–929.

* Rai, A., S. Borah and A. Ramaprasad (1996), 'Critical success factors for strategic alliances in the information technology industry: An empirical study', *Decision Sciences*, **27**(1): 141–155.

Rajagopalan, N., A. M. A. Rasheed and D. K. Datta (1993), 'Strategic decision processes: Critical review and future directions', *Journal of Management*, **19**(2): 349–384.

Reuer, J. J. (2001), 'From hybrids to hierarchies: Shareholder wealth effects of joint venture partner buyouts', *Strategic Management Journal*, **22**: 27–44.

Reuer, J. J. and M. P. Koza (2000), 'International joint venture instability and corporate strategy', in D. Faulkner and M. de Rond (eds), *Cooperative Strategies: Economic Business and Organizational Issues*, Oxford: Oxford University Press, pp. 261–280.

Ring, P. S. and A. H. Van de Ven (1992), 'Structuring cooperative relationships between organizations', *Strategic Management Journal*, **13**: 483–498.

Ring, P. S. and A. H. Van de Ven (1994), 'Developmental processes of cooperative interorganizational relationships', *Academy of Management Review*, **19**(1): 90–118.

* Robson, M. J., C. S. Katsikeas and D. C. Bello (2008), 'Drivers and performance outcomes of trust in international strategic alliances: The role of organizational complexity', *Organization Science*, **19**(4): 647–665.

Salk, J. E. (2005), 'Often called for but rarely chosen: Alliance research that directly studies process', *European Management Review*, **2**: 117–122.

Salk, J. E. and O. Shenkar (2001), 'Social identity and cooperation in an international joint venture: An exploratory case study', *Organization Science*, **12**: 161–178.

* Saxton, T. (1997), 'The effects of partner and relationship characteristics on alliance outcomes', *Academy of Management Journal*, **40**(2): 443–461.

Schilling, M. A. (2009), 'Understanding the alliance data', *Strategic Management Journal*, **30**: 233–260.

* Seabright, M. A., D. A. Levinthal and M. Fichman (1992), 'Role of individual attachments in the dissolution of interorganizational relationships', *Academy of Management Journal*, **35**(1): 122–160.

* Shenkar, O. and A. Yan (2002), 'Failure as a consequence of partner politics: Learning from the life and death of an international cooperative venture', *Human Relations*, **55**(5): 565–601.

Silverman, B. and J. A. C. Baum (2002), 'Alliance-based competitive dynamics', *Academy of Management Journal*, **45**(4): 791–806.

* Simonin, B. L. (1997), 'The importance of collaborative know-how: An empirical test of the learning organization', *Academy of Management Journal*, **40**(5): 1150–1174.

* Steensma, H. K. and M. A. Lyles (2000), 'Explaining IJV survival in a transitional economy through social exchange and knowledge-based perspectives', *Strategic Management Journal*, **21**: 831–851.

* Subramani, M. R. and N. Venkatraman (2003), 'Safeguarding investments in asymmetric interorganizational relationships: Theory and evidence', *Academy of Management Journal*, **46**(1): 46–62.

* Sullivan, J., R. B. Peterson N. Kameda and J. Shimada (1981), 'The relationship between conflict resolution approaches and trust – a cross-cultural study', *Academy of Management Journal*, **24**(4): 803–815.

Teng, B.-S. (2007), 'Corporate entrepreneurship activities through strategic alliances: A resource-based approach toward competitive advantage', *Journal of Management Studies*, **44**(1): 119–142.

* Thomas, J. B. and L. K. Trevino (1993), 'Information processing in strategic alliance building: A multiple-case approach', *Journal of Management Studies*, **30**(5): 779–814.

Tushman, M. L. (1977), 'A political approach to organization: A review and rationale', *Academy of Management Review*, **2**(2): 206–216.

* Walter, J., C. Lechner and F. W. Kellermanns (2008), 'Disentangling alliance management processes: Decision making, politicality, and alliance performance', *Journal of Management Studies*, **45**(3): 530–560.

Walter, J., F. W. Kellermanns and C. Lechner (forthcoming), 'Decision making within and between organizations: Rationality, politics, and alliance performance', *Journal of Management*, DOI: 10.1177/0149206310363308.

* White, S. and S. S.-Y. Lui (2005), 'Distinguishing costs of cooperation and control in alliances', *Strategic Management Journal*, **26**: 913–932.

Williamson, O. E. (1995), 'Transaction cost economics and organization theory', in O. E. Williamson (ed.), *Organization Theory: From Chester Barnard to the Present and Beyond*, New York: Oxford University Press, pp. 207–256.

Yan, A. and B. Gray (1995), 'Reconceptualizing the determinants and measurement of joint venture performance', *Advances in Global High-Technology Management*, **5B**: 87–113.

* Yan, A. and B. Gray (2001), 'Antecedents and effects of parent control in international joint ventures', *Journal of Management Studies*, **38**(3): 393–416.

Yan, A. and M. Zeng (1999), 'International joint venture instability: A critique of previous research, a reconceptualization, and directions for future research', *Journal of International Business Studies*, **30**(2): 397–414.

* Young-Ybarra, C. and M. Wiersema (1999), 'Strategic flexibility in information technology alliances: The influence of transaction cost economics and social exchange theory', *Organization Science*, **10**(4): 439–459.

* Zaheer, A., B. McEvily and V. Perrone (1998), 'Does trust matter? Exploring the effects of interorganizational and interpersonal trust on performance', *Organization Science*, **9**(2): 141–159.

18 A review of research progress in understanding the acquisition integration process: building directions for future research

Annette L. Ranft, Frank C. Butler and Jennifer C. Sexton

Mergers and (M&As) acquisitions play a major role in corporate strategy as evidenced by the $1.45 trillion spent on M&A activity in the United States in 2007 alone (*Mergers and Acquisitions Report*, 2008). Despite the preponderance of continued acquisition activity, traditional financial, strategic, and organizational perspectives of M&As have failed to explain the generally disappointing value created by these corporate events (King et al., 2004; Larsson and Finkelstein, 1999; Pablo et al., 1996). Scholars have increasingly emphasized the importance of the post-acquisition integration process, where 'the actions of management, and the process of integration, determine the extent to which potential benefits of the acquisition are realized' (Birkinshaw et al., 2000: 397). Indeed, it is during the acquisition integration process that potential synergy in an acquisition is realized (Larsson and Finkelstein, 1999). A major challenge then, for both managers and scholars, is to identify and manage integration processes that can lead to post-acquisition success. While there is a rich body of research on mergers and acquisitions,[1] research specifically examining process issues during acquisition integration is more limited and somewhat disjointed.

A theoretical process perspective of acquisitions was developed and introduced by Jemison and Sitkin (1986). This perspective considers the overall acquisition process as a series of decisions and behaviors from early stages of the due diligence phase, to deal construction, to the post-deal integration phase. Subsequent process perspectives focused on fundamental dimensions of the acquisition integration phase as identified in seminal work by Haspeslagh and Jemison (1991). At this foundational level, the primary, yet competing dimensions of the integration process were identified. These dimensions of (1) the need for strategic interdependence between the acquired firm and the acquirer and (2) the need for autonomy post acquisition for the acquired firm were highlighted and described. The need for strategic interdependence reflects pressure to combine resources and break down organizational boundaries to create new value with the newly merged firm. The need for autonomy creates a potentially opposing pressure to spend time learning about the acquired firm and its resources and operations prior to combining resources and organizations.

Articulation of these fundamental dimensions of the integration process spurred additional more fine-grained acquisition integration research. The need for strategic interdependence has been extended in research that specifically examines resource exchange in acquisition integration (Capron et al., 1998; Capron, 1999; Saxton and Dollinger, 2004). The focus of this research has been to examine resource transfer, or resource reconfiguration in the newly merged firm. The influence of the nature of resources to be transferred or reconfigured on other dimensions of the integration process, such as autonomy and speed of change, has also received some attention in the literature (Puranam et al., 2006; Ranft and Lord, 2002; Schweizer, 2005). Other research examining the importance of communications (Marks and Mirvis, 2001; Schweiger and DeNisi, 1991), the retention of key employees (Cannella and Hambrick, 1993; Krug and Hegarty, 1997, 2001; Ranft and Lord, 2000), and organizational learning (Vermeulen and Barkema, 2001; Barkema and Schijven, 2008a,b) has further extended our view of the acquisition integration process.

In this paper, we set out to synthesize and review the empirical strategy literature examining post-acquisition integration process dimensions. In doing so, we reviewed literature since 1986 in recognition of Jemison and Sitkin's (1986) seminal conceptual paper highlighting a process perspective of M&A. In the next section, we first describe our literature review search process. Next, we summarize and integrate the major acquisition integration dimensions found in the literature. We conclude with a discussion of the state of research in this area and suggestions for future directions for acquisition integration process research.

RESEARCH EXAMINING ACQUISITION INTEGRATION PROCESSES

We began our review of the literature using the ABI-INFORM Global database. We conducted a key word search using 'acquisition integration' or 'acquisition implementation' for all scholarly articles since January 1986. Despite the extensive time period of over 20 years, and the recognized importance of the acquisition integration process during acquisition implementation, this broad-based search revealed only 69 research articles published in the scholarly literature that examine post-acquisition integration processes. In addition, these articles were published in a wide range of journals, with no journal seeming to have a majority of articles.

We further refined our search to focus on eight mainstream, top-tier theoretical and empirical journals in the field. The eight journals we examined were the *Academy of Management Journal, Academy of Management Review, Administrative Science Quarterly, Journal of Management, Journal of Management Science, Journal of International Business Studies, Organization Science,* and *the Strategic Management Journal.* These journals were selected for their broad-based recognition as leading research journals in the strategic management field with both US-based and international journals included in the set. This search for published top-tier research resulted in the identification of only 13 articles that focused on post-acquisition integration processes.

Given this very small set of top-tier articles, we conducted a second key word search using 'acquisition and process' as our search term, again focusing on these eight top-tier journals. Careful review of the results of this search revealed an additional 31 articles that examined post-acquisition integration process issues as opposed to such issues as selecting acquisition targets or growth initiatives. Overall, we identified a total of 44 articles that were relevant for our examination of post-acquisition integration process research. Table 18.1 provides a synopsis of the final set of articles specifically used to review the state of the literature examining post-acquisition integration processes.

In reviewing these articles, and as shown in Table 18.1, we identified four specific areas of focus that represent different dimensions of the acquisition integration process. These four dimensions are: (1) resource reconfiguration during integration, (2) autonomy and speed of integration, (3) learning, retention, and communication, and (4) sensemaking and behavioral considerations. Research for each of these four dimensions is discussed in turn in the following sections.

RESOURCE RECONFIGURATION

As can be seen in Table 18.1, well over half the articles we reviewed examined resource transfer or reconfiguration in some way. From a strategic management perspective, financial resources, managerial resources, production resources, knowledge-based resources, and other resources possessed by an acquired or acquiring organization can influence synergy realization in an acquisition (Larsson and Finkelstein, 1999). Resource transfer and reconfiguration address the transfer of resources to or from the target (Capron and Pistre, 2002). As resources are transferred and

Table 18.1 Research examining acquisition integration processes

Journal	Authors	Year	Acquisition integration dimensions			
			Resource reconfiguration	Autonomy and speed	Learning, retention, and communication	Sensemaking and behavioral
Academy of Management Journal (8 articles)	Cording et al.	2008		XX		
	Barkema and Schijven	2008a	XX		XX	
	Puranam et al.	2006		XX		
	Schweizer	2005		XX		
	Vermeulen and Barkema	2001			XX	
	Pablo	1994				XX
	Schweiger and DeNisi	1991			XX	
	Bruton et al.	1994	XX			
Academy of Management Review (2 articles)	Jemison and Sitkin	1986		Foundational theory piece		
	Nahavandi and Malekzadeh	1988		XX		
Administrative Science Quarterly (1 article)	Haleblian and Finkelstein	1999			XX	
Journal of International Business Studies (4 articles)	Birkinshaw et al.	2010			XX	
	Zander and Zander	2010			XX	
	Nadolska and Barkema	2007		XX	XX	
	Bresman et al.	1999			XX	

Table 18.1 (continued)

Journal	Authors	Year	Acquisition integration dimensions			
			Resource reconfiguration	Autonomy and speed	Learning, retention, and communication	Sensemaking and behavioral
Journal of Management (7 articles)	Barkema and Shijven	2008b			XX	
	Saxton and Dollinger	2004	XX		XX	
	Porrini	2004			XX	
	Coff	2002	XX		XX	
	Bergh	2001			XX	
	Pablo et al.	1996	XX			XX
	Lei and Hitt	1995	XX		XX	
Journal of Management Studies (3 articles)	Meyer and Lieb-Doczy	2003	XX	XX		
	Vaara	2003				XX
	Birkinshaw et al.	2000	XX	XX	XX	
Organization Science (5 articles)	Paruchuri et al.	2006	XX	XX		
	Ranft and Lord	2002	XX	XX	XX	
	Finkelstein and Haleblian	2002			XX	
	Larsson and Finkelstein	1999	XX	XX	XX	
	Greenwood and Hinings	1994	XX	XX	XX	

416

Strategic Management Journal (14 articles)

	Year					
Ellis et al.	2009					XX
McDonald et al.	2008	XX			XX	
Puranam and Srikanth	2007			XX		
Homburg and Bucerius	2006			XX		
Graebner	2004			XX	XX	XX
Zollo and Singh	2004				XX	
Capron et al.	2001	XX				
Krug and Hegarty	2001	XX			XX	
Capron et al.	1998	XX				
Krug and Hegarty	1997			XX	XX	
Cannella and Hambrick	1993			XX	XX	
Datta	1991	XX		XX		
Walsh	1989			XX	XX	
Walsh	1988			XX	XX	

reconfigured, they can be redeployed to new productive use and create new value for the firm. Redeployment of resources allows for acquirers to take advantage of resources or capabilities specific to the acquirer or target and utilize them to remain competitive or change strategic focus (Capron et al., 1998).

Tangible resources, knowledge-based resources, and external financial resources have been shown to lead to more related diversification, whereas internal financial resources lead to more unrelated diversification (Chatterjee and Wernerfelt, 1991), often achieved by acquiring other firms in related and unrelated industries. In both related and unrelated acquisitions, resources are reconfigured. How the resource profile complements or is redundant between an acquiring and target firm influences how resources are managed post-acquisition (Datta, 1991). Resources are reconfigured and redeployed during acquisition integration to new and alternative uses.

Resource redeployment has been defined as the 'extent to which a target or acquiring firm uses the other firm's resources. . . [and] may involve physical transfer of resources to new locations or sharing resources without physical transfer' (Capron, 1999: 988). Capron et al., (1998) found that firms often redeploy resources in horizontal acquisitions. This redeployment of resources allows organizations to evolve to match changes in the business environment. Following redeployment of resources, asset divestiture is also likely (Capron et al., 2001). Capron et al. (2001) found that the direction of resource redeployment led to divestiture of assets by the receiving unit. Overall, acquisitions provide the organization with a means of reconfiguring resources in an organization, through both combining and divesting particular resources (Bruton et al., 1994; Capron et al., 2001). However, the divestiture of resources following an acquisition can be risky. Redeployment of target resources, followed by the divestiture of specific assets, may have a negative impact on acquisition performance (Capron, 1999).

Following this line of research, Capron and Pistre (2002) found that acquirers tended to earn abnormal returns when resources were transferred to the target. There was no evidence of abnormal returns when resources were transferred from the target to the acquirer. The authors suggest that this is the case because competing bidders can all see the value in the target, and therefore are able to bid away any gains from the acquisition. However, when transferring resources to the target, only the bidding firm has intimate knowledge of how its resources would work with the target firm. Capron and Pistre (2002) examined the occurrence and results of transferring marketing capabilities, innovation, and managerial resources. While this research confirms and highlights the importance of transferring, reconfiguring, and redeploying resources during the acquisition integration process, it does not, however, examine the process itself. In other words, *how* resources are reconfigured, and the decision-making, behavioral, and political processes surrounding the reconfiguration of resources, are not considered in this research.

One study by Saxton and Dollinger (2004) begins to examine decision-making and behavioral elements related to resource redeployment in acquisitions. This study examined the selection and deployment of resources in acquisitions and assessed managerial satisfaction with the acquisition as perceived by the acquiring firm managers. Selecting resources was found to be based, in part, on the perceived reputation of the acquired resources. Positive perceptions of target reputation increased the perceptions of acquisition satisfaction (Saxton and Dollinger, 2004).

Much of the research identified in the literature focuses on what resources to exchange, or which resources were important to the success of the acquisition. Little emphasis, however, has been placed on the process of how resources are transferred or reconfigured. Rather, challenges to effective transfer have been identified. One such challenge often articulated is the need to reconfigure and redeploy resources in the newly merged firm juxtaposed with the need to give some degree of autonomy to the acquired firm (Haspeslagh and Jemison, 1991). Often, autonomy slows down the integration process and the rate at which performance benefits are achieved. Autonomy, however, may be necessary to create a period of learning needed prior to effective redeployment of resources (Ranft and Lord, 2002). In the next section, we discuss the literature that examines autonomy and the speed of acquisition integration.

AUTONOMY AND SPEED OF INTEGRATION

The degree to which acquired and acquiring organizations are integrated is a major strategic decision post-acquisition. Differences in organizational cultures, technology, nature of resource, and motives for the acquisition can influence the degree of autonomy of the acquired organization. Balancing the need to integrate and transfer resources with the degree of autonomy required for the acquired firm is a complicated process. Too much autonomy can make it difficult for the acquiring firm to benefit from the acquisition while too much integration can destroy resources and capabilities in the acquired firm (Puranam et al., 2006; Ranft and Lord, 2000).

Early research highlighted differences in organizational cultures as a major influence on how much autonomy between acquired and acquiring firms exists (Nahavandi and Malekzadeh, 1988). The more similar the cultures, the more the target can be integrated. As the organizational cultures differ, however, integration becomes more difficult and more autonomy may be beneficial to reduce the disruptions that can occur (Nahavandi and Malekzadeh, 1988). More recent research has linked this to intangible resources and capabilities that are often embedded in organizational culture and human capital. Specifically, greater autonomy is necessary to help preserve tacit knowledge in the target organization that may be integral to the performance of the acquisition (Ranft and Lord, 2002).

Autonomy essentially slows the acquisition integration process significantly. Often pressures for a quick return and pressures to recoup an acquisition premium make rapid integration desirable (Jemison and Sitkin, 1986). Yet, the need to slow the process to preserve resources through acquired firm autonomy counters this pressure. Jemison and Sitkin (1986) outlined how escalating momentum can lead to pressures to complete the integration process quickly. Therefore, care is needed to prevent acquisition integration from occurring too quickly. The required speed of the integration process is suggested to be dependent on the characteristics and motives of the acquisition (Homburg and Bucerius, 2006; Ranft and Lord, 2002).

Some scholars have examined the need to support exploration or exploitation of the knowledge and capabilities of the target firm (Greenwood and Hinings, 1994; Puranam and Srikanth, 2007). In a study of small technology-based targets acquired by larger organizations, Puranam and Srikanth (2007) found that when acquiring to exploit the innovative capability of a target, rapid integration allows exploitation. Consistent with Ranft and Lord (2002), however, when acquiring a firm to continue or leverage its exploration capability and subsequent innovation, autonomy remains high at the target and slows the integration process. In a separate study of acquisitions in the pharmaceutical industry, a hybrid approach to the acquisition integration process was recommended (Schweizer, 2005). This hybrid approach indicates that short- and long-term motives of the acquisition should moderate the speed of integration. For example, if the motive is to have continued innovation by the target, a slower integration process through providing significant autonomy is necessary. This hybrid approach prevents disturbance in the process of exploration. Quicker integration is pursued when required capabilities such as marketing and regulatory approval expertise reside in the acquiring firm.

Homburg and Bucerius (2006) also examined how speed of integration can be beneficial or detrimental to an organization from a customer perspective. Speed can be an important factor in acquisition integration in order to reduce customer uncertainty. They found that speed is most beneficial when external relatedness is low and internal relatedness (organizational fit) is high. Slower integration has also been shown to be beneficial when establishing links across operating units (Birkinshaw et al., 2000). By allowing the operating units to integrate first, they can achieve acceptable performance before taking the next step to integrate across the units. By integrating too quickly, responsibilities may be unclear and essential employees could resign. Also, the integration of the human capital is by its very nature very slow and difficult (Birkinshaw et al., 2000), but important to a successful integration. By integrating at a slower pace, retention of key employees occurs, and the success of operating units is also ensured. This can lead to greater knowledge transfer and combination, and in turn identify synergies from the combination of the organizations.

While the integration of acquisitions can be an opportunity for organizations to learn and transfer knowledge, the speed at which these organizations are integrated can influence the ability to transfer tacit knowledge (Ranft and Lord, 2002). One of the best documented dangers in quickly integrating an organization is a loss of productivity in the scientists of the corporation (Paruchuri et al., 2006; Ranft and Lord, 2000) or the loss of key managers (Cannella and Hambrick, 1993; Graebner, 2004). Disruptions in the productivity or leadership of these individuals can occur as a result of a loss in social status and centrality in the combined organization. Because learning is often linked to human capital, and rapid integration is associated with high turnover in an acquired firm, the speed of the integration can be important to organizational learning from acquisitions.

LEARNING, RETENTION, AND COMMUNICATION

Acquisitions have been examined from a learning standpoint from two different perspectives (Barkema and Schijven, 2008a). The first learning perspective describes the development of acquisition capability over time and through experience with other acquisitions. The second learning perspective focuses on learning about the acquired firm and its resources for effective integration and value creation.

Learning about how to manage acquisitions and develop acquisition integration capabilities through prior acquisition experience has received some attention in the literature. For example, Zollo and Singh (2004) examined the US banking industry and focused on how acquisitions can create knowledge-based capabilities specific to managing the acquisition process. They found that when acquisition experiences are codified, subsequent acquisitions perform better.

Finkelstein and Haleblian (2002), however, found that such learning outcomes are not always positive in acquisitions. Specifically, negative transfer effects may occur as a result of taking lessons learned from a previous acquisition and trying to apply them to a new subsequent acquisition (Haleblian and Finkelstein, 1999). As an organization undertakes more acquisitions, however, these authors argue that over time the organization should be able to identify the differences across acquisitions and not misapply the knowledge that was gained in previous acquisitions.

Other research has looked at alliance experiences prior to acquisitions as a source of learning how to manage an acquisition. Specifically, Porrini (2004) found that previous alliance experience did lead to better post-acquisition performance, especially between firms that shared R&D, technology transfer, manufacturing, and marketing alliances by improving integration and synergy realization. Prior acquisition experience is key from this learning perspective as it posits that firms learn how to integrate new acquisitions from their previous acquisition experiences.[2]

The second learning perspective focuses on learning about the acquired firm's resources. Learning about the acquired firm may include learning about new international markets (Birkinshaw et al., 2010; Nadolska and Barkema, 2007; Zander and Zander, 2010) or about newly acquired resources including tacit knowledge and capabilities (Lei and Hitt, 1995; Ranft and Lord, 2002). From this perspective, the role of human capital is key as capabilities and knowledge-based resources are embedded in organizational cultures and routines dependent upon individuals. However, M&As affect individuals at all levels of an organization, especially in the target firm.

At the top management team level of the acquired firm, roughly two-thirds of acquired executives leave within five years after the acquisition has occurred (Walsh, 1988). This departure rate is amplified when the acquiring firm is a foreign multinational (Krug and Hegarty, 1997) or when the takeover was deemed to be hostile (Walsh, 1989). Similar results are found throughout the organization with key employees in other areas of the firm (Paruchuri et al., 2006; Ranft and Lord, 2000).

From a resource-based or knowledge-based perspective, top manager and key employee retention is necessary for acquisition success because of their knowledge of the acquired organization, its culture, systems, relationships, and resources (Cannella and Hambrick, 1993; Coff, 1999, 2002; Ranft and Lord, 2000). At least through the integration phase of an acquisition, acquired managers may be important to effectively integrate the firms and create value (Bergh, 2001; Graebner, 2004; Ranft and Lord, 2002). From a resource-based perspective, the top managers of an acquired firm are considered to be a valuable component of the acquired firm's resource base (Castanias and Helfat, 1991). Research has shown that the top management team may possess tacit knowledge and have social relationships that can improve strategic decision-making (Amason, 1996). Top managers may also be considered intangible assets that can directly contribute to a firm's performance (Michalisin et al., 2004, 2007). Finally, Saxton and Dollinger (2004) found a strong relationship between top management team retention and acquisition satisfaction. Top managers and key employees, then, are important to resource reconfiguration, especially when these resources are knowledge-based and embedded in social relationships within an acquired firm.

Acquiring and integrating tacit and socially complex resources is a complex undertaking. Findings suggest that retention of key employees, appropriate levels of autonomy, and rich communications help in integrating knowledge from a target (Ranft and Lord, 2002). This is consistent with a hybrid approach to autonomy with regard to short- and long-term objectives (Schweizer, 2005).

Graebner (2004) explicitly found that the retention of top managers can aid in the identification of potential opportunities for resource combinations. Through the retained top managers, the identification of how resources can be recombined led to serendipitous value creation in the acquisition. This was especially true when the top managers were retained and integrated into the upper echelons of the combined firm. Other benefits from the retention of top managers include the ability to retain key employees as well as the ability to communicate expectations to employees within the acquired firm.

Communication in the acquisition integration process can help reduce potential dysfunctional outcomes such as increases in stress and uncertainty, and a decrease in satisfaction (Schweiger and DeNisi, 1991). Clearly articulating acquisition expectations through a realistic merger preview reduced these negative effects. The retention of target top managers can also help with communication at the acquired organization, as acquired employees will first turn to these managers for information. The retention of these managers can help minimize the negative reactions and emotions of the employees (Graebner, 2004).

In addition to reducing uncertainty of the human resources in the organization, communication can reduce the turnover of top managers at the target (Krug and Hegarty, 2001). Post-merger communications reduced the uncertainty felt by top managers, which in turn reduced the turnover of these top managers. Perhaps as importantly, communications processes have been shown to reduce ambiguity surrounding knowledge-based acquired resources. Rich communications processes can both elucidate the resources and build trust between acquired and acquiring employees (Ranft and Lord, 2002).

Recent research has begun to examine the characteristics and experiences of directors in acquisition outcomes. Acquisition experiences of directors have been shown to lead to positive acquisition outcomes (Kroll et al., 2008). Directors with these experiences may help with the integration of the acquired organization based on their prior experiences with acquisitions, as they may be able to provide advice and guidance on the possible pitfalls that can arise. This becomes particularly true with regards to director experiences and their experiences with related and unrelated acquisitions (McDonald et al., 2008). This line of inquiry is still in the early stages of being explored with regards to acquisition integration. Further research is needed to assess the role that directors play in the integration process.

In sum, learning processes about how to integrate an acquired firm, and learning processes designed to understand acquired resources and transfer knowledge and capabilities, are intimately connected to the human capital of the firm. As such, retaining acquired employees and clear and rich communication processes are critical to successful acquisition integration where resource reconfiguration is necessary to create value.

SENSEMAKING AND BEHAVIORAL CONSIDERATIONS

Despite the importance of individual-level processes and behaviors for acquisition success, research examining decision-making and behavioral issues in acquisitions has been somewhat sporadic, perhaps because of the difficulty of research design and access. Some exceptions are notable, however, and highlight important elements of the acquisition integration process.

For example, grounded in a decision process perspective, Pablo used a policy-capturing research design and highlighted the importance of decision sequencing and risk in post-acquisition integration processes (Pablo et al., 1996). Cording and colleagues highlighted that in addition to sequencing and risk, ambiguity during acquisition integration can be reduced by setting intermediate and clearly sequenced goals (Cording et al., 2008). In a sample of 129 acquisitions, intermediate goals of first reorganizing internal structural elements prior to setting goals regarding market expansion had strong impacts on acquisition performance (Cording et al., 2008). In addition to these advances from a decision-making perspective, scholars have begun to take political and social perspectives as well, and to examine processes and sensemaking efforts that may not fit traditional rational decision-making process models.

One such study focused on organizational justice. Organizational justice refers to perceived fairness in a firm setting (Ellis et al., 2009). Research in organizational behavior has identified four types of justice in the organizational environment: distributive justice, procedural justice, informational justice, and interpersonal justice (Colquitt et al., 2001). Ellis and colleagues examined the role of procedural and informational justice in the integration process and found that both types of justice can have important implications for acquisition integration outcomes in related acquisitions (Ellis et al., 2009). They found that procedural justice was important for realizing market position improvements (as measured by a factor of sales growth, market share, and innovation/research and development) in the post-integration phase. In addition, they found that informational justice was important during both the integration and post-integration phases, especially with regards to financial returns (a factor measured by profitability and stock price).

A second study takes a direct sensemaking perspective and presents a Finnish furniture manufacturer's acquisitions of three smaller Swedish furniture companies (Vaara, 2003). Through direct observation, sensemaking processes regarding ambiguity, cultural confusion in social interaction, and communication, hypocrisy and politicization were identified.

DISCUSSION

This paper set out to review the literature examining the post-acquisition integration process. In doing so, it became apparent that limited research has been done. It is interesting to note that of the 44 articles presented in Table 18.1, 27 were published in the last decade, a significant time lag from Jemison and Sitkin's seminal process theory published in 1986. Despite the limited research, several dimensions of integration have been identified and studied to varying degrees. Yet perhaps because the research is limited, or perhaps because of the complex and interrelated nature of the dimensions identified, how these dimensions work together as a system and are managed over time remains a critical question. Many of the pieces of the integration puzzle have been identified in the literature. But 'despite all these insights into what needs to be done, . . . many firms do not quite seem to know how to do it' (Barkema and Schijven, 2008a: 595). How the puzzle pieces fit together and the process of putting them together remain relatively untapped.

For example, in the area of resource reconfiguration, research that examines the resource exchange process (Capron et al., 1998; Capron, 1999; Saxton and Dollinger, 2004) and the interactive influences of different types of resources with autonomy and speed of change (Puranam et al., 2006; Ranft and Lord, 2002; Schweizer, 2005) stops short of identifying which resources to transfer in what order, or how the steps of the process should unfold. This implies that sequencing of actions may be an important area of research to more fully understand the acquisition integration process and interrelationships between dimensions of the process. The use of primary data collection techniques and experimental designs may be helpful in this regard.

Other research emphasizes the importance of communications (Marks and Mirvis, 2001; Schweiger and DeNisi, 1991) and the retention of key employees (Cannella and Hambrick, 1993; Krug and Hegarty, 1997, 2001; Ranft and Lord, 2000) for a successful process, but again this research highlights the elements necessary for success, not how these elements should be managed or developed.

Research examining organizational learning (Vermeulen and Barkema, 2001; Barkema and Schijven, 2008b) begins to move closer to the spirit of studying process, yet much of this research looks at prior organizational experience and ultimate organizational performance outcomes and attributes the relationship to learning. Alternatively, some research has taken the perspective of learning about the resources acquired (Graebner, 2004; Ranft and Lord, 2002) rather than learning associated with building acquisition integration capability (Zollo and Singh, 2004). Very little of this research takes a true process perspective such as a sense-making view (Vaara, 2003).

Much of the literature examining acquisition integration processes is grounded in the strategic management or finance tradition. As a result, a concern for organizational performance outcomes and the use of cross-sectional research designs built using archival data dominates the literature with few exceptions (e.g., Graebner, 2004; Ranft and Lord, 2002; Saxton and Dollinger, 2004). To study process and behaviors, future research should take a more behaviorally theoretically grounded approach to examining acquisition integration processes. This may require research designs that incorporate survey data, simulations, and qualitative studies.

Research on learning during acquisitions should also begin to explore the micro concepts of acquisitions and acquisition integration. While transfer effects and learning curves have been studied (Barkema and Schijven, 2008a), often this research has focused on macro concepts in acquisitions. Organizational learning research during the acquisition integration process should explore such concepts as the development of an emotional capability, or even an organizational justice capability and applications of these capabilities in future acquisitions. Turning our attention to behavioral processes and away from specific acquisition integration dimensions may lead to a more generalized theory of acquisition integration.

For example, key employee retention has been cited as one important dimension of the integration process (e.g., Graebner, 2004; Ranft and Lord, 2000). The concept of justice can be extended to this line of research to help determine whether the different types of justice can influence key employee retention. Also, the notions of organizational justice should be extended to more than just related acquisitions. A lack of procedural justice in an unrelated acquisition may lead to managers from the target organization not participating in the integrative processes of the acquisition, or lead to turnover of top managers from the target organization. In addition, procedural and information justice may be able to mitigate the issues that employees may experience in an acquisition context (e.g., merger syndrome: Marks and Mirvis, 2001). Clearly articulating what the motives of the acquisition are and making the employees feel as if they are a part of the process may help mitigate the fear and anxiety that can come with the unknown to the employees of a target organization. Beyond the two types of justice explored by Ellis and colleagues, interpersonal and distributive justice may play key roles in the acquisition process, especially with regards to the management of negative reactions that may occur in an acquisition (Marks and Mirvis, 2001).

As M&As can create a host of negative reactions to an acquisition, especially emotional responses (Fugate et al., 2002), the ability of an acquirer to manage emotions may also be important. An acquirer that is aware of the relationships between emotions and organizational behavior and has developed a capability to manage emotions, or emotional capability (Huy, 2002), may be in a better position to offset the negative reactions and emotions to an acquisition and in turn lead to better knowledge transfer, worker effectiveness, and job satisfaction during the integration process. Future research should explore how the management of emotions during the integration process can improve the integration of the target firm.

Larsson and Finkelstein (1999) emphasize the importance of these behavioral and sensemaking factors in realizing synergy in an acquisition but they also note the disconnected nature of research from a behavioral perspective and the strategic objectives of an acquisition. Further integrating these dimensions into a more complete view of post-acquisition integration processes will help further both theory and practice.

CONCLUSION

While extant research has helped identify certain dimensions of post-acquisition integration processes, there are significant gaps in our understanding of how these dimensions work together and how these dimensions can be effectively managed for acquisition success. In studying the process of acquisition integration, more research should take longitudinal, qualitative, or experimental design approaches to identify these relationships. Current research provides many pieces of the acquisition integration puzzle but we urge scholars to begin to turn their attention to how the pieces of the puzzle fit together for effective integration.

NOTES

1. See Haleblian et al. (2009) for a recent comprehensive review of the M&A literature.
2. See Barkema & Schijven (2008b) for a recent comprehensive review of this perspective of organizational learning in the M&A literature.

REFERENCES

Amason, A. C. (1996), 'Distinguishing the effects of functional and dysfunctional conflict on strategic decision making: Resolving the paradox for top management teams', *Academy of Management Journal*, **39**: 123–148.

Barkema, H. G. and M. Schijven (2008a), 'Towards unlocking the full potential of acquisitions: The role of organizational restructuring', *Academy of Management Journal*, **51**: 696–722.

Barkema, H. G. and M. Schijven (2008b), 'How do firms learn to make acquisitions?: A review and an agenda for the future', *Journal of Management*, **34**: 594.

Bergh, D. D. (2001), 'Executive retention and acquisition outcomes: A test of opposing views on the influence of organizational tenure', *Journal of Management*, **27**: 603–622.

Birkinshaw, J., H. Bresman and L. Hakanson (2000), 'Managing the post-acquisition integration process: How the human integration and task integration processes interact to foster value creation', *Journal of Management Studies*, **37**: 395–425.

Birkinshaw, J., H. Bresman and R. Nobel (2010), 'Knowledge transfer in international acquisitions: A retrospective', *Journal of International Business Studies*, **41**: 21–26.

Bresman, H., J. Birkinshaw and R. Nobel (1999), 'Knowledge transfer in international acquisitions', *Journal of International Business Studies*, **30**: 439–462.

Bruton, G. D., B. M. Oviatt and M. A. White (1994), 'Performance of acquisitions of distressed firms', *Academy of Management Journal*, **37**: 972–990.

Cannella, A. A. and D. C. Hambrick (1993), 'Effects of executive departures on the performance of acquired firms', *Strategic Management Journal*, **14**: 137–152.

Capron, L. (1999), 'The long-term performance of horizontal acquisitions', *Strategic Management Journal*, **20**: 987–1018.

Capron, L. and N. Pistre (2002), 'When do acquirers earn abnormal returns?', *Strategic Management Journal*, **23**: 781–794.

Capron, L., P. Dussauge and W. Mitchell (1998), 'Resource redeployment following horizontal acquisitions in Europe and North America', *Strategic Management Journal*, **19**: 631–661.

Capron, L., W. Mitchell and A. Swaminathan (2001), 'Asset divestiture following horizontal acquisitions: A dynamic view', *Strategic Management Journal*, **22**: 817–844.

Castanias, R. P. and C. E. Helfat (1991), 'Managerial resources and rents', *Journal of Management*, **17**: 155–171.

Chatterjee, S. and B. Wernerfelt (1991), 'The link between resources and type of diversification: Theory and evidence', *Strategic Management Journal*, **12**: 33–48.

Coff, R. W. (1999), 'How buyers cope with uncertainty when acquiring firms in knowledge-intensive industries: Caveat emptor', *Organization Science*, **10**: 119–133.

Coff, R. W. (2002) 'Human capital, shared expertise, and the likelihood of impasse in corporate acquisitions', *Journal of Management*, **28**: 107–128.

Colquitt, J. A., D. E. Conlon, M. J. Wesson, C. O. L. H. Porter and K. H. Ng (2001), 'Justice at the millennium: A meta-analytic review of 25 years of organizational justice research', *Journal of Applied Psychology*, **86**: 425–445.

Cording, M., P. Christmann and D. R. King (2008), 'Reducing causal ambiguity in acquisition integration: Intermediate goals as mediators of integration decisions and acquisition performance', *Academy of Management Journal*, **51**: 744–767.

Datta, D. K. (1991), 'Organizational fit and acquisition performance: Effects of post-acquisition integration', *Strategic Management Journal*, **12**: 281–298.

Ellis, K. M., T. H. Reus and B. T. Lamont (2009), 'The effects of procedural and informational justice in the integration of relation acquisitions', *Strategic Management Journal*, **30**: 137–161.

Finkelstein, S. and J. Haleblian (2002), 'Understanding acquisition performance: The role of transfer effects', *Organization Science*, **13**: 36–47.

Fugate, M., A. J. Kinicki and C. L. Scheck (2002), 'Coping with an organizational merger over four stages', *Personnel Psychology*, **55**: 905–929.

Graebner, M. E. (2004), 'Momentum and serendipity: How acquired leaders create value in the integration of technology firms', *Strategic Management Journal*, **25**: 751–777.

Greenwood, R. and C. R. Hinings (1994), 'Merging professional service firms', *Organization Science*, **5**: 239–258.

Haleblian, J. and S. Finkelstein (1999), 'The influence of organizational acquisition experience on acquisition performance: A behavioral learning perspective', *Administrative Science Quarterly*, **44**: 29–56.

Haleblian, J., C. E. Devers, G. McNamara, M. A. Carpenter and R. B. Davison (2009), 'Taking stock of what we know about mergers and acquisitions: A review and research agenda', *Journal of Management*, **35**: 469–502.

Haspeslagh, P. C. and D. B. Jemison (1991), *Managing Acquisitions: Creating Value through Corporate Renewal*, New York, NY: Simon & Schuster Inc.

Homburg, C. and M. Bucerius (2006), 'Is the speed of integration really a success factor of mergers and acquisitions? An analysis of the role of internal and external relatedness', *Strategic Management Journal*, **27**: 347–367.

Huy, Q. N. (2002), 'Emotional balancing of organizational continuity and radical change: The contribution of middle managers', *Administrative Science Quarterly*, **47**: 31–69.

Jemison, D. B. and S. B. Sitkin (1986), 'Corporate acquisitions: A process perspective', *Academy of Management Review*, **11**: 145–163.

King, D. R., D. R. Dalton, C. M. Daily and J. G. Covin (2004), 'Meta-analyses of post-acquisition performance: Indications of unidentified moderators', *Strategic Management Journal*, **25**: 187–200.

Kroll, M., B. A. Waltersand and P. Wright (2008), 'Board vigilance, director experience, and corporate outcomes', *Strategic Management Journal*, **29**: 363–382.

Krug, J. A. and W. H. Hegarty (1997), 'Postacquisition turnover among U.S. top management teams: An analysis of the effects of foreign vs. domestic acquisitions of U.S. targets', *Strategic Management Journal*, **18**: 667–675.

Krug, J. A. and W. H. Hegarty (2001), 'Predicting who stays and leaves after an acquisition: A study of top managers in multinational firms', *Strategic Management Journal*, **22**: 185–196.

Larsson, R. and S. Finkelstein (1999), 'Integrating strategic, organizational, and human resource perspectives on mergers and acquisitions: A case survey of synergy realization', *Organizational Science*, **19**: 1–26.

Lei, D. and M. A. Hitt (1995), 'Strategic restructuring and outsourcing: The effect of mergers and acquisitions and LBOs on building firm skills and capabilities', *Journal of Management*, **21**: 835–860.

Markides, C. C. and P. J. Williamson (1996), 'Corporate diversification and organizational structure: A resource-based view', *Academy of Management Journal*, **39**: 340–367.

Marks, M. L. and P. H. Mirvis (2001), 'Making mergers and acquisitions work: Strategic and psychological preparation', *Academy of Management Executive*, **15**: 80–92.

McDonald, M. L., J. D. Westphal and M. E. Graebner (2008), 'What do they know? The effects of outside director acquisition experience on firm acquisition performance', *Strategic Management Journal*, **29**: 1155–1177.

Mergers and *Acquisitions Report* (2008), 'Covering M&A, distressed situations and other corporate restructurings', December: 1.

Meyer, K. E. and E. Lieb-Doczy (2003), 'Post-acquisition restructuring as evolutionary process', *Journal of Management Studies*, **40**: 459–482.

Michalisin, M. D., S. J. Karau and C. Tangpong (2004), 'Top management team cohesion and superior industry returns', *Group & Organization Management*, **29**: 125–140.

Michalisin, M. D., S. J. Karau and C. Tangpong (2007), 'Leadership's activation of team cohesion as a strategic asset: An empirical simulation', *Journal of Business Strategies*, **24**: 1–27.

Nadolska, A. and H. Barkema (2007), 'Learning to internationalize: The pace and success of foreign acquisitions', *Journal of International Business Studies*, **38**: 1170–1187.

Nahavandi, A. and A. R. Malekzadeh (1988), 'Acculturation in mergers and acquisitions', *Academy of Management Review*, **13**: 79–90.

Pablo, A. L. (1994), 'Determinants of acquisition integration level: A decision-making perspective', *Academy of Management Journal*, **37**: 803–846.

Pablo, A. L., S. B. Sitkin and D. B. Jemison (1996), 'Acquisition decision-making processes: The central role of risk', *Journal of Management*, **22**: 723–746.

Paruchuri, S., A. Nerkar and D. C. Hambrick (2006), 'Acquisition integration and productivity losses in the technical core: Disruptions of inventors in acquired companies', *Organization Science*, **17**: 545–562.

Porrini, P. (2004), 'Can a previous alliance between an acquirer and a target affect acquisition performance?', *Journal of Management*, **30**: 545–562.

Puranam, P. and K. Srikanth (2007), 'What they know vs. what they do: How acquirers leverage technology acquisitions', *Strategic Management Journal*, **28**: 805–825.

Puranam, P., H. Singh and M. Zollo (2006), 'Organizing for innovation: Managing the coordination–autonomy dilemma in technology acquisitions', *Academy of Management Journal*, **49**: 263–280.

Ranft, A. L. and M. C. Lord (2000), 'Acquiring new knowledge: The role of retaining human capital in acquisitions of high-tech firms', *Journal of High Technology Management Research*, **11**: 295–319.

Ranft, A. L. and M. D. Lord (2002), 'Acquiring new technologies and capabilities: A grounded model of acquisition implementation', *Organization Science*, **13**: 420–441.

Saxton, T. and M. Dollinger (2004), 'Target reputation and appropriability: Picking and deploying resources in acquisitions', *Journal of Management*, **30**: 123–147.

Schweiger, D. M. and A. S. DeNisi (1991), 'Communication with employees following a merger: A longitudinal field experiment', *Academy of Management Journal*, **34**: 110–135.

Schweizer, L. (2005), 'Organizational integration of acquired biotechnology companies into pharmaceutical companies: The need for a hybrid approach', *Academy of Management Journal*, **48**: 1051–1074.

Vaara, E. (2003), 'Post-acquisition integration as sensemaking: Glimpses of ambiguity, confusion, hypocrisy, and politicization', *Journal of Management Studies*, **40**: 859–894.

Vermeulen, F. and H. Barkema (2001), 'Learning through acquisitions', *Academy of Management Journal*, **44**: 457–476.

Walsh, J. P. (1988), 'Top management turnover following mergers and acquisitions', *Strategic Management Journal*, **9**: 173–184.

Walsh, J. P. (1989), 'Doing a deal: Merger and acquisition negotiations and their impact upon target company top management turnover', *Strategic Management Journal*, **10**: 307–322.

Zander, U. and L. Zander (2010), 'Opening the grey box: Social communities, knowledge and culture in acquisitions', *Journal of International Business Studies*, **41**: 27–37.
Zollo, M. and H. Singh (2004), 'Deliberate learning in corporate acquisitions: Post-acquisition strategies and integration capability in U.S. bank mergers', *Strategic Management Journal*, **25**: 1233–1256.

19 Internationalization process*
Alvaro Cuervo-Cazurra

INTRODUCTION

The number of multinational companies (MNCs) has increased significantly in recent times. The United Nations Conference on Trade and Development (UNCTAD) *World Investment Report* indicates that in 1992 there were 35 000 MNCs, or firms with assets abroad, while in 2008 there were 78 817 (UNCTAD, 1992, 2008). This increase in the number of MNCs has been facilitated by technological advances in transportation and information and communication technologies, as well as by the liberalization of investment and trade that accompanied the structural reforms of the last third of the 20th century. Companies have moved out of their national borders in search of new markets, new and better inputs and new sources of knowledge.

Theoretical advances explaining the internationalization process of firms, the sequence of events that a firm follows as it expands outside its country of origin, have not kept pace with real world events. More than three decades have passed since the key theoretical models explaining a firm's internationalization process were developed: the innovation-related models (Bilkey and Tesar, 1977; Cavusgil, 1980; Czinkota, 1982; Reid, 1981), the incremental internationalization model (Johanson and Wiedersheim-Paul, 1975; Johanson and Vahlne, 1977) and the product cycle model (Vernon, 1966). Although these models have been refined and updated over time, they have been challenged by new phenomena, such as the rapid internationalization of small high-tech firms (Knight and Cavusgil, 2004; Oviatt and McDougall, 1994). Additionally, further advancements in the world economy, such as global supply chains and offshoring and the internationalization of developing-country firms, are providing additional challenges to existing arguments that need a theoretical explanation.

Therefore, this chapter takes stock of where we stand regarding the internationalization process, summarizing what we currently know about the topic, discussing challenges to traditional arguments and identifying new areas of research that have not been properly studied yet. Such a review and identification of new research areas will help researchers better understand the current state of knowledge and direct their attention and effort to areas that have promising prospects of impact. The review will also help managers learn from a distillation of advances in theory and practice in the area of internationalization process.

To do this, the chapter is organized in four parts, of which only the first has received attention in previous reviews of the literature. The first part briefly reviews the traditional models of the internationalization process (innovation-related, incremental, product cycle). The second part summarizes two challenges to traditional models that have appeared in the literature: the internationalization of high-tech firms and learning through networks. The third part analyses emerging phenomena that need to be incorporated into internationalization process research: global supply chains and offshoring and developing-country MNCs. Because such phenomena are not fully analysed, this third part provides some suggestions for how to conduct future studies. The chapter concludes with an indication of areas that need additional research to have a complete understanding of a firm's internationalization process: the process of transformation from a small and simple to a large and complex MNC, the process of reducing foreign expansion, and the relationship between internationalization process and performance.

TRADITIONAL MODELS OF THE INTERNATIONALIZATION PROCESS

The internationalization process of the firm is a complex phenomenon that has multiple dimensions. As a result, several models have appeared in the literature. Although these traditional models seem to offer alternative explanations, in most cases they offer complementary ones because the models focus on related but different dimensions of the process. To clarify the arguments of the traditional models I organize them by the research question they answer: how to become an international firm, how to enter a country and how to select among countries to enter. Such organization helps establish the complementarities among models and illustrate the complexity of the internationalization process of the firm. All these models have an underlying motivation of a firm expanding abroad to sell; later I review emerging arguments that do not have such underlying motivation.

The present review briefly outlines the key arguments of the models. Readers interested in more detailed explanations are encouraged to read the original sources and other reviews, which this one complements by taking a different focus, such as Melin (1992), Andersen (1993, 1997), Kumar and Subramaniam (1997), Blomstermo and Sharma (2003) and Cuervo-Cazurra and Ramos (2004).

There are other arguments and theories that explain the international expansion of a firm but that are not process models because they do not provide a prediction regarding the sequence of events in the firm's internationalization. One is the eclectic paradigm or ownership–location–internalization (OLI) framework (Dunning, 1977, 1995), which proposes that a firm will select among countries in which to set up production facilities depending on the location advantage that the country provides, on the ownership advantage that the firm has and on the internalization advantage that the firm may gain from controlling such production facility. However, it does not provide a prediction on the sequence of countries a firm may enter because the selection depends on the specific advantages the firm can realize at the time of the decision. Another is the internalization theory of the multinational (Buckley and Casson, 1976) and related transaction-cost model (Hennart, 1982), which explain why a firm internalizes cross-border relationships rather than using market mechanisms in its foreign operations. A firm selects among license, exports, sales subsidiary or production subsidiary to serve the country based on which method is better for it to achieve its objective while reducing internalization and transaction costs the most (Anderson and Gatignon, 1986; for a review see Datta et al., 2002). I will not review these models further in this chapter. For a detailed review of them see Dunning (2001) and Hennart (2001).

Becoming an International Firm: Innovation-Related Models

The first set of models explains how a firm changes from being a purely domestic company to becoming an international firm, with an underlying explanation based on managerial knowledge and attitudes. Several researchers have analysed the steps taken by firms as they move from only having domestic sales to exporting (Bilkey and Tesar, 1977; Cavusgil, 1980; Czinkota, 1982; Reid, 1981). These analyses are called innovation-related models because they explained the internationalization process of the firm in similar terms to the adoption of an innovation (Andersen, 1993). The models have a common theoretical basis on behavioral economics, proposing that internationalization is the outcome of an information-processing approach, with managerial knowledge of and attitudes about foreign markets changing with the involvement of the firm in foreign markets. Although each model provides slightly different steps, an abstraction of all of them is the following process. The firm is initially uninterested in exporting because managers know little about foreign markets and their attention is focused on the home country. However, sporadic orders from foreign markets place demands on managerial attention. The firm starts exporting to serve these requests for products from foreign countries, but this is done in a passive way. However, increasing requests from foreign markets create a conflict with the attitudes of domestically oriented managers. This conflict and the experience gained serving foreign markets induces managers to revise their expectations regarding foreign markets and refocus their firms to become active exporters.

Although useful for understanding how and why a domestic firm becomes an international company with sales abroad, these models provide a limited explanation of the internationalization process beyond exports. They are not designed to explain how the firm becomes an MNC with value-added operations abroad.

Entering a Country: Incremental Internationalization Model

An answer to how to enter a country is provided by the incremental internalization model, which is a true process explanation of the internationalization process because it provides a logic and a sequence of steps to follow when entering a country. The incremental internationalization model developed by Johanson and Wiedersheim-Paul (1975) and Johanson and Vahlne (1977) explains the entry into a country and the selection of countries; I review the entry into a country now and the selection among countries later. The model builds on behavioral economics and assumes that managers are risk averse and have bounded rationality, and that lack of knowledge is an important obstacle for expanding abroad. It proposes that managers' lack of knowledge and their risk aversion result in the firm following an incremental internationalization, gradually increasing its commitment and investments in a foreign country. Incremental internationalization enables managers to learn about the foreign country through direct experience and reduce risks as they increase commitment toward it. The firm internationalizes incrementally by increasing its commitment in the country in stages: no export activities, exports via independent representatives, a sales or marketing subsidiary and finally a production subsidiary.

Later studies provided additional depth by discussing how managers' lack of three types of knowledge induces them to follow the sequential approach because of the perceived costs of operating abroad (Eriksson et al., 1997, 2000): (1) internationalization knowledge, or knowledge about how to manage the increase in complexity and diversity associated with the overall foreign expansion; (2) foreign business knowledge, or knowledge of clients, markets and competitors abroad; and (3) foreign institutional knowledge, or knowledge of government, institutional frameworks, rules, norms and values prevalent in foreign countries.

The incremental internationalization model has become one of the cornerstones of the explanation of the internationalization process. However, its prediction regarding the sequence that the firm will follow in the foreign country has received criticisms of being overly deterministic. Nevertheless, many of the criticisms are directed more toward the specific sequence than toward its underlying logic (Hadjikhani, 1997). Thus, as I discuss later, some of the criticisms can be accommodated within the theoretical basis of the model by modifying its view of knowledge in the firm.

Selecting among Countries: Product Cycle and Incremental Internationalization Models

A third set of models tackles the selection among the countries a firm would enter first and those it would enter later. Two process models have provided answers to this question: the product cycle model, which has explained the spread of innovations around the world, although it has limitations explaining the behavior of firms nowadays; and the incremental internationalization model, which in addition to explaining the entry in a country I reviewed earlier also provides an explanation of the selection among countries.

Product cycle model
The product cycle model (Vernon, 1966) builds on the concept of the product life cycle, or the stages that a product innovation goes through – introduction, growth, maturity and decline – and uses these to describe the location of sales and production across countries over time. The model views innovations being generated in developed countries and gradually spreading to developing countries. The model proposes that in the introduction stage, a firm located in a developed country innovates and introduces the innovative product in the home country to serve the needs of customers there. It undertakes some exports in order to gain economies of scale. These exports are directed to other developed countries that are similar to the home country in terms of demand. In the growth stage, the firm increases exports and later establishes some foreign production facilities as demand builds in other developed countries. Pressures for cost efficiency increase as imitators enter into the industry and the production method becomes standardized. As foreign demand continues to increase, demand becomes more price elastic while labor costs become a concern due to the standardization of technology. Thus, in the maturity stage, developed-country markets saturate, the product becomes standardized and production moves to countries with low-cost labor. Finally, in the decline stage, production in the home country stops as demand declines and the now standardized product is imported from less-developed

economies. Vernon (1979) revised the model to accommodate developments in international business that limited the scope of its applicability, such as the shortening of life cycles or the existence of firms that introduced innovations in developed and developing countries simultaneously. However, although the model is useful for explaining the movement of innovations across countries at the industry level (Wells, 1972), it has limited predictability for explaining the internationalization process at the level of the firm (Melin, 1992).

Incremental internationalization model

The incremental internationalization model also explains the selection of countries in which to internationalize. This is based on the concept of psychic distance, which is defined as 'the sum of factors preventing the flow of information from and to the market. Examples are differences in language, education, business practices, culture, and industrial development' (Johanson and Vahlne, 1977: 24). Psychic distance limits the transfer of information across national borders and reduces managers' ability to understand information from the foreign country and apply their knowledge there. Because of managers' lack of knowledge about foreign markets and their risk aversion, the firm internationalizes sequentially based on the psychic distance between the home and destination country. The firm first expands into countries that are close to the country of origin in terms of psychic distance. This enables managers to reduce risks by using knowledge developed in the home market in a similar environment. The firm then enters more distant countries as managers gain experience operating in the initial foreign country.

The model has been challenged in its application. Although the concept of psychic distance has been widely used, in many studies it has been analysed as cultural distance (for example, Barkema et al., 1996; Benito and Gripsrud, 1992; Kogut and Singh, 1988; see Shenkar, 2001, for a review). Moreover, it is not clear that entering a country with a low psychic distance will always result in a successful operation (O'Grady and Lane, 1996; Mitchell et al., 1994).

CHALLENGES TO TRADITIONAL MODELS

Although the traditional models reviewed have been updated and modified over time, two lines of research have emerged to challenge their predictions: the rapid internationalization of small high-tech firms and learning about foreign markets through networks. These two lines of research challenge the sequences that a firm may follow in its internationalization process, but they are not necessarily in contradiction with previous arguments on a theoretical level. All have as a common theoretical basis the notion that managerial knowledge and attitudes, in particular the stock of knowledge and its transfer to and from abroad, affect a firm's internationalization process. The traditional models and new research lines highlight different aspects of this relationship. The internationalization of small high-tech firms highlights how advances in information and communication technologies and the reduction of barriers to international trade have, for some firms, reduced the cost of obtaining knowledge about foreign markets and using knowledge abroad, thus facilitating their internationalization. Learning through networks highlights the ability of the firm to obtain knowledge about foreign markets indirectly from network partners rather than having to obtain it directly through its own experience, thus also facilitating its internationalization. Hence, these two research lines complement previous arguments and explain new phenomena not considered in the traditional models.

Rapid Internationalization of Small High-Tech Firms

The rapid internationalization of small high-tech firms has been presented as a challenge to existing models. These firms, usually referred to as born-global firms – 'business organizations that, from or near their founding, seek superior international business performance from the application of knowledge-based resources to the sale of outputs in multiple countries' (Knight and Cavusgil, 2004: 124) – have received much attention in the literature (Knight and Cavusgil, 1996, 2004; Oviatt and McDougall, 1994, 1997; see the reviews in Rialp et al., 2005, and Zahra and George, 2002). Born-global firms appear to challenge both the innovation-related models and the incremental internationalization model. First, in contrast to the predictions of the innovation-related models, born-global firms do not first sell in their domestic market and later become international firms. Instead, they become international firms right at the start of their existence; their managers are focused on foreign markets from the beginning. Second, in contrast to the predictions of the incremental internationalization model, born-global firms do not first enter countries that are close in psychic distance and later enter countries that are far away. Instead, these firms do not appear to be constrained by psychic distance and start selling in a myriad of countries; their managers do not appear to be affected by differences in knowledge across countries.

Although born-global firms challenge the sequences of previous models, they do not fully challenge their theoretical foundations; instead, they can be seen as identifying theoretical boundaries in terms of the existence and use of managerial knowledge abroad. First, some firms have managers with knowledge about foreign markets and experience in serving them before the companies are created. These managers have developed the knowledge and attitude needed for serving foreign markets in previous jobs (for example, Reuber and Fischer, 1997). When they join the company they already have the needed attitude and knowledge that enable the firm to internationalize from its inception. Second, some firms face low or no psychic distance in their exporting thanks to technological advances and reductions in barriers to trade. Many of the firms studied are in information and telecommunication industries (for example, Bell, 1985), where the internet has reduced the influence of psychic distance by making irrelevant the location of producers and consumers: the products are transferred in digital form, payments are also done in digital form, and producers and consumers use a common language. Thus, managers' lack of knowledge on internationalization, business and institutions that induces firms to follow a sequential model may not apply to some small high-tech firms. Third, many analyses of born-global firms highlight the speed at which these firms internationalize. As such, these analyses bring to the fore another dimension to consider in the internationalization process of the firm: timing of internationalization. Traditional models have tended to focus on how rather than when to internationalize.

The born-global firms argument is not free from limitations. First, it is focused on the initial internationalization of the firm through exports, but does not explain well the continued expansion of the firm using foreign direct investment or other methods to serve foreign markets. Second, however, it does highlight the use of intermediate methods, such as alliances, to internationalize; many of these firms ally with other companies to internationalize because they have a limited resource set. Third, it is difficult to assess the time when the firm was created and when it started serving foreign markets. Thus, it is not clear whether firms are global from creation or merely internationalize very quickly after creation (Moen and Servais, 2002). Finally, there are still firms that do not internationalize from inception, even in recent times. The born-global firms argument cannot be generalized to all firms.

Learning about Foreign Markets through Networks

Several studies have argued that managers and their firms can learn about foreign markets indirectly from firms in their network of relationships, resulting in changes to the predicted internationalization sequence. The studies are not commonly viewed as being part of an overarching model, but they can be grouped because they build on a common explanation of learning through networks affecting the internationalization process. These studies propose viewing the firm as part of a network of relationships from which managers are able to obtain knowledge about foreign markets (Ghoshal and Bartlett, 1990; Johanson and Vahlne, 2003; see Petersen et al., 2003 for a review of learning in the internationalization process). This extended view of the firm sees managers as active learners who can obtain knowledge about foreign markets not only through direct experience, as proposed in traditional models, but also through indirect experience from its relationships with others.

Studies that analyse learning about foreign markets through networks can be grouped into two sets. First, managers can learn about foreign markets before their firms venture abroad from networks in the home country, such as from business relationships (Johansen and Vahlne, 2003; Luo and Peng, 1999), competitors (Knickerbocker, 1973; Delios et al., 2008; Henisz and Delios, 2001; Meyer, 2006; Shaver et al., 1997) or firms that belong to the same business group (Guillen, 2003). Managers internalize the experiences and knowledge of others about foreign countries, increase their stock of knowledge on foreign operations and countries, and reduce psychic distance. Second, managers can also learn about foreign markets from networks in other countries once the firm has expanded abroad. Existing operations in foreign countries become part of the learning network of the firm, with the firm using knowledge developed in other countries to enter distant countries (Barkema and Drogendijk, 2007), using alternative methods of entry as it continues expanding (Barkema et al., 1996; Nadolska and Barkema, 2007) and expanding within the foreign country (Aharoni, 1966; Chang, 1995; Kogut, 1983; Song, 2002; Tong et al., 2008).

Many of these arguments are in line with the theoretical basis of the incremental internationalization model. However, they provide additional depth and nuances that were not discussed in the initial proposition of the model (see Forsgren, 2002, for a review of learning in the incremental internationalization model).

EMERGING EXTENSIONS

In addition to these two challenges, new phenomena that affect the internationalization process need to be theoretically explained: offshoring and global supply chains and the internationalization of developing-country firms. The incorporation of these phenomena into the internationalization process requires additional modifications because they are built on a different theoretical assumption than existing models and extensions.

Instead of assuming that the firm expands abroad to sell as the models and challenges discussed so far do, these emerging extensions assume that the firm internationalizes to acquire: acquire access to low-cost factors of production in the case of offshoring and global supply chain internationalization, or acquire access to advanced capabilities in the case of a developing-country firm's internationalization. These phenomena do not mean that a firm will no longer expand abroad to sell, but that in some of its foreign expansions it would not aim to sell but to buy instead. Since the reasons for internationalizing differ, the explanations need to be altered.

Access to Low-Cost Factors of Production: Offshoring and Global Supply Chains

Reductions of barriers to international trade and advances in information and telecommunication technologies have resulted in the globalization of supply chains. The rise of Asian countries, notably China, and some Latin American and Eastern European countries as bases for low-cost manufacturing, and the recent rise of Asian countries, notably India, and some Eastern European countries as the bases for low-cost provision of services, have resulted in a different type of internationalization process that needs explanation. Firms in developed countries have taken advantage of these opportunities and moved into developing countries to access these low-cost factors of production, giving rise to global supply chains and the offshoring of manufacturing and services. This has resulted in a heated debate (Bhagwati et al., 2004; Harrison and McMillan, 2006) and an emerging literature in international business explaining this phenomenon (Doh, 2005; Espino-Rodriguez and Padron-Robaina, 2006; Farrell, 2005; Pyndt and Pedersen, 2006).

The process by which a firm expands abroad to access low-cost factors of production would therefore need a new explanation. One could build on the logic of the incremental internationalization process and modify it to account for this phenomenon. This would require discussing two sequences, one for selecting the country from which to supply and another for entering the country. I outline some of the logic and sequences; future research can take this outline and explain the relationships in more detail.

First, to select among the countries from which to supply, two new concepts – factor distance and access distance – would be needed. Factor distance refers to the differences in factor costs between home and host countries, while access distance refers to the differences in access to the desired factors between home and host countries. The idea of first entering countries with low psychic distance discussed in traditional models loses relevance because the firm is seeking countries with differences in endowments to benefit from such differences in its purchases, rather than countries with similarities in environments to benefit from selling to similar customers. However, similarly to traditional models, managers' perceptions and knowledge about differences in factor costs and ease of access affect the firm's internationalization process. When evaluating countries from which to supply, managers would need to balance the differences in the cost of the factor they seek to obtain for their firms with the ease of access. Although some countries have the lowest cost factors, they may not necessarily be the optimal location because of the difficulty in accessing such factors. The interaction between these two distances can result in a sequence of expansion whereby the firm first moves into countries with lower factor distance but lower access distance and continues into countries with higher factor distance and higher access distance as its managers gain experience in solving the challenges of accessing factors of production abroad.

Second, to analyse the sequence of entry into a country to access low-cost factors of production, the theoretical basis of the incremental internationalization model can be adjusted. Managers' lack of knowledge on foreign markets, risk aversion and potential transaction costs induce them to internationalize their firm's supply chain gradually. Managers start the process by first buying foreign inputs and intermediate products in the home country from importers. As managers learn about foreign inputs and their sources, they can start importing directly from the country using intermediaries, especially if the input is important to the production process. Once managers have gained experience about how to buy directly from abroad, they can then contact the producers in the country directly and set up supply chain centers in the host country, bypassing intermediaries and achieving direct access to multiple producers in the host country; some of these producers may not have been considered by the intermediaries, which gives the firm a broader set of suppliers in the host country. This sequence may be altered when there are no local providers of the inputs at the level of technological sophistication that the firm requires. In such a case, the firm will have to jump the proposed sequence and invest directly with its own supply facilities, accessing local pools of factors of production and exporting them, or the product they embody, to its home country.

Access to Advanced Capabilities: Internationalization of Developing-Country MNCs

Another challenge to existing models is the internationalization process of developing-country firms when they enter developed countries not to sell there, but to purchase higher-quality factors of production and capabilities to complement and upgrade existing operations in the home country. This argument explains some, not all, of the foreign expansions of Asian and Latin American firms (for example, Cuervo-Cazurra, 2007, 2008; Luo and Tung, 2007; Mathews, 2006), which enter developed countries as sources of high-quality inputs.

These foreign expansions of developing-country firms require a different explanation of the process because the firms do not move abroad only to sell as traditional models and their extensions argue, but also to buy advanced capabilities. Managers of developing-country firms lead their firms to enter developed countries not only to access superior factors of production, but also to access the superior capabilities of specific firms there. As a result, the process of selecting among countries and the process of entering a particular country vary.

First, when assessing the selection of countries where to access advanced capabilities, managers need to be concerned about sophistication distance, the difference in quality or sophistication of factors of production in the host country, rather than psychic distance as in traditional models. Sophistication distance differs from the factor distance discussed earlier because instead of cost, quality is the dimension that matters to managers who are seeking to upgrade the firm's capabilities. Additionally, managers would need to be concerned with the ease of absorption, in terms of the ability of the firm to use the advanced capabilities accessed abroad. This differs from the ease of access discussed before, in the sense that what matters to managers is not only whether it is easy to access the advanced capabilities, but also whether the company can use such capabilities to upgrade its own capabilities. As a result, in the selection of countries managers would have to balance sophistication distance with ease of absorption. This balancing may result in firms first entering countries with an easier absorption although not a high sophistication distance and, as the firm updates its capabilities and builds its absorptive capacity, later entering countries that are at a higher sophistication distance.

Second, when considering the sequence of actions to enter a country to obtain advanced capabilities, managers face a situation similar to the one discussed in the analysis of global supply chains. The logic differs slightly because managers are seeking to obtain advanced capabilities for their firms. These advanced capabilities take the form of knowledge available in other countries, but knowledge is difficult to access and transfer across countries (Kogut and Zander, 1992; Nonaka, 1994). As a result, the sequence is driven by an increase in the acquisition of relatively more tacit knowledge, which is also more difficult to transfer across countries, and the subsequent upgrading of capabilities. This would result in a sequence that takes the following form. The firm starts in the home country by purchasing knowledge from foreign providers there; this enables managers to access knowledge that is explicit and can be easily transferred across countries. Once the firm improves its capabilities, it can go to the host country to obtain licenses from providers of knowledge and capabilities there, gaining access to still explicit but more difficult to transfer knowledge. Once managers and employees in the firm have mastered the explicit knowledge, they can obtain the tacit knowledge embedded in the capabilities of firms that have them, establishing tight relationships with or acquiring existing operations in the host country. In contrast with the case of low-cost factors, advanced capabilities have poorly developed markets, and are instead embedded in companies, requiring the firm to access them by establishing tight links with firms in the host country.

ADDITIONAL EXTENSIONS

Finally, there are other areas of research that would benefit from additional analyses to gain a better understanding of the complete internationalization process of the firm. These areas include: the transformation of a firm from a small and simple MNC to a large and complex one, the process of reducing internationalization, and the relationship between internationalization process and performance.

From Small and Simple MNC to Large and Complex MNC

We need additional analyses to understand how the firm moves from being a small and simple MNC to become a large and complex MNC. Most analyses of the internationalization process are focused on predicting the behavior of firms as they become MNCs and start selling and operating in a few countries. At the same time, there is a large literature analysing the behavior of large and complex MNCs (Bartlett and Ghoshal, 1989; see reviews in Tallman and Yip, 2001, and Westney and Zaheer, 2001). The intermediate stages have received less attention. The challenge in analysing the intermediate steps is that the increase in complexity in the firm also requires a complex theoretical apparatus that can explain not only the entry in multiple countries, but also the building of relationships among operations in countries.

Some literature has explored this middle area, but there is need for additional analyses to gain a better understanding of the process. For example, studies on learning from networks discussed earlier have analysed how a firm uses existing foreign operations to continue expanding abroad, and how a firm may extend operations beyond the initial area of entry in the country. There are also some developments in the area of the structure of the firm and how it changes over time as the operations of the firm become more complex, moving from having an international division, to organizing operations by markets, to creating a matrix structure (Malnight, 1995; Stopford and Wells, 1972; see Westney and Zaheer, 2001, for a review). There are also developments in the analysis of the transformation of subsidiaries and their position within the network of subsidiaries as they gain competencies (Birkinshaw and Hood, 1998; see Birkinshaw, 2001, for a review). The challenge for future literature is to develop a process analysis of the middle stage that explains the complexity that arises.

Process of Reducing Internationalization

Reducing internationalization is another area that has received less attention. The vast majority of research has focused on analysing the expansion of the firm across countries, implicitly assuming that a company will continue expanding abroad. However, firms do reduce their international presence. There is some literature on this topic (for example, Benito, 1997; Benito and Welch, 1997; Henisz and Delios, 2004; Hennart et al., 2002; Mata and Portugal, 2000) but the topic has barely been analysed, especially from a process perspective. Future research can study the process of reducing operations in a country and the process of fully exiting from one or multiple countries. Even though exit tends to be viewed as failure, it may not always be so. The conditions of operation in the country evolve and the firm may have achieved the objectives it set out to obtain with the operation in the country. In this case, exit is not failure but success. However, exit may turn such success into failure if the process is not done properly. Unfortunately, we know little about why and how to successfully exit a country.

Relationship between Internationalization Process and Performance

The link between internationalization process and performance is another area that has received comparatively little attention despite the importance of this question. Some researchers have focused on a related but different question of how the degree of internationalization affects performance (Contractor et al., 2003; Hitt et al., 1997; Lu and Beamish, 2004; Tallman and Li, 1996), explained by the ability of firms to learn and solve liabilities of foreignness (Zaheer, 1995; Zaheer and Mosakowski, 1997; see Cuervo-Cazurra et al., 2007, for a review of the causes of the difficulties in internationalization). Few researchers have focused on the relationship between internationalization process and performance; the exception being work such as Vermeulen and Barkema (2002), who have discussed how the speed, scope and degree of internationalization affect performance. We need further analyses in this area to be able to provide suggestions to managers on which internationalization process is likely to result in better performance.

CONCLUSIONS

This chapter reviewed the literature on internationalization process, identified new areas of research and provided suggestions for future research. There is a large body of literature analysing internationalization process, but most studies analyse parts of the process and do not provide a holistic view. The review and ideas presented in this chapter could be summarized into an integrative model that Figure 19.1 illustrates. The model has managers and their knowledge and attitude as the key drivers of the internationalization process followed by the firm. Their knowledge and attitude determine how the characteristics of the firm, the network of the firm, the country of operation and the conditions of the world affect the internationalization process of the firm. This process takes different dimensions depending on the question answered: (1) Why internationalize, with two main drivers, selling abroad, which is the underlying assumption in most studies of the internationalization process, and buying from abroad, which is the assumption of new phenomena such as offshoring and some of the expansions of developing-country MNCs. (2) What to do in the internationalization process, which includes not only the start of internationalization and increase of commitment in a country, but also the diversification of operations in the country and, in some cases, exit. (3) How to internationalize, which refers to the discussion of selecting between

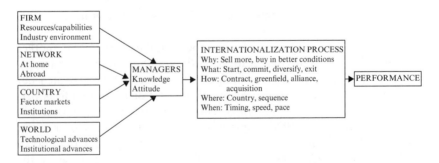

Figure 19.1   Integrated model of the internationalization process

methods such as contracts, greenfield operations (internal development), alliances and acquisitions. (4) Where to internationalize, which refers to the decision of selecting in which countries to operate first and in which countries to operate later. (5) When to internationalize, which refers to the timing of internationalization in terms of speed and pace. The final step of the integrative model is the analysis of the impact of the internationalization process on performance.

The review indicates that the models developed to explain the internationalization process of the firm have been the basis of a large literature, literature that has continued evolving as new phenomena and theoretical advances have entered the field. At the same time, the review highlights the need for additional research on the topic, not only because new phenomena require explanation, but also because there are topics in this area of investigation that have not received sufficient attention. The continued expansion of firms around the globe and the changes in the environment of operations are a reminder that this topic is not only relevant for managers, but its analysis is far from being settled. Whereas we seem to reach agreement on certain aspects of the internationalization process of the firm, new aspects emerge, providing additional opportunities for theoretical and empirical analyses. I hope that a future review of the topic will show both answers to the questions posed in this review and new questions that can result in interesting and useful research.

NOTE

* The paper benefited from suggestions from the editors, Franz Kellermanns and Pietro Mazzola, Anabella Davila, Luis Dau, Annique Un, Jorge Wise and participants at a research seminar at EGADE at the Tecnológico de Monterrey. The financial support of the Center for International Business Education and Research at the University of South Carolina, the Moore School of Business Research Grant Program at the University of South Carolina, and the Chair on Firms' Internationalization Schemas at the Tecnológico de Monterrey are gratefully acknowledged. All errors are mine.

REFERENCES

Aharoni, Y. (1966), *The Foreign Investment Decision Process*, Boston, MA: Division of Research, Graduate School of Business Administration, Harvard University.

Andersen, O. (1993), 'On the internationalization process of firms: A critical analysis', *Journal of International Business Studies*, 24: 209–231.

Andersen, O. (1997), 'Internationalization and market entry mode: A review of theories and conceptual frameworks', *Management International Review*, 37: 27–42.

Andersen, E. and H. Gatignon (1986), 'Modes of foreign entry: A transaction cost analysis', *Journal of International Business Studies*, 17: 1–26.

Barkema, H. G. and R. Drogendijk (2007), 'Internationalising in small, incremental or larger steps?', *Journal of International Business Studies*, **38**: 1132–1148.
Barkema, H. G., J. Bell and J. M. Pennings (1996), 'Foreign entry, cultural barriers, and learning', *Strategic Management Journal*, **17**: 151–166.
Bartlett, C. A. and S. Ghoshal (1989), *Managing Across Borders: The Transnational Solution*, Boston, MA: Harvard Business School Press.
Bell, J. (1985), 'The internationalisation of small computer software firms: A further challenge to "stage" theories', *European Journal of Marketing*, **29**: 60–75.
Benito, G. R. G. (1997), 'Divestment of foreign production operations', *Applied Economics*, **29**: 1365–1377.
Benito, G. R. G. and G. Gripsrud (1992), 'The expansion of foreign direct investments: Discrete rational location choices or a cultural learning process?', *Journal of International Business Studies*, **23**: 461–476.
Benito, G. R. G. and L. S. Welch (1997), 'De-internationalization', *Management International Review*, **37**(Special issue): 7–25.
Bhagwati, J., A. Panagariya and T. N. Srinivasan (2004), 'The muddles over outsourcing', *Journal of Economic Perspectives*, **18**: 93–114.
Bilkey, W. J. and G. Tesar (1977), 'The export behavior of smaller Wisconsin manufacturing firms', *Journal of International Business Studies*, **9**: 93–98.
Birkinshaw, J. (2001), 'Stratergy and management in MNE subsidiaries', in A. M. Rugman and T. L. Brewer (eds), *The Oxford Handbook of International Business*, New York: Oxford University Press, pp. 380–401.
Birkinshaw, J. and N. Hood (1998), 'Multinational subsidiary development: Capability evolution and charter change in foreign-owned subsidiary companies', *Academy of Management Review*, **23**: 773–795.
Blomstermo, A. and D. D. Sharma (2003), 'Three decades of research on the internationalization process of firms', in A. Blomstermo and D. D. Sharma (eds), *Learning in the Internationalization Process of Firms*, Cheltenham, UK and Northampton, MA, USA: Edward Elgar, pp. 16–35.
Buckley, P. J. and M. Casson (1976), *The Future of the Multinational Enterprise*, New York: Holmes & Meier.
Cavusgil, T. S. (1980), 'On the internationalization process of firms', *European Research*, **8**: 273–281.
Chang, S. J. (1995), 'International expansion strategy of Japanese firms: Capability building through sequential entry', *Academy of Management Journal*, **38**: 383–407.
Contractor, F. J., S. K. Kundu and C. C. Hsu (2003), 'A three-stage theory of international expansion: The link between multinationality and performance in the service sector', *Journal of International Business Studies*, **34**: 5–18.
Cuervo-Cazurra, A. (2007), 'Sequence of value-added activities in the internationalization of developing country MNEs', *Journal of International Management*, **13**: 258–277.
Cuervo-Cazurra, A. (2008), 'The internationalization of developing country MNEs: The case of Multilatinas', *Journal of International Management*, **14**: 138–154.
Cuervo-Cazurra, A. and M. Ramos (2004), 'Explaining the process of internationalization by building bridges among existing models', in S. W. Floyd, J. Roos, C. Jacobs and F. Kellermanns (eds), *Innovating Strategy Processes*, Oxford, UK and Malden, MA, USA: Blackwell Publishing, pp. 111–122.
Cuervo-Cazurra, A., M. Maloney and S. Manrakhan (2007), 'Causes of the difficulties in internationalization', *Journal of International Business Studies*, **38**: 709–725.
Czinkota, M. R. (1982), *Export Development Strategies: US Promotion Policies*, New York: Praeger.
Datta, D., P. Herrman and A. A. Rasheed (2002), 'Choice of foreign market entry models: Critical review and future directions', *Advances in International Management*, **14**: 85–153.
Delios, A., A. S. Gaur and S. Makino (2008), 'The timing of international expansion: Information, rivalry and imitation among Japanese firms, 1980–2002', *Journal of Management Studies*, **45**: 169–195.

Doh, J. (2005), 'Offshore outsourcing: Implications for international business and strategic management theory and practice', *Journal of Management Studies*, **42**: 695–704.

Dunning, J. H. (1977), 'Trade, location of economic activity and the MNE: A search for an eclectic approach', in B. Ohlin, P. O. Hesselborn and P. M. Wijkman (eds), *The International Allocation of Economic Activity*, London: Macmillan, pp. 395–418.

Dunning, J. H. (1995), 'Reappraising the eclectic paradigm in an age of alliance capitalism', *Journal of International Business Studies*, **26**: 461–493.

Dunning, J. H. (2001), 'The key literature on IB activities: 1960–2000', in A. M. Rugman and T. L. Brewer (eds), *Oxford Handbook of International Business*, Oxford and New York: Oxford University Press, pp. 36–68.

Eriksson, K., A. Majkgard and D. D. Sharma (2000), 'Path dependence and knowledge development in the internationalization process', *Management International Review*, **40**: 307–328.

Eriksson, K., J. Johanson, A. Majkgard and D. D. Sharma (1997), 'Experiential knowledge and cost in the internationalization process', *Journal of International Business Studies*, **28**: 337–360.

Espino-Rodriguez, T. F. and V. Padron-Robaina (2006), 'A review of outsourcing from the resource-based view of the firm', *International Journal of Management Reviews*, **8**: 49–70.

Farrell, D. (2005), 'Offshoring: Value creation through economic change', *Journal of Management Studies*, **42**: 675–683.

Forsgren, M. (2002), 'The concept of learning in the Uppsala internationalization process model: A critical review', *International Business Review*, **11**: 257–278.

Ghoshal, S. and C. A. Bartlett (1990), 'The multinational corporation as an interorganizational network', *Academy of Management Review*, **15**: 603–625.

Guillen, M. F. (2003), 'Experience, imitation, and the sequence of foreign entry: Wholly owned and joint-venture manufacturing by South Korean firms and business groups in China, 1987–1995', *Journal of International Business Studies*, **34**: 185–198.

Hadjikhani, A. (1997), 'A note on the criticisms against the internationalization process model', *Management International Review*, **37**: 43–66.

Harrison, A. E. and M. S. McMillan (2006), 'Dispelling some myths about offshoring', *Academy of Management Perspectives*, **20**(4): 6–22.

Henisz, W. J. and A. Delios (2001), 'Uncertainity, imitation, and plant location: Japanese multinational corporations, 1990–1996', *Administrative Science Quarterly*, **46**(3): 443–475.

Henisz, W. J. and A. Delios (2004), 'Information or influence? The benefits of experience for managing political uncertainty', *Strategic Organization*, **2**: 389–421.

Hennart, J.-F. (1982), *A Theory of Multinational Enterprise*, Ann Arbor: MI: University of Michigan Press.

Hennart, J.-F. (2001), 'Theories of the multinational enterprise', in A. M. Rugman and T. L. Brewer (eds), *Oxford Handbook of International Business*, Oxford and New York: Oxford University Press, pp. 127–149.

Hennart, J.-F., T. Roehl and M. Zeng (2002), 'Do exits proxy a liability of foreignness?: The case of Japanese exits from the US', *Journal of International Management*, **8**: 241–264.

Hitt, M. A., R. E. Hoskisson and H. Kim (1997), 'International diversification: Effects on innovation and firm performance in product-diversified firms', *Academy of Management Journal*, **40**(4): 767–798.

Johanson, J. and J. E. Vahlne (1977), 'The internationalization process of the firm: A model of knowledge development and increasing foreign market commitments', *Journal of International Business Studies*, **8**: 23–32.

Johanson, J. and J. E. Vahlne (1990), 'The mechanism of internationalization', *International Marketing Review*, **7**: 11–24.

Johanson, J. and J. E. Vahlne (2003), 'Business relationship learning and commitment in the internationalization process', *Journal of International Entrepreneurship*, **1**: 83–101.

Johanson, J. and F. Wiedersheim-Paul (1975), 'The internationalization of the firm: Four Swedish case studies', *Journal of Management Studies*, **12**: 305–322.

Knickerbocker, F. T. (1973), *Oligopolistic Reaction and the Multinational Enterprise*, Cambridge, MA: Harvard University Press.

Knight, G. A. and S. T. Cavusgil (1996), 'The Born Global firm: A challenge to traditional internationalization theory', in S. T. Cavusgil (ed.), *Advances in International Marketing*, Greenwich, CT: JAI Press, **8**: 11–26.

Knight, G. A. and S. T. Cavusgil (2004), 'Innovation organizational capabilities and the born-global firm', *Journal of International Business Studies*, **35**: 124–141.

Kogut, B. (1983), 'Foreign direct investment as a sequential process', in C. Kindleberger and D. Audretsch (eds), *The Multinational Corporation in the 1980s*, Cambridge, MA: MIT Press.

Kogut, B. and H. Singh (1988), 'The effect of national culture on the choice of entry mode', *Journal of International Business Studies*, **19**: 411–432.

Kogut, B. and U. Zander (1992), 'Knowledge of the firm, combinative capabilities, and the replication of technology', *Organization Science*, **3**: 383–397.

Kumar, V. and V. Subramaniam (1997), 'A contingency framework for the mode of entry decision', *Journal of World Business*, **32**: 53–72.

Lu, J. W. and P. W. Beamish (2004), 'International diversification and firm performance: The s-curve hypothesis', *Academy of Management Journal*, **47**: 598–609.

Luo, Y. and M. W. Peng (1999), 'Learning to compete in a transition economy: Experience, environment, and performance', *Journal of International Business Studies*, **30**: 269–295.

Luo, Y. and R. L. Tung (2007), 'International expansion of emerging market enterprises: A springboard perspective', *Journal of International Business Studies*, **38**: 481–498.

Malnight, T. W. (1995), 'Globalization of an ethnocentric firm: An evolutionary perspective', *Strategic Management Journal*, **16**: 119–131.

Mata, J. and P. Portugal (2000), 'Closure and divestiture by foreign entrant: The impact of entry and post-entry strategies', *Strategic Management Journal*, **21**: 549–562.

Mathews, J. A. (2006), 'Dragon multinationals: New players in 21st century globalization', *Asia Pacific Journal of Management*, **23**: 5–27.

Melin, L. (1992), 'Internationalization as a strategy process', *Strategic Management Journal*, **13** (Winter Special Issue): 99–118.

Meyer, K. (2006), 'Globalfocusing: From domestic conglomerates to global specialists', *Journal of Management Studies*, **43**: 1109–1144.

Mitchell, W., M. Shaver and B. Yeung (1994), 'Foreign entrant survival and foreign market share: Canadian companies' experience in United States medical sector markets', *Strategic Management Journal*, **15**: 555–567.

Moen, O. and P. Servais (2002), 'Born global or gradual global? Examining the export behaviour of small and medium-sized enterprises', *Journal of International Marketing*, **10**: 49–72.

Nadolska, A. and H. G. Barkema (2007), 'Learning to internationalise: The pace and success of foreign acquisitions', *Journal of International Business Studies*, **38**: 1170–1186.

Nonaka, I. (1994), 'A dynamic theory of organizational knowledge creation', *Organization Science*, **5**: 14–37.

O'Grady, S. and H. W. Lane (1996), 'The psychic distance paradox', *Journal of International Business Studies*, **27**: 309–333.

Oviatt, B. M. and P. P. McDougall (1994), 'Toward a theory of international new ventures', *Journal of International Business Studies*, **25**: 45–64.

Oviatt, B. M. and P. P. McDougall (1997), 'Challenges for internationalization process theory: The case of international new ventures', *Management International Review*, **37**: 85–99.

Peterson, B., T. Pederson and D. Sharma (2003), 'The role of knowledge in firms' internationalization process: Wherefrom and whereto?', in Anders Blomstermo and Deo D. Sharma (eds), *Learning in the Internationalisation Process of Firms*, Cheltenham, UK and Northampton, MA, USA: Edward Elgar.

Petersen, B., L. S. Welch and P. Liesch (2002), 'The internet and foreign market expansion by firms: Theoretical questions and three predictions', *Management International Review*, **42**: 207–221.

Pyndt, J. and T. Pedersen (2006), *Managing Global Offshoring Strategies*, Copenhagen: Copenhagen Business School Press.

Reid, S. D. (1981), 'The decision-maker and export entry and expansion', *Journal of International Business Studies*, **12**: 101–112.

Reuber, A. R. and E. Fischer (1997), 'The influence of the management team's international experience on the internationalization behavior of SMEs', *Journal of International Business Studies*, **28**: 807–825.

Rialp, A., J. Rialp and G. A. Knight (2005), 'The phenomenon of early internationalizing firms: What do we know after a decade (1993–2003) of scientific inquiry?', *International Business Review*, **14**: 147–166.

Shaver, J. M., W. Mitchell and B. Yeung (1997), 'The effect of own-firm and other-firm experience on foreign direct investment survival in the United States, 1987–92', *Strategic Management Journal*, **18**: 811–824.

Shenkar, O. (2001), 'Cultural distance revisited: Towards a more rigorous conceptualization and measurement of cultural differences', *Journal of International Business Studies*, **32**: 519–535.

Song, J. (2002), 'Firm capabilities and technological ladders: Sequential foreign direct investments of Japanese electronics firms in East Asia', *Strategic Management Journal*, **23**: 191–210.

Stopford, J. M. and L. T. Wells (1972), *Managing the Multinational Enterprise: Organization of the Firm and Ownership of the Subsidiaries*, New York: Basic Books.

Tallman, S. and J. Li (1996), 'Effects of international diversity and product diversity on the performance of multinational firms', *Academy of Management Journal*, **39**: 179–196.

Tallman, S. B. and G. S. Yip (2001), 'Strategy and the multinational enterprise', in A. M. Rugman and T. L. Brewer (eds), *The Oxford Handbook of International Business*, Oxford and New York: Oxford University Press, pp. 317–348.

Tong, T. W., J. J. Reuer and M. W. Peng (2008), 'International joint ventures and the value of growth options', *Academy of Management Journal*, **51**: 1014–1029.

UNCTAD (1992), *World Investment Report 1992*, New York: United Nations.

UNCTAD (2008), *World Investment Report 2008*, New York: United Nations.

Vermeulen, F. and H. Barkema (2002), 'Pace, rhythm, and scope: Process dependence in building a profitable multinational corporation', *Strategic Management Journal*, **23**: 637–650.

Vernon, R. (1966), 'International investment and international trade in the product cycle', *Quarterly Journal of Economics*, **80**: 190–207.

Vernon, R. (1979), 'The product cycle hypothesis in a new international environment', *Oxford Bulletin of Economics and Statistics*, **41**: 255–267.

Wells Jr, L. T. (ed.) (1972), *The Product Life Cycle and International Trade*, Boston, MA: Harvard University Press.

Westney, E. D. and S. Zaheer (2001), 'The multinational enterprise as an organization', in A. M. Rugman and T. L. Brewer (eds), *The Oxford Handbook of International Business*, Oxford and New York: Oxford University Press, pp. 349–379.

Zaheer, S. (1995), 'Overcoming the liability of foreignness', *Academy of Management Journal*, **38**: 341–363.

Zaheer, S. and E. Mosakowski (1997), 'The dynamics of the liability of foreignness: A global study of survival in financial services', *Strategic Management Journal*, **18**: 439–464.

Zahra, S. A. and G. George (2002), 'International entrepreneurship: The current status of the field and future research agenda', in M. A. Hitt, R. D. Ireland, S. M. Camp and D. L. Sexton (eds), *Strategic Entrepreneurship: Creating a New Mindset*, Oxford, UK and Malden, MA, USA: Blackwell, pp. 255–288.

20 Constructing power to drive strategy processes in multinational firms
Markus Venzin

Over the years, subsidiaries have gained importance as sources of competitive advantage in many multinational companies (MNCs). Various subsidiary types have emerged (Birkinshaw and Hood, 1998): some subsidiaries are pure sales units, while others are hubs with a global mandate to undertake R&D, marketing, production or other value-creating activities. As a result of the geographically dispersed allocation of productive capabilities, most MNCs attempt to facilitate the peripheral development of knowledge, competences or other sources of competitive advantage. In order to unleash this potential, headquarters must learn how to involve subsidiaries in strategic decision-making processes, and find the right balance between subsidiary initiatives and central control.

This chapter explores the role of power in strategy processes. How does power work in strategy processes that attempt to encourage subsidiaries to develop autonomous strategic initiatives rather than following induced strategic guidelines? Many headquarters feel a need to choose between a paternalistic management style in which power is fairly static and based on expert knowledge located at the headquarters and a liberal style in which power is more dynamic and dispersed in order to find the optimal position between decentralized decision making and central control. This chapter shows that these two management styles can co-exist. Firms need to learn how to switch from one style to another depending on the desired knowledge process. Furthermore, complex firms need to manage the dilemma that results from the opposing tendencies of stability and change.

FREEDOM WITHIN BOUNDARIES

In general, headquarters defines the boundaries of subsidiaries' strategic decision making in five principal ways: (1) by influencing the strategic agenda-setting process, (2) by allocating resources, (3) by defining subsidiary charters, (4) by selecting top management team members, and (5) through monitoring and rewarding.

Strategic Agenda Setting

Corporate headquarters is legitimized to set the strategic agenda of a firm and its subsidiaries. It is responsible for quickly identifying and responding to relevant events and trends in the various markets. Strategic issue management (Ansoff, 1980; Dutton and Duncan, 1987) has been identified as one of the key roles of headquarters in relation to subsidiaries. A strategic issue is a 'forthcoming development, either inside or outside the organization, which is likely to have an important impact on the ability of the enterprise to meet its objectives' (Ansoff, 1980: 133). To ensure early identification and fast response to strategic issues, strategic issue management systems steer the selection of strategic issues as they come to the attention of decision makers and are addressed by the organization. The legitimization of strategic issues and associated administrative routines, such as meetings and conferences to process the issues, are of focal interest. National cultures influence the perceptions of environmental uncertainty and organizational control, thereby altering the interpretation of and response to strategic issues (Schneider and Meyer, 1991). A corporation's headquarters needs to be sensitive to local interpretations of strategic issues, since such local interpretations trigger different decision processes and behaviour.

Resource Allocation

Internal competition for scarce resources and management attention plays a central role in the life of the MNC (Birkinshaw and Lingblad, 2005). The resource allocation process in a multinational firm can start at the top (allocating surplus cash) or among the subsidiaries (applying for additional resources to follow up on strategic initiatives). Several methods can be applied to help make resource allocation decisions: portfolio matrixes, past-performance tracks, net present values of expected future cash flows or real options models. Subsidiaries can attempt to influence resource allocation decisions by leveraging a central position in the MNC network, which could, for example, arise from the dependence of headquarters and other subsidiaries on a subsidiary's unique resources. The higher the knowledge intensity (i.e., the knowledge output from the subsidiary to other MNC units) of a subsidiary, the higher its bargaining power will be (Mudambi and Navarra, 2004).

Definition of Subsidiary Charters

The evolution of a subsidiary depends on the enhancement of a subsidiary's capabilities and the explicit changes in the subsidiary's charter. The subsidiary role can be measured in terms of specific businesses or elements of the business the subsidiary undertakes, and for which it has responsibility (Birkinshaw and Hood, 1998: 775). Three factors determine the subsidiary role and, thereby, its evolution: (1) head-office assignments, that is, decisions regarding the allocation of activities to the subsidiary; (2) subsidiary choices regarding those activities; and (3) local environment determinism, perceived as environmental influences on subsidiary and head-office decisions.

Top Management Selection

Corporate headquarters often selects the top management team members for subsidiaries, thereby influencing the dominant coalition within the subsidiary. Since complex strategic decisions are frequently more influenced by behavioural factors than economic optimization (Cyert and March, 1963), the composition of the top management team has a decisive influence on organizational outcomes. The decision of whether to appoint local managers or use expatriate managers from the corporate centre illustrates the impact top management selection has on subsidiary performance and on the subsidiary–headquarters relationship.

Monitoring and Rewarding

Corporate headquarters influences strategy processes and strategic decisions through the establishment of monitoring and control systems. Grant (2003) reports that the focus of strategic control systems shifted in the late 1990s from the content of strategy (i.e., behavioural control) to outcomes in terms of performance items (i.e., output control). Negotiating, monitoring and rewarding the achievement of financial performance goals became the dominant theme in strategy meetings between the headquarters and geographical divisions of many MNCs. As a consequence, strategy plans became less detailed on the qualitative side and more focused on the quantitative parts.

This short description of how headquarters – together with subsidiaries – constructs the boundaries of strategic decision making helps to illustrate that the creation of strategy is to a large extent driven by power plays. Process of strategic agenda setting, resource allocation, definition of subsidiary charters and top management team selection as well as the creation of a system for monitoring and rewarding will most likely be influenced by power structures rather than an objective and aseptic process. For example, consider a case in which subsidiary A wants to convince headquarters to adapt a specific product to local customer needs. Headquarters insists on cross-border standardization and central control of product innovation. Subsidiary A demonstrates that local competitors have higher market shares because they are able to better serve client needs. Headquarters responds by pointing out that the benefits of increased market share would be offset by higher product variation costs. Such discussions between headquarters and subsidiaries are hard to objectify. Personal beliefs and the power to impose those beliefs on the discussion partner play an important role when new ideas are introduced in the strategy processes of an MNC. The strategic context, or, in other words, the way power is exercised in such processes, has a great influence on their outcomes. The next section looks at how power influences strategy processes.

THE ROLE OF POWER IN STRATEGY PROCESSES

The mechanism allowing for the generation of new ideas and their integration into the strategic thinking process of an MNC may be defined as strategic context determination (Burgelman, 1983). In most firms, managers need to be able to play power games, as described by Mintzberg (1983) or Westley (1990), if they want to achieve their goals. Managers are usually legitimized by their organizations to use their power to run operations efficiently. Power also plays a pivotal role in strategic conversations about resource allocation, new market-entry plans, the selection of new management, the redesign of organizational structures, decisions about alliance partners and the development of new marketing concepts. Common sense suggests that the power dynamics of conversations that deal with daily business should differ from the power dynamics of strategic conversations. However, in general managers do not appear to change the way they use power according to the type of conversation in which they are engaged.

Birkinshaw and Hood (2001) report that the dominant model of headquarters–subsidiary interaction in MNCs in the first half of the twentieth century was 'paternalistic' – headquarters aimed to ensure that home country innovations would be introduced across affiliated subsidiaries. As some MNCs grew, subsidiaries were also used to scan the environment for new ideas and technologies. The designation of 'competence centre' was assigned to some subsidiaries, signalling to other units that the subsidiary in question had a mission to innovate in a certain area. Although this second model of organizing the MNC worked well during the 1970s and 1980s, Birkinshaw and Hood (2001) proposed a new governance model for the MNCs – a model that should be based on 'liberalism'. The basic ideas of this proposal are that new knowledge can emerge from everywhere in the MNC, and that headquarters needs to adopt a more democratic approach to its pursuit of new opportunities. In contrast to the centre-dominated view of the MNC, the liberal perspective suggests that subsidiaries are capable of developing strategies on their own, rather than relying exclusively on the role assigned by headquarters, and that they be encouraged to develop such strategies (Delany, 2000).

POWER IN A PATERNALISTIC STRATEGIC CONTEXT

Most of the literature on power in the fields of organizational studies and strategic management is embedded in an economic model of organizations. In this model, power is seen as a force that can be used to pressure someone to do something that he or she would otherwise not have done (Dahl, 1957; Salancik and Pfeffer, 1977). Power is a resource that a person possesses based on formal authority, control over scarce resources or control over technology: 'Power is the medium through which conflicts of interest are ultimately resolved. Power influences who gets what, when, and how' (Morgan, 1986: 158). If the distribution of power becomes legitimate, power is transformed into authority.

Knowledge is Power

Bacon's statement that 'knowledge is power' is probably the best-known description of the relationship between power and knowledge. Knowledge as a power base − expert knowledge − has been treated extensively (French and Raven, 1960; Reed, 1996). The widespread positive view of power that is based on knowledge, at least in comparison to other kinds of power, might have contributed to the increased interest in expert power. Expert power is closely linked to managers' abilities to cope with uncertainty. Therefore, knowledge is more relevant if it can be applied to a specific task that is crucial for the company's survival (Salancik and Pfeffer, 1977). Consequently, the pre-condition for expertise to become a source of power is that it must be attributed to a specific task or domain. This implies that power structures change if the perception of the task's importance to the organization changes, assuming that expertise is closely linked to a specific organizational function, that managers have different experience levels in different domains, and that there are conditions of task dependency and non-substitutability (Emerson, 1962).

Power is Static

The task dependency of expert power requires a certain stability of power structures. Although task assignments and their related power can be easily transferred, power distribution is relatively static within organizations. The more stable the crucial task system of the company is, the more stable the power distribution will be. This statement is valid only if we assume that knowledge development is augmented by positive feedback loops, rather than negative feedback loops, to some extent (Arthur, 1994: 3). If knowledge development is generally characterized by reinforcing mechanisms, it would be almost impossible for a newcomer to outstrip an established expert in a specific field, because knowledge can be easily developed through information gathering that focuses on the specific task.

Power is Easy to Detect

The stability of power structures might be one reason for the ease with which power can be detected and observed, because a particular picture of existing power structures can be tested on several occasions over a relatively long period of time. Accordingly, Pfeffer states that 'power may be tricky to define, but it is not that difficult to recognize' (1981: 3). Consequently, if power is a force that individuals feel when they are urged to do something they would not have done otherwise, then it might be easy to detect power, at least for the individual that is the target of the exercise of power. On the other hand, one could assume that organizational members can also recognize whether they are exercising power, given that there is an intention behind most individual action in organizations. Although this seems trivial, power in use seems to be easier to detect than potential power, at least for people involved in power games.

Power is Clustered

As tasks or responsibilities are important factors that influence the political landscape, power centres around points in the organization where critical tasks are congregated. An analysis of organizational forms is therefore necessary because the structure influences the opportunities for agents to make choices and pursue strategies (Lukes, 1977: 29). In organizational forms based on the organizing principles of a bureaucracy, power increases the higher one climbs the hierarchical ladder because the tasks at the top have a different scope. Along with more tasks and responsibilities comes an increasing amount of information to which top managers have access.

As a result, the expert power of the group leader in relation to group tasks is very likely to take precedence over that of the group members.

LIBERAL STRATEGIC CONTEXT

In a liberal strategic context, traditional sources of power lose some of their significance. If conversations are not limited to current business issues but aim to create new opportunities, formal authority and the control over scarce resources are no longer bases of power. If existing knowledge is at stake, knowledge is not a pre-determined object that can be obtained through information-gathering processes. If knowledge is not a target of a social legitimization process, then apparently legitimized knowledge cannot be a source of power. In conversations that attempt to venture into new knowledge areas, existing knowledge might lose its importance as a source of power. Consequently, assuming conversations cannot take place in a power vacuum, power in strategic conversations might come from other sources, including different types of knowledge (i.e., knowledge that has not yet been legitimized).

A deeper investigation of French and Raven (1960) reveals that the subjectivity of knowledge in strategic conversations would make the described power bases obsolete. Referent power, coercive power, reward power, legitimate power and power from expert knowledge are all based on and anchored in objective knowledge. These power bases drive knowledge development towards a legitimization of knowledge that is closely related to existing knowledge and should therefore be reduced because it would limit knowledge development. However, if power is a natural force in social processes that shapes what is perceived as reality (Foucault, 1977; Gergen, 1995), what other bases of power can be imagined?

Gergen's (1995) description of 'centripetal power' and 'centrifugal power' is a first important distinction that will increase our understanding of power in strategic conversations. Gergen describes centrifugal power as predominant in situations where one group tries to achieve power over another group. Centripetal power, on the other hand, 'is achieved within a group when they can achieve their own goals according to their own definitional terms' (Gergen, 1995: 39). Consequently, Gergen argues that the existence of a singular hierarchy, as suggested by the classical work on power, must be replaced by the notion of multiple power clusters according to different ontology and value systems (pp. 39–40). Still, power is closely linked to a specific value system or to an understanding of these value systems that leads to an increased ability to know facts and structure objects in the world (Dachler and Hosking, 1995: 17). Leaving this system would basically mean losing the power base and, with it, the impact on the conversation. Therefore, in strategic conversations, power comes, on the one hand, from the ability to call the dominant frame of reference into question and to rethink the current knowledge stock, and the ability to facilitate the sense-making process on the other. The ability to question the dominant logic is based on embrained knowledge and the ability to drive the sense-making process is based on encultured knowledge. Both knowledge categories that are described in the following paragraphs permit knowledge with a low legitimization level to receive attention. Embrained and encultured knowledge represent the ability to generate understanding to a large extent, which may be defined as the most profound form of knowledge because it arises when principles and connections of (social) systems are recognized (Wikström and Normann, 1994: 12).

Power from Embrained Knowledge

Embrained knowledge (Blackler, 1995: 1023–1024) is the conceptual skills and cognitive abilities that allow an individual to rethink objectives and assumptions that were previously taken for granted. The ability to recognize and understand complex rules and causation is a major part of embrained knowledge, but such an understanding is especially difficult when subsidiaries are culturally distant and use different languages. Blackler (1995) connects this notion of embrained knowledge to Argyris and Schön's (1978) work on 'double loop learning' and to Senge's (1990) achievements in organizational-learning theory. Consequently, power stems from the ability to discover new knowledge streams and to connect them creatively with existing knowledge, along with the ability to unlearn or forget, and to make distinctions and connections that have little legitimization within the organization. Emphasis on embrained skills is most evident in symbolic-analyst-dependent organizations, such as software consultancies – organizations that focus on solving unique problems. Embrained knowledge therefore involves the ability to recognize, understand and rearrange patterns throughout different scales.

Power from Encultured Knowledge

Another source of power in strategic conversations stems from the ability to formulate statements in such a way that the discussion partners can easily connect and create their own meaning. Power means knowing how to convey an idea to conversational partners that live in a cultural context distinct from the one where the idea has been developed. Blackler (1995: 1024) describes this ability as encultured knowledge, which refers to the process of achieving shared understanding and meaning. However, as meanings develop through connections with past experiences, they are idiosyncratic in nature because individuals have different past experiences. Hence, in order to share meaning, managers have to talk about their shared experiences in close proximity to their occurrence, and hammer out a common way to encode and talk about them (Weick, 1995: 188). Power, therefore, depends on the ability to extract specific events from past experiences and to connect them with the current event. Hence, power consists to a large extent of the ability to coordinate attention.

Power is Dynamic rather than Static

In a liberal strategic context, power is not a property and is not static, since powerless experts and powerless bosses probably exist in all organizations (Moch and Huff, 1983). Along with the disconnection of knowledge and tasks comes the increased dynamics of power, as power in a liberalistic strategic context does not develop from formal power through task assignments but through the capacity to sense and convey new knowledge to fellow managers. Foucault (1977: 4) expands this idea – he perceives power as neither an institution nor a structure. Furthermore, he does not attribute power to a certain personal strength. Power, in Foucault's opinion, is attributed to a complex strategic situation in a particular society. Foucault expresses the view that power is dynamic because a strategic situation is complex, that is, consists of several interconnected components that change over time, as the following statement extracted from an interview with him shows: 'If one tries to erect a theory of power one will always be obliged to view it as emerging at a given place and time and hence to deduce it, to reconstruct its genesis' (Gordon, 1980: 199). Therefore, power is dynamic. The level of power depends on the embrained and encultured knowledge of the individual and on the specific context in which the conversation takes place. The ability to recognize and rethink the basic assumptions of a specific group in a specific area, as well as the facilitation of meaning creation, requires a certain degree of involvement with the group, on the one hand, and the cognitive skill to interpret these shared experiences on the other. In strategic conversations, power positions are, therefore, embedded in a field of relationships in which every position is contestable, because they are not institutionalized but depend on specific and changing contexts.

Power is Invisible and Therefore Not Easy to Detect

The dynamic character of power is one reason power is difficult to detect. Another reason is connected to the attribution of power to a change of existing knowledge. Power derives from the ability to facilitate individual meaning creation − from the ability to endure a change in deeply rooted convictions. This process is characterized by a narrow borderline between interpretation of data and the inheritance of information. Karl Weick states: 'We would expect to find less sensibleness in traditional bureaucracies where formalization, tradition, and centralization reduce the occasions of choice. Participants in bureaucracies inherit explanations of what they are doing rather than construct them continually' (1995: 160). In liberalistic organizations where power is more dynamic and distributed than in traditional bureaucracies, we could expect employees to form their own interpretations more independently rather than forming interpretations that are close to the inherited explanations or the dominant way of thinking.

Power is Distributed, Not Clustered

As markets become more complex to manage, bureaucratic organizational forms are increasingly replaced with other structures described as 'infinitely flat', 'spider's web' or 'inverted' (Miles and Snow, 1986; Quinn, 1992: 113–135). They are characterized through the destruction of formal hierarchies and self-organization. Ciborra even argues that the current pace of competition calls for a 'platform organization', which is a 'shapeless organization that keeps generating new forms through frequent recombination' (1996: 104). Bennis (1993: 20) argues that under certain conditions democracy is a more 'efficient' form of social organization, and because today's business environment is increasingly approaching these conditions, he perceives democracy as 'inevitable'.

In modern organizational forms, critical tasks assignments do not always go hand in hand with the formal position. These tasks cannot always be aggregated and formally assigned to a senior person in the company. In the short run, power might be clustered in organizations. Power is useful and necessary for the functioning of organizations (Kraus, 1984: 132) but in the long run power is established from inside or from the bottom up (Kögler, 1994), because power constructs organizational reality and, thereby, the identity of the individual. The knowledge worker (Drucker, 1993) is now more independent of the organization in the long run than he or she was some decades ago. In contrast to the 1970s and 1980s, employees own an important part of the resources: knowledge. Equipped with knowledge that is valuable not only to their own company but also to other companies, individuals can more easily decide over their long-term employment. If the employees were not part of strategic conversations, they might decide that the created organizational reality did not suit them in the long run, which might lead them to plan to leave the company in a few years. Although inclusion in strategic conversations alone does not guarantee satisfaction (Westley, 1990), the creation of strategic options for all organizational members – to 'enlarge the pie' for all – might be more important in strategic conversations than favouring the organizational reality of the dominant coalition over another, thereby merely 'slicing the existing pie'. Consequently, the exercise of power in a liberal strategic context is not a zero-sum game. In the long run, the size of the 'pie' is not fixed.

This leads to the perspective that potential power is distributed among those in the organization, because everybody can contribute to a certain extent to the expansion of the 'pie'. Perrow (1986) therefore suggests focusing on how power can become a 'non-zero-sum' game. As organizations tend to facilitate the generation of zero-sum power, he suggests putting more emphasis on the development of the 'pie' than on slicing it. This will essentially happen if 'the amount of power generated within an organization could vary from low to high' (Perrow, 1986: 258). Power is more likely to be a non-zero-sum game if access to power is guaranteed for all members of the organization in order to support the sustainable development of the employees, own value and belief systems.

Table 20.1 summarizes how power works in the paternalistic and the liberal strategy contexts.

BALANCING STABILITY AND CHANGE

As suggested at the start of this chapter, strategic context determination refers to the mechanism through which the generation and integration of new ideas into the strategic thinking process of the MNC takes place. The strategic context plays a fundamental role in the processes of knowledge exploitation and knowledge exploitation. A paternalistic strategy context favours efficient knowledge exploitation and dissemination but may limit knowledge development. On the other hand, a liberal strategy context promotes the knowledge-generating role of the subsidiary network but may obstruct its global application. As a result, firms tend to either concentrate on adaptive processes that refine exploitation more rapidly than exploration, which may lead to improved short-term results but could be self-destructive in the long run (March, 1991), or on exploration processes, thereby withdrawing the resources needed for engagement in advancement activities. Levinthal and March (1993) therefore describe the balance between exploitation and exploration as essential for a company's long-term survival. They state that companies either tend to overemphasize

Table 20.1   Perspectives on power and knowledge

	Paternalistic strategic context	**Liberalistic strategic context**
Issue 1 Sources of power	Power is based on the ability to reward, the reference to internalized shared values and the amount of expert knowledge. Power increases with the importance of the assigned task and the possession of critical resources (e.g., information)	Traditional sources of power lose their effect because knowledge is subjective and not directly connected to a specific task. The ability to recognize, understand and rearrange patterns (embrained knowledge) and the ability to attract attention to selected strategic issues (encultured knowledge) become more important as sources of power
Issue 2 Dynamics of power	Power is task dependent. As tasks are relatively stable over time, power is also relatively static. The building of dominant coalitions reinforces the static character of power because the behaviour of the person in power leans towards keeping strict, strong control over task assignments and resource allocations	If power does not come from actual task assignments and control over critical resources, but instead depends on individuals and context-dependent characteristics (i.e., embrained and encultured knowledge), it becomes more dynamic
Issue 3 Evidence of power	Potential power and power in use can be detected by analysing the sources of power. In addition, the observation of decision-making processes, whereby individual goals are clearly stated, makes the ex-post and ex-ante analyses of power easier	As power bases are inherent in the individual and context dependent, rather than objective, it is hard to detect power. Although traditional power bases no longer count, they may still be embedded in legitimized behavioural patterns
Issue 4 Distribution of power	The centralization and clustering of tasks is one reason for the emergence of power centres. The reinforcing mechanisms of power enhance this tendency	In the long run, organizational members are free to create their own reality. If they see that they have no influence on the development of the organization or if they have no voice in the development of new knowledge, they might leave the company

Table 20.1   (continued)

	Paternalistic strategic context	**Liberalistic strategic context**
Conclusion The nature of power	Knowledge development is controlled by an elitist group and is driven by static and clustered power, which reinforces existing knowledge	Knowledge development is a shared responsibility and is driven by dynamic, dispersed power, which enables management teams to abandon internalized convictions

knowledge exploration (failure trap) or knowledge exploitation (success trap). Yet, in most cases organizations need to stimulate exploration and restrain exploitation because learning tends to sacrifice the long term to the short term, tends to favour effects that occur close to the learner, and overemphasizes success and underestimates failures (Levinthal and March, 1993: 107–110).

Exploration aims to ensure 'advancement', which entails the development of knowledge and consists of the development of distinction and norms, the scaling of knowledge, the development of knowledge connectivity, self-referencing and languaging (von Krogh et al., 1994: 64). Knowledge exploration concerns itself with developing options for the organization through activities such as search, variation, risk taking, experimentation, play, flexibility, discovery and innovation (March, 1991: 71). In sum, it is about generating options for the organization (March, 1991: 71). Therefore, *strategy-making processes usually require more knowledge exploration than exploitation.*

Exploitation, on the other hand, aims to ensure survival by turning existing resources into money, namely by realizing some of the options created by exploration activities. Traditional managerial activities, such as planning, organizing, controlling or product-market positioning, are in the foreground. Exploitation, or survival, is therefore about 'refinement, choice, production, efficiency, selection, implementation, execution' (March, 1991: 71). Therefore, *strategy implementation and operations usually require more knowledge exploitation than exploration.*

This chapter suggests that power works differently in situations of knowledge exploitation and exploration. The power mode embedded in a strong, static hierarchic mode of thought is more commonly applied in knowledge exploitation. This power mode refers to the paternalistic strategic context and most often leads to discussions of who gets what or how to 'slice the pie'. This power mode is well learned and internalized, in contrast to power processes that aim to 'make a bigger pie'. Because it

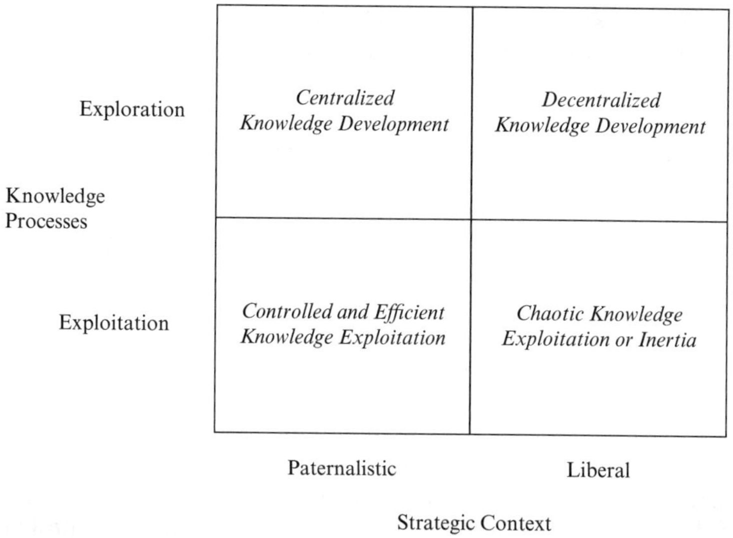

	Paternalistic	Liberal
Exploration	*Centralized Knowledge Development*	*Decentralized Knowledge Development*
Exploitation	*Controlled and Efficient Knowledge Exploitation*	*Chaotic Knowledge Exploitation or Inertia*

Knowledge Processes (left axis, spanning Exploration and Exploitation)

Paternalistic   Liberal

Strategic Context

Figure 20.1   The impact of the strategy context on knowledge processes in the MNC

might be difficult to change this power mode, it seems to be more expedient to exploit knowledge than develop new knowledge. Therefore, the way in which we are accustomed to exercising power might be one reason why companies often have problems in striking a balance between knowledge exploitation and exploration. In sum, choices have to be made between 'gaining new information about alternatives and thus improving future returns (which suggests allocating part of the investment to searching among uncertain alternatives), and using the information currently available to improve present returns (which suggests concentrating the investment on the apparently best alternative)' (March, 1991: 72).

As Figure 20.1 shows, power modes can be combined with different knowledge processes. Although the distinction between exploitation and exploration is an analytical/theoretical distinction, because it may always be hard to clearly distinguish between them, one knowledge process prevails in some contexts.

To find a balance between exploitation and exploration, MNCs construct strategic contexts as either paternalistic or liberal. Figure 20.1 shows that a paternalistic strategic context probably works best in daily operations when knowledge needs to be exploited. Consider the following example: a cement plant in Uruguay breaks down and a roller mill component needs to be replaced. The same problem recently occurred in Sweden.

Therefore, the knowledge to solve the problem in Uruguay already exists and is best applied through a paternalistic strategic context: someone at the centre of the organization makes sure that the best practice developed in Sweden is transferred to Uruguay.

But what effect does a paternalistic strategic context have on knowledge exploration processes? A dominant group of people at the headquarters (or a competence centre) develops new knowledge in a controlled, efficient way. Nokia and Apple, for example, use a few R&D centres to develop new products. Subsidiaries have little impact on the process. It would probably be too costly to adapt products and a liberal strategic context would make the knowledge development process too inefficient. Therefore, in these organizations, power is static, clustered and based on expert knowledge.

In industries that require substantial local adaptation and offer fewer benefits for cross-border integration, liberal strategic contexts allow subsidiaries to engage in autonomous strategic initiatives. The likelihood that new ideas, business concepts or products will be generated in subsidiaries and legitimated throughout an MNC increases if a liberal strategic context is created. Unilever's innovation gate model, for example, encourages subsidiaries to come up with new ideas and evaluate centrally developed inventions. The food and beverage business requires higher levels of local adaptation. As a consequence, power is more dynamic, dispersed and based on the ability to recognize new customers' needs.

However, Unilever's detergent business requires more cross-border aggregation. Therefore, the company runs the product innovation process in a more paternalistic way. This business requires that subsidiaries engage more in knowledge exploitation than in knowledge development processes. A liberalistic strategy context would hamper the fast, efficient development and implementation of a new product.

IMPLICATIONS FOR THE DESIGN OF STRATEGY PROCESSES IN MULTINATIONAL FIRMS

This chapter has made several points. First, strategic initiatives adopted by subsidiaries are potentially value generating, but need to be carefully controlled and integrated. Second, multinational firms design their strategic contexts – the mechanisms that allow new ideas to be generated and integrated into the strategy process. This chapter has described how power is exercised in a paternalistic strategic context, as opposed to a liberalistic strategic context. Third, it has been argued that liberalistic strategic contexts generally favour decentralized knowledge exploration and, therefore, the development of autonomous subsidiary initiatives. Paternalistic strategic contexts, on the other hand, favour knowledge exploitation and, therefore, the efficient development of economies of scale through cross-border integration. Fourth, to successfully design and implement strategies, multinational firms need to actively construct the strategic contexts and be able to switch from one power mode to another.

These reflections have several implications for the design of strategy processes in multinational firms:

1. *Distinguish strategy creation from strategy implementation.* Knowledge processes related to strategy development require a different strategic context than knowledge processes related to strategy implementation. If an MNC aims to encourage subsidiaries to adopt autonomous strategic initiatives, it needs to create a liberal strategic context.
2. *Distinguish among different levels of globalization.* MNCs that operate in geographical markets with higher levels of cross-border integration (i.e., payment services, the turbine market) can afford less decentralized strategic initiatives and need a more paternalistic context. MNCs that recognize that the world is not 'flat' but separated by many cultural, administrative, geographical and economical differences will probably achieve better results with a more liberalistic strategic context.
3. *Uncover strategic contexts in use.* Prior to constructing an appropriate strategy context, MNCs need to understand how power is currently used in strategic processes. There are various sources of power and ways to exercise them. One simple way to uncover power in strategic conversations is to check the possibility of 'reversing action' (Bochum, 1990). For example, if a leader slaps a subordinate on the back but the opposite action (i.e., the subordinate slaps his leader on the back) is not appropriate, then power resides in the leader. As power is not always tied to a formal position, there are some instances in which power is more difficult to detect and recognize. In addition, in some instances the reversibility of an action is a useful method for uncovering power. If a statement starts with 'I know exactly what you mean', would it be possible to reply similarly? Is it always the same person who defines management practices, routines, conversational rules or seating orders in strategic meetings? Would it be possible for a subordinate to invite his boss to his office for a conversation? Are subordinates viewed as rude if they do not agree with the opinion of the CEO? Is it possible to know what the outcome of a conversation will be before it even starts? The answers to these and similar questions determine whether a firm uses a more liberalistic or a more paternalistic strategic context.

4.   *Design the strategic context.* The last step aims to bridge the gap between the desired and the current strategic context. As suggested by Burgelman (1983), the mechanisms for integrating autonomous strategic behaviour into the current strategy need to be defined. If, for example, a multinational management team discovers that to increase its competitiveness it has to shift away from knowledge creation centralized in headquarters to encourage subsidiaries to more actively bring in new knowledge, this would require a reconstruction of the power mode from a static, clustered (paternalistic) mode to a dynamic and dispersed (liberalistic) one. Such a change requires that formal leaders be able to construct the power mode and to 'step back for advancement' if necessary. As Zand states: 'Effective triadic leaders use their power appropriately. They know when and how to be directive or to delegate. They know how to review and to evaluate constructively. They know how to be consultants, providing guidance rather than issuing commands' (1997: 4).

CONCLUSION

This chapter demonstrates that different power modes are needed for strategy creation and strategy implementation. While bureaucracies are more likely to lead to efficient knowledge exploitation and strategy implementation, organized anarchies (Olsen, 1976) tend to be more effective in knowledge exploration and strategy creation. Managers are invited to reflect on the effects that static and clustered power have on knowledge exploration if this mode is applied. If a managerial team agrees that this power mode would limit the scope of knowledge exploration, a self-control mechanism might come into effect if team members start to judge their own behaviour and the behaviour of their colleagues in terms of knowledge management. It might not be enough to introduce well-known control mechanisms, such as brainstorming techniques, methods of avoiding 'groupthink', anonymous conversations by computer, or the like. If the basic attitudes towards knowledge and power do not change, these instruments may be limited in their efficiency.

REFERENCES

Alvesson, M. (1996), *Communication, Power and Organization*, Berlin and New York: Walter de Gruyter.

Ansoff, I. (1980), 'Strategic issue management', *Strategic Management Journal*, 1(2): 131–148.

Argyris, C. and D. A. Schön (1978), *Organizational Learning: A Theory of Action Perspective*, Reading, MA: Addison-Wesley.

Arthur, B. (1994), *Increasing Returns and Path Dependence in the Economy*, Ann Arbor, MI: University of Michigan Press.

Bennis, W. (1993), *An Invented Life*, Reading, MA: Addison-Wesley Publishing Company, Inc.

Birkinshaw, J. and N. Hood (1998), 'Multinational subsidiary evolution: capability and charter change in foreign-owned subsidiary companies', *Academy of Management Review*, 23(4): 773–795.

Birkinshaw, J. and M. Lingblad (2005), 'Intrafirm competition and charter evolution in the multibusiness firm', *Organization Science*, 16(6): 674–686.

Birkinshaw, J. and N. Hood (2001), 'Unleash innovation in foreign subsidiaries', *Harvard Business Review*, 79(3): 131–138.

Birkinshaw, J., C. Bouquet and T. Chini (2006), 'Managing executive attention in the global company', *Business Strategy Review*, 17(3): 4–9.

Blackler, F. (1995), 'Knowledge, knowledge work and organizations: An overview and interpretation', *Organization Studies*, 16(6): 1021–1046.

Bochum, A. (1990) Macht, *Arbeitspapier Bochumer Arbeitsgruppe für Sozialen Konstruktivismus und Wirklichkeitsprüfung*, Nr. 9.

Borum, F. (1980), 'A power-strategy alternative to organizational development', *Organization Studies*, 1(2): 123–146.

Burgelman, R. A. (1983), 'A process model of internal corporate venturing in the diversified major firm', *Administrative Science Quarterly*, 28: 223–244.

Ciborra, C. (1996), 'The platform organization: Recombining strategies, structures, and surprises', *Organization Science*, 7(2) (March–April): 103–118.

Cyert, R. M. and J. G. March (1963), *A Behavioral Theory of the Firm*, Englewood Cliffs, NJ: Prentice-Hall.

Dachler, H. P. and D.-M. Hosking (1995), 'The primacy of relations in socially constructing organizational realities', in D.-M. Hosking, H. P. Dachler and K. J. Gergen (eds), *Management and Organization: Relational Alternatives to Individualism*, Aldershot: Avebury.

Dahl, R. (1957), 'The concept of power', *Behavioral Science*, (2): 201–215.

Delany, E. (2000), 'Strategic development of the multinational subsidiary through subsidiary initiative-taking', *Long Range Planning*, 33: 220–244.

Drucker, P. (1993), *Post-Capitalist Society*, New York: Harper Business.

Dutton, J. and R. Duncan (1987), 'The creation of momentum for change through the process of strategic issue diagnosis', *Strategic Management Journal*, 8: 279–296.

Emerson, R. (1962), 'Power-dependence relations', *American Sociological Review*, 27: 31–41.

Finkelstein, S. (1992), 'Power in top management teams: dimensions, measurement, and validation', *Academy of Management Journal*, 35(3): 505–538.

Foucault, M. (1977), *Der Wille zum Wissen: Sexualität und Wahrheit*, Frankfurt am Main: Suhrkamp.

French, J. and B. Raven (1960), 'The bases of social power', in D. Cartwright and A. Zander (eds), *Group Dynamics: Research and Theory*, Second Edition, New York: Evanston, and London: Harper and Row, pp. 607–23.

Gergen, K. J. (1995), 'Relational theory and the discourses of power', in D.-M. Hosking, H. P. Dachler and K. J. Gergen (eds), *Management and Organization: Relational Alternatives to Individualism*, Aldershot: Avebury, pp. 29–50.

Gordon, C. (ed.) (1980), *Power/Knowledge*, Brighton: Harvester Press.

Grant, R. M. (2003), 'Strategic planning in a turbulent environment: Evidence from the oil majors', *Strategic Management Journal*, 24: 491–517.

Kögler, H. H. (1994), *Michel Foucault*, Stuttgart and Weimar: Metzler.

Kraus, W. A. (1984), *Collaboration in Organizations: Alternatives to Hierarchy*, New York: Human Science Press.

Levinthal, D. A. and J. G. March (1993), 'The myopia of learning', *Strategic Management Journal*, **14**: 95–112.
Lukes, S. (1977), *Essays in Social Theory*, Hong Kong: Sung Fung Printing.
March, J. G. (1991), 'Exploration and exploitation in organizational learning', *Organization Science*, **2**(1): 71–87.
McClelland, D. and D. Burnham (1995), 'Power is the great motivator', *Harvard Business Review*, January–February: 126–139.
McNulty, T. and A. Pettigrew (1996), 'The contribution, power and influence of part-time board members', *Corporate Governance*, **4**(3): 160–179.
Miles, R. E. and C. C. Snow (1986), 'Network organizations: New concepts for new forms', **28**(3): 62–73.
Mintzberg, H. (1983), *Power In and Around Organizations*, Englewood Cliffs, NJ: Prentice-Hall.
Moch, M. and A. S. Huff (1983), 'Power enactment through language and ritual', *Journal of Business Research*, **11**: 293–316.
Morgan, G. (1986), *Images of Organization*, London: Sage.
Mudambi, R. and P. Navarra (2004), 'Is knowledge power? Knowledge flows, subsidiary power and rent-seeking within MNCs', *Journal of International Business Studies*, **35**(5): 385–406.
Olsen, J. P. (1976), 'Choice in an organized anarchy', in J. G. March and J. P. Olsen (eds), *Ambiguity and Choice in Organizations*, Oslo: Universitetsforlaget, pp. 82–139.
Perrow, C. (1986), *Complex Organizations–A Critical Essay*, 3rd edn, New York: Random House.
Pettigrew, A. and T. McNulty (1995), 'Power and influence in and around the boardroom', *Human Relations*, **48**(8): 845–873.
Pfeffer, J. (1981), *Power in organizations*, Marshfield, MA: Pitman.
Prahalad, C. K. and R. A. Bettis (1986), 'The dominant logic: A new linkage between diversity and performance', *Strategic Management Journal*, **7**(6): 485–501.
Quinn, B. (1992), *Intelligent Enterprise*, New York: Maxwell Macmillan.
Reed, M. (1996), 'Expert power and control in late modernity: An empirical review and theoretical synthesis', *Organizational Studies*, **17**(4): 573–597.
Salancik, G. R. and J. Pfeffer (1977), 'Who gets power and how they hold on to it: A strategic contingency model of power', *Organizational Dynamics*, (5): 3–21.
Schneider, S. C. and A. D. Meyer (1991), 'Interpreting and responding to strategic issues: The impact of national culture', *Strategic ManagementJournal*, **12**: 307–320.
Senge, P. (1990), *The Fifth Discipline: The Art and Practice of the Learning Organization*, London: Century Business.
von Krogh, G., J. Roos and K. Slocum (1994), 'An essay on corporate epistemology', *Strategic Management Journal*, **15**: 53–71.
Weick, K. E. (1995), *Sensemaking in Organizations*, London: Sage.
Westley, F. (1990), 'Middle managers and strategy: Microdynamics of inclusion', *Strategic Management Journal*, **11**: 337–351.
Wikström, S. and R. Normann (1994), *Knowledge & Value: A New Perspective on Corporate Transformation*, London: Routledge.
Zand, D. (1997), *The Leadership Triad: Knowledge, Trust, and Power*, New York and Oxford: Oxford University Press.

21 Perceptions, processes and performance during organizational decline
Michael R. Braun and Scott F. Latham

INTRODUCTION

This chapter focuses on the strategy process during situations of organizational decline, or when firms experience a substantial, absolute decrease in their resource base that occurs over time (Cameron et al., 1987). While research on organizational decline has long been part of the strategic management literature, interest in the topic remains variable for several reasons. Traditionally, researchers tend to shy away from this relatively gloomy subject matter, opting instead to turn their attention to what makes firms grow and succeed (Cameron et al., 1988). During times of economic prosperity, decline scholars are often deemed pessimists or even veritable Cassandras for drawing attention to firm malfunctions, whereas in times of hardship the topic of decline takes a backseat to the power of positive thinking. Furthermore, as early researchers discovered, real challenges exist in gaining access to data on organizational decline since managers, more often than not, avoid engaging in discussions on the subject. Indeed, as a popular saying so aptly notes, success has many fathers but failure is an orphan.

Mirroring the strategic management literature in general, strategy process research contextualized to organizational decline remains relatively sparse. While scholars maintain a low yet steady output of studies investigating causes and consequences of organizational decline, the manner in which the strategic process unfolds within declining organizations remains, to a large degree, underexplored. More specifically, we observe a research void in how managers come to formulate and implement strategies to stem deterioration in firm performance. Therefore, the present chapter aims to appraise what we know and what remains to be explored about the influence of initial conditions and managerial perceptions on the strategic process within the context of declining organizations. We rely on the integrated framework presented in Figure 21.1 to organize various aspects of decline-related causes, processes, and outcomes for our discussion. The framework will also permit us to advocate for a more holistic approach to the study of strategy process in the context of

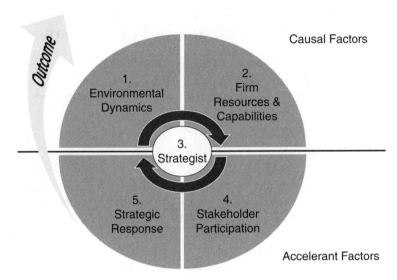

Figure 21.1   Causes, processes, participants and outcomes of organizational decline

organizational decline. Last, we will use the framework to engage in a selective review of relevant literature and offer avenues for future research on the topic.

In the first section, 'Impact of Firm Decline on Managerial Perceptions', we draw attention to the first two components of our framework (i.e., Environmental Dynamics and Firm Resources and Capabilities). We do so by first attending to a definition of organizational decline, followed by an examination of different causes of decline (both internal and external to the firm), and how these causes can differentially impact decision-makers' perceptions and framing of strategic responses to initiate turnaround. We believe this perspective to be central to our treatise since the broader strategy process literature highlights the effect of the strategist's unique cognition on the formulation and implementation of strategy. In the next section entitled 'Linking Managerial Perceptions and Strategic Processes' we delve more deeply into the accelerant factors, such as decision-makers' characteristics, predispositions, and cognitive models, that shape the decline process. Within our framework, the focal point is on the strategist and stakeholder participants and their combined influence on decisions and actions in response to organizational decline. Specifically, we consider various decision-making processes to attempt turnaround, especially as risks to the firm and its stakeholders become amplified under circumstances of organizational decline. Decisions concerning firm resources, leadership, governance, and other strategic elements, along with their underlying theoretical rationale, are contextualized within various scenarios of organizational decline. We also consider the extent to which various stakeholders, such as middle management, suppliers, and competitors, can have a bearing on the sequence of actions to accomplish turnaround. In the last section, 'Strategy-Making Processes and Firm Performance', which attends to strategic responses and outcomes in our framework, we bridge the discussion of strategy process to strategy outcome. We theorize to what extent the relationships between managerial perceptions, strategic formulations, and organizational actions are influenced by additional considerations internal and external to the firm and how those dynamic interactions affect firm outcomes. To make strategy process research in the context of decline more pragmatic, it is vital to follow the decisions made and courses of action taken by management to their conclusions. As we will attempt to highlight throughout this chapter, causes of organizational decline, which are numerous and multi-faceted, dictate managerial interpretations, evaluations, and implementations. These, in turn, do not lead to universal outcomes. We will illustrate that organizational decline is a messy affair, impacting one firm differently from the next, and, as such, no one strategic process fits all declining firms.

IMPACT OF FIRM DECLINE ON MANAGERIAL PERCEPTIONS

We begin by focusing on a firm's environmental dynamics, its resources and capabilities, and the dynamic interplay among these causal factors on management's cognition of decline and, subsequently, its level of commitment to the problemistic search of a solution. Since the last seminal collection of academic writings on the topic (see *Readings in Organizational Decline: Frameworks, Research, and Prescriptions*, by Cameron et al., 1988), an abundant body of work has contributed to our understanding of the causes and consequences of decline. For one, scholars have clearly distinguished firm decline from other organizational phenomena, including stagnation (Grinyer et al., 1988), crisis (Milburn et al., 1983), bankruptcy (Daily and Dalton, 1994), organizational change (Armenakis and Bedeian, 1999), and organizational failure (Amburgey et al., 1993). Furthermore, studies relying on linear, time-sequential approaches (Lohrke et al., 2004; Arogyaswamy et al., 1995; Robbins and Pearce, 1992) have succeeded in isolating various stages of the turnaround process that inform on intermediate steps between causes and consequences. Yet much of the literature continues to treat decline predominantly as a situational artifact, without much consideration as to why and how the firm arrived at that particular state of decline to begin with. If, as Hutzschenreuter and Kleindienst (2006) maintain, 'antecedent factors influence a strategist's cognition', then it becomes important to draw attention to causes of organizational decline in efforts to understand management's 'awakening' to the firm's problems and its potential solutions. While the majority of investigations on firm strategy thus emphasize the effective alignment of a firm's internal strengths and weaknesses to environmental opportunities and threats, Sheppard and Chowdhury (2005) consider the study of decline to involve a firm's misalignment of these factors. As such, we can better understand strategic shortcomings by bringing awareness to internal and external causes of decline.

Causes of Decline

In what decline scholars designate as r-type decline, firms experience a reduction in resources as they flounder in healthy markets. More specifically, despite growing product/service demand, some firms experience sub-par performance compared with their peers by failing to fit their internal resource base with the external opportunities necessary to achieve competitive advantage. Alternatively, k-type decline involves firms struggling due to changes or deteriorations in their respective macro-niche or industries. However, it is important to note that decline can also be instigated by a combination of internal deficiencies and externally caused disruptions (Barker, 2005; Lohrke et al., 2004), resulting in 'double whammy' situations for firms. As we will expound on this facet in later sections, these types of situations require strategic renewal initiatives into growth segments for an organization to achieve long-term competitive advantage.

The challenge for management remains in effectively scanning for, and interpreting the nature of, decline; that is, r-type vs. k-type. At a general level, r-type decline entails internally generated failures, including physical, managerial, behavioral, and financial causes (McKiernan, 2002); for example, product failures are representative of physical shortcomings whereas lack of leadership indicates a managerial deficiency leading to the firm's decline (McKiernan, 2002). K-type decline, on the other hand, can be caused by technological disruptions, deregulation, recessionary demand shocks, or other economic shifts, as well as increasing competitive pressures. Barker (2005) notes that the combination of internal and external sources of decline and the information processing overload gives rise to decline misdiagnoses that often lead to formulations and implementations of ineffective solutions. Furthermore, sources and outcomes often are inextricably intertwined, making the search for a firm's source of deterioration a chicken-and-egg problem (Sheppard and Chowdhury, 2005). Causal ambiguity represents an additional obstacle to management's effective information gathering and processing. More specifically, decision-makers perceive their level of influence to vary over different types of negative events and situations. Chattopadhyay et al. (2001) differentiate between managerial interpretations of control-reducing threats and threats of potential loss to tangible resources, and how these interpretations result in distinct categories of strategic action. On one hand, internal, controllable factors are more apt to receive immediate attention than external factors that management perceives to reside outside its locus of control (Barker and Barr, 2002). Moreover, threats involving resource losses are likely to instigate externally oriented organizational actions, such as product-market development initiatives, whereas internal strategic responses align with causes of decline that reduce management's sense of influence (Chattopadhyay et al., 2001). Thus, economic recessions, for example, which are viewed largely as uncontrollable events that 'can only be tolerated – they cannot be fought' (Thurow, 1996: 217), prompt managers to focus on domains over which they have greater control, including financial conservatism and cost cutting.

Causal Interpretations of Decline

Aside from having to identify *what* erodes the firm's resource base, managers need to be attuned to *how* those resources put the firm at risk. For k-type causes of decline, the magnitude of a firm's decline is influenced by environmental munificence, or a firm's ability to access critical resources in the external environment (Castrogiovanni, 1991), dynamism (Sharfman and Dean, 1991), including the volatility in product, market, and competitive environments (McArthur and Nystrom, 1991), complexity, and uncertainty. Decline originating from r-type sources, on the other hand, is shaped by organizational factors such as structural misfit (organic versus mechanistic; see Burns and Stalker, 1961), rate of resource loss (Chowdhury and Lang, 1993), insufficient slack (Cyert and March, 1963), as well as harmful firm culture, politics, and values, among many others (Rosenblatt and Mannheim, 1996). These dimensions not only affect the severity of decline, but can hinder and even forestall firm participants' scanning behaviors and their subsequent diagnostic abilities, decisions, and actions that determine the timing, content, and process of their turnaround efforts. As our discussion suggests, the multitude of decline causes and their underlying dimensions induce high levels of complexity and biases into managerial scanning and interpretation, thus easily obfuscating problems affecting the firm and delaying triggers for action. More so, the implication is that such differential effects of causal attributions of firm decline are likely to greatly influence subsequent managerial decisions and actions pertaining to adopted strategic processes (Goncalo and Duguid, 2008). In the next section, we move our discussion to the participants in the strategy process during decline.

LINKING MANAGERIAL PERCEPTIONS AND STRATEGIC PROCESSES

The previous section touched on an array of decline issues and how they can differentially influence management's reaction to poor performance and the problemistic search for solutions. As our diagram indicates, at the core of the strategy process lies the issue, the strategist, and the sequence of decisions and actions that determine how a strategy is formulated, implemented, and changed (Hutzschenreuter and Kleindienst, 2006; Chakravarthy and White, 2001). As Finkelstein (2005) so aptly notes, if you want to understand strategy, study the strategist. We therefore turn our attention to the strategist by attending to the actors and participants in the strategy process during decline, and the extent to which they influence the shaping and execution of turnaround efforts.

The CEO as Decline Strategist

As the firm's primary leader, the CEO is responsible for gathering and processing information, developing firm strategy, and subsequently directing its implementation throughout the firm (Montgomery, 2008). In this role, the CEO holds the necessary decision-making authority and power to enact strategic change in face of declining firm performance (Finkelstein and Hambrick, 1996; Boeker and Goodstein, 1993; Tushman and Romanelli, 1985). Much work has been done to explore the relationship between the CEO's static characteristics and their relationship with an organization's strategic reorientation. Relying on upper echelon theory (Hambrick and Mason, 1984), researchers link CEOs' demographic traits, functional backgrounds, and experiential bases to the extent of organizational adaptation and change. These studies also inform on the causes of strategic inertia in face of an organization's adaptive potential. For CEOs, sources of this strategic inertia are often rooted in what Starbuck and Hedberg (1977) identify as 'success breeds failure' complacency. That is, CEOs operating within a bandwidth of success using industry recipes come to rely on a dominant logic concerning their firm's competitive advantage that guides the strategy process. This dominant logic, in turn, can give rise to cognitive inertia and change constraints wherein CEOs and their managers become overly reliant on their mental maps of heuristic and standardized procedures (Amason and Mooney, 2008). As such, not only are CEOs disadvantaged in their capacity to recognize sources of decline but are further hindered when formulating discontinuous, 'frame breaking' shifts necessary at times to enact decline-stemming strategies (Tushman et al., 1986). Similarly, Barker (2005) and others make the case that CEOs' aptitudes to formulate appropriate strategic responses are misdirected by their experiential, personality, and attribution biases, self-serving causal interpretations, and data-filtering capabilities. In short, strong evidence exists to support bounded rationality arguments suggesting limits in CEOs' cognitive efforts when making strategic choices.

TMT Involvement During Decline

Research on CEO influence on the strategy process during decline using upper echelon theory, attribution theory, and other perspectives has been extended to examine top management teams' (TMTs') vital involvement in effecting turnaround. Making the case that CEOs rarely engage in strategic decisions in isolation, these studies focus on TMTs' demographics (background, education, tenure, etc.), for example, to demonstrate that functional heterogeneity can provide the firm with organizational learning necessary to enact strategic reorientation. In situations of deteriorating performance, a diverse TMT is more likely to question the validity of prior strategies (Milliken and Lant, 1991). As a result, managerial learning may be enhanced via complex cognitions and flexible information-processing capabilities inherent in a heterogeneous TMT, thus allowing the organization to respond more quickly and effectively with appropriate solutions (Greening and Johnson, 1996). In contrast, TMTs, including boards of directors, can also impede the turnaround process due to managerial entrenchment (Wiersema and Bantel, 1992), groupthink (Whyte, 1989), or a group's failure to communicate their concerns about a turnaround solution (Westphal and Bednar, 2005). For example, longer tenured top managers have been shown to induce rigidity in decision-making processes and actions needed to combat decline (Greening and Johnson, 1996). These studies, among numerous others (for an extensive review, see Lohrke et al., 2004), call attention to the importance of top management's role in the turnaround strategy process.

Additionally, literature on workplace conflict informs on the incompatibilities of participants' goals and aspirations and their influence on the behavioral integration in teams and groups necessary to accomplish organizational transformation. That is, as firms deteriorate, stress and emotions of organizational participants often heighten due to loss of organizational identity, stigmatization, and political vulnerabilities, consequently impairing managerial information gathering and analysis, communication quality, and task clarity. Aside from evaluating TMT compositions and configurations, this research reaches beyond structural considerations to link task and affective inputs of conflict to individual-, group-, and organizational-level manifestations of behavior and decision making (Korsgaard et al., 2008). In addition, over the past decade, scholars have built a robust body of work on workplace aggression (Douglas et al., 2008), although how it unfolds in the context of organizational decline and the task environments and leadership qualities needed to stabilize unraveling organizations has not received attention.

Risks in Decision-making

While the strategist represents a potential cause of organizational decline (Barker, 2005; Arogyaswamy et al., 1995), the decision-maker can also influence the strategy process by either stemming or hastening the firm's ensuing performance. Two opposing theoretical perspectives have emerged within the decline literature attending to the strategy process in response to deteriorating performance and the underlying risk and rationality of those decisions. The rigidity perspective is predominantly grounded in Staw et al.'s (1981) threat rigidity theory which predicts that managers, when faced with adverse circumstances, will adopt conservative strategic behavior. Staw and colleagues argue that when confronted with external threats, managers tend to make their decisions on initiatives of efficiency, tighter budgets, cost cutting, and increased accountability. That is, poorly performing firms will narrow their scope of strategic actions and thus potentially become less innovative in their strategic response. In short, threat rigidity predicts that managers faced with performance threats are likely to reduce both the scope and nature of their innovation. The invention perspective, on the other hand, draws heavily from the precepts of prospect theory, as developed by Kahneman and Tversky (1979; see other joint publications as well), to suggest that decisions based on risk differ depending on whether a decision-maker resides in a domain of gains or losses. That is, decision-makers evaluate outcomes against some reference point, subsequently becoming risk averse when outcomes are above that particular reference point (i.e., a domain of gains), but increasingly risk seeking when outcomes fall below the reference point (i.e., domain of losses). These underpinnings of prospect theory have significant implications for understanding the strategic decisions of declining firms: in contrast to threat rigidity, managers faced with firm performance residing in the domain of losses may engage in higher-risk initiatives such as innovation in the hope of 'hitting a home run' to effect turnaround.

Decline studies using these competing frameworks remain equivocal, prompting researchers (e.g., Latham and Braun, 2009b; George et al., 2006) to focus on a variety of environmental, organizational, and managerial contingencies. This stream of research provides an increasingly comprehensive picture not only of the factors that affect decision making, but also the circumstances under which various responses help or hinder turnaround efforts. For instance, our empirical examination (Latham and Braun, 2009b) on the relationship between managerial risk profiles and risk taking with firm resources in poorly performing firms indicates that managers with low ownership participation and few slack resources tended to 'bet the farm' when facing organizational decline, thus lending support to the prospect theory view. However, within our particular context, risk taking by managers in poorly performing firms led to what Chowdhury and Lang (1993: 10) identify as an 'escalation of resource commitment to an unsuccessful course of action', thus hastening their eventual demise.

Middle Management and Other Stakeholders

Other decline studies focus on additional stakeholder participants and their differential impact on organizational turnaround. Wooldridge et al. (2008), for example, specify several dynamics relating to middle management's cognitive capacity in the context of organizational change. For one, while middle managers' strategic buy-in is critical to turnaround success, it is nevertheless contingent on their comprehension of the strategy, its objectives, and the availability of relevant skill sets to implement the strategy. Thus, senior managers must be sensitive to middle management's cognitive perspective to garner support. Also, middle managers often have a strong grasp of their firm's core competencies and capabilities and are therefore more likely to recognize the advantages and limitations of a new strategy. In this process, middle managers deliberate the strategic challenge, arrive at a consensus, and subsequently reshape the strategy to increase its prospect for success. Nevertheless, middle management involvement and participation can also impair the strategic reorientations. For example, participation can complicate the strategic decision-making process, slow managerial action and implementation, and give rise to factionalism (Ashmos et al., 1998). In similar fashion, studies attending to outside stakeholder involvement in the turnaround process highlight the importance of a firm's exchange relationship with external constituents to access resources and rebuild core capabilities (e.g., Pajunen, 2006; D'Aveni and McMillan, 1990). The underlying argument is that firms facing descent experience weakening interorganizational linkages and loss of legitimacy among investors, suppliers, buyers, and other strategic players within the organization's system. Using the resource dependence perspective (Pfeffer and Salancik, 1978) to examine the nature of the resource relationship and, increasingly, social network theory (Powell, 1990) to define stakeholders' structure-based influence, this research examines how the quality and structure of social ties among various stakeholders shape organizational decisions and actions by broadening or restricting their strategic opportunities. McDonald and Westphal (2003), for instance, demonstrate the extent to which CEOs' advice-seeking network with other executives influences perceived diagnosticity of organizational problems and the validity of decline-stemming strategies. Similarly, Pajunen (2006) provides a more comprehensive model on the direct and reciprocal impact of a variety of primary stakeholders that hinder or enhance the company's turnaround process.

From this brief appraisal of the relevant literature, it quickly becomes apparent that the relationships between the strategist and other participants both within and outside an organization have considerable bearing on the nature of the strategic process. Commenting on the strategy process in general, Chakravarthy and White (2001: 190) maintain that 'strategies represent a stream of decisions made by multiple levels of decision-makers, over time'. Indeed, under circumstances of decline, more recent research suggests that these dynamics hold true even more as key participants sever their relationships with weakened firms while other governing stakeholders become increasingly involved.

Dynamic Interactions during Decline and Turnaround

Aside from the participative complexity in the strategy process, it is important to consider additional dimensions that inform on the types of decision characteristics and the sequence of actions necessary to stem decline. We want to draw attention to several potential feedback and feed-forward paths between the strategist and stakeholders. For one, the issue of relevant human capital to enact turnaround initiatives becomes paramount in declining firms. Apart from the necessary skill set among top managers, middle managers, and the extended network of stakeholders, organizations require the culture of turnaround that encourages reinterpretations of problematic routines and, subsequently, facilitates learning and understanding of effective solutions. Early work by Whipp et al. (1989), for instance, highlights the need for managerial nurturing of organizational cultures and shared meaning (i.e., the collection of beliefs, values, and assumptions of organizational participants) when attempting strategic change. Castrogiovanni et al. (1992) and others place the onus of developing and managing corporate change culture on executives, with Cameron (1994) providing an expansive list of related dimensions, including boosting morale, building trust, facilitating communication, and promoting teamwork. In the absence of effective culture, Rosenblatt and Sheaffer (2001) argue, firms suffering decline become highly vulnerable to 'brain drain' – the loss of talent central in shaping and carrying out turnaround strategies – due to work overload, dwindling compensation and incentive schemes, limited internal career opportunities, and the probable stigma of bankruptcy (Rosenblatt and Sheaffer, 2001; Bedeian and Armenakis, 1998). As such, the ensuing leadership anemia precipitates further decline by changing the inherent capabilities and cognitions of those left to deal with the sinking ship. Failing organizations are additionally destabilized as a negative 'bandwagon effect' spurs subsequent departures by organizational members, thus placing the firm on a path towards its downward spiral.

Decline and Leadership

A discussion of the strategy process during decline is incomplete without attention to the role of executive leadership. Numerous turnaround successes have been attributed largely to one central figure: IBM's Lou Gerstner moving the company into IT services, Steve Jobs' reorientation of Apple towards digital media convergence, and Lee Iacocca's rescue of Chrysler with the introduction of the minivan. These accounts highlight the importance of turnaround 'artists' with the necessary vision, sense of urgency, speed of decision, and level of commitment to achieve strategic renewal and long-term competitive advantage. Nevertheless, they provide only a partial picture of executive leadership. Strategic change and renewal studies point to differences between incremental change strategies and those involving radical reorientations (Kuwada, 1998; Tushman and Romanelli, 1985); their distinctions have been variably defined as incremental versus disruptive (Tushman et al., 1986), frame bending versus frame breaking (Nadler and Tushman, 1986), and incremental versus radical innovation (Dewar and Dutton, 1986). These categorizations prompt a closer study of the cognitive capabilities, experience bases, and internal control systems needed to align appropriate strategic responses to decline. Depending on root causes and whether decline situations call for drastic initiatives or gradual improvements, there is a clear need for executives, as change agents, to possess the leadership characteristics, qualities, and capabilities suitable to the practices, routines, structures, and technologies for each strategy. To date, only a handful of researchers have attended to distinct managerial profiles and requirements relevant to each category of change strategy needed to halt decline.

STRATEGY MAKING PROCESSES AND FIRM PERFORMANCE

The last part of our dynamic diagram draws attention to outcomes of turnaround efforts in declining firms. Process scholars have called attention to the importance of linking strategy process research to strategy outcomes in efforts to increase its pragmatic value to managers (Hutzschenreuter and Kleindienst, 2006; Chakravarthy and White, 2001; Pettigrew, 1997). This shortcoming is evident in the decline literature where processual work remains largely descriptive in nature. More scholarly work is required that offers theoretical insight, as well as managerial guidance, into the linkages between the underlying strategic process adopted by managers and the fate of the firm. Having discussed in previous sections the various aspects of decline origins, the strategist, and other firm participants, we now focus on the process–content–outcome link.

Modes of Outcomes

At a general level, a recovery effort is dictated by the firm's present and future domain (i.e., customer segment, product lines, etc.), the scope of its strategic actions, and the strategic contours involved with turning around the firm (Sheppard and Chowdhury, 2005). These, along with the availability of necessary resources and capabilities, may be viewed to provide the firm with three strategic outcomes: retrenchment, renewal, and replacement (Walshe et al., 2004). Retrenchment is the product of largely short-term actions (e.g., fiscal conservatism, cost reductions, and operational improvements) needed to stabilize the firm, curtail its resource losses, and to attend to immediate problems which have precipitated its decline (Robbins and Pearce, 1992). In contrast, firms pursuing renewal aim to reorient their strategic direction via 'a fundamental review of the activities of the organization and their long-term prospects [and] a detailed analysis of the culture and leadership of the organization and a concerted effort to change the way that it works' (Walshe et al., 2004: 204). Third, a firm's performance deterioration and survival threat can prompt top management team replacements as a catalyst for organizational adaptation and strategic change (Karaevli, 2007; Barker et al., 2001; Boeker and Goodstein, 1993). We proffer an illustration that attends to all three responses. For instance, technology disruptions represent k-type, or externally generated decline threats, that destabilize established competitors. Falling victim to the migration of customers to new competitors' superior (i.e., *disrupting*) products and services, these established firms often react with internally oriented responses such as product upgrades and process efficiencies of the disrupted technology. In what Christensen (1997) identifies as the 'technology mudslide hypothesis', managers of incumbent firms strain to remain operationally efficient while demand in the mainstream market dwindles. For firms already on the path of decline, their managers may opt to retrench even more rather than take a competitive position within the newly created market. To provide an example, Dell, the early innovator in built-to-order PCs, continues to experience eroding profitability and shrinking market share due to competitor mimicry in supply chain management and cost advantages from more sizeable players such as HP. Furthermore, with consumer preferences migrating to smaller, more versatile, and more cost effective communication devices such as smartphones and netbooks, Dell's performance deterioration is further precipitated by reduced demand in its core product.

Adner (2002: 684) maintains that in light of technology disruptions, 'consumers with sufficiently satisfied functional requirements are more concerned with differences in absolute price than with differences in price/performance points'. Faced with steep price erosions and larger cost-based players, Dell's competitive priority, as per its CEO's 2008 letter to shareholders, is on 'costs across all processes and organizations'. In other words, Dell is currently engaging a retrenchment response to combat unfavorable competitive dynamics and eroding internal core competencies. As discussed earlier, Apple, facing similar dynamics in the late 1990s, opted for a renewal strategy by reorienting its core business towards consumer electronics. Today, Apple enjoys market domination by continuously innovating next-generation electronic devices. As was the case with both Apple and Dell, poor performance also precipitated the removal of key members of the leadership and management of the organization, with succession either from within the firm or outside hires. As Mueller and Barker (1997) argue, the intent of replacement is to overcome the strategic inertia arising from the old guard's narrow perspective on decline problems and solutions and its psychological commitments to failing courses of action (Hambrick et al., 1993). Nevertheless, succession scholars argue that critical firm- and industry-specific skills may be lost, and that new CEOs, lacking adequate institutional knowledge, may engage in premature and uninformed changes (Karaevli, 2007). While we discuss these three strategic responses independently, as the Apple and Dell examples suggest, they are not mutually exclusive.

Measuring Outcomes

The outcomes of managerial responses to decline are, in the most simple terms, recovery success and failure. However, difficulties arise in evaluating these successes and failures since turnaround measures entail a multitude of dimensions, including longevity of success, strength of firm resources, competitive position, distance from bankruptcy, and, at a basic level, firm survival (Sheppard and Chowdhury, 2005). Furthermore, most operationalizations of both decline and turnaround remain heavily focused on economic measures of efficiency (Arogyaswamy et al., 1995). While the variety of indicators in the extant literature provides for a varied picture, Hambrick and D'Aveni (1988) make a strong case for both economic and non-economic dimensions to capture the intermediate steps in the turnaround process. For example, we know little about the circumstances under which managers at declining firms are likely to realize performance gains from dedicating finite resources to the risky endeavor of innovation, and when they are better served to conserve those resources, as well as to pursue more conservative, efficiency-driven strategies. The notion of feedback loops (Latham and Braun, 2009a) has significant repercussions for advancing our understanding of organizational decline because management's cognitions, evaluations, and affective reactions to performance shortcomings are likely to either accelerate (i.e., destabilize) or impede (i.e., balance) the decline (Lindsley et al., 1995). Obviously managers expect any innovations they make in response to decline to reverse the decline process, but the literature suggests that is not always the case (Hambrick and D'Aveni, 1988). More specifically, the best intended strategies can compound an already bad situation; as Cameron et al. (1988: 8) acknowledge, 'choosing the wrong strategy, or implementing the correct strategy poorly, can decrease organizational adaptation and further hamper the flow of resources'. As such, we anticipate a distinction between self-correcting outcomes, wherein management engages decision and actions that promote an incremental turnaround effort with a long-term prospect of success, and self-reinforcing feedback loops that lead to downward spirals and, if not arrested, eventual organizational collapse.

CONCLUSION

Throughout this chapter, we have touched on various aspects of the relationship between antecedents, processes, and outcomes in the context of organizational decline, to lay bare the intricacies in this type of research and to provide an impetus for scholars to engage this timely topic. In doing so, we have also exposed several unresolved and neglected issues in the strategy process literature on decline. Numerous opportunities exist for researchers to take up the reins studying how strategies unfold during decline. We attend to our framework to highlight some areas with strong potential for future explorations.

For one, causal factors of decline require more in-depth treatment. Indeed, while performance deterioration may represent the independent variable in this type of research, the extent to which effective turnaround strategies can be formulated will depend on managers possessing appropriate cognitive and experiential skills to meet particular causes of decline. For example, our brief mention of recession-induced decline represents an opportunity for researchers to engage in one of the most important but overlooked areas in the strategic management field (Pearce and Michael, 2006). As is evident from the current economic crisis, recessions affect most industrial sectors, making it difficult for firms to seek refuge from the accompanying fallout. In this case, the combination of external demand shocks and low environmental munificence presents managers a unique challenge of timing the eventual economic recovery, maintaining slack resources and employee morale, and opportunistically scanning for potential acquisitions or innovations. These recessionary effects and the subsequent managerial strategic issue framing and decisions required to weather economic downturns stand in stark contrast to our earlier previous example of managers facing decline as a consequence of technological disruptions. Hence, the distinction between internal and external causes of decline is an important first step to clarifying the subsequent strategy process to turnaround since it forces a deeper understanding of the interactions between various causes of decline and the firm's missing resources and capabilities or dysfunctional processes necessary to bring about realignment. Additional dimensions of interest include the temporal aspects of decline causes, contrasting, for example, Bear Stearns' rapid collapse due to loss of investor confidence to GM's slow downward spiral in a series of strategic product missteps, as well as exploring causes, interpretations, and subsequent turnaround responses between service and manufacturing businesses, as well as cross-cultural and cross-border treatments of strategy processes in faltering firms. In general, however, only by specifying internal and external causes of decline and linking their dynamic interaction can researchers and practitioners receive a more comprehensive understanding of how to interpret this complex phenomenon.

The human element of organizational decline requires additional inquiry as well. While reaching beyond static data (e.g., functional background, gender, education, etc.) on managers poses great challenges, we perceive a void in research peering inside the mindsets of those affected by decline. As

Van de Ven (1992: 181) puts forth, 'if the purpose of a study is to understand how to manage the formulation or implementation of an organizational strategy, it will be necessary for researchers to place themselves into the manager's temporal and contextual frames of reference'. In the case of decline, various trigger events are bound to be framed and processed differently, thereby impacting participants' nature and strength of cognitive, evaluative, and affective reactions. How these individual, group, and organizational interactions play out and to what extent they help or hinder decision-making processes and effective turnaround remain unclear. In some cases, as Westphal and Bednar (2005) and others put forth, task-related dissension can help organizational participants detect underlying performance problems, evaluate the merits of various turnaround actions, and build consensus concerning effective implementation of strategies.

Similarly, research exploring stakeholder influences and their positive outcomes or conflicts in troubled firms has gained increasing treatment from management scholars (Arogyaswamy et al., 1995; Pajunen, 2006, 2008). Indeed, creditors, suppliers, consumers, and so on, are viewed to both help and hinder recovery courses of action, depending on their motivations, dedications, and perceptions of risk and future prospects. Future research avenues include exploring, at the individual, group, and organizational level, issues of trust, mutual benefit, collaboration and interdependence, and degrees of formal and informal relationships of stakeholders involved in formulation and implementation procedures. Indeed, we envision multiple scenarios of stakeholder conflicts where suppliers or creditors, for instance, would rather see an organization perish than prosper. These may be explained by particular configurations of relational and structural embeddedness, as well as resource dependencies and strategic networks. Furthermore, managerial sensitivities and orientations, perceptions of urgency, and means of communication to decline may differ for public versus private firms, as well as across other types of organizational forms encompassing different sets of stakeholders and related demands and expectations (e.g., family firms).

In our chapter, we provide avenues for additional research attending to issues of strategic content and outcome in underperforming firms. However, turnaround responses and actions cannot be studied in a vacuum since 'strategic decisions are shaped by a variety of contextual influences' (Bateman and Zeithaml, 1989: 59). Our framework indicates that researchers take a more holistic and dynamic view to the study of organizational decline processes wherein the disparate parts interact with each other. Given the confluence of participants, environments, systems, and processes to support turnaround efforts, it is common for stages of decline to 'slop over' (Greinger in Van de Ven, 1992), or even to occur at multiple junctures in an organization's efforts to stabilize. As such, it becomes important to distinguish between sequential and non-recursive developments when taking struggling organizations under consideration. In fact, in much of the decline process literature to date, we perceive an over-reliance on stage theories (Walshe et al., 2004) and linear process models (Arogyaswamy et al., 1995), which lead researchers and practitioners to overlook potentially overlapping stages of decline that can differentially impact managerial perceptions and related processes. While recent studies have identified important managerial, organizational, and environmental contingencies, what is becoming increasingly evident is that causes and consequences of decline entail a multitude of attributes that interact to destabilize an organization. In step with Child's (1972) long-standing view that a firm's performance represents both an input as well as an outcome, and that the combination of internal and external elements influences the constraints of managerial decision making, we believe that an understanding of the decline and turnaround process can be greatly enhanced by adhering more closely to specific developmental process models. Just as defining the meaning of process in general drives the family of theories to be employed and the subsequent appropriateness of research designs and methodologies (Van de Ven, 1992), it is necessary for decline scholars studying the formulation and implementation of strategic change to specify relevant paradigms when exploring causal relationships, identifying process constructs, or attempting to uncover progressions of incidents or activities. Beyond employing traditional event sequence analyses of process models, scholars can also draw on configurational theories (Meyer et al., 1993), thereby side-stepping issues of uni-directional relationships and separate constituent parts to acknowledge the disorder and diversity of sources that destabilize an organization and the actions and decisions needed to reestablish its wellbeing.

Lastly, as mentioned, decline research over the past two decades has successfully teased apart various aspects of organizational decline (e.g., crisis, stagnation, change, etc.). While these conceptual classifications have produced robust theoretical and empirical research streams, we concede that the domain of organizational decline is today lacking in coherence and focus. For a theme receiving widespread academic attention in the 1980s, a cursory search through two decades' worth of academic journals indicates fewer than eighty published papers with mention of 'organizational decline' in their abstract. This dearth stands in stark contrast with the topic of mergers and acquisitions, for instance, with thousands of published studies. This is not to say that our understanding of organizational decline is not significantly enriched; rather, we maintain that many topics, including turnaround, bankruptcy, and organizational death, intrinsically fall under the general purview of organizational decline. As such, organizational decline, as an investigative domain and a delineated branch in the management literature, can be enhanced by strategy process and content researchers explicitly acknowledging this domain and, more importantly, bringing together disparate aspects of strategy process and content in underperforming firms under the overarching theme of organizational decline. The body of knowledge concerning this fascinating and ever-present phenomenon can be revived and buttressed by recognizing its fractured state and actively bringing it to the forefront of the management discipline's attention. While managerial efforts in turning around poorly performing firms may be inherently complex and messy, the scholarly community can bring vital understanding to this timely topic.

REFERENCES

Adner, R. (2002), 'When are technologies disruptive? A demand-based view of the emergence of competition', *Strategic Management Journal*, **23**: 667–688.
Amason, A. and A. Mooney (2008), 'The Icarus paradox revisited: How strong performance sows the seeds of dysfunction in future strategic decision-making', *Strategic Organization*, **6**: 407–434.
Amburgey, T., D. Kelly and W. Barnett (1993), 'Resetting the clock: The dynamics of organizational failure', *Administrative Science Quarterly*, **38**: 51–73.
Armenakis, A. and G. Bedeian (1999), 'Organizational change: A review of theory and research in the 1990s', *Journal of Management*, **25**: 293–315.
Arogyaswamy, K., V. Barker and M.Yasai-Ardekani (1995), 'Firm turnarounds: An integrative two-stage model', *Journal of Management Studies*, **32**: 493–525.
Ashmos, D., D. Duchon and R. McDaniel (1998), 'Participation in strategic decision making: The role of organizational predisposition and issue interpretation', *Decision Sciences*, **29**: 25–51.
Barker, V. (2005), 'Traps in diagnosing organizational failure', *Journal of Business Strategy*, **26**(2): 44–50.
Barker, V. and P. Barr (2002), 'Linking top manager attributions to strategic reorientation in declining firms attempting turnarounds', *Journal of Business Research*, **55**: 963–979.
Barker, V., P. Paterson and G. Mueller (2001), 'Organizational causes and strategic consequences of the extent of top management team replacement during turnaround attempts', *Journal of Management Studies*, **38**: 235–269.
Bateman, T. and C. Zeithaml (1989), 'The psychological context of strategic decisions: A model and convergent experimental findings', *Strategic Management Journal*, **10**: 59–74.
Bedeian, A. and A. Armenakis (1998), 'The cesspool syndrome: How dreck floats to the top of declining organizations', *Academy of Management Executive*, **12**: 58–63.
Boeker, W. and J. Goodstein (1991), 'Organizational performance and adaptation: Effects of environment and performance on changes in board composition', *Academy of Management Journal*, **34**: 805–826.
Boeker, W. and J. Goodstein (1993), 'Performance and successor choice: The moderating effects of governance and ownership', *Academy of Management Journal*, **36**: 172–186.
Burns, T. and G. Stalker (1961), *The Management of Innovation*, London: Tavistock.
Cameron, K. (1994), 'Strategies for successful organizational downsizing', *Human Resource Management Journal*, **33**: 189–211.

Cameron, K., D. Whetten and M. Kim (1987), 'Organizational dysfunctions of decline', *Academy of Management Journal*, **30**: 126–138.

Cameron, K., S. Sutton and D. Whetten (1988), 'Issues in organizational decline', in K. Cameron, S. Sutton and D. Whetten (eds), *Readings in Organizational Decline: Frameworks, Research and Prescriptions*, Boston: Ballinger, pp. 3–19.

Castrogiovanni, G. (1991), 'Environmental munificence: A theoretical assessment', *Academy of Management Review*, **16**: 542–565.

Castrogiovanni, G., B. Baliga and R. Kidwell (1992), 'Curing sick businesses: Changing CEOs in turnaround efforts', *Academy of Management Executive*, **6**: 26–39.

Chakravarthy, B. and R White (2001), 'Strategy process: Forming, implementing and changing strategies', in A. Pettigrew, H. Thomas and R. Whittington (eds), *Handbook of Strategy and Management*, London: Sage, pp. 182–205.

Chattopadhyay, P., W. Glick and G. Huber (2001), 'Organizational action in response to threats and opportunities', *Academy of Management Journal*, **44**: 937–955.

Chowdhury, S. and J. Lang (1993), 'Crisis, decline and turnaround: A test of competing hypotheses for short-term performance improvement in small firms', *Journal of Small Business Management*, **31**: 8–18.

Child, J. (1972), 'Organizational structure, environment, and performance: The role of strategic choice', *Sociology*, **6**: 2–22.

Christensen, C. (1997), *The Innovator's Dilemma: When New Technologies Cause Great Firms to Fail*, Boston, MA: Harvard Business School Press.

Cyert, R. and J. March (1963), *A Behavioral Theory of the Firm*, Englewood Cliffs, NJ: Prentice Hall.

Daily, C. and D. Dalton (1994), 'Bankruptcy and corporate governance: The impact of board composition and structure', *Academy of Management Journal*, **37**: 1603–1618.

D'Aveni, R. and I. McMillan (1990), 'Crisis and the content of managerial communications: A study of the focus of attention of top managers in surviving and failing firms', *Administrative Science Quarterly*, **35**: 634–657.

Dewar, R. and J. Dutton (1986), 'The adoption of radical and incremental innovations: An empirical analysis', *Management Science*, **32**: 1422–1433.

Douglas, S., C. Kiewitz, M. Martinko, P. Harvey, Y. Kim and J. Chun (2008), 'Cognitions, emotions, and evaluations: An elaboration likelihood model for workplace aggression', *Academy of Management Review*, **33**: 425–451.

Finkelstein, S. (2005), 'When bad things happen to good companies: Strategy failure and flawed executives', *Journal of Business Strategy*, **26**: 19–28.

Finkelstein, S. and D. C. Hambrick (1996), *Strategic Leadership: Top Executives and Their Effects on Organizations*, Minneapolis/St. Paul, MN: West Publishing Company.

Floyd, S.W. and B. Wooldridge (1997), 'Middle management's strategic influence and organizational performance', *Journal of Management Studies*, **34**: 465–485.

George, E., P. Chattopadhyay, S. B. Sitkin and J. Barden (2006), 'Cognitive underpinnings of institutional persistence and change: A framing perspective', *Academy of Management Review*, **31**: 347–365.

Goncalo, J. and M. Duguid (2008), 'Hidden consequences of the group serving bias: Causal attributions and the quality of group decision making', *Organizational Behavior and Human Decision Processes*, **107**: 219–233.

Greening, D. and R. Johnson (1996), 'Do managers and strategies matter? A study in crisis', *Journal of Management Studies*, **33**: 25–51.

Grinyer, P., D. Mayes and P. McKiernan (1988), *Sharpbenders: The Secret of Unleashing Corporate Potential*, Oxford: Basil Blackwell.

Hambrick, D. and R. D'Aveni (1988), 'Large corporate failures as downward spirals', *Administrative Science Quarterly*, **33**: 1–23.

Hambrick, D. and P. Mason (1984), 'Upper echelons: The organization as a reflection of its top managers', *Academy of Management Review*, **9**: 193–206.

Hambrick, D., M. Geletkanycz and J. Fredrickson (1993), 'Top executive commitment to the status quo: Some tests of its determinants', *Strategic Management Journal*, **14**: 401–418.

Hutzschenreuter, T. and I. Kleindienst (2006), 'Strategy-process research: What have we learned and what is still to be explored', *Journal of Management*, 32: 673–720.

Kahneman, D. and A. Tversky (1979), 'Prospect theory: An analysis of decision under risk', *Econometrica*, 47: 262–291.

Karaevli, A. (2007), 'Performance consequences of new CEO "outsiderness": Moderating effects of pre- and post-succession contexts', *Strategic Management Journal*, 28: 681–706.

Korsgaard, M., S. Jeong, D. Mahony and A. Pitariu (2008), 'A multilevel view of intragroup conflict', *Journal of Management*, 34: 1222–1252.

Kuwada, K. (1998), 'Strategic learning: The continuous side of discontinuous strategic change', *Organization Science*, 9: 719–736.

Latham, S. and M. Braun (2009a), 'Organizational decline and innovation: Closing the loop', Paper presented at Academy of Management Meeting, August, Chicago, IL.

Latham, S. and M. Braun (2009b), 'Managerial risk, innovation, and organizational decline', *Journal of Management*, 35(2).

Lindsley, D., D. Brass and J. Thomas (1995), 'Efficacy-performance spirals: A multilevel perspective', *Academy of Management Review*, 20: 645–678.

Lohrke, F., A. Bedeian and T. Palmer (2004), 'The role of top management teams in formulating and implementing turnaround strategies: A review and research agenda', *International Journal of Management Reviews*, 5(6): 63–90.

McArthur, A. and P. Nystrom (1991), 'Environmental dynamism, complexity, and munificence as moderators of strategy–performance relationships', *Journal of Business Research*, 23, 349–361.

McDonald, M. and J. Westphal (2003), 'Getting by with the advice of their friends: CEOs' advice networks and firms' strategic responses to poor performance', *Administrative Science Quarterly*, 48: 1–32.

McKiernan, P. (2002), 'Turnarounds, in D. Faulkner and A. Campbell (eds), *Oxford Handbook of Strategic Management*', Oxford: Oxford University Press.

Meyer, A., A. Tsui and C. Hinnings (1993), 'Configurational approaches to organizational analysis', *Academy Management Journal*, 36: 1175–1195.

Milburn, T., R. Schuler and K. Watman (1983), 'Organizational crisis. Part I: Definition and conceptualization', *Human Relations*, 36: 1141–1160.

Milliken, F. and T. Lant (1991), 'The effect of an organization's recent performance history on strategic persistence and change: The role of managerial interpretations', in J. Dutton (ed.), *Advances in Strategic Management*, Greenwich, CT: JAI Press, pp. 129–156.

Montgomery, C. (2008), 'Putting leadership back into strategy', *Harvard Business Review*, January: 54–60.

Mueller, G. and V. Barker (1997), 'Upper echelons and board characteristics of turnaround and nonturnaround declining firms', *Journal of Business Research*, 39: 119–134.

Nadler, D. and M. Tushman (1989), 'Organizational frame bending: Principles for managing reorientation', *Academy of Management Executive*, 3: 194–204.

Pajunen, K. (2006), 'Stakeholder influences in organizational survival', *Journal of Management Studies*, 43(6): 1261–1288.

Pajunen, K. (2008), 'The nature of organizational mecahnisms', *Organizational Studies*, 29: 1449–1468.

Pearce, J. and S. Michael (2006), 'Strategies to prevent economic recessions from causing business failure', *Business Horizons*, 49: 201–209.

Pettigrew, A. (1997), 'What is a processual analysis?', *Scandinavian Journal of Management*, 13: 337–348.

Pfeffer, J. and G. Salancik (1978), *The External Control of Organizations: A Resource Dependence Perspective*, New York: Harper & Row.

Powell, W. (1990), 'Neither market nor hierarchy: Network forms of organization', in B. M. Staw and L. L. Cummings (eds), *Research in Organizational Behavior*, Greenwich, CT: JAI Press, pp. 295–336.

Robbins, D. and J. Pearce (1992), 'Turnaround: Retrenchment and recovery', *Strategic Management Journal*, 12: 287–309.

Rosenblatt, Z. and B. Mannheim (1996), 'Organizational response to decline in the Israeli electronics industry', *Organization Studies*, **17**: 953–984.

Rosenblatt, Z. and Z. Sheaffer (2001), 'Brain drain in declining organizations: Toward a research agenda', *Journal of Organizational Behavior*, **22**: 409–424.

Sharfman, M. and J. Dean (1991), 'Conceptualizing and measuring the organizational environment: A multidimensional approach', *Journal of Management*, **17**: 681–700.

Sheppard, J. and S. Chowdhury (2005), 'Riding the wrong wave: Organizational failure as a failed turnaround', *Long Range Planning*, **38**: 239–260.

Starbuck, W. and B. Hedberg (1977), 'Saving an organization from a stagnating environment', in H. Thorelli (ed.), *Strategy + Structure = Performance*, Bloomington, IN: Indiana University Press, pp. 249–258.

Staw, B., L. Sandelands and J. Dutton (1981), 'Threat-rigidity effects in organizational behavior: A multilevel analysis', *Administrative Science Quarterly*, **26**: 501–524.

Thurow, L (1996), *The Future of Capitalism*, New York: Penguin Books.

Tushman, M. and E. Romanelli (1985), 'Organizational evolution: A metamorphosis model of convergence and reorientation', *Research in Organizational Behavior*, **7**: 171–222.

Tushman, M., W. Newman and E. Romanelli (1986), 'Convergence and upheaval: Managing the unsteady pace of organizational evolution', *California Management Review*, **29**: 29–44.

Van de Ven, A. (1992), 'Suggestions for studying strategy process: A research note', *Strategic Management Journal*, **13**: 169–188.

Walshe, K., G. Harvey, P. Hyde and N. Pandit (2004), 'Organizational failure and turnaround: Lessons for public services from the for-profit sector', *Public Money and Management*, **24**: 201–208.

Westphal, J. and M. Bednar (2005), 'Pluralistic ignorance in corporate boards and firms' strategic persistence in response to low firm performance', *Administrative Science Quarterly*, **50**: 262–298.

Whipp, R., R. Rosenfeld and A. Pettigrew (1989), 'Culture and competitiveness: Evidence from two mature UK industries', *Journal of Management Studies*, **26**: 561–585.

Whyte, G. (1989), 'Groupthink reconsidered', *Academy of Management Review*, **14**: 40–56.

Wiersema, M. and K. Bantel (1992), 'Top management team demography and corporate strategic change', *Academy of Management Journal*, **35**: 91–121.

Wooldridge, B., T. Schmid and S.W. Floyd (2008), 'The middle management perspective on strategy process: Contributions, synthesis, and future research', *Journal of Management*, **34**: 1190–1221.

22 An institutional view of process strategy in the public sector*

P. Devereaux Jennings, Paul A. Zandbergen and Martin L. Martens

> Scholarly strategy process research goes on, perhaps more than ever, suggesting that there is something fundamental and deeply interesting and profound about how strategies are made, where they originate, and how the process of strategy-making impacts the performance of organizations. (Szulanski et al., 2005: xv)

In their 2005 compilation, The Strategy Process, Szulanski, Porac and Doz summarized the development of the process strategy field. They maintained that the field, though highly fragmented, has been held together by research choices around four theoretical issues: 1) the meaning of process, 2) the type of study, 3) the primary level of analysis, and 4) the locus of action. Past process strategy researchers emphasized emergence as process and detailed emergence via in-depth, intra-organizational case studies of strategic decision making, often at the top management team level. Current strategy researchers have chosen to view the strategy process as a more complex phenomenon, best studied at multiple levels of analysis with comparative cases or longitudinal analysis to capture a shifting locus of action.

This chapter is part of this newer strain of process strategy research. Strategy is conceptualized as being multidimensional, involving hot and cold issues as well as aligned and unaligned interests. The strategy process is also studied from multiple levels of analysis and via over-time qualitative (historical) and quantitative analysis in order to capture the shifting locus of action. However, unlike much strategy process research, our work is devoted to theorizing and testing concepts about process strategy in the *public sector*. In the wake of Enron, Parmalat, Lehman Brothers and the broader economic shocks experienced by the financial system, there has been a call by practitioners and strategists alike for more attention to strategy in the public sector (Collins, 2001; Dobbin and Baum, 2000; *Economist*, 2009). The public sector refers to the domain occupied by governmental, non-governmental, and not-for-profit organizations (Vago, 1994). The public sector also includes activities of private organizations that are formally regulated by a governmental organization (Landy and

Levin, 1995; Perkmann and Spicer, 2009). While public sector organizations and their strategy processes have many features that are consistent with private sector organizations and their strategy processes, public sector organizations also differ substantially in a few. Strategy in these organizations is normally derived first from its network of stakeholders and external controlling agencies and then from its top management team – not the other way around. In addition, these public sector organization strategies rely heavily on formal legitimacy. At the very least, then, the strategy process in the public sector offers researchers a more extreme case of power dynamics (March and Olsen, 1989; Stryker, 2000; Wilson, 1989).

The perspective on which we rely to make our contributions to process strategy research is institutional theory. In keeping with process strategy research, institutional theory emphasizes the emergence of threads of idea, belief, and action. Institutional theory also works at multiple levels of analysis and argues that the process and outcomes are often unintended, not involving either efficiency or technical criteria. However, as some process strategy researchers have begun to realize (Farjoun, 2002), institutional theory has a set of mechanisms that appear to work well with notions of strategy emergence, such as the formulation of new strategies via contested logics in the field (Lounsbury, 2002; Seo and Creed, 2002) and the adoption of new strategies due to coercive, normative, and mimetic forces (Mizruchi and Fein, 1999; Ruef and Scott, 1998). Institutional theory seems particularly useful as a means of understanding public sector strategy, because, by definition, such sectors are more institutional in nature than private sector ones (Meyer and Scott, 1983; Scott, 2001).

Yet we do simply transport institutional theory into the process strategy domain. We also try to offer insights and evidence to help address some critical, unsolved problems within institutional theory. One is how inter-organizational mechanisms sort out competing field-level logics (Marquis and Lounsbury, 2007). Another is how boundary objects, like policy statements, offer points of reference for change in the institutional system (Bechky, 2003). Yet another is how social movements are reflected in new policy initiatives (Hoffman and Bertels, 2009). These issues are explored using our long-term research on water law and regulation (Jennings and Zandbergen, 1995; Jennings et al., 2002, 2005; Schulz et al., 2008).

AN INSTITUTIONAL MODEL OF PROCESS STRATEGY

Institutional theory does not have a single agreed-upon set of arguments about the formation and adoption of strategy. Nevertheless, there is some agreement on terms, levels of analysis, potential loci of action, and mechanism involved in institutionalization (Scott, 2001). We describe a generic institutional model of process strategy, applicable in multiple sectors, then adapt and refine this model to describe process strategy in the public sector.

From an institutional perspective, strategy refers to what organizational members construe an organization's strategy to be. This means that the label 'strategy' is an important signifier. In addition, strategy is the set of related practices (repertoires, rites, underlying activities) that are part of the firm's formally recognized plan (Barry and Elmes, 1997). Thus, strategy for an institutionalist fits with Mintzberg's famous dictum: strategy is both plan and action, intended and unintended (Mintzberg, 1987).

The plan and its processes are embedded in a much broader social and cultural milieu. This broader milieu can be viewed as comprising two groups of organizations: 1) the field of relevant organizations, and 2) the task environment around the focal organization. The field involves all organizations dependent on similar social and economic forces for economic survival and legitimacy, which includes populations, industries, networks, and communities or organizations (Powell and DiMaggio, 1991). The field is also held together by deeper schemas of values and acceptable patterns of action, what Friedland and Alford (1991) call 'logics'. The task environment involves the buyers, suppliers, competitors, governmental units, and other organizations with which the firm has interaction (Scott and Davis, 2005). Unlike the field, the operation of the task environment involves much more explicit power process based on the resource dependencies among firms. The 'mezzo' level encompasses not only the task environment but also the linkages from these actors to the field and from the mezzo actors down into their focal organizations; that is, the cross-level linkages depicted in Figure 22.1.[1]

From an institutional view, 'process strategy' (not simply 'strategy') entails not only the focal firm's strategy but the related sets of strategies pursued by organizations around the firm (the linked stars in Figure 22.1). A strategy is created by a key field member and then adopted by some, but not all, field members, leading to differences in their success (Martens et al., 2007). The strategy of diversification was first adopted by centrally networked, powerful Fortune 500 firms, and then diffused across key industries in the economy, especially manufacturing, but not in resource and utilities (Chandler, 1980). The diffusion accounted for the success of these firms in the 1930–1960 era, relative to competitors who were not as diverse and multidivisional (Fligstein, 1990).

This diffusion process is rarely smooth because it is based on the competitive positioning and counter-positioning of firms, each trying to garner

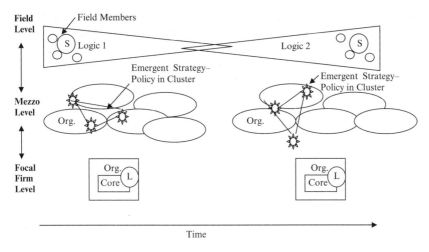

S = the State; L = leader.

Figure 22.1   An institutional model of process strategy

social legitimacy and/or economic success (Scott et al., 2000; Leblebici et al., 1991). The diversification strategy and multidivisional form diffused in various industries because of highly networked actors, who had some economic similarities but, more importantly, shared similar social and intellectual circles (Palmer et al., 1993). In addition, there is research that shows that clusters or niches of adopting firms must jointly enact strategy in order to make it work well. In their study of Scottish knitwear, Porac et al. (1995) show that the producers of wool and the crafters of sweaters form product-oriented groups, controlling output and maintaining the brand, while allowing each subgroup to jockey for more market share in this closed community. A fundamental translation has occurred in the meaning of apparel manufacturing when one discusses 'Scottish knit-wear': this interpretation helps build the market system (not the reverse), and subsequent knitwear designs must build off of this understanding. In Figure 22.1's terms, the cluster of networked organizations adopting and promoting a strategy in the first time period must endure until the second if the strategy is to be successful.

In fact, each focal firm in an interorganizational network must interpret and translate a strategy into its own terms (Sahlin and Wedlin, 2008). As Rao et al. (2003) have shown, this re-mixing tends to draw on new cultural categories and sets of understanding, potentially creating a new strategy in the process, as *nouvelle cuisine* did with traditional French cooking. Part of the strategy-making process is building narratives that cobble together these pieces (i.e., use 'bricolage') in convincing ways for those who provide tangible and intangible resources for the firm (Gioia and Thomas, 1996; Lounsbury and Glynn, 2001; Martens et al., 2007). This makes organizational leaders and social groups in the focal firm important in the bricolage effort (Maguire et al., 2004). These actors are depicted as 'L' within the focal firm in Figure 22.1. It also implies that each star in Figure 22.1 is a focal firm-specific version of a strategy and not completely equivalent.

Process Strategy in the Public Sector

The unique aspects of process strategy in the public sector can be understood by examining the institutional model in Figure 22.1 vertically and horizontally. From a vertical, top-down perspective, all organizations in the public sector have been shown to rely more heavily on legitimacy from the State ('S') than they do in the private sector (DiMaggio and Powell, 1983; Oliver, 1991). The dependence on the State, whether at the regional, national or international level, means that the type of strategies adopted must, first and foremost, be acceptable to any oversight agencies from the State. For example, hospitals adopted more budget-based planning starting in the 1980s because State agencies required better accounting practices during this newer era, even though accounting practices had always been important for the technical operation of hospitals as very expensive physical plants (Scott et al., 2000).

At the field and organizational level, there is a great deal of interpretation and translation of State policies, but often in quite a different way than among private sector organizations. Research has shown that organizations in this sector tend to loosely couple their core practices and to adopt strategies symbolically, while pursuing really important strategies or practices elsewhere (Dobbin and Sutton, 1998; Edelman, 1992). Thus, in Figure 22.1, we see the core of the focal organization ('Core') is normally buffered by its periphery from its task environment (March and Olsen, 1989; Meyer and Rowan, 1977).

Recent institutional work on public sector organizations has also demonstrated significant 'push-back' from the focal firm on the government-controlled field. In Figure 22.1, this push-back is depicted by the two-headed arrow from the focal firm to the mezzo and field levels as well as by the relationship among the organizations that negotiate strategy and policy at the mezzo level. For instance, laws governing practices like tax breaks for child care or civil rights in the workplace are re-interpreted significantly by interested and mobilized actors at the mezzo level (Kelly,

2003; Pedriana and Stryker, 2004). Indeed, at key junctures in economic development, regulations itself derives from competing models of business practice fought out among financers, the government, and shareholders at the mezzo and field levels (North, 1990; Dobbin and Dowd, 2000; Selznick, 1949).

This implies that the critical level of analysis and locus action in the public sector is the mezzo one where policies are formed and interpreted in networks (Dobbin and Baum, 2000). In traditional terms within policy theory, these are the overarching policies in the system that incorporate political objectives, interests, and techniques, and guide governmental bodies at the micro level (Landy and Levin, 1995). From an institutional theory standpoint, these policies include the formal and informal policies that are actually pursued in practice, something we term 'policy initiatives' (see 'Policy' in Figure 22.1) in order to distinguish it from policies as institutional logics (Hoffman and Vantresca, 2002). Business models fostered by governmental policy, law, and action can thus be construed roughly as extensions of policy initiatives (Dobbin and Dowd, 2000; Perkmann and Spicer, 2009). It is these policy initiatives in the interorganizational networks that form the core of the public sector strategy process.

From a horizontal perspective, the enactment of the policies at one point in time normally leads to different but related policies at a second point in time (see the horizontal time axis in Figure 22.1). Unlike the private sector, the adopted set of strategies (i.e., policy initiatives) tends to be re-cast more often in order to maintain political mandates and track with current issues. The deeper meaning of the initiatives remains, even if the label changes. For example, the notion of cooperation remains while labels like 'stewardship' are replaced by 'partnership'. Yet the label helps differentiate the policy and attract more adherents while not losing the cluster of supporting organizations.

The outcome or effects of these policies over time is more complex than in the private sector. First, the outcome is based on mandates and missions, which tend to be broad and thus require sequential attention to performance measures (March and Olsen, 1989). Second, the outcomes are negotiated by the policy cluster, in accordance with the time period and logic (Fligstein, 1990; Thornton, 2004). Third, the outcomes adjust for prior performance and mission. While systematic study of performance adjustment models in the public sector is not known to us, detailed case work has shown that strong mission-type agencies are likely to keep their strategies as part of their focus, regardless of results, while weaker mission agencies are likely to be issue driven, and thus be perceived as achieving some target, even if not the original one (Espeland, 1998; Wilson, 1989).

APPLYING AND EXTENDING THE INSTITUTIONAL MODEL

To elaborate these arguments and demonstrate how a reader might use our model to do research, we examine public sector process strategy in one policy domain: water management. Water management has been studied by other institutional theorists (e.g., Espeland, 1998; Russo, 2001; Selznick, 1949), for it enables economic and social growth in regions and typically involves large sets of complex organizations (De Villiers, 2000). We concentrate on a twelve year period (1985–1997), during which the policy of the environmental agency, the British Columbia Ministry of Environment, Land and Parks (BCMOELP), was transformed (Jennings et al., 2002). We also draw on our more general knowledge of water law and its evolution from 1900–2005 (Jennings et al., 2005).

Policy Initiatives in BC Water Management

In the institutional approach, policy initiatives depend on the overarching logic in the field. The logic provides the taken-for-granted understanding that frames policy initiatives. The initiatives themselves are negotiated among the cluster of key actors at the mezzo level, but in light of these logics. For instance, a legalistic logic for handling environment management frames discussion around a variety of possible related policy initiatives, including command-and-control rigid enforcement regimes and gradual compliance regimes. Then it is up to the set of actors at the mezzo level to work out the specific policies and their applications. Institutional leaders at the mezzo level are particularly important for adding in their own interpretations and selecting among possible initiatives (e.g., see Bansal, 2005; Zan, 2005).

Turning to our case at hand, research has shown that the environmental management logic at work in the late 1980s in the US was regulatory (legalistic) but then evolved a logic based on corporate social responsibility (CSR) (stewardship) logic (Hoffman, 1997). Work by Schofer and Hironaka (2005) and Frank (1997) has shown that this switch in logics occurred in several nations; Harrison recorded a similar shift for western Canada, where the regulatory ideology moved from 'command and control' to 'cooperation' (Harrison, 1999). Hence, we expect a regulatory logic to exist in BC water management in the late 1980s, followed by a CSR–stewardship logic in the 1990s.

The organizational actors involved in interpreting and applying these logics in the BC water management system were, first and foremost, the BCMOELP, whose mandate was water management. In addition, there were the related sets of policy organizations in the government, especially the Fraser Basin Management Program (FBMP), and other Environmental non-Governmental Organizations (ENGOs), notably the West Coast Environmental Law (WCEL) Association (Jennings et al., 2002). Finally, the regulated actors and their associations were part of the negotiated response system, as they are in most regulatory systems (Hawkins, 1984, 2002).

The policies pursued by this group of actors in the cluster formed around the BCMOELP in the water management system are shown in Table 22.1. The table contains the archival and interview materials involving the actors. Following on Hoffman (1997) and Thornton (2004) key events and power shifts around the Ministry were used to demarcate policy eras.

1985–1988 was a period of opposing forces, some for the status-quo and others for reform. Two conservative governments were elected during the time period, but water management bureaucrats and scientists also conducted several large studies in the late 1970s and early 1980s that showed drastic declines in local water quality (Dorsey, 1991). As a result, new water-related laws, in particular the Waste Management Act (1983) and the Pesticides Control Act (1986), were put in place. This reformist approach was taken in one of the most traditional and intractable industries, pulp and paper (Krahn, 1998). There a policy of education for two years followed by a six year period of increasing enforcement was formally instituted. Indeed, a glance at the Deputy Minister's year-end message about Ministry initiatives shows the Ministry to be quite interested still in promoting the public's use of natural resources (wildlife, fisheries, recreation areas) along with devoting funds to scientific study of water and diffusion of water quality objectives (BCMOELP, 1984/85–86/87). Hence, the emergent policy initiatives in this three year period appear to be to 'Educate and gradually regulate' (Policy A in Table 22.1).

In 1988 and 1989 a switch is noticeable due to unforeseen events: the Nestucca oil spill on the West Coast of Vancouver Island and, not long after, the Exxon Valdez spill in nearby Alaska. Both were discussed in the opening message of the annual reports by the Deputy Minister. The Ministry created two task forces, one on environment and economics, and another on solid waste (BCMOELP, 1989/90: 9). Land and Parks was split out of the Ministry of Environment, ostensibly to separate recreation and resource usage from monitoring and enforcement. In pulp and paper, education also ended and enforcement began (Krahn, 1998). In 1991, the Deputy Minister reflected that 'certain program sections grew into full fledged branches, and out of necessity, certain regulations and activities to enforce them were made stronger and tougher' (BCMOELP, 1990/91: 11). In a comprehensive interview about water policy, management, and enforcement, the chief conservation officer said that during this three year period 'we were running a "Blitzkrieg".' Such actions were made possible because the conservative government was discredited in late 1989 by scandal. Thus, 'Regulate and enforce' best describes the emergent policy initiatives covering early 1988 to early 1991 (Policy B in Table 22.1).

In the spring of 1991 a new, more progressive government (the NDP) took over. The new government publicly pledged itself to a long-term vision for environmental stewardship (Blake, 1996; Dyck, 1995). Land and Parks was re-incorporated in the Ministry of the Environment, making it again BCMOELP, and long-term planning began (BCMOELP, 1991/92: 15). Several strategic policy initiatives were released: 'Environment 2001 – Strategic Directions for British Columbia', the 'Protected Areas Strategy' and the 'Provincial Clean Area Strategy'. Equivalently broad water policies were not developed, though there were water-related initiatives in 'Environment 2001' and in the 'Protected Areas Strategy'. Instead, regional stewardship and consultation initiatives in water management were pursued under the rubric of 'partnership'. The most notable example was the FBMP, which was designed to coordinate water quality objectives, assessment, and management, and aid ministry enforcement for the Lower Fraser Basin, the most populated area of BC. All in all, this set of emergent policy initiatives can be labeled as 'Partner, Please' (Policy C in Table 22.1).

The period following this planning was highly tumultuous. In 1993/94 and 1994/95 the Forest Practice Code was developed out of the Protected Areas Strategy, with great protest by corporations and rural communities, creating such conflict that one author has called it 'The War of the Woods' (Zietsma et al., 2002). In water management, this contestation was apparent among the policy initiatives pursued. In the first *State of the Environment Report* (1994) and in the 'Deputy Minister's Message' in the annual report, the success of enforcing pulp and paper regulations and the need for compliance with water quality objectives were both highlighted. At the same time, there was a continued claim that planning, partnership, and cooperation were needed to achieve these ends (BCMOELP, 1993/94: 8). This tension between enforcement and cooperation was aptly put by one officer, who was confused about her roles: 'are we biologists or police?' Hence, we labelled this set of policies 'Cooperate or else' (Policy D in Table 22.1).

The Effects of the Emergent Water Policies

Process strategy models are clear that strategy's effects, like strategy itself, are emergent and complex (Szulanski et al., 2005). The effects cross

Table 22.1 *Emergent water management policies in BC, 1985–1997*

Admin. Year	Relevant historical event	Key industry reports	Agency annual report	Agency interviews
		A: 'Educate and gradually regulate' policy		
1985/86	SOCRED Bill Bennett in third term. Recession starts to end, more serious action on pollution issues and waste occurs (Rankin and Finkle, 1983)	D: development of water standards groups in late 1970s leads to WMA (1983); creation K: 1983–1986 P&P voluntary	Focus is on technical management; first joint Federal and provincial flood management and fisheries systems	Period for enactment and development of water regulations Chief CO: we 'needed to do something.' (1994)
1986/87	Pesticides Control Act (1986); SOCRED Bill Vander Zalm elected; rule of law platform (Blake, 1996)	D: further professionalization and formalization of water management K: 1986–1989 P&P code	Concern is with wildlife and parks	
1987/88	Env. Canada, DFO, BCMOELP initiative on P&P	developed; D: FREMP starts.	Substantially increased interest in environmental quality noted and wildlife focused upon	
		B: 'Regulate and enforce' policy		
1988/89	Exxon Valdez spill and local Nestucca spill; Environmental Protection Act adopted (CEPA, 1988)	D: environmentalism as an ethic affects multiple industries K: 1989 mandatory P&P Enf; H: max. enforcement of P&P	Deputy Minister discusses Valdez and need for clean-up in LFB Canadian adopted; FRAP	Chief CO: 'During this time we were running a "Blitzkrieg"' (1994) Org: 'We had to spend the money, even if it wasn't scientifically justified' (1994)
1989/90	Battle over pulp and paper combining forest and water interests; Spring 1989 march for environment			

Table 22.1 (continued)

Admin. Year	Relevant historical event	Key industry reports	Agency annual report	Agency interviews
1990/91	SOCRED Scandal; battle over P&P continues; env. legislation squelched (Dyck, 1995); SOCRED premier resigns		Spills, pulp and paper, lots of waste initiatives, plus the clean up of Expo 1986 sites	
		C: 'Partner, please' policy		
1991/92	NDP Elected. NDP initiatives based on partnerships and alliances in govt. (Blake, 1996; Dyck, 1995)	K: 1992 P&P code finally in place and working 5 Yr FBMP program	Development of protected parks and Forest Practice discussed. Partnership and alliances	Senior CO: 'Our issue was developing new regulations and approaches' (1996)
1992/93	Press discusses issues over Forest Practice Code (*Vancouver Sun*)		Start of the Forest Practice Code; strategic planning in Ministry continues	
		D: 'Cooperate or else' policy		
1993/94	Forest companies and Green Peace still battle; on the water maintaining Pacific fisheries is the issue	Z: 'War of the Woods' heats up; Forest Alliance unravels H: In fish, dykes, wells, agri. are issues	Dep. Min. applauds P&P reduction; discusses broader programs. Water becomes secondary issue	Officer: Are we 'biologists or police?' (1996: 2) Org: 'They wanted cooperation but. . .' (1999)
1994/95	NDP scandal; agriculture's contamination of groundwater. NDP Premier resigns		AR combined for 2 years:	
1995/96	NDP re-elected with new Premier, Glenn Clarke	K: FRAP & P&P code final effects	Dep. Min. discusses 'cooperation and stewardship'	

502

Notes:

Codes & Acronyms* Reference

D	Dorsey (1976, 1991)
H	Healey (1999)
K	Krahn (1998)
Z	Zietsma et al. (2002)
AR	Annual Report (of BCMOELP and its various incarnations)
BCMOELP	British Columbia Ministry of Environment, Land and Parks – BC's main environmental agency
CEPA	Canadian Environmental Protection Act
CO	Conservation Officer
DFO	Department of Fisheries and Oceans
Dep. Min.	Deputy Minister
Env. Canada	Environment Canada – Canada's main environmental agency
FBMP	Fraser Basin Management Program
FRAP	Fraser River Action Plan
FREMP	Fraser River Estuary Management Program
NDP	New Democratic Party
Org.	Organization (interview)
P&P	Pulp and paper
SOCRED	Social Credit Party
WMA	Waste Management Ac

503

levels, linking the macro to the micro (Burgelman, 1996; Ocasio and Joseph, 2005), and the effects include intended and unintended outcomes (Mintzberg, 1987, 1994). Institutional theory's view of effects is in keeping with process strategy's, particularly where unintended effects are concerned (e.g., Selznick, 1949; Gouldner, 1954; Meyer and Rowan, 1977).

These specific effects of the emergent policy initiatives can be measured in several ways, for example in terms of internal efficiency changes, budget fluctuations, or switches in mandates (Vago, 1994). In the case of water management, we concentrate on one of the agency's own major indicators of performance: its level of regulatory enforcement. There are three outcomes of interest: referrals, charges, and penalties (BCMOELP Interview #1, 1996; Hawkins, 1984). These represent inputs, throughputs, and outputs of the enforcement system. In each annual report enforcement activities are discussed at length, often near the end of the report, as an assessment of performance (BCMOELP, 1985–1997).

Below, we model the impact of the four different emergent policy initiatives (A–D in Table 22.1) on each outcome, with 'Partner, please' as the omitted baseline category. Controls are included for standard factors that affect agency performance (Hawkins, 1984; Vago, 1994): the transition in the government ('lame duck periods'), agency load, and agency resources. We have also included controls for potential competing explanation of interorganizational effects: the attention given to the issue by a key policy actor (March and Olsen, 1989; Sabatier, 1975). In this case, we focus on the levels of attention from the environment ministry and the regional media to water as an issue (see Jennings et al., 2002). Figure 22.2 displays their interest level, compared with those of an important ENGO member and a large important regulated firm. All variables are lagged back one month. Stationary time series are used to examine interval level changes in number of referrals per month (i.e., differences) and negative binomials are used to examine the number of charges and penalties per month (i.e., counts). These are standard analyses for such data and designs, according to Greene (2003). Further details on these measures and analyses are available from the authors.

Model 1 of Table 22.2 shows that policies of educate then regulate and of regulate and enforce both lead to lower levels of referrals, but tend to lead to higher levels of charges and/or penalties than the omitted baseline emergent policy of 'Partner, please' and the included emergent policy of 'Cooperate or else'. One would expect that policies of command and control (regulatory policies) would lead to higher levels of legal outcomes (charges and penalties), so this is not surprising. Indeed, such expected results are comforting.

The more surprising, emergent strategy type of result generated by

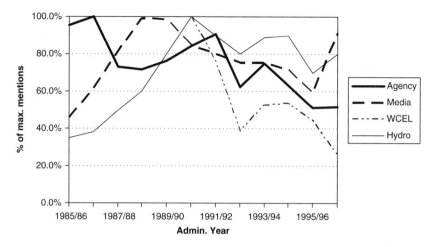

Figure 22.2.   Attention to water issues from different actors, 1985–1996

taking our institutional approach is that 'Cooperate or else' leads to higher levels of referrals and to reasonable levels of charges compared with the omitted category and relative to either regulatory logic-type policies. In other words, contrary to what some policy analysts would argue (e.g., Harrison, 1999; King and Lenox, 2000), the emergent policy of cooperation between the government ministry and local regulated organizations *increased* the amount of review of local water management activities and also put more pressure on these firms to comply or face consequences. From an institutional theory standpoint, this means that the normative and informal coercive pressure among the actors in the system that are involved in the 'Cooperate or else' policies has increased to the point that the actors are now behaving in a way that they might under more formal regulatory systems.

A second surprising finding from taking this approach is that while several controls work (e.g., for lame duck period and agency load), the alternative explanation of issue-interest group attention does not explain much variance. The agency's and media's attention do not have net positive effects on enforcement rates (Models 1–3). In fact, media attention is negatively related to referrals and charges. Why? In part, because the media's attention tends to peak only occasionally, meaning most rates are not related to monthly variations in rates. In addition, in our sample, this peak came mid-way through the regulatory period. As referrals, charges, and penalties gradually increased in the latter years, it meant the decline in interest was negatively related, on average, to these enforcement rates. Clearly, emergence of an identifiable policy became more important than

Table 22.2   Stationary time series and negative binomial results of emergent policy effects on regulatory agency performance, 1986–1997

	Model 3: Referrals (stn. time series)	Model 1: Charges (neg. bin.)	Model 2: Penalties (neg. bin.)
Constant	141.689***	4.112***	−2.593*
	(24.705)	(.994)	(1.816)
Govt. in transition	−17.551**	−.288[†]	0.089
	(6.461)	(0.214)	(0.382)
Agency load	−24.796[†]	−1.841**	1.340
	(19.476)	(.766)	(1.317)
Agency resources	4.507	.262*	.604**
	(5.357)	(.124)	(0.193)
Agency attention	−1.109	−.065	.045
	(2.820)	(.080)	(.140)
Media attention	−10.592*	−.594**	.436
	(5.751)	(.191)	(.364)
Policy: educate, grad. reg.	−44.779***	.455[†]	.783
	(10.436)	(0.381)	(.778)
Policy: regulate and enforce	−32.766***	.207	1.959***
	(6.481)	(0.242)	(.553)
Policy: cooperate or else	33.253**	1.296*	−.630
	(13.865)	(0.513)	(0.997)
Overall *F*	24.88***	–	–
Log likelihood	–	−357.853***	−175.744***
Number of months	105	124	138
(Number of cases)	(11,461)	(931)	(145)

$p = ^† \leq .10, * \leq .05, ** \leq .01, *** \leq .001$; one-tailed t-test for directional hypotheses.

just having interorganizational groups temporarily mobilized around that policy.

DISCUSSION AND DIRECTIONS FOR FUTURE RESEARCH

Returning to process strategy more generally, we can now assess some of the contributions of an institutional approach, especially for examination of strategy in the public sector. Table 22.3 contains a synopsis of the major

Table 22.3   A comparison of private versus public sector process strategy research

Theoretical elements	Private sector	Public sector
Strategy	Planned and recognized strategy along with unplanned, emergent strategy	Emergent policy initiatives, including the formal policies and brokered policy used in practice
'Strategists'	TMT and managers at various levels in organization who affect key choices	Disembodied 'agency' loosely cohering around organizations and leaders
Objectives	Assigned or imported from board or field, often via TMT	Stakeholder mandates and interest realization
Organization	Private firm	Interorganizational networks enmeshing agency or NGO
Environments	Interactive macro–micro environments	Mezzo level and its connection to macro and micro levels
Key processes	Operations vs. administration across roles and functions; path of firm prior investments; learning	Interpretation and translation of field policy; communication and sensemaking; building of support
Intended outcomes	Partial adaptation and survival in changing environments	Building and maintaining legitimacy; changes in mandate, regulatory policy, and key personnel
Unintended outcomes	Ever moving performance targets and permanently failing organizations	Goal displacement and problem embodiment

TMT = top management team.

dimensions tying together process strategy today, discussed by Szulanski et al. (2005). We will try to identify the differences as well as discuss each dimension. To avoid creating a 'strawman' when setting up our contrast, we will rely on what seem to be core ideas in the most current process strategy research on private sector firms (e.g., Burgelman, 1996; Farjoun, 2002; Labianca and Fairbank, 2005; Regner, 2005), rather than just more traditional work (e.g., Mintzberg, 1987, 1994; Grant, 2003). We also believe that many of the contrasts are more a matter of degree than absolute.

In the case of the concept of *strategy*, the institutional view still incorporates the private sector process approach, that is, the focal organization's emergent strategy is an object of study. Yet the institutional approach broadens it by including whatever current policy and related practices (implemented initiatives) are guiding the network of organizational actors. Institutional theory also narrows the construct of strategy. Public sector strategy requires legitimation from several actors, and ultimately the State. Thus, the policy initiatives (public sector strategies) are those in the subset that have gradually emerged and endured (Lounsbury and Glynn, 2001). In water management, these policies lasted between two and four years. Yet many private sector firm strategies, especially those in small start-up firms in competitive markets, change more rapidly (Martens et al., 2007).

The meaning of '*strategists*' also differs in private versus public sector process strategy research. Mintzberg (1987, 1994) was instrumental in persuading the field that the strategists and strategy were inseparable in a deep way. Recent work has explored cognitive schema and emotional process as dynamic capabilities affecting strategy formulation (Huy, 2005), pushing this intra-subjective link even deeper. The institutional approach seeks to put the strategists in context and not valorize them as primary sources of action. Instead, they are viewed as carriers and interpreters of field-level strategy; this is particularly true of strategists in the public sector. The members of the public sector are frequently searching for the next motivating concept or ideal, meaning many members must be involved in trying to formulate policies that can get traction – that is, 'hot' policies. These actors are likely to come from different organizations, such as ENGO, consulting firms, and other government agencies, as well as from different levels in these organizations (Hoffman and Bertels, 2009). In addition to these 'strategists', there are actors who have less directly observable access to rule creation and interpretation. Some are legislators on powerful committees; others are judges in national courts. These actors shape policy by setting up the rules and regulations underpinning it (March and Olsen, 1989; North, 1990; Schulz et al., 2008).

The *objectives* of the strategists and their strategies differ less in the process strategy and institutional approaches. In current strategy process research, objectives are often imported or adopted via some form of consensus, otherwise resistance will be created. The same is true in the public sector according to institutional theory. A difference is that public sector objectives must directly involve mandates from the field and State. For instance, in the private sector, an agreed upon objective among top managers may be to 'become a leader in innovation' even though this may not fit with the opinion of its widely dispersed, weakened shareholders. But in the public sector, policy initiatives like 'cleaning up our polluted environment' must build a mandate – in this case, appealing to the broad base of voters rather than specific corporate interests.

The *organization* and its *environments*, two highly related but separable dimensions, show a sharper contrast between the two perspectives on process strategy. In new process research, the macro environment is interpreted by some as the task environment around the firm and by others as the field (Ocasio and Joseph, 2005), and the micro environment ranges from the units with the firm down to intra-individual processes (Huy, 2005). In the case of the institutional approach, the main environment is at the mezzo level. Highly cognitive and subjective processes are considered important, but only collectively; that is, as an understanding among clustered organizations, one that might lead to a new translation or development of a new policy initiative (Marquis and Lounsbury, 2007).

In terms of key processes, the process strategy and institutional approach are more similar than different. Over the years, dozens of processes have been identified by each. For instance in the *Handbook for Process Strategy*, Ocasio and Joseph (2005) have boiled the relevant firm-level ones down to operations and administration, distributed around roles and functions at different levels in the firm. This distinction builds off work from Burgelman (1996) and harkens back to March and Simon (1958). Process theorists taking a more political or critical approach (e.g., Pettigrew et al., 2002) add in the importance of power. Power dynamics involve the top management team, but also key resources and stakeholders (Chakravarthy and White, 2006). An institutional approach to process strategy in the public sector is quite similar to critical theory in this regard, emphasizing resource mobilization as being critical. Nevertheless, institutionalists also give primacy to translation, interpretation, sensemaking, and communication in the public sector as a means of understanding the strategy of an agency, NGO or other public organization (Sahlin and Wedlin, 2008). As Weber noted many years ago (Weber, 1919/1947), in public sector bureaucracies, operational rules within the technical core are less critical than the interpretation and application of administrative rules for mandate building.

In terms of intended outcomes, traditional process strategy theory still views performance as control to the strategy process. The types of intended outcomes are not simply financial, but include survival and variance and adjustment over time (Mintzberg, 1994). Public sector outcomes are naturally even less identifiable than private sector ones, but common to all, according to an institutional perspective, is that the outcomes involve legitimacy. As part of the ongoing legitimation process, there are mandate shifts, regulatory policy changes, and the movement of key personnel (Hawkins, 1984, 2002). A 'successful' agency is one that increases its mandate, aligns its policy, and garners valuable personnel under a new authority regime (March and Olsen, 1989; Scott, 2001). Whether it hits specific budget targets is secondary.

As for *unintended outcomes*, process strategy's strength as a research area is in showing how targets move, aspirations track downward, and organizations permanently fail (Grant, 2003; Tamuz et al., 2004). In this sense, new research on the strategy process is more similar to than different from work on strategy from an institutional perspective. Nevertheless, institutional research on public sector organizations has also described even more extreme cases. One is goal displacement due to co-optation by one narrow, external interest (Selznick, 1949). Another is becoming the embodiment of the problem the organization is designed to solve (Gouldner, 1954), a version of Orwell's Ministry of Peace designed to carry out war (Orwell, 1949).

Directions for Future Research

Based on Table 22.3 above and the preceding discussion, there are at least three areas for process strategy that seem ripe for further exploration: the nature of policy initiatives, the identification of strategy agents, and the modeling of endogenous effects.

The nature of policy initiatives
Given that policy initiatives are the mezzo-level construct that best matches with the notion of 'strategy', it is important to understand the nature, types, interaction, and effects of policy initiatives. Political scientists have their own methods of examining policy initiatives, some of which have been alluded to above (e.g., based on type of interests and the distribution of costs and benefits). Organization theorists have adopted and built upon these, assessing the interests and issue groups in governments (Laumann and Knocke, 1987; March and Olsen, 1989). But organizational strategists would probably be able to identify others based on competition and cooperation models over mandates. Without being too simplistic, policy initiatives might be divided into diverse, specific, and broad appeal policies, based on the ways in which the policies enable actors to compete for mandates and legitimacy. Diverse policies capture a complex mandate based on many different actors; specific policies secure mandates offered by a few highly committed and discriminating interest groups; and broad appeal policies rely on one or two policies to capture a relatively thin but similar mandate across apparently different interest groups.

Given this simple scheme, a process theorist would be intrigued to see how a diverse set of policy initiatives might lead an organization in intended and unintended directions, compared with a specific or broad appeal set. National environmental agencies in many countries appear to rely on diverse policies, covering many environmental issues simultaneously and somewhat co-equally (e.g., a focus on clean air, water quality, park and wildlife protection, etc.). But given their limited resources and their diverse mandate, these agencies typically can only attend to policies and objectives in sequential and superficial fashion (March and Olsen, 1989; Hoffman and Bertels, 2009). Thus, in periods like 2003–2009 when one overall issue, like climate change, arises, the diverse policy set will be insufficient, compared with a broad policy on this single issue.

The identification of strategy agents
There has been a move to 'bring the manager being back in' to strategy and to focus on practice (Lovas and Ghoshal, 2000). This is most apparent in Mintzberg's recent popular book, *Managers, Not MBAs* (Mintzberg, 2005). This work is consistent with other process strategy work that views managers, especially those in the middle and lower level of the organization, as the source of real strategy (Burgelman, 1996). However, in the public sector it is not managers within the organizations but the collective, disembodied agency that is the source of action. In a given policy era, this disembodied agency might be anchored loosely around a new leader in a ministry, along with her contacts in industry and one well-known NGO; but it is just as likely to be embedded in the set of rules and interpretations from a prior set of deputy directors and the four or five bell weather regulated firms in the domain that have crafted their strategies around these rules. In keeping with process strategy research, the investigator will have to examine the interorganizational network and find the threads of action around policy to determine the real networks generating strategy. Hoffman and Bertels (2009), for instance, are currently examining all issues and actions taken by ENGOs and mapping out their overlapping activities to establish different agents in the environmental policy network. He has identified four types: portals, liaisons, peripherals, and isolates. While Professor Hoffman has not yet proposed examining the impact of the networks, it would be an intriguing (and natural) next step.

Modeling endogenous effects
Process strategy has been ahead of the strategy field on the issue of endogeneity. Most process models see strategy and its outcomes at least as co-determined by within-firm activities, and not just as a result of shocks or pressures from an external environment (e.g., see Farjoun, 2002; Lovas and Ghoshal, 2000). Several studies of organizational learning capture the simultaneous endogenous and exogenous effects of strategy and firm

processes on performance and adaptation (Greve, 2003; Schwab and Miner, 2008). Such studies require many observations and time periods, along with interorganizational environments that vary, yet in ways that can be systematically modelled. Such change can occur via the evolution of the industry structure (Dobrev et al., 2006) or new patterns among network participants (Gulati, 1995).

Public sector strategy is viewed as even more endogenously conditioned than private sector strategy, because the source of political mandates, the agents of action, and the adjudged outcomes are often all interacting within the same interorganizational network at the mezzo level. This makes it even more imperative to consider reciprocal effects and feedback loops within the public sector. Unfortunately, there are far fewer studies of public sector organizational initiatives modelling exogenous and endogenous drives, in part because the interorganizational situation is more changeable and complex, requiring more assumptions and a narrower focus. March and colleagues have probably done the most work in this regard. Their early work examined intra-organizational decision dynamics under various conditions of uncertainty and co-determinacy (see March, 1994 for a review). A recent extension of this work to the public sector has been made by Schulz and colleagues in a study of factors underlying legal rule changes in water law (Jennings et al., 2005; Schulz et al., 2008). This work fits with other institutional theory research that emphasizes the importance of courts and legislatures in identifying and interpreting key legal rules guiding policy and sector changes (Dobbin and Sutton, 1998; Edelman, 1992; Edelman et al., 1999). We expect to see other studies on public sector policy in this area in the near future.

CONCLUSION

This chapter has drawn on recent advances in process strategy research and extended them to public sector strategy using an institutional perspective. We have argued that strategy in this sector should be understood as emergent policy initiatives among groups of interorganizational actors. The policy formation process is both formal and informal in nature, and shaped by the institutional logics and sources of legitimacy in a field during a particular period. The effects of these emergent policies are likewise highly contingent on the actors, the logics, and the period, often producing surprising outcomes.

The institutional perspective on public sector process strategy extends current theory by focusing researchers on policy initiatives and the complex set of actors involved in their emergence. In addition, the institutional view extends current theory by examining outcomes from multiple levels of analysis and interpretation. The organization's intended and unintended is part of that analysis, but so is the implication of that performance in the wider system (e.g., of regulation). This malleable, multilevel, interpretive and emergent nature of policy and its effects in the public sector makes us wonder if Mintzberg's famous refrain about strategies might be re-phrased as:

> Not to our *realities*[2]
> – may they mostly fall
> as fast as they rise –
> but to the wonders of *fantasy*.

NOTES

* We would like to thank our co-authors on our water management and water law research, Martin Schulz, David Patient, Ke Yuan, Caroline Gravel, and Jennifer Jennings, for allowing their work to be discussed and cited in this chapter. Any untoward extensions, inconsistencies, or factual errors, however, should be ascribed to the lead author.
1. The 'mezzo' level is also dubbed the 'interorganizational' level in the text, but with the caveat that the mezzo level includes not just the horizontal linkages among those organizations, but their vertical linkages with the field and focal organization.
2. Italics for the words switched (reality and fantasies) added for emphasis and focus.

REFERENCES

Bansal, P. (2005), 'Evolving sustainability: A longitudinal study of corporate sustainable development', *Strategic Management Journal*, **26**(3): 197–218.

Barry, D. and M. Elmes (1997), 'Strategy retold: Toward a narrative view of strategic discourse', *Academy of Management Review*, **22**(2): 429–452.

BCMOELP (1984–1999), *British Columbia Ministry of Environment Lands and Parks. Annual Reports*, BC Government Document, Victoria, BC, www.gov.bc.ca/elp/.

Bechky, B. A. (2003), 'Sharing meaning across occupational communities: The transformation of understanding on a production floor', *Organization Science*, **14**(3): 312–330.

Blake, D. E. (1996), 'The politics of polarization: Parties and elections in British Columbia', in R. K. Carty (ed.), *Politics, Policy, and Government in British Columbia*, Vancouver, BC: University of British Columbia Press, pp. 67–84.

Burgelman, R. (1996), 'Process of model of strategic business exit: Implications for an evolutionary perspective on strategy', *Strategic Management Journal*, **17**(Summer): 193–214.

Chakravarthy, B. S. and R. E. White (2006), 'Strategy process: Forming, implementing and changing strategies', in A. Pettigrew, H. Thomas and R. Whittington (eds), *Handbook of Strategy and Management*, London: Sage Publications, pp. 182–205.

Chandler, A. D. (1980), *Managerial Hierarchies: Comparative Perspectives on the Rise of the Modern Industrial Enterprise*, Cambridge, MA: Harvard University Press.

Collins, J. (2001), *Good to Great*, New York: Harper Collins.

De Villiers, M. (2000), *Water: The Fate of Our Most Precious Resource*, Boston, MA: Houghton Mifflin Company.

DiMaggio, P. and W. W. Powell (1983), 'The iron cage revisited: Institutional isomorphism and collective rationality in organizational field', *American Sociological Review*, **48**(2): 147–160.

Dobbin, F. R. (1994), *Forging Industrial Policy: The United States, Britain, and France in the Railway Age*, New York: Cambridge University Press.

Dobbin, F. R. and J. A. C. Baum (2000), 'Economics meets sociology in Strategic Management', *Advances in Strategic Management*, **17**: 1–26.

Dobbin, F. R. and T. J. Dowd (2000), 'The market that antitrust built: Public policy, private coercion, and railroad acquisition, 1825 to 1922', *American Sociological Review*, **65**(5): 631–657.

Dobbin, F. R. and J. Sutton (1998), 'The strength of a weak state: The rights revolution and the rise of human resources management divisions', *American Journal of Sociology*, **104**(2): 441–476.

Dobrev, S., A. Witteloostuijin and J. A. C. Baum (2006), 'Ecology and strategy', *Advances in Strategic Management*, **23**: 1–26.

Dorsey, A. (1976), *The Uncertain Future of the Lower Fraser*, Vancouver, BC: Westwater Research Centre, University of British Columbia Press.

Dorsey, A. (1991), *Water in Sustainable Development: Exploring our Common Future in the Fraser River Basin*, Vancouver, BC: Westwater Research Centre, University of British Columbia Press.

Dyck, R. (1995), *Provincial Politics in Canada: Towards the Turn of the Century*. 3rd edn, Scarborough, ON: Prentice Hall, Canada.

Economist (2009), 'The other worldly philosophers', *Economist*, 18–24 July: 65–69.

Edelman L. B. (1992), 'Legal ambiguity and symbolic structures: Organizational mediation of civil rights laws', *American Journal of Sociology*, **97**(6): 1531–1576.

Edelman, L. B., C. Uggen and H. Erlanger (1999), 'The endogeneity of legal regulation: Grievance procedures as rational myth', *American Journal of Sociology*, **105**(2): 406–454.

Environmental Protection Agency (EPA) (2004), *Compliance and Enforcement*, http://www.epa.gov/compliance/.

Espeland, W. N. (1998), *Politics, Rationality, and Identity in the American Southwest: The Struggle for Water*, Chicago, IL: University of Chicago Press.

Farjoun, M. (2002), 'Towards an organic perspective on strategy', *Strategic Management Journal*, **23**(7): 561–594.

Fligstein, N. (1990), *The Transformation of Corporate Control*, Cambridge, MA: Harvard University Press.

Frank, D. J. (1997), 'Science, nature, and the globalization of the environment, 1870–1990', *Social Forces*, **76**(2): 409–437.

Fraser River Action Plan (1998), *Final Report*, http://www.rem.sfu.ca/FRAP/introe.pdf.

Friedland, R. and R. Alford (1991), 'Bringing society back in: Symbols, practices, and institutional contradictions', in W. W. Powell and P. J. DiMaggio (eds), *The New Institutionalism in Organizational Analysis*, Chicago, IL: University of Chicago Press, pp. 232–266.

Gioia, D. and H. Thomas (1996), 'Identity, image and interpretation: Sensemaking during strategic change in academia', *Administrative Science Quarterly*, **41**(3): 370–403.

Gouldner, A. (1954), *Patterns in Industrial Bureaucracy*, Glencoe, IL: The Free Press.

Grant, R. B. (2003), 'Strategic planning in a turbulent environment: Evidence from the oil majors', *Strategic Management Journal*, **24**(6): 491–517.

Greene, W. H. (2003), *Econometric analysis*, 4th Edition, New York: Macmillan.

Greenwood, R., C. Oliver, K. Sahlin and R. Suddaby (2008), 'Introduction', in R. Greenwood et al. (eds), *The Sage Handbook of Organizational Institutionalism*, London: Sage, pp. 1–44.

Greve, H. (2003), *Organizational Learning from Performance Feedback: A Behavioral Perspective on Innovation and Change*, Cambridge, UK: University of Cambridge Press.

Gulati, R. (1995), 'Social structure and alliance formation patterns: A longitudinal analysis', *Administrative Science Quarterly*, **40**(4): 619–652.

Harrison, K. (1999), 'Talking with the donkey: Cooperative approaches to environmental protection', *Ecology*, **2**(3): 51–72.

Hawkins, K. (1984), *Environment and Enforcement*, Oxford, UK: Oxford University Press.

Hawkins, K. (2002), *Law as Last Resort: Prosecution Decision-Making in a Regulatory Agency*, Oxford, UK: Oxford University Press.

Healy. M. (1999), *Sustainability Issues and Choices in the Lower Fraser Basin: Resolving Dissonance*, Vancouver, BC: Westwater Research Center, University of British Columbia Press.

Hoffman, A. J. (1997), *From Heresy to Dogma: An Institutional History of Corporate Environmentalism*, San Francisco: The New Lexington Press.

Hoffman, A. J. and S. Bertels (2009), 'Structure and role heterogeneity, in organizational fields: Evolving board interlocks in the environmental movement', Manuscript under review at *Organization Science*.

Hoffman, A. J. and M. J. Vantresca (2002), *Organizations, Policy and the Natural Environment*, Stanford, CA: Stanford University Press.

Huestis, L. B. (1993), 'Enforcement of environmental law in Canada', in G. Thompson, M. L. McConnell and L. B. Huestis (eds), *Environmental Law and Business in Canada*, Aurora, ON: Canada Law Book, pp. 243–274

Huy, Q. N. (2005), 'An emotion-based view of strategic renewal', in G. Szulanski, J. Porac and Y. Doz (eds), *Strategy Process: Advances in Strategic Management*, New York: Elsevier, pp. 3–39.

Jennings, P. D. and P. A. Zandbergen (1995), 'Ecologically sustainable organizations: An institutional approach', *Academy of Management Review*, **20**(4): 1015–1052.

Jennings, P. D., P. A. Zandbergen and V. Clark (1999), 'The role of organizations in the lower Fraser basin's water quality: An institutional approach', in Michael Healey (ed.), *Sustainability Issues and Choices in the Lower Fraser Basin: Resolving Dissonance*, Vancouver, BC: Westwater Research Centre, University of British Columbia Press, pp. 64–105.

Jennings, P. D., P. A. Zandbergen and M. L. Martens (2002), 'Complications in compliance: Variations in enforcement in British Columbia's lower Fraser basin, (1985–1996)', in A. Hoffman, and M. Vantresca (eds), *Organizations, Policy, and the Natural Environment: Institutional and Strategic Perspectives*, Stanford, CA: Stanford University Press, pp. 57–89.

Jennings, P. D., M. Schulz, D. Patient, C. Gravel and K. Yuan (2005), 'Weber and legal rule evolution: The closing of the iron cage?', *Organization Studies*, **26**(4): 621–653.

Kelly, E. (2003), 'The strange history of employer-sponsored child care: Interested actors, uncertainty, and the transformation of law in organizational fields', *American Journal of Sociology*, **109**(3): 606–649.

King, A. A. and M. J. Lenox (2000), 'Industry self-regulation without sanctions: The chemical industry's Responsible Care Program', *Academy of Management Journal*, **43**(4): 698–716.

Krahn, P. K. (1998), 'Enforcement versus voluntary compliance: An examination of the strategic enforcement initiatives implemented by the Pacific and Yukon Regional Office of Environment Canada, 1983–1998', *Department of Environment, Fraser River Action Plan: Regional Action Report, 98-02*, Victoria, BC: British Columbia Government.

Labianca, G. and J. F. Fairbank (2005), 'Interorganizational monitoring process, choices, and outcomes', in G. Szulanski, J. Porac and Y. Doz (eds), *Strategy Process, Advances in Strategic Management*, New York: Elsevier, pp. 117–150.

Landy, M. K. and M. A. Levin (1995), *The New Politics of Public Policy*, New York: Johns Hopkins Press.

Laumann, E. and D. Knocke (1987), *The Organizational State: Social Choice in National Policy Domains*, Madison: University of Wisconsin Press.

Leblebici, H., G. R. Salancik, A. Copay and T. King (1991), 'Institutional change and the transformation of interorganizational history of the U.S. radio broadcasting industry', *Administrative Science Quarterly*, **36**(3): 333–363.

Lounsbury, M. (2002), 'Institutional transformation and status mobility: The professionalization of the field of finance', *Academy of Management Journal*, **45**(9): 255–266.

Lounsbury, M. and M. A. Glynn (2001), 'Cultural entrepreneurship: Stories, legitimacy, and the acquisition of resources', *Strategic Management Journal*, **22**(6/7): 545–564.

Lovas, B. and S. Ghoshal (2000), 'Strategy as guided evolution', *Strategic Management Journal*, **21**(9): 875–896.

Maguire, S., C. Hardy and T. B. Lawrence (2004), 'Institutional entrepreneurship in emerging fields: HIV/AIDS treatment advocacy in Canada', *Academy of Management Journal*, **47**(5): 657–679.

March, J. G. (1994), *A Primer on Decision Making: How Decisions Happen*, New York: Simon and Schuster.

March, J. G. and J. P. Olsen (1989), *Rediscovering Institutions: The Organizational Basis of Politics*, New York: John Wiley.

March, J. and H. Simon (1958), *Organizations*, New York: John Wiley.

Marquis, C. and M. Lounsbury (2007), 'Vive la resistance: Competing logics and the consolidation of U.S. community banking', *Academy of Management Journal*, **50**(4): 799–820.

Martens, M. L., J. E. Jennings and P. D. Jennings (2007), 'Do the stories they tell get them the money they need? The role of entrepreneurial narratives in resource acquisition at IPO', *Academy of Management Journal*, **50**(2): 1107–1132.

Meyer, J. W. and B. Rowan (1977), 'Institutionalization and organizations: Formal structure as myth and ceremony', *American Journal of Sociology*, **83**(2): 340–363.

Meyer, J. W. and W. R. Scott (1983), *Organization and Environments: Ritual and Rationality*, Stanford, CA: Stanford University Press.

Mintzberg, H. (1987), 'The strategy concept: The five P's for strategy', *California Management Review*, **30**: 11–24.

Mintzberg, H. (1994), 'The rise and fall of strategic planning', *Harvard Business Review*, Jan–Feb.: 107–114.

Mintzberg, H. (2005), *Managers, Not MBAs*, San Francisco, CA: Berrett-Koehler Publishers.

Mizruchi, M. S. and L. C. Fein (1999), 'The social construction of organizational knowledge: A study of the uses of coercive, mimetic, and normative isomorphism', *Administrative Science Quarterly*, **44**(4): 653–683.

North, D. (1990), *Institutions, Institutional Change and Economic Performance*, Cambridge, UK: Cambridge University Press.

Ocasio, W. and J. Joseph (2005), 'An attention-based theory of strategy formulation: Linking micro- and macroperspectives in strategy processes', in G. Szulanski J. Porac and Y. Doz (eds), *Strategy Process (Advances in Strategic Management Series*, New York: Elsevier, pp. 39–61.

Oliver, C. (1991), 'Strategic responses to institutional processes', *Academy of Management Review*, **16**(1): 145–179.

Orwell, G. (1949), *Nineteen Eighty-Four. A Novel*, New York: Harcourt, Brace and Co.

Palmer, D., P. D. Jennings and X. Zhou (1993), 'Politics and institutional change: Late adoption of the multidivisional form by large U.S. corporations', *Administrative Sciences Quarterly*, **38**(1): 100–131.

Pedriana, N. and R. Stryker (2004), 'The strength of a weak agency: Enforcement of Title VII of the 1964 Civil Rights Act and the expansion of state capacity, 1965–1971', *American Journal of Sociology*, **110**(3): 709–760.

Perkmann, M. and A. Spicer (2009), 'The institutional work of creating, maintaining and disposing of business models', Working paper submission to the University of Alberta Business School Conference on Institutions.

Pettigrew, A. (1992), 'The character and significance of strategy process research', *Strategic Management Journal*, **13**(Winter): 5–16.

Pettigrew, A., H. Thomas and R. Whittington (eds) (2002), *The Handbook of Strategy and Management*, London: Sage Publications.

Porac, J., H. Thomas, F. Wilson, D. Paton and A. Kanfer (1995), 'Rivalry and the industry model of Scottish knitwear Producers', *Administrative Science Quarterly*, **40**(2): 203–227.

Powell, W. W and P. J. DiMaggio (1991), *The New Institutionalism in Organizational Analysis*, Chicago, IL: University of Chicago Press.

Rankin, M. and P. Finkle (1983), 'The enforcement of environmental law: Taking the environment seriously', *UBC Law Review*, **17**: 34–57.

Rao, H., P. Monin and R. Durand (2003), 'Institutional change in Toque Ville: Nouvelle cuisine as an identity movement in French gastronomy', *American Journal of Sociology*, **108**(4): 795–843.

Regner, P. (2005), 'Adaptive and creative strategy logics in strategy process', in G. Szulanski, J. Porac and Y. Doz (eds), *Strategy Process, Advances in Strategic Management*, New York: Elsevier, pp. 189–212.

Ruef, M. and W. R. Scott (1998), 'Multidimensional model of organizational legitimacy: Hospital survival in changing institutional environments', *Administrative Science Quarterly*, **43**(4): 877–904.

Russo, M. (2001), 'Institutions, exchange relations, and the emergence of new fields: Regulatory policies and independent power production in America, 1978–1992', *Administrative Science Quarterly*, **46**(1): 57–86.

Sabatier, P. (1975), 'Social movement and regulatory agencies: Toward a more adequate – and less pessimistic – theory of clientele capture', *Policy Sciences*, **6**(3): 301–342.

Sahlin, K. and L. Wedlin (2008), 'Circulating ideas: Imitation, translation and editing', in R. Greenwood et al. (eds), *The Sage Handbook of Organizational Institutionalism*, London: Sage, pp. 1–44.

Schofer, E. and A. Hironaka (2005), 'The effects of world society on environmental protection outcomes', *Social Forces*, **84**(1): 26–47.

Schulz, M., P. D. Jennings and D. Patient (2008), 'Cleaning up the Water Act: A problemistic approach rule change', *Academy of Management Annual Meeting Proceedings*, Anaheim, CA.

Schwab, A. and A. S. Miner (2008), 'Learning in hybrid-project systems: The effects of project performance on repeated collaboration', *Academy of Management Journal*, **51**(6): 1117–1149.

Scott, W. R. (2001), *Institutions and Organizations*, Thousand Oaks, CA: Sage Publications.

Scott, W. R. and G. Davis (2005), *Organizations: Rational, Natural and Open Systems*, Stanford, CA: Stanford University Press.

Scott, W. R., M. Ruef, P. Mendel and C. Carona (2000), *Institutional Change and Healthcare Organizations: From Professional Dominance to Managed Care*, Chicago, IL: University of Chicago Press.

Selznick, P. (1949), *TVA and the Grassroots*, Berkeley, CA: UC Berkeley Press.

Seo, M. and W. E. D. Creed (2002), 'Institutional contradictions, praxis and institutional change: A dialectical perspective', *Academy of Management Review*, **27**(2): 222–247.

Stryker, R. (2000), 'Government regulation', in E. F. Borgatta and R. Montgomery (eds), *Encyclopedia of Sociology*, 2nd edn, New York: Macmillan, pp. 1098–1111.

Suddaby, R. and R. Greenwood (2005), 'Rhetorical strategies of legitimacy', *Administrative Science Quarterly*, **50**(1): 35–67.

Szulanski, G., J. Porac and Y. Doz (eds) (2005), 'Introduction to the strategy process', *Strategy Process, Advances in Strategic Management*, New York, Elsevier, pp. xiii–xxxv.

Tamuz, M., E. Thomas and K. E. Franchois (2004), 'Defining and classifying medical error: Lessons for patient safety reporting systems', *Quality and Safety in Health Care*, **13**(1): 13–20.

Thornton, P. (2004), *Organizational Decisions in Higher Educational Publishing*, Stanford, CA: Stanford University Press.

Vago, S. (1994), *Law and Society*, 4th edn, Englewood Cliffs, NJ: Prentice Hall.

Weber, Max (1919/1947), *The Theory of Social and Economic Organization*, Edited and introduction by Talcott Parsons, New York: The Free Press.

Wilson, J. Q. (1989), *Bureaucracy: What Government Agencies Do and Why They Do It*, New York: Basic Books.

Zan, L. (2005), 'Future directions from the past: Management and accounting discourse in historical perspective', In G. Szulanski, J. Porac and Y. Doz (eds), *Strategy Process, Advances in Strategic Management*, New York, Elsevier, pp. 437–490.

Zietsma, C., M. Winn, O. Branzei and I. Vertinsky (2002), 'The war of the woods: Facilitators and impediments of organizational learning processes', *British Journal of Management*, **13**(S2): S61–S74.

23 Public sector and strategic management: the case study at the US Army Corps of Engineers*

Anil Patel

INTRODUCTION

Many scholars (Chakravarthy and Doz, 1992; Huff and Reger, 1987; Pettigrew, 1992) have written extensively about strategic processes in private sector firms. But recently, scholars from the field of strategy and organization management have challenged researchers to begin taking public sector organizations more seriously (see *Academy of Management Journal*, Special Issue, December 2005). According to Hambrick (2005: 961), 'as management scholars, it is our job – collectively – to know more than anyone else about how organizations work and how they can be improved . . . For the sake of society we mustn't just pass our knowledge around among ourselves. We must step out of our monastery.' Using Hambrick (2005) as our guide, I ventured outside the 'monastery' to examine how a federal government organization adopts strategic management concepts. Despite these calls, there is little evidence that the academic community has heeded these challenges, as can be inferred from the lack of publications in the most prominent management journals.

Within the public sector literature, the philosophical underpinnings to policies regarding managing the organization have been drawn from the writings of Dewey (1948) and other researchers such as Kaplan (1974) and Lasswell and Kaplan (1950) from the public policy field. To focus on strategic management, Kelman (2005: 69) states that 'the traditional field called public administration and a new one called public management is relatively primitive in its research methods'. Therefore, solving complicated management problems in the public sector requires drawing from business researchers.

Despite this background, a thorough examination of the strategic management processes has barely been examined in the public sector, given the prevalence of these processes within organizations in modern societies (Montanari and Bracker, 1986). Only a handful of studies have contributed to public sector strategic management (Bryson, 1981, 1988; Roberts and Wargo, 1994; Barzelay and Campbell, 2003; Simone et al.,

2005). It may be asserted that one of the likely reasons for limited inclusion of public sector strategic management writings in business management literature is that scholars in the field of strategy and business, in general, seem to lack awareness about the practice within the federal departments/agencies as well its applicability to public policy issues. Another likely reason is that while much of the strategy influences is deeply rooted in institutional theory (Chandler, 1962; Rumelt, 1974; Quinn, 1980), industrial organization economic theory (Porter, 1980; von Neumann and Morgenstern, 1947) and administrative behavioral theory (March and Simon, 1958; Simon, 1958, 1991; Lindblom, 1959), there is a lack of conceptual connection or even application between the disciplines of strategic management and public policy. This weak linkage stems from far too few exchanges between management scholars located in the schools of business, organizational theorists in the political science department and public policy academicians in the school of public affairs (Ring et al., 2005). Another rationale for this feeble link is that there is little interest from the field of business to work on problems that lie at the intersection of multidisciplinary theories across fields such as history, economics, ecology, psychology, sociology, biology, systems, military studies, engineering and political science. These likely reasons let readers infer about why very few scholarly articles about strategic management have been published in the management journals or organizational case studies have been written and/or used in the business literature.

Thus, the general goal of this chapter is to provide a clear linkage between the key concepts of strategic management and the inner workings of a public sector entity. Specifically, because the focus of this book is on strategy process, this chapter describes in great detail the strategic management system as an interlocking set of strategic processes – plan–program–budget–execute–control – in a United States federal government organization. Through the approach of case analysis about the United States Army Corps of Engineers (USACE), this chapter provides an in-depth account of how strategic management concepts are applied inside a public sector entity. It shows that these concepts allow the organization to execute its command policy by adopting strategic management processes, thereby enabling the multiple levels within the organization to achieve alignment, also known as 'internal fit' within the organization as well as 'external fit' (Venkatraman, 1989; Venkatraman and Camillus, 1984; Siggelkow, 2001, 2002) with applicable statute(s) enacted by the United States Congress, executive orders mandated by the Executive Office of the President, and directives and guidance issued by the Departments of Defense and Army. This chapter offers three contributions to the strategy process literature. First, it provides a descriptive view about the inner workings of the strategic management system within the USACE, thereby helping strategy scholars to understand the flow and interconnectivity of various processes from a multi-level strategic management perspective, necessary for alignment in any organization. This illustration is consistent with the strategic management concepts proposed by Hax and Majluf (1984, 1996) in which they suggest that the hierarchical strategic process is based upon the diversity of businesses within the organization. The second contribution focuses on the idea that the strategic management principles developed and applied by the private sector could be helpful to not-for-profit organizations, including the public sector (Kelman, 2005; Wortman, 1979). Finally, one of the most unique contributions of this chapter is that unlike most strategy process scholars who observe the organization from the outside, the author of this chapter has been deeply involved in the development of the strategic management system and policy with the help of several project team members within the USACE, allowing readers to obtain an insider's rather than an outsider's viewpoint, as is the case in most situations.

The remainder of this chapter is outlined as follows. The first section focuses on the historical roots of strategic management in US federal governmental departments/agencies. The second section discusses the methodology chosen for this chapter, including the rationale about the appropriateness of this research setting at the USACE. The third section provides a framework for data collection, analysis and synthesis for each stage of the strategic management system. The fourth section is broken up into three parts, with each part describing a specific aspect of the USACE strategic management system. The first part pertains to strategic planning; the second explains strategic implementation through programming, budgeting and executing; and the third covers strategic control. In the fifth section, the general discussion focuses on broad implications and future research. In the last section, a summary about this chapter is provided as the conclusion.

STRATEGIC MANAGEMENT IN FEDERAL GOVERNMENT: A RETROSPECTIVE

Since the mid-1940s, the federal budget of the United States has included identification of major goals and program objectives, a systematic analysis of supplies and needs for both military and civilian purposes, and a long-range plan of national projects. Its origins are rooted in the Budgeting and Accounting Act of 1921, where a distinct relationship was drawn between budgeting and program planning. In the Post-World War II period, social scientists began to play a major role in the decision-making process, with simulated analytic techniques such as systems analysis and operations research (Radin, 2000). As early as the 1950s, researchers from the public policy discipline recognized that there was an inherent difficulty in setting goals and objectives among governmental agencies and, as such, the governmental departments and/or agencies practiced 'the science of muddling through' (Lindblom, 1959: 79–88) to manage their operation regarding the formulation and implementation of policy.

In 1964, President Lyndon Johnson introduced the planning–programming–budgeting system to the Department of Defense for the purpose of improving the department's ability to decide among competing proposals and requests for capital projects as well as to evaluate actual performance of the departments/agencies. President Nixon followed with an effort called management-by-objective (Drucker, 1976), in which the administration attempted to identify goals of federal programs so that it was easier to determine what results were expected of each program and where programs were redundant or ineffective. President Ford commenced initiatives that were designed to reduce spending for public programs, including consolidating overlapping programs and 'zero based budgeting' (Pyhrr, 1970, 1974; Schick, 1966, 1978), return decision-making and responsibility to state and local governments, and eliminate red tape and outrageous government regulations. With the introduction of the concept of zero-based budgeting, President Carter forced each government program to prove its value each year. 'It's not enough to have created a lot of government programs. Now we must make the good programs effective and improve or weed out those that are wasteful or unnecessary,' he told the Congress and the American people in his 1978 State of the Union address (Carter, 1979). President Reagan sought to make government more efficient by reducing waste and improving administrative systems. President Clinton sought government reinvention with National Performance Review (Clinton, 1993), National Partnership for Reinventing Government (US Office of Management and Budget, 1997; Kamensky, 1999) and Reinventing Government II (Kamensky, 1996). Finally, President Bush focused on improving government management and delivering results with five government-wide and nine specific agency-wide initiatives. These attempts by various administrations and the involvement of several presidents indicate that the political leadership was sowing the seeds for improving management practices in public administration.

In the 1990s, the adoption of strategic management got a boost with the passage of several key legislative acts and issuance of executive orders (The Government Performance Results Act of 1993 (GPRA) (US Congress, 1993); The Government Management and Reform Act of 1994 (GMRA)

(US Congress, 1994); The Chief Financial Officer's Act of 1990 (CFOA) (US Congress, 1990); The Federal Managers' Financial Integrity Act of 1982 (FMFIA) (US Congress, 1982); The Federal Financial Management Improvement Act of 1996 (FFMIA) (US Congress, 1996a); The Clinger–Cohen Act of 1996 (CCA) (US Congress, 1996b); and The Office of Management and Budget Circulars A-19, A-11, A-123 and A-136 (US Office of Management and Budget, 1979, 2008, 2004a, 2009)). Following these policy drives, the focus shifted to the President's Management Agenda (US Office of Management and Budget, 2004b), supplemented by the Program Assessment Rating Tool (US Office of Management and Budget, 2004c), a central element of strategic control that was used to monitor institutional performance within the executive branch of government.

RESEARCH METHODOLOGY

The Research Question

Although a substantial amount of literature is available about public policy and executive action, researchers argue that there is a major empirical gap in linking strategic management processes to public sector organizations (Ferlie, 1992, 2002). This gap is evident despite the legislative acts and executive orders that have been issued throughout the past several decades and the flurry of papers that have appeared mainly in the journals of public administration and public policy, as well as numerous books that have been written by scholars from the public policy academies (for examples please see, Berry, 1994; Osborne and Gaebler, 1992; Kamensky, 1996, 1999; Radin, 1998, 2006; Kettl, 2002; Thompson, 2000; Moynihan, 2005; Simone et al., 2005). Therefore, the primary question is: how does strategic management work inside a federal government organization?

The Approach and Method

To investigate the manner in which the USACE strategic management process works, I adopted qualitative methodology. This method was chosen for two reasons. First, the major objective is to assimilate a descriptive account about the contemporary practices related to strategic management inside a public agency. Second, there is minimal scholarly writing about strategic management with a focus on US federal departments/agencies. By providing one of the first comprehensive descriptions in the governmental sector about the inner workings of strategic management, I have attempted to fill the gap in the strategy literature.

This case study research is based upon the framework developed by Gibbert et al. (2008). Their scholarship was underpinned originally by Cook and Campbell (1979) and later adapted by Eisenhardt (1989) and Yin (1994). The method for this case research project took the following steps. First, my search began by looking for examples of single case settings in the strategic management literature, as part of the internal validity activity. Some of the cases that were relevant included Siggelkow's (2002) longitudinal case study about developmental processes at Vanguard, focusing on organizational configuration and fit; Siggelkow's (2001) case analysis about external fit at Liz Claiborne; Allison's (1971) study of the Cuban missile crisis; and Intel's case experience about strategy-making and its evolution as a strong force in the computer industry crafted by Burgelman (2002). While some of these cases provided a comprehensive description about strategic planning, none of them took a strategic management stance from an organizational system perspective, especially in a public sector setting. However, researching these cross-cases did assist in the external validity activity (Gibbert et al., 2008), particularly in drawing the implications for this case. Second, I conducted research about the appropriate strategic management framework from the literature by pattern-matching from two sources: (a) the theoretical construct documented by another author (Hax and Majluf, 1996) and (b) the legal construct reported in Congressional documents (US Congress, 1990, 1993). For internal validity (Gibbert et al., 2008), this framework became the basis for the third step: data collection, analysis and synthesis. In this step, I collected data through various means and sources – direct observations, participatory workshops, one-on-one interviews, and post-meeting conversations and archival data. Next, I reviewed the draft reports prepared by peers and key staff members on the project committee. Then, I conducted an independent analysis and synthesis activity during which data explanations were noted from the reconciliation analysis work and comparisons of earlier drafts of the command's strategic management policy. This activity was followed by a validation and verification activity by cross-functional team members in smaller groups to explain the data analysis and synthesis and to seek their agreement on the content in the command policy. These activities involved data triangulation, multiple reviews and data explanation so that the construct validity requirement was met (Cook and Campbell, 1979; Yin, 1994; Gibbert et al., 2008). In the last step, I used inductive logic to identify practical insights (Siggelkow, 2007). To validate the discussion in this section, I scanned the management literature as well as approaching key employees and external experts so that relevant phenomena could be documented from other cases.

The Research Setting

There are several reasons that contributed to selecting the USACE as a case example for demonstrating how strategic management works inside a federal government agency. First, the USACE has a rich and long history. It has its origins in the Continental Army and was established in 1802. From its permanent establishment in 1802 to the Civil War, the USACE provided much of the engineering talent in the United States, and the US Military Academy at West Point was the first, and for a while the only, engineering school in the country. Thus, the formal training and historical tradition instilled discipline and rigor in the methodical approaches taken by the Army engineers to solve complex engineering and organizational problems.

Second, the USACE is the world's largest public engineering organization, with an annual budget of over $40 billion and an approximate count of more than 37,000 personnel that includes both civilians and military. Its civil works and military program areas in art executed through 9 divisions, 45 districts (sub-units of divisions that serve a general purpose), 1 laboratory, 2 specific purpose centers, 4 field-operating activities and 1 engineer battalion. The USACE serves the United States, Asia and Europe and extends its reach to 90 countries as a force multiplier in military engagements.

Third, the USACE is complex in its operating structure when compared with other federal bureaucracies in Washington. To use a private sector analogy, the USACE is a diversified conglomerate with a 'multidivisional structure' (Chandler, 1962; Rumelt, 1974) resident in two key areas – civil works and military programs – each with broad missions that contain multiple lines of business which cuts across geographical areas of operations. Like private sector entities, the functional areas play a supporting role to the program areas. In this complex operating structure, the majority of the workforce is civilian. Complexity is also inherent in the USACE mission scope, stakeholder diversity, constituency demands and sources of authorities. A description of the reporting structure within the USACE is provided in Appendix 1.

Fourth, while most civilian departments/agencies have been involved in strategic management activities for the past decade or so, the USACE, like the US military, has been steeped in this practice for a long time. This factor is largely due to the military establishment's commitment and familiarity with the works of Napoleon (Paret, 1986), Sun-Tzu (Griffith, 1963), Molkte (Paret, 1986) and von Clausewitz (von Clausewitz, 1976; Paret, 1986), as well as the nation's demand to solve complex military and engineering problems. As a result, the USACE was an early adopter of sophisticated toolkits such as scenario analysis, gaming and simulation, and forecasting for the Department of Defense (Baldwin, 1985).

Finally, the accessibility to information was a critical factor in selecting the USACE. This access was convenient because the author played a vital role in leading an interdisciplinary and cross-functional command-wide team to formulate the strategic management system as well as craft the strategic management policy. As a result of the access, readers will gain from the rich process descriptions in this case study that they could not have received from an outsider's view.

THE FRAMEWORK

Based on an extensive review of strategic management and public policy literature, the framework for any public organization typically has three major components. These include: (a) strategic planning, in which external and internal context ascertain strategic vision/direction, strategic choices and performance measures; (b) strategy implementation, in which programming, budgeting and executing establish performance plans; and (c) strategic control, in which performance evaluating and reporting functions are related to the strategic and performance plans (US Congress, 1982, 1990, 1993, 1996a; Hax and Majluf, 1996). As discussed earlier, the Congress, President and other related stakeholders set not only the mission but also drive the context for federal departments/agencies. Thus, in accordance with the Congressional statute – the GPRA and applicable executive orders, the organizational mission, vision, goals, objectives, strategies and performance measures are crafted and labeled as strategic planning. The strategic implementation process involves conducting programming, budgeting and executing activities for the USACE missions within the context of specific legislative acts and executive orders that enables formulation of performance plans and annual performance reports. As part of the strategic control process, the evaluating and reporting activities are carried out in accordance with the GPRA, CFOA, FMFIA and FFMIA.

Hax and Majluf (1984, 1996) emphasized the need for an organization to have an appropriate system in place where its degree of planning competence matches its degree of complexity. Strategic fit or alignment applies to the interlocking sets of activities in strategic management (Venkatraman, 1989). In particular, Venkatraman and Camillus (1984: 514) have argued that 'fit has been used to highlight the importance of synchronizing complex organizational elements for effective implementation of the chosen strategy'. The issue of fit becomes very critical for this study because, according to Mazmanian and Nienaber (1979), policy shifts must happen from the legislative to executive branch, and in effect become policy itself. From the strategy researcher's viewpoint (Venkatraman and Camillus, 1984), however, the concept of fit is an integral part to achieving strategies of any organization.

In accordance with the goals of this chapter and book, I have focused on the former – the multiple strategic processes that comprise the organizational system. Therefore, this chapter focuses on the key processes – planning, implementation (programming, budgeting and executing) and control – and not on the organization's structure. Additionally, my focus on processes can be justified because many researchers have also argued that fit is critical for organizational strategy to deliver desired organizational performance because fit allows for the implementation of organizational strategies (Kathuria et al., 2007). Many researchers suggest that in measuring the targeted performance, two kinds of alignment or fit must be considered: namely, horizontal and vertical. In their research paper, Kathuria et al.'s (2007: 505) explanation regarding both kinds of alignments is indicated in the following quote:

> The literature distinguishes between two types of organizational alignment – vertical and horizontal or lateral. Vertical alignment refers to the configuration of strategies, objectives, action plans, and decisions throughout the various levels of the organization. Strategy implementation is effectively carried out in a bottom-up fashion, with an aim to make lower level decisions consistent with the decisions at the upper levels. When this consistency is achieved, vertical alignment has been realized . . . Horizontal alignment can be defined in terms of cross-functional and intra-functional integration. Cross-functional integration connotes the consistency of decisions across functions.

Similarly, Lingle and Schieman (1996: 59) have suggested that a strong link exists between alignment and performance because 'effective organizations are organic, integrated entities in which different units, functions and levels support the company strategy – and one another'. In light of this reference on alignment and performance, the strategic management system must be designed with elements such as organizational competence and complexity while focusing on alignment (vertical and horizontal). At the USACE, these elements of design are taken into consideration before collapsing them into the three components of the strategic management framework. The USACE framework is based upon the strategic process documented in literature by Hax and Majluf (1984, 1996); crafted in the statutes by the US Congress (1982, 1990, 1993, 1994, 1996a,b); documented in the administrative guidelines by the US Office of Management and Budget (1979, 2004a,b, 2007, 2008); and written in the regulations and policies by the departments (US Department of the Army, 1989, 1994,

2009; US Department of Defense, 2003, 2006); these processes have been designed to fit with the organizational characteristics discussed earlier. Therefore the differentiating aspects include: (a) the USACE hierarchical level covers the entire organization (vertical and horizontal) and is not just limited to corporate, business and functional levels shown in the Hax and Majluf (1996) model; (b) unlike Hax and Majluf's (1996) depiction that is applicable for private firms, the components of the USACE strategic management process extend beyond strategic planning to include strategic control so that federal departments/agencies can comply with legislative acts, executive orders and departmental directives; and (c) the manner and direction in which the activities flow within the framework. The key attributes that call for such differentiation are underpinned in the very nature of certain public characteristics such as organic law, constituent expectations, cultural distinctions, institutional history, mission complexity, and organizational scale and scope. These attributes make the inner workings of the framework as well as the processes inside the strategic management system work differently when compared with private sector entities.

THE STRATEGIC MANAGEMENT SYSTEM AT USACE: A DESCRIPTIVE VIEW

This study was performed at three major levels: within each level of the headquarters (command and program areas), divisions and districts, and inside each element of the strategic management process. In this section, the next three parts account for the complexity of multi-level strategic management and illustrate the alignment of distinctive processes with their interlocking elements in terms of how the strategic management system works.

Strategic Planning

At each level, the strategic planning process feeds the strategic implementation processes of programming, budgeting and executing. The point of origination for commencement and formulation of strategic planning is the authorization and appropriations received from Congress as well as guidance, directives and policies issued from the executive branch (in this case, the Office of Management and Budget (OMB), the Office of the Secretary of Defense (OSD), the Office of the Secretary of the Army (OSA) and the Office of the Chief of Engineers (OCE)). In congruence with specific legislation, executive orders, and management directives and departmental regulations, the USACE program areas formulate their strategic plans and develop their business programs. Within the program areas, the process of strategic planning involves synthesis of two approaches: (a) formulating each program area's strategic direction, goals, objectives and strategies by leveraging scenarios and capabilities (Kahn, 1960, 1984; Schoemaker, 1991; US Congress, 1993; US Office of Management and Budget, 2008); and (b) formulating and addressing by various methods emerging and planned issues or specific management problems in which initiatives are dependent upon various stakeholders and chance (Cohen et al., 1972; Mintzberg and Waters, 1984; Lindblom, 1959; Allison, 1971). The functional areas develop their plans by participating in the program area strategic planning process. This two-pronged approach to strategic planning allows the program areas to be prepared with robust capabilities so that the organization can respond to contingency situations.

To formulate the command strategic plan, the corporate strategy group integrates the program area strategic plans and functional area plans through a roll-up procedure that involves a combination of intuition and analysis. During this integration process, the office of the commander may provide additional guidance to the corporate strategy group. This input becomes incorporated into the command strategic plan. The integrated process also involves encapsulating the emerging issues – that is, those issues that may occur outside the regular planning process – into the command strategic plan. Here, 'unplanned emergent' (Mintzberg and Waters, 1984) issues are synthesized with the 'deliberate, crafted strategy' (Mintzberg and Waters, 1984). Through this approach, a strategic thinking climate is fostered due to the deliberation, consensus and commitment among the leadership. The conversations at the strategic forums ensure that the USACE is prepared for various exigencies. To validate robustness, the corporate strategy is proof-tested against a broader set of global defense planning scenarios. This particular activity ensures that the USACE is prepared and ready to execute its mission, within the context of national guidance and higher-authority plans, and in a supporting role that provides for the common defense. Following reviews and approvals by the executive office, the command strategic plan and the consolidated command guidance are issued to all division and district commanders. This activity enables major subordinate command (MSC) to begin formulating their implementation plans.

The major subordinate commands align their strategic planning processes at two levels: the divisions and districts for downstream fit and the command area for upstream fit. The divisions and districts receive their direction from the consolidated command guidance as well as from the command strategic plan following approval from the office of the commander. The guidance and directive art incorporated into the development of the MSC implementation plan. The division addresses local operating issues in its MSC implementation plan with alignment to the command strategic plan. In the districts, the planning process involves estimating the workload and manpower requirements so that the districts can perform their programming and budgeting activity for projects.

Strategic Implementation: Programming, Budgeting and Executing

At each level, the strategic implementation process feeds the strategic control process. In the headquarters, each program area – civil works and military – has a different set of programming, budgeting and executing processes. These differences are largely due to the distinctive characteristics of each program in terms of their uniqueness in mission, stakeholder considerations, organizational reporting, statutory provisions and organizational culture. In the headquarters, the programming–budgeting–executing process includes formulating the annual program and operating budgets, preparing and issuing the program performance and budget guidance, submitting the program area budgets and justifications to higher authorities, and developing the program area annual performance plans in accordance with the Office of Management and Budget and Department of Army guidance. These activities, accomplished by civil works and military programs, are linked to their respective goals and objectives identified during the program area strategic planning process. While the programming, budgeting and executing processes are carried out independently within the program areas, the command resource management group integrates the command budget consisting of program and operating funds. The command budget integration and the command strategic plan contribute to the development of the command performance plan so that the command can focus on delivering superior results.

In the division, the programming–budgeting–executing processes ensure the requirement for balancing the regional business center's project management business processes. Besides creating equilibrium among the business processes – manpower requirements and allocations, operating budget, workload and resource leveling, and acquisition management – these processes must also align with the MSC implementation plan and the district operations plan. In the districts, the programming and budgeting processes involve formulating proposed program/project plans with upstream inputs to the region business planning process and the MSC implementation plans. The district operations plan discusses the executing details for program/projects on the shop floor.

For executing the command strategy, the headquarters staff elements and MSCs develop their implementation plans. This top-down and bottom-up approach creates buy-in and consensus between the division and headquarters staff about executing organizational goals, objectives and strategies. Due to operational configuration and cultural considerations, division commanders are given the latitude to develop and execute their MSC implementation actions. But as the situation on the ground changes with unplanned exigencies, strategic initiatives often need to be updated even in the MSC implementation plans for executing the mission by the districts as designed in local operational plans.

Strategic Control

At the USACE, the evaluating and reporting of performance results are an integral element of strategic control. Performance progress is routinely assessed and reported through external and internal mechanisms by the command, division and district levels. Top management sets stretch-targets, allowing organizational units to be measured on their strategic and operational performance. This approach to management-by-objective fosters an organizational climate in which results do matter with continuous performance improvement. External review takes the form of program area customer satisfaction surveys and stakeholder listening sessions. Each of these assessment methods enables data to be collected, analysed and synthesized by the program areas and organizational improvements to be put into place. Internal reviews, on the other hand, are highly specialized assessments about performance. The command management review assesses organizational performance on a quarterly basis. The command resource management group incorporates the management results into the financial management and internal controls processes. These processes ensure compliance with the CFOA, FMFIA and FFMIA, and OMB circulars A-11, A-123 and A-136 in terms of accurately recording the management analysis discussion and financial information in the Army's Annual Financial Statement so that policy-makers can make informed decisions about the fiscal condition of public programs. Civil works and military programs submit their annual performance plans and reports to higher authorities for tracking results and incorporating their data into higher-level financial reporting and management systems. For example, the focus of the directorate management review is to track program execution and performance while the command management review is aimed at discussing command-wide performance. Similarly, the functional areas engage in a management review process to improve their performance. The headquarters leadership undertakes a command staff review about MSC performance on a regular basis. Division commanders prepare and report their performance upwards. The district review board reports project/program performance issues upward while the district operations board discusses budget and manpower issues. Within the USACE, performance is reported upwards through the division to the headquarters for discussions in directorate and command management reviews.

DISCUSSION

For the most part, in-depth research about strategic management processes and systems in the public sector has been non-existent. Calls by Mintzberg and Westley (1992), Ferlie (2002, 1992), Wortman (1979), Montanari and Bracker (1986) and the writings by management scholars in the *Academy of Management Journal* (2005, Special Issue) are testaments to the importance and extent of management problems facing the public sector. Ring et al. (2005) as well as Hambrick (1994, 2005) argue that the public sector matters.

From this case study, strategy researchers can take away several points. First, we can all learn to invest more time and give our attention to public sector problems because the government affects all sectors of a nation's economy, especially business. With the recent surprises and shocks – the tragedy of NASA's Shuttle Columbia, the catastrophic event of 11 September, natural disasters caused by the Mississippi River, the failure of veterans' care at the Walter Reed Army Medical Center and the global economic crises of 2008 – the spotlight has shifted to the public sector in terms of the federal government's role vis-à-vis states, municipalities and industry. And it is here that we should take Hambrick's (1994, 2005) advice to heart and help out our government. If we don't step up to the plate, who will? Second, this case demonstrates the extent to which public managers are keenly committed to apply the concepts of strategic management and organizational change to tackle complex management challenges. Third, strategy researchers can learn the importance of undertaking case study research as argued by Siggelkow (2007) by going beyond the existing milieu of academics and forming partnerships with non-traditional institutions such as government. Fourth, collaborative journeys between the disciplines (social sciences and management), professionals (academicians and social sector staff), and institutions (public, non-profit and government) can benefit our field greatly by generating and testing new theories from an interdisciplinary perspective and seeding fresh ideas into practice. Fifth, this chapter challenges researchers in strategy to co-create new knowledge by co-experimenting, co-producing and co-disseminating rather than going through the case study research process solo. Lastly, practical research can help build bridges with legislators, oversight authorities and policy implementers.

Implications

First, strategic fit or alignment (Venkatraman, 1989; Venkatraman and Camillus, 1984) is applicable to multiple levels within the USACE and at departmental/agency levels (as part of the executive branch). This study demonstrates the interlocking elements of strategic processes between the headquarters and subordinate units, and with the department/agency levels because the processes operate as a 'system-of-systems' to sustain government performance. In addition, strategic fit between the organization and environment (Venkatraman and Camillus, 1984) is also applicable because of the linkages between the inner context and the outer context – namely, to the statutes, stakeholders and external conditions. Therefore, multi-level strategic management framework is a strong indicator of the success or failure of the public policies pertaining to performance, accountability and management with the government. For the USACE, this implication is captured in the following quote from Mazmanian and Nienaber (1979: 2):

> Legislation and implementing presidential directives unfortunately are insufficient in themselves to effect programmatic changes. Policy changes must filter down to the operating levels of government, the departments and agencies, which not only administer programs, but also apply and interpret and hence in effect make policy. It is at this level of the executive branch that changes in policy either succeed or fail.

Thus at the USACE, the implementation of public laws involves drafting of administrative orders, regulations and circulars for day-to-day program management by agency officials (Oleszek, 2001). Therefore, it is implied that effective multi-level strategic fit calls for paying closer attention to the statutory and executive administrative frameworks that act as boundary spanners while simultaneously ensuring alignment with the organization's systems.

Second, strategic management in large organizations focusing on organizational coordination has relevancy even to the public sector (Grant, 2003). In this case, weaving such coordination with multi-level internal fit requires coordination and interaction between the program, functional and command areas, as well as between the headquarters and field units, so that the compartmentalization of functions is lessened. The basis for effective coordination is openness, collaborative dialog, cross-fertilization of knowledge and trust. This case observes that coordination and collaboration increase transparency and foster shared organizational decision-making. It is implied that fit, external and internal, is a function of organizational interaction and collaboration. Strategic fit also ensures better improvements to performance (Venkatraman and Camillus, 1984; Siggelkow, 2002; Burgelman and Doz, 2001), largely due to changes in operational integration. Thus, operational integration (within public organizations like USACE) necessitates the combining of resources and competencies from various business units so that the maximum strategic opportunity set can be identified and realized (Burgelman and Doz, 2001).

Third, the strategic processes in an organizational system may not operate in a top-down, command-and-control-driven manner (despite being a military-led organization). Instead, decentralization plays a major role in the USACE because it gives managers maximum authority to operate with independence and allows for faster reaction time. With the diffusion of authority, middle and lower managers begin to take on the responsibility of bringing new ideas regarding organizational change to senior executives through the collaborative work process. Process action teams and working committees are the means for collaborative processes. As a result, leadership and staff are motivated to maximize their contribution to the organization. These aspects of operating philosophy make the flow of work multi-directional and multi-connected. Thus, it is implied that organizational cooperative arrangements can be viewed as an aid to 'replication of experiential knowledge such as complex organizational routines' (Stiles, 2001: 130) and fostering consensus, deliberation and commitment for the organization to adapt in dynamic environments.

Future Research Directions

Although this case enriches our understanding about how strategic management is practiced inside a federal government organization, this avenue of research is the beginning of a new stream of study for strategy scholars. In the future, researchers might focus on contexts and drivers that alter the administrative processes of public bureaucracies. For instance, since external context changes over time, researchers might focus on identifying coping mechanisms that public sector entities use to adapt to change. Furthermore, I believe that there is a need to move beyond the traditional case analysis to a quantitative assessment so that we can test implications. Notwithstanding this limitation, it must be acknowledged that this case has provided a rare glimpse to readers about strategy process in the public sector and allowed them to observe the intricacies of practice from an insider's perspective. Furthering such case research will serve to generate and test theories (Eisenhardt, 1989; Siggelkow, 2007).

CONCLUSION

This case study has applied the rigor criteria (Gibbert et al., 2008) within the context of a public organization's strategic management framework. While this chapter offers an insider perspective about the workings of strategic management in a public organization, it demonstrates that public sector managers do apply multi-disciplinary theories from public policy, sociology, political science, psychology and business to the concepts of strategic management. Also, we stand to learn that it is the interlocking nature of processes that makes the concept of fit or alignment espoused by Venkatraman and Camillus (1984) and Venkatraman (1989) work in an unusual setting – namely, the public sector.

NOTE

* This chapter has benefited from the interdisciplinary experience and cross-functional participation of key members in the US Army Corps of Engineers. Their contributions to the development and deployment of the strategic management system and the formulation of the strategic management policy are valued. I am grateful to the senior leadership for its commitment to strategic management and applaud the dedication of many individuals, inside and outside the USACE, who have significantly contributed to the evolution of strategic management. Finally, my personal thanks to Maheshkumar Joshi of George Mason University and Franz Kellermanns from Mississippi State University for offering comments and engaging in insightful discussions.

The views expressed in this paper are those of the author and do not reflect those of the US Government.

REFERENCES

Allison, G. (1971), *Essence of Decision: Explaining the Cuban Missile Crisis*, Boston, MA: Little, Brown.
Baldwin, W. C. (1985), *The Engineer Strategic Studies Center and Army Analysis*, Washington, DC: US Government Printing Office.
Barzelay, M. and C. Campbell (2003), *Preparing for the Future: Strategic Planning in the US Air Force*, Washington, DC: Brookings University Press.
Berry, F. S. (1994), 'Innovation in public management: The adoption of strategic planning', *Public Administration Review*, **54**(4): 322–329.
Bryson, J. M. (1981), 'A perspective on planning and crises in the public sector', *Strategic Management Journal*, **2**(2): 181–196.
Bryson, J. M. (1988), *Strategic Planning For Public and Non-profit Sectors*, San Francisco, CA: Jossey-Bass.

Bryson, J. M. and W. D. Roering (1988), 'Initiation of strategic planning by governments', *Public Administration Review*, **48**(6): 995–1004.

Burgelman, R. A. (2002), *Strategy as Destiny: How Strategy Making Shapes a Company's Future*, New York: The Free Press.

Burgelman, R. A. and Y. L. Doz (2001), 'The power of strategic integration', *Sloan Management Review*, **42**(3): 28–38.

Carter, J. (1979), 'State of the Union Address 1979', Speech delivered on 25 January 1979, jimmycarterlibrary.org/documents/speeches/.

Chakravarthy, B. S. and Y. L. Doz (1992), 'Strategy process research: Focusing on corporate self-renewal', *Strategic Management Journal*, **13**(special issue): 5–14.

Chandler, A. D. (1962), *Strategy and Structure: Chapters in History of the American Enterprise*, Cambridge, MA: MIT Press.

Clinton, W. J. (1993), *Improving Customer Service: Accompanying Report of the National Performance Review*, William J. Clinton Presidential Center, archives.clintonpresident ialcenter.org/?u=090193-national-performance-review-on-improving-customer-service. htm.

Cohen, M. D., J. G. March and J. P. Olsen (1972), 'A garbage can model of organizational choice', *Administrative Science Quarterly*, **17**(1): 1–25.

Cook, T. D. and D. T. Campbell (1979), *Quasi-Experimental Design: Design and Analysis Issues for Field Settings*, Skokie, IL: Rand McNally.

Dewey, J. (1948), *Reconstruction in Philosophy*, Boston, MA: Beacon Press.

Drucker, P. F. (1976), 'What results should you expect?', *Public Administration Review*, **36**(1): 12–20.

Eisenhardt, K. M. (1989), 'Building theories from case study research', *Academy of Management Review*, **14**(4): 532–550.

Ferlie, E. (1992), 'The creation and evolution of quasi markets in the public sector: a problem for strategic management', *Strategic Management Journal*, **13**(S2): 79–97.

Ferlie, E. (2002), 'Quasi strategy: strategic management in the contemporary public sector', in A. M. Pettigrew, H. Thomas and R. Whittington (eds), *The Handbook for Strategy Process Research*, London: Sage Publishers, pp. 279–298.

Gibbert, M., W. Ruigrok and B. Wicki (2008), 'What passes as a rigorous case study?', *Strategic Management Journal*, **29**(13): 1465–1474.

Grant, R. M. (2003), 'Strategic planning in turbulent environment: Evidence from the oil majors', *Strategic Management Journal*, **24**(6): 491–517.

Griffith, S. B. (translated) (1963), *Sun Tzu: The Art of War*, Oxford, UK: Oxford University Press.

Hambrick, D. C (1994), 'What if the academy actually mattered?', *Academy of Management Review*, **9**(1): 11–16.

Hambrick, D. C. (2005), 'Venturing outside the monastery', *Academy of Management Journal*, **48**(6): 961–962.

Hax, A. C. and N. S. Majluf (1984), 'The corporate strategic planning process', *Interfaces*, **14**(1): 47–60.

Hax, A. C. and N. S. Majluf (1996), *The Strategy Concept and Process: A Pragmatic Approach*, 2nd edition, Upper Saddle River, NJ: Prentice Hall.

Huff, A. S. and R. K. Reger. (1987), 'A review of strategy process research', *Journal of Management*, **13**(2): 211–236.

Kahn, H. (1960), *On Thermonuclear War*, Princeton, NJ: Princeton University Press.

Kahn, H. (1984), *Thinking the Unthinkable in the 1980s*, New York: Simon and Schuster.

Kamensky, J. (1996), 'Role of reinventing government movement in federal management reform', *Public Administration Review*, **56**(3): 247–255.

Kamensky, J. (1999), 'National partnership for reinventing government', www.govinfo. library.unt.edu/npr/whoweare/history2.html.

Kaplan, A. (1974), *The Conduct of Inquiry*, San Francisco, CA: Chandler.

Kathuria, R., M. P. Joshi and S. J. Porth (2007), 'Organizational alignment and performance: Past, present and future', *Management Decision*, **45**(3): 503–517.

Kelman, S. (2005), 'Public management needs help', *Academy of Management Journal*, **48**(6): 967–969.

Kettl, D. (2002), *The Global Public Management Revolution: A Report on the Transformation of Governance*, Washington, DC: The Brookings Institution.

Lasswell, H. D. and A. Kaplan (1950), *Power and Society: A Framework for Political Inquiry*, New Haven, CT: Yale University Press.

Lindblom, C. E. (1959), 'The science of muddling through', *Public Administration Review*, **19**(2): 79–88.

Lingle, J. H. and W. A. Schieman (1996), 'From balanced scorecard to IS management', *Management Review*, **85**(3): 56–61.

March, J. G. and H. A. Simon (1958), *Organizations*, New York: Wiley.

Mazmanian, D. and J. Nienaber (1979), *Can Organizations Change? Environmental Protection, Citizen Participation, and the Corps of Engineers*, Washington, DC: Brookings Institution.

Mintzberg, H. and J. A. Waters (1984), 'Of strategies, deliberate and emergent', *Strategic Management Journal*, **6**(3): 257–272.

Mintzberg, H. and F. Westley (1992), 'Cycles of organizational change', *Strategic Management Journal*, **13**(S2): 39–59.

Montanari, J. H. and J. S. Bracker (1986), 'The strategic management process at the public planning unit level', *Strategic Management Journal*, **7**(3): 251–265.

Moynihan, D. P. (2005), 'Goal-based learning and the future of performance', *Public Administration Review*, **65**(2): 203–216.

Oleszek, W. J. (2001), *Congressional Procedures and the Policy Process*, Washington, DC: CQ Press.

Osborne, D. and T. Gaebler (1992), *Reinventing Government: How the Entrepreneurial Spirit is Transforming the Public Sector*, Reading, MA: Addison-Wesley.

Paret, P. (ed.) (1986), *Makers of Modern Strategy: From Machiavelli to the Nuclear Age*, Princeton, NJ: Princeton University Press.

Pettigrew, A. M. (1992), 'The character and significance of strategy process research', *Strategic Management Journal*, **13**(S2), 5–16.

Porter, M. E. (1980), *Competitive Strategy*, New York: Free Press.

Pyhrr, P. A. (1970), 'Zero based budgeting', *Harvard Business Review*, **46**(6): 111–121.

Pyhrr, P. A. (1974), *Zero Based Budgeting*, New York: John Wiley and Sons.

Quinn, J. B. (1980), *Strategies for Change: Logical Incrementalism*, Homewood, IL: Irwin.

Radin, B. A. (1998), 'The Government Performance Results Act: Hydra-headed monster or flexible management tool?', *Public Administration Review*, **58**(4): 307–317.

Radin, B. A. (2000), *Beyond Machiavelli: Policy Analysis Comes of Age*. Washington, DC: Georgetown University Press.

Radin, B. A. (2006), *Challenging the Performance Movement: Accountability, Complexity and Democratic Values*, Washington, DC: Georgetown University Press.

Ring, P. S., G. A. Bigley, T. D'Aunno and T. Khanna (2005), 'Perspectives on how governments matter', *Academy of Management Review*, **30**(2): 308–320.

Roberts, N. C. and L. Wargo (1994), 'The dilemma of planning in large scale organizations: The case of the United States Navy', *Journal of Public Administration Research and Theory*, **4**(4): 469–491.

Rumelt, R. (1974), *Strategy, Structure and Economic Performance*, Boston, MA: Harvard Business School Press.

Schick, A. (1966), 'The road to ZBB: The stages of budget reform', *Public Administration Review*, **26**(4): 243–258.

Schick, A. (1978), 'The road from ZBB', *Public Administration Review*, **38**(2): 177–180.

Schoemaker, P. J. H. (1991), 'When and how to use scenario planning: a heuristic approach with illustration', *Journal of Forecasting*, **10**(6) 549–564.

Siggelkow, N. (2001), 'Change in the presence of fit: The rise, the fall, and the renaissance of Liz Clairborne', *Academy of Management*, **44**(4): 838–857.

Siggelkow, N. (2002), 'Evolution towards fit', *Administrative Science Quarterly*, **47**(1): 125–159.

Siggelkow, N. (2007), 'Persuasion with case studies', *Academy of Management Journal*, **50**(1): 20–24.

Simon, H. A. (1958), *Administrative Behavior*, 2nd edition, New York: Macmillan.

Simon, H. A. (1991), 'Organizations and markets', *Journal of Economic Perspectives*, **5**(2): 25–43.

Simone, R., J. Carnevale and A. Millar (2005), 'A systems approach to performance based management: The national drug control strategy', *Public Administration Review*, **65**(2): 191–202.

Stiles, J. (2001), 'Strategic alliances', in H. W. Volberda and T. Elfring (eds), *Rethinking Strategy*, Thousand Oaks, CA: Sage Publications, pp. 128–139.

Thompson, J. R. (2000), 'Reinventing as reform: Assessing the national performance review', *Public Administration Review*, **60**(6): 508–521.

US Congress (1982), Public Law 97-255: Federal Managers' Financial Integrity Act of 1982, 93rd Congress, 8 September, Washington, DC: US Government Printing Office.

US Congress (1990), Public Law 101-576: Chief Financial Officer's Act of 1990, 101st Congress, 15 November, Washington, DC: US Government Printing Office.

US Congress (1993), Public Law 103-62: Government Performance Results Act of 1993, 103rd Congress, 3 August, Washington, DC: US Government Printing Office.

US Congress (1994), Public Law 103-356: Government Management Reform Act of 1994, 103rd Congress, 13 October, Washington, DC: US Government Printing Office.

US Congress (1996a), Public Law 104-208: Federal Financial Management Improvement Act, 104th Congress, 30 September, Washington, DC: US Government Printing Office.

US Congress (1996b), Public Law 104-106: Clinger–Cohen Act of 1996 in National Defense Authorization Act for Fiscal Year 1996, 104th Congress, 3 January, Washington, DC: US Government Printing Office.

US Department of the Army (1989), Army Long Range Planning System. Army Regulation 11-32, (January). Washington, DC: HQ, US Department of the Army.

US Department of the Army (1994), Army Planning, Programming, Budgeting and Execution System. Army Regulation 1-1 (Jan 1994). Washington, DC: HQ, US Department of the Army.

US Department of the Army (2009), US Army Campaign Plan. Washington, DC: US Department of Army.

US Department of Defense (2003), 'US Department of Defense Planning, Programming and Budgeting System', DoD Directive Number 7045.14, 21 November, www.dtic.mil/whs/directives/corres/pdf/514101p.pdf.

US Department of Defense (2006), 'US Department of Defense: Quadrennial Defense Review Report', www.defenselink.mil/qdr/report/Report20060203.pdf.

US Office of Management and Budget (1979), 'Circular Number A-19: Legislative Coordination and Clearance', www.whitehouse.gov/omb/circulars_default/.

US Office of Management and Budget (1997), 'National Partnership for Reinventing Government', www.govinfo.library.unt.edu/npr/whoweare/historypart1.html.

US Office of Management and Budget (2004a), 'OMB Circular A-123: Management Accountability and Internal Control', www.whitehouse.gov/omb/circulars_default/.

US Office of Management and Budget (2004b), 'President's Management Agenda', www.whitehouse.gov/omb/pma/index.html.

US Office of Management and Budget (2004c), 'FY 2004 budget chapter introducing the PART: rating the performance of federal programs', www.whitehouse.gov/omb/part/index.html.

US Office of Management and Budget (2007), 'Executive Order 13450: Improving Government Program Performance', 13 November, www.whitehouse.gov/omb/assets/performance_pdfs/eo13450.pdf.

US Office of Management and Budget (2008), 'OMB Circular A-11: Preparation, Submission and Execution of Budget', www.whitehouse.gov/omb/circulars_default/.

US Office of Management and Budget (2009), 'OMB Circular A-136: Financial Reporting Requirements', available at http://www.whitehouse.gov/omb/circulars_default/.

Van de Ven, A. H. (1992), 'Suggestions for studying strategy process: a research note', *Strategic Management Journal*, **13**(S2): 169–188.

Venkatraman, N. (1989), 'The concept of "fit" in strategy research: Toward verbal and statistical correspondence', *Academy of Management Review*, **14**(3): 423–444.

Venkatraman, N. and J. C. Camillus (1984), 'Exploring the concept of "fit" in strategic management', *Academy of Management Review*, **9**(4): 513–525.

von Clausewitz, C. (1976), *On War*, M. Howard and P. Paret (edited and translated), Princeton, NJ: Princeton University Press.

von Neumann, J. and O. Morgenstern (1947), *Theory of Games and Economic Behavior*, 2nd edition, Princeton, NJ: Princeton University Press.

Wortman Jr., M. S. (1979), 'Strategic management: Not-for-profit organizations', in D. E. Schendel and C. W. Hofer (eds), *Strategic Management: A View of Business Policy and Planning*, Boston, MA: Little, Brown, pp. 353–381.

Yin, R. K. (1994), *Case Study Research: Design and Methods*, London, UK: Sage Publishers.

APPENDIX 1   ORGANIZATIONAL REPORTING STRUCTURE

The USACE is under the leadership of the commanding general (military rank of lieutenant general, equivalent to chief executive officer) and reports to the Chief of Staff for the United States Army. Reporting to the commanding general is the deputy-commanding general for command operations (military rank of major general, equivalent to chief operating officer). Each program area is headed by a deputy-commanding general (military rank of either brigadier general or major general), who reports through the deputy commander of the USACE to the commanding general and coordinates programmatic matters with their respective assistant secretaries within the Department of the Army. In the field, the division commanders whose rank is brigadier general have command-and-control authority over their major subordinate command (an MSC is comprises a division with multiple districts) with assigned missions in a specific geographical jurisdiction. The division commander reports to the USACE deputy commander. The district engineers (military rank of colonel) report to the division commander and are responsible for specific missions in their area of operations.

24 The OODA loop: a new strategic management approach for family business
Joseph H. Astrachan, Chester W. Richards, Gaia G. Marchisio and George E. Manners

INTRODUCTION

Today, achieving and maintaining strategic competitiveness is one of the most difficult challenges that firms must address. To meet this need, firms develop, either implicitly or explicitly, strategic management processes whose ultimate goal is to achieve the performance outcomes that allow firms to be competitive over time (Habbershon et al., 2003) and to respond to the continuous changes in the competitive environment in an appropriate and timely way (Volberda, 1996). The current crisis and marked uncertainty do not leave much room for long term plans that may not incorporate the speed, flexibility and responsiveness that the current economic environment requires. To survive and prosper, firms must be swift and agile, able to understand the environment quickly, able to spot opportunities and emergent threats immediately, able to make decisions rapidly, able to recognize when change is appropriate, and able to enact such changes without delay to give themselves a competitive edge and achieve decisive results in the marketplace. Thus, decision speed becomes crucial in enabling firms in dynamic environments to exploit opportunities before they disappear (Stevenson and Gumpert, 1985).

To understand how organizations can accelerate their decision speed, thus improving their performance in a challenging environment (Baum and Wally, 2003; Eisenhardt, 1989), it is important to focus theory and research development on strategic management (Sharma et al., 1997), and firm's adaptability and flexibility (Volberda, 1999).

We center our analysis on family firms, a particular kind of organization that appears to dominate the world economy (Debicki et al., 2009), representing a major engine of economic growth and wealth creation (Short et al., 2009). Family firms have unique characteristics derived from patterns of ownership, governance and succession that are argued to influence the strategic processes and, ultimately, the performance of such firms (Anderson and Reeb, 2003; Chua et al., 1999).

Strategic management and adaptation are topics that have been routinely ignored and remain understudied in the family business field (Debicki et al., 2009; Hatum and Pettigrew, 2004; Zahra and Sharma, 2004). While family business research is no longer in its initial phase (Litz, 1997), its research agenda remains quite long. For example, goal and strategy formulation, innovation in and professionalization, resource management, culture and internationalization need to be addressed in greater depth (Zahra and Sharma, 2004).

Family business literature has only recently evolved from a static view of family and business as two interlocking and interacting systems (Hollander and Elman, 1988), differentiating family business from non-family by the degree of system boundary overlap (Ibrahim and Ellis, 1988; McCollom, 1990; Stafford et al., 1999; Whiteside and Brown, 1991); and explaining the competitive tension in strategic plan development (Habbershon et al., 2003), to a view in which the 'family business social system is a "metasystem" comprised of three broad subsystem components: 1) the controlling family unit [. . .]; 2) the business unit [. . .]; and 3) the individual family members' (Habbershon et al., 2003: 454–455). Thus, the performance of family business is not only influenced by business activities, but also by the resources and the actions developed at the family and individual family member levels (Chrisman et al., 2003; Pearson et al., 2008).

Literature on strategy seemed to have abandoned the view according to which 'there is only one version of what strategy is, and instead accept [ed] that there are multiple versions of what constitute strategy, each with its own set of assumptions and related dimensions' (Bhalla et al., 2009: 80). The evolution of the strategic management field, both theory and research, has swung between an outside and inside perspective in an attempt to explain the relationship between the two, and has concluded that future steps should be moved in the direction of integrative approaches, able to capture the new dynamism in the competitive environment (Furrer et al., 2008; Hoskisson et al., 1999).

In an attempt to provide this outside and inside integration in the context of family business, we propose a conceptual strategic management framework that we believe fits family business well and addresses family business' systemic nature, including all three levels, and the challenges imposed by the rapidly evolving and highly uncertain economic environment. The framework we refer to was developed by John Boyd and is often simplified to the 'OODA loop'. Our intent here is not to advocate the validity of the framework, since that has already been done (Osinga, 2007), but rather to introduce the reader to a heuristic yet not well-known tool and explore its fit with family business. John Boyd, the 'fighter pilot who changed the art of war' (Coram, 2002), after retiring from the Air Force, built a comprehensive theory of conflict that was originally directed towards war but which has since been applied to business (Richards, 2004).

Boyd's philosophy emphasizes the importance of avoiding or degrading the power of the enemy rather than just destroying its military. For military purposes, Boyd prescribes methods to attack the ability of opponents to effectively plan, act in a coordinated fashion and maintain group cohesion. Boyd's framework can be applied effectively in a non-military context if we regard businesses as groups of people who must work together under conditions of uncertainty and stress in order to achieve results that are contested by other groups, namely clients that have to be won over and competitors who must be countered.

In a now classic view of strategy (Porter, 1980), strategy must pursue environmental fit. In some cases, strategy means that firms have to react to industry dynamics; in other cases, a firm's strategy may include influencing those dynamics by, for example, pre-emptive pricing moves and accelerating the rate of product introductions.

Time can be viewed as a scarce and unreplenishable resource. Boyd recognized this and concluded that the *timing* of action is often more important than the *magnitude* of the action. In rapidly changing environments, for example, it is quite difficult to maintain alignment between stated strategy and strategic action (Burgelman and Grove, 1996) unless organizations become agile decision makers. To make such a strategy work, organizations must seek to minimize delays due to internal processes so that opportunities can be seized while they are still opportunities.

In the early 19th century, the great Prussian strategist and general, Carl von Clausewitz, called all causes that promote a focus on internal processes and internal dynamics, things that delay decisions and implementation, 'friction', and insisted that friction distinguishes 'real war from war on paper', that is, actions from plans (Clausewitz, 1968). In a similar vein, some current thinking in business strategy has followed advances in physics and suggests a major task is decreasing entropy; energy that is present in an organization but not available for accomplishing organizational goals, such as endless meetings, processes that don't 'add value' and layers of bureaucracy (Peters, 1987). Boyd's ideas are very consistent with this view and the success of his framework for strategic decision making depends on an organizational culture that seeks to minimize Clausewitzian friction.

The remainder of this paper is divided into three sections. The first section explores a brief review of the literature about the key concepts adopted in the paper: family business and Boyd's strategic concept. The second section provides a description of the OODA loop framework as developed by Boyd. In the third section, we explain the reasons we believe the framework fits family business' characteristics and dynamics better than other strategic management approaches; and we discuss contributions and implications for family businesses and researchers, as well as limitations and future steps.

LITERATURE REVIEW

Family Business as a Context

Since the late 1980s, defining family firms has been 'the first and most obvious challenge' (Astrachan et al., 2002: 45). Authors have recognized that if practically it seems easy to recognize what is meant by the term 'family business', from a theoretical point of view, in the attempt of articulating a precise definition 'they quickly discover that it is a very complicated phenomenon' (Lansberg et al., 1988: 1). Authors have been trying hard to conceptualize 'family business', and they have actually produced over 30 definitions (Litz, 2008), although none have been widely accepted (Klein et al., 2005). Among them, some definitions focus on ownership, some on ownership and management involvement of an owning family, and some on generational transfer or on family business culture (Astrachan et al., 2002).

One of the biggest issues authors have been struggling with is the attempt to create an inclusive view that could comprise the broad range of family businesses and their variability (Distelberg and Sorenson, 2009). If defining 'family business' is still challenging researchers, a growing consensus has been emerging around some characteristics that have been considered unique. It is believed that the interaction among family, business and individuals creates unique systemic conditions and constituencies that can build (or destroy) competitive advantage and impact the performance of the family business' social system (Habbershon et al., 2003). In particular, we believe there are four distinctive characteristics and dynamics within family businesses that might also influence the strategic management process in family firms (Chrisman et al., 2005; Sharma et al., 1997).

First, family businesses have a systematic nature; family and business are separate but overlapping systems, or using system terminology, they are 'independent and interdependent subsystems' (Distelberg and Sorenson, 2009: 66). In the early stage of the field, a dual interlinking closed-system approach was used (family and business), while subsequently a more complex and open approach has been introduced (family, business and individual) (Pieper and Klein, 2007). This systemic nature of family businesses requires a holistic view when dealing with them (Distelberg and Sorenson, 2009).

Second, the family business system aims to survive in the long run, trying to pass the firm to the following generation (Ward, 1997), and having committed shareholders providing patient capital (Zellweger, 2007). Also, practice shows plenty of examples where family businesses are particularly conscious of long term survival (Trostel and Nichols, 1982). They represent the most lasting type of business: it is not uncommon, in fact, to find family businesses that are hundreds of years old. The oldest still-running family business in the world is in Japan, founded in 718, and run today by the 46th generation. Companies lasting over several centuries are not rare exceptions among family businesses. The phenomenon is so widespread that there are two clubs whose members are businesses that have been trading continuously for at least 200 (les Hénokiens) or 300 (The Tercentenarians) years and more, while retaining links with the founding family. For these firms, survival and continuity have become their ultimate objectives.

The third characteristic family businesses have is the pursuit of several goals, which go beyond mere profit maximization: 'Wealth creation is not necessarily the only or even primary goal of all family firms. [. . .] Value creation captures multiple goals and a purpose that transcends profitability, better than wealth creation that really represents the means rather than the ends of family enterprise or enterprising families' (Chrisman et al., 2003: 468).

Last, research has shown that family businesses have a strong culture: in fact, family-controlled firms can have a strong distinct, performance-enhancing culture (Denison et al., 2004), able to develop a strong sense of belonging among both family and non-family (Geus, 1997).

Overall, it has been recognized that family firms are more complex than non-family firms (Pieper and Klein, 2007). Researchers have been dealing with this complexity for almost 50 years now. Family business, in fact, is a relatively young field: its emergence in the 1960s can be attributed to the proactive approach of a small number of individual practitioners who realized that many businesses had members from the owning families involved with the business (Astrachan and McMillan, 2006). After these beginnings, nearly 20 years elapsed before the first academic publications recognized family businesses and called for the attention of multiple researchers, disciplines and approaches (Heck et al., 2008). In the last 20 years, the field has grown greatly. Researchers remain convinced that family involvement makes a family business different from one with no family ownership or involvement.

An early approach to describing family businesses used a three-circle Venn diagram, showing overlap and independence of the subsystems of family, business and owners (Tagiuri and Davis, 1996). This approach, though popular among practitioners, has been criticized mainly because it lacks a dependent variable, which makes it difficult to examine the efficacy of the family business in terms of achieving the goals set by the owning family (Chua et al., 2003b).

Other frameworks have been developed which assist the development of strategic management theory of family firms and theory that explains the effects of family involvement on firm performance (Chrisman et al., 2005). More recently, researchers have proposed frameworks, models and theories such as the sustainable family business model (Danes et al., 2008; Heck et al., 2008; Stafford et al., 1999); F-PEC scale measuring the family influence and control (Astrachan et al., 2002), family embeddedness perspective (Aldrich and Cliff, 2003), agency theory and altruism (Schulze et al., 2003), and the bull's eye model of open systems (Pieper and Klein, 2007).

Two recent approaches are relevant here, one that emphasizes the beneficial effects of family involvement – the Resource Based View (RBV) (Habbershon and Williams, 1999) – and another that explains malevolent family influence – Agency Theory (Schulze et al., 2001). However, both of the approaches are built on the implicit assumption that the primary goal for family businesses is wealth creation. This has been criticized by family business scholars (Chrisman et al., 2003; Sharma et al., 1997), who state that 'wealth creation is not necessarily the only or even primary goal of all family firms' (Chrisman et al., 2003: 468). The authors agree with the view that family businesses have multiple, complex and changing goals (Adams et al., 2004; Sharma et al., 1997), generating value for a wider range of internal and external stakeholders than family only (Tagiuri and Davis, 1992).

Moores (2009: 170) attempted to prove that the family business field has evolved into a scientific discipline and that it now needs to define clear paradigms 'using the integration of accepted theories to better explain the subject body of the phenomena'. One conclusion Moores drew is that theories to be adopted can no longer be based on 'a single objective to be maximized, but rather must embrace the presence of multiple objectives' (2009: 178).

Despite their questionable assumptions, both RBV and Agency Theory have been widely used, mainly because they help explain strategic management issues, relevant for developing a theory of family firms, such as goal and strategy content, formulation, implementation and control, together with leadership and succession (Chrisman et al., 2005). Such a strategic management perspective, in fact, is needed to improve family business practice and performance, which represents the ultimate goal of developing such a theory (Sharma et al., 1997).

In sum, because of the multiple goals of family businesses and their owning families, the complexity of the interactions among multiple systems that may have different normative values and purposes, and the dynamic nature of the family business system through time, a strategic framework for family business must have the capacity to model the complexity of family business over time and be able to account for its systemic nature and multitude of objectives.

The Strategic Theory of John Boyd

Boyd's ideas are compelling. His theory grows from an assumption based in evolutionary science:

> Goal: Survive, survive on own terms, or improve our capacity for independent action. The competition for limited resources to satisfy these desires may force one to diminish adversary's capacity for independent action, or deny him the opportunity to survive on his terms, or make it impossible for him to survive at all. (Boyd, 1987a: 14)

Some regard Boyd as the most important strategist of the 20th century, or perhaps even since Sun Tzu (Osinga, 2007: 3). John R. Boyd is known in the US Air Force as the creator of the energy-maneuverability concept in the 1960s, which continues to influence pilot training and the design of combat aircraft. His theory revolutionized fighter design by emphasizing maneuverability, the ability to change airspeed, altitude or direction (in any combination), instead of focusing on top speed, which had been the primary consideration until Boyd's concept was accepted.

After his retirement in 1975, Boyd generalized the concept of maneuverability from aircraft to organizations. A key idea is the use of change, and particularly the relative rate of change, to influence the ability of an opponent to make and execute timely decisions so as to increase the level of entropy in the opposing organization.

Although Boyd's major work, 'Patterns of Conflict', a survey primarily of ground warfare since the beginning of time (Coram, 2002: 322), was addressed mainly to military organizations around the globe, his work is beginning to influence the business world (Richards, 2004). In the 1980s, a Harvard professor published a paper about a business campaign where the use of time was described as one of the most effective weapons (Stalk, 1988). The reference to war-related concepts reflects a conclusion from the study of military history: time-based strategy can overcome significant disadvantages in size and technology. The aim in business as in war is to avoid conventional, that is, predictable patterns of thinking that (even) in the business world have failed to create competitive advantage.

Within the broader US military, Boyd is appreciated for his 'OODA loop', which emphasizes the role of a shared implicit orientation, or world-view, as the basis of command and control and therefore of effective group activity. He has had particular impact on the US Marine Corps, where his briefing cycle, 'A Discourse on Winning and Losing', provided the theoretical underpinning for the Marines' doctrine of maneuver warfare.

The OODA loop describes an interactive (decision maker and environment), non-sequential process that allows extraordinary adaptability in making critical decisions in unpredictable, constantly changing environments. The OODA loop was developed by Boyd after he reflected on his own experiences as a fighter pilot, examined many wars, battles and engagements, and wondered what it took to win in any conflict. The basic answer he came up with is the concept of 'agility', which he defined in several ways, but settled on the ability to keep one's dynamic worldview more closely matched to the external world than that of any opponent or competitor.

This concept of agility can apply to any form of conflict or competition, including business. The application of war to business is not new. The *Art of War* by Sun Tzu is the world's first known treatise on war, but the key concepts inspired the development of strategy in business. If properly applied, some of the military strategies have proved to be very useful to overcome enormous disadvantages in size and technology (Byus and Box, 2007). It is worth noting that Boyd did not generally talk about 'winning' but wrote instead of surviving on one's own terms and improving one's capacities for independent action in situations where other thinking beings or organizations are trying to do likewise and where there are not sufficient resources for all parties to achieve these objectives (Boyd, 1986: 10). Such situations are ones in which conflict will almost certainly occur. This concept of 'winning' is also as applicable to business as it is to war.

Although Boyd's work is rooted in the study of military history, he follows in the footsteps of other military strategists, including Sun Tzu, Corbett, Fuller and Lawrence, by adopting a holistic approach that draws upon various disciplines to provide insights into the nature of conflict (Osinga, 2007). Osinga labeled Boyd as the first postmodern strategist because 'his approach and his views implicitly are pregnant with postmodern epistemological principles. [. . .] at the heart of Boyd's view resides the view of knowledge as unfolding, evolving as a dialectic process and uncertain' (Osinga, 2007: 242).

Boyd's OODA loop has been characterized as a grand theory because of its elegant simplicity, extensive domain of application and high quality of insights about strategic essentials (Gray, 1999: 91).

THE FRAMEWORK PROPOSED: THE OODA LOOP BY BOYD

Before giving the details of the framework, a premise is needed. In particular, we believe that to fully understand and functionally operate Boyd's framework, there are two fundamental conditions that must be met. These conditions are needed because Boyd's OODA loop can produce the need for rapid change and an organization must be designed to enact rapid change for the OODA loop to have great value. The first condition is the inculcation of four cultural characteristics (for which Boyd often used the German words that originally denoted them): focus and direction (*Schwerpunkt*); deep knowledge (*Fingerspitzengefühl*); trust (*Einheit*); and mission-oriented task ownership (*Auftrag*). The other primary condition is that the organization must develop a harmonized orientation among its members.

Condition 1: The Four Business Cultural Characteristics

Boyd defined four attributes needed for operational success of any organization which dramatically improve the speed of decision making and action taking. He derived them from a deep analysis of the many examples in history where numerically inferior forces were victorious. He borrowed the terminology from the German tactics of *Blitzkrieg*[1] that he studied. According to Boyd, any group of people that have to work together in an uncertain and threatening environment must develop these four conditions (or something equivalent) in order to shape a cultural environment that promotes local autonomy and enables people within the organization to decide and execute faster (i.e. with less friction).

The first attribute is the focus and direction of the effort, which defines what has to be done. It comes from the German term *Schwerpunkt*, and in Boyd's usage indicates any concept that gives focus and direction even in ambiguous situations. It is the main goal for the whole organization, the reason to be and to operate. Once the focus is set, all the other activities of the organization must support it, providing a clear sense of direction and aligning everyone's efforts within the company.[2] A widely shared understanding of the *Schwerpunkt* helps people decide what to do in situations where they do not have previously issued instructions or the ability or time to contact higher levels of authority. It becomes a fundamental tool for motivating people in the organization while harmonizing their energy and efforts to reach the goal. As a result, internal friction is reduced. Goal setting is in fact the most common device for giving people focus and direction (Erez and Kanfer, 1983; Mento et al., 1987).

The second attribute is the development of deep, intuitive knowledge (*Fingerspitzengefühl*), which is the product of years of experience and incessant practice such that skills and a feel for one's job, company and industry become second nature. Only then can people begin to acquire a true intuitive competence by using their skills together in ever more complex circumstances, thereby building an intuitive feel for situations in which there is considerable stress and the answers are not clear. Deep knowledge allows for insight into confusing and chaotic situations. As with the *Schwerpunkt* concept, internal friction is reduced because people know what to do the vast majority of the time (Klein, 1998), increasing decentralization in decision making, which in turn facilitates a firm's adaptability (Hatum and Pettigrew, 2004).

The third attribute is trust; unity and cohesion among the people in the organization (*Einheit*). This condition is most important in situations where, under acute stress, there is no time to check with higher authority. In such circumstances, trust that members of the organization will do the right things is vital. Trust creates the internal harmony that permits implicit communication among team members, where very little needs to be written down. Trust is also positive because it encourages individual initiative.

This kind of trust and unity cannot be assumed; it has to be developed by training and working together, especially on challenging problems over extended periods of times. As Boyd observed:

> Expose individuals, with different skills and abilities, against a variety of situations – whereby each individual can observe and orient himself simultaneously to the others and to the variety of changing situations.
> ? Why ?
>
> In such an environment, a harmony, or focus and direction, in operations is created by the bonds of implicit communications and trust that evolve as a consequence of the similar mental images or impressions each individual creates and commits to memory by repeatedly sharing the same variety of experiences in the same ways. (Boyd, 1987b: 18).

The fourth and last attribute is 'contracting' of the responsibility for accomplishing an objective. Here too the original meaning comes from a German term, *Auftrag*, which can be translated using, among others, such terminology as a mission, a mandate, a mutually agreed understanding. This condition stresses the importance of developing task ownership and a sense of responsibility among the people in the organization, which allows for individual initiative while accomplishing the organization's mission within given constraints. It is a matter of contracting, which requires people in the organization to consider, think and agree, rather than acquiesce.

Once the constraints are agreed upon, total freedom to proceed is given in the organization and accountability is required. Boyd emphasized that:

> As part of this concept, the subordinate is given the right to challenge or question the feasibility of mission if he feels his superior's ideas on what can be achieved are not in accord with the existing situation or if he feels his superior has not given him adequate resources to carry it out. Likewise, the superior has every right to expect his subordinate to carry out the mission contract when agreement is reached on what can be achieved consistent with the existing situation and resources provided. (Boyd, 1986: 76)

The above mentioned conditions are fundamental to making and executing decisions expeditiously. When people have agreed on common goals and have built sufficient trust based on mutual experience, they know what they are supposed to achieve and what they are capable of, and they trust others to do what they agreed to do. Having mutual trust, people can trust supervisors not to order them to do something that they cannot do or that will endanger them without important strategic reasons. This approach stresses the concept of mission over task (German: *Befehl*) and requires two-way communication between the leader and the followers, who have the right to challenge and question the feasibility of a project. In this way, it becomes possible to give freedom to operate within a strong agreed-upon framework, aiming towards a clear goal.

Condition 2: The Big 'O' Orientation

The second condition that allows both a better understanding and successful operation of Boyd's framework is the dynamic mental model that needs to be developed and shared in the organization. Boyd refers to this mental model as *orientation*. Orientation is the lens through which what is observed in the environment is perceived and interpreted. Orientation is a direct result of the environment we occupy, the new information gathered in combination with our past experiences, genetic heritage, cultural traditions and the analysis and synthesis we conduct. Genetic heritage, cultural tradition and previous experience represent the implicit repertoire of psychological skills built over time; while analysis and synthesis are the way to manipulate the information gathered during observation. In Boyd's words: 'orientation is an interactive process of many sided implicit cross-referencing projections, empathies, correlations, and rejections' (Boyd, 1987b: 15).

Orientation is an ongoing, interactive process, whose outcomes at any point in time are images, views or impression of the world, shaped by the above factors. Boyd explained the orientation stage as follows:

> Without our genetic heritage, cultural traditions, and previous experiences, we do not possess an implicit repertoire of psychophysical skills shaped by environments and changes that have been previously experienced.
>
> Without analysis and synthesis, across a variety of domains or across a variety of competing independent channels of information, we cannot evolve new repertoires to deal with unfamiliar phenomena or unforeseen change.
>
> Without a many-sided implicit cross-referencing process of projection, empathy, correlation, and rejection (across many different domains or channels of information), we cannot even do analysis and synthesis. (Boyd, 1996: 1)

This process of observation that allows us to detect events in the environment should be 'continuous and is constituted by the development and maintenance of interaction of various kinds with the environment' (Osinga, 2007: 193). Therefore, in a given organization, orientations among individuals must be harmonized and aligned but never locked; the continuous interaction with the environment is fundamental. In fact, as long as it stays open, groupthink can be avoided and the organization can be successful. A common, implicit orientation among group members is crucial since it shapes the way the organization interacts with the environment, which is at the base of organizational adaptation, that can be defined as the 'ability of an organization to change itself, or the way it behaves, in order to survive in the face of the external changes which were not predicted in any precise way when the organization was designed' (Tomlinson, 1976: 533). According to Boyd, adaptation is essential to survival.

The OODA Loop

Boyd developed the idea of the OODA loop by looking for a common path among the winners in conflict. His conclusion was that operating at a quicker pace than one's opponent can create opportunities to win, even for those who might have a disadvantage in terms of size and technology. His conclusion has many applications in business, particularly for those who intend to grow at the expense of their larger competitors.

The framework, which is usually summarized in the OODA 'loop', consists of four distinctive, although not distinct, activities, as shown in Figure 24.1. Its name, OODA, is the acronym for the four activities: observe, orient, decide and act. One activity is *observation* of the environment, gathering all the possible information about the physical, mental and moral situation, including potential allies and opponents, by whatever means possible. Accurate observation is critical since it is the only input from the environment. According to Boyd, an important task of observation is to search for data and information that do not fit with the current

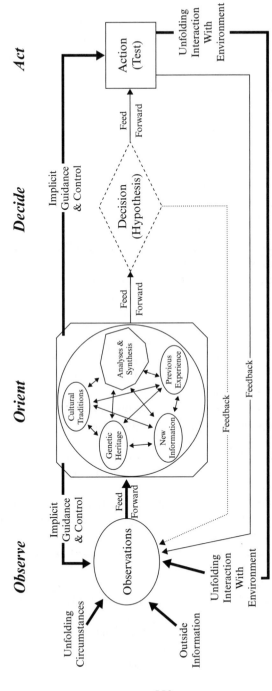

Observe   *Orient*   *Decide*   *Act*

J.R. Boyd, 'The Essence of Winning and Losing', 1996.

Figure 24.1   The OODA loop by Boyd

553

worldview (orientation). In particular, one must spot such mismatches before it becomes too late to understand that the environment, or any of its parts, has changed significantly and adaptive change becomes impossible or prohibitively expensive. Intelligent systems that obtain information from outside and aid in understanding are therefore very helpful to observation. In particular, firms implementing formal and informal mechanisms to scan the environment increase the likelihood of identifying issues quickly, enabling them to be more proactive and change successfully (Pettigrew and Whipp, 1992).

The second element of the OODA loop is orientation, which is the worldview. Orientation is conditioned by several elements, such as genetic heritage, culture and past experiences, that are combined with the new information fed by the observation of the environment, so as to form mental schemes and tacit knowledge about the world. In the business environment, it can be defined from a gap analysis between observation and orientation, which Boyd called 'mismatches'. Mismatches define what is wrong and what needs to be changed.

Although necessary, it is not sufficient for the members of the organization to keep their individual orientations well matched to reality. They must also ensure that their individual concepts of reality are roughly aligned throughout the organization. This is critical to reducing friction and permits the technique that Boyd called 'implicit guidance and control' (Espevik et al., 2006; Klein, 1998). The more the orientation is shared by the people in the organization, the more implicitly and faster decisions can be made, and the better the opportunity to gain competitive advantage. The more harmonized individual orientations are, the less the need to explicitly state a decision, saving precious time and contributing to agility.

Putting all these ingredients together defines a 'control' system that encourages all members of the organization to use their creativity and initiative in ways that further organizational goals and to engage in mission-type management.

According to this theory, organizations that become better at these attributes than their competition will win, that is, achieve their goals at the expense of those who are less adept. This is an ancient idea dating back to Sun Tzu, who provided a list of seven organizational attributes that would serve as a guide for comparison of organizations. Sun Tzu's seven factors for assessing who will win regard: which political leadership has the stronger moral influence; which commander is the more able; which force is better able to use terrain and the weather; in which are instructions and regulations better carried out; which has the stronger soldiers; which has the better training; and which administers rewards and punishments more clearly, consistently and without excess in either (Tzu, 1963, 1988).

Boyd's list may be considered as a direct descendant of Sun Tzu's, and it should be noted that Sun Tzu's is applicable, with minor modifications, to organizations other than armies.

Research is confirming the utility of commonality of orientation for business, particularly for family businesses. Firms with a high degree of commonality among their mental models, for example, are more likely to spot external threats to the business (Kellermanns and Barnett, 2008). A common, aligned and harmonized orientation determines the speed of *decision*, allowing the organization to understand, before others, whether or not it is necessary to act, and how fast.

Research has shown some evidence that decision speed results in enhanced firm growth and performance (Baum and Wally, 2003). More recently, Doz and Kosonen recognized the advantages for a company to be agile, and to stay nimble and flexible, so as to be 'open to new evidence, always ready to reassess past choices and change direction in light of new developments, and willing and able to turn on a dime' (2008: 95).

Because Boyd emphasized the implicit over the explicit 'in order to gain a favorable mismatch in friction and time (i.e., ours lower than any adversary)', it follows that most decision making should occur inside the orientation block (Boyd, 1987b: 22). Such 'intuitive' decision making accords with the concept of 'recognition-primed decision making' (Klein, 1998). Explicit decisions, indicated by the 'decision' block, are needed when the implicit link cannot be used. This situation can arise when people are not sufficiently trained, individually or as an organization (which would indicate a lack of *Einheit*), or when the nature of the decision requires explicit communication, as with financial transactions and the employment of nuclear weapons.

Although people refer to the OODA as a loop, it is not as simple as 'observe, then orient, then decide, then act'. It is definitely not a linear process and some of the activities have to be realized simultaneously. Orientation must always be maintained as more accurate than competitors' orientations. Decisions should generally be made intuitively and communicated implicitly so that the individual or the organization can act more expeditiously. Both decision and action flow from orientation, which has to be continuously compared and contrasted with the environment through observation to avoid even the smallest detachment from reality.

The tempo of execution of the whole OODA loop defines agility: the quicker the OODA loop is executed, in particular, the more quickly errors in orientation can be noticed and corrected, the more agile the organization can be in tracking the environment, in discovering both customers' needs and changes in their preferences, and therefore the organization can be faster than competitors in responding to such changes.

Strategic management literature supports the importance of this idea of strategic agility (Doz and Kosonen, 2008), which is seen as a result of the co-presence of three meta-capabilities strategic sensitivity, leadership unity and resource fluidity.

THE OODA LOOP IN FAMILY BUSINESS

We suggest that Boyd's OODA loop, the framework and his strategic approach might fit very well family businesses' characteristics. In particular, we refer to the base assumptions on which Boyd built his framework.

First, Boyd stressed the importance of the moral bonds that tie an organization together, even during periods of high stress and rapid change (Boyd, 1986: 124–125). We argue that this fits with the systemic nature of family business. Since the beginning of the field, family business has been explored using a systems approach. In addition, families are systems themselves: open, ongoing, goal seeking, self-regulating (Broderick, 1993); unique among social systems in that they may be permanent and are emotional (Borwick, 1986), they have the capacity to be moral and non-political at the level of ultimate control (Astrachan, 2005), where merit is acquired 'when a family member contributes to the welfare of others and the trustworthiness of the family' (Fowers and Wenger, 1997: 155), and where family managers might act in the true interest of the company (Miller and Le Breton-Miller, 2005).

Second, Boyd stated that the ultimate purpose of any system is to survive 'on its own terms' and increase its capacity for independent action in a threatening and confusing world. We believe that 'survival' and 'on own terms' taken together best fit family business' characteristics. In fact, both family business literature and practice show that family businesses are particularly conscious of long term survival (Trostel and Nichols, 1982). Theory shows how family businesses are able to ensure continuity with both family and business (Habbershon et al., 2003; Miller and Le Breton-Miller, 2005); with transgenerational intentionality (Chua et al., 1999), so that the goal of assuring continuity of the owning family is consistent with the business' survival (Miller and Le Breton-Miller, 2005) in the long term (Kreiser et al.,2006). In practice, the presence of the above mentioned clubs of ultra centenaries family businesses shows how, for these firms, survival and continuity become their ultimate objectives. Moreover, these firms set their own survival terms beyond mere profit maximization (Chrisman et al., 2003).

Third, Boyd argues that organizations that want to adopt strategies described by the OODA loop need cultures that both enable rapid action and have an ability to adapt more quickly than their competition. This is possible in the presence of a strong culture and common background that reduce friction and thus facilitate collective action, because organizational culture helps align employees and stimulate their interest in maintaining the organization's ability to be flexible in response to external changes (Zahra et al., 2008). Again, family business can best fit this requirement, and research has shown that strong, distinct, performance-enhancing culture is something families are known for (Denison et al., 2004); they are able to develop a strong sense of belonging among both family and non-family (Geus, 1997). In particular, with respect to the four cultural attributes – main goal, deep knowledge, mutual trust and contracting – we again believe that family business provides a compatible context for their development. Research on successful family businesses led by Miller and Le Breton-Miller (2005) has shown that family firms concentrate on a 'substantive mission attached to a specific social or economic purpose, and don't stray from that purpose' (2005: 518) and that they 'foster a cohesive organizational community because they wish to ensure their personal values and ethics are deeply embedded in their company and reflected in all its behavior' (2005: 521). This shared family vision can be considered a superordinate goal that unites family and inspires family members to manifest the same vision within the organization (Hubler, 2009).

Concerning the second attribute, deep knowledge, family businesses are often described as having competitive advantage rooted in the extensive expertise of family members, since they are often in contact with the business from early childhood onward (Kets de Vries, 1993). In addition, family members can be exposed to tacit knowledge possessed by the founder that represents a potential strategic asset for the business. In family business, this tacit knowledge can be transferred more effectively to family members due to the special relationship between successor and predecessor that goes beyond work and includes personal and family ties (Cabrera-Suarez et al., 2001). Family business literature has long recognized that the intimate knowledge among family members facilitates communication and decision making (Gersick et al., 1997).

The third attribute, to build a strong culture, is a combination of factors described by words like 'trust', 'unity' and 'cohesion', and here family businesses also have a potential advantage. Family businesses are often depicted as 'high trust' organizations (Corbetta and Salvato, 2004; Sundaramurthy, 2008), where trust can remain strong over generations, maintaining high levels of open, honest and consistent communication (Astrachan and McMillan, 2003; Ward, 2004). Researchers suggested that the family system attempts to create and maintain a cohesiveness that supports the family 'paradigm', which is described as the 'core assumptions, beliefs, and convictions that the family holds in relation to its environment' (Gudmundson et al., 1999: 27). Research has also shown that family managers in successful family businesses, due to their ownership status and sense of responsibility to follow the family dream, act in the interest of the company, and their candor helps create cohesion (Miller and Le Breton-Miller, 2005). These cohesive ties in turn promote more trust and cooperation (Coleman, 1988).

Finally, as far as contracting is concerned, family business also can display potential advantage. Miller and Le Breton-Miller (2005) showed how great family businesses are guided by principles that operate as behavioral rules, rather than bureaucratic rules or financial incentives; instead, employees are told what they have to work towards. Family businesses can develop task ownership among employees, training, motivating and engaging them.

Within this framework, we believe that the highest level function the family might serve is as keeper of culture. If they focus on preservation of the firm over the long term, family members can ensure that the culture is passed down not only from one generation of family to the next, but the culture will survive intact through the more frequent changes of managers. Because family members view the firm over the passage of generations, they are uniquely positioned to determine whether the culture is getting stronger, weaker or surviving at all.

On a daily basis, the family is in a good position to ensure that the company's orientation continues to be well matched to the evolving environment and to bring potential mismatches to the attention of management. This is particularly true if the family is large enough to have members who do not participate as line managers or who do not participate in the company at all because, in that case, the family can function as outsiders as well as insiders.

For these reasons, we think that Boyd's OODA loop can represent a highly valuable strategic management approach for family business and that family businesses can represent a viable context in which to apply it. Boyd's framework relies on the assumption that in the presence of a 'higher purpose' groups are more likely to be effective (Boyd, 1986). We suggest that the 'higher purpose' for family business should be reciprocal altruism that, together with willingness to care for significant others, can enhance cohesion in family business (Kellermanns and Eddleston, 2004), which may then ensure family business survival and continuity (Pieper and Astrachan, 2008) and increase strategic flexibility (Zahra et al., 2008). Altruism is noted to be higher among family than non-family businesses (Ling et al., 2001; Schulze et al., 2003).

In that respect, we believe that the development of a *Blitzkrieg* culture in family business can bring several advantages. It can overcome one of the main concerns family members have, which is to prevent non-family members from acting opportunistically (Chua et al., 2003a), reducing the differences between family and non-family firms in terms of both their behavior and performance (Schulze et al., 2003) and decreasing potential for relationship conflict. Finally, through altruism, the family can decide how to use resources (Harvey, 1999), can positively affect strategic decisions (Zahra, 2003) and be willing to supply financial resources to the business (Olson et al., 2003), increasing the business' capability to adapt to the changing environment (Zahra et al., 2008), which is recognized as essential for survival (March, 1995).

To conclude, we believe this approach can have several benefits, both for theory development and for family business practice. From the theoretical point of view, we contribute both to family business and strategic management literature. As far as the former is concerned, we consider Boyd's framework as a positive response to the need for a theory of family firm strategy that is able to consider the systemic nature of family business; to accept the presence of multiple goals (Adams et al., 2004; Castillo and Wakefield, 2007); and to improve its management practice and performance (Sharma et al., 1997).

This approach also suggests a strategic management perspective sought after by family business researchers (Sharma et al., 1997). In the conclusion of their research review of strategic management in family business, these authors called for future studies that could take into consideration the needs of family business research, such as the 'identification, explicit recognition and inclusion of dependent variables to measure the outcome of decisions and actions' (1997: 18); and the inclusion of the importance of the business, and not only of the family. They hope that future studies might suggest 'how the influence of the family can be directed toward more productive and profitable outcomes' (1997: 19). We believe that the framework we propose meets both the above mentioned requests, representing in this way a worthy contribution. In fact, Boyd's approach begins with the recognition of the importance of those dependent variables, however the families want to define them (e.g. as family harmony or economic performance). Secondly, we have described the fundamental role of family in keeping the culture and assuring business results.

We believe another benefit for family business research lies in the notion that this framework might be operationalized, thus allowing for study of actual strategic processes in family business, about which current knowledge is quite limited (Steier et al., 2004; Upton et al., 2001).

More generally, we believe that Boyd's framework can be a valuable first response to the recent call for new approaches in the strategic management field, which is seeking new theories able both to capture the new dynamism and to include the benefits offered by the cross-fertilization of the field with other disciplines (Furrer et al., 2008). We think Boyd's theory can represent an appropriate answer to the needs set by the fast paced changing environment, given his underlying idea of using time as a shaping and exploiting mechanism (Eisenhardt, 1989). Leveraging organizational culture to reduce frictions, and thus make decisions more quickly (Richards, 2004), best fits the current situation characterized by great uncertainty. The role of culture and the four conditions stressed by Boyd are in line both with the meta-capabilities identified by Doz and Kosonen (2008) and with the importance of avoiding locking the company into a sub-optimal pattern when developing only one capability (or according to Boyd, one condition).

We also expect that family business practice can benefit from the implementation of this approach. Previous research shows that family firms can largely benefit from strategic planning (Astrachan and Kolenko, 1994; Ward, 1997). We suggest that family businesses adopt Boyd's framework as a starting point for their strategic planning activity. In fact, Boyd's theory and the development of a *Blitzkrieg* culture can be a successful tool that can allow a family business to create a flexible organization, enabling it to anticipate if not create the future, to know its customers' needs better than do the customers and therefore give the family firm a competitive edge that allows it to shape and reshape its market.

Finally, being such a theoretically innovative approach, we acknowledge the need for empirical research to test its validity. As future steps, we encourage both qualitative and quantitative research on this topic. Qualitative studies might delve into the strategic process of the OODA loop in family business and might identify elements idiosyncratic to family business that the theory might have overlooked. Other qualitative work might include action research on an organization in the process of implementing the required culture and OODA loop. Quantitative studies might aim at measuring performance in family businesses that have introduced both the *Blitzkrieg* culture and that have operated the OODA loop, to determine whether they actually led to superior performance (defined idiosyncratically or at least by survival characteristics). To do that, researchers should first develop a scale to operationalize the four characteristics of the culture. In both types of studies, we recognize that the identification of cases and samples will not be easy given the innovativeness of the approach.

In the end, we are aware that this theoretical introduction of Boyd's framework represents only the first step for the development of a complete theory of family business, but we believe that this step is poised toward the direction established by prior research, and hopefully sets the stage to advance the field.

NOTES

1. *Blitzkrieg* means 'lightning war'. *Blitzkrieg* was first used by the Germans in World War II and was a concept based on speed and surprise. It also needed a military force formed around good communications, and usually employed mobile tank units supported by planes and infantry (foot soldiers).
2. The Marine Corps teaches that an operation can have only one *Schwerpunkt* at any time, and as a rule it is assigned to one of the participating units (U S Marine Corps, 1997: 90). The activities of the other units involved in the operation must support the *Schwerpunkt*. Businesses, by contrast, may find multiple *Schwerpunkts* to be useful tools, so long as they do not conflict or trade off (Richards, 2004).

REFERENCES

Adams, A. F., III, G. E. Manners, Jr, J. H. Astrachan and P. Mazzola (2004), 'The importance of integrated goal setting: The application of cost-of-capital concepts to private firms', *Family Business Review*, **17**(4): 287–302.

Aldrich, H. E. and J. E. Cliff (2003), 'The pervasive effects of family on entrepreneurship: Toward a family embeddedness perspective', *Journal of Business Venturing*, **18**(5): 573–596.

Anderson, R. C. and D. M. Reeb (2003), ' Founding-family ownership and firm performance: Evidence from the S&P 500', *The Journal of Finance*, **58**(3): 1301.

Astrachan, J. H. (2005), 'Editor's notes', *Family Business Review*, **18**(3): V–VI.

Astrachan, J. H. and T. A. Kolenko (1994), 'A neglected factor explaining family business success: Human resource practices', *Family Business Review*, 7(3): 251–262.

Astrachan, J. H. and K. S. McMillan (2003), *Conflict and Communication in the Family Business*, Marietta, GA: Family Enterprise Publisher.

Astrachan, J. H. and K. S. McMillan (2006), 'United States', in F. W. Kaslow (ed.), *Handbook of Family Business and Family Business Consultation: A Global Perspective*, 347–363: Florence, KY: International Business Press Taylor & Francis.

Astrachan, J. H., S. B. Klein and K. X. Smyrnios (2002), 'The F-PEC scale of family influence: A proposal for solving the family business definition problem1', *Family Business Review*, **15**(1): 45–58.

Baum, J. R. and S. Wally (2003), 'Strategic decision speed and firm performance', *Strategic Management Journal*, **24**(11): 1107–1129.

Bhalla, A., J. Lampel, S. Henderson and D. Watkins (2009), 'Exploring alternative strategic management paradigms in high-growth ethnic and non-ethnic family firms', *Small Business Economics*, **32**(1): 77–94.

Borwick, I. (1986), 'The family therapist as business consultant', in L. C. Wynne, S. H. McDaniel and T. T. Weber (eds), *Systems Consultation: A New Perspective for Family Therapy*, 423–440, New York: Guilford.

Boyd, J. R. (1986), 'Patterns of conflict', Unpublished presentation.

Boyd, J. R. (1987a), 'The strategic game of ? and ?', Unpublished presentation.

Boyd, J. R. (1987b), 'Organic design for command and control', Unpublished presentation.

Boyd, J. R. (1996), 'The essence of winning and losing', Unpublished presentation.

Broderick, C. B. (1993), *Understanding Family Processes*, Newbury Park, CA: Sage.

Burgelman, R. A. and A. S. Grove (1996), 'Strategic dissonance', *California Management Review*, **38**(2): 8–28.

Byus, K. and T. Box (2007), 'Guerilla actions as small business strategy: Out-witting is more competitively responsive than out-spending', *Entrepreneurial Executive*, **12**: 51–63.

Cabrera-Suarez, K., P. De Saa-Perez and D. Garcia-Almeida (2001), 'The succession process from a resource- and knowledge-based view of the family firm', *Family Business Review*, **14**(1): 37–46.

Castillo, J. and M. W. Wakefield (2007), 'An exploration of firm performance factors in family businesses: Do families value only the "bottom line"?', *Journal of Small Business Strategy*, **17**(2): 37–51.

Chrisman, J. J., J. H. Chua and R. Litz (2003), 'A unified systems perspective of family firm performance: An extension and integration', *Journal of Business Venturing*, **18**: 467.

Chrisman, J. J., J. H. Chua and P. Sharma (2005), 'Trends and directions in the development of a strategic management theory of the family firm', *Entrepreneurship: Theory and Practice*, **29**(5): 555–575.

Chua, J. H., J. J. Chrisman and P. Sharma (1999), 'Defining the family business by behavior', *Entrepreneurship: Theory and Practice*, **23**(4): 19–39.

Chua, J. H., J. J. Chrisman and P. Sharma (2003a), 'Succession and nonsuccession concerns of family firms and agency relationship with nonfamily managers', *Family Business Review*, **16**(2): 89–107.

Chua, J. H., J. J. Chrisman and L. P. Steier (2003b), 'Extending the theoretical horizons of family business research', *Entrepreneurship: Theory and Practice*, **27**(4): 331–338.

Clausewitz, C. von (1968), *On War*, trans J. J. Graham, London: Penguin.

Coleman, J. S. (1988), 'Social capital in the creation of human capital', *American Journal of Sociology*, **94**: s95–s120.

Coram, R. (2002), *Boyd: The Fighter Pilot who Changed the Art of War*, Boston, MA: Little, Brown Hachette Book Group.

Corbetta, G. and C. A. Salvato (2004), 'The board of directors in family firms: One size fits all?', *Family Business Review*, **17**(2): 119–134.

Danes, S. M., J. T.-C. Loy and K. Stafford (2008), 'Business planning practices of family-owned firms within a quality framework', *Journal of Small Business Management*, **46**(3): 395–421.

Debicki, B. J., C. F. Matherne III, F. W. Kellermanns and J. J. Chrisman (2009), 'Family business research in the new millennium: An overview of the who, the where, the what, and the why', *Family Business Review*, **22**(2): 151–166.

Denison, D., C. Lief and J. L. Ward (2004), 'Culture in family-owned enterprises: Recognizing and leveraging unique strengths', *Family Business Review*, **17**(1): 61–70.

Distelberg, B. and R. L. Sorenson (2009), 'Updating systems concepts in family businesses: A focus on values, resource flows, and adaptability', *Family Business Review*, **22**(1): 65–81.

Doz, Y. and M. Kosonen (2008),*Fast Strategy: How Strategic Agility will Help You Stay Ahead of the Game* (1st edition): Wharton School Publishing.

Eisenhardt, K. (1989), 'Making fast strategic decisions in high-velocity environments', *Academy of Management Journal*, **27**: 299–343.

Erez, M. and F. H. Kanfer (1983), 'The role of goal acceptance in goal setting and task performance', *Academy of Management Review*, **8**(3): 454–463.

Espevik, R., B. H. Johnsen, J. Eid and J. F. Thayer (2006), 'Shared mental models and operational effectiveness: Effects on performance and team processes in sub marine attack teams', *Military Psychology*, **18**: S23–S36.

Fowers, B. J. and A. Wenger (1997), 'Are trustworthiness and fairness enough? Contextual family therapy and the good family', *Journal of Marital and Family Therapy*, **23**(2): 153–173.

Furrer, O., H. Thomas and A. Goussevskaia (2008), 'The structure and evolution of the strategic management field: A content analysis of 26 years of strategic management research', *International Journal of Management Reviews*, **10**(1): 1–23.

Gersick, K. E., J. A. Davis, M. Hampton and I. S. Lansberg (1997), *Generation to Generation: Life Cycles of the Family Business*, Boston, MA: Harvard Business School Press.

Geus, A. D. (1997), *The Living Company*, Boston, MA: Harvard Business School Press.

Gray, C. (1999), *Modern Strategy*, Oxford: Oxford Print University Press.

Gudmundson, D., E. A. Hartman and C. B. Tower (1999), 'Strategic orientation: Differences between family and nonfamily firms', *Family Business Review*, 12(1): 27–39.

Habbershon, T. G. and M. L. Williams (1999), 'A resource-based framework for assessing the strategic advantages of family firms', *Family Business Review*, 12(1): 1–25.

Habbershon, T. G., M. Williams and I. C. MacMillan (2003), 'A unified systems perspective of family firm performance', *Journal of Business Venturing*, 18(4): 451–465.

Harvey, J. S., Jr. (1999), 'What can the family contribute to business? Examining contractual relationships', *Family Business Review*, 12(1): 61–71.

Hatum, A. and A. Pettigrew (2004), 'Adaptation under environmental turmoil: Organizational flexibility in family-owned firms', *Family Business Review*, 17(3): 237–258.

Heck, R. K. Z., F. Hoy, P. Z. Poutziouris and L. P. Steier (2008), 'Emerging paths of family entrepreneurship research', *Journal of Small Business Management*, 46(3): 317–330.

Hollander, B. S. and N. S. Elman (1988), 'Family-owned businesses: An emerging field of inquiry', *Family Business Review*, 1(2): 145–164.

Hoskisson, R. E., M. A. Hitt, W. P. Wan and D. Yiu (1999), 'Theory and research in strategic management: Swings of a pendulum', *Journal of Management*, 25(3): 417–456.

Hubler, T. M. (2009), 'The soul of family business', *Family Business Review*, 22(3): 254–258.

Ibrahim, A. B. and W. H. Ellis (1988), *Family Business Management: Concepts and Practice*, Dubuque, IA: Kendall/Hunt.

Kellermanns, F. W. and T. Barnett (2008), 'Commentary: What were they thinking? The role of family firm mental models on threat recognition', *Entrepreneurship: Theory and Practice*, 32: 999–1006.

Kellermanns, F. W. and K. A. Eddleston (2004), 'Feuding families: When conflict does a family firm good', *Entrepreneurship: Theory and Practice*, 28(3): 209–228.

Kets de Vries, M. F. R. (1993), 'The dynamics of family controlled firms: The good and the bad news', *Organizational Dynamics*, 21(3): 59–71.

Klein, G. (1998), *Sources of Power*, Cambridge, MA: Massachusetts Institute of Technology Press.

Klein, S. B., J. H. Astrachan and K. X. Smyrnios (2005), 'The F-PEC scale of family influence: Construction, validation, and further implication for theory', *Entrepreneurship: Theory and Practice*, 29(3): 321–339.

Kreiser, P. M., J. Ojala, J. Antti-Lamberg and A. Melander (2006), 'A historical investigation of the strategic process within family firms: A cross-cultural analysis', *Journal of Management History*, 12(1): 100–114.

Lansberg, I., E. L. Perrow and S. Rogolsky (1988), 'Editors' notes', *Family Business Review*, 1(1): 1–8.

Ling, Y., M. Lubatkin and W. S. Schulze (2001), 'Altruism, utility functions, and agency problems at family firms', in C. Galbraith (ed.), *International Research in Business Disciplines, Strategies and Organizations in Transition*, 171–190. New York: JAI Press.

Litz, R. (1997), 'The family firm's exclusion from business school research: Explaining the void; addressing the opportunity', *Entrepreneurship Theory and Practice*, 21(3): 55–71.

Litz, R. A. (2008), 'Two sides of a one-sided phenomenon: Conceptualizing the family business and business family as a Möbius strip', *Family Business Review*, 21(3): 217–236.

March, J. G. (1995), 'The future, disposable organizations and the rigidities of imagination', *Organization Science*, 2(3/4): 427–440.

McCollom, M. E. (1990), 'Problems and prospects in clinical research on family firms', *Family Business Review*, 3(3): 245–262.

Mento, A. J., R. P. Steel and R. J. Karren (1987), 'A meta-analytic study of the effects of goal setting on task performance: 1966–1984', *Organizational Behavior and Human Decision Processes*, 39(1): 52–83.

Miller, D. and I. Le Breton-Miller (2005), 'Management insights from great and struggling family businesses', *Long Range Planning: International Journal of Strategic Management*, **38**(6): 517–530.

Moores, K. (2009), 'Paradigms and theory building in the domain of business families', *Family Business Review*, **22**(2): 167–180.

Olson, P. D., V. S. Zuiker, S. M. Danes, K. Stafford, R. K. Z. Heck and K. A. Duncan (2003), 'The impact of the family and the business on family business sustainability', *Journal of Business Venturing*, **18**(5): 639–666.

Osinga, F. P. B. (2007), *Science, Strategy and War: the Strategic Theory of John Boyd*, Florence. KY: Routledge Taylor and Francis.

Pearson, A. W., J. C. Carr and J. C. Shaw (2008), 'Toward a theory of familiness: A social capital perspective', *Entrepreneurship: Theory and Practice*, **32**(6): 949–969.

Peters, T. J. (1987), *Thriving on Chaos: Handbook for a Management Revolution*, New York: Harper Collins.

Pettigrew, A. M. and R. Whipp (1992), *Managing Change for Competitive Success*, Somerset, NJ: Blackwell Pub, c/o John Wiley and Sons.

Pieper, T. M. and J. H. Astrachan (2008), *Mechanisms to Assure Family Business Cohesion: Guidelines for Family Business Leaders and their Families*, Kennesaw, GA: Cox Family Enterprise Center.

Pieper, T. M. and S. B. Klein (2007), 'The bulleye: A systems approach to modeling family firms', *Family Business Review*, **20**(4): 301–319.

Porter, M. E. (1980), *Competitive Strategy: Techniques for Analysing Industries and Competitors*, New York: Free Press.

Richards, C. (2004), *Certain To Win: The Strategy of John Boyd, Applied to Business*, Philadelphia, PA: Xlibris Corp.

Schulze, W. S., M. H. Lubatkin, R. N. Dino and A. K. Buchholtz (2001), 'Agency relationships in family firms: Theory and evidence', *Organization Science*, **12**(2): 99–116.

Schulze, W. S., M. H. Lubatkin and R. N. Dino (2003), 'Toward a theory of agency and altruism in family firms', *Journal of Business Venturing*, **18**(4): 473–490.

Sharma, P., J. J. Chrisman and J. H. Chua (1997), 'Strategic management of the family business: Past research and future challenges', *Family Business Review*, **10**(1): 1–35.

Short, J. C., G. T. Payne, K. H. Brigham, G. T. Lumpkin and J. C. Broberg (2009), 'Family firms and entrepreneurial orientation in publicly traded firms: A comparative analysis of the S&P 500', *Family Business Review*, **22**(1): 9–24.

Stafford, K., K. A. Duncan, S. Dane and M. Winter (1999), 'A research model of sustainable family businesses', *Family Business Review*, **12**(3): 197–208.

Stalk Jr, G. (1988), 'Time – the next source of competitive advantage', *Harvard Business Review*, **66**(4): 41–51.

Steier, L. P., J. J. Chrisman and J. H. Chua (2004), 'Entrepreneurial management and governance in family firms: An introduction', *Entrepreneurship: Theory and Practice*, **28**(4): 295–303.

Stevenson, H. and D. Gumpert (1985), 'The heart of entrepreneurship', *Harvard Business Review* **63**(2): 85–94.

Sundaramurthy, C. (2008), 'Sustaining trust within family businesses', *Family Business Review*, **21**(1): 89–102.

Tagiuri, R. and J. A. Davis (1992), 'On the goals of successful family companies', *Family Business Review*, **5**(1): 43–62.

Tagiuri, R. and J. Davis (1996), 'Bivalent ttributes of the family firm', *Family Business Review*, **9**(2): 199–208.

Tomlinson, R. C. (1976), 'OR, organizational design and adaptivity', *Omega*, **4**: 527–537.

Trostel, A. O. and M. L. Nichols (1982), 'Privately-held and publicly-held companies: A comparison of strategic choices and management processes', *Academy of Management Journal*, **25**(1): 47–62.

Tzu, S. (1963), *The Art of War*, trans. S. B. Griffith, Oxford: Oxford University Press.

Tzu, S. (1988), *The Art of War*, trans. T. Clearly, Boston: Shambhala.

Upton, N.,E. J. Teal and J. T. Felan (2001), 'Strategic and business planning practices of fast growth family firms', *Journal of Small Business Management*, **39**(1): 60–72.

US Marine Corps (1997), *Warfighting*, 20 June, Washington, DC.

Volberda, H. W. (1996), 'Toward the flexible form: How to remain vital in hypercompetitive environments', *Organization Science*, **7**(4): 359–374.

Volberda, H. W. (1999), *Building the Flexible Firm: How to Remain Competitive*, Cary, NC: Oxford University Press.

Ward, J. L. (1997), 'Growing the family business: Special challenges and best practices', *Family Business Review*, **10**(4): 323–337.

Ward, J. L. (2004), *Perpetuating the Family Business: 50 Lessons Learned from Long-Lasting, Successful Families in Business*, Gordonsville, VA: Palgrave Macmillan.

Whiteside, M. F. and F.H. Brown (1991), 'Drawbacks of a dual systems approach to family firms: Can we expand our thinking?', *Family Business Review*, **4**(4): 383–395.

Zahra, S. A. (2003), 'International expansion of U.S. manufacturing family businesses: The effect of ownership and involvement', *Journal of Business Venturing*, **18**(4): 495–512.

Zahra, S. A. and P. Sharma (2004), 'Family business research: A strategic reflection', *Family Business Review*, **17**(4): 331–346.

Zahra, S. A., J. C. Hayton, D. O. Neubaum, C. Dibrell and J. Craig (2008), 'Culture of family commitment and strategic flexibility: The moderating effect of stewardship', *Entrepreneurship: Theory and Practice*, **32**(6): 1035–1054.

Zellweger, T. (2007), 'Time horizon, costs of equity capital, and generic investment strategies of firms', *Family Business Review*, **20**(1): 1–15.

Index

ABI-INFORM Global database 413
Abrahamson, E. 23, 29
Acedo, F. 17
Ackoff, R. L. 187
acquisition integration processes
    412–31 *see also* literature
    autonomy and speed of integration
        419–21
    learning, retention and
        communication 421–4
    research examining 413–14, 415–17,
        425–7
    research configuration 414, 418–19
    sensemaking and behavioral
        considerations 424–5
Adams, A. F. III 546, 559
Adner, R. 483
advertising intensity 31
agency theory 101, 147–8, 166, 179,
    546
Aguilar, F. J. 33
Aharoni, Y. 440
Ahuja, G. 241, 242, 244, 251
Akan, O. 171
Alder, P. 240, 242, 243, 246, 248, 259
Aldrich, H. 22
Aldrich, H. E. 338, 546
Alexander, L. D. 168, 170, 172
Alexander, M. 48
Alford, A. 494
Alford, R. R. 99
Allio, M. K. 168
Allison, G. 58, 524, 529
Alvarez, S. A. 311
Amason, A. C. 423, 477
ambidexterity, volatility and
    performance 240–63
Amburgey, T. 473
Amit, R. 98
analysis, environmental and
    organizational levels of 38
Anand, B. N. 6, 375, 398, 399, 403
Andersen, O. 433, 434

Anderson, E. 434
Anderson, P. 350, 351, 355, 357, 359,
    360
Anderson, R. C. 541
Andrews, K. R. xxiii, 22, 110, 145, 269,
    373
Ansoff, I. xxiii, 110, 112, 373, 453
Antoncic, B. 330, 345
Apple 52, 466, 481, 483
Arend, R. J. 23
Argenti, P. A. 170
Argote, L. 246
Argyris, C. 49, 117, 122, 128, 187, 459
Arino, A. 399, 403
Armenakis, A. 473, 481
Arogyaswamy, K. 473, 478, 484, 486,
    487
Arthur, B. 353, 457
Ashford, S. J. 74, 76, 152, 290, 330,
    331
Ashmos, D. 479
Astrachan, J. H. 544, 545, 546, 556,
    557, 558, 560
Astrachan, J.J. xxxiii
AT and T 198
Atkinson, S. 51
Aufrag 549, 550 *see also* Boyd, J. *and*
    OODA loop
Autoliv 101
awareness
    concept of 36
    option and discretionary set as
        prerequisites for managerial
        discretion 26
Axelrod, R. M. 37, 98
Azar, O. H. xxiv, 5, 17

Bacon, F. 456
Bagby, D. R. 310, 311
Bain 272
Bak, P. 364
Balakrishnan, S. 371
Baldwin, W. C. 526